THIS OLD BOAT

DON CASEY

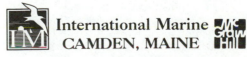

International Marine
CAMDEN, MAINE

This book is dedicated to Judy Casey, who first showed me how
to do much with little.
Thanks, Mom.

International Marine/
Ragged Mountain Press
A Division of The **McGraw·Hill** Companies

15   14   13   12

Copyright © 1991 International Marine, a division of The McGraw-Hill Companies.

Library of Congress Cataloging-in-Publication Data
Casey Don,
    This old boat / Don Casey.
        p.   cm.
    Includes index.
    ISBN 0-07-157993-1
    1. Boats and boating—Maintenance and repair.
    I. Title.
VM322.C37 1991
623.8'223'0288—dc20   91-10174
                                                       CIP

Questions regarding the content of this book should be addressed to:
International Marine
P.O. Box 220
Camden, Maine 04843

Questions regarding the ordering of this book should be addressed to:
The McGraw-Hill Companies
Customer Service Department
P.O. Box 547
Blacklick, OH 43004
Retail customers: 1-800-262-4729
Bookstores: 1-800-722-4726

Typeset by A & B Typesetters, Bow, NH
Printed by Quebecor Printing Co., Fairfield, PA
Design by Janet Patterson
Illustrated by the author
Tables on pages 106 and 224 from *Boatowner's*
Mechanical and Electrical Manual by Nigel
Calder. (International Marine, 1990)
Edited by J.R. Babb, Mary McCormick, Pamela Salomon
Production by Janet Robbins

Contents

Acknowledgments

This book would not exist but for the number of fine boats built in the 60s and 70s by a handful of quality-conscious manufacturers. The contributions to boating of those pioneers in fiberglass boat construction cannot be overstated. I make no attempt to list them, but you cannot be around the docks very long even today – 20 or 30 years later – without hearing their names revered.

I must also acknowledge the builders of the 80s, who have taken the cost of the average new boat well beyond the reach of the entry-level or casual sailor. How many of us can honestly afford a boat that costs more than $100,000? It is the high prices of new boats that make a sound, old boat such a terrific bargain.

As for the specific content of the book, everything I know about boats I learned from someone else. Many who contributed to this book did so in lantern-lit cockpits during convivial evenings in remote anchorages; other ideas came from anchored or docked boats whose owners I never had the good fortune to meet. Many of the ideas and concepts I gleaned from magazine articles and books. My sincere appreciation is extended to all those who, knowingly or otherwise, showed and taught me boatcraft. I take credit only for arranging the words.

The thousands of dedicated hours required to get those words on paper would not have been available without the support of my wife and partner, Olga. She also gave up endless precious hours of her evenings and weekends to wade through the manuscript, her frequent, "I don't understand this part" invariably leading to clearer explanations. Her assistance came not out of obligation, but out of inclination. I wish to acknowledge that assistance for the same reason.

iv

Introduction

The obvious is that which is never seen until someone expresses it simply.
—KAHLIL GIBRAN—

On the wall of my local marine chandlery, above a cash register that spits out bad news like a ticker tape on Black Monday, hangs a small plaque. It was placed there in an apparent effort to cheer the customers through commiseration, and it reads: "boat (bot) *n.* A hole in the water, surrounded by wood, into which one pours money." As I part with all my cash and discover that my purchases will fit into my shirt pocket, *I* am not cheered.

It does cost money to own a boat. But there are ways to make it cost less—a lot less. Take *Nabila*, for example. Billionaire arms dealer Adnan Khashoggi reportedly spent about $90 million to build and equip his dream yacht. But other matters demanded Khashoggi's time and money. Enter Donald Trump. For a mere $29 million, he picked up Khashoggi's old boat. Of course she wasn't exactly the way The Donald wanted her, but with a million here and a million there, she was soon close enough. The cost to duplicate the boat at the time was estimated at more than $150 million!

Even for those of us who think of "a lot of money" in terms of hundreds rather than millions—perhaps especially for us—there is a lesson to be learned from this highly publicized transfer of ownership. When a boat loses the eye of her original owner, is she any less of a boat? Is she any less capable of satisfying the common dreams that dictate pleasure boat design?

In marinas, canals, and boat yards all across the country sit tens of thousands of boats in various stages of neglect. Many were designed with great vision, built with great care, delivered with great optimism. And perhaps once they did satisfy the dreams of their owners, but today their dull finish, greying wood, and tattered canvas fail to ignite excitement.

But you, smart person that you are, know better. You have asked yourself if the boats that manufacturers are turning out today satisfy dreams that much better than the boats they built 20 years ago. And you know that the answer is, in most cases, no. Or maybe you haven't considered this question at all; for you, the guiding factor is strictly economics. Either way, your boat is not new.

Owning a boat you can afford is no reason not to have a boat you are proud of. Starting with an old boat provides an almost unlimited opportunity to "do" the boat in a way that suits you. Changes can be made at one time in an extensive re-fit, or they can be made little by little over a period of years, as time, money, and motivation dictate. If you give the project sufficient thought and effort, you will end up with a boat that satisfies your specific tastes and requirements better than any new production boat could—and you will have poured a lot less money into that watery hole.

Transforming *your* boat from castoff to show-off is what this book is all about. In the pages that follow, you will find guidance for developing and executing a complete plan of improvement, repair, and modification. You will note an emphasis on sailboats; I am a sailor and these are the boats I know. But boats, all boats, are more similar than they are different, so most of the projects in this book, and *all* of the concepts and skills, are applicable to boats of any size, sailboats and powerboats alike.

This book will take you through a logical, orderly process of bringing *your* boat to progressively better condition. It will teach you to give your imagination a free rein; to look at your chalking and streaked hull and see instead the emerald light of some distant lagoon reflected in a mirror finish. It will help you to develop a list of all the changes necessary to give substance to your vision. You will learn how to plan the transformation and how to set priorities. You will find guidance for making intelligent choices among the myriad of possibilities. You will encounter practical solutions to common boat requirements, such as electrical power, and find fresh ideas for dealing effectively with such inherent limitations as scant stowage space.

But project management, consumer guidance, and a source of ideas, as important as these are, are only a small part of this book. Most of the text is devoted to showing how to make the desired changes, repairs, and enhancements. It tells you what tools and materials to use and how to use them.

Even if changing the bulb in a cabin light is the most complicated task you have previously attempted, that is no reason to assume that you cannot give substance to your vision. The skills required are not difficult and we begin most of the chapters with a simple project that allows you to learn and practice those skills. For example, in the chapter on working with fabrics, we begin by constructing a simple skirt to protect the hull from the fenders. If you can sew the seams and hems required for this simple item, you can also make a Bimini top; the skills required are essentially the same. Likewise, if you can cut and install a plywood shelf, you can build an entire cabinet. And if you can paint the inside of a locker, you can refinish a hull.

Clearly it is not possible to detail every imaginable enhancement project, but it is possible to address virtually all of the necessary skills. You need to master only the basic skills illuminated in the following pages to effect the transformation of a sound but tired older boat into a jewel that will turn heads in any anchorage, get you there in safety and comfort, and yield immeasurable pride—and measurable savings.

What more can you ask?

ONE

The Choice

Men have learned to travel farther and faster,
though on errands not conspicuously improved.
This, I believe, is called progress.
−WILLIS FISHER−

In the pages that follow, I will try to provide clear and logical instructions for enhancements that can add to the pleasures of use and ownership of any boat. The specific boat is up to you. If you already own the apple of your eye, perfect in conception and flawed only with age or modesty, this first chapter may not interest you. And there is the risk that my comments will reflect poorly on your judgment (or, from your point of view I suppose, on *my* judgment). Enraptured owners may skip this chapter.

You may also have come to this book not as a sailor but as a dreamer. You stand on the shore on weekends watching the parade of boats, an observer only, prohibited from becoming a participant by the escalating prices of new boats. Perhaps you have considered buying an old boat, but the affordable ones all seem so . . . tired. And if you do buy one, you are afraid of what you might be getting into.

Good news, Bunky. If you really want to get your share of the pleasures of boating, your only obstacle is you. Somewhere out there is a boat you can afford, and with a little time and effort she can also be one you will take pride in.

Not so sure? Then this chapter comes too early for you. Come back to it later after you have had a chance to try your hand at some of the skills needed to refurbish an old boat. For the rest of you, those with that "you-just-show-me-what-to-do-and-I-can-do-it" attitude, I offer a few thoughts on choosing the right boat.

Several years ago, on a cruise through the Bahamas, we were joined for a few days by close friends.

Richard, an avid fisherman and diver, had owned powerboats most of his life and spent almost every weekend on the water. After a few days of the cruising life, he began to talk seriously about buying a sailboat. Like an evangelical preacher, I pointed out to him the "good" boats in the anchorage: an old Pearson Invicta with a powerful sheer; a Hinckley Bermuda 40 with the grace and beauty of a swan; a Morgan 34, related to the later "Out Island" series like Cinderella to her stepsisters; even a stout and capable Westsail. He umm-hmmed politely. Then late one afternoon a new boat came motoring in.

"What is that?"

It was a Coronado 41, to my eye one of the ugliest boats ever to go into production, but before I could voice that sentiment, Richard continued. "Now *that* is the kind of boat I want!"

The appeal of a specific boat is as individual as the person examining her. If you are prowling the docks and boatyards, trying to decide which boat is right for you and frustrated by the vast array of boats available, I suppose you would welcome a list of the "ten best" used boats to buy.

However, this is a *skills* book with the premise that if you master a skill, you can easily adapt it to your particular project. You will not find in these pages, for example, construction plans for *the* dish box. What good would that be? I don't know if you have Melamine for two or Wedgwood for twelve; if the box will be hidden away or a prominent feature of the galley; if it will be horizontal or vertical, or if it lies against a straight bulkhead or the compound curvature of your hull. What I do know is that if you

1

Coronado 41: "She is not fair to outward view . . ."

can learn to visualize, plan, measure, cut, fit, glue, and finish, you can build the dish box that suits *your* needs.

In keeping with this premise, I will not mislead you with a consensus of the so-called *experts* of the "best" old boats. Best for what? There are just too many variables for such lists to have any validity. Instead, I have compiled a list of ten specific considerations that may be applied against any boat to help you determine if she is the *right* boat for you. They are: beauty, cost, use, quality, size, design, accommodations, rig, power, and condition.

BEAUTY

The boat you own should make your heart sing. As you dinghy away from her in the anchorage, she should hold your eye. She should stop you on the dock for one final gaze before you leave her, not to check but to admire. She should be the boat in your fantasy, the one anchored at the base of a verdant forest, tied stern-to in a tiny Mediterranean harbor, rolling off miles in the trades, carrying your family down the bay, leaving lesser sailors in your wake, or rafted with friends on the far side of the lake. In front of others she should make you feel inflated with a sense of pride; alone you should feel humbled by a sense of privilege. If she does not affect you this way, keep looking.

Perhaps it seems odd to you that beauty leads my list of boat selection criteria. Assuming that most boat purchasers intend to sail away from shore farther than they can swim back, shouldn't something like seaworthiness lead the list?

Let's understand this list, shall we? The boat you select should satisfy all ten considerations, seaworthiness included. The purpose of the list is to provide an orderly sequence to the evaluation process, not unlike measure, cut, fit, and glue in the carpentry process. Similarly, every step is required.

I lead the list with beauty because, for most of us, boating—sailing in particular—fills some kind of aesthetic need. There is nothing pragmatic about pleasure boating; it is entirely a romantic endeavor. If the sight of the boat you are considering does not quicken your pulse, she will ultimately prove unsatisfactory no matter how seaworthy, commodious, or practical.

Of course, the burning desire to get out on the water can be so strong that you would welcome any lump of a boat if she gets you out there sooner. That is a compromise you may choose to make, but remember that no matter how wisely the galley is redesigned, how natty the new canvas looks, or how shiny the refinished topsides, the one thing that stays the same will be her lines. If you are going to devote the time, effort, and money to restoring an old boat, pick one that merits your devotion.

COST

If owning a boat puts too great a strain on your budget and prevents you from doing other things that were previously an important and pleasurable part of your life, discontent with boating cannot be far behind. Buying too large a boat, too fancy a boat, or too complicated a boat leads far more quickly to discontent than buying too small, too plain, or too simple.

Because of statements similar to those in the previous paragraph, I have occasionally been referred to as a minimalist. Not true. I see nothing whatsoever wrong with owning the largest boat you can *both afford and use*. But if paying for her keeps you from the enjoyment of using her, either in the physical sense for lack of time, or in the mental sense from budget strain, what is the point?

Boating is a leisure time activity. It should

require only discretionary income, and not all of that. Maybe you think that if you only had the right boat, *you* would spend every free minute on the water. The odds are against you. Take a walk through any marina on a perfect Saturday and compare the number of empty slips to the number with boats still tied in them. I assure you that the owners of all those boats intended to use them every weekend, certainly every sunny weekend. What happened?

Reality. A sunny weekend is also perfect for tennis. Or golf. Or a cookout with friends. Or working on the lawn. Or a drive to Grandma's. There are also concerts and weddings, sporting events and sales. And there are weekends when it is rainy, or cold, or you just don't want to do anything.

Vacations aboard? Of course, but what about Yellowstone and Yosemite, Las Vegas and Disney World, the Rockies and the Alps, London and Paris, the Calgary Stampede and Mardi Gras, or Mom and Dad?

If living aboard is your objective, you can add housing costs into the equation. If you are preparing for an extended cruise, you might also commit additional dollars, but you should never lose sight of the fact that every dollar you spend unnecessarily on the boat either postpones or shortens the cruise.

For the rest of us there is a number that represents the dollars that we can sensibly commit to boating. Aside from the cost of the boat, those dollars must also be sufficient to pay monthly dockage or storage fees, insurance, fuel, and upkeep, with some money left over to fund the cost of restoration and enhancement. You must be scrupulously honest in determining what that number is for you, and equally vigilant in holding the line in the ensuing search for a boat that fits your budget constraints.

There is a tendency to let the ceiling creep up, to look at incrementally more expensive boats in the search for just the right boat. The most effective way to combat this is to avoid boats priced above your limit, but since there is often a big difference in the asking price of a used boat and her ultimate selling price, it may be unwise to overly restrict

Typical marina scene on a perfect day for boating.

yourself. The risk is that the cost of the boat you choose will not be sufficiently negotiable to meet your budget requirements. If this happens to you, you may be able to lower the monthly cost with longer-term financing, electing a mooring rather than a dock, or some other creative action. If not, keep looking. There are a slew of old boats out there.

USE

The Miami-bound plane was still climbing through the clouds over Atlanta when the well-dressed guy in 11-G noticed the sailing magazine I was reading and struck up a conversation. In his second sentence, he told me that he had just bought a new sailboat. His breathless urgency to share that news with a total stranger marked the purchase as a BIG EVENT.

I asked the obvious question and from his briefcase he produced a color brochure for a Valiant 40.

A bluewater boat. I reconsidered my accent-based assumption and asked if he lived in south Florida.

"No," he drawled. "Atlanta."

"And where," I inquired, "will the boat be kept?"

"Lake Lanier."

Lanier is a long, inland lake rarely more than three miles wide, hardly a challenging body for a 40-foot cruising boat. In a few years, he told me, he *hoped* to be able to go cruising and he wanted to have the boat to do it in. Meanwhile, he had saddled himself with a boat that was ill-suited for the kind of sailing that he *would* be doing.

An extreme example? Not really. We often make our selection more on the kind of boat we want rather than how we intend to use her. My frequent-flyer friend wanted a "real" cruising boat even though he knew his sailing would be limited to weekends on a lake. In my own marina is a dynamite little racer whose enamored owner cannot understand why his wife and daughters have lost interest in spending cramped weekends aboard. And there is a heavy, steel ketch, built to survive a navigational oversight in reef-strewn waters, but which leaves the dock only once a year for the yard where her live-aboard owners wage a mechanical and chemical war against rust, corrosion, and electrolysis.

Before you begin looking at boats, you should know how you will use the one you select. Will you be racing, cruising, daysailing, or entertaining at the dock? Do you see yourself creaming along on sunny days or squinting into rain and spray with your feet planted on the coaming? Will you be sailing to St. Louis, St. Michaels, St. Thomas, or St. Helena?

Be wholly truthful with yourself, but—are you watching?—here comes the sleight of hand. Don't be too certain that you know the whole truth. Until you have eaten the meal, how can you know which course you prefer? A fast boat may arouse in you a competitiveness that you did not know existed. A capable boat may tempt you far beyond imagined horizons. A commodious boat may lead you to forsake shore life altogether.

Of course the boat you choose should be suitable for the use you anticipate, but utility is not a particularly good selection criterion. As quintessential yachtsman Arthur Beiser has sagely observed, you're not buying a truck. Allow your imagination into the equation. What kind of boating do you *want* to do? My traveling companion from Atlanta let this consideration dominate his decision. I would have counseled him to buy a boat more suitable for sailing on the lake, waiting to buy a heavy cruiser until he had a better grasp of how cruising might fit into his life, but if owning a bluewater boat keeps the dream alive for him, then I would be wrong.

The best approach, I think, is to give your imagination a free rein or, more accurately, a long rein, but not longer than three or four years. If you think there is even the slight possibility that you may sail for the South Seas within the next three years, by all means buy a boat capable of taking you there. But if the realities of work and mortgages and family have you thinking more in terms of a few weekends away, even though you may be dreaming of a voyage someday, the best boat to buy now is one that maxi-mizes the enjoyment you will get from the boating you anticipate doing now. Maximizing enjoyment is, after all, what boating is about.

QUALITY

Determining the true quality of a boat is not always a simple matter. You can inspect the boat, looking for obvious clues like broken or replaced deck hardware, undersize rigging and attachments, rusting and corroding metal fittings, springy decks, gelcoat blisters, hull and deck separation, or evidence of water below. But the worst sins are often hidden behind attractive joiner work or a glossy inner liner.

One of the benefits of buying an older boat, particularly a stock boat that has been produced a hundred, two hundred, or five hundred times is that a lot of inspection has already been done. And most of the chronic problems will have already surfaced. Consequently, the boat will have a reputation.

Talking with owners of the kind of boat you are considering will help you to ascertain that reputation. Locally, you can find them by spending a few weekends prowling the docks. If you are using a broker, he may be able to come up with the names and telephone numbers of recent purchasers. For a broader cross section, try writing to the "Another Opinion" column in *Cruising World* magazine.

Owners can provide valuable information about quality (and other things, such as speed), but their opinions are just that—opinions. The more owners you talk with, the more accurate will be the picture that emerges. Ask why they selected this particular boat, what other boats they considered, and why those were rejected. (Some of the other boats may be on your list of considerations.) It will also be valuable to find a couple of former owners who will likely not feel the same sense of loyalty that may be coloring the opinions of current owners.

Magazine evaluations can also provide valuable information about the quality of a particular boat, but keep in mind that because magazines are dependent upon advertising dollars, they almost never run a negative evaluation. Sometimes (but not always) you can learn more from what was not said than from what was. One notable exception is the "Used Boat Survey" done by *Practical Sailor*. Since *Practical Sailor* is a consumer-type publication without advertising, its evaluations are generally more candid.

It may be obvious that if you want to buy a boat to win races in a series, you will first determine what kind of boats are collecting the silver. Less obvious is the application of this same logic when your interest in boating is more cruise oriented. Read as much as you can, both books and magazines, about the kind of cruising you want to do, and pay attention to kinds of boats already out there doing it. Don't consider just the authors' boats, but examine the accompanying photos and try to identify the other boats in the harbor. Unlike racing boats where you will get a feel for relative performance, the repeated appearance of a particular type of cruising boat in the text and photos of cruising literature is a fair barometer of quality.

Remember that we are not talking about condition. Quality has only to do with the materials and workmanship that went into the original construction of the boat, not with how she has been maintained.

The purchase of a boat of poor quality, regardless of how fast, spacious, or pretty she is, or how well her cheap price fits into your limited budget, is *always* a mistake. In the first place, if the boat suffers a major failure, you cannot simply walk home. And even if your luck holds on that score, such a purchase is a bad financial decision. While improvements made to a quality boat typically add more value than their cost, the money you spend on a bum boat, no matter how well considered and beautifully executed your improvements are, does nothing to alter the boat's reputation and will have little, if any, impact on the resale value. You really will be throwing money into a hole in the water.

When you have narrowed the field and start asking about a particular boat, if you don't consistently hear "great," or at least "good," no matter how attractive *you* find the boat, pass her by. You can't make a silk purse from a sow's ear.

SIZE

In America, we like BIG. We like big houses, even if the mortgage puts our health at risk and the only time we go into some of the rooms is to clean them. We like big cars, even if they cost us twice as much to get us from Point A to Point B, are difficult to wrestle through increasingly congested traffic or into compact parking spaces, and squander limited natural resources. We watch big heroes on our big-screen televisions. Even our elected officials wear lifts and stand on boxes to be big enough to get our votes. Big is good. Small is less.

Listen up. There are some very good reasons for buying a big boat. Space is one. If you have a family of six, you are not likely to find long-term contentment with a 19-foot Typhoon. Ditto if you want all your friends to join you in various ports around the world. Or if you want to have the board of directors aboard for cocktails.

Speed may be another reason. The bigger the boat, the faster she should be. The maximum hull speed of a displacement boat is generally calculated by multiplying the square root of the waterline length by 1.34. Using this formula, we can determine that in ideal sailing conditions, a 30-foot sailboat with a 24-foot waterline will have a hull speed of 6.6 knots while a 40-footer with a 32-foot waterline will be almost exactly 1 knot faster. In a race, the bigger boat will cross the finish line first, although on corrected time the smaller boat may be declared the winner. The big boat also will reach a cruising destination first, but my guess is that *most* weekend destinations are less than 20 miles away. That means that the crew of the 40-footer will still be setting the anchor when the smaller boat arrives. An extra knot may be very important for long passages, but if weekend cruising is your objective, fractionally higher hull speed is not going to be a very persuasive argument for selecting a larger boat.

A persuasive argument *can* be made on the basis of comfort. Greater interior volume allows for more shorelike accommodations—regular beds, real chairs, a kitchen-size galley. The larger the boat, the more likely it is to have an auxiliary generator. This opens the door to air conditioning, microwave ovens, color televisions and VCRs. For liveaboard comfort, there is no substitute for space.

Comfort offshore is another advantage of big boats. The bigger and heavier the boat, the slower and more comfortable will be her motion at sea. Do not confuse this *seakindliness* with *seaworthiness*. Seaworthiness is a function of design and construction, not size.

Often the consideration having the most sway is status. If you are buying a boat to impress your friends, particularly non-boating friends, buy the biggest boat you can afford. Period. Big impresses.

There are some equally compelling reasons to buy a small boat. The obvious one is cost. A quick comparison of listings will disclose that a 40-footer costs three times as much as a 30- footer of equivalent design and quality. And beyond the purchase price, the smaller boat will be cheaper to operate, cheaper to dock, cheaper to maintain, and cheaper to insure.

Ease of handling is another advantage of a small boat. Alain Colas raced the 235-foot *Club Mediterranee* across the Atlantic singlehanded, and a lot of cruising couples are competently plying the world's oceans in 50-footers and larger, but don't let anyone convince you that a "properly rigged" 50-footer is as easy to handle as a 25-foot boat. 'Taint so, McGee, and you know it. Think about getting the main down and furled in a squall. Will it be easier to deal with 150 square feet of 5-ounce cloth or 600 feet of board-stiff 10-ounce? Right. Which one would you prefer to sail to the dock? And if you blunder into shallow water, which boat will be easier to get afloat?

Speaking of shallow water, smaller boats will take you a lot of places that a larger boat simply cannot reach. If your sailing area is shallow, draft will be a major consideration, and all things being equal, smaller boats have shallower draft.

Simplicity may be the biggest advantage of a small boat. Larger boats are, almost by definition, more complex, and every additional winch, pump, and head requires attention. Besides the smaller boat having fewer such complications, the maintenance and repair jobs that are necessary will be smaller, thus requiring less time. If your primary objective is spending the maximum time on the water, you should consider buying the smallest boat that will safely carry you and your crew to your intended destinations.

DESIGN

If your objective is speed, you want a design that minimizes wetted area. If you are going offshore, you want a hull that has plenty of reserve buoyancy in the ends. If you plan to live aboard, internal volume is a prime concern. *All* production designs are a compromise, an attempt to strike a balance between speed and comfort, between upwind and downwind abilities, between light air performance and heavy-weather competence, between responsiveness and ease of handling, between function and beauty.

In the search for an appropriate old boat, some design considerations are fairly obvious. For example, the lack of directional stability inherent in most fin-keel designs will have the helmsman (or the autopilot) working constantly, which may not be a problem if you are racing on Wednesday nights, but is a point to keep in mind if long passages are in your future. If your sailing will be in an area of typically light air, bypass heavy-displacement boats. Conversely, if you are planning a long cruise, the weight of the necessary equipment and supplies will severely compromise the performance of a light-displacement hull. But what about features with less obvious implications? Are full bilges better than slack ones? Are overhangs good or bad? Is a canoe stern more seaworthy than a transom? What about a reverse counter? Does a clipper bow offer advantages over a spoon bow? What about a plumb bow? What are the benefits and drawbacks of a centerboard? Of tumblehome? Of high freeboard?

Volumes have been written about the science and subtleties of yacht design. I don't want to discourage you from doing your homework before you select the design that is right for you, but the fact is that even the most knowledgeable naval architects occasionally turn out a design that far exceeds their expectations. The whole exceeds the sum of the parts. And it is the whole you are interested in.

Beyond a sense of light versus heavy and fin keel versus full keel, you do not *need* to predetermine what other hull features you should be searching for in a stock boat. The designer has already considered all the trade-offs and made choices based on how he expected the boat to be used. If he designed the boat to win races and she does, his choices—whatever they were—were correct.

You are interested in how successful the *whole* boat is, not in individual design features. Just be sure to select a design that has a history of being successfully used the way you want to use her.

ACCOMMODATIONS

For many years, I held onto a brochure for a 34-footer that proudly proclaimed "sleeps nine." It is not false advertising: the boat has two settees that each become a double berth, two pilot berths, a quarter berth, and a Vee-berth. But since there is no place left to stand when the settees are extended, I suppose everyone changes into their jammies out in the cockpit. And with nine people sharing one head, God help you if dinner disagrees with anyone.

You might have nine aboard if you were racing the boat, and the designers of the "racer/cruisers" of 25 years ago loaded the interior with bunks for that reason. But dealers soon discovered that how many people a boat "slept" was inevitably the first question of new buyers. More was better. The tendency to evaluate a boat based on the number of bunks she contains is ridiculous. Most of us would have difficulty comfortably accommodating eight guests in our homes, much less in a space smaller than a normal bedroom. (For Sale: Ranch style 3/2, sleeps 218.) Family cruising does require a bunk for every member, but it can be difficult enough keeping everyone interested in the enterprise without sleeping accommodations that are little more than a padded version of an old slave runner's hold.

How you evaluate accommodations will depend upon what kind of alterations you are willing to undertake. It is possible to strip the interior of an old boat of all furniture and bulkheads and reconstruct the accommodations to your own design. If that is your intention, then your only interests will be the volume of the cabin space and the structural limitations of the existing bulkheads. But very few choose this course, and for good reason: it can be enormously difficult and time-consuming.

More modest cabin modifications, remakes that require no bulkhead removal and, to the extent possible, use the existing furniture, are easily undertaken by almost anyone. And in most cases they make better sense. With such alterations in mind, the interior requires a better-considered evaluation. In later chapters, we will consider specific features in more detail, but in a general overview of accommodations, there are six main considerations: berths, seats, the galley, the head, atmosphere, and stowage.

The question is not how many berths there are, but if there are a sufficient number and if they are long enough. Location and width become considerations if you expect to use the berths while the boat is underway: sea berths should be narrow and located in the center or after part of the boat.

Berths often do double duty as settees, with mixed success. Since you will likely spend as much time below sitting as reclining, comfortable seating is imperative. If the layout is workable, ergonomically shaped cushions can be added to provide the comfort.

The longer you expect to be aboard, the more important the galley is. A good galley is compact, but with adequate counter space. A deep sink, a quality stove, and a well-insulated cold box are all pluses, but they are a matter of cost. Galley space that is inadequate or poorly located is much more difficult to correct.

The head compartment must either be workable or of adequate size to allow the necessary modifications to make it workable. In all but the smallest boats, that means the toilet must face forward or aft, not athwartship. The compartment should at least be large enough to pull your pants up without opening the door. A shower is an advantage only if the boat has ample water tankage to support it.

Atmosphere is important too, and by atmosphere, I mean light, air, and temperature. I have never been aboard a boat that was *too* bright below. The more portholes, the better, and if they all open, that is even better still. In warm weather, the more opening hatches the boat has, the cooler the cabin will be, and if they are transparent, or at least translucent, rainy days below will be far less gloomy. In cold weather, comfort will depend upon a safe and efficient source of heat.

All of the equipment essential to the operation of the boat should have space allocated for stowage; you should not have to share bunk space with it. There should also be space for cookware, dishes, linens, towels, clothes, food, fishing and diving gear, tools, spares, and the myriad other items that you will take aboard. The longer you intend to be away from the dock, the more stowage space you will need. You can make numerous modifications to make stowage more efficient, but only if the space is there to work with.

I cannot leave this subject without touching on safety. Adequate strong handholds, sturdy construction, and an absence of sharp corners will vastly reduce the likelihood of injury below. If these are not features of the boat you are considering, you will have to make the necessary modifications or look elsewhere.

Like hull design, the accommodation plan of a production boat is a series of compromises. There

Fixed portholes: It is 90 degrees outside--how hot is the cabin?

is almost nothing below that cannot be changed, within the constraints of the volume of space available, but the more closely the existing layout matches your concept of the ideal layout, the less money and effort you will spend in achieving that ideal.

RIG

If you are looking at production sailboats that are 15 years old or older, you are going to encounter two rigs—sloop and ketch—with a smattering of yawls and maybe a cutter or two thrown in to confuse the issue.

Conventional wisdom is that the sloop goes to weather better than the other rigs and is the least complicated. The ketch offers the advantage of breaking the sail area up into smaller, more easily managed sails, but it is not quite as efficient on the wind. The cutter accomplishes the same thing, but without the penalty in windward ability. No one is quite sure what the purpose of the yawl is. And schooners hang on because they make the heart go pitty-pat.

If you start your search with a driving partiality to a particular type of rig, unless it is a sloop or a ketch you are severely restricting your possibilities. If this preference is firmly based in your own experience, I won't try to change your mind. But if it is based on what you have read, or what your sailing friends tell you, listen up. Every type of rig has good points and bad points. When the architect matched a particular rig with his hull design, it was because he thought that rig was, on balance, the best for that boat. If you find a design that is right for your use, you will probably find the rig she carries satisfactory as well.

POWER

If you are looking for a powerboat, you probably know more about engines than I do. The vast majority of powerboats continue to be delivered with gasoline engines, despite the inherent danger. The reasons are higher speeds and lower prices, both compelling arguments in the power boat market.

In contrast, it is almost impossible to buy a new sailboat today with an inboard gasoline engine. That's good. A diesel is much better suited to the displacement speeds and infrequent use an engine gets aboard a sailboat, and it is less likely to send you to the next life.

But most older production sailboats were delivered with gasoline auxiliaries because suitable small diesels were perceived as prohibitively expensive. Twenty years ago, the sailboat market was also race-oriented—even cruising boats were billed as racer/cruisers—and the considerable additional weight of diesel engines then available had a detrimental effect on performance under sail.

Many of the old Grays and Atomic Fours have gone on to motor heaven, often replaced by new generation, lightweight diesels. But in an old boat sitting forlornly in the back of the yard or neglected at a rickety dock—the kind of sound old boat that can be purchased at a bargain price—what is most likely to be found crouched over stale bilge water is the original gasoline engine.

That may not be all bad. The absence of a diesel is, in today's sailboat market, a major negative. Shrewd negotiations may achieve a price reduction sufficient to repower with a diesel. Even if the original gasoline engine has been well maintained and still seems to do its job well, any serious improvement plan will call for diesel power. Conversion is a major expense, a fact that you should have clearly in mind.

Of course, some of the boats built two decades ago did have diesel power. Robust and slow-turning, these engines, if well maintained, were designed to deliver at least 5,000 hours of service before requiring a major overhaul. To put this number in perspective, few weekend sailors log more than 200 hours annually, most less than 100. Consequently the diesel in a 20-year-old boat may have another 20 years left in it. If it does have a high number of engine hours, it should still be less expensive to rebuild than it is to repower, and far less complicated.

CONDITION

The previous nine considerations can be applied to all the boats of a specific type: if one Morgan 34 meets your requirements, then all 347 built meet them (allowing for some differences in interior layout, rig, and power). Condition, on the other hand, must be evaluated boat by boat.

Old boats vary widely in condition—from above improvement to above average to above water. The ones offered for sale will more often fall into the lower end of this spectrum.

There should be a direct relationship between condition and purchase price—the poorer the condition of the boat, the less she should cost. This is the relationship we are counting on when we choose to purchase an old boat rather than a new one. But the cheapest boat is not necessarily the best bargain. A great deal depends upon exactly what is wrong with the boat. Before you purchase any boat, she should be thoroughly surveyed, and you should have a close estimate of what it will cost to correct every major deficiency. Otherwise, what appears to be a terrific bargain can turn into a very costly mistake.

A close friend of mine owns a boat-painting business. Regularly he is asked to estimate the cost to refinish the hull and the deck of someone's just-purchased old boat. When the painting estimate turns out to be higher than the purchase price, more than the hull suddenly loses its gloss. Of course, as we will see in a later chapter, the cost of painting a boat does not have to be astronomical if you do it yourself, but you should know how you are going to deal with every *major* deficiency and the approximate cost *before* you buy the boat.

A professional survey is usually money well spent. When you find a boat that captures your imagination, you may be inclined to overlook her flaws. There is nothing like a written survey report to drag you back down to earth. The survey can also be a good bargaining tool. The psychology of a "subject to survey" contract is such that the seller is often willing to pick up the repair tab on significant survey findings in order to keep the deal alive. And if you plan to insure the boat, most underwriters will require a recent survey anyway.

With a big enough bank account, virtually any old boat can be reconditioned, but few of us have such deep pockets. Your objective here is to end up with the most boat for the smallest investment—in both money and time. An accurate assessment of the initial condition of any boat you are considering is essential if you are to meet that objective.

When you find the boat that best satisfies all ten selection criteria, buy her. Then give the left side of your brain a rest. It is time to close your eyes and contemplate the possibilities that your new boat will present to you.

TWO

The Dream

*Many men go fishing all their lives without
knowing that it is not fish they are after.*
–THOREAU–

Let's get started. The concept of this book is the transformation of *your* old boat—but into what? That determination does *not* begin with assessing the condition of the gelcoat, or choosing a color for the new sail covers, or buying new cabin lamps. You will eventually get to all of those things, but before you decide *what,* you need to know *why.* I realize that a dull finish, frayed canvas, and poor lighting answer the "why" for those items; that is not the why I am talking about.

THE INITIAL QUESTION—WHY?

Why did you decide on this boat? Broader, why buy *any* boat? Broader still, why do you want to be out on the water at all? Forget about the boat as an object. What does it represent? Exactly how do you expect your life to be enhanced by boating? You have spent your money, perhaps a lot of money, on a boat and now you are about to reach even deeper into your pockets. Why?

Ancient man got involved in boating by some compelling need to get to the other side of some body of water. It is not difficult to imagine Og and his tribe starving on one side of a river while game drank along the opposite shore. When one of Og's lowbrow clan noticed a log floating across the water, the rest was, as they say, history.

We still use boats to get to the other side, but presumably the *why* for you is more than that. Most Americans buy boats for recreation, more specifi-cally as a diversion for weekends. Boating is a counterpoint to the demands of the week, a way to "get away," a source of fun. You, no doubt, answered part of the *why* when you decided on the type of boat you would buy. If you imagined yourself out at daybreak, trailing enough fishing lines to keep the transom in shade, your choice of boat was different than it might have been had you pictured yourself driving the bow through a shower of diamonds on a fast close reach, or cutting the dawn chill with a mug of steaming coffee in some distant, fogbound cove.

Not that a single boat cannot be used in different ways, but if your primary interest was fishing, you bought a fishing boat; if it was sailing, you bought a sailboat; and if it was cruising, you bought a cruising boat. Those are pretty straightforward choices, but they still do not answer the total *why.* What is your underlying agenda? Besides "fun," what is it that you want from your boat? Let's look at some of the possibilities and how they might affect your enhancement plan.

Differing Requirements

Boats are often purchased in the hope that boating will be an activity that the entire family can enjoy together. It is an admirable objective. The concept of boating as a family activity, something more than a Sunday afternoon on the water, suggests more than just an adequate number of bunks. Does every member have some space of his or her own? Can meals be as good as (or better than) those at home? Is the boat a comfortable platform for *each*

12

family member's favorite water activity — swimming, fishing, scuba diving, and sailboarding? Can a family member especially sensitive to the sun find shade? Can "best friends" be accommodated?

In contrast, maybe your boating is a solitary activity, an opportunity to spend time alone. Is the boat easily singlehanded? Are the items important to your comfort close at hand? With no assurance of assistance, is your personal safety adequately addressed?

Perhaps you expect your boat to serve as your "summer cottage." Small shortcomings, easily ignored on weekends, will have to be corrected. Is there adequate space for clothes? For food? Are you (and everyone else aboard) giving up television for the summer? What about videos? Your hair dryer? Your computer? Is refrigeration a requirement? Do you expect to have guests?

Forsaking brick and mortar to move aboard permanently raises requirements to another level. Is your "bed" better than adequate? Can the head accommodate daily ablutions for everyone aboard? Is there room for *all* of your clothes? Can you roast a Christmas turkey? Keep ice cream? Host a formal dinner? Stay warm in winter? Cool in summer? Are you an architect? Or a pianist?

Long-term cruising brings a different set of priorities. Self-sufficiency becomes the watchword. Can you carry ample water? Fuel? Tools and spare parts? Does generating capability exceed power consumption? Can you get the anchors up in adverse conditions? Can you stay dry underway? Do you have adequate ventilation?

If you imagine your boat anchored in the Papetoai Bay, beneath the verdant peaks of Moorea, new priorities emerge. Can the hull stand the rigors and uncertainty of the open ocean? What about the mast and rigging? Is the deck joint strong and watertight? Are there good sea berths? Is the galley serviceable at 30 degrees of heel? On both tacks? Can the dodger shed green water? Are the cockpit drains large enough?

It is essential that you understand your own motivation. The same old boat can be transformed into a weekender, a floating home, or a world cruiser, but the modifications necessary are substantially different in each case.

Around-the-World Misconception

Too many boat owners, sailors in particular, believe that if the modifications that they make are guided by the requirements for ocean voyaging, by virtue of such intense preparation the boat will handle the lesser demands of more modest use in a superior manner. Wrong!

Part of the reason for this fallacious belief probably has to do with boating literature. There are not a lot of books on library shelves about weekend cruising. Almost all are about voyaging, typically about circumnavigating, this despite the fact that the overwhelming majority of sailors will never attempt anything more daring than an overnight passage in fair weather. But we *read* to go beyond what we *do,* and publishers know that a book titled, for example, *Between Hell and High Water: Rounding Cape Horn* will probably sell much better than *A Perfect Day on Biscayne Bay.*

The authors of all these voyaging books are anxious to share with the reader the lessons learned during their adventure. (If you are preparing to take off for the South Seas, you would be wise to study as many of these accounts as you can.) And while their opinions on specific issues vary, many of the lessons of voyaging are universal — the need for adequate rest, the need for tasty and nourishing meals, the need to stay dry, the need to keep the mast up, the need for hull, deck, hatch, and porthole integrity, the risk of a large cockpit, and so on. A kind of dogma has resulted that dictates much of what the sailing public sees as "proper."

As a result, sea berths may occupy the best space aboard even though the owner never intends to take the boat outside of the Chesapeake; a side galley may be rejected out of hand without considering how rarely it may actually see use underway (or the fact that it may be ideal in every instance except one tack); or a doghouse may be added without regard to the detrimental effect it has on performance or on

Books about ocean voyaging crowd the shelves.

the exhilaration of the breeze in your hair during a brisk afternoon sail.

Matching Function and Feature

The requirements of a yacht intended for more modest use are not just less; they are different. For long passages, additional tankage for water and fuel may be a desirable modification. On a coastal cruise, extra tanks will only forestall an occasional marina stop, and for weekending additional tankage has no value at all. Meanwhile the tanks add weight if they are full, and waste space if they aren't.

Converting drawers in the main cabin to easily accessible stowage for a broad array of tools is not a bad concept for the sailor heading off on an extended cruise. But for weekends aboard with children, convenient toy stowage will yield greater benefits.

Good sea berths do take on extreme importance if the boat will be underway for more than 36 hours. A "good" sea berth is always a single berth, however, and does little to contribute to connubial bliss aboard. On most boats, even cruising boats, a com-fortable double berth will contribute far more than a sea berth toward making the time aboard pleasant.

Few voyagers headed for the remote atolls of the South Pacific would give the installation of a microwave oven a second thought—occupies too much space, requires too much power, and what would you cook in it anyway? Yet aboard the same boat in Marina Del Rey, serving as home to a professional couple, is there any other galley enhancement with more benefit potential?

This yuppie couple may lament limited space in the hanging lockers, perhaps finding a way to augment the boat's "closet" space. Aboard the voyaging sister ship, the effect on clothes left hanging for a 2,000-mile passage can be approximated by running them in a tumble dryer for about three weeks. The space occupied by the hanging locker is better utilized for some other purpose.

Even if your dream *is* running down your westing in the trades, resist modifications that are not compatible with the kind of boating you are doing now until you have a time frame in hand. Concentrate on projects that enhance your current activity. Besides offering a better short-term return, the quality of your later improvements will benefit from the delay, both in concept and in execution. As your boating objectives evolve or solidify, deficiencies and weaknesses will surface in both the boat and your planned changes, siring new and better improvement ideas.

If shortcomings are serious enough, they may lead you back into the marketplace. If this is your first boat, keep in mind that almost no one finds long-term contentment with his initial selection. The first-boat ownership experience is on-the-job training. Some learn well and their second boat becomes a fixture of their lives for half a century; others change boats like calendars. Whatever the case, embarking upon too ambitious a program before you have spent sufficient time with your old boat risks wasting the effort.

QUESTION NUMBER TWO – WHAT?

Once you have answered *why,* it is time to think about *what.* Reconditioning can be as simple as cleaning and painting, as complex as dismantling and reconstructing. The time required may be little more than a weekend, little less than a lifetime. You may choose to restore, modify, or completely redesign.

A restoration suggests that you have found a boat that fits your dream in virtually every detail. No design improvements are required and you are only interested in bringing the boat back to new condition. A true restoration, one motivated by a sense of history, can be an arduous undertaking because of the difficulty of locating suppliers for replacement parts identical to the originals. Here I use restoration in a less restrictive sense to indicate that the design of the boat is unaltered and improvements are cosmetic or reparative in nature.

Modification is a more likely path. You have chosen a particular boat because you like most of her features but there are a few things that you would like to change. You find the standing rigging too light for your intended use. The gasoline engine is unacceptable. You favor a wheel over a tiller. Lockers need shelves and dividers. You prefer additional galley space to a second quarterberth. You want refrigeration rather than an ice chest.

When the number and extent of your modifications become extreme, you have crossed the threshold from modification to redesign. A few features of the boat hold great attraction – hull shape and performance, perhaps – but you find much of the rest of the design ill-suited for your intended use. You might also be trying to make do with the boat you already own, a course shaped mostly by economics. In either case, you are willing to make extensive changes to the boat, restrained only by structural limitations and your own ability.

How you label your efforts is not that important. We are more concerned that you not limit yourself with some arbitrary restriction on your abilities. In the dream stage, assume that you can do anything. Can't make that leap yet? Then imagine yourself as a modest winner in the state lottery. (Not the top prize – I don't want you flying off to Finland to place your order for a new Swan.)

Generating a List

Time to get specific. With the picture of your "perfect day on the water" held clearly in your mind, write down every change that occurs to you to fit your old boat into that picture. Don't trust the fruit of this deliberation to your memory. You need a list, something you can physically look at, evaluate, manipulate, refer back to. I like a spiral-bound notebook for this purpose, but whatever you use, capture every want and idea permanently on paper.

Get all your senses involved. Do you *see* the wavering, luminous plaid of light reflecting from the hull? Write down "paint hull." Do you *hear* the reassuring diesel throb reflected off wooded banks? Write down "new engine." Do you *feel* the tendrils of a warm breeze probing the half-sleep of an afternoon nap? Write down "cockpit cushions." Do you *smell* fresh bread baking in the galley? Write down "replace two-burner stove." Do you *taste* Greek table wine at a quayside cafe in Corfu? Write down "rub rails."

Give your mind free reign. Write down everything that occurs to you. Don't worry about getting your thoughts into any kind of order—we will deal with that in the next chapter. For now, you just want to try to capture that picture in your mind. It might help to spend a couple of hours aboard.

Walk around the deck. Are the lifelines adequate? In good condition? What is the condition of the rigging? Are the anchors well stowed? Is there a good platform for handling ground tackle? Are the bow chocks adequate? What about the cleats? Are the running lights too small and ridiculously placed? Are there adequate strong handrails? Are the winches large enough and well placed? Is the cockpit comfortable? Is it protected from wind and spray? From too much sun? Is the nonskid nonskid? Is the canvas crisp and bright? Is the gelcoat in good condition? Is this old boat the same color as the one in your vision?

Go below. Did you have to step on the galley counter? Was your footing secure? Does the cabin feel open or gloomy? Does the layout work? Are there ample secure handholds? Are fixtures substantial enough to arrest a lurch, rounded enough to do it gently? Is the head accommodating or disgusting? Are the settees comfortable? Are the bunks large enough? Is there adequate counter space in the galley? Can you heat the cabin? Keep it cool? How is the lighting? Is there a great spot to sit and read? One for every crew member? Can you bake lasagna? Chill beer? Make ice? Where do the charts go? The fishing rods? Extra sails? Wet rain gear? Tools? The wok?

Open everything. Are the lockers efficiently divided or open maws? Are there proper seacocks on every through-hull fitting? Can you close them? Any signs of leakage? Can the drawers open accidentally? The locker doors? Does the chain locker drain into the Vee-berth? Are there spaces behind the furniture without access? Where is the wiring? Is the electrical panel neat and accessible? Is there good access to the engine compartment? What is the condition of the engine? Is the bilge clean or coated with black mayonnaise? Are the bilge pumps adequate?

Look around. What about aesthetics? Does it feel warm below or as cold as a hospital room? Is there adequate brightwork? Too much? Did the builder substitute wood-grain plastic laminate for honest veneer? Is there a liner? Is it attractive? Does the countertop show years of wear? Is it ugly? What about the upholstery? Good color? Good texture? Good quality? Good condition? Is the sole attractive? Safe? Are the cabin lamps unobtrusive or as eye-catching as a wart?

What should emerge from this exercise is a long and undisciplined list of everything about your old boat that you would like to repair, replace, change or improve. The list may get so long that it becomes paralyzing. Relax. This is not a contract. You are just trying to make sure that the changes you do make are the best ones. The more complete your list, the better.

THE THIRD QUESTION—HOW?

Knowing *what* you want to change is only half of the process. Exactly *how* do you want to change it? This step is considerably more difficult. Let's select at random a few of the deficiencies that may have surfaced in the previous exercise and see how you might go about determining the best solution.

Take anchor handling, for example. Scratches and gouges in the hull at the bow are clear evidence that you need a better way to get the anchor back aboard. But how?

The molded-in nonskid on the deck wasn't all that great when it was new, but now it is downright dangerous. How do you correct it?

There are seven bunks below, but barely counter space for one pot and a salt shaker in the galley. Somehow the cabin space needs to be apportioned better. How?

Every seacock aboard is frozen or it leaks, or both. Can they be reconditioned or is replacement

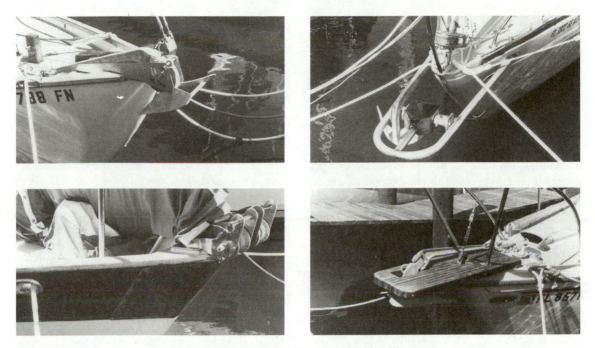

The docks offer numerous ideas for anchor handling.

the only alternative? There are several types now; how do you determine which type to install?

Every bulkhead is surfaced with wood-grain plastic laminate and you hate it. (So do I.) How can you eliminate it?

It is time to reupholster below. Will your favorite color go with varnished mahogany? Should the pattern be large or small, or should you select a solid? How do you choose the kind of material?

There are answers to all of these questions. In some instances the answer is clear-cut, black-and-white, the only appropriate conclusion. In others your course of action will hinge entirely upon your own preference. Often past experience will provide the answer, particularly if you are not new to boating. For novice and old salt alike, common sense can point you in the right direction. But when you are not sure that you know the answer, or that your answer is the best one, where do you find the answers you need? There are numbers of very good sources.

Looking at Other Boats

Try the docks. Walking out the finger piers of a sizeable marina can be an enlightening experience. Get a specific problem in mind and go for a stroll to see how others have solved it. Take your anchor scarred bow, for example. As you walk along the dock, you will see a broad array of individual solutions to the very same problem. Will a bow roller work on your boat, or does an anchor davit seem like a better idea? Is a bowsprit a possibility, or perhaps an anchor platform? If all of these appurtenances seem likely to spoil the sweet lines of your classic, keep looking. You will probably see at least one boat with an anchor lining, a polished stainless sheathing at the bow to protect the hull from the anchor.

The docks don't offer much help for below-deck problems unless you can get invited aboard other boats—not that that is all that difficult. Meeting as many other owners as you can will provide you with the opportunity to go aboard various boats to see how they are laid out, equipped, and adorned. And other owners are always willing to share their insight on a particular subject. One word of caution: sailors are notoriously opinionated, and sometimes the most opinionated are the least informed. Always get a second opinion, preferably from someone whose knowledge and judgment you trust.

Another way of going aboard a lot of boats is to attend a boat show. While I am not so sure that boats have made substantial improvements in the quality of construction over the last couple of decades, there can be no doubt that there have been some design improvements. Almost all of them can be adapted to an older boat. The trick is not to just think, "Wow, what a great idea!" but rather, "How can I adapt this to my own boat?"

Pearls in Print

A third source of ideas is books, including this one. In later chapters, as we develop each skill, we will consider a number of ways to use that skill toward the enhancement of your boat. The number of potential projects I have included is considerable,

The best time to go to a boat show is when you already own a boat.

but by no means exhaustive. In bookstores, marine stores, and libraries you will find numerous other volumes, all with the potential to have just the right solution to a specific deficiency of your old boat.

Magazines are another excellent source of ideas. Most boating magazines run a number of articles every year on maintenance and improvement projects, often providing step-by-step instructions. Many even have monthly columns detailing enhancement projects. The photographs that accompany the other, nontechnical articles provide an opportunity to examine a vast number of boats, each photo revealing features that you may want to adapt. In addition, manufacturers often tout new design features in their advertising. An afternoon spent with a stack of boating magazines can be very productive, indeed.

If you are not yet familiar with catalog suppliers of marine equipment, take time out now to become familiar with them. They can provide you with a broad array of items that you may be unable to obtain locally, and often they can do so at discount prices. Just as important, they are an endless source of ideas. The most common boat problems have almost all been addressed commercially, and those solutions are illustrated and offered for sale in the various catalogs—items such as solar-powered ventilators for your mildew problem, attractive and efficient cabin lamps, teak bookshelves, nonskid deck covering, refrigeration conversions, and brushable urethane paints. Snap-apart hinges, Y-valves, and deck plugs may kindle your own original solutions.

Material Answers

Materials can stimulate ideas. Wood is one of the most inspiring. Learning to shape, smooth, and finish wood has led many a person into woodworking as a lifelong leisure-time activity. With a few shop tools, the possibilities are unlimited, but even with no more than common hand tools, a block of wood can be shaped into a piece of furniture or a work of art. Plywood is less inspirational, but no less useful. Bulkheads, fixtures, counters, and shelves are easily fabricated from a sheet of plywood. Wood veneer can change an unremarkable surface into a thing of beauty.

Plastics do not enjoy the same reverence as wood, but in many applications no other material works as well. Fiberglass boats are more appropriately called glass-reinforced plastic. With a can of polyester or epoxy resin and a piece of glass cloth, you can repair a fiberglass hull, strengthen it, or attach virtually anything to it. Plastic laminates (Formica and others) are available in an incredible array of colors and patterns, providing an attractive and extremely durable covering for counters and other flat surfaces. Clear acrylics are the only choice for portholes, and the best choice for hatches because of the light they introduce below. Dark acrylic doors

can modernize a dated galley, and plastic mirrors can be used to expand a cabin.

As incongruous as it may sound, a walk through a good scrap metal yard can fire the imagination. Aluminum round stock might be just the thing to replace those rotten spreader tips. A bin of stainless tubing may suggest a custom-fabricated boarding ladder. A stack of sheet brass could prompt a solution to wear spots on the cap rail.

Chemicals such as cleaners, paints, and varnishes suggest their own use. As do soft goods—leather, rubber, carpet, and fabric. Acrylic canvas, for example, is virtually the only material used to make sail covers and spray dodgers, and for good reason. It is strong, it resists rot, mildew, water,

Boating magazines full of fresh ideas abound.

fading and ultraviolet damage, it dries quickly, it is easy to sew, it comes in bright colors, and it looks damn nice. Considering these characteristics, it is not hard to imagine other uses for acrylic canvas. We will examine several possibilities in a later chapter.

Serendipity

The ancient Romans recognized one more source of ideas with the proverb, *mater artium necessitas* – necessity is the mother of invention. A musician friend moved aboard a 27-footer with no fewer than three guitars. Tired of moving them every time he wanted to sit down, he was at a loss for a good solution – until one awakened him in the middle of the night. The next day he attached padded chocks to the underside of the foredeck, above the Vee-berth, and strapped the instruments in place. Easily accessible yet safe and completely out of the way, it was a harmonious solution in every way. Odd requirements and unusual problems often suggest their own solutions if you keep your mind open to them.

In this chapter, I have tried to get you to unleash your imagination, to let your dream drive your actions. Your specific expectations from boating are unique, and the better you understand them, the easier it is to distinguish between boat features that contribute and those that detract.

Examining the specific features of your boat in the light of your own expectations should have led to a comprehensive list of deficiencies. The search for the best way to address each of those deficiencies does not end with the end of this chapter. Much of the remainder of this book offers ideas for your consideration. And new ideas appear every day – on other boats, in magazines, in books, in your daily routine.

Having determined *why, what,* and, at least in some cases, *how,* it is time to address the fourth question: *When?*

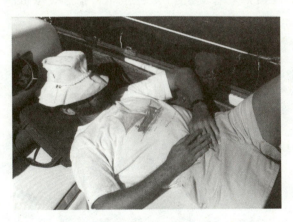

Keeping an open mind.

THREE

The Plan

You must know for which harbor you are headed
if you are to catch the right wind to take you there.
–SENECA–

Examining your boat from stem to stern is not a bad plan, but reconditioning it in that order leaves much to be desired, especially if the work will take place over a lengthy period of time. In this chapter, we will try to bring a plan to the project.

I have known sailors, wealthy to a man, who have had a classic old boat professionally reconditioned, but most of us would find the expense prohibitive. The plan we will be developing is based on the assumption that you do not intend to have your yard do all the work in a matter of a few weeks. This is not exactly clairvoyance. You surely did not come to this book just so you could make sure the yard was doing it right. Holding down the cost is, at the very least, almost always one of the attractions of buying an older boat. For a lot of sailors it may be the main attraction.

BAD ORDER

If you are among this last group – don't feel bad, you have plenty of company – there is a tendency to do projects in dollar order, getting what the pop culture calls the most bang for the buck. This is a self-defeating course of action. When you first start the work, you will be bubbling with enthusiasm, and the frequent gratification of completing improvements keeps that enthusiasm stoked. As time drags on, the same high level of enthusiasm becomes more and more difficult to maintain. And just when you could most use the encouragement of moving closer to completion, the remaining items on the list will be those requiring more and more money, increasing the time between visible signs of progress. There is a very real risk of losing interest in the project altogether.

Limited time can lead to a parallel tendency to do the "easiest" tasks – those requiring the least amount of time – first. (The most kick for the tick?) And for similar reasons, this scheme will make the project increasingly difficult to complete.

A BETTER PLAN

I am not suggesting that you forgo a quart of varnish, a brass barometer, or a new sail cover while you save up for a new engine. Nor am I saying that doing a two-hour project when you have just two hours to devote is a bad plan. Clearly, both money and time will have an influence, but there are other considerations.

Safety is one. If the swaged end fittings on the shrouds are cracked, replacing them tops the list regardless of the potential cost or time required. The same applies to fragile lifelines, a faulty bilge pump, a loose rudder, or frozen seacocks. The first rule of boating is don't screw around with safety. We all have an inclination, especially when money is tight, to spend what is available on things we expect to add to our pleasure rather than on preventive measures or on items we never expect to use. To give in to that inclination is to risk your boat, your life, and the lives of those who sail with you.

The season is another consideration. I don't necessarily mean summer and winter, although on a day when even the mercury has better sense than to venture out of the bulb at the bottom of the thermometer, painting the hull is probably not a good idea. Weather aside, the season I am referring to is the boating season. Why deprive yourself of the opportunity to take advantage of those perfect weekends by decommissioning your boat in the heart of the season? Concentrate on items that allow you to work on the boat and use her, too, saving incapacitating projects for the off season. This is an especially strong consideration if your boat sits in a cradle half the year anyway; but even where the weather allows boating year-round, there will be months when it is typically too hot, too cold, too windy, or too something for boating. But not for boat work.

Special requirements are also a consideration. For example, a tricolor running light at the masthead can be installed from a two-blocked bosun's chair, but the anxiety factor is much lower if the mast is lying horizontally on horses. If rerigging plans call for pulling the stick later, put off the light installation until then. Similarly, the day *after* you have completed your annual bottom job and relaunched is not the time to realize that the Loran you planned to install requires a dedicated underwater ground plate.

These last two examples really illustrate a specific aspect of the broader concept of appropriate order. The building contractor makes sure that all plumbing lines are in place before pouring the concrete slab, that all wiring is complete before installing wallboard, that all painting is finished before laying carpet. We need to bring the same kind of order to reconditioning a boat. If oilcanning at the bow is a problem, strengthen the hull before you hide it behind some kind of ceiling. Water stains on interior joiner work should lead to finding and stopping the leak before revarnishing is contemplated. The icebox should be adequately insulated on all sides before the refrigeration system is installed. After the new cushion covers have been fitted is a bad time to wish for thicker foam.

It is this need for order that necessitates a plan.

You can take the helter-skelter list of desired changes from the previous chapter and let time, money, and whim determine the order of completion. Or you can organize the list, taking into consideration, in addition to time and money, the safety imperative, conflicting boating objectives ("a time to work, a time to play"), how each change relates to others on the list, and the importance of each to your vision. A little time spent now organizing the list can save you a great deal of irritation and disappointment later on.

OTHER BENEFITS

Besides order, there are at least four other reasons to develop a master plan. The most obvious one is to allow you to generate a valid estimate of the money you'll need. This is the time to find out the price tag of your unrestrained vision, not when the money runs out. If you add up the dollars now and the total shocks you, you can moderate the project, plan to stretch it out over a longer period of time, or come to grips with the reality and ante up. Go blindly forward only to be stranded by insolvency in the middle of the project and you have committed the metaphorical equivalent of impaling your boat on a reef. It is a matter of navigation.

Time estimates are just as important. Most owners of old boats never really complete the transformation—there are always a few more things to be done. An estimate of the total time required is not that crucial—except as it relates to impending plans like a cruise next year, or a growing or shrinking family. The time a specific enhancement will require *is* important. Can that new hatch be fitted and installed in a day, or will you have to devise some way to close the opening to weather and uninvited guests? If you start stripping and bleaching the brightwork, will you get the new varnish on before the end of the weekend? Will one week in the yard be long enough to do all the bottom work you have planned?

Estimating time is more difficult than estimating cost. You can look in a catalog for the price of a refrigeration system, but how do you know how long it will take to install? Your problem is particularly knotty if you have never done anything similar before. Still, when you consider a job, some time estimate will come to mind. The best advice I can give you is to multiply that number by 2½. Over the years, I have found that most boat owners (including *moi*) are ridiculously optimistic in estimating how quickly they can accomplish a new task, regardless of how experienced they may be in other aspects of boating. Make your best guess, then multiply it by 2½, and you usually won't be very far off. Keep a written record of estimates and actual times if you want to fine tune your estimating ability, but don't expect stopwatch accuracy.

A third reason for a master plan is to provide continuity over the long haul. A comprehensive reconditioning can easily stretch over months or years. The plan assures that modifications made 18 months from now will be just as consistent with your vision as those made today.

The fourth reason is to enhance your sense of accomplishment. A few years ago, I tried my hand at building a house. A unique design with no attic and no crawlspace, it necessitated running all the wiring inside the walls. On the first day I installed the breaker panel and felt pretty good. On the second day, I drilled dozens of holes in the wall studs and ran two circuits into the kitchen. On the third day there were three additional circuits, on the fourth a couple more.

By the end of the week, there were wires running all over the house and the results of my daily labor ceased to have any noticeable effect on the way the house looked. By the end of the second week, there was no joy in Mudville. In the third week, suicide seemed like the only way out. But while I was trying to decide whether the 14-gauge wire would take my weight or I should use the 10-gauge, I was suddenly finished.

When the things you are doing don't seem to move you any closer to achieving your vision, crossing out one more item on the master plan can provide much-needed positive reinforcement. I could have made my wiring job much more pleasant if I had listed all the circuits before I started and crossed

off each as I completed it. This ploy works so well on my own need for direct gratification that before I start any job, I break it down into elementary components and list them. As I cross off each step, that little boost of a visible accomplishment keeps me involved in the job until every item has been struck off.

ESTABLISHING ORDER

As important as these four additional functions of the master plan are, all could be accomplished almost as well with the random list of changes generated in Chapter 2. It is the need for bringing order to the project—for giving priority to safety concerns and emphasis to other significant changes, for accommodating interlocking relationships among the changes, and for reconciling time available with time required—that compels us to develop a more disciplined plan.

It is helpful at this point to think of your boat in terms of layers. The initial layer is the hull and deck, hatches and portholes, structural bulkheads, rigging, sails, and engine—those components central to the boat's integrity and essential for her to function. This is the basic *structure* of your boat.

The second layer is bonded, screwed, or bolted to the first. This layer includes built-in furniture and accommodations, appliances, lights, cleats, winches, handrails, electronics, and cushions. These *features* add comfort, versatility, and perhaps security.

The top layer is the finish—the gelcoat or paint on the hull and deck; the laminate on the bulkheads and counters; the oil or varnish on the teak; the fabric on the cushions. The *finish* layer has two functions: to preserve whatever is underneath and to improve its appearance.

Now with the list of desired repairs, modifications, and enhancements on one hand and a blank sheet with three columns labeled *structure*, *features*, and *finish* on the other, you are going to place every item on the list into one of these categories.

If your boat has a problem with the hull-to-deck joint, the planned repair goes in the *structure* column. If the porthole frames are badly corroded, their replacement is structural. The installation of a new hatch is structure. So is a new internal tank, or repairing or strengthening the hull. Rerigging, engine replacement, and new sails all go into the *structure* column.

Planning to add a new bow roller? Write it in the *features* column. Adding or replacing winches? Installing refrigeration? Converting the starboard quarterberth to a chart table and stowage? Dividing lockers? Adding bookshelves? New stove? Additional handrails? A spray dodger? All of these should find their way into the *features* column.

Painting the hull and varnishing the brightwork are obvious entries to the *finish* column. Less obvious perhaps is the installation of nonskid material on the deck. Or reupholstering the cushions. Or polishing the stainless and brass. A new cover for the mainsail goes into the *finish* column.

Distinctions among each of these categories—structure, features, and finish—are not always clear. For example, because of the implications of their failure, I am inclined to think of repair or replacement of seacocks as structural—an essential part of the hull. But a valid argument could be also be made for considering seacocks as a feature. Similarly, I would place the addition of a cockpit grating into the finish category, not unlike carpet on the cabin sole, but it might equally well be thought of as a feature.

For our purposes, these distinctions among the three categories are of no real importance. We are merely trying to divide and conquer, to break a long list into more manageable pieces. This choice of categories is intended to give some order to that division. Clearly, structural changes should happen first, refinishing last. If you consider the three columns, you should be able to conclude that, *generally*, the items in the first column should be addressed before those in the second column, those in the second column before those in the third. So if you think replacing a seacock belongs in column two, put it there. And if rearranging the layout seems more like a structural change than a change in features, by all means include it in the first column.

Although it is not apparent yet, we are on our way to developing a very simple matrix. Toward that objective, relabel the three columns *A*, *B*, and *C*. With your original list now divided into three groups, you already have a better handle on the project. Safety was one concern. Most items that represent a real risk to the boat should be in column *A*. Decommissioning was another concern. The items in columns *B* and *C* may involve significant inconvenience, but typically they will not put the boat completely out of service for very long. And while *all* the issues of appropriate order are not resolved, categorizing your list this way does point out many of them.

ASSIGNING PRIORITY

Okay, so you have brought some order to the list, but perhaps this is not the order you want to follow. Maybe you want to paint the hull first, before anything else. Maybe replacing the engine would be nice, but the old engine is running fine. Maybe you included a mizzen staysail on your list because the one on Irving Johnson's last *Yankee* looked nice, but unless you come into unexpected money you are not likely to actually spring for one. Fine. Taking into account your preferences is our next step.

For this step, you need an oversize sheet of blank paper—something about 18 inches to a side. Four sheets of typing paper taped together will serve. An inch or so down from the top draw a line across the sheet. Do the same an inch in from the left edge. These two lines give us a small margin for labeling. Now, with two horizontal lines and two vertical lines, divide the remaining blank area into nine more or less equal rectangles. In the margin down the left side, label the rows *A*, *B*, and *C*. (Look familiar?) In the top margin, label the columns *1*, *2*, and *3*.

The letters are obvious, but what about the numbers? They simply represent the priority, from first to third, that you assign to each item, regardless of category.

Specific improvements that you want to make

now will be listed in the first column. If painting the hull is a top priority for you, as you write it into the appropriate row (*C*), it goes in the first column.

Priority 2 items are somewhat less urgent. Still essential for satisfying your vision, their cost or the time required justifies a certain amount of delay. Or the reason for the change has not yet developed. A working gasoline engine might incline you to place your plan to install a new diesel into this group. It would be listed in the second block in row *A*.

Priority 3 means "someday." This is where that mizzen staysail that you think "would be nice" belongs. If your budget is very limited, any number of changes that occurred to you in imagining the possibilities may, in the harsh light of reality, belong in the third priority. And if your dream has a "someday" aspect—someday you are going to take your boat from the English Channel to the Mediterranean Sea through the canals of Europe—changes specifically for that purpose can wait for more concrete plans.

Go through your entire list and place every item in the appropriate box. You should end up with a sheet that looks similar to the one illustrated. Every item on your original list now has a two-character designation. Replacing a stranded forestay is an *A1* matter. An urgent desire to refinish the hull is a *C1*. Strengthening the bow for the rigors of Tierra del Fuego is probably an *A3*. For a San Diego based boat, a refrigeration conversion might be a *B2*, radar a *B3;* a San Francisco skipper is likely to reverse these priorities.

FINE TUNING

Converting the original list into a matrix like this serves two important functions. First, a picture of the most effective order for the project begins to emerge. *A1* items need to be done first, followed by *B1*, then *C1*, then *A2* and so on, ending with *C3*. Dependencies or direct relationships should always be vertical in the matrix, never diagonal. It makes no sense to have "redesign galley" in the *B2* block, and "relaminate countertop" in *C1*. Either the new

	PRIORITY		
	IMMEDIATE	LESS URGENT	SOMEDAY
	1	2	3
STRUCTURE A	New Forestay / New Tiller / Repair Damaged Stern / Replace Spreader Tips / Replace Chainplate - Port Upper / New Thru-Hull Fittings / Restitch Mainsail	New Mainsail / Convert to Roller Furling / New Cutlass Bearing / Replace Toe-Rails	Rub Strake / Water Tank Under V-Berth
FEATURE B	Rebuild Head / Larger Bilge Pump / Service Winches / Dish Rack / Anchor Platform / Install Dodger	Masthead Tri-color / Remove Pilot Berth / Redesign Galley / Install Refrigeration / Closed Cell Cockpit Cushions / Cockpit Table	Solar Panels / Anemometer / Sat Nav / Liferaft / Solar Still
FINISH C	Bottom Paint / Repair Deck Gelcoat / Polish Hull / Refinish Teak	Paint Hull / Paint Deck / Headliner in Fwd. Cabin / Reupholster Bunks & Settees / Cockpit Cushion Covers	Refinish Mast / Teak Veneer Bulkheads / Cockpit Grating

(left label: TYPE OF ALTERATION)

Putting it all in order . . .

galley has to have a higher priority or the new countertop a lower one. The matrix also gives you a picture of how effectively you are planning this transformation. If everything seems to be in the first column, you have avoided the hard decisions. You must decide which items are the most important, which are less important, and which are the least important. Assigning a rough estimate of the cost to every entry may help you make those decisions. You are trying to end up with a more or less even distribution among the columns.

The relationship among the three rows is also informative. If most of your planned changes fall into row *B*, you may be giving insufficient attention to your boat's structural integrity. If the C blocks are the fullest, your old boat must be exceptionally well designed and well maintained. If *A* and *C* have the lion's share of entries, you could be overlooking opportunities to make the boat better suited to your use. A sparsely inscribed row in the matrix, like an empty restaurant, does not necessarily indicate a problem, but it should make you wonder.

This matrix is an extremely useful planning tool and we go through the step of creating it primarily for its visual impact. It displays, in the most conspicuous manner, an overview of the entire transformation you have envisioned, and the anticipated order of its completion. Insufficient planning is immediately apparent, and the effect of corrective measures shows up instantly. However, as useful as it is, it does not provide the most convenient means of tracking your progress.

As you progress from planning the project to administering it, you move from blueprint to ledger. The most convenient ledger in this case is your trusty spiral-bound notebook. By labeling nine pages *A1* through *C3* and copying the lists of items from the blocks of the matrix into the appropriate pages of the notebook, you can transfer the information the matrix contains into a more usable format.

BUT WAIT! Before you do that, we need to readdress the issue of safety.

SAFETY REVISITED

Repairs and additions that are essential to safety need to be attended to first—period. The matrix accommodates that imperative to a degree by allowing you to assign safety initiatives a high priority, but even though you have labeled the replacement of a stranded forestay *A1*, your plan does not clearly show the importance of doing this particular *A1* job first. And a faulty bilge pump might be categorized *B1*, but its replacement cannot await the completion of all the other *A1* and *B1* items. The solution is to give deficiencies that represent a risk the VIP—Very Important Priority—treatment.

On a separate page, which I might label *S1*, list all the entries from the matrix that represent a response to an unacceptable safety risk. This does not necessarily include *all* safety-motivated changes you may be contemplating. Installing handholds on either side of the companionway, a depth sounder, or an intermediate lifeline all represent safety enhancements, yet few would characterize sailing without them as an unacceptable risk. But a boat with questionable standing rigging, a cracked engine mount, weak or broken lifelines, or a loose

rudder should not leave the dock. And corroded through-hull fittings, broken hose clamps, and sticky bilge-pump switches can sink your boat in the slip. Problems such as these *must* be corrected *first*.

BACK TO THE BOOK

After you have extracted the urgent safety concerns and grouped them first, you can copy the remaining entries from the matrix into the appropriate pages of the notebook. When you finish, your notebook should contain ten separate lists in descending order of anticipated completion. You know that the most urgent jobs are in the *S1* list, followed by *A1*, *B1*, and so on. If one weekend you have a sudden impulse to complete a *B3* job even though you have been working your way through the *B1* list, there is nothing to keep you from doing that. This is a plan, not a contract. Its purpose is to keep you on track, but not to deprive you of spontaneity. Part of the attraction of upgrading an old boat is that the process itself is satisfying. If you restrict it too rigidly, it becomes too much like, God forbid, a job. It is called *pleasure* boating, remember.

KEEPING TABS

I mentioned the word *ledger* earlier, and that is exactly how you should use your notebook. With the entries down the left side of the page, the right side should be empty. With the help of a straight-edge, divide this space into seven columns, each approximately as wide as the space between the page's lines. With an abbreviation (*E$* in this case), head the first column *Estimated Cost*. The second column is *Estimated Time* and the third is the *Expected Start Date*. The next three columns are *Actual Cost*, *Actual Time*, and *Start Date*. The seventh column is to note that the item has been *Completed*.

I find the three estimate columns useful in planning the project. The actual cost lets me keep up with expenditures, and the actual time helps me with future estimates. The start date simply tells me at a glance that this item is underway. I usually write

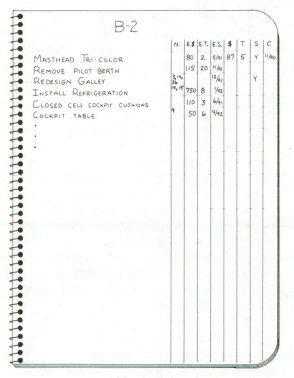

	N	E.$	E.T.	E.S.	$	T	S	C
MASTHEAD TRI-COLOR		80	2	5/91	87	5	Y	11/90
REMOVE PILOT BERTH		115	20	11/91				
REDESIGN GALLEY	3,14,26			12/91			Y	
INSTALL REFRIGERATION	14,15	750	8	1/92				
CLOSED CELL COCKPIT CUSHIONS		110	3	6/91				
COCKPIT TABLE	9	50	6	4/92				

. . . and keeping it in order.

a date in the *Completed* column, but a check mark would serve.

You may think that seven columns represent entirely too much bookkeeping, but I encourage you to give it a try before you reject it. It isn't necessary to fill in every block. I rarely fill in a cost estimate for the small jobs unless I just happen to know the price. The same applies to time estimates. And I typically enter start dates only a month or two in advance except for tasks that are related to some scheduled event–a haulout, for example. I am pretty good about keeping up with dollar expenditures, less diligent about time. My start column usually just has a *Y* (yes) in it.

You may be satisfied with less detail, or you may find that more is preferable. A blank for notations can be useful if you have space; if not, just add a *Notation* column. Notes about parts ordered, or sudden flashes of genius, or whatever, can be written on another page, numbered, and the number entered into the column alongside the item to which it pertains.

The process of categorizing every change and repair, anticipating interdependencies, and assigning priorities does take some time, but once you have the notebook set up, very little time is required to keep a handle on the entire project. Checking off completions and noting expenditures (if you so choose) provides a thorough record of how the project is progressing. Referring to the notebook periodically has the added benefit of keeping you in touch with the entire project, not just the part in process.

As new changes and improvements occur to you (and they will), it is not necessary to go through the matrix process to get them into the notebook. You will know immediately what category they belong in and what priority you want to give them. Just add them to the appropriate list in the notebook and they are immediately integrated into the plan.

KNOWING YOUR HAT SIZE

There are two additional lists that I keep. The first is a shopping list. I am not talking about a list of paint, or wood, or screws that I need for the job I am about to start. Items on this list are for changes scheduled sometime in the future. For example, if there is no real urgency, but I know that I am going to rerig, using Sta-Lok or Norseman mechanical end fittings, I will determine now what type, what size, and how many terminals I need and put them on my shopping list. I also list the size and amount of wire I need. If I have already seen the cabin lamp that will be perfect over the new table I am constructing, I put the lamp on the list. If my mind is already made up for a specific Loran unit, I write the manufacturer and model number on my list. Small items also make this list. If my prop shaft will require a 1-inch zinc collar at the next haulout, I put the collar on my list. If I plan to put some spare V-belts aboard, I note which ones and how many. The one requirement of my shopping list is that the entries are specific—not "refrigeration belts," but "3 Gates 41350 belts or equivalent."

My shopping list serves two functions. First, it lets me take advantage of opportunities. I had planned to add reading lights to my own boat and saw at a boat show some elegant ones fashioned entirely from teak that would be perfect—except that they were $49.95 each and I needed four. I wrote them on my shopping list to await their claim to two of the limited number of hundred dollar bills that float into my hands. Two years later, browsing through a kind of marine trading post, I saw them again, this time for $15. Discounters, salvage outlets, classifieds, bulletin boards, flea markets, garage sales, other sailors, sale flyers—all are potential sources of marine products at substantial savings, but only if you know exactly what you are looking for.

In its second function, I use the list to juice my enthusiasm. When my zeal begins to wane a bit, or nothing seems to be getting done, I dig out a catalog and order an item or two. I get a lift when I fill out the form and mail it, and a second one when the item actually arrives. Blondie (Dagwood's wife, not the rock singer) was onto something all those times she lifted her spirits with a new hat.

LAST LIST (WHEW!)

One of my local marine suppliers gives away little thin notebooks, about the size of a checkbook register, and I almost always have one with me. On a single page—a note card or a blank piece of paper will work just as well—I write down my plan of attack for my next visit to the boat. If I am going to the marina on Saturday and I plan to do several small jobs, I list them. If I have one project planned, I break it into steps and list the steps. On the opposite page, I list all the tools and supplies that I expect to need.

This daily list serves four functions. It keeps me focused all week on the jobs planned for the weekend. When I arrive at the boat there is very little wasted motion; I know exactly what I am going to do. I have all the tools and supplies with me when I get to the boat. And as each job or step is completed and crossed out, I feel the vision getting closer.

A good plan will help you to achieve your vision with the least amount of wasted time. The least amount of wasted money is an equally important objective—perhaps more important. That issue is next.

FOUR

Dollars and Sense

I'm living so far beyond my income that we may
almost be said to be living apart.
–H.H. MUNRO–

There is little value, I think, in talking about expenses in absolute terms. With the dollars required just to replace the engine in an old Columbia 50, one could bring a neglected Cape Dory Typhoon back to new condition–and beyond. Fitting out for an open-ended cruise to Polynesia will certainly cost more than a few comfort enhancements for weekends aboard. And when heiress Elizabeth Meyer decided to restore the 130-foot J-Boat *Endeavour,* you can bet your last buck she didn't start looking around for a do-it-yourself yard.

How much you are going to spend is a function of how big your boat is, her initial condition, the complexity of your vision, and the size of your bank account.

I don't know about your boat or your vision, but I am going to make a wild guess about your net worth: T. Boone Pickens doesn't call you when he is looking for takeover capital. How am I doing?

Thrift is a major element of the philosophy and the projects in this book. It is a good word, *thrift.* The dictionary defines it as "wise economy" in the management of money and other resources. It comes from the Old Norse word for prosperity.

Cheap is another thing altogether. *Cheap* means relatively low in cost; inexpensive. It can also mean of small value or poor quality. You need to be cautious about always taking the *cheap* route. You may be getting exactly what you are paying for.

In the pages that follow, wise economy is our objective.

ECONOMY

A restrictive bank balance is usually a key element in the purchase of an old boat. It is also a key element in reconditioning her. Typical sentiment is that "a few bucks and a lot of TLC" will bring her back. TLC translates into substituting time for money. There are at least three reasons to do as much of the work required yourself; saving money is the one that comes to mind first.

If you *can* do the job, it will almost always cost you less than if you pay someone else to do it for you, often far less. When you hire someone to do something for you–boat-related or otherwise–you are paying for three distinct elements: time, materials, and knowledge or skill. Time and materials show up on the bill, but it is really the knowledge required, or the presumption of knowledge required, that determines the cost.

If your doctor tells you your health problem can only be corrected with delicate brain surgery, you don't pick up a couple of medical texts and a selection of surgical tools for your significant other, no matter how much the surgery is projected to cost. The risks are too high, the requirements too precise, the knowledge required too complex to offer any hope of success.

But boat repair is not brain surgery. Remember that. Hang around a boatyard for day or two and you will discover that there is virtually nothing going on there that is beyond the capability of a reasonably handy boat owner.

That is not to say that you should shun professional help. A true professional can do the job quicker, perhaps better, sometimes cheaper, and his depth of experience can provide a sense of assurance that may be lacking from your own first-time efforts. For example, if you start the job not knowing a pintle from a gudgeon, you will feel a lot less tentative about your rudder repair if you have a knowledgeable boatwright at least check it out. The absolute certainty required on a job that has safety implications may demand professional assistance.

When safety is not an issue, or when you are confident that you can deal with the safety implications, doing the job yourself can have a startling effect on its cost. A few years back, in the middle of a wild and wooly winter night, I put the helm over and as the aged and overstressed genoa backwinded against the spreader tip, the sail ripped from head to foot. New sail time.

Conditioned to think of sailmaking as only marginally less difficult than brain surgery, I visited seven different professional sailmakers, providing each with exactly the same specifications. The results were instructive. There was no clear consensus among the sailmakers on *any* of the basic parameters—not on weight, not on weave, not on cut, and not on cost. The prices ranged from $800 to more than $1,900, and averaged around $1,300.

I knew nothing about building a sail, but apparently there was not a "right" way. The more I looked into it, the less complicated it seemed. Knowing my way around a sewing machine from other canvas jobs, I decided to give it a go. Whether the sail I constructed is better or worse than the seven professional offerings is debatable, but it more than satisfied my requirements and my total cost was under $200!

This is not to say that *you* should make your own suit of sails. We will explore that question fully in Chapter 16. The point is that doing it myself saved me as much as $1,700 on a single sail, with no compromise in quality—I used the same materials as the sailmakers—no disappointment in performance, and no safety risk.

KNOWLEDGE

This experience also illustrates the second reason for doing a job yourself. I learned more about sail shape in one week than I had in a couple of decades of tweaking sheets. I had read a little about sail theory before this experience, but the responsibility of giving the sail the correct amount of draft in the right place converted all that hazy theory into working knowledge.

The more you do yourself, the more you will know about your boat. The knowledge you gain can be more important than the money you save. A sailing acquaintance, approaching the Bahamas in the dark after four days offshore from North Carolina, ran onto the reef east of Abaco. Bad weather was building and every effort to free the boat failed. Water below signaled the beginning of structural damage.

In a desperate effort to escape, the owner made a first-dawn decision to release the keel bolts. Removing the necessary access panels, he and a crew member began removing the nuts, releasing the last two simultaneously. The boat leaped from her ballast and while the crew member drove wooden plugs into the now-open holes, the owner piloted the lightened boat across the reef and into protected waters. Several days later, in calm weather, the ballast was retrieved and the boat was made whole again on the ways at nearby Man-O-War Cay. The owner credited the fact that *he* had recently replaced the keel bolts with providing the knowledge required to take his boat-saving action.

You can never know too much about your own boat, and the farther you stray from boatyards, mechanics, and riggers, the more valuable that knowledge becomes. When you step off the companionway ladder into ankle-deep water, knowing exactly where every seacock is can make the difference between mopping up or swimming to shore.

QUALITY

The third reason you may find yourself doing your own work is that it may be the only way you can get a task done right. Because the truth in this statement typifies a worn spot in the fabric of our society, it saddens me to acknowledge. This is not a blanket indictment of everyone working in the marine trades; there are still some fine craftsmen working on boats, some skilled workmen who take pride in their expertise, some boatyard supervisors who understand how unforgiving the ocean can be. But their numbers are diluted by those whose skill is marginal, whose pride in workmanship is nonexistent, and whose concern for your well being lasts only as long as it takes your check to clear.

I have seen a mechanic forget to refill the engine with oil, a fiberglass "expert" patch a hole in a hull with a mixture of polyester resin and *sand*, a well-known canvas shop deliver an expensive new dodger with a patch in the top. For most of the items on your list, your own lack of expertise is a far less serious risk than such indifference. If you *care* enough, you can acquire the necessary skill.

This is not to say that you must do everything yourself. Quite the contrary, there may be a number of items on your list that you *should not* attempt. How many such jobs, and which ones, depends upon you.

NO APTITUDE

You should not attempt repairs and enhancements for which you clearly have no aptitude. If every time you have tried to give your car a tuneup it had to be towed out of your driveway, attempting a major engine overhaul is probably not a good idea. If your last encounter with a band saw shortened two fingers on your left hand, a finishing sander may be the only power tool you should consider handling. If your efforts on a sewing machine always result in something that resembles the start of a loop-pile rug, you are not likely to be satisfied with a dodger of your own construction.

But be sure that your problem *is* aptitude, not simply that no one has ever gotten you off on the right foot. We will examine this distinction in much greater detail in the next chapter.

MATERIAL INTENSIVE

Some jobs on your list may be material intensive; that is, the cost of the materials required represents a significant portion of the cost of the job. An engine-driven refrigeration system pre-engineered for your boat costs, let's say, around $2,000. The dealer will give it to you in a carton for that price, or installed for $2,200. For 10 percent more, the dealer assumes the aggravation and, more importantly, the responsibility of seeing that the system works. It could be $200 well spent, especially if you can persuade the mechanic to give you a running commentary while he does the job.

The relationship of material cost to labor cost may not be the issue; the absolute cost of the materials may indicate the need for professional assistance. It is one thing to feel your way through the installation of a $250 VHF radio, quite another to risk a $2,500 SSB unit. In some instances, the materials are forgiving; if the seam in a new cushion cover is not quite right, pull it out and do it again. In others, you can make a practice run; a scrap lumber mock-up will pinpoint problems *before* you cut that expensive piece of teak. But you only get one chance to connect the SSB set, one opportunity to cut the hole in the cabin top for the new hatch, and you cannot stop the chemical reaction once you mix the catalyst into a two-part paint. If you are tentative about a project in which an error will be costly, you may want to get help.

NO TIME

The time required to complete a job may indicate that you should pay someone else to do it. Keep in mind that we are talking strictly about the economics of your project.

Remember my story in the last chapter about wiring a new house. What took me almost a month to accomplish, a skilled electrician could have done in half that time, maybe less. What makes that significant is that I gave up a job that paid more than most electricians earn in order to do the job myself. In purely economic terms, it was not a good decision. The cost of materials aside, by doing the job myself, I neither earned nor spent any money. If, instead of pulling wire, I had stayed employed in my own specialty, I would have had to pay the electrician, but would have earned enough in the four weeks to do that and still have more than half my earnings left over.

It is true that I got quicker with each circuit, but by the time I really got the hang of it, I was finished. And the value of acquiring the skill is questionable since I am never likely to use it again.

If you are tempted to give up gainful employment, take a leave of absence, or just turn down overtime in order to complete major modifications to your boat, take a hard look at the numbers. You may be financially wiser to do what you do and pay a specialist to do what he does.

This kind of reasoning has no application to the smaller tasks on your list. If you pay someone $100 to install your new anchor windlass, you cannot justify that expenditure based on your potential earnings unless doing the job yourself would actually result in the loss of those earnings. This is a job you could easily have done on the weekend instead of watching the Trojans take on the Fighting Irish. Your income for the week is unchanged either way, but it costs you $100 *not* to do the job yourself. If economy is important, *you* should have done it.

SPECIALIZATION

A number of items on your list may be so specialized as to preclude you from attempting them yourself. Electronics repairs come immediately to mind. If the autopilot corrects only to port, few of us are equipped to pinpoint the problem and correct it. A trained technician is required.

With today's electronics, even the technician often makes no attempt to actually locate the problem—he simply replaces the entire circuit board. With a selection of circuit boards, you could probably deal with most of your own electronic failures, but unless you are going to be out of reach of any service facility and your electronics are essen-

tial, the expense of such an inventory probably cannot be justified.

Some jobs require special precautions. Safety or health risks may make doing it yourself a poor choice. While the two-part polyurethane paints that have revolutionized boat refinishing in the last decade are relatively benign when applied with a brush or a roller, when they are applied by spraying they are extremely dangerous. If you decide to spray polyurethane on your hull, you should leave that job to someone who understands the nature of the risk and has the equipment necessary to deal with it.

Equipment alone (and the skill to operate it) can be the issue. While most of the work necessary to complete an engine overhaul is well within the capacity of most boat owners, reconditioning the cylinder head requires the services of a machine shop. If the engine is a diesel, repairs to the injection pump are even beyond the capacity of most machine shops; they will send the unit to a shop that specializes in the minimal tolerances the pump demands. A need for special tools and expensive equipment may eliminate doing it yourself as an option.

TOOLS

However, just because your toolbox does not include the needed tools is not always a good reason not to attempt a job. If you need a special hand tool, a torque wrench, for example, you can probably find someone in the marina or boatyard willing to loan you one. Expensive or very specialized tools can often be rented. If you will need the tool more than once, you should consider purchasing it.

Buying tools is a good place to learn the difference between *cheap* and *thrifty*. Quality tools are not cheap, but they are the definitive example of "wise economy." Most of my hand tools are 25 years old, and still as good as the day they were purchased. The few cheap tools I acquired broke or froze and were discarded years ago. I have usually selected Craftsman hand tools because of their availability and lifetime warranty but there are others just as good. There is absolutely no need to pay a higher price for hand tools specifically marketed for the marine environment. If a standard Craftsman tool will last "forever," how do *marine* tools improve upon that?

The extent of your tool inventory will depend upon how extensive your planned modifications are. Typical refurbishing projects require amazingly few tools, and most that are necessary are not terribly expensive. We will examine specific tool requirements in later chapters, but a few comments are appropriate here about tools that do represent a significant expense.

Before you hire work done because the tools required are expensive, you should evaluate that decision carefully. I have never owned any shop tools—lathe, table saw, band saw, jigsaw, drill press, disk sander, or the like—and most boat projects can be done quite well, thank you very much, without them. But if I were planning to rip out the interior of my own old boat and rebuild it, my first action would be to buy a *good* table saw. And I might also spring for a band saw. With patience and care, a circular saw and a high-quality saber saw can be coaxed into doing the job, but why? The time that would be wasted in setup and in fitting the less accurate pieces cut with hand power tools easily justifies the expenditure.

Besides, if you buy quality tools in the used market, you should have every reason to expect virtually every cent to come back to you when you sell them . . . if you sell them. After you have discovered what you can do with a table saw, you may be unwilling to give it up.

The same holds true with a good sewing machine. A decade ago, my wife bought me a new commercial sewing machine. I am not supposed to know, but the cost was more than $600. It seemed like a lot of money at the time, but among the projects for our old ketch I have somehow found the time to complete in the subsequent ten years are new cushion covers below, cockpit cushions, three sails, two sail covers, hatch covers, winch covers, a dodger, a rain awning, two wind scoops, numerous

bags and pouches, and a fish-shaped wind sock to bring luck to our little ship. The fish has never failed us, and the savings on just the sails and the dodger were well over $3,000. I married well.

SHOPPING

You save on labor costs by doing some or all of the job yourself. You save on materials by shopping around. The assumption that a specific product will cost "about the same" regardless of where you buy it is wrong. As I write this, I have a note on my desk from calling five different local suppliers about a specific item. Incredibly, the prices ranged from a high of $67 down to $16. Between two stores literally across the street from each other, one was *206 percent higher* than the other.

How can that be? Because prices are based not on how much an item costs the seller, but on how much he thinks a buyer will be willing to pay. I recently needed a bell bracket. This is a small piece of sheet brass, slightly wedge shaped, with a rolled edge on the two converging sides. The price from my nearest supplier? Six dollars! I passed, fabricating one from scrap in about 10 minutes, but that is not the point. I encountered the same piece of hardware a few weeks later priced at under $2.

I am not advocating driving all over town to save four bucks. What I am suggesting is comparison shopping. Remember the shopping list I described in the last chapter. With that in my pocket, I am prepared to note prices whenever I vist a different supplier. Usually, I find that a pattern emerges. It will come as no surprise that the purveyor of the $6 bell bracket is almost always the most expensive in my area on other items as well. How does the company stay in business? They are in an area of million-dollar yachts, and their very complete inventory is more important than their prices to the professional captains they attract.

Be sure you are comparing oranges to oranges. Before leaving on a cruise, I decided to buy a spare galley foot pump to back up the two aging ones aboard. The Whale pumps had given excellent service, and a nationally known marine supply house sold a pump that was identical in appearance to a Whale pump except that it carried an in-house brand sticker. Probably a way to discount Whale pumps, I thought; so I saved $10 and bought one. As it turned out, it was almost two years before I had occasion to install my "bargain." When one of the old pumps failed, the new one leaked so badly that I was forced to dismantle it, only to discover that it was not made by Whale, and the quality was so poor that the leak could not be stopped. Significantly, I rebuilt the Whale pump using some salvaged parts from an even older pump, and it served for the rest of the trip. When considering costs, brand and model comparisons are the only valid ones.

SELECT QUALITY

My experience with the pump illustrates another tenet of thrift: select good quality. Instead of "saving" $10, my choice actually cost me $30, and a lot of aggravation. Had I examined the pump more carefully initially, I could have seen that it was a cheap knockoff. In the end, I did what I should have done to start with; I bought the genuine article.

The consequences of selecting poor quality can be far more serious than a trickle of water across the cabin sole. A sailing friend, distressed at the prices of turnbuckle toggles, found some of unknown pedigree at a discount supplier. What could go wrong with a toggle? He found out four hundred miles from Bermuda when one failed and the mast went over the side. How can you tell whether a toggle, or a turnbuckle, or an anchor shackle is strong enough? Not by looking at it! You are dependent upon the manufacturer's testing and quality controls. If a part is critical to the safety of the boat, be sure that it is backed by a reputable manufacturer.

A DISTANT DRUMMER

There is a footnote to the cheap toggle story. My friend went to this particular marine supplier for some other item, but when he ran across the toggles, he bought them because they were less than half the price of Merriman hardware—the list price. Ironically, more than one mail-order supplier discounts Merriman marine hardware. A postmortem revealed that the cheap toggle that sent the mast over the side and sounded the death knell for his Atlantic crossing was only a couple of dollars less than the mail-order price for one of top quality.

When you are comparing prices, don't stop with the suppliers near your marina, or in your home town. A vast quantity of boating products is sold through catalog outlets, often at significant savings. Picking a couple of items at random, a Barient winch that lists for more than $1,400 can be purchased from a catalog outlet for less than $900, a $74 cooling water strainer for $52.95. Even a $10.95 cartridge of sealant is priced at $7.50.

Remember my shopping list? Whenever I add an item to it, I always consult two or three of the marine supply catalogs that are a permanent fixture on one corner of my desk. The catalogs give me a good idea of what is available and at what price. If I already know *exactly* what I want, I note on my list the best price and who has it.

The catalogs may also point out the variety of options that are available. For example, when my submersible electric bilge pump began to show signs of expiring, the first catalog I consulted offered nine pumps from three different manufacturers; the second catalog listed 21 pumps from five different manufacturers. It was clearly time to do a bit of research. I surveyed a couple of sailing friends, read a comparison test in a back issue of *Practical Sailor,* factored in my own experience with products from a couple of the manufacturers, and came to a decision. The brand, model number, catalog, and price were duly noted on my shopping list. After comparing that price to the price of the pump locally, I called in my order.

Is mail order always less expensive? No. The shipping charges on heavy or oversize items can make the *delivered* price higher than the local price. Savings in state sales taxes used to more than offset shipping charges, but more and more states are passing laws requiring out-of-state merchandisers to collect and remit sales tax. Some of the catalog companies have local outlets, giving customers catalog prices and saving them the shipping charges. To compete, local marine suppliers are sometimes willing to "meet" mail-order prices. Sales, boat-show specials, and the like can provide lower prices than the fixed ones in catalogs; the same sealant that is $7.50 by mail is often on sale for $6.95 at my local hardware store.

Specialty houses and wholesale suppliers are often a lower-cost alternative. When I need hose, I go to an industrial hose supplier and find the prices about 50 percent less than the best price from any marine source. When I need acrylic canvas, a local distributor invariably has the best price. When I was wishing for a sewing machine, I had my eye on one recommended by a sailmaker who also sold mail-order sailmaking supplies—including this particular machine. At the time, the price of the sewing machine, "packaged" for the sailor, was $995. My resourceful wife bought the identical machine from a local commercial sewing machine company for 60 percent of that price.

WARRANTIES

A concern I have often heard expressed about mail-order shopping is "What if I have a problem with the item?" Deal with a reputable mail-order company, and the answer to that question is "Pick up your telephone and call customer service." My experience has always been that catalog suppliers are just as eager for repeat business as the storefront variety.

Warranties are usually placed on items by their manufacturer, not the retailer, so warranty work should be more or less the same. At least one major mail-order outlet for marine electronics *doubles* the manufacturer's warranty as an incentive. My own experience is that if properly installed (which also means protected from the elements) modern marine electronics work when you initially turn them on, they are unlikely to develop a covered problem during the warranty period—but a longer warranty can't hurt.

Unless you have to pay additionally for it! The manufacturer either stands behind the product or he doesn't. "Extended" warranties are a way of increasing the profit from the sale and I find them distasteful. There has been a trend, for example, for boat manufacturers to warrant the hull for one year or, for an additional charge of as much as several thousand dollars, to *extend* the warranty to three years. I don't want a hull that is going to need warranty work; I want one that is going to be trouble free. If the manufacturer doesn't expect the hull to develop problems, then he is ripping me off with a charge for nothing. If, on the other hand, the charge is intended to offset the warranty work he expects the hull to require during the three-year period, I am not interested in his product.

The length of warranties is often *customary*, rather than having any direct correlation with the expected life of the product. That means that there is no reason to be particularly concerned about a 90-day warranty, if that is what other manufacturers place on similar equipment. But if everyone else warrants for a year? . . . Conversely, if your item of choice has a significantly longer warranty, it could be a reflection of higher quality, but it may be nothing more than marketing strategy. A great warranty is no assurance that the item will perform when you need it. *Look for quality, not promises*.

ME, INC.

A decade ago, my wife and I shared an anchorage with a beautifully finished Brown trimaran. We were soon invited aboard, and the nickel tour included a photo album of the boat under construction, blanketed in some of the pictures with heavy Michigan snow. Mike told me that he had formed a boatbuilding company before starting the construction. That involved little more than having letterhead stationery and business cards printed, and obtaining a tax number from the state—a total investment of less than $50. As a result, he was usually able to obtain equipment and supplies at their true wholesale price.

Back home, I decided to give Mike's method a try. With a package of transfer letters, a copy machine, and a few sheets of linen paper, *Don's Nautical Services* was born. Commissioning was our business. I wrote to a major manufacturer of galley stoves, inquiring about a specific model, and they promptly responded with a wholesale price list. The shipping was FOB and COD, and a commercial address was necessary (I had the stove delivered to my employer's address), but the transaction presented no problems and I saved about $300 compared to the list price.

You will find that not all manufacturers, importers, and suppliers will deal with you. Someone may have a territorial exclusive in your area, and the manufacturer will simply refer you. A supplier may want to "qualify" you by sending a representative to determine how much business you are likely to represent. The manufacturer may require a minimum order, an established line of credit, or an occupational license number. I never advocate being anything less than *absolutely honest* with a potential supplier. If your transaction does not present a conflict or require special handling, most are happy to have the business. If you expect special service, you are out of line.

Should you find something inherently dishonest about this, reconsider. Mike was definitely in the boat building business, and I was just as certainly commissioning. If the boats Mike and I were working on were not our own, the concept of a small business would be a natural, even as a weekend-only occupation. Does the supplier care who owns the boat you are working on? No. If you meet *their* qualifications—which often are as simple as walking through the door—they will do business with you. But remember that you are not buying a carload of their product. You have no reason to protest if they say "no."

RECYCLING

When you recondition an old boat, you will probably be trying to make use of all of the hardware and equipment that is still "good." So what could be more natural on an old boat than taking advantage of the savings available on used items.

When I replaced my galley stove with one with an oven, I tried to sell the old one. The new price was $425, and presumably there was some demand since the manufacturer was still making the stove. My old one was polished and perfect, but I would have happily taken $40 for it if a buyer had come along. And I would have thrown in a folding oven.

The biggest problem with used marine equipment is getting the buyer and seller together. Larger items—engines, outboards, liferafts, etc.—may be advertised in the classified section of magazines and newspapers, but the cost of classified advertising often excludes inexpensive items. Weekly "shoppers" are a notable exception. Yacht-club and marina bulletin boards often display an array of items being offered for sale. In a heavy boating area, there is usually at least one boat salvage-yard or used-equipment outlet. In my town there is a dealer who handles used gear on consignment. Pawnshops near the waterfront take in marine items. Garage sales and flea markets often include marine equipment. In some boating areas, flea markets for marine equipment only are staged periodically. If you don't see the item you are looking for displayed or advertised, your own "wanted" card on the bulletin board, or ad in the shopper, may exhume it from the bottom of someone's sail locker.

If a used item is not worn out, you might ask, why is the owner getting rid of it? A lot of reasons. Getting out of boating. Changing boats. Needing money. Salvage: bronze fittings outlast wooden planking. Upgrading: my old stove was on the market because I wanted one with an oven. Newer technology: when self-tailing winches hit the market, the used market was flooded with excellent standard winches. Reevaluation: a friend vacillated on the installation of an anchor windlass for several years before selling it—in the original carton—at a fraction of its cost.

You do want to be certain that you are not buying a defective item. Flea markets often sport a number of used marine radios and depth finders, none of which I, personally, would buy. That doesn't mean I would not buy any used electronics. A charter captain I know, in need of additional channels, replaced his crystal-controlled ICOM M-25 with a synthesized unit. The sailor who bought the old ICOM knew exactly what he was getting—a great radio at a giveaway price. He also knew *whom* he was buying from and *why* the item was for sale. Knowing both is your best protection in the used market.

Used gear can be as good as new. Sometimes the quality of the old stuff is even better than that of today's goods. If you search actively, you may be surprised at what you will find. Just remember, as with all secondary transactions, *caveat emptor.*

But maybe you aren't interested in all this savings stuff. T. Boone does call you when he hears about a Fortune 500 buyout opportunity, and you are taking on this project only as a hobby—sort of model building on a grander scale. You just want to get on with it. Fine. Then let's.

FIVE

Starting Small

Eighty percent of success is showing up.
–WOODY ALLEN–

Before we actually start cutting and painting and gluing and stuff, let's take one short detour. The purpose of this digression is illustrated by the old story of the burly mountain man who comes into town to replace his worn-out whipsaw. The salesman at the hardware store points out how much more efficient a chainsaw is, and sells him one. A month later the mountain man returns to the store so wasted away that his shirt hangs on him like a plaid choir robe, drops the new saw on the counter, and demands his money back. "Don't cut half so good as my old one," he tells the salesman. Puzzled, the salesman gives the cord a pull and over the rip of the exhaust, he hears the mountain man yell, "What's that noise?"

The remainder of this book is a tool, and you will surely use it more efficiently if you know how to pull the cord. In the dozen or so chapters that follow, the objective is *not* to provide you with step-by-step instructions for a few generic enhancements to your old boat. The bookshelves are already full of such books and while they are informative and useful, typically only a few of the projects they contain will be just right for your boat.

Not that there aren't any projects in this book. Quite the contrary. In the pages that follow you *will* find detailed instructions for dozens of enhancements and improvements, some of which are likely to fit your specific needs. I have made every effort to select only those with broad application. If you follow exactly the instructions provided, the physical result will be a specific item or improvement, but teaching you how to build that specific item is not

really the purpose of the instructions. I am focusing on the "big project," the metamorphosis of your old boat into the one in your vision. You are not likely to find every change on your list detailed in the pages that follow, but if I have succeeded in what I set out to do, you will find detailed illustrations of every skill necessary to make those changes. The projects included are a means to that end.

To be more specific, the purpose of the initial projects in the following chapters is to illustrate certain skills and to provide the opportunity to learn by doing. They represent a low level of difficulty, making success likely even for someone with no prior related experience. They are also low in cost, making failure, if not palatable, at least cheap, and affording the opportunity to give it another go. In most cases, the project will result in legitimate enhancement, but even if you find the "thing" not especially useful, the exercise will be.

In the more advanced projects the dominant purpose becomes exemplifying what is possible. You can take a project whole, duplicating it and changing only the measurements to fit your boat. This is the probable approach to the installation of nonskid deck covering detailed in Chapter 14. Or you might utilize only the idea, changing the project entirely. If you build a galley-locker divider exactly like the one in Chapter 10, *my* pots will fit into *your* locker perfectly. You may also reject both the specific project and the general idea, extracting only the possibility. A thorough understanding of the techniques of canvas work demonstrated in the various projects in Chapter 15 will enable you to effect many more enhancements than the few I have illustrated. I will often suggest other possibilities, but this book is about achieving your vision, not mine.

THE BASIC EIGHT

If the transformation of your old boat is to be at your own hands, you will need to be competent in eight basic skills: fiberglass work, rigging, mechanics, carpentry, electrics, plumbing, painting, and sewing. Some of these skills you undoubtedly bring with you; the others you will need to acquire. None of them are particularly difficult.

How difficult? If you can wet out a T-shirt with a paint brush and a cup of water, you can do fiberglass work. If you can measure accurately, you can rerig. If you can get the cap back on the toothpaste tube, you already have the skill to handle most of the mechanical jobs aboard. If you can trace a straight line alongside the edge of a ruler, boat carpentry will present you with few problems. If you connected the speaker wires to your stereo system, you can handle onboard electrical connections. If you have ever installed new end fittings on a garden hose, you are equipped to do boat plumbing. If you can drive a car, you can drive a sewing machine. And anyone can paint.

Oversimplification? Perhaps, but not by much. Few, if any, of the skills required to refurbish an old boat will tax the abilities of the average sailor. I am not suggesting competence with the cap on the toothpaste qualifies you to rebuild a diesel engine. But recognize that the toothpaste cap threads onto the tube in exactly the same way as the bolts that attach the water pump, the nuts that hold the cylinder head to the block, and the cap screws that clamp the connecting rods around the crankshaft. If you have mastered removing and replacing that cap, then you can learn to dismantle and reassemble virtually any mechanical item found aboard a boat.

STEP BY STEP

Notice that I said *learn*. I have already pointed out that in the chapters that follow, the emphasis is on teaching, on expanding basic skills to encompass a broader range of possibilities. Each chapter usually begins with a project that illustrates the fundamental elements of the subject skill. Unless you already have experience in that skill, I recommend that you take the time to actually *do* the initial project. If it does not, in your particular case, lead to a useful enhancement, it is perfectly acceptable to alter the project to fit your needs. But even if your boat cannot directly benefit from the project in any form, you will. The most effective way to learn is by doing.

Following the initial project, each chapter typically provides detailed instructions for what I would call intermediate projects. Equipped with the knowledge and experience gained from the initial effort, you should find these more complex projects manageable. As the projects become more complex, instructions become less specific; by the time you are reconstructing the furniture below, it should no longer be necessary to tell you how deep to set the saw blade nor to remind you to drill pilot holes for the screws.

You will probably not be surprised to discover that the last projects in each chapter (or occasionally in a supplementary chapter) are the most advanced. They require the most expertise in the subject skill, often in combination with one or more of the other skills. They also require the most ingenuity in adapting the illustrated concept to your specific requirements in the most effective way.

There is nothing particularly revolutionary about this crawl-before-you-walk approach. It is how you learned to read, to write, and to spell. It is also how you learned to run a computer, to cut hair, to cook *coq au vin à la Bourguignonne*, to pilot a 747, to close a deal, or whatever else it is that you do. With the same approach and the same dedication to learning boat enhancement skills, there is little reason not to expect an equal level of competence.

ME OR VERN?

I was in the yard recently for a new coat of bottom paint and to my starboard side sat a not-so-old

Endeavor 37. One afternoon a rusted-out VW bus showed up and the scruffy-looking driver pitched a power cord over the lifelines and went aboard. Fifteen minutes later he asked me to hold the outside part of a new through-hull fitting while he tightened the seacock from the inside. In another ten minutes he was gone. When the owner popped by after work to check on the job, he came back down the ladder muttering obscenities.

"Problems?" I asked, wondering about my participation.

"That *@#@*! I told him exactly what I wanted and the stupid *@#@* still did it wrong."

If I had a dollar for every time I have heard an owner say something similar, I could pay to hire my own work done. He took me aboard to show me.

"Look at that! Do you see any caulk squeezing out of here, or there?" He was pointing at the flange of the seacock. "And the damn thing is just threaded on; what does the *@#@* think those ears are for? And why right smack in the middle of the locker? Now that the hole is there, I guess I'm stuck with that, but I'll have to get somebody else out to reinstall the fitting."

"Why don't you just do it yourself?"

"Me? No-no." His hands waved in the air in a crossing motion. "It would leak for sure if I did it."

Here was a guy that obviously knew everything he needed to know to install the new through-hull fitting. Yet he had hired some hardcore underachiever living in an old hulk out in the free anchorage to do the job for him. Why?

Lack of confidence. The psyche is a strange thing. It is often easier to have unfounded confidence in someone else than to have justifiable confidence in yourself. The guy you hire only has to say, "Sure, I can do that," and you turn your boat, and perhaps your personal safety, over to him. In Mr. Spock's words, "It is illogical, Captain."

Had I needed someone to install a through-hull fitting and had to choose either the owner or the guy he hired, it wouldn't even be close. The owner clearly knew more than the self-proclaimed "expert," but even if the owner did not know the first thing about through-hull fittings, he still would have been my choice. Why? Because of his character. He expected the work to be good, not just *good enough*.

I guessed this even before I talked to the owner. How? The way he dressed. The way his car looked. The condition of his boat. The shine on his shoes. The way he left those shoes at the ladder when he went aboard. Those things contrasted starkly with the filthy jeans and the grimy, junk-laden van of the man he hired, with the way that person tossed the sharp-pronged cord into the cockpit, and with the way he carelessly walked through the blue mud of wet-sanding on his way to boarding.

Of course boat work can be a dirty job. Sure a rusty old VW bus is perfect for hauling around boat parts. But I don't want someone that looks like he just played huggy-bear with a transmission working in the cabin of my boat. And if the inefficiency and poor aesthetics of years of accumulated junk don't bother him, how can I expect him to be sensitive to the efficiency and aesthetics of my boat? I certainly don't want someone who has so little concern for my boat that he chips my gelcoat and leaves blue footprints on the deck, companionway, and cabin sole.

Disclaimer time again. I am not saying that there are no competent people working on boats. *Au contraire*, in the same yard, at the same time, was another person whose skill and workmanship made my brown eyes green. (Significantly, he carried around a small album of photos of his own boat.) I am also not saying that you are somehow less worthy if you do not do your own work. What you hire done and what you do yourself are choices only you can make.

However, if you want to do your own work, or if your financial situation is such that you *need* to do the work yourself, but you are deterred by a personal lack of confidence, you should reconsider. And if you turn the job over to someone on the strength of *his* confidence, you are deluding yourself. Give yourself a break. You didn't get to be vice-president of Widgets International because you were unusually dense. And the typical Mr. Fixit isn't working on boats to fund his research into nuclear fusion.

LEARNING THE ROPES

The modest project that leads each chapter introduces you to each new skill. By doing that project, you will discover that there is nothing mystical about the skill. With each subsequent project, you become more knowledgeable in that skill area. By the time you complete the last project in the chapter, you will have advanced your knowledge to the point that the first project, no matter how difficult it may have seemed to you to start, now has a "See Spot run" quality to it.

If you already have experience in the skill addressed by a specific chapter, the first part of the chapter may seem too elementary. For that I apologize, but it is important to start with the basics for those boat owners who do not have the benefit of your experience. The tedium of the instructions should not prevent the initial project from having the same potential usefulness for your boat. And you may find the step-by-step instructions to be a useful review. In any case, the subsequent projects build on the earlier ones, assuming an ever-broader understanding of the subject skill. The projects later in the chapter should challenge even the most experienced.

DRESS REHEARSAL

Learning a skill in the least stressful manner is not the only benefit to starting small, but before we look at some others, we need to take time out to clarify terms. Thus far I have been using the word *skill* to represent a specific type of endeavor. Carpentry is a skill. Painting is a different skill. Needlework is different from both. If we so choose, we can break needlework into canvas work, sailmaking, and upholstery; carpentry into rough carpentry, finish carpentry, and cabinetry, but regardless of how broad or narrow our definition, *the* skill refers to the endeavor. Skill used this way must not be confused with skill used to mean proficiency or expertness, referring to the quality of the work, not the type.

Proficiency comes with practice; the more you do something, the better at it you should become. So we start small to give you the opportunity to practice, to allow you to develop the necessary "feel." I cannot tell you how tight to tighten a wood screw. I can say "tight," or "snug," or "until you feel significant resistance" but you won't really know what those terms mean until you have the screwdriver in your hand, until you give it that last twist, maybe not until you twist just a little too hard and the screw suddenly turns freely.

The more you practice, the more proficient you will become—but refurbishing your old boat is not a contest, not a championship. You are only trying to achieve competence, not renown. Once you have tightened a few screws, once you know what "tight" means, screws installed by you will be indistinguishable from those put in by a master carpenter. He may be faster than you, may know intuitively what size screw is appropriate and what size pilot hole to drill, but the end result will be the same, provided you have sufficient aptitude.

CRITICAL REVIEW

Determining aptitude is a third reason to begin our treatment of each skill with an elementary project. I have already stated unequivocally that most boat owners can learn to do everything required to transform an old boat into a thing of beauty and source of pride. I did not say *every* boat owner. The reality of individual differences is that some of us will excel in some of the skills required, and be less adept in others. Frustration can be avoided by the recognition and acceptance of a low aptitude, but truly prohibitive deficiencies are rare.

Initial difficulty with a new concept does not necessarily signal a lack of aptitude. Learning is always a series of failures, and mastering the skills required for boat enhancement is no different. If you attempt the initial project and the results are less than stellar, try it again. Failure is far more likely to stem from unfamiliarity than from an innate aptitude deficiency. Yet we are too often like the child that takes one look at a new dish and says, "I don't like it." We claim to have a lack of aptitude without really having any idea whether we do or we don't. Put those prejudices aside and give the initial project your best effort. It may be that all you need is the right tools and clear instructions.

Of course, if you struggle to get the cap off the toothpaste tube, and once it is removed you throw it away to save further aggravation, enhancements that require wrenches and sockets and screwdrivers may be difficult for you no matter how clear the instructions. Or if you gave away the electric knife after your second trip to the emergency room, your confidence in your potential prowess with saw and router may be misplaced—and dangerous. The initial projects in each chapter allow you to fail as well as succeed; to discover or confirm an inability to master a specific skill while failure is more inconvenience than disaster.

BUILDING CONFIDENCE

Fortunately you are far more likely to discover a talent than inability. Success in a small project will provide the boost in confidence you need to take on a larger project. As the projects become larger and more complex, confidence grows. Ultimately you should come to a point where no aspect of the rejuvenation seems beyond your abilities.

Confidence, if it is justified, is a wonderful thing. It opens up whole new vistas of possibilities. If you reach a point where you truly believe that you are capable of doing anything to your old boat that you can imagine, your project is then limited only by your imagination—and practical considerations such

as time and money. Developing that kind of confidence is our objective.

CHAPTER ORGANIZATION

The first step in the restoration of a long-neglected old boat is to insure her seaworthiness. That means evaluating the hull and deck—including portholes and hatches—and correcting any deficiencies. Since we have already established that this old boat is fiberglass, the initial skill required is working with polyester resin and other plastics.

Once you know your old boat is not going to sink in the bay or at the dock, there is little reason why you cannot enjoy using her even while you are modifying and restoring her. The only requirement is that you establish the integrity of her rig if she is a sailboat, or the dependability of her engine if she is a power boat. Thus rigging and mechanics are the second and third skills covered.

Major modifications are the next likely step, requiring carpentry skills. Only after bulkheads and furniture are in place are you ready to tackle wiring, plumbing, or refrigeration. Painting and varnishing comes next, followed by upholstery and canvas work.

This order should generally agree with the order of the jobs listed on your matrix. When it doesn't, simply skip to the chapter that you need.

In the succeeding pages, I can only share with you the knowledge required, push you to test your abilities, provide you with a program for honing your skills, and hope that these things nourish your confidence. If they do, I will accept some of the credit for the accompanying sense of satisfaction. But for the source of any sense of pride that may result, look to the man in the mirror.

SIX

Scratch and Itch

Sometimes it is not good enough to do your best;
you have to do what's required.
–WINSTON CHURCHILL–

Giving substance to your vision for your old boat should begin with learning to work with the basic boatbuilding material, plastic. Wood held this distinction from hairy man through Harry Truman, but, in 1947, boat builders began to experiment with glass-reinforced plastic—fiberglass—as a more economical material for hull construction. Within two decades, virtually all of the production boats built in America featured molded fiberglass hulls and decks. Many fine old wooden boats are still around, and a handful (relatively speaking) of custom builders continue to build in wood, but for the last 25 years, fiberglass has been the dominant material in boat construction.

WHY FIBERGLASS?

For me, at least, this is a good thing. I have spent about three of the past 10 years on the water. That may sound like a lot, and it certainly means that my boat has seen more use than most boats in the marina. But if you look at that statement from the other side, you realize that it also means that 70 percent of the time I was not using the boat. And when I am not using my boat, I want to be free of it.

When I am not sailing, I tend to give my boat about as much attention as I give my tennis racquet when I am not playing tennis. The racquet sits patiently in the closet, completely unaffected by my indifference. My fiberglass boat is not unaffected, but when I do return to it, if I demonstrate my remorse with some extra attention it tends to forgive

my neglect. The souls of wooden-hulled boats are more fragile, and if you ignore one for very long, it will commit suicide before you have the chance to make up. And that is exactly what most neglected old wooden boats have done.

This fact makes the purchase of a neglected wooden boat a much greater risk than rescuing a back-of-the-yard fiberglass one. In fact the two concepts are opposites. The construction of a 25-year-old fiberglass boat is likely to be stronger than that of similar boats built today because early builders were unfamiliar with the medium and added a few extra laminates "just to be sure." Given just neglect and not severe mistreatment, there is little reason to expect the hull to be less sound than the day it left the builder's yard. With some cosmetic work and a few upgrades, you should end up with a better boat than you can buy at a fraction of the new boat cost.

However, unless a wooden hull has been maintained impeccably, any assumption of seaworthiness is pure folly. And if it has been impeccably maintained, then it is not the kind of boat we are talking about in this book. Catch-22. Clearly you should survey any old boat you are considering investing your time and money in, regardless of the construction material, but a neglected wooden boat is far *more* likely to have serious structural deficiencies that require skilled repairs, and far *less* likely to represent a financially sound investment. Wooden-boat owners find compensating spiritual rewards in their craft, and I am not trying to convert anyone. But for the rest of us, the restoration of an old boat is viable *because of* the ability of fiberglass construction to shrug off years of neglect. It is a matter of practicality, not prejudice, that I am assuming hull and deck construction of fiberglass. Besides, the safest course for someone short on experience is to select a production boat with a great reputation, and for the last 25 years that means fiberglass.

Fiberglass boats are, of course, not without problems. The hull and deck of an older fiberglass boat are likely to suffer from one or more of eight possible conditions. They may be dirty, dull, scratched, cracked, blistered, weak, delaminated, or (impact) damaged. We are going to look at the resolution of each.

DIRTY

I know you don't need my help with this one, but allow me to give you a bit of advice. Buy your cleaning supplies at the Piggly-Wiggly. Marine supply shelves are loaded with dozens of overpriced proprietary "boat cleaners" promising miraculous results, but a squirt bottle of Joy, a spray bottle of Fantastic, and a nice, fat sponge are probably all the cleaning supplies your lazarette needs to contain. A *soft* bristle brush works better on some types of nonskid, but stick with the sponge on the smooth stuff.

If you run up against a stain that shrugs off the Fantastic, squeeze a little lemon juice on it. Really. Next try kerosene, or a cloth dampened with acetone. If that fails, trot down to your nearest Ace Hardware for a quart of *brush cleaner.* This is a water-soluble, toluene-based product, not to be confused with the mineral spirits or paint thinner that you may have used to actually clean brushes. If the stain persists, one proprietary product that I have often heard recommended is FSR (Fiberglass Stain Remover). The name is all business, anyway.

If you get to this point and you still have a stain that you cannot remove, it is probably because the gelcoat has become porous and the stain has penetrated. Your only remaining option is to remove the offending layer of gelcoat and the stain with it.

DULL

The treatment for a deep stain and for a dull finish are exactly the same because they stem from the same problem—porous gelcoat. If the gelcoat is thick enough and it is not porous all the way through, you may be able to bring back the original gloss, and the original color, by removing the "dead" gelcoat with polish, rubbing compound, or even sandpaper.

Typically gelcoat is applied to a thickness of about 20 mils (.020 inch), or about the thickness of four pages of this book. But it is probable that a 20-year-old boat has already seen the business side of a polishing cloth a few times, so you may have less to work with than you think. In any case, you do not want to remove any more of the gelcoat than is absolutely necessary. If you are just trying to remove a stain, try a cleaner/polish first. This is the least abrasive, and it usually contains a mild solvent to assist in the stain removal. Now rub until the stain is gone and the gelcoat looks new, or until your arm falls off into the dirt.

If the gelcoat is more than a dozen or so years old, polish is probably going to be too wimpy to restore a shine to the whole boat. Something a bit more abrasive is needed. In my adolescent years, we used to shoehorn huge V-8 engines into depression-era Ford coupes, and paint these hot rods with 12 or 15 or 20 coats of lacquer. When the paint cured, we would rub most of it off with rubbing compound. The results were nothing short of spectacular; finishes that were as flawless and as deep as a mirror. Rubbing compound will do the same for gelcoat.

Attacking the Problem

Using rubbing compound. Rubbing compound is more abrasive than polish and removes the old gelcoat much more quickly, so you first need to test your technique and the thickness of the gelcoat. In some inconspicuous spot, wipe the surface with the toluene-based brush cleaner mentioned above to remove any silicone or wax, then rinse away the cleaner with water. Just because it is apparent that the boat has not been waxed in years, do not omit this step. Despite the fact that wax you apply to your car seems to evaporate before the swelling goes down in your elbow, 20-year-old gelcoat may still have traces of the original mold-release wax.

You use the rubbing compound just like the polish, rubbing with heavy pressure at first, then with progressively less pressure until the finish is glassy. Older gelcoat will probably require the extra abrasion of fiberglass compound #2. For even faster surface removal, try an automotive compound. Formulated for the enamel paint on cars, it will quickly cut the much softer gelcoat, but extra care is required.

A couple of power-tool manufacturers have begun marketing reasonably priced orbital polishers for the yuppie set to use on their BMWs, and if you are pleased with the results on the test spot and intend to compound the entire hull and deck, you might want to buy one, or borrow your brother-in-law's. *Do not* chuck a sanding disk into your old drill and fit it with one of those drawstring polishing bonnets; it will eat right through the gelcoat, or you will burn the drill up running it slowly.

A couple of safety notes are in order. For any gelcoat restoration requiring more than hand polishing, the boat must be out of the water. I have seen boats machine polished in the water, but even if you are lucky enough not to be electrocuted, you will establish yourself as the marina idiot. Power tools around a boat are risky enough without hanging head down over the rail with one in your hand.

The entire hull must be wiped down with toluene (acetone will do if you are *sure* that the hull has never been waxed with a silicone product) before you compound. You will save the risk of immediate skin irritation, and who knows what future horrors, if you put on rubber gloves before you use these or any other chemicals. Throwaway gloves are the best choice because they are not sticky or messy when you start, and you are not tempted to use them after they are holed. At a discount home sup-

ply, I buy packages of 20 gloves for under a dollar. Big deal.

The last hope. If the gelcoat is in bad shape, you could still be compounding this time next year. It's time to bring in the big guns. You are going to *sand* away the dead gelcoat. The exact schedule will depend upon the condition of your gelcoat, but if compounding has failed, start with a sheet of 220-grit *wet-or-dry* sandpaper. The lower the number, the coarser the grit. You can keep that straight if you think of the grit designation as the number of chunks of abrasive material it takes to fill the sheet.

Back at the inconspicuous spot, wipe the surface down again to remove the wax deposited by the rubbing compound. Quarter the sheet of sandpaper. You can apply pressure with your fingers, but the paper will cut faster if you wrap it around a sanding block. Rubber sanding blocks, sold in all hardware stores, are better because they adapt somewhat to the contour of the hull, but if your budget is tight, a scrap of 1 × 2 will serve.

Keep a trickle of water running on your sanding area by holding the hose against the hull above where you are working. Use a piece of *soft* hose with the brass fitting removed to keep from marring the hull. Do I need to tell you not to cut off the end of a hose supplied by the boatyard?

Sand the test spot until the gelcoat has a uniform appearance. It will not be shiny, just smooth and evenly dull. Now switch to 400 grit wet-or-dry until the surface is again uniform in appearance. You may have better results if you abandon the block. Next switch to 600 grit wet-or-dry. Finally, wipe the spot dry and polish it to a high shine with the rubbing compound. If this does not work, it is time to get out your old bugle and play taps. Your gelcoat is dead—period.

Power assistance. If you do end up with a beautiful spot but it took you half a day, which doesn't bode well for the time it will take to do the entire hull, there is a way to do it faster. You will need a finishing sander, and I recommend without reservation Makita's palm sander. Using regular 120 grit sandpaper, test this method of surface removal in another inconspicuous spot. Remember that the sander is working at about 200 orbits per *second*, about a hundred times faster than your hand-powered sanding block. Don't let the sander sit in one spot; keep it moving. And don't sand too long—a few seconds will be sufficient for your test spot. Switch to 220-grit paper and run the sander over the surface again. Then wet the spot and *hand-sand* the surface with 400-grit and then 600-grit wet-or-dry paper. NEVER, NEVER WET SAND WITH A POWER SANDER. Finish by compounding.

Where power sanding is the only timely way to restore the gloss, don't lose sight of the fact that if you are the least bit inattentive, you will cut all the way through the gelcoat. Don't run the sander over any high spots in the hull, or around any corners, such as the bow or where the quarter meets the transom. The sander will strip away all the gelcoat in an instant. Even block sanding is not a good idea; use finger pressure to gently sand these areas.

If the results of your testing are disappointing, do not be too surprised. Gelcoat will hold its color and gloss for about ten years, perhaps twice that long if it has been kept clean and waxed regularly. But eventually it reaches the end of its useful life, and the only way to make the hull shine again is to apply a new finish.

It is possible to apply a new layer of gelcoat to the hull and deck, but this is almost never done. The original gelcoat was applied by spraying it onto the interior surface of a highly polished mold. The bottom surface of the gelcoat mirrored the mold's slick surface, and became the glossy exterior of the hull when the hull was removed from the mold. The top surface of the gelcoat was not smooth, but this texture made for good adhesion to the fiberglass laminates that were applied over the sprayed coating. This inherent unevenness is not such a good thing when the gelcoat is being applied as an exterior coating. To obtain a mirror finish requires sanding the coating to remove the texture and other imperfections, then polishing the surface to produce the desired gloss. Paint, on the other hand, when

applied with reasonable care, dries to a smooth, glossy finish. Not surprisingly, painting is the usual method of refinishing, and we will detail the process of paint selection and application in Chapter 14.

SCRATCHED

The vulnerability of the hulls of pleasure boats, especially sailboats, to disfiguring damage from even the lightest kiss of a piling or seawall is shameful. Pleasure boat manufacturers could learn from a visit to a commercial dock, where robust rub strakes allow workboats to lie alongside the meanest wharf without damage. Meanwhile, the genteel yachtsman is expected to protect his boat's fine finish with ridiculous little inflatable fenders—eight inches of protection for 40 feet of hull. The result is usually a road map of scratches and gouges.

The appropriate method of scratch repair depends upon the severity of the scratch and the overall condition of the gelcoat. Light scratches in the surface of a good gelcoat can be polished out with rubbing compound or, if they are somewhat deeper, sanded smooth and then polished. Deep gouges will require filling, then recoating with gelcoat. If the gelcoat is beyond redemption and you plan to paint the hull (or deck), you only need to fill and smooth the scratch before painting.

Like stains or dullness, a shallow scratch is a surface flaw and the treatment is the same; but if the scratch is too deep to sand and compound out, it will have to be filled. You have three choices of filler: gelcoat putty, polyester resin, and epoxy resin. All three will do the job in most conditions, but each is better in certain circumstances.

Attacking the Problem

Resin. Fiberglass is the marriage of glass fibers and a polymer resin. The liquid polymers used in fiberglass construction are called resins because of their visual similarity to the sticky amber liquid of the same name that drips from trees and ages into a hard, brittle, translucent substance. Fiberglass resins are not organic but chemical in nature. When cured they form a hard, brittle, translucent plastic, a most unlikely material for boat construction. But if this liquid resin is used to saturate a mat or cloth of glass fibers, it binds the fibers together and cures into a tough, flexible material with more tensile strength than steel.

Chemists have concocted numerous polymer resins for different purposes, but the only two used in boat construction are polyester resin and epoxy resin. Unless you *know* otherwise, it is safe to assume that your boat was laminated with polyester resin since not one boat in a thousand is epoxy laminated. Epoxy is stronger and more adhesive than polyester, resulting in a superior fiberglass, but it is difficult to work with, highly toxic, and costs about five times as much as polyester. Only when cost is secondary to high performance are fiberglass hulls laminated with epoxy resin.

For repair work, cost is less of a factor and epoxy resins are commonly used where extra strength and superior adhesion are desired. Nevertheless, polyester resin, in some form, dominates repair work also, although to a lesser degree. Gelcoat is a polyester resin with pigment added for color and UV resistance, and other additives to protect the cured surface from abrasion and water.

Gelcoat putty.　Back to the scratch repair: when the surface blemishes are minor and the rest of the gelcoat is in good condition, gelcoat putty is your best choice. Repair kits with putty, hardener, and a selection of tints are available. For more extensive repairs, make your own gelcoat putty by mixing a thixotropic (an egghead word for thickening) agent into white gelcoat. When you ask your supplier for a thickening agent, if he gives you a bag of something that looks like talcum powder, don't be surprised; that's probably what it is.

If the hull is any color other than white, you will need to tint the gelcoat. Inorganic pigments in a resin base (color resins) are available in $1/4$-ounce tubes for this purpose. Time to play mad scientist. Pour exactly one ounce of gelcoat into a small, unwaxed paper cup and add one drop of color resin. Stir. Too light? Add another drop. Stir. Repeat this

process, counting the drops carefully, until the color matches the old gelcoat. When the color of the gelcoat calls for more than one tint, your task is more difficult, but the process is the same. Try to enjoy this process, not let it frustrate you, and resign yourself to the fact that a perfect match is unlikely. You should end up with a formula. For example, maybe every ounce of gelcoat requires seven drops of green and two of yellow to achieve the right color. Write this information down in your notebook so that you can easily mix gelcoat for future scratches.

Now is a good time to mix in the thickening agent to see if it has an impact on the color. You want to thicken the gelcoat just enough so that it will stay in place, especially if it is to be applied to an overhead or a vertical surface. Now put a lid on the cup and set it aside until you have the scratches ready to be filled.

If the scratch is thin, you may have to open it somewhat by dragging the corner of a screwdriver blade along its length. You only want to open it enough to allow you to get the putty into the bottom of the scratch, and to bevel, or *chamfer*, the edges to give the putty a better surface for adhesion. If the gouge is already wide enough, just smooth and chamfer the edges with a canted scraper blade (or a screwdriver if you don't have a scraper). Clean the surface thoroughly with a fresh rag dampened with acetone, and the scratch is ready. Rewaxing the hull below the scratch will make removing any runs or drips easier.

Before you start, you need to know if the gelcoat will cure in air. Polyester resins, including gelcoat, are usually air-inhibited, meaning that the surface of the resin does not cure quickly if left exposed, but remains tacky. The tacky surface provides an ideal base for subsequent laminates, thus air-inhibited resin may also be called *laminating* resin.

Non-air-inhibited resin, or *finishing* resin, will dry in free air. It is the same as laminating resin, but with a wax added. The wax, or tack-free additive (TFA), floats to the surface and seals the resin from the air, allowing it to cure. If your gelcoat is air-inhibited, you can add a small quantity of TFA to the mix, or

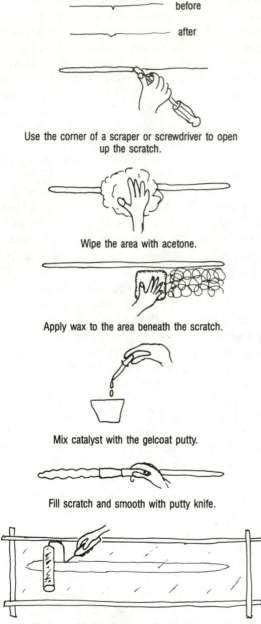

before

after

Use the corner of a scraper or screwdriver to open up the scratch.

Wipe the area with acetone.

Apply wax to the area beneath the scratch.

Mix catalyst with the gelcoat putty.

Fill scratch and smooth with putty knife.

Cover repair with plastic wrap and roll it smooth.

Repairing a scratch

you can simply seal it off from the air with a piece of plastic kitchen wrap.

Adding the catalyst. It is time to add the hardener to your pigmented gelcoat. The most common catalyst is methyl ethyl ketone peroxide (MEKP), not to be confused with the solvent MEK. The gelcoat manufacturer will supply the appropriate hardener and the instructions regarding the amount to be added. Generally, polyester resin requires about one percent of catalyst, by volume—more to hasten the curing process, less to retard it. In hot weather, the gelcoat (or resin) will require less hardener.

So what happens when the instructions say add the contents of the bottle of hardener to the can of gelcoat, but you are only mixing one ounce of gelcoat? I suppose you could draw a line on the bottle at the halfway point, then divide the halves in half, then the quarters in half, and so on until you had the bottle marked into 32 divisions (because the quart can has 32 ounces in it). But that might be difficult on a tiny, 10-cc bottle.

In small amounts, you will be better off catalyzing gelcoat and resin by counting drops. If the hardener is not in a dropper bottle, you will need a small eyedropper. The number of drops in an ounce of catalyst will vary with its viscosity, but you will not be far off if you assume it to be about 700. That means to catalyze one ounce of gelcoat (at one percent) requires about seven drops of catalyst.

Because of the effects of temperature, light, and humidity, the best way to determine the "right" amount of catalyst is by mixing up a test batch. Pour out an ounce of gelcoat—not the colored and thickened putty you have mixed up—and add six or seven drops of hardener. Stir the hardener in thoroughly. Watch the time and check on it every few minutes. You don't want it to go off, to begin to harden, in less than 30 minutes. If it does, reduce the amount of catalyst and run another test. Hardening in about two hours is probably about ideal, but unless the waiting is holding you up, overnight is just as good. Always err on the side of too little hardener.

Now that you know the proper ratio, add the

hardener to your gelcoat putty. It is difficult to expose all of the thickened putty to the catalyst, so think puree and keep stirring until you are sure the two are evenly blended. If they aren't, portions of your repair will be an uncured, sticky mess.

Work the catalyzed putty into the scratch(es) with a small putty knife. With the knife relatively flat, drag it across the top of the scratch to compress the putty and to smooth the surface. The putty will bulge a little behind the knife, but that's okay; it is going to shrink when it cures and you want a little convexity anyway to allow you to fair the surface. Clean up any putty that is not in the scratch.

Give the gelcoat time to begin to cure, then place a sheet of plastic wrap over the repair. Tape one side, roll the plastic smoothly onto the putty, then tape the other side.

That's it. When the putty has cured, peel away the plastic and sand the spot smooth as detailed previously. If your progression through the various grits starts with an electric finishing sander, keep the pressure very light or you will sand away the old gelcoat on either side of the repair. Compound the spot and polish it to a mirror finish. If you have done a reasonably good job of matching the color, the repair should be virtually undetectable.

Repairing deep gouges. For deeper scratches, using gelcoat putty can be less than satisfactory because the unreinforced resin is quite brittle. It is a better idea to do the repair in two steps. Strengthen a quantity of polyester resin by adding an equal amount, by volume, of chopped fiberglass. You can make your own chopped glass by snipping the ends of a piece of glass cloth. Mix in enough thickening agent to make a putty. Catalyze the putty and fill the gouge to the *bottom* of the old gelcoat. Do not cover with plastic. If you prefer, you can use polyester auto body putty (Bondo or the like) for this step.

After the filler has cured, tint a quantity of gelcoat, and thicken slightly if necessary. With a small brush, paint the remaining depression flush (or slightly convex) with the gelcoat. Seal with plastic wrap. When it has cured, sand and polish to finish. Save the brush by cleaning it in brush cleaner.

Epoxy putty. Despite its greater strength and better adhesion, epoxy putty is not a good choice when it will be coated with gelcoat. While epoxy adheres tenaciously to polyester resin, the reverse is not true; gelcoat will not bond well to an underlayer of epoxy. But if your old gelcoat is beyond redemption, meaning that you intend to paint the surface after all blemishes are repaired, you should consider using epoxy putty.

You cannot adjust the cure time of epoxy by varying the amount of hardener, as you can with polyester resin. Epoxy is a two-part mixture, and the parts must be combined in the specified ratio. Mix up only as much as you can use within the cure time given on the package.

You can mix your own putty from epoxy resin, using chopped glass and a thickening agent, but unless you also intend to do some laminating with epoxy resin, you may be better off to buy the epoxy in a putty form. You will be hard pressed to find a proprietary product with a better reputation than Marine-Tex. This epoxy putty is not inexpensive, but its versatility is legendary. I have been told that the gray is stronger than the white. It is also cheaper, but if you are on a "patch now, paint later" program, the white can be less obtrusive.

Filling a gouge with epoxy putty is not much different than filling it with polyester, except that you will not need to seal the surface; the epoxy will cure in air. (Some epoxies will even cure under water.) You also do not want the putty to bulge above the surface. Draw your putty knife over the repair a second time to make the repair as flush as possible. Epoxy doesn't shrink in curing and, because it is harder than the surrounding gelcoat, any bulge will make it difficult to sand it flush. Remember that epoxy is much more toxic than polyester; ventilate well and wear protective gloves. Clean your tools with—right—brush cleaner.

CRACKED

You may think that repairing a crack is exactly the same as repairing a scratch. You might be wrong. It

Use the corner of a scraper or screwdriver to put a smooth chamfer on the sides of the gouge.

Wipe the area with acetone.

Apply wax to the area beneath the gouge.

Thicken polyester resin with an equal volume of chopped fiberglass.

Mix catalyst with the thickened resin.

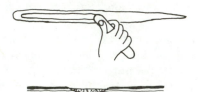

Fill the gouge to the *bottom* of the old gelcoat.

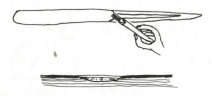

After the resin cures, paint the remaining depression with gelcoat.

Cover repair with plastic wrap and roll it smooth.

Filling a deep gouge

is important to understand what caused the crack before attempting any repair; otherwise the crack may return.

Cracks in the gelcoat are caused by movement. The flexible fiberglass laminates bend, but the brittle gelcoat cannot, so it cracks. If the flexing is a one-time event—like the time our friend released the wrong halyard and the wind generator crashed to the foredeck like a kamikaze helicopter—a sur-

face repair is all that is required. The nature of a crack fosters the temptation to try to "paint" it out with gelcoat, but such a repair is rarely successful because the gelcoat does not fill the crack, just bridges it. You must open the crack somewhat—with the corner of a screwdriver or the point of a nail—to allow the gelcoat to penetrate and to provide more surface area for adequate adhesion.

Often, however, cracks are not the result of a

specific event, but indicate some weakness in the construction. If cracks radiate out from beneath every stanchion base, there is an underlying problem. Parallel cracks along the corner where the foredeck turns up into the cabin trunk suggest flexing of the deck. Similar cracks around the perimeter of the cockpit sole point out another common problem area. A lasting repair can only be made by correcting the weakness. In the case of the stanchions, a larger backing plate might be an adequate solution, but in the other cases, and in most cases, stress cracks can be repaired permanently only by stiffening the underlying laminate *before* executing cosmetic repair to the gelcoat.

Crazing. Older boats may show crazing—tiny random cracks in the gelcoat—in the hull and deck, and from stem to stern. Often this condition is the result of good intentions gone wrong. The builder began the layup process with an extra heavy layer of gelcoat, and followed that with more laminates than were absolutely necessary. But unlike the extra laminates, which are one of the attractions of older boats, the thicker gelcoat was not a good idea. It resulted in a surface that was prone to crazing. Flexing was not strictly required; just the expansion and contraction of hot days and cool nights were sufficient, over time, to crack the gelcoat.

When the gelcoat is badly crazed, the only practical solution is painting. The preparation of a crazed surface for refinishing is detailed in Chapter 14. Less extensive crazing and cracking may be repaired like any other surface blemish, but the permanence of the repair depends upon correcting the weakness that caused the cracking.

WEAKNESS

In its most elementary form, strengthening involves adding laminates to the weak area. In order to do that, you need to be familiar with laying up fiberglass laminates. You could pick an inconspicuous spot inside the hull, someplace where you need extra laminates, and try your hand at fiberglass layup. But fiberglass work can be a sticky, gooey, messy proposition, prone to forgotten steps and incomplete preparation. If you stay away from the boat, you can practice layup technique virtually risk free until you master it.

Fiberglass layup is layers of fiberglass material *saturated* with polyester (or epoxy) resin. Nothing more. The fiberglass material is exactly what it sounds like, a weave of glass fibers. For boat construction and repair, the glass comes in chopped strand mat, unwoven roving, woven roving, and cloth.

Attacking the Problem

Chopped-strand mat. Chopped-strand mat looks like swept-up pieces of discarded thread. Irregular lengths of glass strands are combined randomly and glued together, not woven. Sometimes called CSM, the mat is sold from rolls, like other fabrics. It comes in various weights, but always select $1\frac{1}{2}$ ounce mat unless you have a specific reason to do otherwise. Generally speaking, mat is the easiest fabric to shape, gives the best resin-to-glass ratio, yields the smoothest surface, is the most watertight, and is the least subject to delamination. Unfortunately, the short fibers do not provide high tensile strength, which requires the continuous fibers of roving.

Roving. Unwoven roving is made up of parallel, flat bundles of strands, cross-stitched together. These straight, continuous strands in unidirectional roving add excellent strength, but only in one direction; they add little strength perpendicular to the strands. This shortcoming is overcome through "biaxial" or even "triaxial" composites, or by simply laying alternating laminates crosswise.

The more common solution, the one used by most boatbuilders, is to use woven roving. In this fabric, the flat bundles of strands are loosely woven into a coarse, open weave material offering full strength in two directions, and good strength in all directions. Roving, both unwoven and woven, when laminated together, is unacceptably easy to peel apart. When a layer of chopped-strand mat is used between each layer of roving, the combination is highly resistant to separation. Don't miss the significance here; in every fiberglass layup that I can imagine, *every other layer should be chopped-strand mat.*

Manufacturers alternate the layers of mat with woven roving, but for most of the fiberglass work that you will become involved in, fiberglass cloth will be a better material.

Fiberglass cloth. Fiberglass cloth looks somewhat like shiny canvas, but it is not woven as tightly as canvas and the thread is strands of glass. Cloth is stronger for its weight than roving and less prone to pulling and unraveling in the laminating process. The finished product looks nicer.

Cloth is commonly available in weights from four to 20 ounces. That sounds heavy relative to 1½-ounce mat, but don't be confused. Weight designations for mat are per square foot, while for cloth and roving they are per square *yard.* Leave the calculator in the drawer – 1½-ounce mat weighs the same as 13½-ounce cloth. For any boat over 15 feet, there will be little, if any, fiberglass work that you cannot do with 1½-ounce mat and 10-ounce cloth. Be sure the cloth is chrome treated, which removes manufacturing oils and waxes. If you have a choice, buy it in 38-inch width.

Other materials. Unless you know what you are doing–and you won't learn it here–stay away from the "exotic" materials. They include polypropylene, xynole-polyester, dynel, kevlar, ceramic, and graphite. Each of these has specific strengths and weaknesses which you should fully understand before using them, and none of them are essential to the restoration of an older fiberglass boat.

I have also failed to mention chopper-gun construction. Instead of wetting out chopped-strand mat, some manufacturers use a machine that sprays chopped strand roving and polyester resin at the same time. Manufacturers usually claim that the gun gives them better control over the mix of glass and resin. Maybe so, but that is not the reason they are using a chopper gun. You get one gue$$. Chopper-gun layup goes very quickly, but unless the operator is very skillful, and very attentive, the "perfect" mix will be thick in some places, not so thick in others. Chopper-gun construction does not enjoy an unsullied reputation.

Learning by doing. The best way to develop some familiarity with hand layup is by doing it. Instead of working on the boat, we are going to lay up a small fiberglass part; failures will not require any corrective action but may simply be tossed into the can. The item illustrated is an instrument box. When instruments are installed in the aft end of the trunk, the rear of the instrument intrudes into the cabin. A fiberglass cover gives the installation a finished look.

I have selected a round instrument box because it provides an opportunity to deal with an array of difficulties that are likely occur in other fiberglassing jobs. You may use the same technique to construct a square box, or any shape that fits your need.

The list of materials you need is short: a quart of polyester laminating (air-inhibited) resin, a yard of 1½-ounce chopped-strand mat, a yard of 10-ounce fiberglass cloth, a couple of 1½-inch throwaway bristle brushes, a small quantity of mold release (poly vinyl alcohol), and a quart of acetone. This is far more glass and resin than you need, but it is the smallest practical amount you can purchase; and if you do any other fiberglass work, these are the materials you will be using.

You also need a Cool Whip tub or a plastic refrigerator container, a piece of thick cardboard (foam-filled backer board is perfect), some adhesive caulk, a canister of modeling clay, a roll of waxed paper, and a package of throwaway gloves. You'll also need a strawberry shortcake; you can't just waste a whole tub full of Cool Whip!

Building a mold. First, construct the mold. Cut the plastic tub to the appropriate depth, determined by the protrusion of the instrument being covered. Now cut two squares of the backer board 4 inches wider than the diameter of the tub. Invert the tub onto the center of each of the squares and trace around it. Carefully cut this circle from the center of one of the squares. On the other square, draw a second circle about ⅛ inch outside the first one and cut out this larger circle.

Place the inverted tub on a flat surface and drop the first square (the one with the smaller hole) over the tub so that it also lies on the flat surface. Join the two together with a bead of adhesive caulk and allow the adhesive to set. Hot melt adhesive can speed the process.

Turn the mold over and center the square with the larger circle over the attached square and glue it in place. Now fill the step created by the two circles with modeling clay and shape it into a smooth radius. You should end up with a gentle curve between the vertical side of the tub and the horizontal surface of the cardboard. Some tubs have a radius at the bottom, but if you are using a container that has a sharp corner at the bottom, radius it with a fillet of clay; run the edge of a coin around the fillet to get the radius uniform. We are doing all of this because fiberglass cloth does not conform easily to sharp corners.

We now have a mold. Before we can use it, we

Cut Cool Whip tub to appropriate height.

Cut circle out of stiff cardboard, slip over inverted tub, and glue in place.

Glue second square of cardboard with larger circular opening on top of first square.

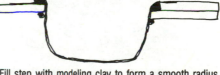

Fill step with modeling clay to form a smooth radius.

Heavily coat mold with wax.

Coat waxed mold with PVA.

Cut three pieces of fiberglass material for each laminate.

Laying up an instrument cover (continued on next page)

Coat the mold with gelcoat (optional).

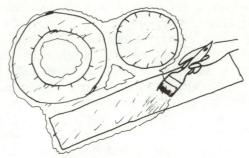

Saturate the pieces of fiberglass with resin.

Put the first strip of material around the inside of the mold, overlapping the ends.

Put the bottom piece in the mold, overlapping the strip.

Put the flange piece in place, overlapping the strip.

Repeat the last three steps for each laminate. After the final laminate brush on extra resin for a smoother finish. After the resin kicks, coat the surface with PVA.

When the resin has cured, flex the mold to pop the cover out.

Trim the flange to size while the fiberglass is still "green."

Laying up an instrument cover (continued)

need to coat it with wax to keep the resin from adhering to it. Almost any soft wax will work, and four coats are not too many.

Cutting the cloth. Next cut the fiberglass to fit. A couple of layers of 1 1/2-ounce mat would be adequate for this particular part, but to learn more from the exercise, we are going to follow a four laminate schedule: two layers of mat, followed by a layer of 10-ounce cloth and another layer of mat. Now is a good time to get those gloves on.

Each layer will require three pieces of fabric: a round piece slightly larger than the bottom of the mold, a straight strip as wide as the mold is deep and half an inch longer than the circumference, and a round piece two inches wider in diameter than the top of the mold. Small notches around the edge of the bottom piece will allow the glass to turn up the sides more easily. Cut the center from the large circle (which will become the flange for attaching the box) to form a ring 1 1/2 inches wide. At 1-inch intervals, cut narrow notches half an inch into the inside edge of the ring, to allow the glass to turn down into the mold. Check the pieces for fit, then duplicate them twice from mat and once from cloth.

The layup process. Now paint the mold with the poly vinyl alcohol (PVA), a parting agent that will insure that the resin will not adhere to the mold. Let the PVA dry to a protective film. If you have gelcoat and want to use it, paint the inside of the mold and the flange with an even coat—not too heavily, about the thickness of four sheets of paper. Let the gelcoat set before proceeding. It is not necessary to use gelcoat, and any imperfections in the molded part will be easier to fair if the surface coat is paint.

In place of the gelcoat, or after it has solidified, paint the surface with catalyzed resin. Lay the parts for the first two layers of mat on a piece of scrap cardboard and saturate them with resin, using a brush to *gently* apply the resin. Properly saturated, the fabric will be uniformly transparent; if the material still appears white, add more resin. When the pieces are wet through, pick up one of the strips and put it around the inside of the mold, overlapping the

ends. Use the brush to smooth it in place. Next apply the circle to the bottom of the mold so that the notched perimeter turns up onto the strip already in place. Using the end of the brush, without adding any resin, stipple the mat into the corner and the two pieces together, working out any voids or bubbles. Lay the saturated ring of mat on top of the mold and fold the inner edge down onto the strip. Smooth the ring and stipple the ring and the strip together. While the first layer is still wet, repeat the process with the second layer. If extra resin begins to puddle in the bottom of the mold, remove it with your brush.

Generally speaking, it is a good idea to apply fiberglass two layers at a time. A single layer may generate insufficient exothermic heat to cure quickly, while too many layers may build up enough heat to "cook" the resin, severely weakening it. On a small part like this one, we could get away with doing all four laminates at once, but you are never wrong doing two at a time.

When the first two layers have hardened, paint their surface with catalyzed resin, saturate the remaining pieces of cloth and mat, and repeat the steps above. Apply the layer of cloth first. You will find that the cloth is a bit more difficult to work with, tending to wrinkle on anything but a flat surface, but a little patience will usually prevail.

After the last layer of mat, brushing on a small quantity of additional resin may give you a nicer finish. It is not important in this case, but it will be for any modifications you may have in mind for your boat.

Because laminating resin is air-inhibited, the surface will remain tacky unless you seal it from the air. On a flat surface, a sheet of plastic wrap will serve, but for a piece that is all curves and corners, a coat of PVA is somewhat easier. Wait until the resin has started to kick (harden), then coat it.

After the resin has hardened, simply pop it out of the mold. This is a good time to trim the flange to the size you want. If the glass is still green, you can trim off the excess with snips without shattering the cut edge. Now drop the piece back into the mold and leave it for a couple of days to reach its full cure.

If the plastic tub had a dimple in its center, the instrument box will also. You can fill the dimple, or any other imperfections in the surface, using polyester putty or thickened resin (or thickened gelcoat if the surface is gelcoat). Be sure to wipe the part thoroughly with an acetone-dampened rag first to remove all traces of mold release and wax. After the putty cures, sand the part and drill the mounting holes in the flange, and any other holes that are necessary for the wires or cables that connect the instrument. Finish the cover with a couple of coats of paint. That's it.

That is all there is to laying up fiberglass. Don't try to make it more complicated than it is. If you had no problem with this exercise, you know all you need to know to handle 95 percent of the fiberglassing jobs you are likely to contemplate. If you don't know how the part might have looked because you can't get it out of the mold, if the brush is permanently attached because the resin kicked while you were still smoothing the glass, if the vertical pieces are bunched at the bottom like an old gym sock, if the "smooth" surface is more like a bad spike haircut, or if you had any other problems, do it again. Figure out what went wrong and correct it. The only expense will be the cost of a couple of brushes.

If you want to go for the advanced degree, put a few blobs of glue on the bottom of the mold and glue it to the underside of a low table. Wait until dark. Now crawl under the table, and by the light of a flashlight, lay up the instrument box in the inverted mold. This exercise will serve you well when you attempt to add laminates to a weak side deck, or reinforce the cockpit sole.

Adding strength.   We started this exercise as a discussion of weakness. The truth is that a springy hull or deck may not be weak at all, but that bouncy feeling does not fill one's heart with confidence. And even if you know that the laminate is plenty strong, flexing is murder on the gelcoat. More often than not it is stiffness we are after, not strength. We will deal with that later. But if you are after strength, you get it by adding laminates. You should already be clear on laying up fiberglass, but there are some other considerations when you are adding laminates to a long-cured hull or deck.

First, resist the temptation to try to lay a single piece the size of a tablecloth; anything bigger than a square yard will be more trouble than it is worth. If you are doing a big area, cut the fabric into several small pieces and overlap them a couple of inches. You will probably be adding more than one layer and you want the edges to taper, not only because it will look neater, but also because you do not want to create a hard spot that can lead to a destructive flexing pattern. To achieve the taper, cut each piece an inch or so larger than the previous one, laminating the smallest piece first and finishing with the largest one. This makes for a neat job, and it gives each layer some direct bond to the original surface instead of making all the laminates entirely dependent upon the bond of the first.

Grinding is essential.   Keep in mind that new

cloth   mat

Alternate layers of mat with layers of roving or cloth, always beginning with mat and generally finishing with cloth. Making each successive laminate larger than the previous one gives each layer a *direct* bond with the original surface and provides a tapered edge, which avoids a hard spot and is more attractive.

Adding laminates

laminates will not adhere to a fully-cured surface unless you grind it. When you are using laminating resin, you can add additional laminates without grinding *because the resin does not fully cure*. That is what air-inhibited means. But if the previous laminates were laid up with finishing resin, or if they were sealed and allowed to cure, or if they are "old," you must grind the surface before adding any laminates. To prevent a maddening itch, wear protective clothing. (And don't wash it later with your BVDs.) Protect your eyes with goggles, and wear a dust mask—not one of those worthless throwaway kind, but a rubber one that seals against your face. Your lungs ought to be worth a sawbuck and change. Now wipe the surface *first* with acetone, then hold the largest of the laminates to be added in place and mark the outline. Chuck a sanding disk into your drill, stick on a #36 grit disk, and take the shine off everything inside the outline. Hold the grinder so that the dust is thrown away from you.

With the surface ground and the precut pieces of glass laid out on scrap wood or cardboard, the process is exactly the one I have already described. If the area being reinforced is large, you can work faster if you use a short-nap paint roller instead of a brush to wet the surface with catalyzed resin. Use the roller also to saturate the fiberglass before lifting it from the cardboard and positioning it. If the surface is relatively flat, the roller can also smooth the laminate into place and force out any bubbles. For more complex surfaces, use the heel of a brush, or try a rubber squeegee. Wipe up the excess resin that is compressed out.

Apply two layers at a time and allow the resin to kick before proceeding. Alternate materials, always starting with a layer of mat and always finishing with a layer of cloth. Do not be tempted by the superior strength of cloth to forgo the weaker mat; it is essential to binding the laminates together permanently. A combined layer of 1 1/2-ounce mat and 10-ounce cloth adds about 1/10 inch to the thickness, and about 10 ounces per square foot in weight. Remember that in order for the last laminate to cure tack-free, you must seal it with plastic wrap pressed in

place and taped around the edges, or with a coat of PVA.

Hat-shaped stiffeners. When it is stiffness you are after, additional laminates are not usually the best way to achieve it. Reinforcing members—ribs and stringers—will add more stiffness and less weight. The ease of flexing a wooden yardstick one way and the difficulty of flexing it the other illustrate the concept of stiffening members. If we put the edge of the yardstick against the springy laminate and fiberglass it in place, we will make the laminate near the reinforcement rigid. We could then extract the yardstick because the fiberglass—molded with a hollow in the middle, like a hat—would provide the stiffness alone. Because of this, hat-shaped reinforcements are often formed over foam, or even cardboard, instead of wood. To stiffen a larger area, we add more reinforcing members.

What you use as a form for the fiberglass hat you are going to construct is up to you. Possibilities are narrow strips of plywood, half-round molding, split cardboard tubing, V-folded corrugated pasteboard, split vinyl hose, plastic pipe, or strips of foam. Cut a strip of mat as long as the reinforcement and wide enough to cover the form and extend out on both sides at least 3 inches. Cut a strip of cloth the same length and an inch wider. Two layers are adequate for a tophat stiffener up to about 3 inches high, but if you want the assurance of additional strips, cut each succeeding one an inch wider.

Grind the old fiberglass, then tack the form in place with hot glue or quick setting epoxy. If the form is wood, the ends should be tapered to avoid a hard spot. Paint the surface with catalyzed resin, saturate the mat strip, and center it over the form. Put the saturated cloth over the mat, overlapping a half inch on both sides. Use the heel of the brush to smooth the glass to the contour of the form and to compress the two layers. (If you are doing additional layers, you can probably do up to four layers in a single layup without a problem.) Seal the surface with PVA or plastic wrap and allow the resin to cure.

Attaching mounting blocks. You use the same layup technique to attach other things to the hull.

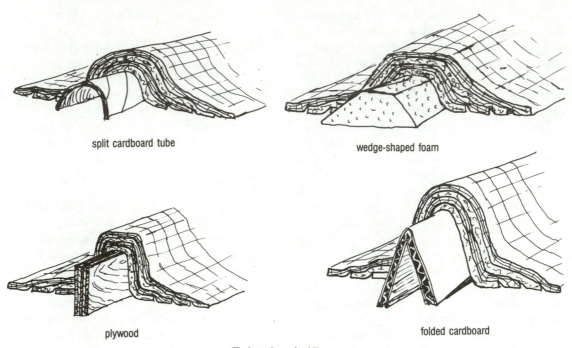

split cardboard tube

wedge-shaped foam

plywood

folded cardboard

Tophat-shaped stiffeners

Say you want to install a foot pump in the galley. In the age of wooden construction, boats had plenty of ribs and stringers that could be drilled for the mounting screws. But where do you drill the mounting holes when the hull is fiberglass? Where you *don't* drill the holes is directly into the hull. The correct way is to bond a wooden block to the hull and mount the pump to the block.

You can use any kind of wood, but I like oak because it holds a screw well and resists rot. Shape the block to fit the contour of the hull (see Chapter 10). You could simply grind the hull and glue the block in place with epoxy, but the block will eventually release. A better choice is laminating the block to the hull.

Grind an area a couple of inches larger than the block. Cut a piece of mat ½ inch larger than the *bottom* of the block. Cut a second piece of mat large enough to contour over the block and extend out onto the hull two inches or so all around. Cut a

square out of each corner so that the material will, in effect, strap the block down in both directions. Cut a piece of cloth to the same shape, but with added length and width so that it will extend beyond the mat laminate about an inch.

Wet the sanded hull with catalyzed resin. Saturate the small piece of mat and smooth it in place where you want the block to be located. Paint the entire surface of the block with resin, taking care to saturate any end grain. Put the block in place and push it down into the mat. About ¼ inch of the mat should peek out from under the block all the way around; this will provide some support for the radius that will be formed when the covering laminates turn out onto the hull. Wet out the second piece of mat and smooth it in place over the block. Next comes the saturated piece of cloth. Smooth all of the laminated surfaces, brushing up any excess resin. With the tip of the brush, stipple the inside corners where the block meets the hull. If the resin is air-inhibited, seal the surface. When the resin has cured, drill through the laminates into the block and mount the pump.

Tabbing bulkheads. Shelves, dividers, furniture, and bulkheads are attached to a fiberglass hull in almost the same manner. Successively wider strips of mat and cloth are laid along the joint, extending out onto the hull several inches and up onto the part a similar distance. (Fiberglass tapes with finished edges and in a variety of widths are available specifically for this use. You will have to cut the mat for the intermediate layers.) The number of layers depends upon the strength required—perhaps two layers would be adequate to anchor a locker divider, while six layers on both sides might not be too many for a major bulkhead. To accommodate the curvature of the hull and make the strips lie smoothly, you may have to notch them as we did the fabric pieces for the instrument box.

Attaching parts in this way is called *tabbing* (sometimes *taping*), and it differs from the way we attached the mounting block in that the fiberglass does not encapsulate the member, but rather adheres to it. This is an important distinction: while the bond between laminates of fiberglass is, for all practical purposes, permanent, the bond between fiberglass and wood most assuredly is not. Wood shrinks and swells with changes in humidity, while the fiberglass is relatively unaffected. Release is inevitable.

But since there is not a practical alternative, tabbing is the standard way of mounting parts to a fiberglass hull. Done carefully, a tabbed joint can last a long time, but before you offer your old boat as an example of just how long, take a flexible, thin-blade knife (or a feeler gauge) and see if you can run it between the fiberglass tabbing and the bulkheads. Don't blanch if you discover a bulkhead that is no longer attached.

Reattaching loose tabbing. When the tabbing has released, there are two good ways to fix it. The most obvious one is to grind away the old tabbing and lay up new fiberglass along the joint, as though you were tabbing the piece in place for the first time.

The alternative is to reattach the bulkhead mechanically. Typically the tabbing has released from the plywood bulkhead, but the leg on the hull is still firmly attached. In this case, an effective repair can be made by prying the gap open a bit and filling it with a polyurethane adhesive (3M #5200), then fastening the flap to the wood with a staggered row of screws. This is a strong, permanent repair.

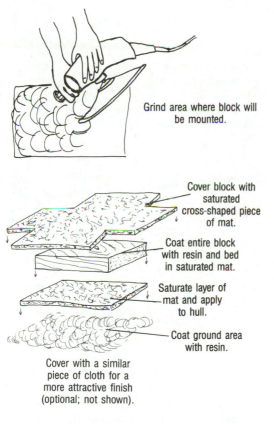

Grind area where block will be mounted.

Cover block with saturated cross-shaped piece of mat.

Coat entire block with resin and bed in saturated mat.

Saturate layer of mat and apply to hull.

Coat ground area with resin.

Cover with a similar piece of cloth for a more attractive finish (optional; not shown).

The finished block.

Glassing a mounting block

If you want to retab the piece, or tab a new part to the hull, there are some techniques you can use to give the joint a longer life. Be sure that you grind the fiberglass well where the tape will be attached. If the part being attached is covered with plastic laminate, you will have to grind that away. Paint or any other covering must be removed. Even raw plywood must be sanded to clean and roughen the surface, providing for better adhesion.

After being shocked by the effect of a strong bleach solution on my precious teak, I began bleaching plywood before laying fiberglass on it. The bleach eats away the soft pulp, leaving the tougher part rough and honeycombed—perfect for good resin adhesion. I suppose it will be 20 years or so before I know if this process is worth the effort, but if you try it, bleach at least a week before tabbing to be sure the plywood is thoroughly dry.

Permanent tabbing. To make the attachment truly permanent, you need to take adhesion to wood out of the equation. You can do this by *slotting* the bulkhead. Drill two $3/8$-inch holes $3 1/4$ inches apart and one inch from the edge of the bulkhead. With a saber saw, make two straight cuts between the two holes, creating a $3/8$-inch slot. Round the bottom edge of the slot with a router or sandpaper. Cut similar slots every 6 or 8 inches along the edge to be attached. Paint the bottom of the slot and the sides of bulkhead beneath it, and the hull, with catalyzed resin. Begin with a 3-inch-wide strip of saturated mat long enough to pass through the slot, down the bulkhead and at least an inch out onto the hull on both sides of the part. (Lay the end of the saturated fiberglass onto the end of a strip of stiff cardboard to simplify threading it through the slot.) Each additional layer of glass should be a couple of inches longer than the previous one. Now tab the space between the slots in the usual manner, with the same number (and combination) of laminates. Finish the joint neatly with an additional laminate or two covering both the slotted and the unslotted tabbing.

You have already discovered that fiberglass does not like to conform to sharp corners; filling the corner where the surfaces intersect with polyester

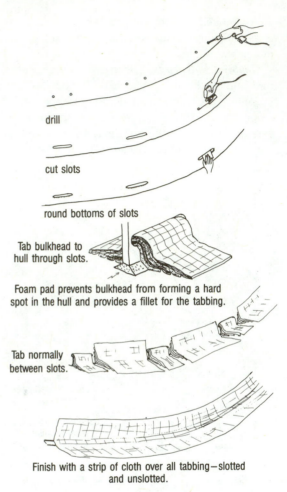

drill

cut slots

round bottoms of slots

Tab bulkhead to hull through slots.

Foam pad prevents bulkhead from forming a hard spot in the hull and provides a fillet for the tabbing.

Tab normally between slots.

Finish with a strip of cloth over all tabbing—slotted and unslotted.

Tabbing bulkheads

putty or polyurethane caulk will make the tabbing easier and neater. A better solution is a tent-shaped (with the top sliced off to the width of the bulkhead) pad of polyurethane foam *between* the part and the hull. In addition to providing the desired fillet (easing the angle), the foam will prevent the joint from causing a hard spot in the hull.

BLISTERED

Anything I say about blisters will probably be obsolete soon since this subject continues to get a great deal of attention. A couple of years ago, for example, the standard treatment was to strip the gelcoat and apply a barrier coat of epoxy. Lately there is evidence that the epoxy may ultimately make the blistering more severe. Next year . . . who knows?

The best scientific minds agree (this year) that the cause of blisters, or *boat pox*, is water penetration through a porous gelcoat. The water dissolves any unbound chemicals—solvents, accelerators, fabric binders, and other impurities—forming an acidic solution, which sets up an osmotic flow of more water through the gelcoat. The effect is to make your gelcoat into a water balloon. It's bad enough if it stops there, but over time the acid may also attack the resin beneath the gelcoat.

Not all boats develop boat pox, but no one knows exactly why not. Orthophthalic gelcoat resin seems to be more prone to blistering than isophthalic resin; boats in the water all year more prone than ones wintering in a cradle; boats in warm climes more prone than those in cold; boats in fresh water more prone than those in salt water; boats from one manufacturer more prone than those from another. A lot of old boats have never developed blisters, perhaps because the gelcoat was thicker, or fewer additives were used, or pre-OPEC resins were better, or there was more pride in workmanship, or less air pollution, or more rain forest. Whatever the reason, blistering seems to be less of a problem with older boats—more like pimples than pox.

Contrary to what your boatyard manager may be telling you, I think it is a mistake to remove all the gelcoat at the first sign of blistering. That's like burning down the barn to get rid of rats. With just a few blisters, deal with them one at a time.

Open each blister completely and let it drain. Wipe it out with brush cleaner. Use a disk sander to grind the blister into a shallow depression, then use a brush to scrub the depression squeaky clean with fresh water and TSP (trisodium phosphate), available at any hardware store. Rinse thoroughly. Rinse thoroughly. Rinse thoroughly. Let the spot dry for a couple of days.

There is enough evidence now to suggest that epoxy is not a good choice for repairs to the under-water portion of the hull. The curing agents in epoxy seem to aggravate the blistering problem. Automotive body putty is also a poor choice unless you know that it contains no hollow fillers (such as microballoons). Either polyester resin or gelcoat resin, thickened with chopped glass, is the best choice. Fill the depression and seal it with plastic wrap. After it has cured thoroughly, fair it, and give it three coats of an *alkyd-based* topside enamel.

To prevent future blisters, you must stop water from penetrating the hull. It is epoxy's resistance to water penetration that accounts for its popularity as a preventative coating, but when the water does eventually penetrate, the epoxy coating exacerbates the problem. Recent studies indicate that three coats of alkyd-based topside enamel will prevent blisters from forming for as long as an epoxy coating, and if water does penetrate the surface, blistering will be less severe. So the current cure for boat pox is painting, not fiberglassing. We will treat the subject in greater depth in Chapter 14.

DELAMINATED

The separation of the layers of a fiberglass laminate generally stems from one of three conditions: overbending the laminate, water penetration, or poor construction. Overbending, usually related to impact, requires the laminates to slide over one another (flex a paperback book sharply to get the idea), causing the laminates to sheer apart. Water penetration is most destructive when the laminate includes an absorbent core—plywood or balsa, for example—but the water may also combine with unbound chemicals in the laminate to form an acidic solution that actually attacks the resin. And if the laminates were not saturated thoroughly or rolled down properly in the layup process, the bond between laminates may be fragile rather than robust.

How do you know you have internal delamination? The two places you are most likely to encounter it are in the deck and behind severe hull blisters. In the first case, you will hear it; in the second, you can see it. If you suspect delamination elsewhere—

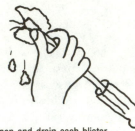

Open and drain each blister.

Wipe the cavity with brush cleaner.

Grind the blister into a shallow depression.

Scrub vigorously with TSP.

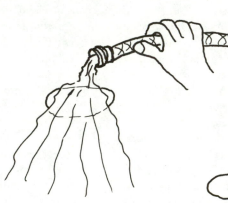

Rinse. Rinse. Rinse.

Allow blister to air dry for several days (or longer).

Thicken gelcoat or polyester resin
with chopped glass.

Add catalyst.

Fill depression.

Gelcoat blister repair

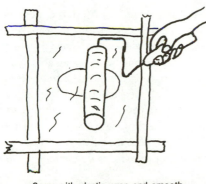

Cover with plastic wrap and smooth.

Paint area with three coats of alkyd-based enamel.

Gelcoat blister repair (continued)

in a dent or soft spot, or at the point of an impact—you can confirm or refute your suspicions by tapping the area with a light mallet and listening for a difference in the sound.

Attacking the Problem

Resin injection. Occasionally—maybe rarely is a better choice—you can repair delamination by injecting resin into the void. Bore two holes into the highest part of the void, one to let the resin in, the other to let the air out. If the void is in the hull, you may be able to drill the holes from the inside, leaving the gelcoat unmarred. For delamination in the deck, the holes must be bored from the top surface. Resin is fed into one hole until it flows out of the other one. Simple.

Except that we already know that new resin does not adhere well to a cured surface, which is what we have inside the void, and grinding is obviously out of the question. The void may also be irregular in shape, forming air pockets that will still be delaminated when the repair is finished. And moisture inside the void will defeat this effort entirely.

We can increase the likelihood of a good bond by using epoxy resin instead of polyester. The epoxy will get a more tenacious grip on the unsanded surfaces inside the void and will be less affected by moisture. Putting the resin under pressure will also help. This is accomplished by hot gluing a 2-foot

length of hose to the feed hole, supporting the hose vertically, and feeding the resin through it. When all the air has been displaced, the vent hole must be plugged. Feeding the resin with a 2-foot column will add about a pound of pressure per square inch.

For an irregular void, exploring with a piece of wire or a 90-degree pick (a small Allen wrench works well) can help in accurately mapping the void. Additional vent holes will facilitate the resin flow.

When moisture has penetrated the void, it must be removed if the repair is to succeed. In the case of delamination between layers of fiberglass, flushing the void with acetone should do the job, but if there is a core involved and it is wet, forget it. Injection is no longer an option.

Delaminated core. Delamination of cored decks is all too common, particularly when the core is balsa or plywood. This should not surprise anyone; the bond between fiberglass laminates and wood is never permanent. The release is often accelerated by water penetration. How does water get into the core? Every drilled hole in the deck is a potential spigot: mounting holes for cleats, stanchions, and tracks; openings for chainplates, ventilators, and deck pipes; screw holes for trim rings, anchor chocks, or teak decks.

A delaminated deck will usually snap and pop when you walk on it. A few test holes will tell you if the core is wet or dry. If it is dry, epoxy injection will

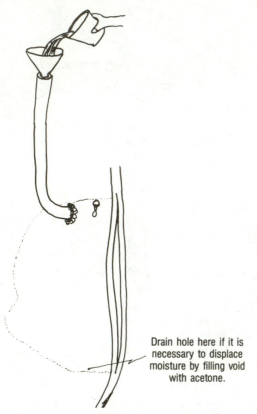

Drain hole here if it is necessary to displace moisture by filling void with acetone.

Hot-glue hose over drilled fill hole to put resin under pressure. Fill void *and* hose with *epoxy* resin, plugging vent hole when all air has escaped and epoxy begins to run out.

Injecting a void with epoxy resin

Excising the damage. Map the delaminated area by sounding the deck with a light mallet. Outline the area with straight lines. Using a circular saw with a fiberglass-cutting blade (or an abrasive cutoff wheel), set the cutting depth to the thickness of the top skin and cut along the outline. Whenever possible, make the cuts through the smooth part of the deck rather than across any molded-in nonskid pattern. This will make it easier to make the repair to the deck unnoticeable. Remove the top skin and set it aside.

The core will almost certainly be either plywood or balsa. If it is not too wet, you may be able to let it air dry, or help it along with a hot air blower. If the core is thoroughly saturated, drying could take months. Unless you are willing to wait that long, replacement is the appropriate course.

Set the saw deeper and cut around the saturated core. If the core is plywood, the repair will be stronger if the joints for the new core and the joints where the top skin is replaced are staggered. This is less of a concern with end-grain balsa. Don't get too bold with the depth setting on the saw; you want to be sure that you do not cut the bottom skin. Remove the old core and use a chisel to clean up the bottom and the edges. Grind the bottom skin, and the underside of the top skin that you set aside.

Replacing the core. Cut two pieces of mat to the size of the repair. Cut and fit new core material. The new core should be $1/8$ to $3/16$ inch *thinner* than the original, because you are going to join it to the old skins with additional laminates, and you want the finished thickness to be the same. You can duplicate the original core, or substitute nonabsorbent PVC foam (Airex) or a honeycomb product (Nomex). If you are using wood or plywood, sand both sides to improve the bond. The other core materials are more easily crushed, and if you are using them, plywood or solid laminate should be substituted under any through-bolted items that will sit on the repair.

Maybe I don't need to say this, but *never, never* use anything but marine grade (or void-free exterior grade) plywood for any work on your old boat, including *core* replacement. The glue in interior-

be the easiest route to repair. Keep in mind that the core may have released on both sides, so you will have to inject resin below the core as well as above it. If your feed hole passes through the core—but not through the bottom skin—you can rebond both sides at the same time.

If the core is wet, it will have to be dried, and that invariably means removal of one of the skins. Few old boats have cored hulls, so this problem most often has to do with the deck. If you can get to the underside of the deck easily, you can do the repair without damaging the exterior finish of the boat. Unfortunately there is usually a molded headliner between you and the underside of the deck, making on-deck repair the only reasonable choice.

Cut around the outline of the faulty core, taking care not to cut the opposite skin. Set aside removed skin.

Use a chisel to clean up bottom and edges.

Grind bottom skin and underside of top skin.

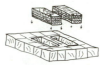

Cut new piece of core material. If you are using balsa, substitute plywood in all areas where hardware will be mounted.

Saturate two layers of mat. Apply one to the bottom of the new core material and the other on the bottom skin. Stipple lightly with a brush to remove bubbles and insure contact, then fit core—mat-to-mat—into cut-out. Weight to improve bond.

With new core bonded in place, fill all voids and saturate core with resin.

Using as many layers of saturated mat as necessary to achieve a flush fit of the top skin, bond the skin to the core and apply weight.

Grind all joints into a shallow V with a 15:1 bevel on each side.

Fill the beveled joints with alternating layers of mat and cloth.

Core repair

grade plywood is not waterproof; when moisture gets to the plywood, it will come apart.

Remove the fitted core and the pieces of mat from the repair. Turn the core upside down on scrap cardboard, and paint it with epoxy resin. Saturate the mat. Thickly paint the bottom skin and the edges of the core that remains in the deck. Lay one layer of saturated mat against the bottom skin. Stipple *lightly* with the end of the brush to be sure that the mat is in contact with the skin and no air bubbles are trapped. Apply the second layer of mat to the bottom of the core in the same manner. Do not compress either layer with a squeegee or a roller; the new core is not likely to fit perfectly against the bottom skin and the uncompressed mat will help fill the irregularities. Turn the new core back over and put it in place, compressing the two layers of saturated mat together and weighting the core evenly until the resin kicks.

Reattaching the outer skin. With the new core now in place, saturate it with epoxy resin until all voids are filled and the cells of the core material are virtually encapsulated in resin. After the resin has kicked, put the original top skin in place and, pressing it down, measure how far below the adjoining skin it sits. (You made the new core thinner, remember?) A single layer of 1 1/2-ounce mat can be compressed to about 1/32 inch, so if the loose piece sits, for example, 1/16 inch below the rest of the deck, you will use two layers of mat beneath the skin.

Cut the necessary layers of mat to size. Paint the surface of the new core and the underside of the piece of top skin, and saturate the pieces of mat. Apply one piece of mat to the underside of the skin. The remaining layers are laid up on the new core. Only the top piece is exempt from rolling to smooth and compact the layers. Put the skin in place, compressing the two layers of saturated mat together and weighting the skin evenly.

It would be nice if you could just putty the cut around the repair and gelcoat or paint it; but if you did, you would end up with a repair only marginally stronger than the strength of the bottom skin *alone*. This would become manifestly clear when you stepped off the cabin top and found yourself standing on the Vee-berth. You have to *strongly* reattach the cut piece to the rest of the top skin. That means laminating the piece in place.

For a strong joint, you need a scarf. I am not talking about laminating with strips of your paisley ascot. A scarf is a way of joining two pieces by cutting their ends at an angle and overlapping them. It is somewhere between a butt joint and a lamination, serving the purpose of the former with the strength of the latter.

Clearly the cut-out piece is not going to overlap the remaining skin when reinstalled. To achieve a scarf joint requires a new piece of skin scarfed to *both parts*. You do this by grinding the joint into a shallow V. A joint as strong as the original laminate usually requires a 15-to-1 bevel, but for a skin no more than 1/4 inch thick, a 10-to-1 bevel is appropriate. In other words, the bevel on a 1/4-inch skin should be 2 1/2 inches. But we are scarfing the new piece of laminate to both pieces, so the width of the V would be 5 inches.

Once the perimeter of the repair has been bev-

eled, cut alternating strips of mat and cloth to fill the joint. The first layer of mat should be about 2 inches wide, and subsequent layers of glass should be 1 inch wider than the preceding one. You could duplicate the original laminate schedule, but it is not necessary. Simply lay in laminates until the V is flush, or slightly indented if you want to finish with gelcoat. You can estimate the number of laminates required by knowing that one layer of 1 1/2-ounce mat and one of 10-ounce cloth, compacted and cured, will have a finished thickness of slightly more than 1/16 inch.

If the joint was not visible—on the inside of the hull, for example—you would carry the last laminates out onto the skin surface beside the bevel. But on deck, we want to confine the repair to the already-big-enough-thank-you-very-much bevel. The top strips of fabric should be no wider than the bevel. Heavily waxing the surface next to the bevel, taking great care not to let any wax get onto the ground surfaces, will assist in the containment effort.

Concealing the repair. After the laminates have cured, all that remains to be done is to blend the repair into the deck. For a deck that has required major surgery, the easiest way to hide the scar is to cover the deck with rubber nonskid overlay (Tread Master), and as a side benefit, you get what is arguably the most secure footing. Overlay installation is detailed in a later chapter. When the repair will be hidden beneath an overlay, it may be easier to simply lay up an entirely new top skin rather than grafting the old piece in place. The perimeter of the cutout should still be beveled 10 to 1, then increasingly larger pieces of mat and cloth are laid up on the new core and out onto the bevel.

If you want to maintain the original nonskid, but plan to paint the deck after it has been repaired, you will need to sand the new seams smooth, filling any imperfections with epoxy putty. Using mat for the top layer or two of the new laminate will make the smoothing process easier. When the repair cuts across a nonskid panel, symmetry can be reestablished by taping off a matching pattern on the opposite side of the deck and filling the molded nonskid pattern with epoxy putty. Painting is detailed in Chapter 14.

It seems unlikely to me that the gelcoat of a badly delaminated deck will be in such good shape that you will want to try to match it after the repair. In that event, however, the new laminates should not quite reach the level of the old surfaces, allowing for the application of 20 mils of gelcoat. Alternatively, you will have to grind the new laminates slightly below the adjoining surfaces. The depression is filled with gelcoat, and as it begins to kick, it is sealed from the air. After the new gelcoat has thoroughly cured, there is a great deal of sanding, compounding, and polishing to be done to achieve a glassy finish.

It is also possible to match the nonskid by taking

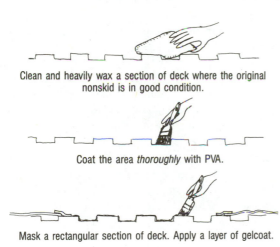

Clean and heavily wax a section of deck where the original nonskid is in good condition.

Coat the area *thoroughly* with PVA.

Mask a rectangular section of deck. Apply a layer of gelcoat.

When the gelcoat hardens, add three layers of saturated mat.

Remove the cured lamination from the deck, invert, and use as a mold to lay-up nonskid identical to the original. Wax the mold and coat it with mold release (PVA) before applying gelcoat and the appropriate schedule of laminates.

Matching molded nonskid

a mold from the original. Clean and heavily wax the spot on deck that you select as the pattern for the mold, and then coat it with PVA—you want to make absolutely sure that the resin will not adhere. Mask around a rectangular section of the waxed deck and paint it with gelcoat. When the gelcoat has hardened, paint it with resin and add about three layers of saturated mat. When fully cured, the mold is removed. The process is now repeated, this time onto the gelcoated surface of the mold rather than the deck. The gelcoat used this time should be tinted to match the original nonskid, and the number of layers of mat reduced to two. Don't forget to wax the mold and coat it with PVA. The new piece of laminate will be an exact copy of the original surface and it can be cut to the size required and bonded to the repair with epoxy putty. Handle it gently until it is in place to keep from cracking the gelcoat. The results of this process will generally be less detectable if you allow a smooth margin around the new piece rather than butting it against other nonskid.

After you have gone to all of this trouble to replace a delaminated deck, you certainly do not want it to happen again. To insure against water penetration, drill every mounting hole that passes through core material 1/8 inch oversize, tape across the bottom of the holes with mylar tape (several layers for stiffness), and fill the hole with epoxy putty. When the hole is redrilled to the proper size, the core will be sealed away from the hole. Proper bedding is still essential to prevent water from entering the boat and as double protection from core penetration.

STRUCTURAL DAMAGE

Thus far, we have been focusing on internal delamination, either the release of the core in a cored deck, or a modest void inside single-skin fiberglass. More severe damage to fiberglass construction almost always results in delamination as well, but it requires a different response. When the delamination is associated with some type of hull or deck

Drill hole 1/8" oversize.

Tape the bottom of the hole closed and fill with epoxy putty.

When epoxy cures, redrill hole to correct size.

Waterproofing mounting holes

Attacking the Problem

Severe boat pox. Boat pox is almost always a cosmetic problem, but occasionally the solution inside the blisters begins to attack the polyester resin, causing the fiberglass to delaminate. In the worst case, the integrity of the hull can be severely compromised, but don't start biting your nails—your hull is more at risk from surfacing submarines.

That does not mean you can ignore blisters on the hull. Quite the contrary, blisters should be drained and repaired as soon as you are aware of them, and steps should be taken to prevent the problem from recurring.

In the event that you open a large hull blister and find the fiberglass behind the domed gelcoat beginning to delaminate, filling the cavity with polyester putty is no longer the appropriate course. Where delamination has taken place the hull has been weakened, and the unreinforced putty does not provide sufficient strength to restore it. You will need to reconstruct the damaged portion with new laminates.

The first steps of the treatment are the same as for a surface blister. Open the blister completely and let it drain. Put on your gloves and wipe out the open blister with a rag moistened with brush cleaner. Put a #36 grit disc on your grinder and grind out all the loose laminates. Be careful not to grind any *deeper* than the damage has penetrated. The sides of the ground depression should have at least a 10-to-1 bevel to insure that the joint with the new laminates will be adequately strong.

Once you have the damaged material ground away, use a light mallet to sound all around the spot to make sure that the delaminated area was not larger than it appeared. When you are satisfied that all the surrounding fiberglass is sound, scrub the excavation vigorously with a TSP solution and rinse thoroughly. Now pick up the tools, lock the boat, and take that trip to Europe you have been thinking about.

Drying the hull. Here comes the bad news. Underwater delamination associated with a blistering problem invariable indicates that the hull is satu-

trauma, there is little reason to attempt to rebond the damaged laminates. Instead, the damaged area is cut away and discarded and the area is reconstructed with new laminates.

Remove all damaged material, grinding the damaged area into a depression with a 10:1 bevel.

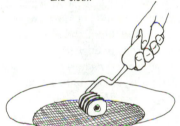

When the hull is sufficiently dry, wipe the depression with an acetone-dampened rag and fill it with alternating layers of mat and cloth.

Compact each layer of fiberglass with a roller.

Begin with a layer of mat. Finish with two layers of mat for better impermeability. Seal top layer with plastic wrap.

Repairing deep blister damage

Baja California in July, but where most of us have our boats, we are talking two to six months. In northern climates, tenting and using a dehumidifier is not overkill.

I could try to cheer you by pointing out that you are not likely to be going to all this trouble for a single blister, but the satisfaction from that knowledge may be elusive. In actual fact, drying the hull should be part of the larger effort to cure your boat of pox, not just to repair the latest blisters.

That cure is detailed in Chapter 14, but hey, you're in no particular hurry now anyway, right?

Filling the cavity. When the hull is dry, and you are back from Paris, the repair of the excavated blister is straightforward. Clean away the legacy of air pollution by wiping the spot to be repaired with a clean cloth *dampened* with acetone. Span the spot with a springy strip of brass, or aluminum, or plastic, and use a ruler to measure the depth of the depression. Generally speaking, for every $1/32$ inch, you will need one layer of fabric—mat or cloth.

Cut a piece of mat the size of the outside diameter of the ground spot. This will be the top laminate. Cut a second piece of mat to the same shape, but $1/2$ inch smaller in diameter. Finishing the repair with two layers of mat will make it less water permeable. Cut the remaining pieces, alternating between cloth and mat, each $1/2$ inch smaller than the one before. The smallest piece, the bottom laminate, should always be mat.

It is a good idea to mask the hull beneath the depression to keep excess resin from making vertical chines on your previously smooth underbody. Paint the depression with catalyzed polyester resin and saturate the first two layers of fabric. Press each layer in place, using the brush to compact the layers and remove excess resin.

If the spot is large enough, a 3-inch trim roller will make compacting quicker. Paint suppliers will be glad to sell you 3-inch covers, but save yourself a bit of money by buying standard (9-inch) throwaway covers from a discounter and cutting them into thirds. If a lot of fiberglass work is in your future, consider investing 15 bucks in a 3-inch grooved

rated. It sounds crazy to me, too, but once water has breached the barrier of the less permeable gelcoat, it is slowly absorbed by the fiberglass. When the hull becomes fully saturated, blistering begins, followed by delamination. Any legitimate attempt to correct this condition requires leaving the boat out of the water for long enough for the hull to dry out. Two weeks may be long enough if you haul out in aluminum roller. Made just for this purpose, a grooved roller requires cleaning, but it is used over and over. And if you forget to clean it, the cured resin can be burned off with a torch.

After the resin has kicked on the first two layers, lay up two more, repeating the process until the repair is flush with the surrounding surface. Small areas can be laid up three or even four layers at a time without risk of cooking the resin. Remember to seal the final layers from the air by taping a piece of plastic over the repair.

If you want to gelcoat the repair, the last layer of laminate should finish slightly below the surrounding surface, leaving a shallow (20 mils) depression for the gelcoat putty. Do not seal the repair from the air until after the gelcoat has been applied and it begins to kick. To seal the hull from further water penetration, you will be painting it, so gelcoating the repair is not essential. Nevertheless, I like the idea of providing fresh laminates with the added protection of a layer of gelcoat. It is your call.

Impact damage.   There is a marker in Biscayne Bay that my wife invariably comments on as we sail by it, a not-so-subtle reminder that when she disagrees with me, it does not necessarily mean she is wrong. On a warm afternoon some summers ago we approached the same marker, and as it became apparent that we were not going to pass it on the correct side, I pinched up tighter on the light breeze. The gurgle at the bow faded. "Tack," my devoted mate counselled, but I had the bow pointed well clear of the marker and hung on. Unfortunately, the current did not care where the bow was pointed, and we took the piling just abaft the starboard genoa winch. A stout rubstrake limited the damage to some splintered teak and a crushed ego, but in a different boat the consequences of my foolishness would have been far more serious.

Repairing damaged fiberglass is surprisingly easy. We have already seen how to repair damage that does not penetrate all of the laminates. When the area is broken or holed, the process is only slightly more complex.

Begin by cutting away the damaged glass. If the area is large, use a circular saw with a fiberglass-cutting blade or an abrasive cutoff wheel. For a smaller area, a saber saw is the tool of choice. Keep in mind that the impact that caused the hole undoubtedly caused some delamination. Sound the area with your mallet and outline the damage. Now go back and smooth that outline into a circular or oval shape. This is the piece you are going to cut away.

Before you begin cutting, go inside the boat and see if there is anything in the way of your repair. If, for example, a bulkhead or a cabinet is attached across the damaged area, you will have to decide how to deal with it. Usually the best way is to cut away the member that is interfering.

Now go back outside, take a deep breath, and cut around the circular outline. Fiberglass will eat up cheap saw blades, so buy rugged ones rated for cutting fiberglass, and cut slowly to keep from overheating the blade. Once the piece is removed, carefully examine the cut edge for any signs of delamination that your sounding may have missed. If you find any, enlarge the cutout until all edges are sound.

Working from the inside.   You repair blister damage from the outside, because that is where the damage is, but damage that results in a hole all the way through the fiberglass gives you a choice. You want to make the repair from the inside if at all possible.

There are two reasons for this preference. The first is that for a repair to fiberglass more than $1/4$ inch thick, you are going to bevel the edge of the hole 15 to 1 to give adequate strength to the joint between the old laminates and the new ones. If the hull is $1/2$ inch thick, the bevel will run back from the edge about $7^1/2$ inches all the way around. That means that for a 5-inch hole, you are going to grind away an area 20 inches in diameter. Need I say more?

The second reason you want to make the repair from the inside is because you have to back the hole on one side or the other to provide a surface on which to lay up the laminates. The backing in effect provides a mold, and if the backing is smooth the cured resin will mirror that surface. It is outside where we need that smooth surface, and backing

Cut away the
damaged laminate.

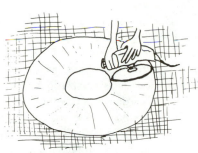

Bevel the fiberglass around the hole from
inside the hull to 15:1.

Tape a flexible piece of acrylic or
plastic laminate over the hole to back
the repair. If the backer is too small,
it will not assume the proper contour.

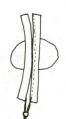

Compound curves require
the backing in strips. Use
dividers to mark the edge
of one strip onto the
adjoining one.

Trim along the
marked lines.

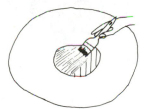

Tape all the strips over
the hole and mark
them so they can be
put back in exactly the
same position.

Remove the strips and
wax around the hole.

Wax the inside of the
strips and retape them
over the hole.

Tape all seams with
cellophane to
contain gelcoat.

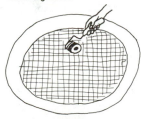

Fill any gaps between the backing
and the edge of the hole with
modeling clay.

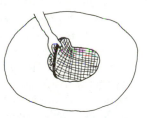

Apply a 20-mil coat of gelcoat.

Lay up alternating layers of mat
and cloth.

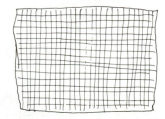

Thoroughly compact
each laminate.

When the repair is complete, grind all
ridges and irregularities off the
inside surface.

Apply a final layer of mat and cloth.

Use a finishing
sander to remove
any imperfections
from the
outside surface.

Compound and
polish the
repair.

Structural damage repairs

the hole on the outside means doing the layup from inside.

Backing the hole. After you have cut out the damage and beveled the hole from inside the boat, backing the hole is the next step. If you back the hole hastily and poorly, you will be filling and sanding, filling and sanding, and filling and sanding in a frustrating effort to get the surface fair. Do it carefully and well, and the repair will require a minimal amount of fairing and polishing.

Any hard, flexible material can be used as a backing. Plastic laminate (Formica) or thin clear acrylic (Plexiglas) work especially well because they will readily take on the curve of the hull and they can be held in place with duct tape. Stiffer backing, like coated hardboard, is better when the damaged area is large, but the backing may have to be screwed to the hull to hold it in position.

If you are fortunate enough that the damage is in a relatively flat spot, or in an area where the curvature is in only one direction, backing the hole should present no problem at all. Cut the backing material about 8 inches larger than the hole, hold it in place, and tape the edges down tightly. If you fail to cut the backing sufficiently oversize to carry out onto the hull several inches, it will lie flat across the hole rather than taking the hull's curvature, and the resulting repair will be flat.

With the backing in place, check the hole from the inside. The backing should rest tightly against the edge of the hole all the way around. If it does, you are ready go ahead with the reconstruction; if it doesn't, then there is probably a compound curvature (curving in two directions at the same time) in the hull in the area of the damage. If you consider the distance between the hull and the backing as a crack rather than space, filling it with a bit of clay will be all that is required, except for brushing in a second layer of gelcoat on either side of the hole near the clay filling. The extra gelcoat will accommodate the additional sanding that will be required to fair the raised sides.

If the compound curvature is more pronounced, you can abandon any effort to force a single sheet of backing to take on the correct shape; it will not bend in two directions at once. Cut the backing into 3-inch-wide strips and run the strips diagonally across the hole, butting their edges. Because of the different curve each strip will assume, you may find that they do not fit together well. Do not try to force them to mate. Tape both strips in place and with a compass (the kind that draws circles, not the one that points north) held parallel to the ground, trace the edge of one of the strips with the point, allowing the pencil to duplicate that curve onto the adjoining strip. Remove the marked strip and trim it along the pencil line. When you tape it back in place, it should fit nicely.

Sounds easy enough, but when you try it, it may put you in mind of one of those gizmos that, in the TV commercial, slices, dices, chops, grates and juliennes every fruit and vegetable known to man. Unfortunately, when *yours* arrives home, you can't force an overripe banana through it. Both the Formica and the Plexiglas can be trimmed with tinsnips, or even heavy scissors, but the Formica tends to chip and the thin Plexiglas tends to crack. If you run into this problem, sanding the contour or cutting it with a router will solve it.

Trim each strip and tape it in place. When all the strips are in place, check inside to make sure they lie tightly against the edge of the hole all the way around. Don't worry about imperfections in the fit between strips. Go back outside and draw a horizontal line across all the strips and onto the hull to ensure that you can put them back in exactly the same attitude; then remove them.

Heavily wax the outside of the hull around the hole, especially beneath it. Resin will find its way between the hull and the mold, and you want to be sure that the runs do not permanently attach to the hull. If you have PVA, apply a coat over the wax. While you have the strips off is also a good time to wax them and apply the releasing agent; it is more convenient and you will not accidentally get wax on the ground surfaces. If you are using Formica as a backing, it should have a shiny surface, not one of the more popular textured ones.

Inside the boat, grind a rectangular area a few inches larger than the beveled hole. The top layers of laminate may carry out beyond the bevel, and the final step in the layup will be to lay a piece of cloth over the repair to give the interior a finished look. Wipe down all the ground surface, including the bevel, with a clean cloth dampened with acetone.

Now go back outside and put the strips back in place, taping them carefully and tightly to the hull with duct tape. The seams between the strips will likely not be entirely free of gaps, but do not be too concerned—any small ridges that result can be ground away easily. With cellophane tape, tape all the seams *on the outside* to contain any resin that finds its way into the seams. You might also fill the seams from the inside with clay, but I think you run the risk of trading a ridge for a depression; the ridge is much easier to deal with. You *will* need to fill any gaps in the seams at the bottom of the hole to block the flow of resin.

Making the repair. With the backing securely in place, waxed, and coated with a releasing agent, begin the actual repair by coating the mold with matching gelcoat to a uniform thickness of about 20 mils. You can check it using toothpicks as dipsticks. Compare the coated tip to the $1/32$ markings on your scale. A 32nd of an inch is about 30 mils.

Measure the thickness of the piece you cut away to estimate the number of laminates you will need. If you are using $1\,1/2$-ounce mat and 10-ounce cloth, you will need approximately one layer for every $1/32$ inch of thickness. Unless you are repairing a very large area, there is no valid reason to be concerned about duplicating the original laminate schedule—it just adds an unnecessary complication. On a more modern hull, the laminate schedule may be "engineered" to yield strength in a specific direction, but older boats were simply laid up with mat and woven roving to a specified thickness. The manufacturer selected roving because it was cheaper and built up faster. You can do the same, but whether you use 20-ounce roving or 10-ounce cloth is not particularly important. It is far more important that you mix the resin properly, grind the old surface well, mate the old to the new with a 15 to 1 scarf joint, work out all air bubbles, and compact the new laminates.

Cut the first piece of mat 1 inch larger than the hole; it should overlap the bevel by about $1/2$ inch all the way around. Using the cut piece as a pattern, cut a second piece of mat $1/2$ inch larger than the first all around. You want to start the patch with two layers of mat because they will make the laminate somewhat more waterproof, and they will prevent the pattern of the cloth (or roving) laminates from ever "printing through" the gelcoat. Cut the remaining layers of alternating cloth and mat, each overlapping the previous one by $1/2$ inch all around.

Begin the laminates by saturating the first two layers of mat and a layer of cloth with catalyzed resin. Paint the hardened gelcoat and the first couple of inches of the bevel with the resin, then lay up the three layers and smooth them in place. You want to do three layers so that the top layer is cloth, which is less fragile than saturated mat and easier to roll or squeegee smooth. When the first layers have kicked, you continue the laminate process until you have rebuilt the damaged area to the original thickness. You can probably apply the laminates four at a time without a problem, but if this is your first major repair, take the safe route and apply only two, allowing them to harden and cool before adding two more at a time.

When the repair to the hole has been completed, grind all of the ridges and irregularities off the interior surface of the patch. Then apply a final layer of mat and cloth to hide the repair and to give it a professionally finished look. Protect the final layer from the air to allow a tack-free cure.

Outside the hull, carefully peel the mold away. There will probably be thin ridges of gelcoat where the backing strips adjoined, and around the perimeter of the repair. A finishing sander should make short work of these. Slight imperfections can be corrected with thickened gelcoat. Finally, compound the repair if necessary, then polish it or paint it to match the surrounding area. Ta da!

Working from the outside. You can make an equally sound repair working from the outside. An inner liner, tankage, or complex cabinetry may make working from the inside impractical. In that case, grind the bevel on the outside and treat the repair in a similar manner to that outlined for blister damage. Of course, since the hole penetrates the hull, you will have to back the hole before you can make the repair.

When you cannot get to the back side of the hole, try some variation of the following. After the damage has been cut away and the area around the hole beveled, reach through the hole with a piece of very coarse sandpaper and hand sand an inch or two of the inside of the hull around the hole. If the damage is large, stick a #36 pad on the wrong side of a drill-mounted sanding disk, chuck it, insert it into the hole, and grind the interior surface close to the edge.

Cut a 3-inch-wide strip of cloth into short pieces; the exact length will depend upon the size of the hole you are attempting to back. Lay each piece on a piece of stiff posterboard *cut to the same size*. Now saturate the pieces with resin and paint resin around the inside of the hole as well as you can. Pick up fiberglass and cardboard together, insert them in the hole, and flatten the strip of glass against the inner surface so that half of the cloth (about 1½ inches) will bond to the inner surface, the other half protruding out into the opening. Using the other pieces of saturated cloth, repeat this procedure until you have formed a series of tabs all the way around the hole, each almost touching its neighbor. (Don't make them overlap.) The purpose of the posterboard is simply to support the otherwise limp cloth.

While the tabs cure, cut a piece of mat and a piece of cloth to the size of the cut-out hole. Lay the two pieces on waxed paper and saturate them with resin. Put the cloth on top of the mat and compact the two. When both the tabs and the laminate have hardened, peel the laminate from the wax paper, trim it if necessary, then with catalyzed resin, bond it in place against the tabs. When the resin kicks, the hole is backed and you are ready to proceed with the repair.

Unless a freighter blows down on you, crushing

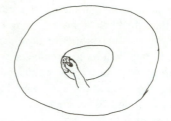

Sand the inside surface around the hole.

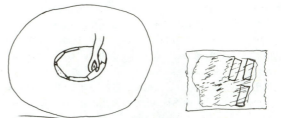

Saturate cardboard-backed, 3-inch-wide strips of cloth and press them against the inside surface around the perimeter of the hole.

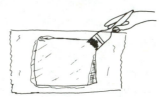

Lay up a piece of mat and a piece of cloth large enough to cover the hole.

Cut the cured laminate to the size of the hole.

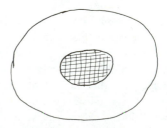

Bond circle of laminate to the cured tabs with polyester resin. Proceed with the repair.

Making repairs when inside access is limited

your boat against the quay, this is likely all you'll ever need to know about fiberglass repair. Even then, bigger damage just means a bigger repair, not a different one. Spend time to get the backing really right, and the repair will come out well every time.

Considering the advantages of glass-reinforced plastic in the construction of boats, it should not be surprising that a number of other plastics have found their way into marine use. These other plastics are the focus of the next chapter.

SEVEN

Windows and Walls

Let there be light.
–GOD–

Plastic had already taken over boat construction when I first realized how much more world was open to you if you had a waterborne conveyance. I chose a sailboat because the sort of limitless horizon aspect of sailing appealed to me; a person of ordinary means could untie his sloop in San Diego, and by the time his credit card bills were past due, he could be lying on an ebony beach, engulfed by the sweet scent of frangipani, sipping from a coconut, and basking in the warm smile of a bronze-skinned South Seas maiden. We buy the sizzle, not the steak.

I was lucky with my first boat. I chose a 27-footer from the board of Carl Alberg, built by New England craftsmen who viewed this new material with a jaundiced eye. Their distrust made her heavy but, with her sweet lines, the weight affected her only in the lightest conditions. I bought her used, but there was an advertising brochure aboard and it called her accommodations "light and airy." I had little quarrel with that characterization until the first rainy summer afternoon.

The airy part is self-explanatory; the rain necessitated closing all portholes and hatches. In south Florida, that is approximately equivalent to putting the lid on a slow cooker. Except that the lid is glass, so at least a lamb chop has plenty of light when getting ready for dinner.

Not so with most older boats. The hatches, like the boat, are constructed of fiberglass. What happens to the light when the weather forces you to close the hatches? Consider this. The total area of the portholes in my old 27-footer, excluding those in the head and the hanging locker, which did not contribute to the illumination of the cabin, was about 3 square feet. The combined area of the forward hatch and the companionway was about 13 square feet. So with the hatches open, the total area admitting light below was about 16 square feet, but put in the boards and close the hatches and the area admitting outside light drops to 3 square feet—a reduction of *more than 80 percent*! And that does not take into account the poor light-gathering characteristics of openings in the side of the cabin compared to those in the overhead. The only thing light and airy about most old boats is the advertising copy.

Ventilation is not about hatches; it is about openings, and we will consider the subject more closely in Chapters 10 and 15. But there is no reason for the daylight below to depend upon open hatches. It carries the old fiberglass boat/refrigerator analogy a bit too far—close the door and the light goes out.

I recall wondering why the forward hatch in my boat was the color of toxic waste, in disgusting contrast to the pristine white of the cabin top and deck around it. It turned out to be an industry-wide response to the primal screams of sailing nyctophobes. And a pathetic response it was. Manufacturers simply omitted the gelcoat in laying up the hatches. After all, the hatch was already glass; leave off the gelcoat and it becomes translucent, right? God made eyelids more translucent, and their purpose is to shut light *out*.

Boat manufacturers eventually "saw the light,"

and newer boats are almost all delivered with transparent hatches, in effect bringing the light below. Part of the reason was the development of a water-clear polycarbonate resin called Lexan.

Clear plastics–Plexiglas, Lucite, Acrylite, and other acrylics–have been used in boat portlights for three decades. They are almost twice as strong for the same thickness as the tempered glass they replaced, but the brittle nature of acrylic makes it something of a risk for an opening the size of a hatch. More than a few manufacturers simply elected to overlook the fact that the purpose of the hatch is to keep the *ocean* out. Responsible companies addressed the problem with hatches constructed with surprisingly thick clear plastic. But acrylics have another drawback: many have a tendency to develop a spider web of internal cracks as they are subjected to the stresses of age and movement. These cracks weaken and cloud the plastic. A better material was needed.

That material was Lexan. Don't think of Lexan as just a more expensive Plexiglas. It *is* more expensive, costing about 2 1/2 times as much, but it is no more like acrylic than gin is like water. Incredibly tough and structurally stable, Lexan is the perfect material for portlights and hatches.

Where polycarbonates and acrylics are alike is in how you go about fabricating them into the item you want. They are deceptively easy to work with, and great fun. Once you have made an item or two and discovered how easy it is, the biggest risk you run is in getting carried away with the possibilities. In almost any boat, there are some excellent applications for clear plastic, but too much can look really tacky. I don't want to be a party to that, so if you can't exhibit some self-restraint, skip this section.

No, I haven't forgotten that I was discussing hatches and portlights. I will be back to that subject soon enough, but as I promised from the start, I first want to give you a chance to work with clear plastic on a low-cost, low-risk project. To keep the cost as low as possible, we will be working with clear acrylic; the added expense of Lexan is only justified where strength is essential.

ACRYLIC ACCESSORIES

Acrylic is an inexpensive material. Sheet plastic comes in 4-foot by 8-foot sheets. At this writing, the full sheet price of 1/4-inch clear is around two dollars per square foot, but you don't have to buy a full sheet. The supplier will be happy to provide you with whatever size you need, but expect to pay a cutting charge, more per square foot than the full-sheet price, or both. Every cloud has its silver lining; because the supplier provides cut sizes, almost every supplier has a scrap bin–the smaller pieces left over from filling an order. Often the scrap pieces are at giveaway prices. And for cabin accessories, small pieces are exactly what you need. Isn't it great how things work out?

Cabin accessories are usually fabricated of 1/4 inch clear acrylic, but if you want extra strength you might select a 5/16-inch thickness. There are different types of acrylic–Plexiglas comes in more than half a dozen different varieties–but for most onboard projects special characteristics are unnecessary. You just need standard clear acrylic, or whatever you find in the scrap bin.

Creating in Acrylic

Mounted on the bulkhead above the head of my bunk is a clear acrylic bin. I did not make it or install it–it was an enhancement of a previous owner–but it is a shoo-in for my list of the 10 most useful items aboard. At any given time, it holds sunglasses, lip-block, Blistex, keys, pens, a pad, rubber bands, change, an extra Croakie, a lighter, a penlight, gum, sunscreen, and a dozen other items. Ostensibly a teak bin would serve the same function, and we have such a bin right by the companionway–part of the original cabinetry. The teak bin is an equally convenient receptacle for small essentials, but the difference comes in the effort required to locate and retrieve an item. The search for a loose key that might be in the teak bin usually leads to removing almost all the items and putting them on the settee while holding my forehead against the bulkhead to peer down into the bin. With the acrylic bin, I look directly into it, then reach in and pull out the item I want, regardless of whether it is on the top or the bottom. Acrylic is an especially good material for bins and racks because of its transparency.

To construct the acrylic bin detailed, you will need a piece of ¼-inch clear acrylic about 9 inches wide and 22 inches long. Cutting and drilling requires no special tools. You can cut acrylic with almost any hand saw, and with most power saws, but for cutting irregular shapes, a saber saw is usually the tool of choice. Use a blade designed for cutting plastics—a common item and available from the plastic supplier or any hardware store. Drilling holes requires a drill, hand-powered or electric, and the appropriate bits. Special plastics bits are available, but any high speed drill bit used carefully will do the job. To finish the sawn edges, you will need an old hacksaw blade, some fine sandpaper, and a tube of toothpaste.

Constructing a strip heater. Bending acrylic requires heating the plastic, and it is much easier

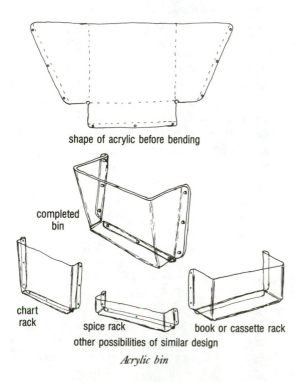

shape of acrylic before bending

completed bin

chart rack

spice rack

book or cassette rack

other possibilities of similar design

Acrylic bin

with a special tool—a strip heater. For around $15, you can buy a flexible, 3-foot heating element, called a *heat strip*, where you bought the acrylic. To assemble a heater from the heat strip, you will also need a plank or a piece of plywood about 40 inches long and 6 inches wide, a couple of 3-foot strips of ¼ inch plywood, 2½ inches wide, some heavy-duty foil, and some high-temperature insulation paper (oven liner paper—available in hardware stores). The plywood strips are set about ¾ inch apart and nailed to the plank, forming a narrow channel for the heating strip. (The heating element must never touch the acrylic.) Two layers of foil cover the strips and the sides and bottom of the channel. For safety, a ground wire is attached to the foil with a screw. Two layers of insulation paper are stapled over the top of the foil; dampen the paper to get it to follow the contour of the channel, and put the staples in the sides or bottom of the heater so they will not scratch the plastic. The heating element lies in the channel, tied tightly between small nails at either end of the plank.

A versatile design. With the heater assembled, you are ready to proceed. The detailed bin is 12 inches wide (excluding the mounting flanges), but you can make yours as long or as short as you like, depending upon how you want to use it and where it is to be mounted. If the bin will be a catchall, I would caution against making it more than 6 inches deep so you can easily retrieve items from the bottom. Making the bin wider at the mouth also makes access easier.

The first step is to construct a mock-up from stiff posterboard. Use the illustration to duplicate the flat shape, adjusting it to any changes in dimension that may be appropriate in your case. Draw in the fold lines and the location of mounting holes. Cut around the outline and fold it to shape. Try it for fit where you intend to mount it.

When you are satisfied with the mock-up, flatten it out again and use it for a pattern. The acrylic will have a protective film of masking paper covering both surfaces. Leave that in place while you are cutting and drilling the plastic. Lay your pattern on

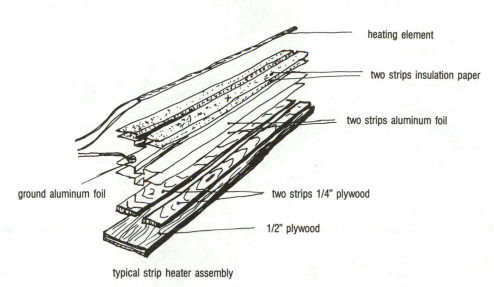

heating element

two strips insulation paper

two strips aluminum foil

ground aluminum foil

two strips 1/4" plywood

1/2" plywood

typical strip heater assembly

Strip heater

the paper covering and trace the outline. Puncture the pattern at the center of the marked mounting holes and use a sharp pencil to transfer their location to the paper.

Cutting and drilling. Acrylic can be cracked if it is mishandled, but adequate caution will prevent such an occurrence. It is less brittle when it is warm, so if you are working in the winter, work inside. Inside corners will be less prone to crack if they are drilled before being cut, and that is how we will start the bin. Laying the acrylic on a plank or a scrap of plywood, use a 1/4-inch bit to drill a hole at the apex of both inside corners. If you let the bit get too big a bite, it will crack the plastic, especially as it exits the hole at the bottom, so feed the drill slowly.

Feed slowly applies to the saw as well. Saw around the marked outline with the saber saw, supporting the acrylic as close to the cut as possible by placing it on a flat surface, like the top of a workbench, and running the saw blade just beyond the edge of the bench, repositioning the piece as necessary. The acrylic will chip if you let it bounce or chatter when you are cutting it; clamp it in place with a board on top if necessary. If the piece being cut off is large, support the cutoff as well. Use moderate blade speed, or if your saw is not variable-speed, stop

occasionally to let the blade cool. If the blade gets too hot, it will begin to melt the plastic and bind. Lubricating the blade with beeswax or bar soap will help reduce this tendency.

Lay the cut-out piece on your scrap of wood, and carefully drill the marked mounting holes. The edge of a hole should be no closer to the edge of the acrylic than 1.5 times the thickness of the plastic— 3/8 inch in this case. The bit should penetrate the wood beneath. It is in the process of drilling holes that you are most likely to crack the plastic, so go slowly and keep the pressure light. The plastic may also crack after it is mounted if it cannot expand and contract with temperature changes. For this reason, always drill mounting holes *one size larger* than the screw or bolt that will pass through the hole.

After all the holes are drilled, clamp or hold the piece vertically and draw the *back* of a hacksaw blade (not the side with teeth) along the cut edge to remove the melted slag and most of the saw marks. If the edge was to be glued, the importance of keeping it flat and square might necessitate buying a special edge scraper. The square edge is not necessary or even desirable on an exposed edge. Hand sand, or use a finishing sander if you have one, to put a smoother finish on the edges and to round their corners slightly. Use a buffing wheel (*not* a disk) and a stick of buffing compound to finish the edges. With enough time, the same thing can be accomplished with a rag and a blob of white toothpaste.

Bending. That is the end of the difficult part. Bending the acrylic into the desired shape is all that is left, and that is easy. Your pattern has six fold lines marked on it. Snip a ¼-inch notch in the pattern at both ends of each line. Peel away the adhesive covering from both sides of the acrylic and lay the notched pattern on one side. Using a grease pencil or felt-tip marker, transfer the notched locations to the acrylic. It is not necessary to connect the marks with a straight line; laying the heat strip in a straight line between the marks will be sufficient. But you can make all the marks and notes on the acrylic you want; isopropyl alcohol will easily remove all traces of the marks.

Bending acrylic has three steps: heat, bend, and hold. You want to be sure you are making the bend in the right direction, and sometimes the sequence of the bends is important, but that is as complicated as it gets. I hope that doesn't disappoint you.

For the bin, it will be necessary to bend the sides first, then the flanges. Preheat the strip heater for five minutes. Lay the acrylic on top of the heater, lining the heat strip up with the two marks that define the bend to form the bottom. To contain

small, loose items, you want to minimize the space between the bottom and the sides, so be sure to make the bend high enough, but not higher than the two holes. *Before* the plastic gets hot, dampen a tissue with isopropyl alcohol and clean away the two marks.

It will take the strip about 15 minutes to heat ¼-inch acrylic to the proper temperature. When the plastic is hot enough, it will be rubbery and soft, bending without any strain. A scrap of acrylic placed on the heater at the same time will allow you to check without disturbing the position of the actual item. Keep track of how long heating took; the bends will all be similar if you heat them for the same amount of time.

When the plastic is hot enough, leave the shortest side lying on the flat surface of the heater and quickly bend the rest of the piece up to a position about 5 degrees beyond the angle desired. Overbending counteracts the "memory" of the plastic, relieving some of the stresses in the bend. Now back the bend up to the desired angle, in this case a little less than ninety degrees. The short angle is made because the face of the bin slants away from the bulkhead. To get the angle correct, refold the pattern and tape it in shape before you heat the plastic. Then lay the softened acrylic over the mock-up and hold it in place until the plastic cools and the bend sets—probably about a minute.

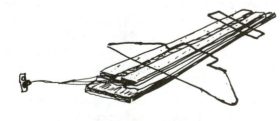

Align bend line of part over heating element. Place scrap of same material over element to allow you to check bend readiness without disturbing part.

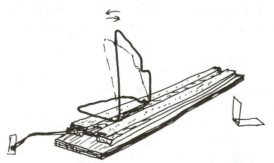

When test piece bends without effort, bend part 5 degrees beyond desired bend, then back to correct angle. Remove from heat and hold in position for 1 minute.

Bending acrylic

Line up the heat strip with the marks for one of the sides. Remove the marks with alcohol. When the acrylic is hot enough, overbend by about 5 degrees, then back the bend up to vertical (90 degrees) and hold it there for about a minute. Repeat the process for the opposite side.

The next step is to bend the flanges. Note that these bends are in the opposite direction of the ones you have already made. For the smoothest bend, you generally want to bend *away from* the heated side, but that is not always possible. In this case, it would require the inside of the bin to lie flat on the heater, but the bends you already have prevent that. So you will have to bend toward the heated side.

Using the two marks for the bottom flange, position the acrylic over the heat strip. Remove the marks. When the plastic is hot enough, turn it over and make the bend. Span the corner of your work table and press the flange flat on the top surface, overbending by 5 degrees, then returning the bend to an angle of 90 degrees with the bottom. Hold it in position until the plastic cools. Repeat the process for the other two flanges.

After the last bend, check the flanges on a level surface. See how flat they sit. (If they don't, fix them by reheating the bend that seems to be wrong. You don't have to tell anyone it took you two tries.)

When you mount the bin, remember to use screws one size smaller than the mounting holes. *Never countersink acrylic or Lexan;* if you do, the screw will act like a wedge and crack the plastic. Guaranteed. The best choice is oval-head screws used with finishing washers. The finishing washer spreads the compression out away from the hole and it gives the mounting a professional look. If you don't want to spend the three pennies for a finishing washer, then use round-head fasteners.

Other acrylic accessories. You can use this bin design, with the dimensions altered, to make a spice rack, a chart rack, a magazine bin, a kitchen wrap holder, a shelf for cassettes or paperback books, or to provide utility space on the inside of cabinet doors.

If your taste runs to acrylic toothbrush stands, paper towel holders, and wine racks, you can do those, too. Large holes are cut in acrylic with a drill and a standard hole saw. Just keep the drill straight and cut slowly and you should have no difficulty.

If an item requires joining two pieces of acrylic, buy a tube of acrylic cement from your plastics supplier. It is not really a glue, but a solvent, softening the two pieces and causing them to actually fuse together. The surfaces to be joined must mate well, but when they do, the solvent yields a very strong joint.

Once you are comfortable with sawing and drilling acrylic, you can move on to the more expensive polycarbonates. And that takes us back to our discussion of hatches and portholes.

LEXAN HATCHES

No change adds more to the livability of an old boat than replacing an opaque or a translucent hatch with a transparent one. The effect on cabin illumination cannot be overstated, but the virtues of a clear hatch extend beyond just that. You are, after all, out on the water to enjoy nature, not to be shut off from it. A transparent hatch will inevitably lead to the association of nights aboard with the wonder and beauty of a star-crowded sky. If corporate politics have dulled your romantic sensibilities, think of it as getting an office with windows.

Manufactured Hatches

In the case of the forward hatch, one option that may be available is to replace the hatch with a manufactured one. Catalog suppliers list a wide variety of designs and sizes, most of which are constructed of smoked Lexan in an aluminum frame. These are ideal for installation as an *additional* hatch, for example in the cabin top to provide light and ventilation over the salon table. However, an irregular opening, molded coamings, excessive deck camber, or other complications may preclude the easy substitution of a manufactured hatch for the original one.

If you use a manufactured hatch, select a brand with a reputation for quality; there are several. The manufacturer will provide detailed installation instructions with the hatch. In general terms, you will use a saber saw to cut an opening to the size of the included template. Mounting holes are marked and drilled. The hatch is placed in the opening and bolted in place, sandwiching the deck between a trim ring that is installed from inside the boat and the flange of the hatch frame outside.

In concept, that is all there is to it. In reality, some shimming is usually required to accommodate differences in camber between the deck and the hatch. If the deck is cored, it is imperative to seal the cut edges with a thick layer of epoxy. Also seal the mounting holes by drilling them oversize, filling them with epoxy, then re-drilling them smaller. Bed the frame generously; sealing compound should squeeze from beneath the flange all the way around the hatch. Assuming a metal frame—the only kind you should consider—use either a polysulfide or a polyurethane sealant.

Modifying a Fiberglass Hatch

An easier and lower cost course to a transparent forward hatch is to modify the existing hatch. The idea is to cut away the top of the hatch and replace it with a piece of clear plastic. If the hatch is flat or only slightly curved, this should not present any difficulty. If a square of hardboard can easily be made to assume the shape of the top of the hatch, you can proceed.

The first step is to select the material. Acrylic is the lower-cost alternative, but it is a false economy. My experience with acrylic is that sooner or later it will crack—usually sooner. In contrast, I have a Lexan hatch over 15 years old that has not shown a hint of failure despite abuses that included a wrench dropped from the masthead. For hatches, Lexan is the only choice.

Thickness will depend upon the size of the hatch and what you expect it to resist. Thicker is better, but a piece of 1/2-inch Lexan large enough to cover a typical forward hatch can easily cost more than $50—significantly cheaper than a new hatch, but a lot of money for a little piece of plastic. If you are

going offshore, pay the money. For lake and coastal boating, 3/8-inch Lexan will be plenty strong.

The choice of clear or smoked is up to you. Most people find smoked more attractive. It enhances daytime privacy, and it may actually screen out some UV, but when the sun is that strong, the hatches are probably open anyway.

Remove the hatch from its hinges, lay it upside down on the masked piece of Lexan, and trace around the outside perimeter. Keeping the saber saw blade outside of the line, cut the Lexan to size. If the Lexan is not from the scrap bin, and *if the sides of the hatch are straight and parallel*, measure carefully and let the supplier cut the piece to size for you. Round the corners with your saber saw. Scrape the edges, then sand them, gently rounding the edge that will be on top, but leaving the bottom edge square. Polish the edge.

Aligning the new top. Now pay attention. You are eventually going to attach the Lexan with machine screws, but you want to be sure that the screws don't interfere with closing the hatch. Put the hatch back in place, then go below and trace the coaming onto the inside of the hatch. Remove the hatch and measure the width of the coaming. Using that measurement, draw a second outline on the inside of the hatch to approximate the outside of the coaming. Crosshatch the area between the two outlines. This is where the hatch rests on the coaming, and unless there is 3/4 inch or more between the crosshatched area and the edge of the hatch—not very likely—fasteners for the new top will have to be countersunk into the bottom of the hatch.

To locate the mounting holes, draw a line on the underside of the hatch parallel to one side and about an inch in from it. The holes can be closer to the side if necessary, but no closer to it than 1.5 times the thickness of the Lexan panel you are installing— 9/16 inch for 3/8-inch Lexan. Measure from the adjoining side 2 inches along the line and mark the point. Do the same on the opposite end of the line. Now, measure the distance between the two lines and divide that distance into equal divisions between 4 and 5 inches long, marking the divisions.

Outline coaming on underside of hatch.

Remove hatch and trace top on Lexan.

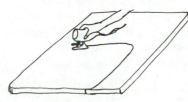
Cut out new top.

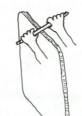
Scrape slag with back of hacksaw blade. Sand and polish edge.

Drill mounting holes in hatch. Countersink each hole.

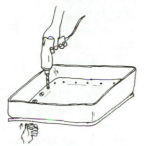
Using the hatch as a pilot, drill mounting holes in Lexan in sequence, fitting each hole with a bolt before drilling the next hole.

Lubricate each hole in the Lexan and redrill 1/16 inch oversize.

Drill the hatch inside the four corners of the coaming outline.

Cut away the old top between the four holes.

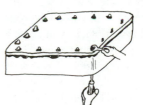
Clean remaining flange with acetone and coat with silicone sealant.

Remove protective paper from Lexan and bolt in place using stainless steel flat-head machine screws with flat washers and cap nuts.

Trim away excess sealant after it cures.

Installing a Lexan top on a fiberglass hatch

For example, on a 20-inch hatch, the distance between the end marks is 16 inches, which can be divided into four equal divisions of 4 inches. Repeat this process for the other three sides. Using a $^3/_{16}$-inch bit, and taking care to keep the drill perpendicular, drill the mounting holes through the old hatch.

Three-sixteenths-inch machine screws are a good size for this application. Were there space to do so, you would use an oval head with a finishing washer on the top, and a cap nut with a flat washer on the bottom, but this is not usually possible because the mounting holes are in the area where the hatch contacts the coaming. Instead, you will be inserting flathead screws from the bottom. To allow them to sit flush, countersink the holes from the underside of the hatch.

With the stainless steel screws, cap nuts, and flat washers at hand, place the piece of Lexan *exactly the way it goes* on top of the old hatch. Holding the two together, turn them over and lay the Lexan on a wood surface. Using one of the holes in the hatch as a pilot, gently drill a $^3/_{16}$-inch hole through the Lexan. Insert one of the screws through the hatch and into the plastic. Check again to make sure that the Lexan is properly aligned. In the same side as the first hole, drill the next hole and insert a second screw. Check one more time for alignment. Now drill in sequence the remaining mounting holes along that side and insert the screws. Lift the assembly, push the screws through the plastic, put the washers in place, and hand-tighten the nuts.

Lay the assembly flat again, with the line of nuts just beyond the edge of the support surface. Drill the nearest hole on the two adjacent sides. Insert the screws and tighten by hand. Drill and fasten the next two holes, repeating the sequence until both sides are completely fastened. Drill the holes in the remaining side, inserting screws; it is not necessary to put the nuts in place.

I don't want to make this task tedious, but perfect hole alignment is essential. If the holes don't quite match on a piece of wood, tightening the fastener crushes some of the wood fibers until all is in alignment. The plastic will not adjust; it will crack.

With all holes drilled, disassemble the two parts, taking care to mark the Lexan so you can put it back in exactly the same way. Lay the top of the Lexan on the wood surface and put a small amount of beeswax in each of the holes. Run a $^1/_4$-inch drill through each; as with acrylic, always drill mounting holes in Lexan oversize. The wax will leave the holes with a smoother finish.

Now you are going to cut away the center of the old hatch. You do not want to disturb the way the hatch rests on the coaming, so the cutout will be the size of the hatch opening, which is the only place you need transparency anyway. You have already marked the opening on the bottom of the hatch. Drill a $^3/_8$-inch hole in each corner of the outlined cutout, making the holes *tangent* to the two lines. The holes will give the corners an attractive radius and allow you to insert your sabersaw blade for making the cuts. With the center removed, smooth the edges of the cutout with coarse paper on a finishing sander or a sanding block.

Assembling the hatch. Using acetone, clean the top of the hatch that remains. Peel away the masking paper from the Lexan, noting how it aligns with the hatch *before* you tear away your notations. Place the Lexan top down on a pad of newspaper. Heavily coat the remaining top surface of the old hatch with silicone sealant. White will give a more attractive joint. Do not use polyurethane or polysulfide sealants on Lexan.

Put a bit of sealant in each of the mounting holes in the Lexan. Carefully place the hatch on the Lexan and insert several screws to hold the two in position. Following a sequence similar to that of the drilling, insert and tighten the screws by hand. You want the silicone to squeeze out all around the outside and the inside, but you do not want to squeeze it all out. The idea with silicone sealant is to create something like a rubber gasket. After the sealant has hardened for a day or two, you can tighten the nuts, but just slightly (a quarter turn).

If the hatch has significant camber (curvature), the silicone will squeeze out of the middle before the sides are sufficiently tight for the sealant to contact both surfaces. Counteract this situation before installing the Lexan by running a bead of silicone 3 or 4 inches long in the center of the front flange. Do the same at the rear of the hatch. Flatten the beads to about $1/16$ inch with a strip of waxed paper and let the silicone cure. Now install the Lexan as previously outlined. The precured silicone will keep the two pieces from squeezing too tightly together in the middle.

Do not try to wipe away the excess silicone sealant; it will just smear. After the sealant has fully cured, carefully trace the inside edge of the cut-out with a new single-edge razor blade. Cut all the way through the beaded silicone and it will pull away cleanly. Use the blade to slice away the excess sealant around the outside of the hatch.

Lexan on Wood Frames

Wooden hatches can be modified in almost the same manner. Instead of cutting an opening in the top, the top is generally removed and replaced with a piece of Lexan. If the top is put on with screws, they will be hidden beneath round wooden plugs. Drill a small hole in the plug and thread a screw into it. As the point of the screw encounters the screw head beneath the plug, it will lift the plug out of the hole.

On a wood frame, attach the Lexan top using oval-head #10 wood screws with finishing washers. The screws should penetrate the wood at least $1/2$ inch. Drill the Lexan and the pilot holes in the frame at the same time, using a #33 drill. Then turn the Lexan over, put wax in the holes, and enlarge them to $1/4$ inch. Bed the joint with silicone sealant.

A Lexan Companionway

The reasons for a transparent main hatch are equally compelling, and the modification is essentially the same as that for the forward hatch. If the hatch slides into a sea hood, or if you plan to construct one, be sure that there is clearance for the probable extra height of the Lexan and fasteners.

Clear drop boards for the companionway are another excellent onboard application for Lexan. If you want to replace the original wood boards, the Lexan should be similar in thickness, cut to size using the original boards as patterns. You can bevel or rabbet the plastic just like the wood—see Chapter 10. If you just want a clear alternative for a rainy day at anchor, cut a single piece for the opening from $1/8$-inch Lexan. It will easily store under a bunk. If you have difficulty cutting thin acrylic or polycarbonate, try sandwiching the piece between two pieces of scrap plywood and cutting all three layers.

REPLACEMENT PORTLIGHTS

If your fiberglass boat is more than 15 years old, you can be relatively certain that the fixed portlights are acrylic. You may find tempered glass in the opening ports, but the fixed ones will be plastic. Quarter-inch Plexiglas was pretty standard, replaced in recent years by $1/4$-inch Lexan. If your boat has the original acrylic portlights, the view through them is almost certainly obscured by surface scratches and internal crazing. Replacement can be a breeze, or it can incline you to hang yourself from the starboard spreader.

The determining factor will be the condition of the portlight frames. On most older boats, they are aluminum. Often the outside half of the frame is threaded for mounting bolts installed through the inside half. After a decade or so, the mounting bolts are either welded to the outside frame, or the threads have turned into a white powder. Either way, when you take them apart, you cannot simply put them back together.

Expect problems with the screws. If the whole frame disintegrates in your hands, you will have to chase down the original supplier (the boat manufacturer, if still in business, can give you that information), have new frames machined locally, or find a similar frame and modify the cabin-side opening to fit. Problems with reattaching the original frame are less complicated and far less expensive. Forget about rethreading the outside frame; it was a bad idea to start with. Redrill the once-threaded holes through the frame and after the new portlight is in place, through-bolt both halves with oval-head machine screws and cap nuts.

Use the old portlights as a pattern for new ones of the same thickness cut from Lexan. Be sure all the old bedding has been removed from the opening and the frames, and wipe both with acetone. Assemble the new window and modified frames to check for any fit problems. Disassemble and remove the masking paper from the plastic. Apply a thick layer of clear silicone sealant to the inside of both halves of the frame. Insert a mounting screw in each end of one half, and insert the screws through the appropriate holes in the cabin side to locate the frame. While the mate holds the frame in place, carefully put the new window in place from the opposite side. Slip the other half of the frame over the two extended screws and press it in place.

Thread nuts onto the two screws. Install the remaining screws and tighten the nuts evenly, working outward from the center of the frame and alternating across the portlight. Be sure that sealant squeezes out of all edges of the frames, but do not overtighten. Again, you are not trying to glue the window in place, but to provide a flexible gasket.

Do not try to wipe up excess silicone; after it is fully cured, trace the frame with a razor blade and peel off the cut-away sealant. Tighten the mounting screws an additional turn to tightly compress the new gasket. See how easy it is!

PLASTIC LAMINATES

Another plastic product that has found its way into boats is decorative laminate. Often referred to as

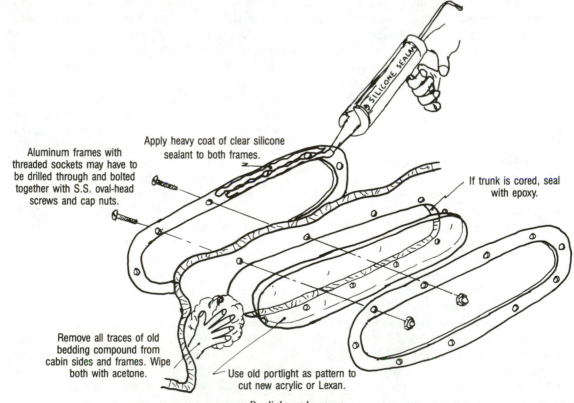

Portlight replacement

Formica, after a well-known brand name, decorative laminate covers the countertops and brightens the kitchen cabinets of most of the houses built in America in the last half of the 20th century. It is manufactured of layers of kraft paper soaked in phenolic resin—reminiscent of fiberglass construction. The penultimate layer is colored or printed paper, beneath a surface layer of tough, clear melamine. Decorative laminate is attractive, tough, incredibly versatile, and very easy to use.

Unlike acrylic, decorative laminate has to be bought in a full sheet, but the cost is usually reasonable. A standard sheet of plastic laminate is 4 feet by 8 feet. Most patterns will be available in both the standard horizontal grade ($1/16$ inch thick) and in a vertical grade ($1/32$ inch thick), intended for surfaces that will get little wear. The most likely uses of plastic laminate aboard an old boat are to resurface the counter in the galley, which requires horizontal grade, and to cover bulkheads and cabinets, where vertical grade is appropriate.

If your ultimate project is a countertop, select the color and pattern you want from among the scores of samples the supplier will show you. Be cautious about being too trendy; you may find yourself dissatisfied with your choice in a short time. A "butcher block" pattern, for example, was all the rage a few years ago. Now it just says, "1982." Not that recovering is all that difficult, but removing and replacing the wood trim that typically accents galley counters can be. If your boat sees regular use, you will reupholster a couple of times before the laminate begins to show age. Buy a color and pattern that will allow you to change the cabin decor if you choose to.

On a sheet of plain paper, sketch out the shape of the surface you plan to cover, and write the dimensions on the sketch. Now turn the paper over and trace the lines from the other side, giving you the same shape, but in reverse. Write *bottom* in the center of the outline, and write in the dimensions. You will be marking and cutting the laminate from the bottom, and drawing the piece as it looks from the bottom will keep you from getting confused.

Draw out the piece or pieces you need on the bottom of the sheet of laminate. If the back of the counter butts against a cabinet and is not covered with trim, lay out the piece to take advantage of the sheet's finished edge. Add about $1/4$ inch to each cut edge to allow for trimming. Don't cut anything yet! You are just trying to "reserve" the laminate for what you bought it for.

A First Project

Now open the cabinet below the counter and remove one of the plywood shelves. If there aren't any, get one out of the cockpit lockers, or out of the lazarette. If you don't have any shelves on the boat, read Chapter 10 and build one. Lay the shelf—top down—on a section of the laminate not already designated for the counter. Hold your marker at an angle to trace an outline around the shelf about $1/4$ inch larger on all sides. Also outline a straight strip $1/2$ inch longer than the front edge of the shelf and $1/2$ inch wider than its thickness.

All decorative laminate has a tendency to chip when it is cut, which is why it is always cut slightly oversize. The thinner grade can be cut with tin snips or special scissors (a paper cutter does a nice job on smaller pieces), but it is prone to tear. It can also be scored with a special tool and broken—like glass. Cut horizontal grade with your saber saw.

Supporting *both sides* of the cut as close to the blade as possible, cut out the two pieces of laminate for the shelf. Using a special blade for laminates will minimize chipping. Do not cut out any of the other pieces.

Put a square of coarse sandpaper on your finishing sander, and run it over the top and front edges of the shelf. If the shelf has been previously painted, take the gloss off the paint, or remove it altogether. When applying new laminate over old laminate, be sure there are no loose edges, and heavily sand the old surface (using a belt sander if you have one) to give the glue a good bonding surface. Fill and sand any holes in the surface. When applying plastic laminate to any surface, that surface must be smooth (not slick), clean, and dry.

Using a paper pattern or the actual item, outline the piece on the *back* side of the laminate. Cut about 1/4" outside of the outline.

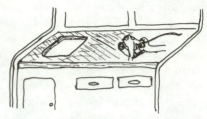

Sand the old surface with a disk or belt sander.

Cover sides first, then front, and finally top. In this example, coat the front edge of the counter and the back of the strip of laminate with contact cement.

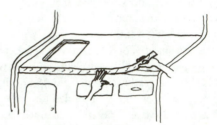

After the glue dries, press the strip in place, taking great care with the alignment.

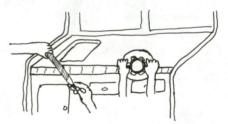

Apply pressure with your thumb to compress the joint when the strip is narrow.

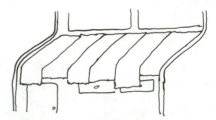

Trim away the excess width with a file or a router.

Coat the top of the counter and the back of the laminate with contact cement.

When the glue dries, cover the entire surface with waxed paper.

Installing plastic laminate

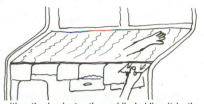

Position the laminate, then while holding it in the correct position, slide the paper out.

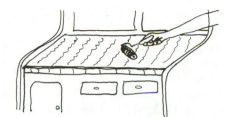

Compress the bond with a rubber roller.

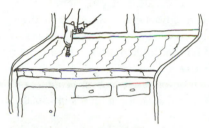

Drill a hole in each cut-out to allow the router bit to penetrate.

Rout cut-outs and untrimmed edges. Use the file to trim edges inaccessible to the router.

Installing plastic laminate (continued)

Contact cement. Plastic laminate is glued in place with contact cement. For obvious reasons, you do not want the water based variety. Unfortunately the "right" contact cement–petroleum based–is also extremely volatile. You can take the shelf and the pieces of laminate out to the cockpit to coat them, but you cannot do a counter or a bulkhead that way. When you are gluing below, be sure that you have lots of ventilation and everything that has a flame or might generate a spark is *off.* Don't even think about smoking; the Surgeon General is right. The stuff is also toxic, so as soon as you have the parts coated, get out of there until it dries.

Use a throwaway bristle brush to coat the bottom of the laminate and the surface it will cover. One coat on both surfaces is usually enough, but new wood can sometimes absorb the cement, requiring a second coat. Fold a paper towel in half and roll it tightly to make a cheap "brush" for small jobs.

Start the shelf by coating its front edge and the back of the cut strip. The edge of the shelf will probably require two coats. After the cement has dried tack free, line up the strip with the edge, overlapping on all sides. Do not let the glued sur-faces touch or the shelf will grab the strip out of your hand like something running amok in a Stephen King novel.

When you have the piece lined up, press it in place. It is a good idea to compress large areas with a rubber roller, but a roller tends to crack the overlap on a narrow surface, so compress the strip with your thumb.

Trim to fit. Trimming away the overlap is next. The cheap way is with a mill file. Support the shelf vertically and file away the excess. You can use the file much like a saw, holding it flat to the surface of the shelf and cutting the laminate with the edge of the file. If you will be doing all the trim with a file, you want to hold the overlap to no more than is absolutely necessary. Measure the width of the worst chip on the pieces you have already cut, and reduce the overlap on future pieces (from the same material cut with the same saw) to that width plus $1/16$ inch.

If you have very much to cover with laminate, buy or borrow a router. It will change the task from drudgery to fun. A flush-trim blade makes short work of trimming the laminate; run the router around the perimeter of the piece being trimmed and that's it. The roller guide gives a perfect edge every time. Inside corners, or an inability to run the router around the *entire* perimeter of a fixed surface, may necessitate some filing.

After the front piece is trimmed, evenly coat the top of the shelf and the bottom of the cut piece of laminate from edge to edge with contact cement, taking care not to leave any of either surface uncoated. To minimize the visibility of the seams, the usual sequence of installation is: sides (in this case, there is no point in covering the sides of an interior shelf); then the front; and finally the top. Let the glue dry tack free. If the can the cement comes in provides different instructions, follow them.

Preventing premature adhesion. Dry contact cement will stick only to other contact cement. To make positioning a large piece of laminate easy, lay waxed paper over the coated surface, covering every inch of it. Place the laminate in place on top of the paper and position it correctly. Without moving the laminate, carefully slide the paper partially from between the two and press the parts together. Now slide the paper out completely and compress the bond with a rubber roller or by hand. Install the laminate on the shelf in this manner and then run the router around the perimeter, and the shelf is finished.

Removing trim molding. The only difference in the shelf and a counter top or a bulkhead is the trim and molding that you may have to deal with. All the wood trim will have to be removed. If it was installed with finishing nails, your task will not be difficult. Look at the trim carefully and you will see where the nail holes have been filled. Use a 1/16-inch nail set to drive the nails completely through the molding. When all the nails have been located and driven through, the molding will come free.

Unfortunately (for the purpose of easy removal) the trim is usually glued in place as well. In this case, sharpen the edge of a stiff, 3-inch-wide putty knife and, after the nails have been driven through, drive the blade under the edge of the molding to release the glue bond. You may have to separate every inch of the trim, but be patient and you will be able to remove it without damaging it.

A new counter top. With the trim removed, you should be ready to resurface the counter top. The rear of a counter top, and sometimes the sides as well, may not hide the edge of the laminate under any trim, necessitating a finished edge on the laminate *before* it is installed. If you cannot cut out the piece to take advantage of the edge of the sheet, clamp the piece slightly overlapping a *straight* plank, and put a finished edge on it by running the router along the edge.

A seam is never a good idea on a counter top, and rarely necessary. If your counter is unusually large,

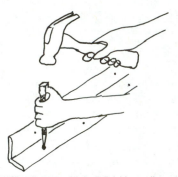

Use a 1/16" nail set to drive all finishing nails completely through the molding.

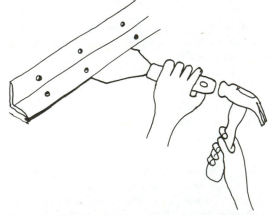

Sharpen the edge of a 3-inch-wide putty knife and drive it under the edge of the molding to release the glue bond.

Removing counter and bulkhead trim

check to see if your supplier can get you an oversize sheet—5 feet by 12 feet. If a seam is required, try to locate it in an inconspicuous spot and prerout the edges of the laminate to a precise fit. After both pieces are installed, cover the seam with a dishtowel and run a *warm* iron over it to soften the cement and embed the edges more securely. Heat, from an iron or a heat gun, is also useful in coaxing the laminate into sharper curves.

Covering Bulkheads

Vertical-grade laminate in some shade of white is the ideal covering for cabin bulkheads. Laminate is an improvement over paint because it resists stains and marring, can be scrubbed repeatedly, and should last a couple of decades. White bulkheads are traditional in appearance, contrasting nicely with oiled or varnished trim; they make the cabin seem larger, and they brighten it.

A lot of boat manufacturers recognized the benefits of plastic laminate, and your old boat probably has laminate-covered bulkheads. But many of those same manufacturers failed to see the advantages of white. Woodgrain was their choice.

Woodgrain laminate is fabricated by taking a photograph of a *real* piece of wood, printing it on a 4 by 8 sheet of paper, and using that print as the penultimate layer in the laminate. The last time I was in San Diego, my wife and I had a Polaroid taken arm in arm with a cardboard cutout of Ronald Reagan. The Reagan Republican we sent the photo to was astonished, but no one on the sidewalk mistook the cutout for the real thing. No one will be fooled by woodgrain laminate either, except in a photograph. Sound snobbish? It is unintentional. I think decorative laminate is a great product; I just don't care for it when it pretends to be something it isn't. Maybe it's just a matter of taste.

If all the edges of the counter or bulkhead are covered with wood trim wide enough to hide any chipping, cutting the laminate oversize may be unnecessary. Simply cut the piece to size, laying it in place to check for fit. Then coat both surfaces to be joined with contact cement, allowing the glue to dry. Keep the coated surfaces separated with waxed paper until they are positioned, then extract the paper and compress the laminate onto the surface being covered. Rout cutouts—the sink opening, the ice-chest opening, electrical outlets, etc.—after the laminate is glued in place. A drilled hole will admit the flush-trim router bit.

When the laminate is installed and trimmed, reattach the trim with finishing nails. The plastic laminate is very hard, so pilot holes may be necessary. Sink the nails below the surface of the trim with a nail set. Fill the nail holes, the new ones and the old ones, with matching wood putty. When the filler dries, sand away the excess, and refinish the trim (Chapter 14). Move on to the next challenge.

SEALANTS

When the various parts of a boat are assembled, we generally want the junctions to be water tight. Stockholm tar has been out of favor for a long time, but when our old boats were new boats, the most popular bedding compound was an oil-based gook that came in a can and looked exactly like peanut butter. Until it dried out.

Polymers—and monomers, if you really care—changed all that. Today's sealants come in tubes and cartridges and can last 20 years or longer without drying out. In fact, they never really dry out; like the rest of us, they just lose their grip.

There are scores of products from a couple of dozen manufacturers vying for your bucks. It all seems very confusing. Relax. For marine use, there are really only three types of sealants.

Polysulfide

Probably the most versatile sealant is polysulfide based. A two-part variety has been used for a long time to caulk teak decks, but it is a pain to use. One-part polysulfides changed all that. As durable as the two-part, although slower to cure, one-part polysulfide sealant is used right out of the tube or cartridge. It bonds well to most surfaces and the cured sealant is rubbery, allowing some give and flex. Life

Calk, a popular polysulfide sealant from Boatlife, comes in white, black, and wood colors. It cures tack-free in about 48 hours and reaches full cure in about a week.

Polysulfide can handle almost every caulking and sealant requirement aboard your old boat. Its versatility extends beyond bedding deck hardware. It can be used to seal items below the waterline as well—transducers and through-hull fittings, for example. It will adhere well to wood, although in the case of oily woods, such as teak, a primer is usually indicated. Ironically, about the only time that polysulfide would not be a good choice is as a bedding for plastic hardware or a sealant for plastic portlights. *Polysulfide: for bedding everything except plastic.*

Polyurethane

Polyurethane sealant is more appropriately thought of as an adhesive. When you bed an item with polyurethane sealant, consider that you have glued the item in place. For installing underwater through-hull fittings, or resealing a hull-to-deck joint, it is the best choice. But be cautious about using polyurethane on deck fittings and hardware; if you ever need to remove it (ever hear of Murphy's Law?), it will be very difficult, and any item at all fragile will break before the polyurethane bond releases.

Cure times for 3M's highly regarded 5200 sealant are similar to those of polysulfides, but other polyurethane formulations, such as Sikaflex 241, skin in as little as half an hour and reach final cure in 72 hours. Polyurethanes come in colors similar to those of polysulfides, but unlike the sulfides, white polyurethane does not tend to yellow with age.

Polyurethanes will adhere tenaciously to teak without priming, but it is not a good idea to use polyurethane on unvarnished teak because teak cleaners tend to soften the sealant. Polyurethanes are also incompatible with many plastics, particularly ABS and Lexan. Even when compatibility is not a problem, a plastic item bedded with polyurethane probably cannot ever be removed in one piece. *Polyurethane: for a permanent bond.*

Silicone

The third sealant is silicone. Most of us were first introduced to silicone when Dow put a candy-kiss shaped blob of it on the outside of all of their blister packages. We pulled and tugged on that little blob and were suitably impressed. We should have been; it is a terrific product. But many people have become disillusioned with silicone, mostly because their expectations were wrong.

Despite the grip that little blob had on the package, silicone sealants are not very adhesive. As a caulk—where you run a bead around the edge of a joint and expect it to seal—silicone is rarely satisfactory. It soon releases, and if you pull on one corner, the entire bead will peel away as a single strand of cloudy rubber, a giant rubber band.

It is this elasticity that defines the appropriate use for silicone sealant. When used properly, it forms wonderfully resilient gaskets that are impervious to almost any chemical assault. The gasket formed can even be used multiple times. Silicone makes an excellent insulating barrier between dissimilar metals. It is compatible with almost all marine materials, including plastics, but it should not be used below the waterline. *Silicone: to form a flexible gasket.*

APPLICATION TECHNIQUE

None of these sealants will work well unless you give them a chance. If you crank down on the mounting bolts until you squeeze all the sealant out, you might as well put the parts together without sealant. The correct technique is the same for all three sealants.

Rule 1. Both surfaces must be clean and dry. That means peeling or scraping away every bit of old caulking and wiping the surfaces with acetone. If you try to caulk right over the old caulking, it will leak. I promise. The only exception is an intact silicone *gasket*. A thin coating of fresh silicone sealant on both sides of the gasket will renew its grip on both parts.

Rule 2. Apply the sealant liberally. If it does not

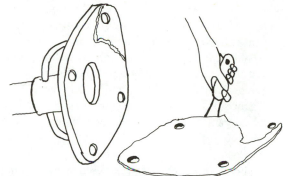

Scrape away all old caulking.

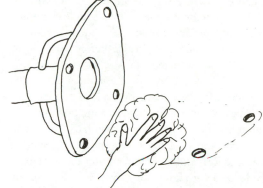

Wipe both surfaces with acetone.

Liberally apply sealant to one surface and around fasteners.

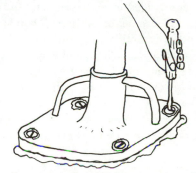

Snug mounting screws until sealant squeezes out on all sides; do not over tighten.

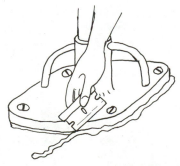

After sealant cures, trim away excess.

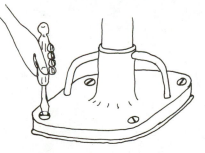

Tighten screws to put "gasket" under pressure.

Proper sealant application

squeeze out all the way around the joint, you are going to have to do it again. There is no reason to be miserly; the sealant you save is almost certain to harden in the tube or cartridge before you use it, anyway. If you are using silicone, allow any excess sealant that squeezes out of the joint to cure fully, then slice it free with a razor blade. For the more tenacious poly sisters, put tape around both sides of the joint before bedding, then smooth the ooze with your finger and peel the tape promptly, leaving a neat edge. Remember to seal around the fasteners.

Rule 3. Learn to "snug" the mounting screws after applying sealant, not tighten them. You want to pull both parts sufficiently together so that both surfaces are bedded in the sealant and the excess begins to squeeze out on all sides. Then leave the part undisturbed until the sealant cures. The lower flexibility and higher adhesion of polyurethane suggests a thinner seal. To make a reusable silicone gasket, wax the surfaces of both parts lightly or cover them with wax paper.

Rule 4. Put the seal under compression. After the sealant has cured, tighten the nuts of the mount-ing screws (turning the screws will break the seal around them). This will ensure a watertight seal even if the sealant does lose its grip.

Rule 5. If you suspect a fitting is leaking, don't even think about a sloppy repair job. Remove the fitting, clean the surfaces, and bed it right. Your diligence will ultimately save you time and money, and probably a great deal of aggravation.

There are many other plastics that have found their way aboard. You are not likely to have occasion to fabricate or repair most of them: ABS housings, Teflon bushings, Delrin sheaves, nylon impellers, polyethylene containers, and PVC ventilators. You will be cutting and fitting PVC hose in Chapter 12, and perhaps working with PVC-coated cloth in Chapter 15. Dacron dominates the chapter on sail construction and repair (Chapter 16), and you will also get some hands-on experience with plastic foams when we examine iceboxes and refrigeration in Chapter 13. But for now, let's desert the Space Age in favor of the Bronze Age.

EIGHT

Forks, Eyes, and Studs

Facts do not cease to exist because they are ignored.
–ALDOUS HUXLEY–

A couple of days ago, as I scanned the cable with some fancy thumb work on the remote control, I paused at an old black-and-white series. The bad guy had just been identified, and his photograph televised. To make the point that *everyone* would now recognize this rat, the director did a split-screen shot: the television broadcast on one side, the roofs of a southern California residential community on the other. The roof shot was a forest of masts and guy wires supporting spiky TV antennas.

Cable TV has changed the residential skyline, but don't miss the point. If you are 30-something, or beyond, you probably have some rigging experience. If a broken wire on your TV antenna led you to call someone, it was because you didn't like heights, not because you didn't think you could handle the complexity of measuring and attaching the wire. Any reluctance to attempt the replacement of rigging on your boat should be for the same reason. Major rerigging suggests lowering the mast anyway.

This chapter is about being your own rigger. It is mostly about the mast and the wires and fittings that hold it up, but you will find a smattering of information about the lines you pull to hoist, trim, and furl.

THE RIG

I am sure that I will be scalded for this heresy, but the type of rig that is popular at any given time is more a matter of fashion than of performance. I don't mean to suggest that the well-equipped skip-

per this year is sporting a Bermudian cutter—at least that isn't exactly what I mean. It also has to do with the *type of sailing* that is fashionable.

Schooners enjoyed immense popularity when yachting was the sport of the wealthy and owners had ample paid crew aboard to pull all the strings. With the entry of the less prosperous into recreational sailing, the economy of the sloop rig endeared it to a generation of sailors. John Hanna's Tahiti ketch design inspired a decade of interest in the ketch rig. Carleton Mitchell shook up the racing community with an incredibly successful yawl, and for the next ten years you could buy a dozen yawl-rigged production boats. Rule changes put the sloop back on top. The phenomenal growth of cruising regenerated interest in the ketch. Then someone coined the phrase "performance cruising", and the sloop reemerged. But as boats got larger, sails got so large that a split rig was obligatory. The ketch was still "out" because it reputedly won't go to weather, so the well-equipped skipper this year sports a cutter rig. Of course, as I write this, *Steinlager 2*, a ketch, has just won the Whitbread Round-the-World Race, calling into question (again) some of the common wisdom about the ketch rig.

Which is the fastest rig? The safest rig? The best rig? To quote Bob Dylan, "The answer, my friend, is blowing in the wind." Quite literally.

If you can resolve the design and engineering issues that are likely to arise, particularly in the case of mast relocation, you can change the way your old boat is rigged. You might decide to convert from a yawl to a sloop, from a sloop to a cutter, or from a cutter to a ketch. You might even install an unstayed mast, or convert to a junk rig. But don't make the change because you have heard that the junk rig is clearly superior. It isn't, not in every circumstance and not in all conditions. Nor is the cat rig, the ketch, the cutter, or the sloop.

The decision to radically alter a boat's designed rig should be based upon dissatisfaction with specific aspects of the boat's performance, not some general sense that a different rig is better. And you need a high degree of confidence that the new rig will correct the performance problems without introducing new ones. This suggests a level of experience that most sailors never reach.

If you want to experiment, go ahead. Sailing is, after all, about going your own way. But what follows is not about type: it is about condition. With the exception of a short segment on adding an inner stay, we will be concentrating on evaluating, strengthening, and renewing the *existing rig* on your old boat.

THE MAST

Your old boat almost certainly has an aluminum mast; relatively few fiberglass boats have been delivered with wooden masts. Unlike wood, anodized aluminum requires very little maintenance—a coat of wax every year and a thorough inspection about every third year.

You cannot do a thorough inspection with the mast erect. It has to come down. If you will also be replacing rigging, be sure you tune the rigging and mark the adjustment of the turnbuckles *before* you slacken and release the stays. Let the boatyard lower the mast. I once dropped and restepped a 33-foot stick at the dock, but I don't recommend it.

With the mast supported on sawhorses and lying on its side, sight down the sail track. There will be some downward sag in the unsupported middle, but don't worry about that. You are trying to ascertain that the mast is straight fore and aft. If you start to hyperventilate trying to decide if it is or it isn't, sit down and breathe into a paper bag. You aren't looking for anything that subtle. Straight is best, but a gentle, regular curvature, preferably *aft*, is no cause for alarm. If the bend is excessive or irregular, seek a professional opinion.

Now turn the mast with the sail track up. Nail or clamp wooden supports to one of the horses to hold the mast in this position. Sight down the track. The mast should be straight—period. If there is some sideways curvature, go to the far end of the mast and move it to make sure the curve is not being induced by the way the mast sits on the horses. Check again. Straight this time? Good, because any significant sideways curvature is bad, very bad. But I knew all along your mast was going to be straight. They almost always are.

Next you want to check for corrosion. You can give the stick a visual onceover, but damaging corrosion is most likely where the aluminum is in contact with a dissimilar metal. That means you need to check the mast beneath any fitting attached with stainless steel screws. But before you start unscrewing things, you need to do a little preparation.

First, using a felt-tip marker, mark the top (toward the masthead) of each fitting you will be removing. On tandem fittings (e.g., spreader bases, shroud tangs) also indicate port or starboard. Make any other notations that will help you to avoid confusion when you replace the removed items.

Next, put a drop or two of penetrating oil around every screw that you will be removing. Some of the screws are going to be frozen and the penetrant will help. Now let the oil do its job while you make a trip to Sears.

You are after an impact driver. This is an ingenious device that translates a hammer blow into torque. Looking like a beefy, steel-handled screwdriver, it will come with interchangeable tips so it can be used either with sockets or for slot-head or Phillips-head screws. Expect to get change back from your twenty.

Corrosion beneath the spreader bases is particularly serious, so that is a good place to start your examination. Far too often, spreader fittings are riveted or screwed to the mast. Both are poor methods of attachment. The considerable leverage exerted by any unfair pressure on the outboard end of the spreader, such as the pressure the genoa exerts when it backwinds against the spreaders in tacking or that the mainsail exerts in running downwind, tends to loosen these fasteners, often cracking the thin wall of the mast in the process. And since spreader bases so attached are held apart only by the thin walls of the spar, the tightened shrouds try to crush the mast.

If the bases are riveted, presumably with aluminum rivets, and you do not want to change the way the spreaders are mounted, you may want to check for signs of serious corrosion elsewhere before you decide to remove the spreader bases. If they are attached to the mast with machine screws, remove the screws and the fittings, and examine the holes carefully for cracks. Don't even try a regular screwdriver on the screws; at least one will be frozen and you will strip the slot trying to free it. Use the impact driver, seating the blade carefully in the slot and turning the grip as far as it will go in a counterclockwise direction. Now give the top of the driver a whack with your hammer. The blow will twist the screwdriver blade with considerable force and at the same time keep the blade from slipping out of the slot. Don't get overzealous with the hammer; you don't want to dimple the mast.

Properly mounted spreader bases will be through-bolted. When you release the nuts, remove one of the fittings before extracting the bolts. The bolts should pass through compression sleeves—thick-wall aluminum tubing as long as the mast is wide—and you don't want the sleeve to fall inside the mast. Without the sleeves, tightening the mounting bolts would tend to pull the opposite sides of the mast together—not good.

If your spreader fittings are not through-bolted, consider altering them. You may be able to use the original fittings, or you may have to have new spreader bases manufactured. Make the base plates as large as possible to spread the load. If you have difficulty locating bolts long enough, get a machine shop to thread the ends of lengths of stainless steel rod. A tubing supply can help you with the stock for the compression tubes.

The holes have to be large enough, at least on one side, to admit the compression tubes, so keep the bolt size modest. Be sure the tubes, not the mast, take all the compression. A four-bolt pattern works well, but two bolts are adequate if the base is broad and the bolts a size larger than those originally fitted. Holes in the mast weaken it, particularly when they are in a line, so try to use the existing holes in the mast, enlarging them as necessary to accommodate the bolts and sleeves. If that is not possible, move the spreader bases up the mast slightly so the new holes will not be among the old ones. This will alter the geometry of the rigging slightly, but the implications are far less serious than drilling additional holes in line with the existing ones.

If your spreader bases were screwed to the mast and the holes are not cracked and there is only minor pitting and the spreader fittings have given no trouble in 20 years and you're not headed around the world and you don't see any reason to change the way the spreaders are mounted and . . . take it easy. Fine. You're right. Don't change them. But if

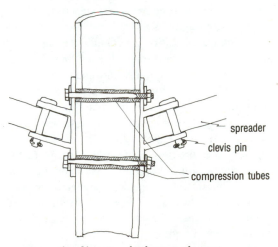

Attaching spreader bases to the mast

spreader

clevis pin

compression tubes

they are loose or if the holes are stressed, don't just put in bigger screws. Fix them right.

We were looking for corrosion anyway, and another likely spot is around the mast step. Typically the mast extrusion slips over a cast heel fitting, which is held in place with three or four machine screws. Free the screws with the impact driver and remove them. With a punch or a screwdriver, tap the heel free. Check inside the mast for corrosion.

If the bottom of the mast is badly corroded, you might cut off the bad section, but shortening the mast will require shortening all the rigging and may be detrimental to the fit of the sails and even to the performance of the boat. Replacing the mast is always a better alternative, and often less expensive. Find the same extrusion (in the absence of an identifying sticker on the mast, call the boat's manufacturer) and replacing the mast is simply a matter of taking the fittings from the old extrusion and installing them on the new one. Otherwise, you will need, at a minimum, new cap and heel fittings. The spar manufacturer will advise you.

Fortunately, the corrosion you find is not likely to be so serious. With a pad of coarse bronze wool, clean away all signs of corrosion. Then paint the inside of the mast as far in as you can reach with a corrosion-inhibiting paint. Be sure it is intended for aluminum. Give the heel fitting the same treatment.

The mast cap will be similar to the heel fitting. Remove it and treat any corrosion. Now is also a good time to service the masthead sheaves. You may be disappointed to find that they are little more than phenolic or aluminum disks rotating on a bolt through the mast. Don't be; bearings are unnecessary in this instance.

Remove the bolt and extract the sheaves and their side plates. With bronze wool (or a soft wire wheel), polish the sides of both the sheaves and the plates. Insert the bolt through the center bushings to check for wear. Replacements can be obtained from a bearing supplier. Coat the bushings and the sides of the sheaves and the plates with a thin layer of water-pump grease.

The mast tangs will also be through-bolted. Re-

move them to check for hidden corrosion in the mast, and to examine the tangs for signs of fatigue. Metal ages, losing some of its resilience (don't we all?) and under stress tiny cracks begin to form. Called *propagating defects*, these cracks will continue to grow and weaken the part until it fails. When that happens with a mast tang, it often results in the loss of the mast.

Any nick, bend, or hole in the part concentrates the stresses, hastening the process. That's bad news. It's also good news, because it means that weakening cracks generally begin on the surface of the part, where they can be detected before they become dangerous.

With good light, examine every square millimeter of the tangs. For about five bucks, the nearest camera shop will sell you an 8-power loupe which will reveal the texture of the surface in great detail. If your magnified examination does not turn up any flaws, the tangs are probably sound.

Probably? Well, the cracks start out microscopic and they may not be visible, even with magnification. But if you do not find a visible crack in any of the fittings (later you are going to examine the chainplates with the same thoroughness), your visual check should be sufficient. Only if you find a crack, or if the fittings are more than 20 years old and/or you are headed over the horizon, will you want to take your checking one step further.

The only way to assess the absolute strength of the fitting is to put it on a hydraulic ram and crank up the tension until the part breaks, but if you do that with all of your tangs and chainplates, then where will you be? Fortunately, the designer specified fittings of adequate strength and the manufacturer fabricated them as specified (we hope), so you are only concerned with weakening defects.

There are three types of nondestructive testing that might be employed. The parts can be subjected to X-ray, but unless the crack is parallel to the radiation it will not show up on the exposure. In any case, given the expense of X-ray, it will probably be less costly to replace the suspect parts.

Magnetic particle inspection, often referred to by

the trade name Magnaflux, is used extensively in industry. The principle involves passing a current through the part. Any discontinuity caused by a surface crack will set up an electromagnetic field. When the surface is coated with a fine metallic powder, the particles are attracted to the field, forming a line that corresponds to the crack. Sadly, magnetic particle inspection can only be performed on ferrous metals, and ferrous metal is an anathema in modern rigging.

That leaves us with dye penetrant inspection. The part is thoroughly cleaned, then painted with a very thin, liquid mixture of dye and penetrating oil. The oil is allowed to "soak in" for a prescribed time before the surface is wiped clean. Finally a "developer", which is a fine powder, is applied to the surface. It draws out any oil that has remained in a crack, resulting in a dark line. A more sensitive version uses a fluorescent dye and the part is examined under ultraviolet light.

Dye penetrant testing is just as easy to perform as it sounds and it can be done right on the boat, sometimes without even necessitating the removal of the suspect item. Dye penetrant kits (Spot Check) are not cheap, but if the testing results in early identification of a flaw that might have otherwise resulted in the loss of the entire rig, or even if the results only assure you that the rig is sound, it will be money well spent.

Whether you remove cleats, winches, and any other remaining fittings from the mast may be determined by what you have already found. If corrosion does not seem to be a problem beneath the fittings already removed, the only reason to remove the remaining items is to be thorough. Use your own judgement.

THE BOOM

Give the boom the same treatment as the mast. Remove fittings to check for corrosion. Check the gooseneck for cracks, using dye penetrant. Also check the bails for the mainsheet blocks. Be sure that all of the fasteners are appropriate and sound.

For a couple of decades, most sailboats were delivered with roller reefing. It was an aberration, and today slab reefing is preferred. Roller reefing does work, so unless you reef often, there is usually no pressing need to get rid of it. I still have roller reefing on my own boat, not because I like it, but because changing it has never migrated into the first priority column of my plan. But roller reefing is more cumbersome, the sail shape is less satisfactory, and the boom adds complications to the rig that are unnecessary if you have a mainsail with reefing points.

Most of the loading on a boom is upward, so a fixed boom will have a vertical section that is deeper than its width. A roller-reefing boom is usually round or nearly round, so it either has an insufficient vertical dimension, which allows the boom to flex and destroys the shape of the mainsail, or it is far wider than it needs to be, adding undesirable weight. Roller-reefing booms must also be free of hardware so that the sail can roll around them smoothly. Consequently, sheeting is at the end of the boom, and a proper vang attachment is not possible.

Unlike replacing the mast, replacing a roller-reefing boom involves more than removing the hardware from the old boom and attaching it to the new one. You do not want the new boom to be configured like the old one; that is the reason you are replacing it. A fixed boom provides unlimited sheeting and vanging possibilities, including mid-boom sheeting and the possibility of fitting a hydraulic vang or a compression strut. There are too many variables to provide specific directions here, but if you are replacing your roller-reefing boom, you should give ample thought to three considerations—sheeting, vanging, and reefing—before you attach any hardware to the new boom.

INTERNAL WIRING

If your mast is rigged with internal halyards, you can replace them now if you like, but having the mast horizontal does not make the job any easier. However, now *is* the time to deal with the electrical wiring inside the mast.

When wires hang loosely down the hollow center of an aluminum mast, the slightest cross-chop sets up an incessant clanging that would easily qualify as a human rights violation under the provisions of the Geneva Convention. One common solution is to seize butterfly-shaped pieces of soft polyurethane foam to the wire every 3 to 4 feet before it is inserted into the mast. The foam keeps the wire away from the walls of the mast. This solution has obvious drawbacks when there are internal halyards. Also, I don't like the idea of damp foam (of course it will be damp) lying against the inside of my aluminum mast. And what happens if you want to add another wire?

A better solution is a conduit inside the mast. While the mast is on horses is the time to install such a conduit. Thin-wall PVC conduit is ideal for this purpose. Select a diameter that will allow the easy passage of all the wires you anticipate running from the masthead and the spreaders—lights, antennas, and instruments. For spreader lights and a tricolor at the masthead, one-inch conduit will be adequate, but add a VHF or Loran antenna and a masthead anemometer, and you will be better served by $1\frac{1}{4}$-inch, or even $1\frac{1}{2}$-inch conduit.

To install the conduit, you need a handful of $\frac{3}{16}$-inch aluminum pop rivets and the installation tool. The rivet length will depend upon the thickness of the mast and conduit walls. Borrow the tool if you like, but it is a good item to add to any onboard tool chest.

The conduit comes in 20-foot lengths; two sections will handle a mast up to about 45 feet. First determine where the conduit will lie. Typically, it will interfere with the tang or spreader mounting if it runs down either side. A bow light may preclude mounting against the front of the mast, and the mainsail track has the same effect aft. Often the best place is in the corner formed by the inside wall of the track and the side of the mast. Be sure that the conduit can run the length of the mast without interfering with anything. Do not overlook any fittings that you may have temporarily removed.

You want to install the conduit in two separated sections to allow the easy exit of wires that run only to the spreaders. Position the conduit alongside the *outside* of the mast to determine the location and the length of the two pieces. The space between the two should be a couple of inches and it should be located where the mid-height wires exit the mast. The top section should reach to within a foot or so of the cap and should be cut accordingly. The bottom piece should stop several inches above where the wires exit the mast. Mark the mast with the proper locations of the ends of the two sections of conduit.

With a felt-tip marker, draw a straight line from end to end on both sections of conduit. Rotate the mast so that the conduit will lie on the "bottom", and insert the top section of conduit into the mast, leaving a short length sticking out. Rotate the conduit until it sits on the black line and draw a corresponding line on the outside of the mast. Extract the conduit and rotate the mast to make the new line convenient. Extend this line the length of the mast, or simply measure its relationship to some full-length feature—e.g., the edge of the sail track or an extruded seam. This is the rivet line; all the rivets that will hold the two sections of conduit in place will be on this line.

Starting about 2 inches below the mark that represents the top of the top section, mark your first rivet location on the rivet line. Mark a second location about 2 inches from the first, toward the base of the mast. From there, place a mark on the line every 18 inches until you near the end of the top section. The final two marks should be 2 inches and 4 inches from the end of the section. Following the same pattern, mark the rivet locations for the lower section of conduit.

Before drilling the marked holes, hold the sections of conduit against the markings to make sure that everything looks right. Carpenters live by the old adage, "Measure twice, cut once." The same applies to drilling holes in your mast. If everything looks right, place the tip of a center punch on each mark and give it an authoritative whack. Now use a sharp $\frac{3}{16}$-inch bit to drill all the holes. If you try to

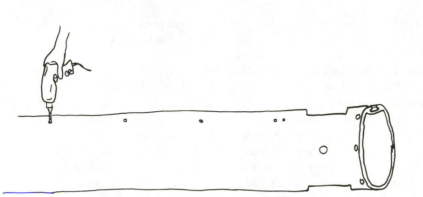

Decide on location of conduit and drill mast for pop rivets approximately every 18 inches.

Draw a straight line the full length of the PVC pipe with a felt marker.

Position mast with holes down and insert pipe with line down. With black line over drilled holes, drill the first hole in the pipe and install a pop rivet. Use an ice pick to jockey the pipe so each drilled hole is through the line. Install the rivet before drilling the next hole.

Mid-mast wires exit at the opening between the two sections of conduit.

Wiring conduit inside mast

drill the holes without using the punch, your drill bit will dance all over the curved surface of the mast.

Drill the first hole in the conduit 2 inches from the end and centered on the black line. Rotate the mast back down and insert the top section of conduit, lining up the hole with the first hole in the mast. With one hand (or the hand of a helper) holding the conduit in place, insert a rivet into the hole in the mast and through the hole in the conduit and squeeze the tool until the stem "pops." Be sure the rivet is long enough to flare inside the conduit. Line the black line up over the second hole and drill the conduit through the hole in the mast. Install the second rivet. Do the same for the third hole.

After the third hole, you will not be able to position the conduit by reaching inside the mast. The black line will probably fall across the hole, but when it doesn't, use an ice pick in the *next* hole to jockey the plastic pipe into position. It is imperative that you line up the black line each time to insure that the rivet grips the two pieces at their point of tangency. The previous rivet will hold the conduit against the wall of the mast, but your drill bit should be very sharp, and you must apply very little upward pressure to keep from pushing the conduit to one side or the other.

After all the rivets are in, check each one. Occasionally the stem breaks above the surface of the rivet, and the last thing you want is a sharp little spike sticking out of the mast beside the sail track. Make sure all of the rivets are smooth.

With both sections in place, simply run all of the mast wiring through the conduit. A length of light ($^3/_{32}$- or $^1/_8$-inch) 1 × 19 wire will serve as an electrician's snake if you do not have access to the real thing. With the mast cap and base both removed, feeding the masthead wiring should present no difficulty. Wiring that exits mid-mast may be somewhat more troublesome. The exit hole in the mast should be large enough to accept a grommet, but leave the grommet out while feeding the wire. Take the sharp edges off the drilled hole with sandpaper or a strip of emery cloth to keep the metal from stripping or nicking the insulation. Coating the wiring with beeswax (or soap) will make it slip past other wiring in the conduit much more easily.

SPREADERS

If the spreaders are wood, now is the time to check them for rot. Even if they look okay, poke them a few times with your ice pick. Don't hold the spreader in your hand while you are doing this; I have seen wooden spreaders so rotten that the ice pick went all the way through. If that happens to you, be glad you have a fiberglass *boat*.

Conventional wisdom is to varnish wooden spreaders rather than paint them so that rot will be immediately visible. The truth is that rot almost invariably begins on the top of the spreader, so looking up from the deck at the still-sound varnished undersides can be disastrously misleading. The other truth is that paint protects the wood better than varnish. If you have aesthetic reasons for choosing varnish, at least add a couple of coats of paint to the *top* of the spreaders; it won't be seen and it will add years to the life of your spreaders.

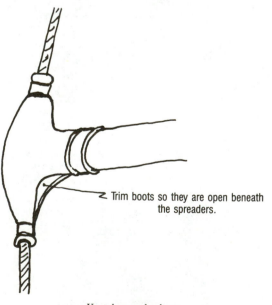

Trim boots so they are open beneath the spreaders.

Vented spreader boots

Aluminum spreaders are not without their own problems, particularly at their outboard ends. Remove all chafe guards and tape to expose the tip. Interaction of the stainless steel shroud with the aluminum tip often results in destructive corrosion. Corrosion is hastened by wrapping the tip with tape because the tape tends to hold water. Rubber boots are preferable. Modify them so that they are as watertight as possible above the spreader, but trim the boots below the spreaders to leave a generous gap in the seam so that any rain that does find its way into the boot can escape or evaporate.

STAYS AND SHROUDS

Every stay and shroud should be checked from one end to the other for broken strands. When a strand breaks, it tends to curl out, forming what is descriptively called a "meathook." If G. Gordon Liddy is your hero, locate the broken strands by running your bare hand down the stays, wrapping your lacerated palm afterwards with gauze. If you're a wimp, wrap the gauze *around the stay* and run it down the wire.

Broken strands mean it is time to replace the wire, and not just the one that is broken. When one shroud starts to go, all the other ones the same age will not be far behind.

You will probably want to replace the old wire with new wire of the same diameter, but it can be very useful to know if that diameter is adequate. Rigging calculations begin with the righting moment (RM) of your boat. In yacht design books, such as *Skene's*, you will generally find a graph providing the RM at 30 degrees for various waterline lengths. The graph has serious limitations. Imagine a paper cup and a straw as a sailboat and mast. Insert the straw through the lid of the empty cup and tilt the cup with pressure against the top of the straw. No problem. Fill the same cup with sand. Instead of tilting the cup, pressure against the top of the straw just bends the straw. Now empty the cup, glue it to the center of a 6-inch cardboard disk, and try to tilt it with the straw. Clearly displacement and beam

affect the RM. The only way to know the RM of your boat is by measuring it. The procedure is called an *inclining test*.

Did I say test? I'm sorry. I meant measurement. And you have to do this measurement while the boat is rigged and in the water, and preferably fully loaded.

Tie a weight—a heavy nut is good—to a length of string and tape the string to the cabin overhead on the centerline of the boat, so that the nut is suspended a couple of inches above the cabin sole. Putting the weight in a bucket of water will dampen (aha!) its motion. Lay a strip of wood across the cabin and next to the string to record the movement of the pendulum.

Now you need a couple of fat and honest friends. Get their accurate weights and ask them to stand on the centerline of the boat. You will be standing on the centerline too, but in the cabin to record the heel. Mark the spot where the line crosses the board. Now ask your big buddies to stand on the rail at the main shrouds. You are going to owe them a big meal for this. When the boat has stopped oscillating, mark where the string crosses the board. If the string hits the side of the bucket, *move the bucket*.

You want to know the angle of heel. You can derive it trigonometrically by dividing the distance between the two marks by the length of the string from the overhead to the board to obtain the tangent of the angle. Look up that tangent in the trig tables, or key it into your fancy calculator to get the angle. If you've never heard of trigonometry, measure the angle with the protractor you keep by the chart table. If the angle is less than 6 or 7 degrees, get some more friends and do it again.

Now multiply the total weight of your assistants times the distance from the centerline to the rail. Divide that number by the degrees of heel to get the righting moment per degree. Traditional calculations use the RM at 30 degrees, so multiply your one degree number by 30. Now multiply by 1.5 to allow for severe conditions that might heel the boat beyond 30 degrees. (Occasionally 2.78 is used rather than 1.5, a good precaution if you are headed

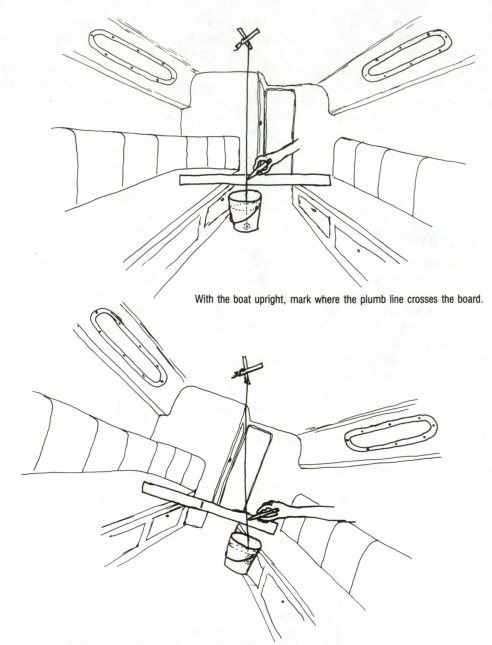

With the boat upright, mark where the plumb line crosses the board.

With a known weight (W) a known distance (D) from the centerline, heel the boat and mark where the plumb line crosses the board. Measure the angle of incline or calculate it by dividing the distance between the marks by the length of the string from the overhead to the board. Divide this angle by (W x D) to get righting moment (RM) per degree.

Rigging load (PT) is calculated by multiplying RM by 30 to get RM at 30 degrees, then by 1.5 to allow for severe conditions. Divide the result by the distance from the centerline to the chainplate to get PT.

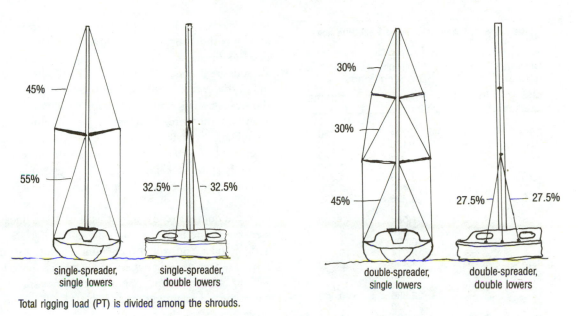

45%

55%

32.5% 32.5%

single-spreader,
single lowers

single-spreader,
double lowers

30%

30%

45%

27.5% 27.5%

double-spreader,
single lowers

double-spreader,
double lowers

Total rigging load (PT) is divided among the shrouds.

Calculating righting moment

for high latitudes, but empirical data suggest that the higher factor is rarely essential under more normal conditions.)

To convert the righting moment to the total load on the chainplate, called PT in the formula, you need only divide by the distance from the centerline of the boat to the chainplate. This assumes that all the shrouds come to a single point on either side. In actuality, the load is divided among multiple shrouds. The distribution varies according to the rig configuration. No single method of calculating shroud loads is universally recognized, but you should get satisfactory results if you assume, for a single-spreader rig, 45 percent of the load on the upper shroud and 55 percent on the lower. With twin lowers, each carries about 32.5 percent of the load. (I know that adds up to more than 100 percent; I don't make the rules, I just report them!) For a double-spreader rig, the upper shroud and the intermediate both carry 30 percent, and the lower gets 45 percent of the load—twin lowers get 27.5 percent each.

We are almost finished. The numbers you have calculated are the *theoretical* loads on each shroud,

but when the boat rolls off a wave and the mast whips, the load on the shrouds goes up. The situation is made worse if the rigging is loose; a thread that cuts a blue line into your fingers when you attempt to break it with a steady pull, pops effortlessly if you subject it to a sudden jerk. The headstay and backstay are subjected to similar load escalation from a pitching motion, or from a shuddering impact with a wave.

By how much does the load increase? I don't know. Neither do the experts. But the best and brightest say that even the worst conditions will not triple the load, so if you use a safety factor of 3, the rig will be strong enough to take whatever Mother Nature hails down on you. Actually, unless you are really planning to challenge the Old Girl, a factor of 2.5 should be adequate. If you are wondering why you should even consider the lower factor, it is because weight aloft is detrimental to both the performance and the comfort of the boat. The stays and shrouds should not be a millimeter larger than *big enough*.

So . . . multiply the calculated shroud loads by 2.5 to get the required strength of the wire. Consult

Typical Breaking Loads for Stainless Steel Wire Rope.

Nominal Diameter (strand size)		1 × 19 Minimum Breaking Load	
MM	Inches	Pounds	Kilograms
2	—	704	320
2.5	—	1,100	500
3	1/8	1,584	720
4	5/32	2,816	1,280
4.76	3/16	3,960	1,800
5	—	4,400	2,000
5.56	7/32	5,295	2,470
6	—	6,336	2,880
6.35	1/4	7,084	3,220
7	9/32	7,810	3,550
8	5/16	10,208	4,640
9	—	12,914	5,870
9.53	3/8	14,476	6,580
10	—	15,950	7,250
11	7/16	19,294	8,770
12	—	22,880	10,400
12.7	1/2	25,630	11,650
14	9/16	31,196	14,180
16	5/8	40,832	18,560
19	3/4	47,564	21,620
22	7/8	63,954	29,070
26	1	89,320	40,600

the table to determine the wire size that provides the strength you need. If it agrees with the size of your old rigging, perfect. If you calculate that lighter rigging would be adequate, consider carefully before you rerig lighter. I know what I just said about the weight aloft, but it is equally true that profit-motivated manufacturers do not incur the extra expense of oversize rigging without a reason. I would not ignore their decision on the sole basis of the above calculation.

Even if you calculate that the original rigging is too small, you may not want to change sizes. If the mast has been standing for a couple of decades, if all the sisterships you have seen still have the same size rigging, and if the sailing you have in mind is not that unusual, the expense of the change and the added weight aloft are probably not justified. Should your future sailing plans develop into something more ambitious, strengthening the rig at that time would be in order.

We have not sized the forestay or the backstay in this exercise. The forestay should be at least as strong as the strongest shroud, and in actual practice the forestay is often one size larger, unless the shrouds are oversize. The extra strength is in recognition of the risk to the crew in the cockpit should the headstay fail, and to allow for the chafe of jib snaps on the wire. From a load standpoint, the (standing) backstay can be a size smaller than the forestay, but since the tension on the forestay depends upon backstay tension, it is better for the two to be the same size. An inner stay can be a size smaller.

If you do not already know this, 1 × 19 stainless steel wire rope is really your only choice for stays and shrouds. You will also encounter 7 × 19 wire rope, used for running rigging because of its flexibility, and 7 × 7 wire rope, popular for lifelines and luff wires. But for standing rigging aboard a fiberglass boat, 1 × 19 is the norm.

Stainless steel wire rope comes in various types. The most common are Type 302 and Type 304, high-carbon alloys offering high strength at relatively low cost. These alloys give long service in a temperate climate, but in the tropics 302 and 304 stainless demonstrate an unsettling inclination to corrode rapidly. Boats headed for the tropics often choose Type 316 stainless for its considerably higher corrosion resistance, but 316 stainless will be as much as 15 percent weaker than 302 and 304. At a slightly higher cost, at least one manufacturer offers a proprietary alloy—MacWhyte's "Sailbrite"—claiming both high corrosion resistance and strength on a par with that of 302 and 304. Type 2213-5, also called Nitronic 50, is stronger and much more corrosion-resistant than any of the other types, but the cost is also much higher. Nitronic 50 is also used in the manufacture of rod rigging.

Rod rigging has been around for a long time, but its tendency to succumb to fatigue and part without warning have made cautious sailors regard it with suspicious eyes. After all, when one "strand" of a rod breaks. . . . Many of the early problems with rod rigging have been engineered out, and there is little reason for properly installed rod rigging to fail, but it remains a less forgiving material than wire rope. Lower elasticity and less windage make rod rigging very attractive to the racing sailor, but for rerigging a 20-year-old production boat, the benefits are not likely to justify the cost—or the potential risk.

If any of the original rigging is still aboard (God forbid!), it almost certainly has swaged terminals. Even if the rigging has been renewed, swaged terminals are likely. Swaged terminals are attached to the wire by a special machine that literally compresses the barrel of the fitting, gripping the wire. In the right conditions, swaged fittings last a very long time. In the wrong conditions, they fail before your insurance man sends you another tacky calendar.

Swages fail because the machine that installed them was not adequate or the operator did not use it correctly. They fail because compressing the metal weakens it. They fail because the die marks concentrate the stresses. They fail because water runs down the wire into the fitting, and the resulting rust expands inside the fitting. They fail because the same water freezes and expands. They fail because any unfair lead or pull tends to pry open the squeezed barrel. They fail.

If you have swaged fittings, check them with dye penetrant. If they fail the test, replace them. When a swage cracks, it is—or soon will be—severely weakened. If they pass, don't just forget about them. They should be checked for cracks *every year.*

Every swaged terminal I have ever owned eventually had to be replaced, while not a single cone-type terminal of the nearly three dozen I have owned has ever been replaced or even given me a moment's concern. You can see where my loyalty lies. And cone terminals have the added benefit of being *intended* for do-it-yourself installation. Cone terminals are, in my opinion, the *only* terminals to even consider. I personally prefer the design of those made by Sta-Lok, but once installed, the Norseman terminals are equally secure.

Each terminal comes with detailed installation instructions, making instructions here redundant, but if you have your palms in the air at the thought of trusting your mast to fittings *you* installed, let me at

least give you a sense of how easy it is. The threaded body of the fitting is slipped over the wire, then the outer layer of wire is slightly unlaid. A small cone with a hole in the center is slipped over the center strands of the wire. The preformed outer strands are allowed to assume their original lay, and a metal cap is placed over the reunited wire ends. The body of the fitting is then slipped back toward the end of the wire and screwed into the end fitting. That's it. Inside, the compression of screwing the two parts together forms the wire into a secure cage around the internal cone, giving you a fitting that is stronger than the wire it is attached to.

Before you begin rerigging, you need to gather all the parts together. If you are just replacing old wire with new wire of the same diameter, preparation involves little more than buying the appropriate terminals—eyes, forks, or studs—and an adequate length of wire. Determine how much wire you need by measuring each of the stays and shrouds you are replacing. Measure from clevis pin to clevis pin to make sure that differences in the end fittings will not leave you short of wire. Add all the measurements together and buy the wire in a single length, ordering a couple of extra feet as cheap insurance.

If you are changing the rig in any way, make sure all of the new parts are compatible. That means you must pre-assemble each piece with whatever it connects to. If you decide to replace the rigging with wire one size larger, the pin size of the fittings will likewise be larger and they will no longer fit the holes in the mast tang and the chainplates. So you just get out your trusty drill and. . . . Wrong again. Drilling out the pin hole to a larger size reduces the amount of metal on either side of the hole, weakening the fitting. Usually, heavier wire will require thicker and wider tangs, and often heavier chainplates.

You can calculate the strength of a tang by multiplying its thickness times the *remaining* width of metal at the hole times the tensile strength of common stainless steel, which is around 80,000 pounds per square inch. This calculation for a one-inch-wide tang fabricated from $3/16$-inch-thick stainless

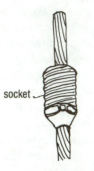

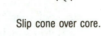
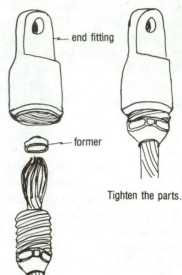

cone

end fitting

socket

former

Tighten the parts.

Slip socket over wire.　Unlay outer layer of wire.　Slip cone over core.　Re-lay outer wires.

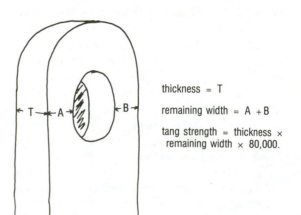

Fit former and end fitting.

Mechanical terminal fitting

drilled to accept a $^3/_8$-inch clevis pin would be $^3/_{16} \times ^5/_8 \times 80,000$, which yields a strength of 9,375 pounds. This is more than adequate for $^3/_{16}$ inch wire with a breaking strength of 4,700 pounds. Step the wire size up to $^1/_4$ inch and the corresponding clevis pin diameter will be $^1/_2$ inch. Drill out the old tang, and the new calculation would be $^3/_{16} \times ^1/_2 \times 80,000$, or 7,500 pounds—inadequate for the 8,200-pound breaking strength of the wire. The tang should be wider and probably thicker. In some circumstances, the load on the tang can be concentrated on one side of the hole, so it is a good idea to make sure the tangs are at least twice as strong as the wire.

Heavier wire also means heavier turnbuckles. Continuing with the above example, $^3/_{16}$-inch rigging requires $^3/_8$-inch turnbuckles. Even if the pin sizes were not incorrect for $^1/_4$-inch wire (which they are), a bronze Merriman $^3/_8$-inch turnbuckle has a rated strength of only 6,500 pounds, far less than the 8,200-pound strength of the wire. A $^1/_2$ inch-turnbuckle with a strength of 10,300 pounds is indicated.

If your rerigging does not require replacement of the turnbuckles, inspect them carefully. It is a very good idea to check the body of each turnbuckle with dye penetrant. If the threads of the turnbuckle, particularly if it is stainless steel, have not been kept

thickness = T

remaining width = A + B

tang strength = thickness × remaining width × 80,000.

Tang strength calculation

lubricated, the threads may have galled; if so, replace the turnbuckle. Also be very suspicious of turnbuckles with an integral toggle. The bottom stud is threaded into the pin of the toggle and water invariably finds its way inside this joint, leading to dangerous and undetectable corrosion. With the fervor of personal experience, I strongly recommend replacing turnbuckles of this type.

With all the pieces in hand, the biggest difficulty in replacing your own rigging is in getting it to come out to the correct length. If you marked the turnbuckles while the rig was properly tuned, your job is much easier. Adjust the turnbuckle to the marks and lay the old shroud on the ground, pulling it straight. If you are working on a dock, drive two stiff nails through the clevis pin holes at each end. If you are working on the ground, nail a couple of scraps of plywood to the ground (it sounds odd, but it works), then put nails through the ends of the stretched wire and into the plywood. The two nails mark the pin-to-pin length—from the mast tang to the chainplate—of the shroud you are duplicating.

Now remove the clevis pin that attaches the end fitting of the wire to the turnbuckle. The turnbuckle is adjusted to the way it was on the boat, but that may not be the way you want it adjusted on the new shroud. Ideally, the turnbuckle should be half extended, so adjust it to that condition. If you are replacing the turnbuckle, it should be the new one you are adjusting.

Is there a toggle under the turnbuckle? If not, you are going to add one. No turnbuckle should ever be installed without a toggle beneath it. Go ahead and install the correct toggle on the lower end of the turnbuckle now. On the upper end of the turnbuckle, install the eye of a disassembled wire terminal (Sta-Lok or Norseman).

On the end of your coil of rigging wire, install the proper fitting, which will be attached to the mast tang. Do not neglect to disassemble the fitting after you have tightened it the first time to make sure that the wires were formed properly and none are crossed. Fill the fitting with clear silicone sealant and apply Loctite or a similar product to the threads before reassembling. Sealant should flow out of the fitting all around the wire.

Hook the just-installed fitting over one of the two nails. Hook the properly adjusted turnbuckle and toggle assembly over the other nail. Uncoil and stretch the wire until it reaches the end-fitting eye attached to the turnbuckle. When the wire is cut to the proper length, you should be able to insert the wire into the endfitting, just touching the bottom of the hole. Mark the wire to this length and cut it.

If you have a 2-foot-long pair of Swiss-made Felco cable cutters handy, or a pair of those nifty Norseman hydraulic jobs, cutting the wire rope will be little more difficult than trimming a thread off your sleeve. Some of the cheaper cutters tend to crush the wire and cut the strands to different lengths. I have used a hammer-blow cutter for many years with excellent results. The main thing is that for maximum strength from the end fittings, the cut must be straight and regular, which rules out clipping each strand separately. A hacksaw will do the job perfectly, but you need a miter box to keep the blade from running all over the cable.

Scrounge up a 4- or 5-inch-long piece of 2 × 4 and drill a hole *lengthwise* through it, near one edge, and slightly larger than the wire rope you want to cut. With a saber saw, make a perpendicular cut in the edge of the block nearest the hole, and deep enough to cut through the drilled hole. Now feed the wire through the hole and, with your hacksaw blade in the slot, cut the wire. If you are working with a long coil of wire, slip the miter block over the wire *before* you install the first terminal.

Perhaps you have heard that the rigging wire stretches when it is placed under a load. That is true. So shouldn't we cut the wire a bit short to allow for this stretch? No. This initial elongation, called "constructional stretch" is typically only about .02 percent in 1 × 19 stainless steel wire rope. That means a 50-foot stay will stretch about $1/8$ inch, not enough to be of concern.

Don't confuse construction stretch with elasticity. In a good breeze with the main and genoa sheets two-blocked, the lee shrouds will be slack. That is because the weather shrouds have stretched. Release the sheets and stand the boat up, and all of

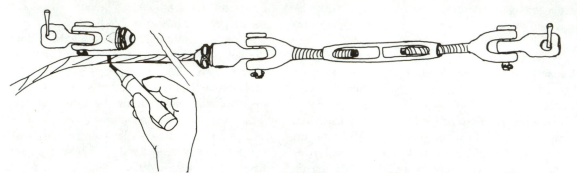

Remove old stay—correctly adjusted—and stretch it between two stiff nails.

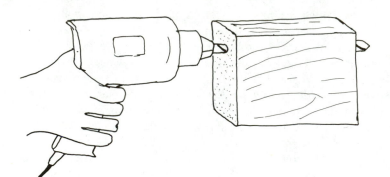

Install one end fitting. Attach it to its associated hardware, then hook the assembly over one of the nails. Hook the end fitting and attached hardware for the other end over the second nail. Pull the wire tight and mark it to correspond with the socket in the fitting. Cut the wire and attach the fitting.

Length determination for replacement shrouds and stays

Miter for cutting rigging wire with a hacksaw

the shrouds will again be tight. Like very strong rubber bands, the weather shrouds return to their original length. The larger the diameter of the wire, the less it will stretch under a given load, and rod rigging has lower elasticity than wire rope. But you do not need to be concerned about this when you are cutting the wire; you made all the accommodations necessary for elasticity when you marked the adjustment of the turnbuckles while the rig was properly tuned.

Back to the matter at hand: install the second end fitting and pin it to the turnbuckle. The shroud assembly is complete and if it matches the nail-to-nail length on the ground, you can be confident that it will be the right length when you step the mast. I prefer this method because it requires no calculations and added toggles or different turnbuckles don't throw you off since they are already in place when you measure the wire.

Some calculations may be required if you are replacing chainplates or tangs and the clevis pin holes of the new ones are not the same distance from the mounting holes. In such a case, it will be simpler to move the nail than to add to or subtract from the wire. Be sure you move the nail in the right direction; if the tang is shorter, the shroud must be longer, and vice versa.

The forestay, and the inner stay, if your boat has one, should also be toggled at the top. The sideways pressure on headsails will put an unfair load on the end fittings, and if the top fitting can articulate in only one direction, the most benign result will be flexing the wire where it enters the fitting, resulting in a shorter life. (I meant the life of the wire, but . . .) If you are adding a toggle to the top of a stay, be sure to assemble it to the end fitting *before* you determine the length of the wire.

CHAINPLATES

If the chainplates are attached to the outside of the hull, you can see what is going on with them. But most of the time, chainplates penetrate the deck and are attached below to the hull, knees, or a bulk-head. On some boats, the below-deck portion of the chainplate is observable. On more, they are hidden behind cabinetry and hull liners.

No matter where they are attached or how inaccessible they are, if you have 20-year-old chainplates they must be removed and carefully examined. Those attached to the hull, because they sit in a fore-and-aft plane while the stresses on them are athwartship, are subject to fatigue, especially where they bend. It is usually not possible to examine the inside of the bend without removing the chainplate.

For those chainplates that pass through the deck, the critical area is that hidden by the thickness of the deck. Often water is trapped against the chainplate in this area, setting up destructive corrosion which can literally eat the chainplate in half. The only way to inspect this area of the chainplate is to extract it.

Some manufacturers have fabricated chainplates in the shape of a T, and fiberglassed them in place. I don't think they chose this method because it is better than bolting. In order to inspect such chainplates, you will have to grind away the capturing fiberglass. If your boat has this type of chainplates, I strongly recommend that you fabricate new chainplates and bolt them in place.

Every chainplate should be inspected visually for surface cracks, and if any are noted (in *any* of the chainplates or in any of the other fittings), *all* of the chainplates should be checked with dye penetrant.

Also inspect the mounting holes in the knees or bulkheads. If they show any elongation, fill them with epoxy putty and redrill them.

After all the chainplates have been inspected, reinstall them. There should be a backing plate on the opposite side of every through-bolted chainplate. If they aren't there, now is the time to fabricate and install them. Bed the chainplates in the deck with polyurethane sealant as you install them. Also apply the sealant generously to the bottom of the deck plates and screw them in place, forcing a bead of sealant out of the slot all the way around the chainplate and out all edges of the plate. Let the sealant cure before trimming the excess.

INNER STAY

The praise heaped on double headsail rigs in magazine articles and books leads many sailors to consider the possibility of converting their own boats to double headsails. The sloop, the ketch, and the yawl are all candidates for this "enhancement," and the addition of an inner stay does not seem all that complicated. My advice? Not so fast.

Why do you want double headsails? They do make the headsails smaller and correspondingly easier to handle. They do provide sail combination possibilities that are not available with a single headsail. And the staysail is regarded as an outstanding heavy weather sail, easier on boat and crew alike.

But if handling the headsail is difficult, more powerful winches or even roller furling gear will likely be a less expensive option than adding an inner stay and associated hardware, buying a new sail, and having the existing jibs appropriately recut. The additional sail combination possibilities do not necessarily translate into better performance of the boat. And a sail intended for heavy conditions cannot be set on a casually rigged stay.

I am not advising against double headsails. On the right boat, in the right conditions, with the right sails, they have much to recommend them; but a sloop with an inner stay does not a cutter make. And the conversion requires more than stretching a wire between a tang on the mast and a deck eye.

Because of the mast location, the foretriangle of a sloop is smaller than that of a comparable, legitimate cutter. Moving the mast aft is usually not a practical alternative, but sometimes the overall length of the boat is extended with a bowsprit and the forestay moved to the end of the sprit. This does increase the size of the foretriangle, but it also alters the balance of the boat. The longer the sprit, the more pronounced the effect.

Since the integrity of the rig, not to mention windward ability, depends upon a securely anchored forestay, the bowsprit must be held down with its own stay attached to the hull. Adding a sprit and staying it to the hull is not a particularly difficult modification, but because of the potential to adversely affect the balance of the boat, and probably because of the way a sprit will alter the lines, most owners contemplating double headsails simply add a second stay inboard of the original forestay.

How far inboard should the inner stay be? Typically the distance between the deck fitting of the two stays will be about a quarter of the distance between the stem fitting and the mast, although there is nothing sacred about this ratio. The foredeck of most fiberglass boats is too flexible for an eye bolted to the deck to be an adequate anchor for the lower end of the stay. When the wind fills the sail, the force will flex the deck upward, causing the stay to sag to leeward and destroying the shape of the sail. Fortunately, most fiberglass boats have a bulkhead between the forward cabin and the chain locker. If this bulkhead sits between 20 percent and 35 percent back from the stem, locating the lower end of the stay at the juncture of the bulkhead and the foredeck will simplify the installation. A chainplate of adequate strength is passed through a slot in the deck and bolted to the bulkhead, effectively spreading the load to the full width of the deck (and to the hull if the bulkhead is strongly bonded in place). It is imperative that the protruding part of the chainplate is properly bent so that the pull of the stay is fair.

If the chain-locker bulkhead does not lie in the right spot, a satisfactory installation will oblige you to use a tie rod (or wire) to attach the underside of the deck eye to the hull. The tie rod should be a straight-line extension of the stay.

If you intend to fly two headsails at the same time, the inner stay should be parallel to the forestay. This allows the two sails to be trimmed for optimum interaction (slot effect) along the full length of the slot between them. Once you have decided how far inboard to set the new stay, this requirement will determine the location of the mast tang.

Before you install the tang and the deck fitting, take a look at your spreaders. If you have double spreaders, the size of the staysail will be limited.

Keep in mind that the staysail will be sheeted *inboard* of the shrouds and that the leech of the sail will pass *under* the spreaders. The lower the spreaders, the more they limit the sail size. If you have a genoa staysail in mind, you might decide to open the slot wider by locating the deck fitting further aft (and the mast tang lower), since the lower spreaders will limit the luff dimension anyway.

The mast tang should be a wishbone-shaped fitting that attaches to the sides of the mast. It must provide a strong attachment point for the stay and a bail for the halyard block that is required. If the tang can be fabricated to be through-bolted to the mast, and incorporate integral (or at least mounted to the same bolt) tangs for the running backstays, so much the better.

Running backstays? That's right. What do you think is going to happen to the mast when you tighten that new stay? Or when 40 knots of wind is filling your new "heavy weather" sail? If your mast has a generous fore-and-aft dimension, you might dispense with the backstays on those lazy days of summer, but if you plan to use the staysail when the wind pipes up, the pressure will pull the mast out of column. Running backstays are part of the package.

You might get adequate support from a second pair of aft lower shrouds attached to the mast at the same height as the new inner stay, but to be effective in resisting the *forward* pull of the stay, the shrouds should form an angle of *at least* 12 degrees with the transverse plane of the mast. Multiply the height of the new tangs above the deck by .21 (the tangent of 12 degrees) to find out how far aft of the upper shroud chainplates the new lowers will have to be located. With a 40-foot mast and an inner stay set inboard 25 percent, the stay will attach 30 feet above the deck. Multiplying 30 by .21 yields 6.3, the number of feet aft a fixed lower will need to attach to the deck. Such a lower is almost certain to interfere with easing the boom adequately for efficient downwind sailing. The solution is running backstays.

If you think of running backstays as no more troublesome than an additional sheet when tacking,

you will not mind this aspect of double headsails. You can set up running backstays with tackles, winches, or levers, depending on your preference, what seems appropriate for your boat, and how much you are willing to spend.

In its simplest form, the new inner stay is connected to the deck eye with a heavy-duty pelican hook or some other quick-release fitting so it can be released and lashed out of the way when sailing with a single headsail. (Otherwise, tacking your big genoa with the staysail in the way is going to be a pain.) With such an arrangement, you might likewise equip the running backstays (rigged at 12 degrees) with quick-release fittings and attach both before hoisting the staysail. From closehauled through a beam reach on either tack, such backstays require no attention. When the wind gets far enough aft for the boom to chafe the backstay, the staysail is probably blanketing the jib anyway and ought to come down. Running backstays that can be tensioned under load are more versatile, but this system is adequate for most uses of the staysail and has the advantage of being less complicated.

Even after you have worked out the backstays, you're still not done. There is a litany of deck-mounted hardware: inboard sail track or at least pad eyes, cars, snatch blocks, winches, and cleats. All things considered, unless your boat has a vast fore-triangle, this seems like a lot of work and expense for scant performance improvement. On the other hand, twin headsails look awfully nice in silhouette against a red sunset.

PROTECTING THE MAST

Meanwhile, back at the boatyard, the disassembled mast still reclines on sawhorses. While it is free of all its hardware is a good time to take protective measures. If the mast is in good shape and the anodized surface is still, for the most part, resisting corrosion, a good coat of wax is all that is necessary. Use a top-quality automotive wax (I have had excellent results with Simonize II), and apply several layers, buffing between coats. It only takes a few minutes to apply a

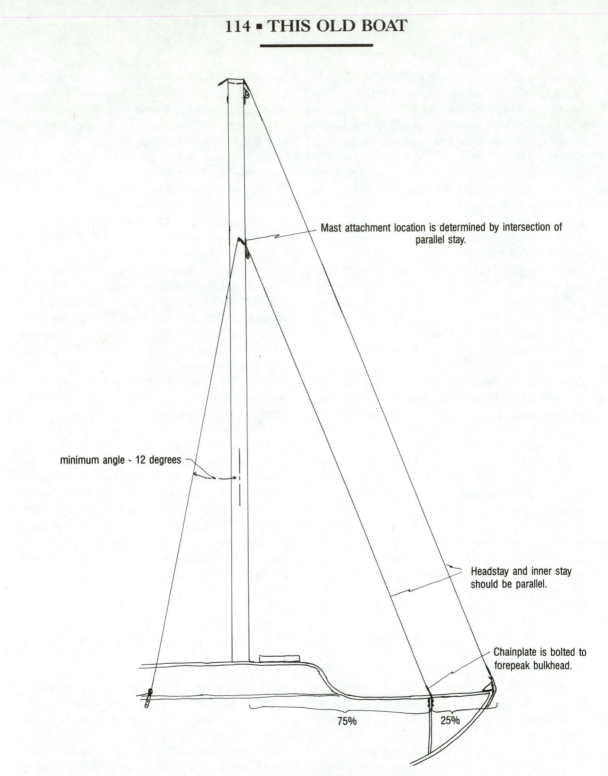

Mast attachment location is determined by intersection of parallel stay.

minimum angle - 12 degrees

Headstay and inner stay should be parallel.

Chainplate is bolted to forepeak bulkhead.

75%

25%

Inner stay and running backstay geometry

coat of wax when the mast is waist-high and horizontal, so get plenty of wax on it while you have the opportunity. This is also a good opportunity to lubricate the sail track.

If the mast is covered with fine white powder, the anodizing has ceased to protect the aluminum. The powdery oxide offers some protection from further corrosion, but it also stains the sails. You might consider having the mast reanodized if you can find a facility with a tank large enough to handle your spar, but currently the cost is around $15 per foot, varying somewhat with the cross-section of the mast. That makes the cost of stripping and reanodizing a 40-foot mast at least $600. Add to that the cost to ship the spar to and from the anodizing facility and you could end up spending more on reanodizing than a new mast extrusion would cost.

A cheaper alternative is wax. Removing the corrosion with a metal cleaner and waxing the mast will protect it even after the original anodizing has given up the battle, but the protection wax alone offers will probably not last beyond about six months. That means a semi-annual ride in the bosun's chair, but it is a good idea to check the masthead fittings every six months anyway.

Painting the mast is perhaps the most cost-effective choice. The mast will not have to be sent anywhere, the cost of painting will be a fraction of the cost of anodizing, and paint will protect the mast as long or longer. On the negative side, paint will chip and scratch, and it does not adhere readily to aluminum. Forget about just spraying the mast with some type of clear coat; the mast will soon drop the coating onto the deck like so many cellophane leaves. Successfully painting an aluminum mast is a very exacting process. Polyurethane coatings are especially durable and in Chapter 14 we will examine this type of coating and how it is applied.

Reassembly

Before you reattach the hardware to the mast, you should "chase" the threads with a tap. Don't run out and buy a set of taps; you will never use most of them. All of the machine screws you have removed from the mast are likely to be only one or two sizes.

Take the screws with you to the hardware store and buy only the taps you need. If you do not have one, you will also need to buy a small tap handle. Now is also the time to replace any of the screws with damaged heads; if you don't, you will be very sorry the next time you try to remove the damaged screw. Be sure the screws you buy are good-quality stainless steel. Clean the threads of the reuseable screws with a wire brush or on a soft wire wheel.

I have never seen a *sheet metal mast*, but some builders still persist in using sheet metal screws in the mast. If there are any in your mast, replace them with machine screws. You will have to clean up the hole with a drill, then tap it. The size of the tap will depend upon the size of the hole, but be sure the machine screws will fit the fitting. Drilling the holes in the fitting *slightly* larger will usually resolve any problems.

Attaching the fittings to the mast is a two step process. First, coat the bottom of the fitting with a layer of silicone sealant. Install the mounting screws and snug the fitting, but not too tight. You want to create a silicone *gasket* that will insulate the fitting from the mast, so be careful not to tighten the screws so much that you squeeze all the silicone out. After the silicone begins to cure, remove each screw one at a time, coat the threads with Loctite or similar thread sealant, and reinstall the screw. Tighten all of the screws evenly. Take it easy when you are tightening screws in the mast; if you put your shoulder into it, you will easily strip the threads in the thin aluminum.

The one fitting that you do not want mounted on silicone sealant is the tang for double lower shrouds. The tang should be mounted on a single through-bolt and it should be free to rotate to prevent fore-and-aft movement of the mast from transferring all the load to a single shroud. Lubricate the tang with Teflon grease or spray it before you mount it.

All nuts on the mast should either be castle nuts, or drilled, so that they may be secured with a cotter pin. There is nothing quite so disconcerting on a black, blustery night as the sound of a nut falling on the deck, let me tell you.

Before you install *any* cotter pin, round the ends

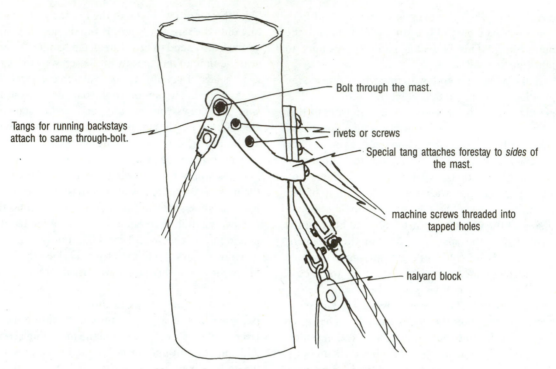

Tangs for running backstays
attach to same through-bolt.

Bolt through the mast.

rivets or screws

Special tang attaches forestay to *sides* of
the mast.

machine screws threaded into
tapped holes

halyard block

Mast attachment of inner stay and running backstays

with a file. After the cotter pin is in place, spread the legs about 20 degrees, but unless the pin represents a genuine risk to a sail, do not tape it. Taping encourages corrosion. But in the event of an unanticipated encounter, the rounded ends will be easier on flesh and sailcloth alike.

Check *every* clevis pin for fit and straightness as you attach the rigging. Any pins that are worn or bent should be replaced. If the problem is an elongated hole in the tang, replace the tang. Be sure that every clevis pin is locked in place with a cotter pin. Check twice.

The threads of all the turnbuckles should be well lubricated. Old salts around the world recommend anhydrous lanolin for this purpose. Make sure all the turnbuckles are turned the same way, preferably with the right-hand threads downward. Also lubricate the toggles so they can do what they were designed to do. In fact, you should lubricate *all* the clevis pins.

If you have eliminated any of the fittings, moved them, or changed the way they are mounted, don't leave the old mounting holes open. Put a screw in each one, coating the threads of screws with thread sealant.

There should be a drain hole at the base of the mast, usually drilled through both the mast and the heel fitting. Be sure that the hole is clear, and if you found significant corrosion inside the mast, enlarge the hole.

After all these years, I am still amazed at all the spreaders I see that are horizontal. Spreaders are designed to withstand compression loading, not leverage. Unless the spreaders bisect the angle between the lower half and the upper half of the shroud, you are inviting spreader failure, with catastrophic implications. Exact adjustment is not critical, but if the spreaders on your mast are not canted upward (above horizontal by about half the angle the shroud forms with the mast—typically around 7 or 8 degrees), you need to modify the base fittings. Seize the upper shrouds temporarily to the tip, but wait to do the final adjustment until after the mast has been restepped.

With the mast in place and the upper shrouds set up loosely, get yourself hoisted to the spreaders. A bevel gauge will help you to position the spreader tip, but if you don't have one, a square of cardboard and a pair of scissors will do the same job. Lay one edge of the cardboard along the centerline of the back of the spreader and trim the adjoining edge to match the lower half of the shroud. Now flip the cardboard over as though it was hinged to the spreader. The upper half of the shroud should also parallel the cut edge. If it doesn't, slide the tip up or down to take out *half* the difference. Retrim the cardboard to take out the other half and check again

to confirm that both angles are the same. Seize the shroud *securely* to the spreader tip with Monel seizing wire. If more than one shroud passes over the tip of a spreader, seize only the upper shroud. Use your cardboard template to position the opposite spreader.

If your mast is keel-stepped, don't forget to slip the boot over the mast *before* it is stepped. A section of tire inner tube will work just as well as a special molded boot. Turn the boot up on the mast inside out and clamp it to the mast with a giant hose clamp (mast boot clamp). Turn the boot over the clamp, as if you were turning down the top of a sweat sock, hiding the clamp. With a second clamp, attach the boot to the deck flange. Protect the boot from the sun with a fabric skirt (see Chapter 14).

RUNNING RIGGING

For the most part, replacing running rigging is no more complicated than buying the right size of braided Dacron, heat sealing the ends, splicing an eye or tying a bowline in one end, and running the other end through the appropriate blocks. You don't need my help. Indulge me anyway.

There has been a tendency in recent years to move away from wire halyards in favor of low-stretch rope. Braid-on-braid polyester (Dacron) is the only choice for sheets, but it is still too elastic for hal-

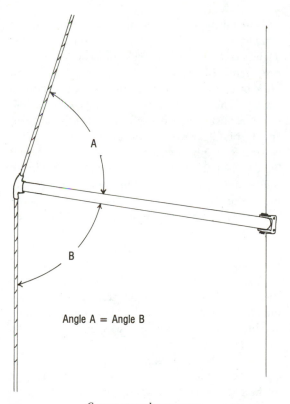

Correct spreader geometry

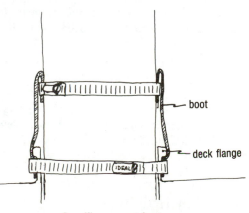

Installing a mast boot

yards. Inexpensive (a relative term, to be sure) low-stretch rope is usually braided polyester over an inner core of braided polypropylene. But low-stretch is not *no-stretch,* and when the wind picks up, the halyard does stretch, causing the luff of the headsail to scallop and destroying the windward performance of the boat. I have noticed a lot more scalloped jibs on the water in recent years, which I have attributed to laziness or ignorance, but maybe it is a reflection of this trend toward rope halyards.

Racing sailors often use braided rope with a core of an aramid fiber called Kevlar. Kevlar is extremely strong and has virtually no stretch. However, the Kevlar fibers are fragile, requiring a minimum sheave-to-rope-diameter of 12 to 1, and they are extremely UV sensitive. Kevlar rope generally has a relatively short life, and at roughly three times the cost of a low-stretch polyester of similar diameter, Kevlar is not a good selection for the average boater.

Another type of low-stretch rope utilizes a core of an olefin fiber called Spectra. Spectra is as strong as Kevlar and much lighter. In addition, the fiber is not fragile, negating the need for high sheave-to-rope-diameter ratios. It is subject to creep, i.e., some stretch over a long period of time under load, but it won't let the luff scallop in a gust. The biggest drawback of Spectra rope is its cost—about four times as expensive as a similar diameter polyester rope.

In light of the realities of low-stretch ropes, wire halyards still have much to recommend them. It is, I think, the necessity of splicing a rope tail to the wire that makes sailors seek an alternative. Yet the tail splice is strikingly similar to a long splice between two pieces of ordinary three strand rope.

Sure it is.

I swear. This is your graduate-level rigging project not because it is difficult, but because everyone *thinks* it is difficult. Skip the game on Monday and give this a try. You will be finished in plenty of time to see the second half.

Splicing Wire to Rope

Start with a length of 7 × 19 wire the diameter you need and an equal length of braid-on-braid poly-

ester rope *twice* the diameter of the wire. (If you are practicing, you need about 8 feet of each. Practice is a good idea.)

Start the splice by tapering the wire. Unlay the six outside strands one at a time, cutting off each one progressively further up the wire. The length of the taper is not particularly important, but making each strand about 2 inches shorter than the previous one works well. Bind the taper tightly with two layers of electrical tape.

Tie a knot in the rope about 5 feet from the end. Wrap the end with tape—not too tight—and cut off the heat-fused end. Slide the cover back at least a couple of feet. Cut a foot off the core, then mark the core about 10 inches from the cut end. Insert the tapered wire into the core until all of the taper is beyond the mark on the core. Wrap the core very tightly at the mark with electrical tape to hold the wire in place.

Unbraid the core below the tape and group the straightened strands into three equal bundles. Tightly tape the ends. Using a metal fid, *carefully* lift *two* strands of the wire where it enters the core. Tuck one of the bundles of rope beneath the two strands. The tuck should be with the lay, i.e., parallel to the next strands of the wire, not perpendicular, and the bundle of rope should be smooth and pulled snug. Lift the next two strands and tuck the second bundle. Lift the last pair of strands and tuck the third bundle. Adjust the bundles until they all exit the wire at the same level. Now take two more tucks with all three bundles, being careful to make each smooth and even.

Is this starting to sound familiar? You thought I was lying to you about the long splice, didn't you?

After the third tuck, cut $1/3$ of the yarns from each of the bundles and tuck them again. Thin the bundles again by $1/3$ and tuck. Thin one more time and tuck. Cut the remaining yarns, allowing them to protrude about $1/8$ inch.

Slide the cover back over the core, burying the core splice. Milk the cover vigorously to be sure that all the slack is out of it. Where the core splice terminates, wrap the cover tightly with tape. Remove the piece of tape on the end of the cover and unbraid the

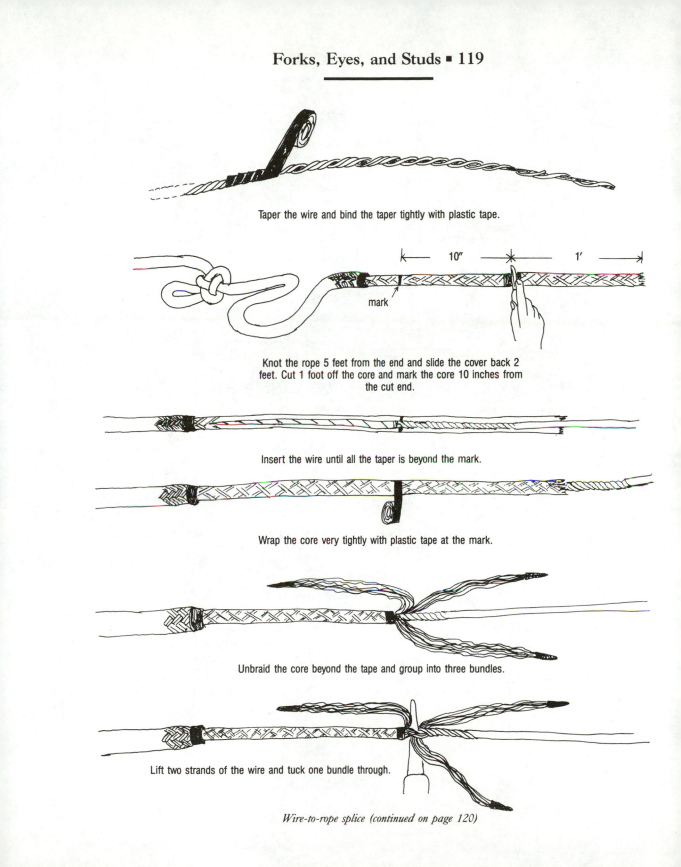

Taper the wire and bind the taper tightly with plastic tape.

mark

10″   1′

Knot the rope 5 feet from the end and slide the cover back 2 feet. Cut 1 foot off the core and mark the core 10 inches from the cut end.

Insert the wire until all the taper is beyond the mark.

Wrap the core very tightly with plastic tape at the mark.

Unbraid the core beyond the tape and group into three bundles.

Lift two strands of the wire and tuck one bundle through.

Wire-to-rope splice (continued on page 120)

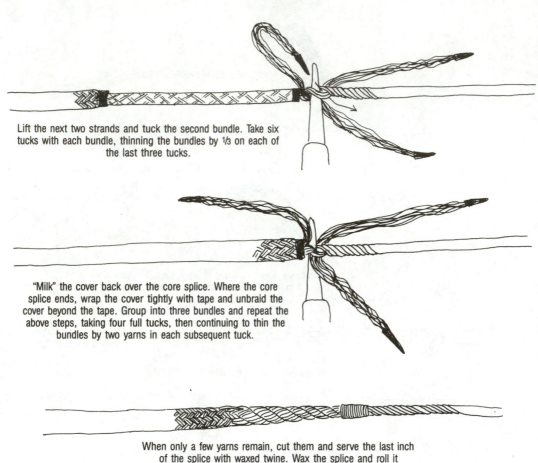

Lift the next two strands and tuck the second bundle. Take six tucks with each bundle, thinning the bundles by ⅓ on each of the last three tucks.

"Milk" the cover back over the core splice. Where the core splice ends, wrap the cover tightly with tape and unbraid the cover beyond the tape. Group into three bundles and repeat the above steps, taking four full tucks, then continuing to thin the bundles by two yarns in each subsequent tuck.

When only a few yarns remain, cut them and serve the last inch of the splice with waxed twine. Wax the splice and roll it between your palms.

Wire-to-rope splice (continued)

cover, gathering the straightened strands into three bundles, just as before.

This time do four complete tucks, taking even greater care to have each tuck snug and smooth. Now cut *two yarns* from each bundle and take another tuck. Remove two more yarns and take another tuck. Continue tapering the bundles and tucking until you have only six or so yarns left. Trim the remaining yarns and serve the last inch of the splice tightly with waxed twine. Remove the tape and smear the splice lightly with beeswax, rolling it between your palms to compact it.

Now go watch the game. You don't need to know anything else about rigging.

NINE

Nuts and Bolts

Think you can or think you can't, either way you will be right.
–HENRY FORD–

Archimedes pushed a pencil, or a piece of charcoal, or whatever it was they wrote with in ancient Greece. But his desk job notwithstanding, he no doubt could have made all necessary mechanical repairs on boats of the time. And despite 22 centuries of "progress," I am absolutely certain (without much fear of being proven wrong) that he could likewise repair the mechanical systems of today's boats, of your boat.

The justification of such an assertion is that Archimedes understood the *five simple machines* that were the basis of all mechanical devices then and now. To understand the principles of the lever, the wheel and axle, the pulley, the wedge, and the screw is to understand the workings of every mechanical device likely to be found aboard a boat, including those occupying the tool box.

Maintenance–the dismantling and reassembly of a device to clean or lubricate it–requires little more than care and audacity. Pay attention to how the device comes apart and you should be able to put it back together. Repair, on the other hand, is not a by-the-numbers process. The insight to repairing a mechanical device comes from understanding how it works.

Perhaps the explanation of mechanical principles by your high-school physics teacher was so spellbinding that it echoes in your ears even today. If your recall is less distinct, it will serve you well in this noble endeavor to become reacquainted.

THE SIMPLE MACHINES

The *lever* is the oldest of the machines, and understanding it is the key to understanding all five. You probably learned about levers on the seesaws of kindergarten. When you sat further from the pivot—the fulcrum—you could lift a bigger kid. The relationship between the two ends of a lever can be defined in simple mathematical terms: the effort arm is equal to the resistance arm. "Arm" is the force (effort or resistance) multiplied by its distance from the fulcrum. On the seesaw, what you lacked in effort (your weight) you made up in distance.

Perhaps this would be clearer if we put some numbers with it. A lever with the fulcrum in the middle does not develop any *mechanical advantage*; to lift an 80-pound weight on one end requires an 80-pound effort on the other. Move the effort twice as far from the fulcrum as the resistance is and you need apply only half the force; four times the distance, 1/4 the force. In other words, if the weight is 1 foot from the fulcrum and the effort 4 feet from the fulcrum, 20 pounds of effort will lift an 80-pound weight ($20 \times 4 = 80 \times 1$). This principle is the same even if the effort and the resistance are on the same side of the fulcrum. A pelican hook comes to mind; a 20-pound effort four inches from the pivot translates into 80 pounds of force 1 inch from the pivot. Of course, this multiplication of force has a price—the additional distance through which the effort must move.

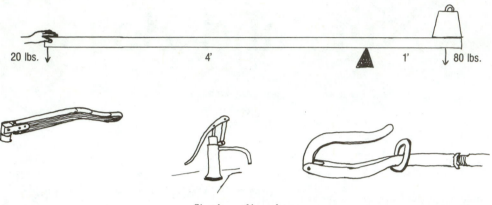

Simple machines: lever

An astonishing number of the mechanical devices aboard are nothing more complicated than applications of the lever principle: the tiller, winch handles, windlass, shift control, snap shackles, pelican hooks, cabinet latches, and oars, to name a few. The lever has an essential function in the operation of hand or foot pumps, the head, seacocks, the control of the mainsail, and the opening and closing of engine valves. It is found among your tools as a pry bar, wrenches, socket handles, pliers, scissors, and cable cutters. The relationship between mast and keel is that of a lever.

The *wheel and axle* is nothing more than a lever that can rotate a full 360 degrees. Mechanical advantage is computed exactly as above, with the radii of the wheel and the axle equivalent to distances from the lever's fulcrum. A 10-inch wheel on a 1-inch axle magnifies force by 10. As with the lever, this magnification of force requires the effort to move through additional distance, and it is this additional distance that is often the main consideration in the design of wheel-based mechanical devices. In this example, a point on the surface of the wheel will travel 10 times as far in a single revolution as a point on the axle. Because both parts complete a revolution in the same amount of time, to make the longer journey the surface of the wheel must be moving 10 times as fast as the surface of the axle.

All three functions find their way aboard. The purpose of the steering wheel is to reduce the amount of effort required to turn the shaft (axle); the larger the steering wheel, the less will be the effort required to steer the boat. Each blade of the propeller (wheel) scribes a circle of thrust with every revolution of the shaft (axle); the larger the prop, the more water it pushes against. The drive-belt pulley (wheel) attached to the engine crankshaft (axle) multiplies the speed of the belt; the larger the pulley, the faster the belt travels. The principles of the wheel and axle are also visible in winches, capstans, roller reefing, roller furling, gears, sprockets, logs, faucets, valves, tap handles and screwdrivers.

Pulley, as it refers to a simple machine, does not mean a drive-belt pulley like those found on your engine, alternator, or water pump. A drive-belt pulley is actually a wheel and axle, a toothless gear. A pulley—the machine—is what a sailor calls a block.

The pulley has no mechanical advantage when it is fixed; lifting an 80-pound weight requires 80 pounds of pull. Its usefulness is in changing the *direction* of the effort; you pull down on the main halyard to hoist the sail. But a *moveable* pulley does

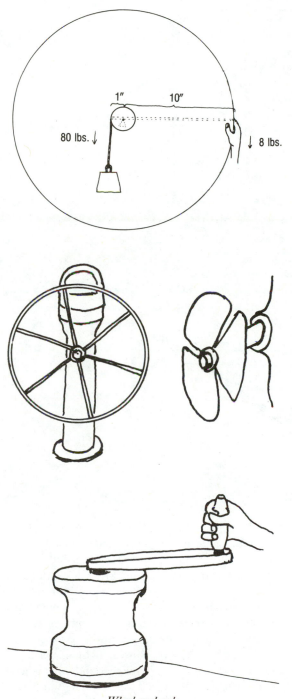

Wheel and axle

provide mechanical advantage. Pass a line around the pulley, anchoring one end. Forty pounds of effort applied to the other end will lift 80 pounds attached to the pulley. The same tradeoff with distance applies; you will have to pull the free end 2 feet to lift the weight 1 foot.

To determine the mechanical advantage of a system of pulleys—the main sheet tackle, for example—you need only count the number of times the line runs to and from the *moveable* block. In the previous example, the mechanical advantage is 2, but if the standing part of the line is anchored to a becket on the moveable block, the advantage becomes 3. A double block provides the opportunity for a mechanical advantage of 4 or, if the standing part is attached to the moveable block, 5. In this instance it only takes 16 pounds of effort on the hauling part, ignoring friction, to exert 80 pounds of pull on the boom, but you will have to pull the hauling part 5 feet for every foot the moveable block travels. An understanding of pulleys is most useful in solving problems with the running rigging.

The fourth of the simple machines is the *wedge*. Every anchor you have aboard is a wedge. Every knife is a wedge. So are the cutting edges of chisels, planes, and hatchets. Punches, awls, fids, needles, and nails are all wedges. The stem of a pop rivet is a wedge. The lobes of the camshaft are wedges. The boat itself is a wedge, splitting the water rather than pushing it.

If you lay a wedge on one of its surfaces, it becomes an inclined plane—a ramp—and the mechanical advantage is easier to fathom. The ratio of the length of the ramp to its height defines the advantage; a ramp 5 feet long and 1 foot high has a mechanical advantage of 5. Again ignoring friction, to lift our 80 pound weight by rolling it up the ramp requires only 16 pounds of effort, but of course we have to push the weight 5 feet to lift it 1 foot.

Diagonally cut a piece of paper, forming an inclined plane. Starting with the wide end, wrap the paper around a pencil. You have just demonstrated the principle behind the *screw*. The mechanical advantage of a screw depends on the pitch (the

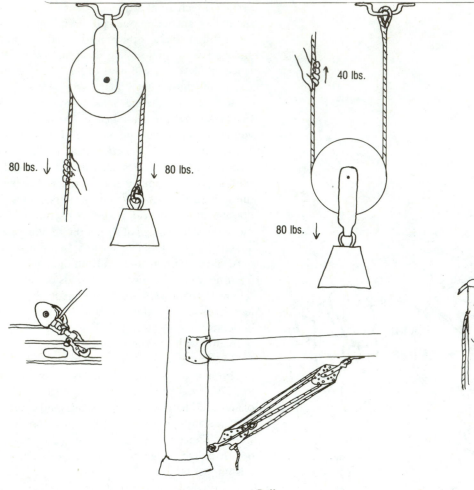

Pulley

incline of the threads) and the lever arm of the effort applied. Turn a screw with threads ⅛ inch apart by applying effort to the end of a 10-inch wrench and you magnify your effort by a factor of 80. With a small pitch (fine threads) and a long lever arm, a screw can provide a tremendous mechanical advantage.

In use, the screw almost always depends upon another machine for its operation—either a lever (such as a wrench), or a wheel and axle (such as a screwdriver). A lot of other onboard items are based on the principle of the screw. The propeller is a screw, threading its way through the water. The tension of the standing rigging is adjusted by the matching screws of turnbuckles. A worm gear (steering) is actually a screw. A screw converts the rotary motion of the handle to the straight-line motion of gate valves and stove burner valves. Screws compress opening portholes against their sealing gaskets. The pressure of a vise or a clamp is applied by a screw. Pipe wrenches and other adjustable wrenches are adjusted with a screw. A drill bit is a sharp screw, as are taps and dies. But by far the most common use of a screw is as a fastener, holding

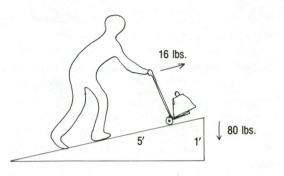

pieces of wood or metal together, and assembling all things mechanical.

TOOLS

Most (but certainly not all) mechanical tools exist for the single purpose of tightening and loosening screws. Their function is no more exotic than the twist knob on a lamp switch, the T-bar on a corkscrew, or the handle on a decorator faucet, yet some people wilt at the thought of using a screwdriver or a wrench. Look around. If you felt the same abhorrence for the handles on the shower, your social standing would surely suffer.

The only "trick" to having success with tools is to be certain that you have the right tool for the job. For the moment we are talking about turning tools, the levers that allow us to turn screws. The lever could be an integral part of the screw but it is not hard to see the problems and limitations such a

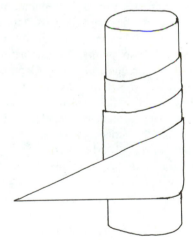

Wedge

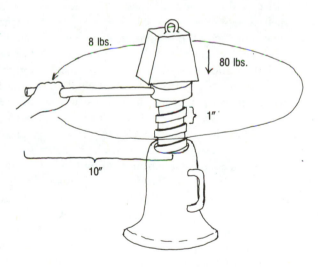

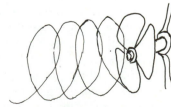

Screw

design would present. Instead, screws are usually manufactured for removable levers. This should present few problems if you think of the screw and the lever as a matched set, like a lock and key; you must have the right key to turn the lock.

Four types of "drives" dominate in all screw applications. A hexagonal-shaped (six-sided) head is most often associated with the word "bolt." Bolt most appropriately refers to a screw that does not thread into the parts being fastened, but passes through them and is held in place by a threaded nut. The head of a bolt is not necessarily hexagonal, but the nut almost always is. Instead of hexagonal, the head of a screw may be round, with a slot machined across the center. This is called standard or slot drive. The screw may also be machined with what appears to be a crossed slot, but is actually a special beveled socket. This is called Phillips drive. The fourth type of drive is also a machined socket in the screw, but in this case, the socket is hexagonal. This is Allen drive, and is most often used on headless screws such as setscrews.

You may run across other types of screws aboard. For example, the deck fill caps for fuel and water are screws and they probably open with a special wrench that fits into two drilled holes in the cap. This is called face pin, or spanner drive. Whenever you encounter a screw with a special drive, you will have to obtain the appropriate tool to turn it.

If the type of drive was the only consideration, you would only need about a dozen hand tools to drive every screw aboard. Hex-head bolts and nuts come in sizes from microscopic to titanic, but those aboard will rarely be smaller the $1/4$ inch, rarely larger than 1 inch. More and more metric-size screws are finding their way aboard newer American-built boats, but unless your old boat has been repowered, the fasteners will be in inch sizes. One quarter to 1 inch in $1/16$-inch increments comes out to 14 different sizes, but a single wrench typically has a socket on both ends so seven wrenches should handle all the possibilities. With fit as the only consideration, the choice of type of wrenches is easy; the shape of the wrench should be identical to the shape of the bolt head—hexagonal. Such a wrench is called a six-point box-end wrench.

For all the screws with slotted heads, you need standard screwdrivers in about three different blade sizes. For the Phillips-head screws, you need Phillips screwdrivers in three sizes—conveniently called #1, #2, and #3. And for the Allen, or *hex key* screws, you need a set of Allen wrenches, which come individually or as a single tool resembling a Swiss Army knife.

Time out. If hex key and Phillips head and box-end and six-point and face pin seem like a foreign language, don't let that put you off. After all, you have mastered bow and stern and port and starboard and chine and sheer and sheet and halyard and helm. The terminology of mechanics is far less obscure than that of boating. Phillips head and Allen wrench and a few others are named after a person or company that developed them, like Stetson, Thermos, or Levis. Otherwise, with rare exceptions— monkey wrench being one—the names of tools and mechanical devices are descriptive. A six-point box-end wrench encloses the hex nut (as opposed to an open-end wrench, which has an open end) and the interior of the box has six points. A combination wrench has a box end on one end and an open end on the other. An offset wrench means the wrench is bent; when the wrench is flat against the surface beneath the nut being turned, the handle of the wrench is clear of the surface. Whatever a tool sounds like, that is probably what it is.

Back to the issue of tool requirements. The type of drive is unfortunately not the only consideration. The location of the screw—its accessibility—often determines the type of tool that is required. In a tight space, a screwdriver with a very short shank, a "stubby," may be required. Conversely, a screw may only be accessible with an extra-long shank. Occasionally, space is so limited that the only tool that will work is the offset screwdriver, a screwdriver with the blades perpendicular to the shaft and operating like a wrench.

Put a wrench on a hex-nut and you often discover that you can rotate the wrench only a short distance before another screw or some other feature interferes. To accommodate this limited rotation, you remove the wrench and reposition it on the nut, swinging the small arc available to you each time until the nut is tight (or loose). But if the arc is less than 60 degrees, you have a problem with your six-point wrenches. Each possible position of the wrench is 60 degrees from the previous one (360 degrees divided by six sides), so if you have less than 60 degrees of swing, you cannot reposition the wrench.

You might assume the same limitation would exist with an open-end wrench, since repositioning it means sliding it onto the next set of *flats*—the parallel sides of the nut. That is still a rotation of 60 degrees. You would usually be wrong because most open-end wrenches have their jaws at an angle of about 15 degrees to the handle. When interference is encountered, the wrench is removed, inverted, and slipped back onto the same flats, turning the nut an additional 30 degrees. If you continue to invert the wrench, you can turn the nut 30 degrees at a time.

Open-end wrenches are popular because of this versatility, the ease with which they are slipped on the nut, and the fact that they can be tilted somewhat to accommodate an awkward reach. But they are second only to the adjustable wrench in their propensity to damage nuts and knuckles. The problem is that all the force is concentrated on two corners of the nut, and the nut is trying mightily to spread the jaws of the wrench. A weak corner or a weak jaw, and the result is a rounded nut, bloody knuckles, and blue air. If at all possible, do not use an open-end wrench to do the final tightening or the initial loosening.

A better choice for limited swing is a 12-point box-end wrench. A 12-point wrench can be repositioned on the nut in 30-degree intervals, just like the open-end wrench, but it distributes the force to all six corners of the nut. The circular (box) construction of the wrench makes distortion unlikely.

When a nut or bolt is accessible only from the top, a socket wrench is indicated. A socket wrench actually has two parts, a socket and a handle. One end of the socket has an opening identical to that of a box-end wrench and may be either six-point or 12-point. A six-point grips the nut more securely. The other end of a socket has a square hole for the handle. Depending upon the size of this hole, the socket is designated as $1/4$-, $3/8$-, or $1/2$-inch square drive.

The simplest socket handle is the hinged handle, or break-over bar. The hinged lug allows the handle to be at right angles to the socket for maximum leverage for tightening and loosening, then moved to a vertical position where it acts much like a screwdriver for quick removal. For screwdriverlike use only, the socket may be fitted to a nut-driver handle, particularly useful for small nuts and bolts. But by far the most common socket handle is the ratchet, and for good reason: it eliminates the need to remove the socket from the nut when swing room is limited and it allows for very rapid turning of the nut. Turning the handle in one direction turns the attached socket, but the handle is free to move in the opposite direction without turning the socket. A reversing lever allows the same handle to tighten and to loosen.

When access is difficult, extension bars can allow you to move the handle clear of interference. If straight access is not possible, a universal joint allows the socket to be driven from an angle. When the item you are working on designates specific torque settings, a torque wrench is required and it is used with your sockets. A socket set is one of the most versatile tools you will encounter, potentially useful in assembling and dismantling any mechanical device, and essential for significant engine repair.

You should be at least acquainted with a few other turning tools. One that is unfortunately included in almost every tool box is the adjustable (crescent) wrench. Adjustable to fit nuts of various sizes, including the occasional odd size, it seems like a great idea. And used properly the adjustable wrench is a wonderful tool, but it is often misused. Its nickname of "knucklebuster" is well-deserved.

The knuckles heal, but the damage done to a nut when the wrench slips can add *hours* to simple repair. Never think of the adjustable wrench as taking the place of a set of box-end or open-end wrenches. It is not rigid enough to grip the nut securely when heavy force is applied. If you use an adjustable wrench for any purpose great care must be taken to insure that the wrench is adjusted for a tight fit; if there is any play in the wrench in either direction, it is not tight enough. Until you consider yourself accomplished in handling tools, you will save yourself a great deal of grief by avoiding adjustable wrenches.

This advice does not apply to adjustable pipe wrenches (Stillson wrenches). Pipe wrenches have a pivoting action that causes the wrench to grip tighter as more force is applied to the handle. The force must always be applied in the direction of the jaw opening. While not particularly designed for gripping nuts, a pipe wrench serves well for tightening the large nuts found on through-hull fittings and stuffing boxes. The wrench always marks the work being gripped, so never use a pipe wrench on a threaded piece or a polished shaft.

Pliers do not belong in a discussion of *turning* tools, but the frequency with which they are misused as turning tools leads me to include them. Pliers are a *gripping* tool, period. Are you paying attention? Pliers have hundreds of legitimate uses—bending wire, crimping sheet metal, holding parts for machining, removing cotter pins, pulling nails, extending reach, the list is endless—but turning nuts and bolts is not among those uses. For appropriate uses, your tool selection should include channel-lock pliers (much more versatile than standard slip joint pliers), needle-nose pliers (ideal for electrical repairs, for reaching into confined areas, and for installing and removing cotter pins), and probably locking pliers (Vise-grip—useful as both a clamp and a portable vise).

I have never understood those who insist on trying to make do with a tool kit consisting of an adjustable wrench, a pair of pliers, and a couple of crooked screwdrivers. Nor is it necessary to fill a seven-drawer cabinet with tools. You should have a modest set of six-point sockets with a ratchet handle and extensions, a set of combination wrenches (six-point box on one end, open on the other), a set of hex keys (Allen wrenches), five or six standard screwdrivers in a variety of blade sizes and shank lengths, a comparable complement of Phillips screwdrivers, a pair of channel-lock pliers, and a pair of needle-nose pliers. These are the tools you will use again and again, and their cost is less than the typical mechanic's bill for a single simple repair.

Don't be misled into thinking that these are the only tools you will need. They aren't, but they are the ones you are *sure* to need. Eventually you will also need a hammer, a center punch, a chisel, metal snips, a file, a hacksaw, and a drill and bits. You might include these in your initial selection, but beyond these, I strongly recommend you purchase tools *as you need them*.

Never hesitate to buy a tool you need. Tools are one of the very few things you can acquire today that will last a lifetime. But if you don't use them, they are just worthless for a lifetime. In the previous chapter, I suggested adding an impact driver, a pop-rivet tool, and a couple of taps to your kit. In the projects to follow, special tool requirements will be noted, but unless these projects have application for your boat, you don't need the tools. Save your money for the tools you do need.

MEASUREMENTS

Once you have the principles of the five basic machines in hand, and you have defeated any sense that the operation of a screwdriver is somehow beyond your genetic capacities, you need one more qualification before you dismantle the gen set. You need a sense of measurement.

A good mechanic can look at the head of a bolt and know instantly if he needs a $1/2$-inch wrench or a $9/16$-inch one. That ability saves a lot of time and frustration, especially when you have to stand on your head in the bilge to get your wrench on the bolt. A good mechanic can likewise look at a socket and tell if it is 1/2-inch or 9/16-inch without consulting the engraving on the side. He can look at a threaded hole and know that it will require a 1/4-inch screw, or look at the thickness of a bracket and ascertain that a 1 inch mounting screw will be too short.

Sure you can measure. I have always thought that it would have been very useful to have a 3-inch ruler tattooed on the palm of my hand between the little finger and the wrist, but after I had the snake done, there just wasn't room. So measuring involves climbing out of the bilge, finding the scale, climbing back in, holding the flashlight in your mouth, contorting your arm painfully to get the scale exactly right, squinting, and then guessing. Wouldn't knowing be easier?

There is no trick to this. Go to the hardware store and buy one each of the following hex-head bolts: #5, #6, #8, #10, #12, 1/4-inch, 5/16-inch, and 3/8-inch. These are the sizes you are most likely to encounter. The length doesn't matter. Now spend an hour with these bolts and the wrenches that fit them until you can identify each by sight.

You should also be able to make a reasonably accurate guess at larger measurements. Is a through-hull fitting 1 1/2-inch or 2-inch? Are 6 inches of aluminum sheet wide enough to cover the opening? Will it take more than 2 feet of hose to reach from the water pump to the heat exchanger?

All it takes is practice. It can be helpful to know the length of your forearm and the width of your hand as a reference. My hand, for example, measures 3 inches across the knuckles, but I've got hands like a concert pianist—if you overlook the snake.

MOUNTING HARDWARE

High noon, Pardner. Time to strap on your tool belt and see if you've got what it takes. (Just kidding about the belt; you are going to make canvas rolls for your tools when we get to Chapter 15.) If you consider yourself to be either an infant or an idiot when it comes to anything requiring a wrench or screw-

driver, begin with something simple. For example, do you have a sufficient number of fire extinguishers? Are they located where they should be, or are they going to be on the other side of the fire when you need them? Perhaps you want to mount an additional extinguisher to the engine compartment bulkhead.

This is a two-screw job. Attach the extinguisher to its bracket, position the unit as you want it—making certain that you have adequate clearance to release it—and outline the bracket on the bulkhead with a pencil. Separate the bracket from the extinguisher. Position the bracket inside the outline and mark the location of the two mounting holes on the bulkhead.

Unless the mounting screws supplied are stainless steel—very doubtful—take them to the hardware store and buy stainless screws just like them. Back at the boat, deep-six the plated screws—if you keep them, you will one day be tempted to use them. Now select a drill bit smaller than the screw for drilling the pilot holes. In wood, a pilot hole should be approximately half the diameter of the screw. But wood screws come in number sizes, not fractional sizes, so without a table handy, how do you select the pilot drill? The simplest way is to hold the shank of the drill bit behind the threaded portion of the screw. If the bit is visible on both sides of the screw, the bit is too large. The right bit will be the same size as the screw's *root diameter*—the diameter of the screw if the threads were ground away.

Before you drill any hole on a boat, *know what is behind where you are drilling*. If there is a tank or a wire or an ocean on the other side, you are in for a most unpleasant surprise. Drill into the ocean with an electric drill, and it could be your last surprise. In this case, check the opposite side of the engine compartment bulkhead, then drill the two pilot holes. Hold the bracket in place and insert the two screws. Be sure you hold the screwdriver perpendicular to the screw head as you tighten.

How do you know which way to turn the screwdriver. Can you say "righty-tighty," boys and girls? Almost all screws have right-hand threads. That means you turn the top of the screw or nut to the right—clockwise—to tighten it. One of the two screws in a turnbuckle has left-hand threads so the screws move in opposite directions when the body of the turnbuckle is turned, but turnbuckle screws will probably be the only left-hand screws you will find aboard. Turn that screwdriver clockwise.

Whenever you have a choice, *select Phillips-head* screws. The screwdriver will hold the screw more securely, you can fit the screwdriver into the screw even when you cannot see it, and you will know immediately what size screwdriver you need. Standard screwdrivers are less secure, and more difficult to fit, and the proper size is less clear. When you are using a standard screwdriver, the blade should be a snug fit in the slot and should be as wide as the screw head, but not wider. If you use a screwdriver that does not fit the slot, the screwdriver is likely to

correct   too small   too large

Choosing a drill size

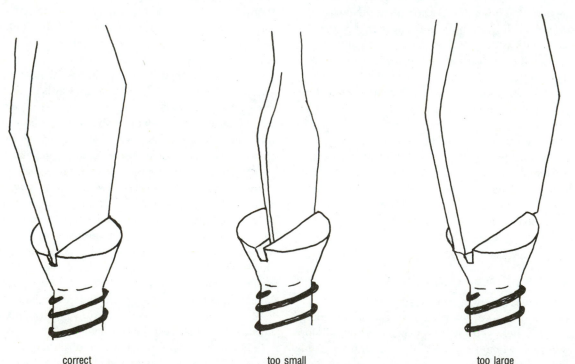

correct   too small   too large

Proper slot screwdriver fit

slip, rounding the slot and making removal of the screw very difficult.

Cleats

Mounting a cleat can present a bit more of a challenge. Stock cleats are almost always too small, and you may decide to replace them with something more substantial. Don't assume that the original placement was well considered; often it wasn't. Most cleats are designed for a load in line with the horns. They should be angled about 15 degrees from the lead of the line that will be attached—far enough to prevent the line from jamming but not far enough to result in unfair loading.

Cleats generally come in two- and four-bolt varieties. Two-bolt cleats of adequate size will work well in any application where the load will always be fair, e.g., cleats intended to secure a halyard or a sheet. But mooring cleats—any cleat primarily intended to secure the boat to an anchor or the dock—will eventually be subjected to severe side loading. Mooring cleats require the added strength and better load distribution of four-bolt cleats.

The mounting holes in the cleat will be countersunk, and the stainless-steel flathead mounting bolts should be the largest diameter that will pass through the mounting holes. They should fit flush with or below the surface of the cleat.

When replacing a cleat, remove the old cleat and run a slightly oversize drill through the mounting holes in the deck to remove all traces of bedding compound. Seal the bottom of the holes with tape and fill them with epoxy putty. Place the new cleat in position and outline the mounting holes with a sharp pencil. Drill a small pilot hole in the *center* of each mounting hole location. Select a drill bit the same diameter as the mounting bolts and drill the new mounting holes through the deck, using the pilot holes as guides. If you are drilling through a cored deck, remember to drill the holes oversize and fill them with epoxy (see Chapter 6). If you have difficulty drilling a straight hole, you can buy an inexpensive drill guide, which will keep the drill perpendicular to the surface you are drilling.

Cleats *must* be through-bolted, and a strong backing plate larger than the base of the cleat is required. Builders often use scraps of the deck laminate. Plywood can be used, but when it is, the through bolts must be fitted with large-diameter washers under the nuts. Aluminum is a better choice. Light and strong, the aluminum doesn't require washers and it will spread the load evenly. The fact that the backing plate is dissimilar to the bolts is actually beneficial in this case since powdery corrosion will immediately "flag" the location of any leaks that may develop.

The most professional installation uses a backing plate of polished stainless steel threaded to accept the mounting screws. The extra effort this approach requires is probably not justified if the backing plate is out of sight, but when it will be seen, a threaded plate looks better. If you elect this route, you should have the plates cut to size where you purchase the stainless steel. You will wear out blades and ears cutting the metal while a good metal salvage yard will have a shear that will slice 1/4-inch stainless like kindergarten construction paper.

With a file or a grinder, round all the corners. Center the cleat on the plate and mark the mounting holes. Check the plate against the underside of the deck to be sure it will fit. Place the point of a center punch in the center of *one* of the marked locations and give it a solid whack with a hammer.

Now you need a taper hand tap the size of your mounting bolts (e.g., 1/4-20; 1/4-inch diameter, 20 threads per inch), a tap handle, and the correct drill bit. It is imperative that you drill the right-size hole; too small and the tap will bind and break, too large and the threads will strip when you tighten the screw. The tap will probably indicate the correct bit. If not, pick up a tap/drill chart at Sears. A 1/4-20 tap requires a 13/64-inch drill bit.

Drilling will be much easier if you grip the backing plate in a vise. On this subject, a momentary digression is in order. You cannot have a more useful tool aboard than a solidly mounted bench vise. Once relatively expensive, vises are now regularly available from discount building suppliers at less

Fill old mounting holes.

Position new cleat and mark holes.

Drill new mounting holes.

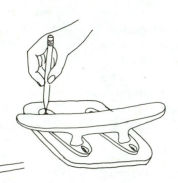
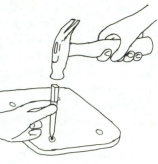

Cut out metal backing plate.

Mark mounting hole locations.

Make an indentation in the center of *one* of the holes.

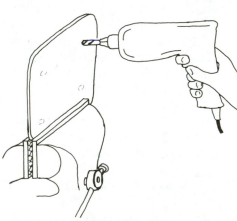
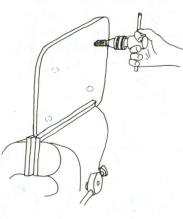

Drill the backing plate at the indention, using a pilot bit first.

Thread the hole.

Mounting a cleat

Mount the plate with one screw. Using the holes in the deck as a template, mark the other holes on the plate with the tip of the drill bit.

Drill the remaining holes at the drilled indentions.

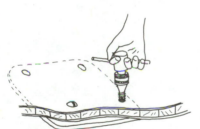

Remount the plate and tap the remaining holes.

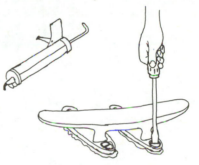

Caulk the cleat and mount it, threading the screws into the backing plate.

than $20 for a 4-inch model, ample for almost all onboard use. The "workshop" aboard most boats, particularly sailboats, is the cockpit and that is where an onboard vise should be mounted. But no one wants a vise permanently mounted in the cockpit, standing proud and rusting. So . . .

Pick a spot over a cockpit locker—not on the locker hatch—and preferably toward the rear of the cockpit, where you will encounter less interference when working on long items. Position the vise and mark the mounting holes. Now open the locker hatch and hold the vise against the underside of the deck in the same place to make sure it can be mounted against the underside with the same bolts. When you are satisfied, drill the mounting holes. Carriage bolts and wing nuts will make solidly mounting the vise a snap. When not in use, fit the carriage bolts with rubber washers (to make them watertight), push them through the deck, and mount the vise *inside* the locker with the wing nuts.

Back to the backing plate: drill a small pilot hole in the center-punched hole; the exact size is not important. You will need first-quality bits to drill stainless steel. And you will need patience; do not try to run the drill too fast or apply too much pressure. The pilot hole will make it much easier for the

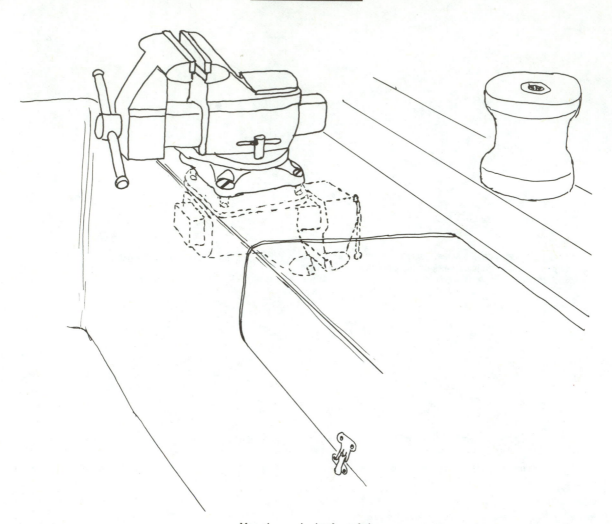

Mounting a vise in the cockpit

correct bit to penetrate and give you a cleaner and more accurate final hole. Drill the hole to the correct size.

Now thread the hole. Using a tap is not difficult, but because the tap is brittle, it does require care, particularly in a hard metal like stainless steel. Chuck the tap securely in the tap handle and put a few drops of engine oil on the cutting threads. Insert the tapered end of the tap into the drilled hole. Exerting inward pressure on the tap, and taking care to keep the tap perpendicular to the plate, turn the tap clockwise. When the tap begins to feel tight, back it up ¼ turn. Turn the tap clockwise again another ½ turn, then back it up ¼ turn. After about two full turns, it will no longer be necessary to keep inward pressure on the tap. Continue the "½ turn forward, ¼ turn back" sequence. If the tap gets very hard to turn, back it out and clean the chips from the tap and the hole. Lubricate the tap and try again. When the tap turns freely, the hole is threaded. Back the tap out carefully and check the hole with one of your mounting bolts.

If the plate is to be mounted to the cleat, you could bolt the two together with the first hole and use the cleat as a drill guide for the other three holes. But there is 1/2 inch or more of deck between the cleat and the plate, and any inaccuracy in your drilling or curvature of the deck will alter the relationship of the holes. For this step, you need a helper. With your helper holding the backing plate in place, insert one of the mounting screws through the deck and into the threaded hole. Tighten. While your helper watches the plate to make certain it does not move, chuck the bit you used to drill mounting holes through the deck. Use those holes as a template, and mark the exact location of the other three holes with your drill. You do not want to drill through the plate—just cut a slight indentation.

Remove the plate and using the indentations as a center punch, drill first a pilot hole and then the tap hole. To minimize alignment problems, bolt the plate in place again and tap the other holes from on deck. When the plate is finished, screw the cleat in place. Mark the screws where they extend through the plate. Remove the screws and cut them at the mark, dressing the cut edge with a grinder or a file. Polish the plate to a mirror shine with metal polish. Bed the cleat generously with polyurethane sealant and run a bead around each of the mounting screws. Position the cleat and thread the screws into the backing plate, tightening until sealant squeezes out all around the base of the cleat. Allow the sealant to partially cure, then finally tighten the mounting screws.

This same procedure is used for attaching any item of deck hardware, from a pad eye to an anchor windlass. Deck gear should *always* be through-bolted, *always* reinforced with a backing plate. You can never mount hardware too securely, only not strongly enough. When hardware under tension rips free, it becomes a deadly missile. I watched an un-backed cleat from a grounded boat miss a small girl by mere inches on its way to burying a horn in the cabin side of a Samaritan's boat, whipped by the tension of a nylon towline. You don't ever want to be part of such a scenario.

OPENING PORTHOLES

Far too many of the opening portholes in boats built in the last decade are virtually all plastic. It is not the plastic I object to (what could be more natural in a plastic boat?), but the frequency that these portholes are plagued with broken hinges and dogs.

The opening hatches in an older boat will likely be bronze or aluminum. There are bronze portholes in service today that were manufactured in the *19th century*. Aluminum doesn't have such a long history, but the aluminum portholes installed in my own boat are well into their third decade of continuous service and give every indication of lasting well into the next century.

Maintenance involves little more than rinsing the frames regularly and applying an occasional coat of wax to retard surface corrosion. Lightly lubricating the screw dogs is recommended. Barring broken glass, the only problem you are likely to experience with a bronze or aluminum porthole is leaking.

If the leak is around the frame, the porthole will have to be removed from the cabin side and rebedded. This involves removing the mounting bolts that hold the two halves of the porthole together (the outside half is called the spigot because of the flange that extends into the opening; the inside half is called the trim ring). Expect recalcitrance from bolts that have not been turned in 20 years—it is habit. Try applying penetrating oil to the nuts for a day or two before you attempt to release them.

Do not be concerned if you break the bolts trying to loosen them; unless they turn freely you should replace them anyway. Frozen bolts are only a problem when they are threaded into some part of the porthole. In such a case, you should drill out the threaded holes and reassemble the porthole using cap nuts. This process was detailed more fully in Chapter 7. Be sure that all traces of the old bedding are removed from the cabin side and the porthole before seating the parts in fresh polysulfide sealant.

If it is the portlight that leaks, the first step is to replace the rubber gasket. Remove the old gasket and clean the corrosion from the channel with bronze wool or a *soft* wire wheel chucked in your drill. Measure the channel and buy new gasket material (sold by the foot). Be sure that you get the right size. Cut one end of the rubber on a 45-degree diagonal and place that end in the channel at the center of the top of the porthole. Press the gasket into the channel, taking care not to stretch the length of the rubber. When you arrive back at the top of the porthole, cut the other end at a diagonal so that the two ends mate in the channel. Close the portlight and dog it down *gently*. Flood it outside with a hose. If it doesn't leak, you are done; if it does, you need to make an adjustment.

On each of the hinges you will find a setscrew. By adjusting the screws in or out, you can adjust how tightly the *top* of the portlight seals against the gasket. For a proper seal, the portlight should seat against the gasket evenly when the screw dogs at the bottom are snugged.

The first step is to determine if the setscrews will turn freely. Select the correct Allen wrench (the screws may also be slotted) and try to turn the screw using finger pressure. Do not force it. If a screw is frozen, apply penetrating oil to both ends and try again in a day or two. Be patient and you should be able to free the screw. You do not want to strip the Allen socket or break one side of the slot. If all else fails, you can apply heat, but caution is required.

Metal (and most other material) expands when it is heated and contracts when it is cooled. You can use this physical property to help you free frozen nuts. If you play the flame of a propane torch around the nut, the nut will expand, often loosening its grip on the screw sufficiently to allow you to turn it. Do not heat the screw; if you do the screw will expand inside the hole, becoming tighter, not looser.

Be very careful with any open flame on a boat. If I have to tell you not to use a torch around a gasoline

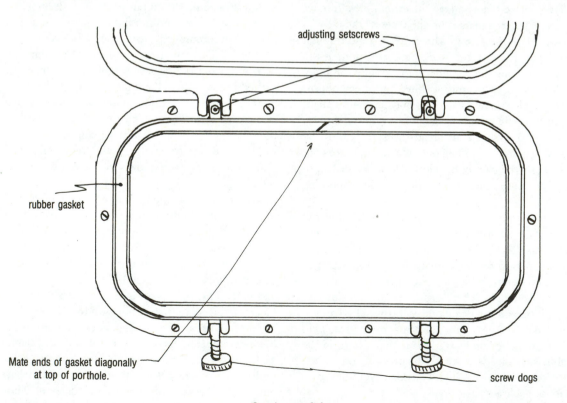

Opening porthole

engine, you should find another interest. In the case of the porthole, if you heat the portlight frame, you will probably crack the glass. Unscrew the hinge pins and remove the portlight. (If the hinge pins are also frozen, your problem is more complicated.) Also remove the rubber gasket. Adjust the torch for a small blue flame and play the blue tip on the hinge around the setscrew. Keep the flame moving, and try the screw every few seconds. If the hinge begins to discolor, stop; you want to heat the aluminum, not melt it. If you were unable to remove the portlight you can still heat the hinge, but hold your fingers on the portlight frame near the hinge and stop if it gets hot. Be careful not to let the flame near the glass.

With the setscrews free, adjustment is a breeze. Loosen the screws until the closed portlight just makes contact with the gasket, then tighten the screws one turn. Coat the rubber gasket with talcum powder, then close and dog the portlight. Flood the porthole outside with a hose, spraying all around the seal. Wipe up the standing water and reopen the portlight. The talcum will show where the leaks occurred. If one side leaked, tighten the setscrew on that side; if the leak was all around, tighten both. Repowder the gasket and check it again. When it is properly adjusted, a couple of easy turns on the screw dogs will make the porthole watertight.

BLOCK REPAIR

To gain a bit of experience in dismantling and reassembly, take a closer look at the various blocks you have aboard. When schooners were king, they carried dozens of blocks—sometimes more than a hundred. On modern yachts, gaffs are gone and winches have replaced the block and tackle for most tensioning applications. Consequently the number of blocks aboard has diminished, but not their importance.

There is an interesting problem with blocks: how do you know if they are working the way they should? A snatch block that turns freely in your hand may not be turning at all under load. And if it isn't, how do you know? If the sheet runs to a winch, there is undoubtedly ample power in the winch to pull the line through the block whether the sheave turns or not. Deck-mounted blocks can be observed, but observation is more difficult for those above the deck. In fact, most of us pay very little attention to the blocks aboard, rarely giving them a second thought.

You can extend the life of the block, the life of the line that runs through it, and probably the life of the person that winches the line by giving blocks just a few minutes of TLC. Care of blocks that are riveted together is limited to flushing them well with fresh water to remove salt deposits and applying a couple of drops of oil to the axle pin (and the swivel if it is a swivel block). Better blocks are screwed together and can be serviced more thoroughly.

I strongly recommend that you dismantle a block for the first time over a towel-covered table. If the block has bearings, they are probably "caged"—held together as an assembly. But if they are not, the towel will keep them from making a break for it.

The most important advice I can give you is to pay attention as you dismantle the block. Is one cheek different from the other? On which side is the nut? How is the head positioned? Which way do the reinforcing straps go? If you have two blocks alike, service one at a time, keeping the other one at hand as a reference.

A single screw fastens the parts of a snatch block together while a conventional block is typically held together with two screws. The screws may thread into the reinforcing strap, or they may be secured with nuts. A single wrench, or a screwdriver, or possibly both, will be the only tools required. Remove the screws and the block separates into pieces. Aside from cleaning all of the parts, you are most interested in the bushing or bearings found in the center of the sheave.

A bushing looks like a short length of metal, phenolic, or plastic tubing. The bushing fits inside the sheave and the axle pin (the center bolt) passes through it. The bushing should be pushed out of the sheave and, along with the sheave and the pin, cleaned with kerosene. When all the old lubricant

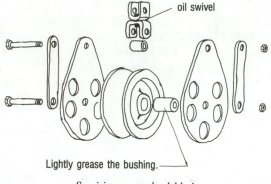

Servicing a standard block

twisted wreckage to some manufacturers, they will recondition the block for you.

WINCHES

There is a perception that winches found aboard boats are somehow complicated pieces of equipment. That perception is wrong. A single-speed winch is a simple wheel and axle, the drum of the winch being the axle, the handle being the wheel (or a 360-degree lever). The mechanical advantage accrues solely from the difference between the two and is calculated by dividing the diameter of the wheel (twice the length of the handle) by the diameter of the axle (the drum). A winch with a 4-inch drum and a 10-inch handle will have a mechanical advantage of 5. Twenty-five pounds of pull on the handle will become 125 pounds of pull on the clew.

The only added complexity is ratchet drive. *Pull* a stick along a picket fence and you get a kid-pleasing click-click-click. Try to *push* the stick and you come to an abrupt halt. The ratchet works exactly the same way. Spring-loaded pawls are pulled over a notched ring as the drum is turned. When the pull of the line tries to turn the drum in the opposite direction, the pawls engage the notches and prevent the drum from turning in that direction. A second notched ring and set of pawls allow the handle to turn the drum in one direction and spin freely in the other. To minimize friction, the drum rotates on a caged roller bearing. The bearing, the drum, and the pawls are all there is.

has been removed and the parts are dry, coat them with a film of grease. I prefer Teflon grease, but any winch grease or water pump grease will do.

Instead of a bushing, the sheaves of higher quality blocks turn on roller or ball bearings. Remove the bearing assembly and soak it in kerosene to dissolve the old grease. Wipe away the residue with a cloth and allow the bearings to dry. Pack them with grease and press the assembly back into the sheave. Reassemble the block. Coat the threads of the screws with a thread sealant (Loctite) before threading them into the strap or installing the nuts. Check the sheave to make sure it turns easily and smoothly.

If you have damaged a block—usually by putting a sideways pull on it—most manufacturers can supply you with replacement parts. Disassemble the block and determine which parts are usable and which require replacement. Order replacement parts from the manufacturer; repairing the block will be less expensive than buying a new one. I probably shouldn't tell you this, but if you send your

More power is obtained from a geared winch. Instead of the handle turning the drum directly, it turns a small gear which engages an idler gear, which engages teeth machined on the inside of the drum. If the small gear has 15 teeth and the drum has 60, the gear ratio (mechanical advantage) is 4. (The idler gear just links the two and has no effect on mechanical advantage.) To get the actual power of the winch, ignoring friction, you have to multiply the advantage gained by gearing by the advantage from the leverage of the handle—in this case 5 × 4, or 20. Now 25 pounds of pull on the handle

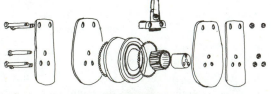

Coat metal bearings with grease. Delrin bearings require no lubrication. Clean only.

Servicing a roller/ball-bearing block

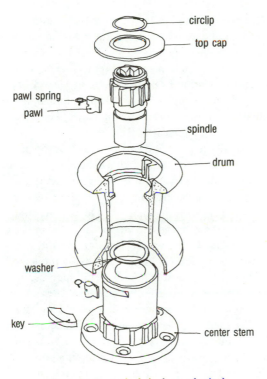

Innards of a typical single-speed winch

ability lull you into complacency. Winches should be dismantled, cleaned, and lubricated every year.

Forget what you have heard about winches flying apart when the drum is removed. Jack-in-the-box was a friend of mine, Senator, and a winch is no Jack-in-the-box. The only springs are the pawl springs and only rarely do they release unexpectedly. If you are the cautious type, clip a towel to the lifelines so flying springs will stay aboard.

You can obtain detailed servicing instructions from the manufacturer of your winch, but you probably don't need them. The first step is to remove the drum, which (depending on the brand and model) is released by loosening a bolt in the bottom of the handle socket, or by *gently* prizing off a snap ring around the top of the shaft. In the latter case, keep your hand over the ring to keep it from flying.

Lift the drum slowly and, as soon as it is above

becomes 500 pounds of pull on the clew. The cost in complexity? Two small gears.

If the winches on your old boat have been updated, they may be two-speed. There are no additional parts in a two-speed winch (unless both speeds are geared, in which case you will find a couple more gears inside the drum). The pawls are just configured to allow the handle to turn the drum directly when cranked in one direction and to turn it through the gear drive when cranked in the other.

A regularly maintained winch is astonishingly trouble-free. The only common failure is a broken pawl spring. Listen to your winches. Pawls operate in pairs and when the spring on one fails, the clicking sound of the winch will change. If you don't replace the spring immediately, you are subjecting the remaining pawl to twice its designed load. Not good, not good at all. And don't let their depend-

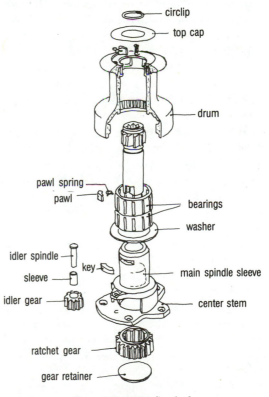

Geared (two-speed) winch

the main shaft, get one hand under it. Often the bearings come up with the drum rather than staying on the shaft, and you do not want them to fall. Now stop and study the exposed viscera of your winch. Pay particular attention to how the pawls are positioned. It is not always necessary to remove them, but if you do it is usually possible to reinstall them in reverse. Get a piece of paper and sketch them the *right* way before you remove them. One other caution: the springs will fly if you don't keep a grip on them when removing the pawls.

Once you have it all figured out, dismantle the rest of the winch. The caged bearings are generally lifted off the main shaft first, but they may be topped or separated by spacers. Laying out the parts in sequence will help you to get everything back together correctly. A more foolproof ploy is to place a tape recorder by the winch and describe what you are doing as you dismantle: "The teflon spacer comes off first, chamfered side up. Next is the top bearing; the ID numbers are up. Now I am removing a thin stainless spacer. Next, the second bearing . . ." and so on. You probably will not need to refer to the recording when you put the winch back together, but if you have parts left over, the answer is at hand.

With the winch completely dismantled, pour kerosene or diesel fuel into a small basin and submerge the parts. While the kerosene is dissolving the old grease is a good time to check the mounting bolts. As inconceivable as it may seem, I know of at least one manufacturer who mounted winches to the decks of his boats with self-tapping screws. Be sure it is not the yard that built your boat. Through-bolt mounting with a heavy backing plate is the only acceptable way to attach a winch. If you find anything less, fix it now.

Remove the parts from the kerosene and, using a lint-free cloth, dry them. If they are not completely clean, put them back in the solvent and use a toothbrush to dislodge stubborn gook, then dry them again.

Now go wash your hands; if you are going to use gritty hands to repack the bearings, you might as well have left the old grease in there. Lubriplate's Marine Lube A is the old standby for lubricating winches, or you can select a proprietary grease from one of the winch manufacturers. Racing crews soften the Marine Lube by mixing in Marvel Mystery Oil (and sometimes STP), but thinner lubricants mean more frequent maintenance. For normal use, stick with regular Marine Lube.

Coat all the parts and surfaces—except the pawls and the ratchet notches—with a light coat of grease. Pack the bearings with grease, but not excessively. Lightly oil the ratchet mechanism—the pawls and the notches—with machine oil. Do *not* use engine oil; the detergents in engine oils will eat into the bronze parts of the winch. Reassemble the winch and give it a spin. I told you it wasn't complicated.

While you are still flushed with success, take your wrenches on a little stroll to the anchor windlass. If it is a capstan type, it should look quite familiar to an old hand at winch maintenance such as yourself. When you remove the drum, it is going to look even more familiar. What about a horizontal windlass, a Simpson-Lawrence or the like? It wouldn't surprise me at all if you found a couple of gears inside. And a bearing. And a couple of ratchet pawls. Are you getting the hang of this?

STUFFING BOXES

The most difficult aspect of stuffing-box maintenance is usually access. I never adjust my own without wondering if it would take the Jaws of Life for the paramedics to extract me if the blood pooled in my head caused me to pass out. Or how many days my feet would stick out of the locker before someone investigated. Or . . . well, you get the picture.

So the first step is to crawl in and figure out how you must lie to reach the stuffing box with *both* hands. You are going to need both hands because there are *two* nuts on the stuffing box, the packing nut and a lock nut, and you are going to have to have wrenches on both, pulling on one while pushing on the other. Unless you have a world class muscle in your thumb, that will require two hands.

The stuffing box seals out water where a rudder stock or a propeller shaft passes through the hull, while still allowing the shaft to turn. In principle it is identical to the packing nut on a common faucet. The shaft passes through a threaded sleeve and a hollow nut. The nut is filled with a packing material—in this case braided flax heavily impregnated with wax and lubricants—and screwed onto the sleeve. As the nut is tightened, the packing is compressed against the shaft, forming a watertight seal.

Some stuffing boxes are rigidly attached to the hull, but more often they are connected to the shaft tube by a length of flexible hose. The hose must be double clamped to the tube and to the stuffing box. These clamps are prone to corrosion, especially at the lowest part of the clamps, and they should be carefully checked for signs of corrosion every time the stuffing box is serviced.

It is perfectly normal, even desirable, for a prop shaft stuffing box to drip when the shaft is turning. You can check it while underway or by simply putting the boat in gear in her slip. With the shaft turning, use a flashlight to assist you in counting the drips. If the stuffing box drips more than, say, 10 drops per minute you need to tighten it. If it is not dripping at all, put your hand on the stuffing box. If it is hot to the touch, the packing is too tight. Please, please, never work around a spinning engine shaft, or any turning part, wearing long sleeves or loose clothing.

To tighten the packing nut, you must first release the lock nut, which is there to prevent the packing nut from turning with the shaft. You will need open-end wrenches to fit the two nuts, or two pipe wrenches. Fit the wrenches and maintain counterclockwise pressure on the packing nut while you turn the lock nut clockwise. If you are using pipe wrenches, remember to apply force only in the direction of the jaw opening. And never try to release the lock nut without a second wrench on the packing nut; you will twist the stuffing box inside the hose, tear the hose, or damage the shaft tube.

With the lock nut released a couple of turns and the shaft turning, tighten the packing nut. Keep the stuffing box from turning by gripping the flange near the flexible hose with your other pipe wrench. When the drip rate is down to one or two drops per minute, tighten the lock nut against the packing nut.

After you have tightened the packing nut a few times, the packing can become so compressed that it loses all resiliency and becomes hard enough to actually wear a groove in the shaft. To avoid such an occurrence, a power boat used regularly should have the packing replaced every two years. A sailboat may not need to have the shaft packing replaced for five years or more, but when the stuffing box begins to feel warm or starts requiring frequent adjustment, it's time.

Release the lock nut and unscrew the packing nut completely and slide it up the shaft. This is a job best done when the boat is out of the water, but if you do it at the dock, wrap the shaft with a towel to direct the incoming water into the bilge, where your pump should have little difficulty keeping up with it. With a piece of stiff wire bent at the end, dig out the first layer of the old packing and take it with you to the chandlery to select the right size. If the old packing comes out in wads of blackened fluff, then measure the space between the shaft and the inside of the packing nut to determine the correct size. Multiplying the diameter of your shaft by 14 will give you the approximate number of inches you need for four layers of new packing—usually sufficient.

Dig *all* the old packing out of the packing nut, taking care not to scratch the shaft. Cut the new packing in lengths equal to 3.14 (π) times the diameter of the shaft. Curl a piece into a ring around the shaft—the ends should just touch—and push it all the way into the packing nut with a thin screwdriver. Push a second ring into the nut on top of the first, staggering the joint about 120 degrees. Add a third layer, again staggering the joint. Screw the packing nut in place and hand tighten.

Now remove the nut again and check to see if there is room to add an additional layer of flax; three

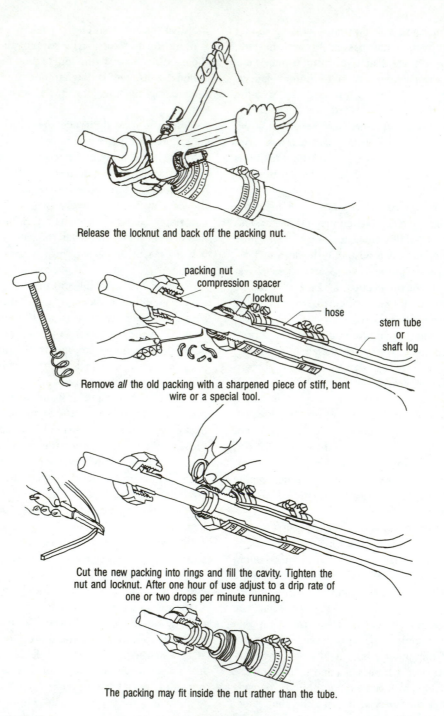

Release the locknut and back off the packing nut.

packing nut
compression spacer
locknut
hose
stern tube
or
shaft log

Remove *all* the old packing with a sharpened piece of stiff, bent
wire or a special tool.

Cut the new packing into rings and fill the cavity. Tighten the
nut and locknut. After one hour of use adjust to a drip rate of
one or two drops per minute running.

The packing may fit inside the nut rather than the tube.

Stuffing box

layers is the minimum, but you should pack the nut until it is full. Retighten the packing nut, adjusting and locking it as previously outlined. After the first hour of use, check again to make sure the adjustment is correct. Some tightening is usually required.

RUDDERS

The stuffing box on the stock of an inboard rudder should be tightened until it does not drip at all. Some water penetration helps to lubricate the spinning prop shaft, but the oscillating rudder stock does not need any additional lubrication.

The constant motion does, however, result in wear, and the exposure of rudders always places them at risk of being damaged. The success of any rudder repairs you undertake will depend upon your understanding of the forces at work on your particular rudder. This is an area where your fresh reacquaintance with the principles of the lever will be helpful.

If you have a spade rudder, all of the bending force exerted on the rudder by the water is concentrated on the rudderstock where it enters the hull. Under normal circumstances, the bending force is manageable; but when, for example, a boat spills sideways off a steep wave, the bending force increases alarmingly. The higher the aspect ratio of the rudder, the greater the bending force. The designer should have taken sea conditions into account when he specified the diameter of the rudder stock. But if it kisses something solid, like a rock or a coral head, the stock of most spade rudders will bend like a pipe cleaner.

Straightening a rudderstock requires the services of a machine shop, and the rudder must be removed from the boat. Before you begin, support the rudder to keep it from dropping when released. Now release the clamp bolts on the tiller arm or the steering quadrant, along with any bearings or collars that may be clamped to the stock, and loosen the packing nut on the stuffing box. On a powerboat, it is simply a matter of lowering the rudder until the

stock comes out of the hull. The length of the rudder assembly makes the problem somewhat more complicated on a sailboat, generally requiring that the boat be lifted.

The only preventative measure available, short of redesign, is to increase the size of the rudderstock. Strength increases with the *cube* of the diameter; double the diameter and the strength goes up by eight. But increasing the size of the stock of a spade rudder comes with its own set of problems. First, it obviously requires the construction of a new rudder, but if the old one has been badly damaged, that may already be necessary. The larger stock also means a new rudder tube, new bearings, new stuffing box, and a new quadrant or tiller clamp.

The biggest problem, however, goes back to the principle of leverage. If you ground the rudder and the shaft is strong enough not to bend, all the leverage bears on the hull. A bent stock is infinitely more desirable than a rip in the hull. Any effort to strengthen a spade rudder must include reinforcing the hull around the rudder tube and include rigid support of the rudder stock as high as possible inside the hull.

If your rudder has a skeg in front of it, the lower end of the rudderstock probably fits into a cast heel fitting at the bottom of the skeg. The rudder is somewhat protected and the rigid skeg reduces the likelihood of a bent rudderstock. The procedure for removing a skeg-mounted rudder is the same as that for a spade rudder, with the addition of unbolting the heel fitting from the skeg. The bolts may not be immediately visible under a dozen coats of bottom paint, but scrape the paint away (or lift it with paint remover), and you will find them.

But if a skeg-mounted rudder is less likely to suffer a bent stock, why would you need to remove it? Because of another leverage-related problem common to inboard rudders of all types. A rudder 2 feet wide with a 2-inch diameter stock is, in effect, a wheel and axle with a 48-inch wheel (twice the width of the rudder) and a 2-inch axle. It has a mechanical advantage of 24. Imagine a 30-foot sailboat making hull speed when a crew member drops a 3-foot-diameter sea anchor overboard, attached to a stern cleat with ⅛-inch flag halyard. What happens when the boat reaches the end of the line? The line snaps like thread. A 500-pound breaking strength is no match for the drag of the sea anchor or the inertia of a 10,000-pound boat moving at 6 knots.

Same boat, same speed, and the rudder described above is suddenly put hard over. The load on the rudder is similar to that on the sea anchor; we could calculate the actual load, but that is not what I am trying to get at. The point is that it is not hard to imagine subjecting the outboard edge of the rudder to 500 pounds of pressure. When we do, we generate *6 tons* of force where the rudder blade is attached to the stock. Far too often, this joint fails.

On powerboats, the metal blade and the metal stock are welded into a single, immensely strong and trouble-free unit. Metal rudders are not often seen on sailboats because sailboat rudders need nearly neutral buoyancy (weighing the same as an equal volume of water). When the boat heels, a metal rudder would tend to sink, causing the bow to pay off. A buoyant rudder would have the opposite effect.

So an inboard sailboat rudder has a metal stock and a wood or composite (fiberglass and wood or fiberglass and foam) blade. The two are joined in various ways, some of which are ludicrous. Commonly, two or three metal rods or narrow plates are welded to the stock, like long fingers, and sandwiched inside the rudder blade. The force on the

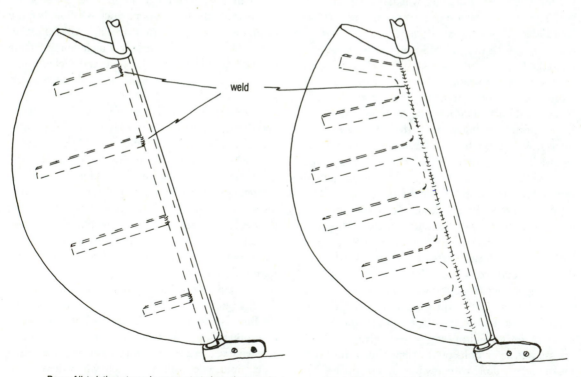

Poor: All twisting stress is concentrated on three or four short welds.

Good: Stress is distributed along the length of the stock.

Rudder detail

rudder is concentrated on these small welds and they eventually fail, allowing the stock to turn inside the blade.

Check your rudder by jamming the wheel or tiller *rigidly* in place with a couple of lengths of wood, then trying to move the trailing edge of the rudder. If the rudder moves and the stock doesn't, you're in trouble. You will have to remove the rudder and grind away the fiberglass that encapsulates the stock. When you have new plates welded to the stock, make them several inches wide and closely spaced. A stronger joint is achieved by welding a broad metal plate to the stock the entire length of the joint. Shape the metal plate like a comb and it will not be necessary to weld the straps needed to spread the attachment to more of the rudder blade.

Once you have a strong attachment system, the decision to reuse the old blade or to construct a new one will depend upon the condition of the old one. The fiberglass almost always encapsulates a plywood or foam core, and rudders are notorious for delaminating. If the core is saturated, you will probably be better off using the old rudder as a pattern for the construction of a new one.

By comparison, outboard rudders are *almost* trouble free. Hanging on the back of the keel like a hinged door, they do not penetrate the hull, have no bendable rudderstock, or vulnerable blade-to-stock joint. The turning force is applied through a robust tiller arm through-bolted to the blade itself. The biggest risk to an outboard rudder is *backing* into a solid object.

Of course, outboard rudders can develop problems. They are just as subject to delamination as any other rudder. The strength of the tiller arm attachment can be inadequate. And the hinge fittings—the pintles and gudgeons—eventually wear from the constant back-and-forth motion. Don't panic when you discover you can shake your outboard rudder. It is not necessary for the fit between the pintles and the gudgeons to be precise—just strong. But if the play has reached a point where it seems excessive to you, it is time to remove the rudder and examine the fittings.

With some outboard rudders, removal is a simple matter of removing the cotter pins through the bottom of the pintles and drafting some help from other sailors in the yard to lift the rudder out of the gudgeons. On others, gudgeons extend into notches in the leading edge of the rudder, and small filler blocks are screwed or bonded in place in the notches beneath the gudgeons, preventing the rudder from lifting. An outboard rudder may also extend under the counter and be prevented from lifting by the hull. In these latter two cases, the rudder is removed by unbolting the fittings from either the rudder or the hull. Like the heel fitting mentioned earlier, pintles and gudgeons should be through-bolted. Some paint removal may be required to find the heads of the various fasteners.

STEERING SYSTEMS

Not much can go wrong with a tiller, and for that reason alone, it has much to recommend it. It requires almost no maintenance—an occasional application of grease or oil to the pivot and a protective coating on the wood. Tiller heads occasionally fail, especially when they are aluminum; installing a stainless steel or bronze tiller head is a wise enhancement. If a tiller breaks or rots, removal is simply a matter of releasing a couple of nuts and extracting the mounting bolts.

Worm gear steering is almost as maintenance free as a tiller. Disassembly is *not* necessary, but the worm screws should be cleaned thoroughly with cloths soaked in kerosene or diesel fuel to remove old grease and grit. When the gears are dry, they should be well coated with winch grease or water pump grease. Any universal joint in the wheel shaft should be packed with grease. All pivots and bearings should be lubricated with nondetergent 30W motor oil. The bearings are lubricated most thoroughly by removing the cap bolts and sliding the inserts clear of the bearing area.

Maintenance of geared quadrant steering is identical to that of worm gear except that it is the pinion and geared quadrant that require cleaning and coat-

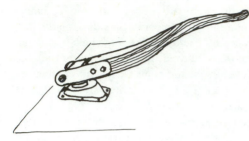

tiller

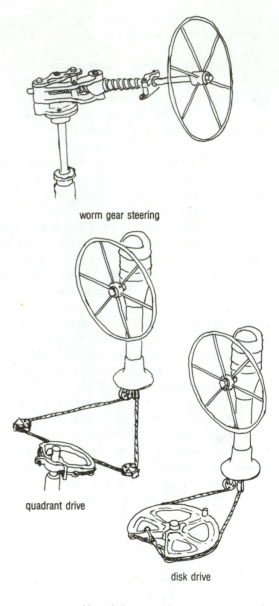

worm gear steering

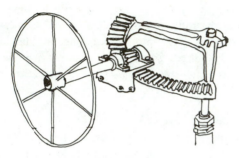

geared quadrant

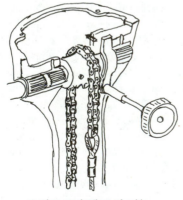

steering mechanism of cable
and sheave system

quadrant drive

disk drive

cable and sheave steering

Steering systems

ing with grease. A geared quadrant may also be adjusted to remove excess play between the gears. On older units, this adjustment is usually made by a screw *beneath* the quadrant where it engages the pinion. A locknut that holds the screw in position is loosened and the screw is adjusted to force the quadrant tightly enough into the pinion to eliminate the play, but not tightly enough to cause the steering to bind or feel tight. Because the quadrant rides on the adjusting screw (or on a plate in later units), the underside of the quadrant should also be coated with grease.

The most common wheel steering on a sailboat is pedestal steering, a system that connects a pedestal-mounted wheel to the rudder with wire cables. In concept, pedestal steering is only slightly more complicated than the simple leverage of a tiller. Imagine a grooved wheel—a pulley—attached to the top of the rudder stock. Now imagine a second wheel mounted horizontally in the cockpit. If we connect the two with a belt, turning the wheel in the cockpit will turn the rudder, which is exactly how pedestal steering works.

Perhaps it troubles you that in this example the rudder turns the wrong way. Picky, picky. So cross the belt, like a figure # eight, and when the steering wheel turns to the right so does the boat. I bet you don't like the horizontal steering wheel either, do you? Bus drivers don't complain about that, but what if we ran the belt through a couple of turning blocks fastened to the cockpit sole and oriented the steering wheel vertically? Happy now?

Instead of a belt, pedestal steering systems use cable which, with the help of sheaves, can be routed in any direction. And since the rudder turns through less than 90 degrees, or a fourth of a circle, we can substitute a quadrant for the pulley on the rudder stock. To prevent any slippage, we use a sprocket instead of a pulley on the steering wheel, and insert a length of bicycle chain into the middle of the cable to run over the sprocket.

While the other three steering systems will shrug off indifferent maintenance for a long time, pedestal steering will not. If you do not give it the attention it requires, it will fail, often spitefully.

Required maintenance begins with regular lubrication of all the sheaves. If you don't know where they are, it is time to climb down into the sail locker and find them. Trace both cables from the base of the pedestal to the quadrant and oil the bearings of each sheave with 30W oil. Manufacturers recommend that you oil the sheaves every month. It really depends on how much you use the boat, but oil them regularly and often.

When you oil the sheaves, you should make sure that all the cotter pins securing the axle pins are in place. Also check all mounting bolts for tightness. The sheaves are subjected to heavy loading by the action of the rudder and must be strongly and securely mounted. Check the rudderstops for wear or any signs of movement. Check also to make certain the cable has not loosened.

Annually (or more often if the boat sees heavy use) more extensive maintenance is required. To gain access to the chain and sprocket in the pedestal, the compass and its housing cylinder have to be removed. Before you unscrew anything, put three lengths of tape irregularly spaced around the pedestal, each beginning on the compass dome and reaching onto the tapered section of the pedestal. With a razor knife, slit the tape where the various binnacle components join. The tape simplifies realignment when you reassemble the parts; the compass should be checked, but adjustment will probably not be required.

Now remove the screws and lift the compass and its housing from the pedestal. If the engine controls are in the pedestal, the control housing will also need to be removed. To do so, remove the cotter pins and slide the pins out of the clevises that attach the levers to the control cables. Clevis pins have a nasty little habit of binding, then releasing with a jerk, so be careful not to let the pins drop inside the pedestal.

With the steering mechanism exposed, squirt *winch grease* into the holes on top of the bearing housing while you spin the wheel. Teflon grease may be recommended by the manufacturer. Oil the chain and sprocket with 30W oil—just like you did with your bicycle when you were a kid. Check the chain-to-wire connections for wear or broken strands. Make sure the master links and clevises are properly secured with cotter pins.

Down below, release the locknut, then back off the adjusting nut on one of the takeup eyes on the quadrant, loosening the cable. With slack in the cable, check each of the sheaves. They should rotate easily and smoothly. If they wobble, replace the axle pins.

Fold a paper towel into a pad and squirt oil in the center of it. Now fold the pad around the cable and slide it back and forth over all of the wire, oiling it lightly and checking for broken strands at the same time. If a strand snags the toweling, replace the cable immediately.

Check the cable attachment to the takeup eyes. The cable *must* loop around a stainless steel thimble and it must be secured to itself with two wire rope clamps. Check the clamps for tightness. Properly installed, the U-bolt of a wire rope clamp always bears against the dead end of the cable and the cast portion bears on the standing part. The two clamps should be separated by about six times the cable diameter.

With the wheel tied or locked, readjust the tension on the cable by tightening the nut on the takeup eye. Proper tension is reached just when the quadrant cannot be moved by hand—no tighter. Lock the takeup eye with the second nut. Recheck the cable tension with the helm hard over in both directions.

Even if you fail to find any broken strands, steering cables should be replaced at least every five years. Cable replacement is a matter of pinning the new cable to the ends of the chain, feeding it through the sheaves, and attaching it to the takeup eyes on the quadrant. With access to a Nicopress tool, there is no reason that you cannot make up your own steering cables from a length of 7 × 19 stainless wire rope.

Installing wheel steering is a common enhancement to older, tiller-steered boats. If you can handle a wrench and a drill, there is little reason why you cannot handle such a retrofit. Some fiberglassing may be also required to reinforce mounting points against the tremendous forces the steering components are subjected to. The steering system manufacturer will be able to assist you in selecting the "right" steering system for your boat and in providing detailed instructions for its installation.

ZINCS

Without sacrificial zincs, the underwater metal parts of your boat are at risk from galvanic action. To protect against this destruction, every underwater metal part should have an electrically conductive contact with a zinc anode. The most direct way to achieve this is to bolt a zinc button directly to each of the underwater parts. On an old boat, hopefully the means of attaching zincs to the underwater parts has already been resolved and you will only need to be concerned with replacing the zinc buttons and collars every year—a matter of removing the mounting screws, discarding the old zinc, fitting the new one, and retightening the screws.

A zinc on one of the pintle fittings protects the attached gudgeon fitting because the metal-to-metal contact is electrically conductive, but it *does not* protect the other pintle fittings. Each fitting requires a zinc. If additional zincs are indicated, the easiest attachment method generally is to remove one of the through-bolts from the fitting and replace it with a bolt long enough to accommodate the two halves of the zinc button like washers on either side of the rudder. An alternative is to drill and thread a hole in the fitting to accept a mounting screw. The shaft and the propeller are both protected by the installation and renewal of a zinc collar, which clamps around the shaft. Be sure you clean away all paint or corrosion beneath the zinc to insure a good electrical contact. Never paint a zinc anode or you will prevent it from doing its job.

Where direct attachment of a zinc button is not practical—bronze through-hull fittings, for example—the unprotected fittings should be connected together by heavy electrical cable (bonded) and to a fitting that *is* protected, typically the prop shaft. The cable is often connected to the engine on the assumption that the engine is electrically connected to the shaft, but if a flexible coupling has been installed, that assumption may be false. In that case, the bonding cable should be attached to the mounting bolt of a through-bolted zinc plate.

PROPELLERS

My guess is that failure to replace the zinc shaft collar is the *second* most common reason for removing the prop on a sailboat; when the blades begin to resemble Swiss cheese, the prop grates the water rather than slicing it. The most common reason for prop removal is an encounter with a line—a trailing sheet, an anchor rode, the dinghy painter. If the wrapped line does not stall the engine before all the slack is spooled, a bent blade is the likely result.

The propeller of a powerboat is much more exposed, and an encounter with the bottom, or a projecting or floating object, precipitates most removals. Mangled propellers are so common that prop reconditioning is a legitimate industry. A bent blade is straightened by heating it white-hot and hammering it into shape against a cast iron form. Straightening it yourself is not a very good idea, except in an emergency.

You might also remove a prop to exchange it for a different size. Just because it has been on there for 20 years is no assurance that it is the best choice. Generally, propellers have a two-number designation. The first number is the overall diameter in inches and the second number is the *pitch*. Pitch is a measurement of how far the prop would travel through solid material in one revolution. A prop stamped 15 × 12 RH is 15 inches in diameter and would push the boat 12 inches with every revolution, except for the fact that water is not solid, and when pushing the boat forward the prop turns to the right (clockwise) as viewed from the stern.

Prop choice is not very exact. Engine manufacturers make recommendations based on horsepower, shaft r.p.m., and displacement, but how you load your boat, how you use it, and the sea conditions you normally encounter are also factors. For example, a prop that easily pushes your boat at hull speed in calm conditions may be too small and turn too fast to push the same boat efficiently against a headwind in a seaway. The prop simply cavitates, losing its "bite" on the water, and the boat slows to an agonizing crawl. If these are your "normal" conditions, a larger prop and slower shaft speed may be a better choice. Some prop shops have loaners so you can experiment with different sizes before deciding.

Other possibilities muddy the picture even more. The idle prop on a sailboat, especially a three-blade prop, is like a small sea anchor. Performance-conscious sailors often exchange it for a two-blade prop which can be locked vertically behind the keel or skeg, or they select a folding or feathering prop. Variable-pitch props that allow for pitch adjustment as different motoring conditions are encountered round out the field.

Whatever your motivation, prop removal is not difficult. Typically the threaded end of the shaft is drilled for a cotter pin. The cotter pin may lock a drilled or castellated nut in position, or it may only prevent a loosened nut from backing completely off the shaft. In either case, remove the cotter pin. Fit wrenches to the two nuts on the shaft and loosen and remove the aft one. Now grip the prop to prevent the shaft from turning and release and remove the second nut.

The hole in the prop is tapered to fit tightly against a similar taper at the end of the prop shaft. Sometimes you can pull a prop from the taper by hand, but it usually requires some type of prop puller. *Never* try to remove a prop by hitting it with a hammer. You will succeed only in destroying the balance of the prop or bending the shaft.

You can rent or borrow a commercial puller—an octopuslike gizmo with hinged arms that grip the hub, or lengths of chain that loop around the blades, and a central screw that tightens against the end of the shaft—or you can make a simple puller from a couple of 6-inch squares, triangles, or disks of $1/4$-inch mild steel. Clamp the two together and drill three evenly-spaced $3/8$-inch holes in a triangular pattern somewhat larger than the hub of the prop. Cut a notch into one of the plates wide enough and deep enough to allow the plate to be slid over the shaft and centered against the hub of the prop.

With the notched plate in place, insert $3/8$-inch bolts through the holes in the plate and between the blades of the prop. Slide the second plate over the bolts and install the nuts, tightening until the aft plate seats squarely against the end of the shaft. Now tighten the bolts evenly $1/2$ turn at a time and the compression will pull the prop. Occasionally a prop will literally leap aft when the taper releases, so

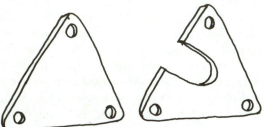

Cut two plates from ¼″ mild steel.

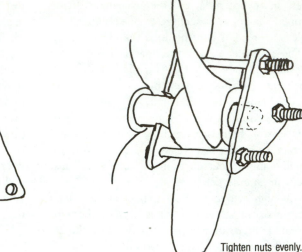

Tighten nuts evenly.

A simple prop puller

be careful. If the prop fails to release after a few turns, hit the aft plate in its center with a hammer. Don't haul off and whang it; you are not trying to impress the crowds at the fair. A single sharp rap should do the trick.

The prop and the shaft are locked together rotationally with a key—a square metal bar—that fits into a machined slot in the shaft and a corresponding keyway in the prop. Be careful not to lose the key, particularly if you are pulling the prop in the water. If the key comes off with the prop, remove it by prying it out of the keyway before you send the prop to be reconditioned; if the key stays in the slot in the shaft, there is no real reason to remove it unless it is in danger of falling out and getting lost.

When reinstalling the prop, be sure the key is in place. Grease the taper lightly to insure that the prop seats fully. Tighten the shaft nut against the hub of the prop, and the locknut against the shaft nut. Insert and spread the cotter pin.

CUTLESS BEARING

The cutless bearing supports the propeller shaft where it exits the hull. There is no maintenance that can be done on a cutless bearing; either it is ok or you replace it.

How do you, a mere novice in such matters, know if it needs replacing? The same way a pro knows; grab the prop and shake the shaft. A little play is fine, but if you can get it moving enough to rattle, it is time for a new cutless bearing.

A cutless bearing is nothing more than a short length of bronze tubing with a grooved rubber liner. The grooves allow water into the bearing; the water acts as a lubricant and it washes out any sand or other abrasive that finds its way onto the shaft.

Replacement varies from boat to boat. In general, the cutless bearing slips into a housing in the stern tube from outside the hull and is held in place by setscrews in the protruding portion of the housing. It may also be held in place by a flange or an

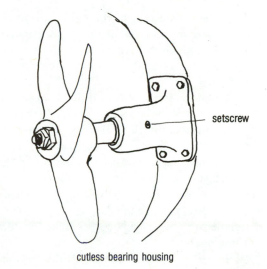

bronze or phenolic sleeve
rubber lining

cutless bearing

setscrew

cutless bearing housing

Cutless bearing

extended housing bolted in place.

The first step in replacing a cutless bearing is to remove the prop. If there is a housing, it should be removed next. The mounting bolts are often well camouflaged by layers of bottom paint, but when they are located and removed, the housing will slide aft and off the prop shaft. The cutless bearing may be contained in the housing. If it is, locate the set-screws in the side of the housing and unscrew them to release the bearing. Tap the old bearing out with a dowel or a pin punch.

A bearing in an internal housing may be partially exposed by the removal of an external collar. In this case, it may be possible to grip the exposed portion of the bearing and extract it by pulling it out of the housing and off the shaft.

With the collar out of the way, if all you can see of the cutless bearing is an end, or if there is no collar and the bearing is held in place with setscrews in the side of an unremovable housing, you will have to drive the bearing out of the tube from inside the boat. That usually means the prop shaft has to be removed.

You will also find cutless bearings in any struts that support the prop shaft, and around the rudder stock where it exits the hull. These bearings are removed and replaced in the same manner.

PROP SHAFT

Cutless bearing replacement is not the only reason you may need to remove the prop shaft. The absence of a zinc collar can lead to destructive corrosion, especially of the threads for the prop nuts. An impact or a wrapped line can bend the shaft, causing severe vibration when underway. The rubber hose attaching the stuffing box to the stern tube can split. (If the hose is old, it is a very good idea to replace it while the shaft is out, split or not.)

The shaft is typically pressed into a flange and a setscrew is tightened against the shaft. The flange is bolted to a similar flange on the rear of the engine, forming the coupling. When the shaft is removed from the coupling, and the compression nut on the stuffing box eased, the shaft will simply slide out of the boat, providing the rudder does not interfere. What could be easier?

Unfortunately, getting the coupling off the shaft is usually a bastard. The first step is to soak the screws, bolts, and the coupling with penetrant and give the fluid time to help you as much as it can. Next remove any setscrews in the coupling and, just for fun, pull aft on the shaft. If it comes free of the coupling, make a large donation to your church. You owe.

For the less favored, the next step is to separate the two halves of the coupling. First, place the point of a sharp center punch on the edge of one of the flanges and tap it *lightly* with your hammer. Make a similar punch mark opposite the first one on the other flange. The two marks will allow you to reassemble the two halves exactly as they came apart. This is a good practice to follow whenever you disassemble parts that could be reassembled in different orientation.

Remove the bolts that hold the coupling together, using a six-point box-end wrench or a six-point socket to be sure the wrench will not slip. Slide the shaft back and note whether the end of the shaft is flush with the face of the flange or recessed. Now find four or five nuts and short bolts of different lengths to use as spacers. Tape the shortest spacer against the end of the shaft and slide the shaft forward, sandwiching the spacer in the middle of the coupling. Insert the coupling bolts and tighten *evenly*. As the flanges are pulled together, the shaft will be pressed out of the flange. Dismantle the coupling and replace the first spacer with a longer one. Reassemble the coupling and tighten. Repeat this procedure with increasingly longer spacers until the shaft comes free. The shaft will be keyed, so try not to lose the key in the bilge. Make sure the key is not still in the shaft when you try to slide it through the stuffing box and cutless bearing.

If the shaft doesn't budge, don't crank down on the coupling bolts until you warp or break the flange. Try expanding the flange with heat from a propane torch. Do not heat the half of the coupling attached to the engine, or you will destroy the rubber oil seal around the drive shaft.

Pressing the shaft back into the flange can be just as difficult. With very fine emery cloth, first polish the shaft and the bore in the coupling free of all imperfections. Insert the shaft through the stern tube and fit the key to the shaft. Spray the shaft and the bore with a lubricant such as WD-40 and slip the flange onto the shaft as far as it will go. From the forward side of the flange, measure the depth to the end of the shaft. While a helper holds the shaft, hold a block of wood against the flange and hit the wood with a hammer. The shaft will move aft despite the helper's grip, but we hope not before the flange slides further onto the shaft. After three or four blows, measure the depth again to see how you are progressing. If the flange is moving, keep pounding on the block until the shaft reaches the original depth in the flange.

You may be tempted to assemble the coupling and hammer the shaft into its bore from outside the boat. Forget about it. The transmission is not designed to be hammered on and is almost certain to suffer damage. But the transmission is designed to handle thrust; after all, it is the prop that pushes the boat. With a scrap timber (4 × 4, or similar) you can build a Rube Goldberg contraption to allow the shaft to be *pressed* into the coupling. Plant the lower end of the timber in an 8-inch deep hole in the ground and lash the upper end against the transom so that the timber stands directly behind the prop shaft and perpendicular to the angle of the shaft. Thread the prop nut onto the shaft to protect the end threads, and wedge a *small* hydraulic jack between the end of the shaft and the vertical timber, using wooden blocks as spacers. Be sure that the jack remains centered; if the timber is far from the shaft, a rigid support for the jack and spacers will be needed. As you pump the jack, the shaft will be pressed into the flange.

If you have difficulty getting the flange to go on the shaft, try packing the shaft in ice for a couple of hours, then heating the flange with a torch just before assembly. The combined effects may just give you the clearance you need. And try not to brand yourself, Pardner.

ENGINE ALIGNMENT

Replacing a cutless bearing or a prop shaft should not alter the engine alignment, but any time you have the coupling apart, you should check the align-

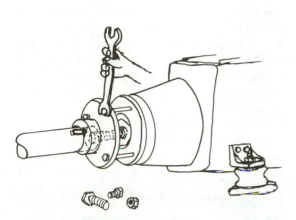

Place "spacers" between halves of the shaft coupling and *evenly* tighten coupling bolts to press out shaft.

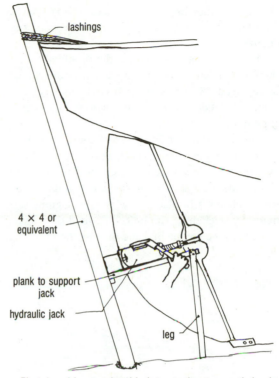

Plant 4 × 4 in ground and lash top to the stern so timber is directly behind the shaft and perpendicular to it. Use hydraulic jack to press shaft into assembled coupling.

Pressing the shaft flange off and on

ment. The fact that the mounting holes in the two halves of the coupling are in alignment is not sufficient. This is called *bore alignment* and it is checked by laying a straightedge across the two flanges at the top and bottom and both sides before the coupling is bolted together. The flexibility of a long, unsupported shaft can make the accuracy of the bore alignment difficult to determine.

Face alignment, the second step in the alignment process, is more exact. When the bolts are *snugged* to draw the halves together (not tightened fully), check the space between the halves. You will need a *feeler gauge,* an inexpensive tool that looks like a pocket knife with 15 or 20 blades. Each blade is etched with its thickness. Insert blades of the gauge

into any space you find until you determine the width of the gap.

If the gap is no more than .001 inch for every inch in diameter of the coupling, i.e., a .004-inch gap on a 4-inch coupling, the alignment is fine. Tighten the bolts, pick up your tools, and head for the light.

Should the gap be significantly wider, don't try to adjust it in the yard. I know you don't want to hear this, but the hull of your old boat distorts when it is lifted out of the water. That distortion may be causing the misalignment between the engine and the shaft. Wait until the boat is back in the water and check the gap again. If an alignment problem is indicated, release the bolts and turn the shaft flange

90 degrees, then bolt it back together and recheck. The location of the gap (relative to the unmoved engine flange) and the width of the gap should be unchanged; if the gap moved, the problem is with the coupling and you will have to have it machined or replaced. A consistent gap confirms face misalignment. You correct it by altering the engine alignment.

Engine alignment is easy to change, difficult to get right. Typically, four brackets on the engine sit over the threaded studs of the engine mounts, with a nut under each bracket to position it and a nut on top to clamp it in place. Side to side alignment is made by slackening the bolts that hold the engine mounts to the engine bed and moving the front, the

back, or the entire engine toward one side or the other. This is another instance in which a small hydraulic jack can be put to good use on a boat to shift the heavy engine incrementally. For vertical adjustments, the top nut on the engine mount is loosened, and the bottom nut is turned to raise or lower—depending upon which way you turn it—one corner of the engine.

If the gap in the coupling is at the top, you need to raise the front of the engine. Remember that you are dealing with thousandths of an inch, so adjustments should be small—$1/4$ of a turn or so. Adjusting the front mounts higher causes the part of the engine behind the rear mounts, including the coupling, to pivot downward. So when the face alignment is right, the bore alignment may now be off. Raising all of the mounts the same distance should correct that problem.

The only special skill required to align your engine is patience. Keep adjustments small and you will zero in on the right combination soon enough. Check the coupling one final time *after* you tighten all the engine mount nuts and bolts; the final tightening often throws the alignment out again. Releasing the top nuts and rechecking the alignment one mount at a time usually reveals which mount needs a little tweaking to make it come in right when it is retightened. See what I mean by patience?

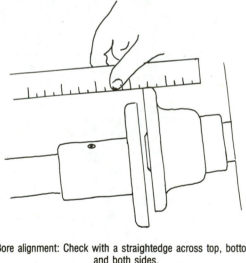

Bore alignment: Check with a straightedge across top, bottom, and both sides.

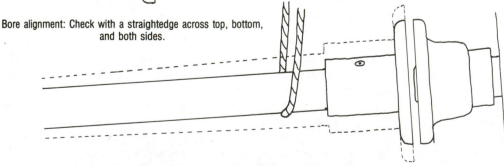

A long, unsupported shaft may "droop," throwing out bore alignment. Flex the shaft up and down to find the center and support the shaft in that position for alignment of the coupling.

Coupling alignment

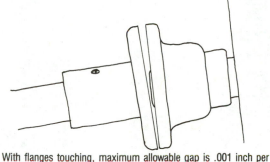

With flanges touching, maximum allowable gap is .001 inch per inch of coupling diameter.

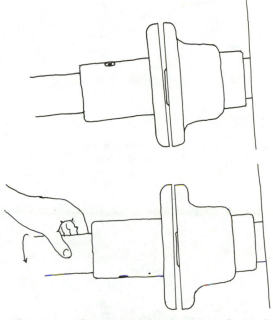

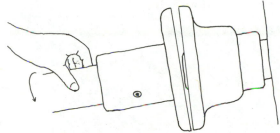

Face alignment: Rotating the shaft should not change the alignment. Correct by raising and/or lowering the engine mounts.

Flange runout: Rotating the shaft moves the gap. Flange will have to be machined or replaced.

Coupling alignment (continued)

ENGINES

Old boat usually means old engine. Old engine suggests more frequent breakdowns, or at least heightened concern about breakdown, but with an adequate maintenance program, this need not be the case. How much of your own engine work you elect to do is up to you, but doing ordinary maintenance and common repairs are no more difficult than servicing the sheet winches.

The objective of this chapter has *not* been to detail every mechanical repair that an old boat may require, but rather to expose you to a sampling of such repairs, illustrating their similarity and the limited number of skills necessary to effect those repairs and innumerable others. Likewise, the objective of the following is to expose you to a sampling of engine-servicing procedures requiring little more than a certain degree of proficiency with hand tools.

Oil Change

The most basic engine maintenance procedure is the oil change and it is no less essential when an engine is older. In an automobile engine, a threaded plug is removed from the bottom of the engine and the oil allowed to drain out. The drain plug on most marine engines is either inaccessible or nonexistent, so the oil is pumped out the dipstick tube.

The standard pump supplied by most engine manufacturers is a small brass piston pump with a length of hose or a reedllike brass tube to insert into the dipstick opening. The agonizing inefficiency of this system has sent many a skipper in search of a better way. Most catalogs carry half a dozen alternative pumps, including one that lists for more than $180.

Save your money. There is nothing wrong with the piston pump. The real problem is the size of the siphon hose; it is like trying to suck molasses

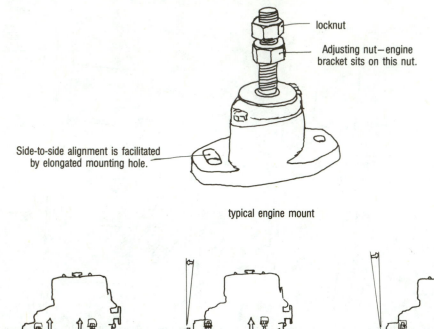

locknut

Adjusting nut—engine
bracket sits on this nut.

Side-to-side alignment is facilitated
by elongated mounting hole.

typical engine mount

Raising front and rear mounts raises the
flange (bore misalignment correction).

Raising front mounts moves the top of
the flange aft (face misalignment
correction).

Lowering front mounts moves the top of
the flange forward.

Adjusting engine alignment

through a soda straw. The solution is available at your hardware store for less than two bucks. Buy a foot or two of ¼-inch copper tubing—you will find it in the plumbing section. Straightened out, it will just slip into the dipstick tube. Be sure it reaches all the way to the bottom of the crankcase, and connect the upper end to the pump with the adapter for the supplied suction hose.

Before you begin an oil change, the engine should be hot. Hot oil is much easier to suck through your copper straw, but the reason for running the engine first is more essential than that. You are changing the oil because it is dirty, and the abrasive impurities cause piston rings and bearings and other internal parts to wear. So periodically you remove the dirty oil and put in clean oil. Except that the dirt in oil is just like dirt in water; leave it undis-

turbed and it will settle to the bottom. Suck out the cold oil and most of the dirt stays behind, immediately contaminating the fresh oil and defeating the whole purpose of the oil change. Run the engine and get all of the contaminants in suspension so they come out with the oil.

Save a plastic milk jug as a receptacle for your old oil. The small opening will keep the outlet hose under control, and the capped jug is convenient for transporting the old oil to the reclamation receptacle in the marina or at a nearby service station. Wrap a thick towel around the pump before you suck hot oil through it unless your past would make the loss of your fingerprints a desirable consequence.

Regardless of the manufacturer's recommendations, change the oil filter every time you change the oil. Most oil filters are the "spin-on" variety and they

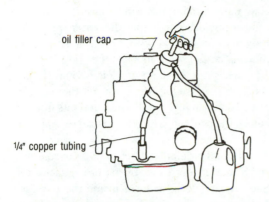

oil filler cap

¼" copper tubing

Pump the old oil out the dipstick tube. Use the largest copper tubing that will fit into the dipstick tube. Engine should be hot.

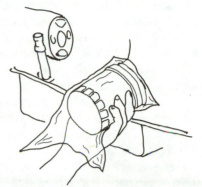

A plastic bag can minimize the mess when removing a spin-on filter . . .

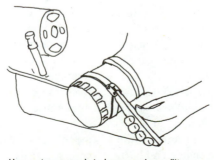

or a cartridge filter . . . .

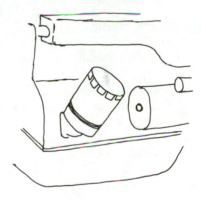

Forget it!

Use a strap wrench to loosen spin-on filters.

Oil and filter change

are simply unscrewed and thrown away. Removing them requires a strap wrench that grips the canister when pressure is applied to the handle. If the wrench slips, take it off the filter and reverse it; it only works in one direction. Lightly coat the gasket of the new filter with oil before screwing it in place. Hand tighten until the gasket makes full contact, then tighten another ³/₄ of a turn.

Some engines are equipped with cartridge-type oil filters. Typically a center bolt holds the filter housing in place. Release the bolt and remove the canister. Empty it and discard the old cartridge. Clean the housing with diesel fuel (or kerosene) and insert the new cartridge. If a separate sealing ring is included with the cartridge, carefully pry the old seal out of its seat by pricking it with a straight pin. Coat the new seal with oil, and push it into position. Reinstall the canister.

Virtually every other kind of filter you will encounter sits vertically so the fluid it contains does not spill when the filter is opened, but for some reason that totally eludes me, engine designers mount oil filters at an angle, horizontally, even upside down. You can guess what happens when you open them. For all but the upside-down variety, you can contain the spilling oil by slipping a freezer bag over the filter and its fitting before you break the seal, unscrewing the filter inside the bag.

Coolant

The heat generated when internal combustion engines burn their fuel would soon evaporate the lubricating oil if the cylinders were not cooled. In a marine engine, cooling is accomplished by circulating water through drilled and cast passages inside the engine. The water absorbs the heat and carries it out of the engine.

Many older engines are raw-water cooled. Raw-water cooling (also called direct cooling) seems like a good idea. After all, the boat is floating in water. What could be easier than drawing in some of the ocean and pumping it through the engine and back over the side? Nothing. The manufacturer did it that way because it was the easiest—not because it was best.

Raw water cooling has three serious problems. The most obvious one is that the water we do our boating in is not always crystal clear and whatever extraneous particles are in the water flow through the engine; some of them are left behind. Intake filters screen out the big stuff, but not the particles in suspension. Enough mud, sand, and bits of weed will block the cooling passages and lead to overheating and damage.

The second problem applies to boats used in salt water. Seawater, corrosive by nature, attacks the engine, causing scale to form inside the passages and chambers. The scale inhibits the transfer of heat from the cylinders to the coolant.

The least obvious and most serious drawback to raw-water cooling is the inability to regulate and optimize engine temperature. Clearly the temperature of the lake or ocean may vary widely, but it is the absence of a thermostat that most limits regulation. The thermostat is a valve that remains closed, restricting most of the coolant flow until the coolant reaches a certain temperature; then the valve opens and remains open unless the temperature of the coolant drops below the specified number. The straight-through nature of raw-water cooling generally prohibits the use of a thermostat, and even when the system is configured to allow its inclusion, it is prone to failure from contaminants.

When a raw-water system does include a thermostat, it is set to open at around 135 degrees Fahrenheit because the rate of scale formation and salt deposits accelerates markedly when the coolant temperature reaches 160 degrees Fahrenheit. Unfortunately, particularly in a diesel engine, this is just trading one problem for two others. To run efficiently, diesel engines need to operate at higher temperatures—around 185 degrees Fahrenheit. Even more serious, the lower operating temperatures cause condensation to form inside the cylinders, and condensation washes the oil from the cylinder walls, contaminates the oil, and forms corrosive acids which attacks the bearings and other internal parts.

If you plan to live with your old engine for a while, give serious thought to converting to indirect or freshwater cooling. As in the system on your car, fresh water circulates through the engine, but instead of dissipating the heat into the air through a radiator, heat is transferred to the surrounding water through a keel cooler or a heat exchanger.

A keel cooler is basically a length of piping attached to the hull below the water. The hot fresh water circulates through it, giving up heat, through the walls of the cooler, to the outside water. Because of the additional drag they represent, the plumbing through the hull, and their vulnerability, I have never seen a keel cooler on a production sailboat, but they are not uncommon in powerboats.

A heat exchanger operates on the same principle except that the cooling tubes remain inside the boat, enclosed in a container that has raw water pumped through it. Pumping the raw water requires an additional pump, but the benefits of freshwater cooling are well worth this added complication. Besides avoiding the disadvantages of direct cooling, a freshwater system allows the introduction of antifreeze and corrosion inhibitors. It also allows the coolant to be held under pressure, which raises the boiling point of the coolant and allows the engine to operate safely at higher temperatures.

Maintaining the cooling system requires little more than keeping the coolant flowing. Raw water, whether it is destined for the engine or the heat exchanger, should first pass through a strainer, and the strainer requires periodic cleaning. New strainers have a screw-off lid and a lift-out basket, but older models require the release of several wing nuts and disassembly of the entire unit. Be sure the inlet seacock is closed before you start. Rinse the screen, scrubbing it with a brush if necessary. Reassemble, being careful to seat the clear body on the rubber gaskets. Tighten the screws evenly. Open the seacock and check the strainer for leaks.

When the seacock is open, keep in mind that the only thing keeping the ocean out of your boat is the thin wall of a rubber hose. Hoses don't last forever, and the consequences of failure can be pretty dramatic. A spongy or brittle hose in the freshwater circuit may not sink the boat, but it certainly puts the engine at risk. You should twist and squeeze every inch of hose in the engine compartment. If a hose feels soft or brittle or shows any signs of swelling or cracking, replace it. Hoses can seem fine from the outside and still be crumbling inside, packing water passages with bits of rubber. If I bought an old boat and did not *know* the age of the hoses, I would replace them all. Waiting does not avoid the expenditure, only delays it, and at considerable risk. Hose replacement is detailed fully in Chapter 12.

Water Pump

On the freshwater side of a cooling system, you may find a centrifugal pump, the same type of pump that is on your car. Centrifugal pumps rarely fail, and when they do—indicated by water dripping from a hole in the bottom of the pump—they are simply replaced. But they are intolerant of foreign matter and are not used as raw-water pumps.

On the raw-water side, you are almost certain to encounter a rubber impeller-type pump. It will pass twigs and pebbles and small pilchards, but stop the flow of water to it and the impeller will shed blades like leaves in an October storm. Why should the flow stop? Someone forgot to open the seacock. The intake sucked in the plastic ice bag you let blow overboard the previous week. Vigorous sailing lifted the intake out of the water, causing an air lock.

Checking the exhaust for spray every time you start the engine can sometimes prevent impeller damage if you react to a dry exhaust quickly, and it can keep you from deserting the security of a dock or mooring only to find yourself dead in the water moments later. But sooner or later the pump will fail despite your vigilance.

Replacing a water pump impeller is usually easier than describing the procedure. With the seacock closed, remove the six machine screws that hold the pump's cover plate in place. The impeller will be exposed and if you can grip it, you can probably slide it out. If you can't grip it, adjust the jaw width of your channel-lock pliers to approximately the diameter of the impeller hub, and grip the impeller. It should come out without too much coaxing.

The shaft is usually splined, but it might have a flat surface or two that mates with similar flats in the impeller hub. Impellers are occasionally keyed or pinned in place. On my engine, a half-round notch in the impeller hub slips over a round pin that sits loosely on a flat spot on the shaft. The pins dive for the bilge every time I pull an impeller, but I have learned to spread a towel under the pump before I start.

If the vanes are broken, the impeller must be replaced. Check at the base of each vane by bending it vigorously; any cracks and the impeller is history. If vanes have torn off, be sure you can account for all the pieces, particularly if the engine is raw-water cooled; if the pieces pass downstream, they will block the water passages and cause damage.

While the impeller is out, check the shaft for wobble. If it seems loose to you, you may need to dismantle the entire pump and replace the bearings and the seals. For the specifics of doing that, you will need to consult a service manual.

Replacing the impeller will be easier if you tie the blades into a folded position with a couple of pieces of 1/4-inch braided line. Tie the lines into two loops and work them over the vanes, one on each side of the impeller. It doesn't really matter which way you bend the vanes; they will arrange themselves on the first revolution of the pump.

Lightly grease the inside of the pump housing with Vaseline to minimize friction on those first few dry turns when the impeller first starts. The Vaseline will also make it easier to slide the new impeller into the housing. Line up the hub with the shaft and push the impeller in place, sliding the loops of line forward as the impeller slides into the housing. Replace the O-ring or the gasket under the cover and screw the cover in place. Open the seacock.

Some pumps, my own included, have dual chambers. A single shaft drives two impellers, one for raw water and the other for fresh water. Instead of a cover plate, the six bolts release the forward half of the pump housing, which slides off the impeller instead of the other way around. Beyond that, disassembly and servicing of this design are the same as those for any other impeller-type pump.

Remove the pump cover.

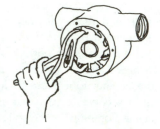

Pull the impeller from the shaft.

Check the impeller for *any* cracks at the base of the vanes.

The new impeller will be easier to install if you collapse the vanes with a heavy rubber band or a loop of line.

Flexible impeller replacement

Fit a new gasket (or O-ring).

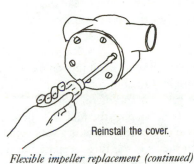

Reinstall the cover.

Flexible impeller replacement (continued)

Water pumps may be either gear-driven or belt-driven. Eventually the seals on gear-driven pumps fail and water begins to flow into the engine, turning the oil into something resembling chocolate milk, and with similar lubricating properties, I fear. New pump-shaft bearings and seals and a couple of back-to-back oil changes can save the day, but exactly what are the future implications?

To prevent a recurrence, or to prevent it from happening in the first place, replace the bearings and seals regularly—every two years, for example. An alternative favored by many is to remove the pump entirely and close the opening with a metal plate. In its place, a belt-driven pump is bracketed to the engine, eliminating the water pump from the list of ways water can find its way inside the engine.

Belt Tension

Whether the V-belt is driving a water pump, an alternator, or a refrigeration compressor, you check the tension by pushing down on the belt in the middle of its widest span. It should deflect about 1/2 inch, less if the span is short. While you are checking, run your fingers along the underside of the belt to make sure it isn't cracked or torn, or visually inspect notched belts. Do I need to point out that the engine is not running when you are messing with V-belts? The back of the belt should be more or less flush with the shoulders of the drive pulleys; if it sits deeply into the pulley, the belt is worn and should be replaced.

Replacement and correct tension are almost always achieved in one of two methods—either by adjusting the position of the driven device or by adjusting the position of an idler pulley. Most often the alternator is hinged to the engine with a single bolt and is held away from the engine with a second bolt through a slotted bracket. Adjustment is accomplished by loosening (not removing) the pivot bolt, the adjusting bolt, and the bolt that attaches the slotted bracket to the engine. With all three loose, the alternator will collapse against the engine, allowing the old belt to be removed and the new one put in its place. Your manual will give you the belt size, or the supplier can determine it from the old one.

Adjustment is a matter of pulling the alternator away from the engine until the belt is tight, then tightening the adjusting bolt. If the adjusting bolt threads into the alternator, this is a simple process, but far too often the adjusting bolt is tightened with a nut. You need one hand for the wrench on the bolt, one for the wrench on the nut, and one to keep tension on the alternator. Unless your last employer was Barnum and Bailey, that is a tall order. You may be able to wedge one of the wrenches in place or wedge the alternator into position.

Limited access to the alternator may make it impossible to exert enough pull on it to achieve adequate belt tension. In such a case, insert a large wrench between the alternator and the engine and use the wrench as a lever to multiply the pull on the alternator. Make sure the end of the wrench rests against the engine block and not on a fuel line, wiring, or a freeze plug. Always tighten the adjusting bolt first, then the other two. Recheck the belt tension after all three bolts are tightened. If you have installed a new belt, check the tension again after the first few hours of engine time.

Some belt-driven devices are rigidly mounted

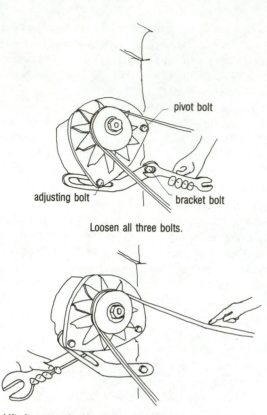

Loosen all three bolts.

Lift alternator, checking belt tension by pressing the center of the belt span. Deflection of ¼ inch to ½ inch is okay.

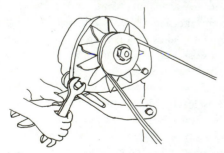

Maintaining tension on the belt, tighten the adjusting bolt, then tighten the other two bolts.

Adjusting belt tension

and belt tension is adjusted with an idler pulley. The idler pulley is mounted on a pivoting arm, and when the mounting bolt is loosened, the arm can be rotated to push the pulley against the belt. An open-end wrench fitted to flats on the pivoting arm

behind the pulley provides the leverage necessary to achieve the desired tension. While the pulley is held in position, the mounting bolt is tightened.

At least once a year, the idler pulley should be removed from the pivot arm and the bearing cleaned in diesel fuel and repacked with water-pump grease. If the pulley is loose or noisy, the bearing should be replaced. Take the old bearing to a bearing supplier and he will match it.

Fuel

It is essential to keep all fuel connections tight, but the primary reasons for this imperative are different for gasoline and diesel engines. When gasoline is the fuel, keeping the fuel *in* is the objective; gasoline leaking inside a boat is a very serious matter. When diesel is the fuel, keeping the fuel in is secondary to keeping *air* out; the slightest leak in the fuel system will stop the engine and it will not start again until the fuel system is airtight.

Weeping around a fuel fitting can usually be corrected by tightening the nut *slightly*. If you really crank down on a flair or compression fitting, you will just distort it and it will leak more. If tightening doesn't stop the leak, dismantle the fitting and clean all the surfaces. A bit of grease on the back side of the flange or ferrule—not on the mating surfaces—can help the nut to compress the fitting more evenly. Reassemble the fitting with a slightly different orientation between the two parts, and tighten. If all else fails, replace the fitting or the line or both.

While a fuel filter on a gasoline engine has much to recommend it, it is a discretionary accessory. Fuel *filters*—plural—are not optional when the engine is a diesel. Gasoline is sprayed into the intake manifold with about the pressure of a cologne atomizer, but diesel is injected directly into the cylinder at the moment that the compression forces in the cylinder are the highest. The tolerances of the pump that puts the fuel under such high pressure are incredibly small, as close as 0.00004 inches, and the holes in injector nozzles are barely larger than a human hair. Any fuel impurities that reach the pump or the injectors are almost certain to cause problems.

Diesel engines almost always come with an

attached fuel filter. It is located between the dia-phragm lift pump (fuel pump) and the high-precision injection pump. The filter's purpose is to arrest the finest particle impurities before they reach the injection system. Despite the fact that it is the only filter supplied by most manufacturers, it is universally referred to as a *secondary* filter. That label begs a question.

The answer is that before the fuel ever reaches the engine, it should pass through a remotely-mounted *primary* filter. The primary filter prevents most particle contaminants from ever reaching the secondary filter, and, perhaps most important, it removes moisture from the fuel. If a droplet of water reaches the tip of an injector, the superheated air of the cylinder will convert it to steam instantly, blowing the tip off like a tiny boiler explosion. Then the tip plays ping-pong inside the cylinder. Oh boy.

To keep this from ever happening, be sure you have a primary filter, be sure it also acts as a water separator (or install a separate water separator in the line) and regularly drain out the water that accumulates in the bowl. The filter will have a plug or a petcock in the bottom. Open it and drain the filter into a container until only fuel runs out, then close the petcock.

Replace the filter elements according to the engine manufacturer's recommendations. Replac-ing a fuel filter is very little different from replacing a cartridge-type oil filter. But before you start, thoroughly clean the outside of the canister and all the area around it; it is essential not to accidentally introduce dirt into the fuel system. As with the oil filters, you can minimize the mess if you slip a freezer bag over the canister before you open it. Wash the canister thoroughly in *clean* fuel before you install the new filter cartridge.

Filter replacement is only one of the ways air can get into the fuel system. A cracked fitting, running out of fuel, heeling enough to uncover the fuel pickup, or just sloshing around in rough conditions are among the other ways. Any time air enters the fuel system, bleeding will be required.

New diesels are often self-bleeding (sounds masochistic to me), but if you have an old engine you will have to bleed it manually. Following a filter change, the first step is to refill the filters with fuel. The standard procedure is to pump the little handle on the lift pump, but it can take a lot of pumps to fill a large primary filter. If you pressurize the fuel tank, you can get the filter to fill easily and sometimes even bleed the entire system without using the lift pump. Forcing air into the vent with a bicycle pump will force the fuel through the lines, provided you open one of the bleed screws so trapped air can escape. Use your imagination on sealing the vent; I

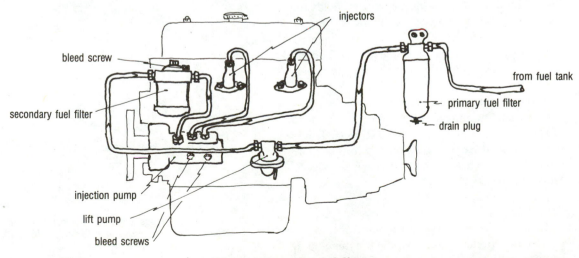

Primary and secondary fuel filters

cut a short section of hose that fits tightly around my round vent fitting and punctured the hose with an ice pick. I inserted a standard inflator needle through the hole and pump. You don't want a lot of pressure; you are not trying to inflate the tank, just put the fuel under pressure.

The lift pump will also do the job. Open the bleed screw on the secondary filter with a box-end wrench. You do not remove bleed screws; just loosen them about ¼ turn. Pump the lift pump handle with firm strokes until fuel begins to run out the open bleed screw. If the pump handle seems to have little or no travel, the engine has stopped with the cam drive holding the pump in the full stroke position; turn the engine a half revolution with the hand crank or by "kicking" the starter.

At first the fuel will bubble and spit from the bleed screw, but you want to keep pumping until the fuel runs out bubble free. When that happens, hold a downstroke on the pump lever and close the bleed screw.

There are usually two bleed screws on the side of the injection pump. Open the one closest to the filter and work the pump handle until clear fuel runs from the screw. Again hold the pump on a down-stroke and close the screw. Repeat the process for the second screw. Now try the engine. If it starts and runs smoothly, you are finished. If it starts and runs roughly you still have air in one of the injector lines. Very carefully, loosen the nut that holds the fuel line to the injector nearest the injector pump. Count to five and retighten it; do not overtighten. Bleed the remaining injectors in sequence. You can stop if the engine smooths out before you have bled them all.

If the engine has failed to start, bleed the entire system again, beginning with the bleed screw on top of the secondary filter. Don't be discouraged—it is not unusual to have to go through the procedure more than once to get all of the air out of the system.

Tune-up

Gasoline engines require periodic tune-ups to continue to perform well. Typically a tune-up is comprised of installing new spark plugs, replacing

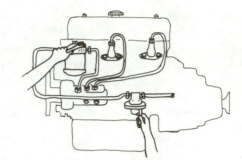

Open the bleed screw on the secondary filter housing and pump the lever on the transfer pump. When clear fuel—without bubbles—runs from the open screw, hold a downstroke on the lever and close the bleed screw.

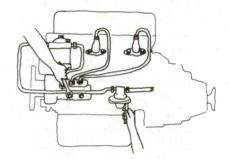

Pump clear fuel from every other bleed screw, beginning with the one closest to the filter.

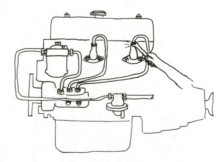

Start the engine. If it runs rough, *carefully* loosen the fuel connection to each injector, allowing it to evacuate fuel for 5 seconds, then retighten.

Bleeding the fuel system

the ignition points and adjusting the gap, checking the ignition timing, and adjusting the carburetor.

To remove and replace spark plugs, you need a plug socket for your ratchet handle. A plug socket is a deep socket with a rubber insert to protect the porcelain part of the plug. They come in more than one size, so take a new spark plug with you when you buy the socket; you probably need the traditional 13/16 inch.

Replacing the plugs one at a time will keep you from getting the wires confused. Pull the wire off the end of the plug. Remove the old plug. Consult the engine manual for the appropriate spark plug gap, and check the new plug with a feeler gauge or a special gap gauge—don't assume that the factory setting is correct. Put a couple of drops of oil on the threads and install the new plug with your fingers; it should screw in easily. Tighten, but don't lean on the wrench—you definitely do not want to strip the threads from the hole.

Slip a screwdriver blade between the distributor cap and the mounting clips and gently twist the screwdriver to release the clips. Lift off the cap and turn it upside down. If the copper terminals inside are not shiny, polish them with a small file; if they are badly pitted, replace the cap.

Pull the rotor from its shaft and polish its tip with a file or, if it is badly burned, replace it. Pull the point wire from its terminal and loosen the screw holding the breaker points. Inserting the screw in the new points before you put them in place will make it easier to reinstall the screw. Snug the screw. Now rotate the engine and you will see the cam-shaped shaft opening the points. Buying a large socket to fit the nut in the center of the crankshaft will make rotating the engine much easier. Stop the engine with the points resting on the apex of one of the high spots; this represents the widest opening of the points. Loosen the mounting screw just enough to allow the points to move. Adjustment is facilitated with a second screwdriver inserted in the notch in the base of the points. Two metal bumps on the distributor plate act as fulcrum points, allowing you to move the points by twisting the screwdriver.

Using the appropriate feeler gauge—check the engine manual—move the base until the feeler gauge just touches both points without moving the movable arm. Tighten the screw and check again; turning the screw often alters the setting. Smear the cam lightly with Vaseline. Put a single drop of oil inside the rotor and seat it on the shaft. Reinstall the distributor cap and snap the spring clamps in place.

Timing is exactly when the spark plug fires. If it fires too soon, the combustion will take place while the piston is still on the way up, actually opposing that motion. If it fires too late, the opportunity to get the maximum power from the combustion is missed. Timing is adjusted by slackening the bolt or nut at the base of the distributor and turning the distributor. The distributor shaft is unaffected by this movement, but you are moving the points, which are screwed to the distributor. It is easy to see that if you move the points in the same direction the shaft rotates, the high point on the cam will reach the points later, causing ignition to be later. This is called *retarding* the timing. Turning the distributor the other direction—opposite the rotation of the distributor shaft—is *advancing* the timing.

A rough adjustment is accomplished by lining up the timing mark on the flywheel or the crankshaft pulley (depending upon the engine) with a pointer. The breaker points should be just opening. The best way to check this is to stop the engine a few degrees before the mark and insert a single thickness of tissue paper. Now rotate the engine slowly, pulling gently on the tissue. When the points release their grip on the tissue—they are just opening—stop rotating. If the timing is correct the pointer and the mark will be in line.

A more accurate way of adjusting the timing requires the use of a timing light, a device that is connected to the engine so that the light flashes at the same time that the spark plug fires. From your disco days, you can probably see the reason for this—the bright flash "freezes" the timing mark. By turning the distributor while the engine is running at a specific speed, you can move the frozen mark until it lines up with the pointer, then tighten the clamp bolt to lock in the setting.

Automotive carburetors from a couple of decades back are nightmares of jets, linkage, pumps, and valves, but you won't find dual quads on an old Atomic Four. Carburetors on old marine engines are short on sophistication, even shorter on complexity. You are faced with only two adjustments—fuel mixture and idle speed.

The needle valve to adjust fuel mixture will be a brass screw in the side of the carburetor. With the engine at normal operating temperature, set the throttle to fast idle—about 800 rpm—and turn the screw counterclockwise about ¼ turn. Turning the screw to the left opens the fuel jet and makes the mixture richer. Wait about 15 seconds to allow the adjustment to affect the engine. If the engine speeds up, give the screw another ¼ turn to the left; if it slows or becomes erratic, turn the screw clockwise back to the original setting and ¼ turn beyond. Continue to turn the screw every 15 seconds until further adjustments fail to increase engine speed, returning to the setting yielding the highest steady engine speed. Now turn the screw counterclockwise ⅛ turn to offset the tendency of the setting to be too lean at slow speeds.

The idle screw is on the linkage and restricts the travel of the throttle; it is screwed against the stop to raise idle speed, backed off to lower it. After you have adjusted the mixture, set the idle to about 600 rpm.

Carburetors should be dismantled and cleaned every couple of years. Disconnect the fuel line, release the control cables, remove the mounting nuts, and pull the carburetor from the manifold. Don't worry about damaging the mounting gasket; the rebuild kit you are going to buy will include a new one along with all the other gaskets and washers you need. Disassemble the carburetor, laying out the parts in order and talking to your tape recorder as you go. Soak all the parts that are not plastic with a powerful carburetor cleaner, using a brush on stubborn deposits. Use gasoline to clean the plastic parts. Make sure all old gasket material has been removed (including any left on the intake manifold). Dry the parts and, if you have compressed air available, blow out all the passages. Reassemble and reinstall, then adjust the mixture and the idle.

Injectors

There is no such thing as a diesel "tune-up." The only thing that might be so considered is servicing the fuel injectors, and that is not something the owner can do properly. What you can do is remove the injectors and take them to an injection shop for cleaning and adjustment.

Before you remove them, clean all around the injector for reasons you already know. Disconnect the high-pressure fuel line; you may have to release it from the injection pump as well to get it out of the way. Also disconnect the return line. Do not lose any of the copper washers that seal these lines. Put plastic tape over the open connections.

The injector is held in place by a metal yoke attached to the engine with two bolts. (Some injectors screw directly into the engine.) Remove the bolts and you should be able to withdraw the injector. If it does not come out easily, run penetrant around the outside and try again in an hour or two. Put a wrench on the flat sides of the injector and twist it back and forth, lifting at the same time. The injector seats on a copper washer; be sure you pay attention to how it comes out.

Once the injector is out, do not disassemble it; take the entire assembly to the injector shop. While the injectors are out of the engine, cover the openings. When you reinstall the injectors, the holddown bolts must be evenly torqued, using a torque wrench. Consult your manual for the correct torque. If your book does not provide this number, torque the bolts to 15 foot-pounds. When you reconnect the feed and return lines, they must fit without any forcing. Thread both ends hand tight before finally tightening either.

Valve Adjustment

You are ready to try your hand at working *inside* the engine. The first thing you need to do is consult your engine manual to see what the valve settings are and if they are set *hot* or *cold*. Hope for cold!

Usually two or more cap nuts secure the valve cover. Remove the nuts and lift off the cover carefully, trying not to tear the gasket beneath it. If the gasket is in good condition and still resilient, you won't need to replace it; if it is brittle, get a new one.

Underneath the valve cover you will discover two rocker arms—looking like little oilfield pumps—for every cylinder, one for the intake valve and one for the exhaust valve. One side of the rocker sits directly on the valve stem and the other side has a screw through it which seats in a cup at the top of the push rod. Valve clearance is adjusted by turning this screw. The bottom of the push rod, which you cannot see, rides on the camshaft which moves the push rod up and down.

Valves should be set when the piston is at TDC (top dead center) on the compression stroke. The easiest way to determine this is to watch the rocker arms while you rotate the engine. When the two arms for a single cylinder are moving at the same time you have *valve overlap*. Overlap only occurs near TDC of the exhaust stroke, when the exhaust valve is just closing and the intake valve is just beginning to open. When overlap occurs, mark the crankshaft pulley with chalk, then rotate the engine one full revolution. That cylinder is now at TDC of the compression stroke and both valves may be checked and adjusted if required.

Simply slip the feeler gauge between the rocker arm and the valve stem on each valve. It should slide between the two with a bit of resistance. If it is too loose or too tight, adjustment is required. If valve clearances are too loose, the engine will not deliver full power and the valves will be noisy. If clearances are too tight, the valves may fail to seat properly, resulting in burned valves and an expensive repair job. Get them set right.

This is another job where three hands would be helpful. Put a box-end wrench on the lock nut and insert a screwdriver in the adjusting screw. Holding the screw in position, release the lock nut. Now turn the adjusting screw while you slide the feeler gauge back and forth between the rocker arm and the valve stem. When the rocker arm begins to "pinch" the gauge, hold the screw in position and tighten the lock nut. Check the setting again and readjust it if you are not satisfied. Adjust the other valve.

Rotate the engine to bring the next pair of valves to overlap, then one full revolution to bring that

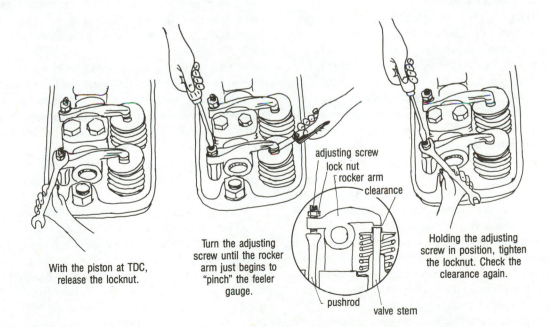

With the piston at TDC, release the locknut.

Turn the adjusting screw until the rocker arm just begins to "pinch" the feeler gauge.

adjusting screw
lock nut
rocker arm
clearance

pushrod   valve stem

Holding the adjusting screw in position, tighten the locknut. Check the clearance again.

Adjusting valves

cylinder to TDC on the compression stroke. Check both valves and adjust as required. Proceed through every cylinder. Reseat the valve cover and tighten the hold-down nuts.

Major Repairs

When it comes to engine repairs, it is time to wake up and smell the coffee. No one *fixes* anything anymore. The offending part is *replaced* or *sent out*. You can do that.

If you are afraid you might screw up the repair, forget about it. Think about the last time you took your car to a "factory-trained" mechanic. You were charged a fair price, every problem was corrected, and you never had to take your car back to have the repair repaired. Yeah, right! Did you ever wonder how a well-known auto company expected to enhance its sales by spending millions to tell us what terrific mechanics they have to fix the product when it breaks down? Would you buy a television from a company that touted the experience of their repair technicians? How about a pacemaker from a company that featured a scrub-wearing and scalpel-wielding Mr. Goodheart?

I'm sorry. Where were we? Engine repair, right? The number of different engines makes detailing specific repairs impossible, and I am not trying to make an engine mechanic out of you anyway. I am only trying to show you that if you want to repair your own engine, regardless of how extensive the repair, the process of dismantling and reassembly will be largely the same as those we have detailed.

The starter fails. A mechanic will check the battery and the switch (which you should have done before calling a mechanic), then remove the three nuts that hold the wires to the solenoid and the two screws that fasten the starter to the engine, and pull the starter out of the engine. He will take it to a starter repair shop and pick it up when the repair is finished. Back on board, he slides it back in place, secures it with the two mounting screws, and reconnects the wires. Is there any part of this repair that requires special training?

Despite a tune-up, your gas engine runs poorly. With the help of a knowledgeable friend, you check the compression of each cylinder and find it low in two. You squirt motor oil into the cylinders and check them again; they still have low compression. Three parts seal the cylinder: the head gasket, the piston rings, and the valves. If the piston rings are worn, the oil will temporarily seal them, raising the compression; if it doesn't, you need a valve job (or there is a problem with the head gasket—either way the head needs to come off).

You need to take the cylinder head to a machine shop to have the valves reconditioned. Removing a cylinder head is clearly more complicated than removing a starter, but most requirements are pretty straightforward. Everything attached to the head has to be removed, including intake and exhaust manifolds; and all the head bolts, most located under the valve cover, have to be loosened and extracted. But some requirements are more subtle. Coolant must be drained at least below the level of the head and the head bolts should be released in a specific sequence. Reassembly requires that each part is returned to its original position—you should never switch around push rods even though they seem identical—and that the head bolts are tightened to a specific torque in a specific sequence. Learn the requirements and the process will not be difficult.

What if the engine is completely worn out? It will have to be removed from the boat to be rebuilt. How complicated is that? The engine is attached to the boat with four mounts, to the shaft with a coupling, and to the exhaust system with a flange, all of which we have already seen how to disassemble. Other connections to the engine are wires, hoses, and fuel lines. Label each when you take them apart and you should be able to put them back together.

What about the actual removal? I removed my own 500-pound engine with a 2×12 and a small hydraulic jack. With the plank wedged under the engine, the jack applied the leverage to lift the engine from the bed. The plank was blocked in position and the jack moved behind the engine and used to push it, sliding the engine along the plank out of the engine compartment and into the main cabin beneath the companionway. A block and tackle from the boom lifted the engine into the cockpit, and the boom was used to swing it onto a wheeled dolly on the dock.

Which only shows that it can be done. The truth is that if money was not a factor, my pianist hands would never be soiled by engine grease. But money is a factor, and there is a second consideration. My boating often takes me far offshore and hundreds of miles from the nearest trained mechanic. It is a comforting feeling to know that if the engine quits, I can almost certainly get it going again.

There is more to being a competent engine mechanic than just skill with tools. You have to be able to diagnose the problem. If you don't know what is wrong, you can spend a lot of time and money on unnecessary repairs. You will be better off to seek professional assistance. With experience, engines and other mechanical devices will hold fewer mysteries. If you understand the problem, you can almost certainly make the repair.

If you do decide to be your own mechanic, the tool that will help you the most is a service manual—not the little owner's brochure that came with the engine, but the detailed manual supplied to service representatives. If there was not one aboard when you bought the boat, contact the engine manufacturer. Don't bitch about the cost; it will be worth every penny.

Repowering

A lot of old sailboats were delivered with gasoline engines. Today it is virtually impossible to buy a new sailboat with a gasoline inboard. There are three reasons for this evolution.

Because of its volatility, gasoline is an inherently dangerous fuel. In an automobile, a fuel line leak drips gasoline on the street. The same leak on a marine engine fills the bilge with explosive fumes, turning the boat into a potential bomb.

Gasoline engines require ignition systems, which do not survive well in the wet environment of boats. Plug the dipstick hole and put a snorkel on the air intake and a diesel engine will run *under* water.

The danger and lack of reliability of gasoline marine engines are recognized by the majority of the boating public and depresses the resale value of gasoline-powered boats. The depreciation (and the difficulty in finding secondary buyers) is greater than the additional expense of equipping the boat with a diesel engine initially.

If you are planning to keep a boat for a long time, it always makes sense to repower with diesel. Even if you plan to sell, repowering *can* add more to the resale value than the cost of the conversion—but not always. Do some price comparison.

Can you do the conversion yourself? If you have discovered that you are reasonably handy, the answer is yes—at least you *can* do most of it.

It would be great if you could just yank out the old gasoline engine and slip the new diesel in place, dropping it onto the old mounts and coupling it to the prop shaft. But it just doesn't work that way. You may have to replace not just the mounts but the entire engine bed. Never mind the coupling; the prop shaft may have to be shortened or replaced with a longer one. And you have to make certain beforehand that the new engine will fit inside the engine compartment.

Selecting an engine that you have seen installed in a boat like your own can allay concerns about fit, and the engine supplier can provide you with all the engineering data. But modifying or replacing the engine bed and locating the new mounts so that when you set the engine in place it lines up perfectly with the prop shaft is not a task to be taken lightly. Expect the job to require at least 50 man-hours and be prepared for it to take twice that.

If you have the inclination and you are willing to commit the time, go for it. Doing the job yourself will save you just about half the cost of having it done, and it will be a tremendous learning experience. Even if what you learn is that you were over-optimistic about your abilities, you can always bail out and pay to have it completed. More likely, you will encounter far fewer problems than you might have imagined and learn more than you might have expected. And, of course, there is the pleasure of a new engine. It is worth considering.

TEN

Chips and Shavings

People love chopping wood.
In this activity, one immediately sees results.
–ALBERT EINSTEIN–

The emergence of fiberglass as the dominant material in pleasureboat construction has not eliminated the need for woodworking skills. Interior fittings–bulkheads, soles, furniture, shelves, and ceiling–are all constructed of wood. On deck of most old fiberglass boats you will find wooden handrails, hatch frames, coamings, toerails, and tillers. You may also find wooden overlay on the decks.

This chapter is about working with wood, but it is not about repairing ribs or replacing planking. It does not contain a comparison of steam-bent versus laminated frames nor an explanation of other structural components. To me, carlings is a beer, knees are troublesome leg joints, and breasthooks are some sort of frightful medieval torture implement. The prevalent uses of wood in the construction, and reconstruction, of fiberglass boats are interior accommodations and exterior trim; we will focus on these two areas.

PLYWOOD

In a word-association test, if you were asked to name the principal wood found on your boat, you would probably say teak or mahogany. It is unlikely that you would say fir, yet there is almost certainly 20, 50, or 100 times more fir than teak or mahogany aboard your boat. Bulkheads, bunks, settees, counters, cabinets, tables, and cabin soles are constructed of thin plies of Douglas fir glued together– plywood.

Why plywood? The builder was saving money at your expense again, right? Not this time. Plywood is just as common in multi-million-dollar yachts whose owners can easily afford to pay for the best. It is widely used because it has advantages over solid wood.

One advantage is strength. Wood cells are long, tubular structures running vertically in the tree. Since the foliage at the top of a tree depends upon moisture and nutrients gathered by the root system, it is not hard to imagine wood cells as bundles of microscopic soda straws. The cells themselves are very tough, but they are held together by a natural adhesive substance called lignin, which is comparatively weak. Consequently, wood is much stronger with the grain than across it.

Clamp 3 inches of a 6-inch length of 1 × 6 in a vise, orienting the grain vertically. Smack the extended half with a hammer; you will probably be nursing a tennis elbow. Now rotate the board 90 degrees and hit it again; it will split like a potato chip. In the manufacture of plywood this inherent weakness of wood is counteracted by orienting the grain of each ply perpendicular to that of the previous ply, yielding a wood product that is rigid and strong in both directions and virtually splitproof.

A second advantage of plywood is its stability. Wood is *hydroscopic*, meaning it readily takes on and gives up moisture. When the cells absorb moisture, they expand, causing the wood to swell. As the wood dries, it contracts, often checking, cracking, and warping. The marine environment often subjects wood to large and repeated changes in moisture content.

Moisture content affects the diameter of the

wood cells but has little effect on their length, meaning that wood tends to swell in width, but not in length. Because of this, the crossed-grain configuration of plywood tends to oppose any swelling or shrinkage that a single ply might undergo. This "balanced" construction makes plywood much less likely to warp, check, or crack than solid wood.

Plywood is nothing new. The ancient Chinese (no surprise here) used the plywood principle in furniture construction. Likewise, early Egyptian furniture reveals plywood construction. Perhaps more interesting, Egyptian mummy cases were fabricated of plywood and veneer. However, it was not until the 1870s with the French invention of the rotary veneering lathe, a machine that *peeled* logs like unrolling a spool of paper, that mass-produced plywood became a possibility.

Use in marine applications had to wait another 60 years for the development of a waterproof glue. Today plywood is the dominant wood product in boat construction. It is the material you will use in any major accommodations changes in your old boat. You will also find plywood well suited for a vast array of smaller enhancements.

Besides being strong and stable, plywood has the additional advantage of being *wide*, a characteristic that makes plywood ideal for large surfaces such as counters, cabinets, and bunks. Plywood has another characteristic that endears it to boat owners: it is *cheap*. You may disagree with this charac-

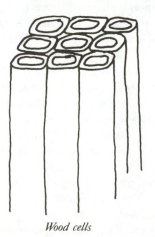

Wood cells

terization if you buy a sheet of teak plywood, but cost is relative and the plywood will be far less expensive than an equivalent amount of solid teak.

Selecting the Correct Grade

Choosing the right plywood for the job can help to hold the cost down. As previously alluded to, common plywood is usually made from Douglas fir. Softwood plywood is graded and given a letter designation of A through D, with A signifying the best quality and D the poorest. The grade, however, pertains to the *surface* veneer *only*. Grade A-A plywood is surfaced on both sides with the best quality veneer, but the inner plies may be pieced and patched grade C. Consequently, the difference in grade A-A plywood and grade A-C, also having inner plies of grade C, may only be in the appearance of one side. If that side is not exposed, there is little point in paying extra for the more attractive surface ply.

Plywood is also classified as interior or exterior (which includes marine grade). Exterior plywood is bonded together with waterproof adhesives and is well suited for the marine environment. Interior plywood, on the other hand, is not waterproof and should *never* be used for any purpose aboard a boat. Do not think that you can protect the wood by sealing it, painting it, or even sheathing it with fiberglass. The cost of such treatment will be greater than the savings on the plywood, and moisture will eventually penetrate anyway. When it does, interior plywood will flake apart.

To understand the difference between regular exterior plywood and what is known as marine grade, you need to understand that unlike the surface plies, inner plies of standard plywood are not necessarily solid. Smaller pieces are butted together to form the inner plies, and there is often space between the pieces, causing small voids in the plywood. For most uses such voids are of no consequence, but for the original purpose of marine plywood—hull construction—voids are intolerable. Marine plywood is free of voids, permits no butted end-grain joints, and all plies are grade B or better. Inner plies are solid in hull-grade marine plywood.

Should you pay the extra money for marine plywood? It depends upon how you are using it, but in most cases the answer is no. For shelves, dividers, counters, and bunks, marine plywood offers no advantages over regular exterior plywood. Buy grade A-A exterior plywood if you will need to finish both sides, A-B or A-C if only one side will be finished.

Hardwood Plywood

For bulkheads and interior furniture, you may want to consider hardwood plywood. Similar in construction to standard fir plywood, hardwood plywood is veneered on one or both sides with a variety of decorative hardwoods. Mahogany and teak are the "classic" boat woods, but by no means the only possibilities. Lighter (in color) woods like oak and ash can brighten and expand a small cabin. I recently went aboard a Beneteau with a chestnut interior that was quite striking.

Properly finished, hardwood plywood has the look of fine furniture—not surprising since much of today's furniture is manufactured from this material. It comes in various types, but the only one appropriate for marine use is Type I, which is laminated with waterproof adhesive. The other types are for interior applications.

Hardwood plywood is also manufactured in several grades. Premium Grade #1 is the best, with no defects in the surface ply, matched veneer, and no contrasts of color. Good Grade #1 also avoids surface contrasts. Sound Grade #2 is still defect-free, but color and grain may not match. The remaining grades have surface defects and are probably not of interest.

OTHER SHEET MATERIALS

Paneling—the wood-grain sheets you nail over the wallpaper in the spare bedroom to convert it to a den—is manufactured in a broad range of qualities. The least expensive are little more than contact paper over cardboard while the best are exquisite wood veneer over thin plywood. All are intended for interior use, but since they are decorative in nature, not structural, they might find uses aboard—such as ceiling or liner panels, for example.

Masonite or hardboard is available in exterior grades with a tough Melamine surface. It is not a very attractive material, but it can be used for drawer bottoms and locker dividers.

Doorskins are another sheet material that can find good uses aboard. These thin (typically $3/32$- or $1/8$-inch) panels are inexpensive and available at almost any lumber yard. Commonly cedar or Lauan, doorskins can be "cold-molded"—laminated in place with epoxy adhesive—to form strong curved surfaces.

Particle board or chip board is used extensively in home cabinet work because it is cheap and it has very little tendency to warp. Covered with decorative laminate, it serves admirably—as long as you keep it dry. But when it gets wet, particle board literally disintegrates. There are no legitimate uses for particle board aboard a boat with less than 10 feet of freeboard.

SOLID WOOD

Solid wood is also graded, but in most cases you will simply pick out the pieces that suit you from among those in the bin at the lumber yard. You should be looking for straight, flat boards with fine grain. Similar coloration will allow you to edge-glue boards into wider panels without the joint being obvious.

Look at the end of the board. If the growth rings are short, almost vertical curves from the top to the bottom, the board was quarter-sawn. If the ring lines form sweeping arches from edge to edge, the board was plain-sawn. Boards that are quarter-sawn shrink about half as much as plain-sawn boards, and they have less tendency to "cup."

Moisture content is another consideration. Green lumber is about half water, and drying is required. When the moisture content drops below 30 percent, the wood begins to shrink. Air drying is preferred, but most wood is kiln-dried because it gets the wood from the mill to the Master Card more quickly. If you were building furniture for your

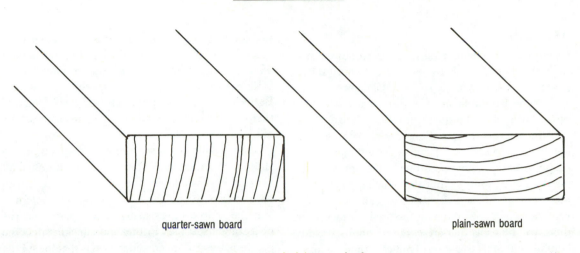

quarter-sawn board   plain-sawn board

Quarter-sawn and plain-sawn lumber

home, the ideal moisture content would be between 6½ percent and 8 percent, but that may be too dry for boat furniture. If the wood is too dry, it will absorb moisture from the air and swell, causing surfaces to buckle, doors and drawers to jam, and joints to split. Too much moisture in the wood means that it will continue to shrink, cracking, warping, and pulling seams apart.

As long as the wood has been dried, you do not need to be especially concerned about the precise moisture content if you are using solid wood for trim, handrails, or other stand-alone items only. But if your plans are for extensive joinery, moisture content is extremely important.

Determining moisture content is not difficult if you have a sensitive kitchen or postage scale. Buy a single board and cut a small section from the center (the wood will be drier near the ends). Weigh the piece carefully, to the nearest fraction of an ounce. Now place it in an oven at about 200 degrees. Periodically remove the piece from the oven and weigh it. When it stops losing weight, it is completely dry. To determine the initial moisture content percentage, divide the weight lost (the initial weight minus the dry weight) by the dry weight and multiply by 100.

An initial moisture content of about 8 percent for interior joinery and about twice that for exterior trim will probably minimize swelling and shrinking problems, but climate, heating, and whether your boat is "wet" or "dry" might alter this. If you are doing extensive reconstruction, cut a piece from the wood being removed, which is presumably in equilibrium with the environment aboard your boat, and determine its moisture content. That will be the correct content for the new wood. If the difference is large, you may want to store the wood aboard for several months before you use it.

Choosing the type of wood will hinge upon its intended use. Teak has the reputation, not undeserved, of being the best choice for boat trim. Teak is a beautiful wood, but it is its resistance to rot that makes it so popular aboard boats. Mahogany's popularity stems from its strength, durability and beauty, but it must be protected with varnish or polyurethane. There are dozens of other woods that, although perhaps not traditional, when similarly protected are equally suitable for use aboard boats, particularly as interior trim.

For framing and cleat stock, do not buy the cheapest wood you can find. That will be *construction grade* lumber and aboard a boat it will warp and rot to beat the band. Clear fir is an excellent choice for a framing material and is especially compatible with fir plywood. It is commonly available and not expensive.

TOOLS

Like quality mechanic's tools, quality woodworker's tools should eventually become part of your estate, passed on to the next generation. Cheap tools just add to the landfill crisis. But you already know to buy good tools. The question is *what* tools?

Almost every woodworking project can be broken into seven distinctive steps—design, mark, cut, shape, drill, assemble, and finish. Design is a primarily mental process, but the remaining six steps represent specific activities that we can use to conveniently categorize the tools required. In each step there will be tools that are essential, tools that are helpful, and tools that offer significant time savings. In the next couple of pages, I will try to help you sort out which are which.

Marking

A pencil is the essential tool. For more accurate marking, a sharp knife is hard to beat. Knowing where to mark almost always requires some means of taking measurements. Choose a 10- or 12-foot metal tape. Select one wide enough to remain rigid when extended a couple of feet.

A 12-inch sliding combination square is also essential for marking cutlines and for squaring during assembly. The combination square can also be used to lay out 45-degree angles, but the odd angles encountered on a boat make an adjustable bevel gauge almost essential. For large projects, a framing square can be helpful. A level isn't much use aboard a boat, unless she is out of the water and has been carefully leveled.

A piece of string and a pencil can be used for marking circles and curved cuts, but a compass is far more convenient. The compass will also help transfer the curvature of the hull onto a new bulkhead, shelf, or divider.

Cutting

This is the step that will probably determine how the rest of the project goes. I have already indicated, 'way back in Chapter 4, that if *I* were beginning a major interior reconstruction, I would buy a table saw and probably a band saw. It is not that either is essential; hand saws will do the job. But the amount of layout time, trim time, and cutting time that the table saw saves more than justifies the expenditure. Besides, if you buy the shop tools used and sell them when you are finished, the actual cost will be minimal.

One problem with shop tools is that you need a shop to put them in. This requirement can limit your options when you live in an apartment, with your in-laws, or on the boat. Another problem is that the shop tool is usually in one place and the boat someplace else. Fitting and checking become problematic. A third consideration is that most boat restorations involve interior modification only, not total reconstruction. For such modest alterations, power tools (the handheld variety) are more than adequate.

The essential cutting tool for doing any significant woodwork aboard is a 7- or 7 1/4-inch circular saw. Forget about handsaws; if God had intended for us still to be using handsaws, He would not have put power outlets on the docks. Hand sawing anything wider than 2 inches crosses the line into masochism, never mind the prospect of ripping an 8-foot sheet of plywood by hand. If you are on a mooring, buy a generator.

If you purchase a new circular saw, throw away the blade that comes with it and buy a carbide-tipped combination blade. Never mind the cost; it will work out to be about $3 per year and a carbide blade is the only kind that will cut teak without scorching it.

For curves and intricate cuts you will also need a sabersaw. Buy one that has variable speed and a heavy-duty and strongly mounted adjustable bevel plate. Skip the other bells and whistles; the basic saw will do everything the more expensive models will.

If you are going to do a lot of trim work, a backsaw and a miter box can help you to get the corners just right. Personally, using a handsaw still seems regressive to me, even for this. In less than 10 minutes, you can build a miter box for your circular saw that will be every bit as accurate and infinitely easier to use. I will outline the details when we get to trim work.

Shaping

Once the part has been cut, some trimming and shaping is almost always required. If the cutting was very accurate, a sheet of sandpaper and a small wooden block may be the only shaping tool necessary, but cutting is rarely that accurate unless you are using shop tools. Even then, the risk of chipping the wood or leaving cut marks leads most of us to cut the piece slightly oversize and trim it to fit.

For trimming straight edges, nothing is better than a *sharp* plane. A woodworking craftsman will own several planes of different lengths, each of which excels in a particular situation, but a single plane is all that is required for our purposes. The best choice is a 6-inch block plane. The small size makes this plane quite handy and allows you to use it with one hand, holding the material with the other (larger planes require two hands to be used accurately, which means the work must be held by a helper or in a vise). The biggest advantage of the block plane, however, is not the size but the low angle of the blade. Typically about 20 degrees—less than half the angle of most other planes—the low angle of the block plane makes it excel at trimming the edges of plywood, and allows the plane to make exceptionally fine cuts, even across the grain.

An alternative to the block plane is the Sur-Form, which looks like a cross between a plane and a cheese grater. Despite its questionable pedigree, it is easy to use for many shaping jobs, but it is not as versatile as a plane.

For putting a radius on corners and trimming curved edges, a belt sander can get the job done in a hurry. If you cut out a simple jig to hold the belt sander on its side, it becomes a bench sander and can be used to shape almost any wooden part, no matter how small. Because the belt is exposed on the front roller, the belt sander can also shape inside curves. A belt sander does not do any better job than a 50-cent piece of sandpaper on a wooden

block, but it does it *much* faster. Whether it is essential depends upon how much shaping you anticipate.

A chisel is an essential shaping tool. Instead of buying a set of five or six, spend the same amount on two chisels of top quality. One with a one-inch-wide blade will get the most use, but you should also have a 1/4-inch chisel for tight work. Also buy a leather mallet to use with the chisels. Chisels are precision tools and should be treated with care. For those inevitable instances when you need to trim something besides wood—such as fiberglass or epoxy—keep a cheap chisel on hand.

The incredible versatility of a router earns it an "essential" designation in all but the most modest alterations. The router opens up a whole new realm of possibilities in working with wood. Spinning a wide variety of razor-sharp blades at 25,000 rpm, a router allows you to do complex and ornate shaping that is simply not feasible with any other tool. It will create fancy moldings or put a simple-but-uniform finish radius on sharp edges. It will trim wood and plastic veneer perfectly every time. It will bevel, rabbet, groove, dado, mortise, and make interior cutouts. With the aid of an inexpensive fixture, it will even do perfect dovetail joints. And to do all these things, the router is no more difficult to use than the circular saw.

As with the saw blade, select only carbide-tipped bits. Initially purchase a 1/4-inch or 3/8-inch straight bit and a 3/8-inch corner round bit with a ball-bearing pilot. If you are installing plastic laminate, add a trimmer bit to your selection. Whether you choose a straight trimmer or a bevel trimmer will depend upon which type of finish you prefer. If you anticipate doing any cabinet work, also take a 3/8-inch rabbet bit. Buy other bits only if the need arises, which is not likely unless you get into fancy carving with the tool.

One other tool that is often essential to the shaping process is a vise. If you installed a machinist's vise as suggested in the previous chapter, all that is necessary to allow it to do double duty for woodwork is a pair of plywood inserts to spread the grip and protect the wood from the jaws. A couple of large C-clamps can be substituted for the vise if you have a rigid surface to clamp to.

Drilling

It is essential to have a hand-powered drill aboard. In many kinds of emergencies one can save your bacon. But hand drills are definitely not the tool of choice for renovation.

If you limit yourself to a single drill, it should be a ³/8-inch variable-speed model. A reversing feature allows backing out a bit when it binds, a situation more likely to occur when drilling metal than wood, but if you have a single drill it will see both uses.

It is true that a fixed-speed ¹/4-inch drill will drill holes just as well at half the cost, but a ¹/4-inch drill will not handle large bits, will not have the power to drive a spade bit or a hole saw, is unsatisfactory for grinding, and cannot double as a screw gun. The limitations of a small drill make it a false economy.

For about five years I have owned a ³/8-inch rechargeable drill. With a fixed speed and a limited use time between recharging, it too lacks the versatility of a variable-speed power drill, but for the jobs for which it is suited, it is infinitely more convenient. As a second drill, it is hard to beat.

A modest set of bits is a good initial choice. Ten or 12 bits will cover most needs. Buy only commercial-quality bits; cheap bits quickly lose their sharpness. High-speed twist drill bits have the point ground at an angle of about 40 degrees, ideal for metal but less so for drilling wood. A sharper angle, about 60 degrees, is better for woodworking, but this makes the bit almost useless for drilling metal. If you will be doing a lot of woodwork, having a separate set of bits reground for wood is not a bad idea, but by no means essential. For combined use, leave the bits alone.

When you buy the bits, also pick up a countersink; you will need it to seat flathead screws. Another worthwhile accessory is an inexpensive drill stand, which will allow you to use your power drill with the precision of a drill press. Other drill accessories such as spade bits and hole saws should be purchased as needed. The same goes for sanding disks and various grinding, buffing, and wire wheels. If you will be doing a lot of "finish" work with teak or mahogany or some other wood, buying a plug cutter for your drill may be less expensive—and better—than buying precut wooden plugs.

One hand drill that will get use at the dock is a push drill. Sometimes called a Yankee drill, the push drill resembles a screwdriver, but the handle is spring loaded and spins the bit as you push it. It is an ideal tool for drilling pilot holes, particularly when the space is confined. A selection of bits come with the drill, stored inside the handle.

Assembly

Most woodworking projects will involve more than a single piece of wood. Nails, screws, and glue—alone or combined—are used to assemble the parts.

The essential tool for nailing parts together is a hammer. Recently, after a loan turned larcenous, I replaced the hammer I had used for more than a decade. At the hardware store, I was confronted with a *wall* of hammers of different weights, shapes, sizes, and construction. A 20-ounce carpenter's hammer is too heavy for cabinet work and a 12-ounce cabinetmaker's hammer is too light for general-purpose use. Select a 16-ounce hammer with a curved claw (better for removing nails). The face of the hammer should be slightly convex, not ground flat. Choose a wood handle or a slightly more expensive fiberglass one. Metal handles, besides transmitting more of the impact to your wrist and elbow, do not do well on boats.

Virtually all of the nails you will use in your reconstruction will be finish nails. Finish nails are driven below the surface of the wood and the indention is usually filled. Setting finishing nails requires a nail set, a punchlike tool with a small tip. A ¹/32 nail set is the most useful for cabinet work, but nail sets are cheap enough to buy two or three different sizes.

In the last chapter we covered the need for three or four standard screwdrivers and a similar complement of Phillips screwdrivers. And we have already pointed out the need for a drill, bits, and a countersink. Assembly with screws requires no additional tools. However, if your plans call for a lot of screws, there are a couple of other tools that you will find quite useful.

The first is a special drill bit that drills the pilot hole, the shank hole, the countersink and the counterbore in a single operation. These combination bits come in various sizes and selecting one for the screws you are using can save a tremendous amount of time.

Driving half a dozen screws with a screwdriver leaves you with a sense of satisfaction; driving a hundred screws leaves you with bandages on your hand. Instead of spending money on gauze and surgical tape, buy screwdriver bits for your variable speed drill. Better yet, buy a cordless power screwdriver; you won't have to remove the drill bit from your drill every time you want to install a screw, and the screw-gun's built-in clutch will keep you from stripping or twisting off screws.

Today's glues are typically stronger than wood fibers, meaning that the wood itself will pull apart before a properly glued joint fails. With glue that holds that tenaciously, there is little need for nails and screws in permanent joints except to hold the glue-coated parts together initially. A great deal of nailing and screwing can be avoided if you have the right clamps. C-clamps are the most useful. They come in sizes from tiny to humongous. The absolute minimum complement of clamps is four 4-inch C-clamps. If you can afford an equal number 6-inch clamps, so much the better. A couple of 2-inch clamps are also likely to earn their way. I never met a woodworker with *too many* C-clamps.

Cabinetmakers often prefer wooden hand-screw clamps because they grip a broader area, do not mark the surface of the clamped item, and can be adjusted so that their jaws are *not parallel* for clamping odd-shaped items. Their bulk is their biggest drawback for boat use; they are awkward or unserviceable in a confined area and they occupy considerable stowage space. Faced with the choice, choose C-clamps.

For edge-gluing planks or assembling cabinets, clamps with a couple of feet or more between the jaws are useful. Bar clamps in widths up to 8 feet or more are available with various jaw depths. A more economical alternative is the pipe clamp. Virtually identical in operation to a bar clamp, a pipe clamp consists of one jaw that screws onto the threaded end of common 3/4-inch steel pipe (1/2-inch sizes are also available, but less powerful) and a second jaw that slides up and down the pipe. With different lengths of pipe, the same clamp can be used to clamp 6 inches or 6 feet. Find a building or house being demolished and the contractor will likely let you carry away all the 3/4-inch water pipe you want. Three pipe clamps should be adequate for most uses.

You should also be aware of spring clamps (good for quickly positioning small parts), edging clamps (for gluing wooden banding to the edge of plywood), and miter clamps (for accurate gluing of miter joints). The usefulness of these will depend upon the type of woodworking you attempt.

Finish

In this chapter, we are going to limit our examination of finishing to the process of preparation. The actual application of paint or varnish or some other coating is detailed extensively in Chapter 14.

Finish preparation essentially means sanding. Once again, a foam or wooden block and a few sheets of sandpaper are the only essentials, but a finishing sander can do the job better and faster. The most versatile is a palm sander with a 4-inch pad to take 1/4 sheet of sandpaper. Making about 14,000 orbits per minute, these lightweight (about 2 pounds) sanders can make short work of almost any sanding project, including minor shaping.

The Makita sander I use came with an attached dust bag that, amazingly enough, actually works. Six punched holes in the sandpaper leading to a high-speed blower act as tiny vacuum cleaners, picking up dust as it is created. The sander is infinitely more efficient when it is not riding on a layer of sawdust. I highly recommend this particular sander.

The problem of sawdust is not limited to clogging sandpaper. If dust is on the surface, it will seriously weaken any glue joints. If it is in the air, it will roughen or ruin paint and varnish. For anything more than minor interior modifications, some type of vacuum cleaner is essential. You might press a home vacuum cleaner with attachments into service, but a shop vac is generally far more satisfactory. Small shop vacs, ideal for onboard use, are now available at a reasonable cost, and they are often placed on sale.

An appealing alternative is the car vac because it is substantially less expensive and it can stay aboard for regular boat cleaning after your renovation is complete. You will need to *sweep* up the bulk of the chips and shavings with a brush and a dust pan before you vacuum, but a good car vac will do an admirable job of picking up the remaining dust. The car-vac made by Black & Decker has dominated the market for a decade—for good reason.

ONE-PIECE PROJECT

Almost any locker on a boat can benefit from a shelf. Dividing the lockers in the galley will allow you to get to the stock pot without removing every other pan and skillet. A shelf in the head cabinet will keep paper products away from the potential dampness of the hull. A shelf in the cockpit locker will provide a flat surface for storage boxes and jerry jugs. A shelf on one side of the lazarette will provide convenient stowage for small cans of paint, oil, polish, and other items.

Even the hanging locker can benefit from shelves. If you live aboard, you may need a place to hang your Brooks Brothers suits, but for most boating, the value of the hanging locker is suspect. It wastes space; hanging clothes are not compactly stowed and there is generally a large amount of unused space in the top and bottom of the locker. It is hard on your clothes; hanging clothes in a boat crashing to windward or rolling downwind is not unlike storing your clothes in a tumble dryer. And if you are hanging your clothes to keep them from wrinkling, take a look inside the locker the next time the boat is heeled; they pile themselves on the hull or the locker door and wrinkle anyway.

The best use for a hanging locker is to convert it to a bureau. Your clothes will do better folded or rolled and stowed in a drawer, and drawers aboard allow for efficient stowage of hundreds of other items as well. Unfortunately, the design of most old boats will not allow for such a conversion; there is insufficient room to open drawers when a deep locker is located across from the head. The next best thing is to build shelves in the locker.

The Design Process

Whether the shelf will be in the galley, the lazarette, or the hanging locker, there is very little difference in construction and installation, but there will be some variation in design. We barely touched on design earlier, yet regardless of how exquisite your craftsmanship, poor design will doom the project.

Come on, you say. How much design can a shelf require? Let's consider that question for a shelf in a galley locker. Obviously you need to know the size of the shelf. You can get that by measuring the locker. But have you given adequate thought to what will be kept in the locker? With the new shelf in place, will the space between it and the bottom of the cabinet *opening* be wide enough to admit the stock pot? Can you remove the saucepan stowed *inside* the stock pot without removing the pot? That requires at least the *combined* height of both between the bottom of the locker and the underside of the shelf. With the shelf in place, will you be able to see what is in the locker? Will you be able to actually *reach* to the back of the shelf? Try holding a board across the center of the opening to see how far you can reach. Does anyone aboard have shorter arms? If you open the cabinet on the wrong tack, is everything on the shelf going to end up on the cabin sole? How heavy are the items you will store on the shelf? Would ventilation be beneficial? Does the shelf need to be removable for access to plumbing, wiring, or hardware? We could go on.

The basic premise is to determine *exactly* how

the shelf will be used and then decide on the design of the shelf, not the other way around. In this case, I am going to assume that you discovered that a "generic" shelf will make storing the large pots more difficult and retrieving small items that migrate to the rear of the shelf nearly impossible. Mounting the shelf higher resolves the first problem, but makes the second one even worse. A shelf that extends from the back of the locker only halfway to the front solves both problems, but if you think about it a little more, you realize that the first time this locker is on the weather side in a decent breeze, or the boat rolls off a steep wave, the half-shelf will dump its contents into the bottom of the locker. What will you do?

The obvious solution is a fiddle rail across the front of the shelf, but that has its own problems. First, if the fiddle is high enough to be effective, it will make seeing the contents of the shelf difficult. Secondly, narrowing the access to the shelf may limit what can be stored on it. But the most serious, at least from my perspective, is that an attached fiddle adds complexity to this first project. The one-piece solution is to mount the shelf with about a 20-degree slant toward the rear. With such a slant, even a 30-degree heel is not likely to spill the contents of the shelf.

The materials list is not very extensive: a piece of plywood and a length of cleat stock. But even here, there are some design considerations. If you are only adding a shelf or two, you do not need to concern yourself with weight, but if you are adding a dozen shelves or reconstructing interior fixtures, weight becomes a major consideration. When weight is a concern, $3/8$-inch plywood will be adequate for shelves, but the better stability and greater rigidity provided by the five-ply construction of $1/2$-inch plywood make it a better choice most of the time. Additional thickness beyond $1/2$ inch offers no advantages. You want exterior grade A-B or A-C plywood.

Cleat stock, if you don't already know, has nothing whatsoever to do with the things the docklines are attached to. Cleat stock is nothing more than a length of wood with a small, square cross-section—ideally $3/4$ inch × $3/4$ inch. You can buy square molding for this use, but a less expensive route is to rip $3/4$-inch strips off a length of clear fir 1-by (1 by 4, 1 by 6, etc.). Forget about "truth in advertising"; 1-by is actually $3/4$ inch thick. The lumber yard may be willing to rip a board for you if you ask.

Measuring begins with drawing a line on one side of the locker to approximate the location of one edge of the shelf. To get us both on the same wavelength, the locker I am describing opens athwartship; in other words, the rear of the locker is the hull. Somehow you have to cut the shelf to the curvature of the hull, but because this shelf does not reach the front of the locker, you can just cut it square and then trim it to fit. So you need two measurements for the shelf.

First you measure between the sides of the locker. Measure across where the front of the shelf will be and where the rear will be to be sure that the sides are parallel. If they aren't, use your square to determine which side is square with the front of the cabinet and make that the square side of your shelf. It can be helpful to sketch the shelf and note the different measurements on the drawing.

You also need a depth dimension. Measure from the point where you want the front of the shelf to the hull along the line you have drawn. If the hull has a pronounced curvature, be sure you measure on the *deepest* side of the locker or the finished shelf will be slightly shorter than you expect.

Making the Cuts

With your two measurements, you are ready to cut the shelf. Sawhorses are very convenient for cutting and other work and inexpensive clamp-on legs are available that allow you to convert a single 8-foot stud (2 × 4) into a pair of horses. For onboard cutting, span the coamings with a couple of 2 × 4's.

To make a straight cut with a circular saw, you need a cutting guide. This is nothing more than a straight edge to run the sole plate against. A new sheet of plywood provides a good opportunity to make a convenient cutting guide. Select the best edge and get your lumberyard to accurately rip a 6-inch-wide strip from the sheet. *Rip* means to cut

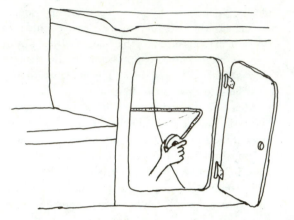

Measure the width.

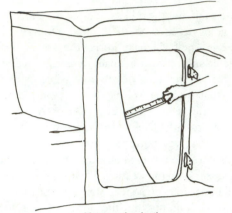

Measure the depth.

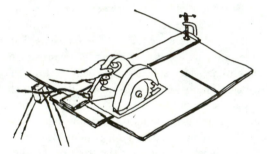

Cut plywood to the measurements.

Cut cleat stock to support the shelf.

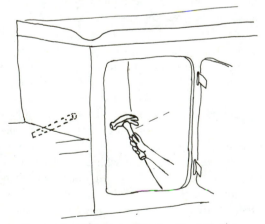

Temporarily nail one support to the side of the locker.

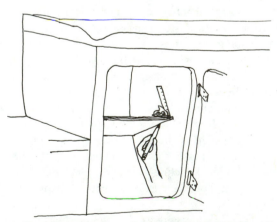

Place the shelf on the support, square it with the side of the locker, and mark the position of the other support.

The basic shelf

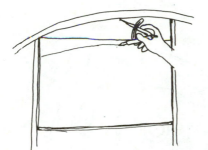

With the shelf temporarily in position, use a compass to trace the curvature of the hull at the back edge of the shelf.

Cut the contour with a sabersaw.

Glue the cleats in position, holding them in place with nails or screws.

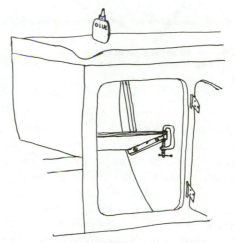

Glue the shelf to the cleats, clamping at the front and applying pressure in the back by wedging a length of cleat stock between the shelf and the top of the locker.

The basic shelf (continued)

with the grain; *crosscut* means to cut across the grain. If the yard cannot do it, it will not be particularly difficult for you to make the cut yourself, especially if your saw has a rip guide.

Start by adjusting your saw. Make sure that it is unplugged, then push the sole plate all the way up, adjusting for the maximum depth of cut. Lay your square against the sole plate and the blade to make sure the blade is absolutely perpendicular, adjusting as required. Do not trust the bevel gauge stamped on the plate. Now put the saw, with the blade against one edge, on the wood you plan to cut.

Adjust the depth of cut so that the blade will penetrate the wood by about half the depth of a tooth. You will need to readjust the depth of cut every time the thickness of the material you are cutting changes; the blade should always penetrate by about half a tooth.

Turn the best face of the plywood *down*. The circular saw cuts with an upward motion with some tendency to splinter the top surface of plywood, so always mark and cut plywood with the best face down.

Install the rip guide on your saw and adjust it so

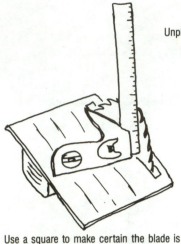

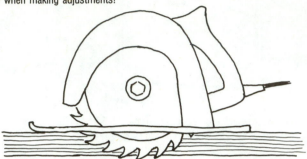

Unplug the saw when making adjustments!

Use a square to make certain the blade is perpendicular to the sole plate.

Set the depth of cut so that the blade penetrates the wood by about ½ the depth of a tooth.

Setting the saw

that the distance between the face of the guide and the blade is about 6 inches. Keeping the guide flush against the best edge of the plywood, run your saw the length of the sheet. Pressing against the rip guide with your free hand will help you to keep it in contact with the edge. Feed the saw slowly and do not worry about cutting the top of the horses.

Measure 18 inches from one end of the strip and use your square to mark a line across it. Readjust the rip guide to 3 inches and rip the strip from the end *through* the marked line, meaning that the center of the blade, not just the front, must reach the line. Remove the rip guide and crosscut the strip at the marked line. You can freehand this cut and it should give you two 18-inch strips about 3 inches wide.

From the uncut end of the 6-inch strip, measure 51 inches and use your square to mark a line. Cut the strip at this line. With this strip and one of the 3-inch-wide strips, you are going to make a cutting guide that resembles a draftsman's T square. You need carpenter's glue (or epoxy), half a dozen inch-long finishing nails, and your hammer.

Place the long strip on a hard surface and coat 3 inches of one end with glue. Center the short strip, placing its edge flush with the end of the long strip

and pressing it into the glue. Drive a *single* nail through the short strip and into the long one. Now, using a square—preferably a large carpenter's square—square the two pieces. Do this very carefully, placing the square against the *inside* edge of the short strip and *both* edges of the long one. Drive a second nail and recheck to make sure that nothing moved. When you are satisfied, drive three or four more nails into the joint and set the guide aside to allow the glue to dry.

This will give you a guide that can be used to make cuts across a full sheet of plywood, but it can

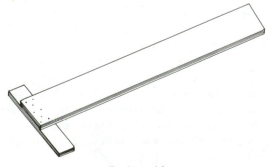

Cutting guide

be somewhat awkward to use when you just want to get a straight cut across a 4-inch plank. Use the pieces that remain to make a second, smaller guide about 15 inches long.

After all this, the shelf itself is a piece of cake. Measuring from the end of the sheet, mark the width of the locker, less about 1/8 inch to assure ample clearance, on the plywood. Measure in from the edge at this mark the approximate depth of the shelf and make a second mark on the plywood. Place the cutting guide about 2 inches (the distance from the outside edge of the sole plate to the blade of most saws) beyond the first mark and seat the crosspiece against the edge of the plywood; a C-clamp on the opposite end will hold the guide in place. Put the outside edge of the sole plate against the guide and run the saw until it just touches the plywood, marking exactly where the cut will be.

Did you just cut off the end of the crosspiece? Relax, Skip. That's what is supposed to happen. Next time you only have to line up the end of the crosspiece with your mark to position the guide.

Adjust the cutting guide so that the saw blade will touch your original pencil mark. Make sure the cut is *outside* of the mark or the shelf will be narrower than you planned by the width of the saw blade. As a rule, if your guide is *on* the part you are cutting, you can line up the end of the crosspiece with your mark. If the guide is *off* the part, you have to allow for the width of the blade. Clamp the guide and cut into the sheet as far as the second mark, this time stopping the cut when the front of the blade reaches the mark.

Since the back of the shelf is to be recut to the contour of the hull, you could freehand the second cut, but this is a good opportunity to trim the other side of the cutting guide crosspiece. Mark the depth of the shelf and place the guide about 4 inches beyond the mark. This time run the opposite edge of the sole—the edge beneath the motor—against the guide. As before, run the saw along the guide until it just nicks the plywood. Adjust the position of the guide, holding it in position with your hand, and make the full cut, stopping when the front of the

blade touches the first cut. Using a sabersaw, complete the two cuts, releasing the shelf from the sheet. The reason for finishing the cuts with a sabersaw is to avoid cutting into the unused plywood, thus conserving it for other uses.

Cut two pieces of the cleat stock about an inch shorter than the depth of the shelf; if the locker sides are tabbed to the hull, you do not want the cleats to reach the radius. Using two finishing nails, tack the cleat in place against the line you previously drew on the side of the locker. Do not drive the nails flush; you are going to remove this cleat later. Place the shelf on the cleat and, using a square against the locker side, square the shelf and trace the underside of it with a pencil on the opposite wall of the locker. Remove the shelf and temporarily tack the second cleat in place using this line as a guide. Put the shelf in place to make sure it sits flat on both cleats. This is also the time to actually try the pots and pans for fit to confirm that the shelf is exactly where you want it.

With the shelf in place, mark the contour of the hull. This is most easily done with a compass. Adjust it slightly wider than the widest gap between the shelf and the hull. Always keeping the line between the point and the pencil approximately perpendicular to the front of the shelf, drag the point against the hull and allow the pencil to trace the contour on the *bottom* of the shelf.

Remove the shelf and cut along the contour line with your sabersaw. Like the circular saw, the sabersaw cuts on the upward motion so mark and cut the plywood from the bottom. There is no depth adjustment on a sabersaw, but the angle of the cut is adjustable. You may be tempted to set the saw for a 20-degree bevel to correspond with the cant of the shelf, but that overlooks the vertical curvature of the hull. To achieve a fairly accurate fit requires measuring the *actual* angle between the shelf and the hull with a bevel gauge and setting the saw to that angle. For the back of a shelf, such accuracy is superfluous.

A sabersaw cannot be counted on to make an absolutely accurate cut anyway because the unsupported blade can be deflected by the wood. Checking the blade initially to make sure it is vertical and feeding the saw slowly will give the best results.

All that is left to finish your shelf installation is to permanently install the cleats and secure the shelf in place. You might drill and screw the cleats in place, but gluing them in place will be much stronger—if you use the correct adhesive.

Selecting an Adhesive

There are half a dozen adhesives you should be familiar with. Everyone has used *Elmer's Glue-All*, the ubiquitous white glue that most of us assume is somehow a dairy by-product but we *really* don't want to know how it is made. Good news, animal lovers; the only dead cattle in this *polyvinyl resin* glue died a couple of million years ago. This glue says "for wood" right on the package, but it has a very low tolerance for moisture and should never be used aboard a boat.

On the same shelf at the hardware store you will find cream-colored carpenter's glue, an *aliphatic resin* adhesive. Aliphatic resin is an excellent adhesive—easy to use, fast setting, long lasting, and it will form a strong bond even when the two parts do not mate well. It is less moisture-sensitive than its white cousin, but if the joint gets soaked, it will fail. Most interior joints will never get that wet, and I recently had to use a chisel to remove cleats that I attached with carpenter's glue more than a decade ago. Still, it should be used selectively; while I might depend on carpenter's glue to hold a shelf containing pots or clothes, I would not trust it with a sextant or expensive electronics.

I have always liked the way the word *resorcinol*, like the name *Spiro Agnew*, exercises all the muscles around the mouth. It is also an elitist word; everyone knows about epoxy but knowledge of resorcinol sets one apart. Totally waterproof, resorcinol is an excellent adhesive, but depends upon a very thin (0.005 inch) glue line for a strong bond. If the parts being joined do not mate perfectly (which generally lets me out) so that a thin glue line can be achieved without excessive clamp pressure, the bond will be weak. The joint must be clamped for at least eight hours. Resorcinol is a two-part adhesive and must be mixed before use.

Plastic resin (actually urea-formaldehyde resin) is another waterproof glue with excellent bonding properties. Many boat carpenters swear by plastic resin. It is not quite as impervious to water as resorcinol is, but it's certainly up to any challenges it might face on a fiberglass boat. The major drawback to plastic resin is that it must be under heavy pressure to bond, always necessitating closely spaced clamping. It sets quickly, which is not always a disadvantage, but it comes in powder form and must be mixed with water before use. The low cost of the adhesive is a definite plus.

A unique plastic resin is *Aerolite 306*. Like other plastic resins, it is a powder that is mixed with water, but what makes it unique is that only one side of the joint is coated with resin. The other surface is coated with an activator and curing does not begin until the joint is assembled. Aerolite does *not* need to be clamped—firm contact is all that is required—and it will fill gaps up to $1/16$ inch and still deliver a strong bond. For boat-related woodwork, Aerolite is hard to beat.

Unfortunately Aerolite 306 is not always easy to find. *Epoxy* is. Common or not, epoxy does the job and does it well. It will readily fill virtually any size gap and requires no clamping other than what may be necessary to hold the two parts in contact. Epoxy is the clear favorite among amateur woodworkers. Available in various viscosities, epoxy adhesive is essentially thickened epoxy resin. In fact, many boat carpenters mix their own from resin by adding fiber filler, silica, graphite powder or simply dry sawdust. The only significant disadvantage of epoxy is the relatively high cost.

Installing the Shelf

When you check the shelf one more time for fit, take notice of whether the cleats extend beyond the front of the shelf; if they do, reposition them so they are slightly recessed. Remove the shelf and outline both cleats on the sides of the locker. Also make a small arrow on each cleat pointing toward the top so you cannot get confused when you glue the cleats in place. Now remove both cleats and coat them and the outlined areas on the locker sides with the glue of your choice. If the inside of the locker has been previously painted, you will need to sand the paint off the area being glued. Nail the cleats back in place, this time driving the finishing nails home. Add more nails as necessary to hold the cleat tightly against the side panel.

If you want to mount the shelf permanently, wait until the glue cures on the cleats, then coat the top of the cleats and the underside of the shelf with glue and tack the shelf in place with finishing nails. You can skip the nails if you can find an alternative way to press the shelf onto the cleats. C-clamps will do the job in the front of the shelf, but there is no way to get a clamp on the back. Measure from the top of the shelf (near the rear) to the top of the locker and cut a couple of pieces of cleat stock slightly longer. Place the lower end of these pieces on the shelf directly above the cleats and wedge the upper end against the top of the locker. Tap the upper end sideways with your hammer to wedge the strut tighter and increase the pressure on the glue joint.

If you want the shelf attached to the hull, keep in mind that, like a bulkhead, the rigid shelf can cause a hard spot on the hull and should be insulated with a fillet of foam. With the foam in place, tab the shelf-to-hull joint with two or three layers of fiberglass. If you are only after rear support for the shelf, fiberglass a cleat to the hull. A short cleat in the center will generally be adequate. Do not attach the shelf to the cleat.

It is sometimes imperative and almost always a good idea to make shelves removable—you might buy a larger stock-pot. The common way is to screw the shelf to the cleats rather than glue it. Two screws to a side are typically adequate. Select a pilot drill by comparing it to the screws you are using; it should be approximately the same size as the screw's root diameter—the diameter of the screw if the threads were ground away. Hold the drill behind the screw to compare. For fastening 1/2-inch plywood, #8 flat-

head screws, 1 inch long, are a good choice. A #8 screw calls for a #40 pilot drill, but if you do not have numbered bits, a 5/64-inch bit will be fine. With the shelf in place drill the four pilot holes through the shelf and into the cleats.

You will find these holes impossible to drill vertically because the bulk of the power drill keeps the bit more than 3/4 inch away from the sides. You can drill the holes at an angle, but this is a good time to use the push drill if you have one. Remove the shelf and drill the holes in it larger. For #8 screws, the shank hole should be 5/32 inch. When you are enlarging a pilot hole, whenever you can, drill the hole *from the bottom*. Few of us can run the second drill right down the center of the first hole with a hand-held drill. The trick is to hold the drill lightly and let the pilot hole dictate the orientation of the drill, but the hole still tends to shift. If you drilled the shank hole from the top and it shifted, the screw may miss the pilot hole, but if you drilled from the bottom, the shank hole and the pilot hole will always align.

Turn the shelf back over and countersink the shank holes from the top. Make sure the entire head of each screw will be below the surface of the shelf. Ideally, you want the top of a flathead screw to be exactly flush with the surface of the wood and you can normally check the countersink without inserting the screw by touching the head of the inverted screw to the hole; when the diameter of the countersink is the same as the diameter of the head, the countersink is correct. In this case, because the screws are installed at an angle, it will be best to check the depth of the countersinks by inserting the screws. When they are correct, screw the shelf in place.

I prefer an alternative method of holding the shelf in place. Cut two pieces of cleat stock, each 1 1/4 inches long, and glue them vertically to the locker sides against the front edge of the shelf and flush with its top. They will prevent the shelf from sliding forward. Tape them in place while the glue sets, making certain that they do not press against the shelf so tightly that they prevent its removal. Next, cut two 6- or 8-inch lengths of cleat stock, centering one along one edge of the shelf, and tacking it horizontally about ¼ inch above the shelf. You are clamping the shelf between the bottom cleat and the top cleat, but you do not want it clamped tightly or you will be unable to lift the opposite side and slide the shelf free. Now drill the other piece for a single screw in its center and screw it to the opposite side of the locker, pressing it tightly against the shelf. A shelf installed this way is very secure but can be removed with a single screw.

If you need to remove the shelf often, you might install this last cleat vertically as a long turn-button and eliminate the necessity of removing a screw. Or you could attach a door hook or even a "bird" catch to the bottom of the shelf.

You may be tempted to sand your new shelf. Don't. When you sand fir plywood, all you succeed in doing is removing the soft fibers, leaving the surface even rougher. Finishing is another chapter, but plywood should always be given a couple of coats of paint or sealer before you attempt to sand it.

Getting Fancy

Before we move on to other projects, let's take a broader look at shelving. If the shelf just completed was in the head or the hanging locker rather than in the galley, ventilating would be a good idea. You could drill the shelf with a pattern of holes with your largest twist drill—probably ³⁄₈ inch—but it will take a lot of holes to be very effective. A better method is to use a spade bit between 1 inch and 1½ inches in diameter and drill far fewer holes.

Using a spade bit is not difficult and it cuts a very neat hole—until it exits. To keep the bit from tearing the bottom ply, do not feed the drill all the way through the shelf. When the point breaks through, invert the shelf and finish drilling the hole from the opposite side.

Another method of ventilating a shelf involves making a series of parallel cuts with the circular saw. This is easily done with your cutting guide. To minimize any impact on strength the cuts should be parallel to the front of the shelf. Draw two lines on the shelf about 1½ inches from the sides; the cuts

will not extend beyond these lines. Clamp the guide in place so that the first cut will be about 1½ inches from the front of the shelf.

You are going to do a *plunge cut*. With the saw in position against the cutting guide, tilt the saw onto the front edge of the sole plate until the blade guard is just above the wood. Pull the guard back with its handle to expose the bottom of the blade. Squeeze the trigger switch, and with the saw running, slowly lower the blade into the wood. When the sole plate sits flush, you can release the blade guard and carefully back the saw until the back edge of the blade touches one of the lines. Now push the saw forward along the cutting guide until the blade touches the other line. Tilt the saw up to extract the blade and release the trigger. Move the cutting guide an inch and make a second cut. Repeat until the entire center of the shelf is vented.

WHAT KIND OF JOINT IS THIS, ANYWAY?

In a lot of applications you will want a shelf to have a fiddle rail across the front. The shelf will still be plywood, but if it is exposed—as in an open (no door) hanging locker—or even if it isn't but you want your work to be "yacht" quality, the fiddle will be solid wood.

Before fabricating the fiddle rail, you need to decide how it will be attached to the shelf. Why not just butt the inside of the rail against the front edge of the shelf? Because such a joint will be very weak.

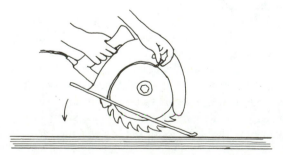

Making a plunge cut

Glue does not bond well to any end grain, including that exposed in the edge of plywood. Mechanical fasteners—nails and screws—are ineffective when driven into the *edge* of plywood.

You can make the joint substantially stronger by placing the rail on *top* of the shelf. In this case, end grain is not involved so the glue joint should have greater integrity. Screws driven from the bottom of the shelf into the solid wood of the fiddle will develop their full holding strength. The butt joint, even in the best of conditions, is the weakest of joints, but certainly strong enough to withstand the assault of seven pounds of escape-minded clothing. The real problem with attaching the rail this way is that it leaves the edge of the plywood shelf exposed. You can do nicer work.

Joining the two parts with a rabbet is your best option. Don't squirm; there is nothing difficult about a rabbet joint. All that is required is a notch along the bottom edge of the fiddle rail. Assuming that the shelf is ½-inch plywood, you want the notch ½ inch wide so that the bottom of the rail will be flush with the bottom of the shelf. The deeper the rabbet is, the stronger it will be, but you don't want to leave less than about ¼ inch of wood at the bottom of the rabbet or the remaining piece may break off. With ¾-inch-thick stock, cut the rabbet to a depth of about ½ inch.

Imagine a saw blade ½ inch wide. If you set the depth of cut to ½ inch and you used a rip guide to place the inside edge of the blade ½ inch from the bottom edge of the rail, a single pass with the saw will give you the ½-inch-deep, ½-inch-wide rabbet you want. This is exactly how a dado blade on a table saw works. The blade on your circular saw is more likely to give you an ⅛-inch-wide cut, but if you move the guide ⅛ inch and make a second cut, you now have a ¼-inch notch. Two more passes and you have the ½-inch rabbet. Actually, after the first cut, you can freehand the following cuts. It is advisa-

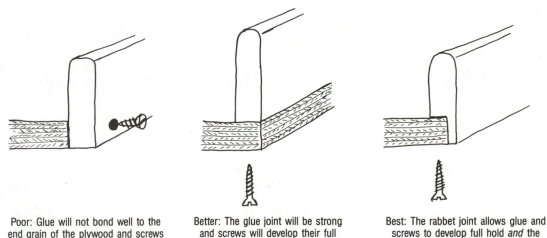

Poor: Glue will not bond well to the end grain of the plywood and screws and nails are ineffective when driven into a plywood edge.

Better: The glue joint will be strong and screws will develop their full hold.

Best: The rabbet joint allows glue and screws to develop full hold *and* the raw edge is hidden.

Attaching a fiddle rail

ble to make the second cut right along the edge of the rail, then remove the wood between the two cuts with additional passes of the saw. This will minimize the risk of chipping when you remove the last of the material.

You can also cut a rabbet with your router. Most piloted rabbet bits are limited to ³/₈-inch width, so use a straight bit. If the router has an accessory guide fence, you can use it to limit the width of your cut to ¹/₂ inch. You can accomplish the same thing by clamping a straight board to the base of the router. Set the depth of the cut to ¹/₂ inch and check both depth and width by making a practice cut on a scrap of material, adjusting the guide and the depth as required.

A word about safety is essential. You *can* drill a hole in your hand with a power drill, but it is not likely to happen unless you hold the material you are drilling from behind. A circular saw is dangerous enough, but the blade guard provides a good deal of protection from momentary lapses of caution. A finishing sander cannot injure you, and if your belt sander runs amok, the consequences will be similar to those of tangling your two left feet on an asphalt tennis court. A router, on the other hand, is about as benign as an angry cobra. The razor-sharp bits are

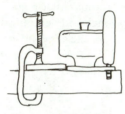  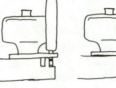 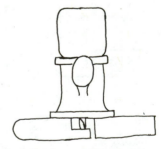

Use a saw guide to make the first cut, accurately defining the rabbet.	Make the second cut along the edge to minimize splintering.	Make additional passes with the saw to remove the remaining material.	The finished rabbet.

Cutting a rabbet with a circular saw

 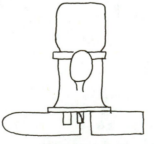

Use the accessory guide fence or a board clamped to the base to make the first cut accurately.	Remove the guide and run the cutter along the edge. Support the "off" half of the router with a piece of the same material.	With the router well supported, remove the remaining material.

Cutting a rabbet with a router

totally unprotected and accelerate from stopped to 25,000 rpm in an instant. *Every time* you change bits, disable the tool by unplugging it, and never, NEVER, rest a router on your leg or in your lap. Accidentally hit the trigger switch while any part of your body is in contact with the bit and you will spend the rest of your life without that part.

Move the router in the direction opposite to the cutter; i.e., the cutter spins in a clockwise direction so you should move the router in a counterclockwise direction. That means left to right on the front of the piece, right to left if you are routing the rear. Routers will cut in either direction, but they are easier to control and the finish will be better in the counterclockwise direction. Always start and stop the router with the bit clear of the wood.

The only trick to using a router is to avoid overloading the cutter. That means you may need to make two or three passes to make the cut. In this case, set both the depth and the width slightly less than 1/2 inch and rough out the rabbet. When you reset the tool to the correct depth and width, the finish cut will be quite smooth.

If you are putting sea rails on several shelves, cut the rabbet in the board *before* you cut it into sections. Any problems that you experience in cutting the rabbet are almost certain to occur while your guide is only half supported—when you start the cut and as you finish it. A single start and finish reduces the opportunity for trouble, and if you screw up anyway, the bad section can be cut away before you divide the board into the lengths you need.

Unless the ends of the rails are to be contoured, radius the top edge before the rabbeted board is cut into sections. The sharp corners can be removed by block-sanding or with a finishing sander, but a more

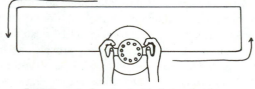

Feed the router in a counter-clockwise direction.

Using a router

attractive edge is achieved with the router and a corner-round bit. A corner-round bit with a ball-bearing pilot is pretty much foolproof. Adjust the depth so that the curve of the bit ends just *above* the router base plate and run the cutter along the edge with the pilot in contact with the wood. Check it on a scrap of the same material. Turn the wood over and run the router against the same edge, giving you an almost perfectly rounded top edge.

From the rabbeted and radiused board, cut a rail to the same length as the width of the shelf. The front edge of the shelf fits into the rabbet. Hold the two parts tightly together and drill pilot holes from the bottom of the shelf into the rail. Space screws between 6 and 12 inches apart. Open up the pilot holes in the shelf to shank diameter and countersink them into the bottom of the shelf. If you have the proper combination bit, you can drill the pilot hole, the shank hole, and the countersink at the same time. Coat both surfaces of the rabbet and the top and edge of the shelf with glue and screw the parts together. The rabbet gives you a strong joint and hides the raw edge of the plywood.

A quick and easy alternative to the rabbet is the glue-block joint. Screw and/or glue cleat stock along the bottom of the shelf flush with its front edge. Screw and/or glue the fiddle rail to the cleat stock. The wood must be wider than the height you want the fiddle by the combined thickness of the shelf and the cleat stock. This joint does not exhibit the same level of craftsmanship as the rabbet joint, but it is equally strong and quite adequate in most applications.

Review of an Independent Board

Sometimes a rail that is not permanently attached to the shelf will be a better choice. For example, instead of canting the shelf in the galley, you might have installed a removable rail in front of it. Such a rail would be effective at greater angles of heel or roll than the inclined shelf, yet not interfere with access to the contents of the shelf when the boat is not underway.

You can make a simple and elegant sea rail quite

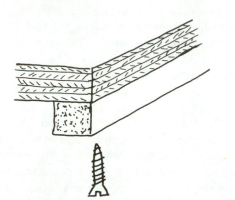

Screw/glue cleat stock flush with the front edge of the shelf.

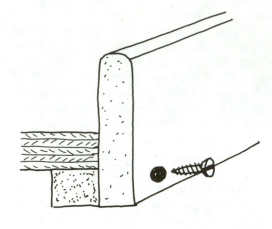

Screw/glue the rail to the cleat stock.

Glue block joint

easily by running the corner round bit of your router along the top and bottom of both edges of a teak or mahogany board. The size of the board will depend upon what the rail is intended to hold in place; for the galley shelf I would use a piece ½- or ¾-inch thick and about 2 inches wide.

All that is required to hold the rail in place is a pair of U-shaped brackets. These may be cut from almost anything. If they will be exposed, you might elect to fashion them from the same material as the rail, but inside a cabinet, ½-inch plywood is a good choice. The depth of the U should be about the same as the height of the rail. In this example, you would lay out (not cut out) a rectangle 2¼ inches wide and about 3 inches long. Place a mark on the centerline of the piece and about 1⅝ inches from one end. Put the point of your compass on that mark and open it until the pencil just touches one of the sides, then swing a half-circle arc to the opposite side. Use a spade bit to drill a ¾-inch hole—the width of the rail—at the mark. Note that the radius of the drill (⅜ inch) added to the dimension from the edge to the mark (1⅝ inches) equals the height of the rail (2 inches). No, that is not a coincidence.

Use your square to draw two lines from the straight end tangent to the drilled hole and parallel to the sides. Cut from the edge to the hole along these two lines with your saber saw, creating the U-shaped cutout. Now cut out the piece by running the saw along one side, around the half-circle arc and back along the other side, releasing the completed bracket. You can fabricate a pair of identical brackets at the same time by clamping two pieces of material together before you start.

Round the sharp edges on the front of the bracket with a sander. Using the rail as a guide, tack the brackets in place, making certain the rail does not bind. When you have them positioned, glue them in place.

Like shelves, rails have numerous applications. Installed across the shelves typically found above bunks and settees, a removable rail fabricated and mounted in exactly the same way provides secure stowage for tall items such as books and bottles.

A rail installed in the icebox or refrigerator corrals breakable items. Sliding countertop items to the back of the counter and dropping a removable rail in front of them when you are getting underway is

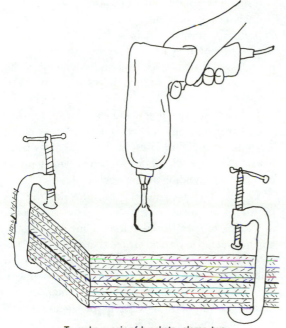

To make a pair of brackets, clamp two boards together. Use a spade bit to bore a hole the width of the rail.

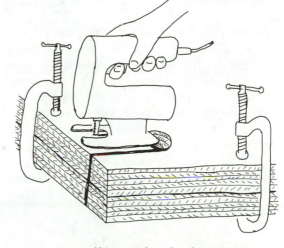

Make a cut from the edge tangent to the sides of the bored hole.

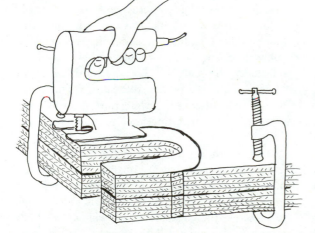

Make a U-shaped cut to complete the brackets.

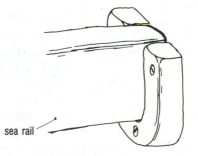

sea rail

Round the front edges, paint, and screw/glue the brackets in position.

Brackets for removable sea rail

easier than finding space for each of the items inside a cabinet.

An effective bunk board is nothing more than a large removable sea rail. A bunk board that drops into U-shaped brackets has the advantage of allowing you to install it on *top* of the cushion so that you can narrow the bunk into a proper sea berth. In port, you want bunks to be as wide as possible, but you will be thrown around at sea if the bunk is more than a couple of inches wider than your shoulders. More than one set of brackets allows the width to be adjusted to the individual off watch. You will not have this versatility with a hinged board or a canvas lee cloth.

CEILING

Ceiling strips are little different from fiddle rails. While newer boats usually hide the inside of the hull with some type of inner liner—not necessarily an improvement—in a lot of older boats the hull is exposed, especially in the forward cabin. Sometimes it is painted like the inside of a bassboat (real nice!), and sometimes it is covered with a piece of carpet or vinyl. A wooden ceiling is easy to install and the difference it makes in the appearance of the cabin is astonishing.

Begin by sawing several 1/2-inch strips from a 3/4-inch-thick board, using your circular saw and its rip guide. Fir will do, but because the strips are going to hold the mounting screws, oak will be better.

Glue these strips vertically to the hull about 18 inches apart, beginning with a strip a couple of inches from the forward edge of the surface being covered, spacing the others equally, and ending with a similar strip a couple of inches from the aft end. If the curvature is not severe, contact cement applied to the strip and the hull will hold the wood in position. Cut a piece of fiberglass mat into 4-inch strips and apply two layers of mat and resin over each strip. Don't forget to grind away the bassboat paint.

Beginning with a wide plank 1 1/2 inches thick and at least as long as the section of hull you are

covering, use your circular saw and rip guide to cut 3/8-inch by 1 1/2-inch slats. Sand each slat and round the edges with a sander or router. Space the slats about 1/2 inch apart and screw them to the fiberglassed strips. Pilot drill and countersink the holes, and use 3/4-inch #6 stainless steel oval-head screws.

Cut each slat to length—and with the appropriate angle—as it is being installed. Take care to keep the screw lines straight. After all the ceiling has been installed, hide any imperfections in fit with a length of matching molding across each end.

Besides looking good, ceiling provides the opportunity to insulate the hull. The traditional method is to glue closed-cell urethane foam to the hull between the vertical strips, then install the ceiling over the foam. A new product from Texcon called Reflectix—a mylar/bubble cap sandwich with an R-value of about six for 1/4-inch thickness—is finding a loyal following (check your local lumberyard). It is installed the same way.

Priming the Pump

Ripping ceiling slats is a lot easier on a table saw and the cuts will be much more accurate. A table saw does a better job on crosscuts, too. If you are doing a lot of woodwork, it is the setup time that kills you. Even with the square guides you made, if you want to cut 10 identical pieces, you must carefully locate the guide and clamp it in position at least 10 times—and the pieces still will vary some. You will save a lot of time in the long run if you will invest a Saturday in converting your circular saw into a table saw.

Begin with a piece of 3/4-inch plywood about 3 feet square. If you have a smaller scrap, you can make the table smaller, but the smaller it is, the more limited it will be. Besides, if it is wide enough to sit across the cockpit seats, it will not need any other support and it will be super handy. The only thing critical about the table is that the sides are straight and parallel and the corners are square.

Fully retract the blade of your circular saw and, with the best surface of the plywood down, place

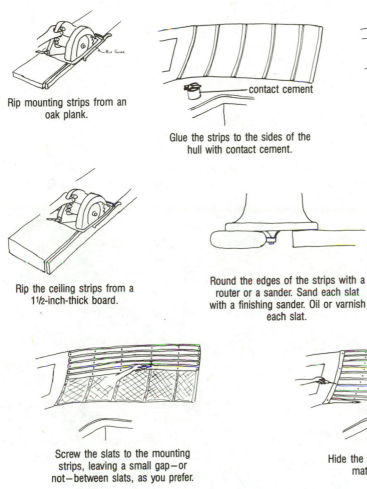

Rip mounting strips from an oak plank.

Glue the strips to the sides of the hull with contact cement.

Apply two layers of fiberglass mat and resin over each strip.

Rip the ceiling strips from a 1½-inch-thick board.

Round the edges of the strips with a router or a sander. Sand each slat with a finishing sander. Oil or varnish each slat.

If insulation is desired, lay it between the mounting strips.

Screw the slats to the mounting strips, leaving a small gap—or not—between slats, as you prefer.

Hide the ends with a piece of matching molding.

Installing ceiling

the saw approximately in the middle of the table. Carefully align the saw parallel to the two sides and outline the base on the plywood. Reset the blade depth and check the blade to make sure it is perpendicular. Align your square guide and carefully make a plunge cut *inside* one of the traced lines, taking care not to allow the blade outside of the outline. Plunge cut the other three sides, then complete the cutout with your saber saw. You want the sole plate to be a *tight* fit, so when you are making the cutout, err on the side of making it too small; enlarge the

hole with a block plane, a chisel, a wood rasp, or sandpaper.

When the saw fits the hole, you will need to fabricate supports to hold it in place. This can usually be accomplished by framing the inside of the cutout with cleat stock, recessed in such a way that the sole plate of the saw is flush with the top of the table. Make sure the saw can be easily installed and removed before gluing the supports to the table.

You are not quite through. Converting a circular saw to a table saw makes the switch inaccessible.

In the center of a 3-foot square of ¾" plywood, outline the base plate of the circular saw.

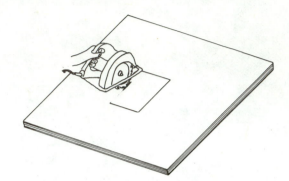

Plunge cut *inside* the outline.

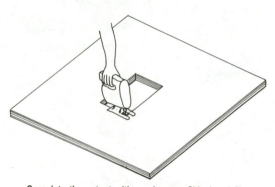

Complete the cutout with a sabersaw. Chisel and file as necessary to allow a *tight* fit.

Nail and glue cleats in the cutout to support the saw so the base is flush with the top surface of the wood.

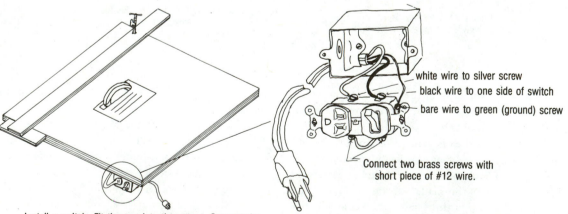

Install a switch. Fit the saw into the cutout. Support the table on horses, a box, or across cockpit seats. Use the cutting guide as shown.

white wire to silver screw
black wire to one side of switch
bare wire to green (ground) screw

Connect two brass screws with short piece of #12 wire.

Switch detail. Plug cord into available outlet. Plug saw into socket. Switch turns off power to adjoining socket.

Converting a circular saw to a table saw

You will have to tape it on, but starting and stopping the saw by plugging it in and out is awkward and dangerous. Go to the hardware store and buy a small outlet box with a cable clamp, a duplex cover plate, an electrical fixture that combines a wall switch and a single outlet, their shortest replacement appliance cord (three-wire) with a molded plug, and a few inches of solid #12 copper wire. Screw the box to the underside of the table near the front—recessed but easily accessible. Thread the end of the replacement cord into the box through the cable clamp. The white (neutral) wire is connected to the silver screw on one side of the outlet. On the same side of the fixture, attach the black (hot) wire to the screw next to the switch. Connect the two screws on the opposite side of the fixture to one another with a short piece of #12 wire. The green wire is attached to the green (ground) screw in the metal part of the fixture. Tighten the wire clamp, screw the fixture to the box, install the cover, plug the drill into the outlet, and attach the new plug to shore power. You will be able to turn the saw off and on by flipping the switch.

Clamp your square cutting guide to the table and run the wood against it and through the saw blade and you can cut similar pieces with a single setup. Adding a sliding top will make your cuts easier, safer, and far more precise. For the slide, you need a piece of 1/4-inch plywood as long as the table and 1 1/2 inches wider. With the best face of the plywood up, lay waxed paper along both sides and center the saw table, top-down, on the slide. Fold the paper up over the table and glue straight cleat stock the full length of both sides of the slide. Clamp the cleats to the slide so that they press against the edges of the table; the waxed paper will shield the table from errant glue and will provide some clearance between the table and the slide when it is removed.

When the glue dries, remove the paper and turn both parts over. The slide rests on the table with the cleats against both edges. You should be able to slide the top back and forth with no sideways movement. If it binds slightly, try coating the inside edge of the cleats and the edges of the table with paraffin or paste wax.

To complete the sliding top, you need two straight sections of 2 × 4 as long as the top is wide. With the 4-inch dimension up, glue one of the boards to the top of the slide along its rear edge. Install the saw in the table and set the blade somewhat higher than 1/4 inch. With the sliding top in place *in front of the blade,* turn on the saw and slide the top into the blade until the cut reaches about two thirds of the way to the front of the slide. Back the slide slightly and turn off the saw. With a carpenter's square, square the second board, also with the 4-inch dimension up, along the front edge of the top. Clamp—do not glue—this fence in place, placing the clamps on the ends so the top will still slide on the table. To avoid cutting all the way through the slide before it is ready, lay a scrap of straight 1 × 4 flat and tightly against the fence and clamp it to the top. Butt a second piece of 1 × 4 against the clamped piece and check the alignment by sliding the top into the blade far enough to cut this piece in half. Invert one half; the cut edges should still meet perfectly.

When the front fence is perfectly square with the blade, turn the top over and drill about six evenly-spaced pilot holes through the plywood and into the fence, countersinking them. Install the screws and then remove them. Unclamp the fence and coat it and the slide with glue, assembling the two with the screws. Remove the clamped 1 × 4. The slide is ready to use when the glue dries.

DIVIDE AND CONQUER

I do not mean to be obsessive about stowage, but I have never seen a boat where everything the owner wanted aboard could be stowed out of sight. I wonder if that's what Mr. Rat meant when he called it "messing about?" I have also never seen a boat that could not gain *usable* stowage with the addition of a shelf or a divider or a cabinet. But the real reason for this emphasis is because these kinds of projects are, for the most part, out of sight—the perfect location for anyone's first attempts to take a sheet or block of wood and shape it into something else.

Dividers are nothing more than shelves turned

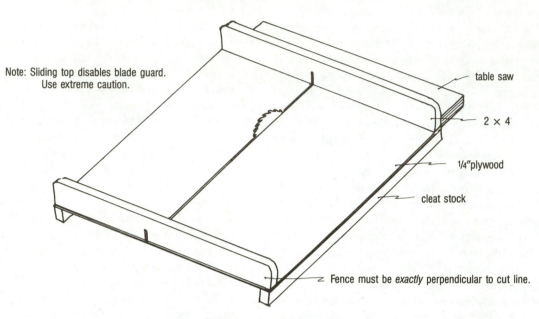

Note: Sliding top disables blade guard. Use extreme caution.

table saw

2 × 4

1/4"plywood

cleat stock

Fence must be *exactly* perpendicular to cut line.

Sliding top for table saw

on end. Any large storage area used for storing small items will benefit from a divider. Drawers, in particular, are more efficient when they are compartmented.

Making a drawer divider requires 1/8-inch plywood and some cleat stock. Determine the width of the divider by measuring the inside width of the drawer. The height of the divider should be about 1/2 inch *less* than the depth of the drawer. Cut the plywood to these dimensions, using a square cutting guide or the table saw slide described above. Cut four lengths of cleat stock to the height of the divider; smaller square stock or 3/8-inch quarter-round molding will be better proportioned for this use than the 3/4-inch cleat stock used for shelves.

Mark the drawer sides with the desired location of the divider. Glue and clamp one cleat on each side against that mark. Wrap a piece of waxed paper across each end of the divider and hold the divider against the two cleats. Glue and clamp the second pair of cleats to the drawer sides, locating the cleats against the divider. As before, the paper protects the divider from accidental bonding and provides clearance between the divider and the sandwiching cleats.

To separate the drawer into four compartments requires a second divider running lengthwise in the drawer. Where the two intersect, each will need an 1/8-inch-wide slot cut halfway through the height dimension. Set your circular saw to full depth to minimize the curvature at the front of the cut. Install the first divider with the slot open at the top. The second divider, with the slot open at the bottom, slips—slot-to-slot—over the first, the uncut portion of each divider fitting into the slot of the other. If you interlock several dividers in this manner, dividing the drawer into additional compartments, you can dispense with the cleats; the interlocked dividers will be sufficiently rigid to stay in place.

Locker dividers are less likely to be square, since most boat lockers lie against the hull. As a result, fitting and attaching a locker divider is slightly more complicated. There are a number of methods of transferring the curvature of the hull to a piece of plywood, and you have already seen how to do it by dragging the point of a compass along the hull while the pencil duplicates the contour on the wood. But to use the compass method, you have to be able to hold the wood in place near the hull. If the shelf you contoured earlier using this method had extended

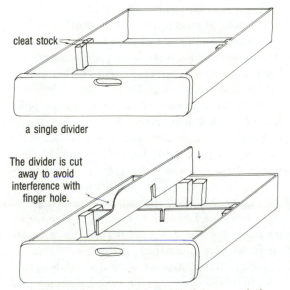

cleat stock

a single divider

The divider is cut away to avoid interference with finger hole.

Where dividers intersect, half-width slots are required.

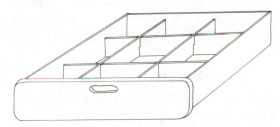

Several interlocking dividers eliminate the need for cleats.

Drawer dividers

all the way to the front of the locker, it would not have fit inside the locker until the contour was cut, but you could not outline the contour until it went inside the locker. Catch-22.

When absolute accuracy is not essential—locker dividers represent a perfect example—the easiest way to transfer the contour of the hull is with a stiff piece of wire. For a full-depth divider, measure the distance from the front of the locker to the hull where the bottom of the divider will be. Measure the height of the divider. Measure the distance from the front of the locker to the hull where the top of the divider will be. Using your square, transfer these measurements to your plywood. You have three

sides of the divider; all that is necessary to complete the outline is a curved line—the same curve as the hull—between the end of the line representing the bottom of the divider and the end of the line representing the top.

Two inches from one end of the wire, put a 90-degree bend in it with the help of your pliers; this bend will help you to keep the wire oriented in the plane of the divider. Place the bent corner where the bottom of the divider will intersect the hull. Shape the wire to the contour of the hull, holding it in place. Check and adjust until the wire lies against the hull its entire length without any pressure. Remove the wire without bending it and lay it on the plywood with the reference corner at the end of the bottom line and the curve crossing the very end of the top line. Trace the contour of the wire onto the plywood. Make the straight cuts with your circular saw, the curved one with the sabersaw. Minor fit problems can be corrected with a plane, rasp, or belt sander.

Install the divider by gluing cleats to the front and the top of the locker and screwing or gluing the divider to the cleats. The easiest way by far to attach the divider to the hull is to run a bead of polyurethane adhesive sealant along the curved edge of the divider before you install it.

In many cases, you may find that you do not want the divider to reach either the front or the top of the locker. Polyurethane adhesive is still a good choice for attaching the divider to the hull, but somehow you must stabilize the front and top. A rail across the front of the dividers several inches above the bottom will hold the front rigid and may be desirable anyway to contain the items that will be on either side of the divider. Either solid wood or 1/2-inch plywood can be used.

Measure the width of the locker and cut the rail to that length. The width of the rail will depend upon its function. Hold the rail in place against the front edge of the divider and trace both sides of it onto the rail. Now cut a 1/8-inch-deep dado between those lines.

What is a dado? For non-woodworkers it's something you shout just before daylight comes (when

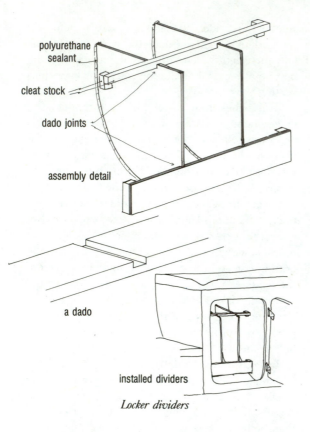

polyurethane sealant

cleat stock

dado joints

assembly detail

a dado

installed dividers

Locker dividers

The cavernous nature of cockpit lockers typically results in wasted space, particularly the space high on the hull close to the underside of the side deck. Use the same methods to cut triangular bulkheads from $1/2$-inch plywood 8 to 10 inches wide at the top and long enough for the vertical fronts to intersect the curvature of the hull. Tab the bulkheads to the hull about every 20 inches, using a layer of mat and a layer of cloth. Rip $1 1/2$-inch-wide strips from $1/4$-inch plywood and screw (and glue) three or four of these slats across the front of the bulkheads about $1 1/2$ inches apart. If you really want to impress the marina set, make the slats from solid teak.

I *know* what I said about fastening and gluing to the edge of plywood, but occasionally there simply aren't any easy alternatives. If you complain about it, I will be forced to point out that you didn't really need to measure between the slats; just use another slat as a spacer. To improve access, you might make the top slat removable. The easiest way is to cut the front edge of the bulkheads with a "crooked finger" to begin with; the slat just drops into the crook.

THE BASIC BOX

In box construction you will again find yourself gluing the edge of the plywood unless you elect to make glue-block joints. And why, exactly, are you building a plywood box? Because the box—sometimes modified to accommodate the curvature

you want to go home). Serious woodworkers use the word dado for the same reason sailors use starboard—to make other people think they're smarter than they are. A dado is a groove, period. Well, technically, I guess, it's a groove across the grain. I suppose that makes you wonder what they call a groove parallel to the grain? A groove. Pretty impressive stuff, huh?

How do you make a dado? If you made the table for your saw and the sliding top, you simply set the blade to cut $1/8$ inch deep, lay the rail against the front fence of the slide, position the marks you made over the saw slot, flip the switch, and push the slide forward.

Glue the edge of the divider into the dado, and attach the ends of the rail to cleats glued to the sides of the lockers. A similar brace across the top of the divider(s) as far toward the front as use will permit will complete the installation.

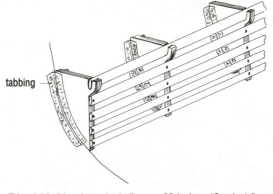

tabbing

Tab mini bulkheads to the hull every 20 inches. "Crooked finger" allows top slat to be removed for easier access.

Cockpit locker stowage

of the hull—is the basic structure of most of the interior features of your boat and several items on deck. It is also the basis for an almost limitless number of additions and modifications.

Consider the chain locker. The chain and line stack or coil into the bottom of the locker. As in the cockpit lockers, the space high in the forepeak—up against the underside of the deck—is typically wasted. Later designs included a box in the top of the chain locker with a hatch on deck for anchor stowage, but you will not find this feature in an old boat. Personally, I prefer the anchors on rollers at the bow, ready to do their job in an instant, but the idea of a box (to stow other items) in the top of the forepeak is still a good one. Instead of compromising the integrity of the deck with a hatch, access should be from below through the forepeak bulkhead.

The forepeak bulkhead usually has an opening into the chain locker. The area of the bulkhead above the opening will determine the maximum box height that will be practical for your boat. Width will be limited by the width of the chain locker, and depth by the curvature of the bow or the location of the chain pipe.

The intended use of the space will also influence the size and shape of the box. Perhaps you would like his-and-her bins for individual stowage of personal items. Maybe a bookcase appeals to you. The broad and deep but short-height aspect of the available space may be perfect for stowing extra charts, the World Atlas (which absolutely, positively will not fit anywhere else on a boat), or the Vee-berth filler board.

Once you have determined the configuration of the box, construction is a breeze. How you measure the parts will depend upon whether available space makes the external dimensions the critical ones or planned contents make the internal dimensions critical. Once again, a quick sketch with the dimensions written on it can help you to avoid confusion.

Half-inch plywood is a good choice for the sides of the box, and 1/4-inch plywood for the back. If you are constrained by the external dimensions, cut the top and the bottom of the box 1/4 inch narrower and

1/2 inch shorter than the finished size you are after. The sides are also cut 1/4 inch narrower, but not shorter. No allowance is required for the back piece.

You can do the job just as well with your circular saw and a cutting guide, but the table saw conversion will make this project go much more quickly. Clamp the square cutting guide in place as a rip fence and run your 1/2-inch plywood against it, cutting a single strip of plywood of sufficient length to provide all four sides of the box. If you are constrained by the external dimensions, the width of the strip should be 1/4 inch (the thickness of the back piece) less than the finished depth you require.

Put the sliding top in place on your saw table and place the plywood strip against the front fence. Square the end by running it through the blade, removing about 1/8 inch of material. Measure and mark the plywood 1/2 inch shorter than the finished width of the box to allow for rabbeted corners. Line the mark up with the slot in the slide. If the piece you are cutting does not extend beyond the edge of the slide, clamp a small block to the fence against the end of the plywood as a stop. Start the saw and make the cut. This piece will be the top of the box. Slide the strip of plywood against the stop, and make a second cut. This will give you an identical piece for the bottom. If you are doing more than one box of the same size, you can cut as many pieces as you need with this single setup.

Mark the plywood for the sides—the same as the desired height of the box—and reposition the clamped stop. Cut the two sides, or as many as you need.

Set the saw blade for a 1/4-inch-deep cut. When you are cutting a rabbet in plywood, you may have better results if you set the blade to finish the cut at the joint between two of the plies. Determine the correct depth by cutting a scrap of the same plywood. Mark the edge of one of the side pieces 1/2 inch from the end. Place the piece against the fence and line the mark up with the slot, with the blade between the mark and the end. Clamp a stop to the fence against the end of the piece.

With the saw running, make the first cut. Now, without disturbing the clamped stop, slide the end

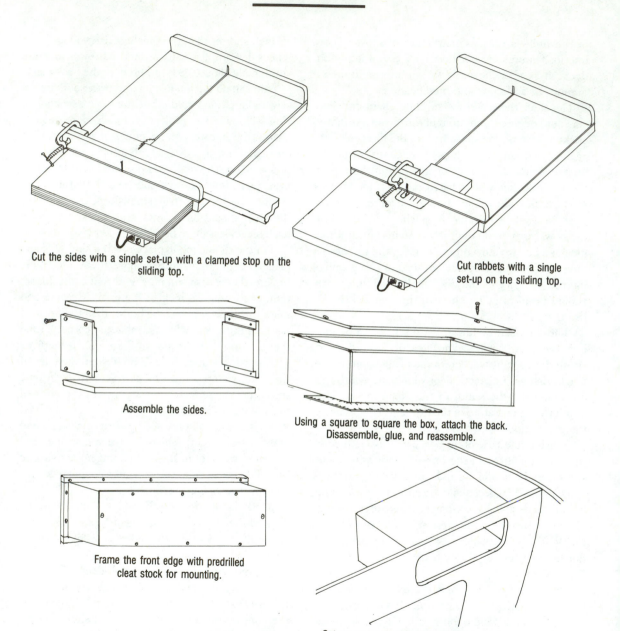

Cut the sides with a single set-up with a clamped stop on the sliding top.

Cut rabbets with a single set-up on the sliding top.

Assemble the sides.

Using a square to square the box, attach the back. Disassemble, glue, and reassemble.

Frame the front edge with predrilled cleat stock for mounting.

Cut an access hole in the bulkhead and mount the box.

Forepeak box

of the piece away from the stop until it is just shy of reaching across the slot and make a second cut. Slide the piece toward the stop by the width of the blade and cut again. Repeat once or twice more until the end touches the stop again. The rabbet is

complete and you should have cut it faster than I have described it.

Turn the part around, butt it against the stop, and rabbet the other end. Rabbet both ends of the other side piece, along with any others, while you have the setup. Finally, cut the back piece from ¼-inch plywood.

Fit the top and the bottom into the rabbets in the sides and drill pilot holes through the sides into the ends of the top and bottom. Hold the two parts against a square while drilling and space the holes 3 to 4 inches apart. Countersink. Use #6 or #8 flat-head screws about 1 inch long to assemble the box. Two screws per corner will be sufficient for this initial assembly. Checking for square, place the back on the assembled pieces and drill a pilot hole through it into one of the sides. Drill a second hole into the opposite side. Attach the back with these two screws, then drill additional widely spaced holes to fasten the back. Label the parts with a pencil to avoid confusion later, then remove all the screws. Coat all the joints with glue, then rapidly reassemble the box, installing and tightening all the screws this time.

After the box is built is the time to cut the access hole in the bulkhead. If the box will be a utility bin, to restrain the contents you will want the hole to be somewhat smaller than the mouth of the box. As a bookcase, on the other hand, the hole and the mouth of the box should probably be the same size. Cutting the hole an inch or two shorter in height than the mouth of the box will have the effect of providing an integral fiddle rail.

Position the box inside the forepeak, allowing room on all four sides for the cleats that you are going to attach it with, and trace the outline. Draw a second outline ½ inch inside the first, representing the mouth of the box, and if the opening will be a different size or shape, draw it also.

Assuming adequate space, make the cutout with your sabersaw. You can start the cut by boring a hole through the bulkhead inside the outline and inserting the blade into the hole, or you can make a plunge cut with a saber saw by tilting it onto the front of the base plate until the blade is almost parallel to the surface. Start the saw and let the blade down until it begins to scratch a groove in the wood. Continue to rock the saw slowly back toward its normal position, also moving it forward slightly to keep the point from jabbing the bottom of the cut.

When the blade penetrates, rotate the saw to the flat position and follow the pencil line to make the cutout.

Two cautions and a truth. Sabersaws are notoriously inaccurate; if your sideways pressure is a bit uneven, and it will be, the cut will be beveled rather than square. And if the face of the bulkhead is covered with plastic laminate, the saw blade is going to leave a chipped edge. The truth, at least in this case, is that since the boxes are being mounted right up against the deck, there may not be adequate room to use the sabersaw to make the entire cut. To address these difficulties, saw the cutout slightly undersize; rout it to the final dimension if there is room, or file and sand it if there isn't. If the space is likewise too limited for your electric sabersaw, you will need the manual equivalent—a keyhole saw.

Cut four pieces of cleat stock to frame the box. To avoid the difficulties of trying to drill straight holes in the cleats after they are attached, predrill and countersink shank-diameter holes 3 to 4 inches apart in the cleats. Glue and clamp the cleats *flush* with the front edge of the box, with the countersinks facing the rear.

Hold the box in place and mark the screw locations on the bulkhead with a prick mark, using a sharpened nail the size of the holes in the cleats. Assuming a ¾-inch bulkhead, wrap several layers of tape around your pilot drill about ½ inch from the point to serve as a depth guide. Be careful not to let the tape be pushed up the bit; you do not want to penetrate the bulkhead. Drill the holes and glue and screw the box to the bulkhead using 1¼-inch #10 flathead screws.

The same basic box can also house your stereo speakers. High-fidelity aficionados will tell you that putting speakers in wooden enclosures will significantly enhance the sound. You never saw a plastic Stradivarius! Since the interior of the box will not be visible, glue-block jointed corners, rather than rabbets, will be easier and adequate.

If the exterior of a box is exposed, use solid wood and/or matching hardwood plywood. To hide the end grain, join the sides with a rabbet block. You will find the rabbet block very easy to make on the sliding table. For a 6-inch-deep box, you need four 6-inch lengths of solid wood with a square cross-section of $1\frac{1}{4}$ inches or a little more. Set the blade to make a $\frac{1}{2}$-inch-deep cut. Using a square, tack a wooden batten to the top of the table parallel to the slot and $\frac{1}{2}$ inch (assuming the box is constructed of $\frac{1}{2}$-inch material) from the far side of the slot. Butt the end of one of the corner blocks against the fence with the side against the batten. Run the block over the saw blade, then make the remainder of the cuts necessary to finish the rabbet.

Pay attention. Rotate the block 90 degrees, so that the rabbet you just made is still on the same side but at the top of the piece. Now, *without lifting it from the table*, turn the part end-for-end. Butt it against the fence and the batten and saw a second rabbet. Cut the remaining three corner blocks the same way. The square ends of the box sides fit into the rabbet cuts, providing a glue block and hiding the end grain at the same time. After the box is assembled, the solid corners can be routed with the corner round bit. Another possibility is to make the rabbet slightly wider than the sides of the box so that the corner block stands out like molding.

How you finish the front of speaker enclosures is up to you. The simplest way is to cut a piece of $\frac{1}{2}$-inch plywood to the size and shape of the front of the box. Cut out the center for the speaker and screw the speaker in place. Wrap speaker cloth—or any open-weave cloth—around the front piece and staple it in place on the back. Screw the front in place with two or four stainless steel oval-head screws in finishing washers. For a cleaner look, snap the front in place by installing a pair of cheap plastic cabinet latches in the box and on the rear of the front piece.

If you want the speaker enclosure to look like fine furniture, frame the front with molding. You can make your own from $\frac{1}{2}$-inch or $\frac{3}{4}$-inch solid stock. Rip the stock to an appropriate width—probably about 1 inch for a small enclosure. Cut a $\frac{1}{2}$-inch-wide rabbet slightly deeper than $\frac{1}{4}$ inch along one edge. With your router, round both corners on the side opposite the rabbet. Miter cut one

end, keeping in mind that the rabbet will be along the inside edge of the frame.

Making an accurate miter cut requires a miter box and a backsaw. Feeling the way I do about handsaws, I usually nail together a miter box for my circular saw. To both edges of a 2-foot length of straight 1×2, I nail two similar pieces, forming a U-shaped channel. I place my saw—with the blade retracted—flat on a 1-foot-square scrap of $\frac{1}{4}$-inch plywood and nail two foot-long lengths of cleat stock against the edges of the sole plate. The plywood sits on the channel with the cleats perpendicular and a single nail is driven—centered between the two cleats—through the plywood and into the front rail of the channel. With this nail as a pivot, I use a combination square to set the angle between the cleats and the channel to 45 degrees, tacking the plywood in position with a partially driven nail *outside* of the cleats. I check the saw blade to be sure it is absolutely vertical and set it to about $\frac{1}{8}$ inch deeper than the distance from the top of the plywood to the bottom of the inside of the channel. With a piece of scrap in the box, I run the saw between the cleats, cutting about halfway across the plywood and stopping the saw as soon as it cuts through both rails. After checking the accuracy of the miter, I can make minor adjustments as necessary by removing the second nail. When the cut is perfect, I fix it with a larger nail.

However, to do a mitered frame, you have to be able to make the cut on both sides of the perpendicular. This can be done with a second miter box, or by pulling the positioning nail and pivoting the plywood on the initial nail to the opposite angle. Once the correct position has been found, it is also fixed with a large nail and either cut can be made by reinserting the appropriate nail. To hold the molding tightly against the rail, use a couple of wooden wedges.

The sliding table can eliminate the miter box altogether. From a piece of $\frac{1}{2}$-inch plywood cut a *very accurate* 45-degree triangle with the base slightly longer than the fence of the slide and tack it in place against the fence with the apex of the trian-

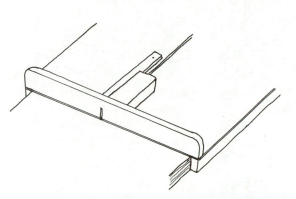

Tack a batten to the sliding top to position the block
for cutting rabbets.

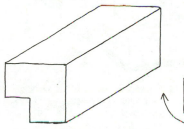

Block after the initial cut.

Rotate 90 degrees.

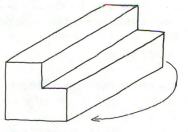

Spin end for end.

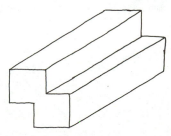

Cut second rabbet to complete block.

Rabbet block

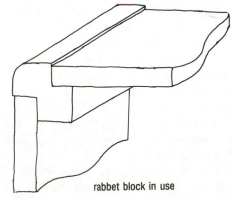

rabbet block in use

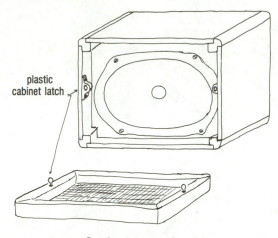

plastic
cabinet latch

Speaker front attachment

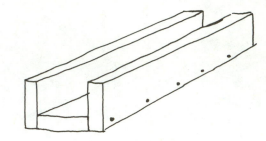

Nail three lengths of 1 × 2 into
a U-shaped channel.

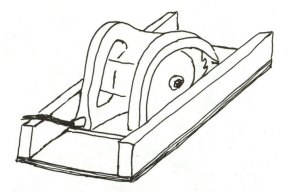

Nail two 1 × 2 rails against the edges of the saw's sole plate
on a scrap of plywood.

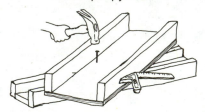

Using the combination square, place the saw channel on top of
the wood channel at a 45-degree angle and nail it tentatively
in position.

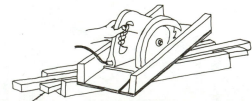

wedges to hold work
against the rear rail

Make a cut with the saw and check the
angle of the cut, adjusting the miter as
necessary. Nail or glue the channels
together when adjustment is complete.

Circular saw miter box

gle centered in the slot. By holding the molding against either side of the triangle (depending upon which way you want the angle) you should get a perfect miter.

Back to business: measure across the completed box and transfer that measurement from the point of the miter along the edge of the molding. The second miter cut is opposite the first one. In the same way, cut the remaining three pieces from the strip.

Gluing mitered parts together is not difficult with special miter clamps or with four bar or pipe clamps. Without these, it requires a little ingenuity. Nail two boards to a flat surface to form a 90-degree corner. Cut four 4-inch pieces of 1 × 2 or 1 × 4 and rip these in half, making the cut at an angle of about 10 degrees so that the two halves are slightly wedge-shaped. Watch your fingers! Assemble the frame with two sides against the two boards and press a pair of wedges near each end of the other two sides. Nail down the outside half of each of the wedge pairs. Now by tapping on the fat ends of the loose halves, you can increase clamping pressure and keep the frame square. So coat the mitered ends with glue and do it.

The center of the speaker enclosure should be cut from 1/4-inch plywood slightly smaller than the dimensions of the rabbeted cutout around the inside

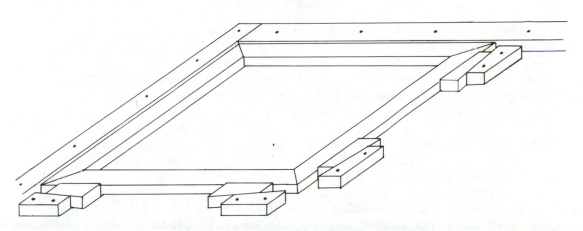

Clamping a mitered frame

edge of the frame. Cut out the speaker opening, mount the speaker, cover the front surface with speaker cloth, and glue the front inside the frame. Mount the front to the box with cabinet latches.

Not to beat a dead horse, but the Dorade ventilator is no more than a box with a baffle or two inside. Most old boats, especially those left closed for long periods, can benefit from a Dorade or two. If you don't object to exposed end grain, you can build the Dorade box from solid wood, butting the parts and joining them with screws. Counterbore the shank holes with a sharp ³/₈-inch drill and plug them with matching bungs after the screws have been installed.

You can cut bungs with a plug cutter, or buy them from your lumber supplier. Put a bit of varnish or glue around the edge of the bung before you install it and try to match the color and the direction of the grain. Gently tap it into the hole as far as it will go. After the glue is dry, place the point of a chisel— beveled side down—against the plug about ¹/₈-inch above the surface of the wood and tap the chisel with a mallet. The top of the plug will split away. Note the lowest edge of the plug. Turn the chisel over and, cutting with the grain from the lowest

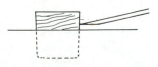

With the bevel of the chisel down, trim the plug about ⅛″ above the surface.

Note the lowest edge of the trimmed plug, and working from that edge, pare the plug nearly flush.

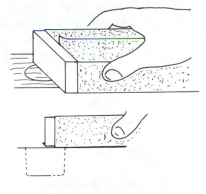

Sand with the grain to finish the job.

Trimming wood plugs

edge, pare away the plug until it is almost flush. Finish the job with sandpaper.

Plugs can be avoided altogether by joining the pieces with glue blocks. Rabbet blocks will allow the sides of the box to be constructed of hardwood plywood, although the top should still be solid wood.

The box may be more attractive if you make the forward face slanted rather than vertical. This is accomplished by cutting the front edge of the sides to the desired angle. To get both sides the same, stack the two pieces and cut them together. The angled front will require that the front piece be somewhat wider than the other three sides and be bevel cut on the top and the bottom. Use one of the sides as a guide to set the bevel of the saw blade. While the blade is set, also bevel the front edge of the top. Do not use the sliding table when the saw blade is not vertical because the bevel cut will alter the slot, making the slide less convenient later for square cuts; use a rip guide instead.

Make the two forward rabbet blocks longer than necessary and, after the four sides have been assembled, trim them to size (and angle) with a sabersaw. Cut a hole at the forward end of the solid top for the cowl ventilator and butt the top to the edges of the sides. You can round three edges of the top with the router, but because of the bevel, you will have to round the forward edge with a sander.

What makes this box a Dorade is the baffle. The rear of the box sits over an opening into the cabin and a cowl vent is installed on the top of the box at the front. Just forward of the opening into the cabin you need a baffle across the interior of the box; it should be flush with the bottom edges and should extend slightly more than halfway to the top. Cut it to fit and install it with glue blocks. The baffle keeps any water that finds its way into the ventilator from coming below, but you need scuppers to let the water out of the box. The easiest way to get them is to use your router and straight bit to cut notches about 3/8 inch deep and an inch long into the bottom edges. Locate the scupper holes in the sides of the box near all four corners of the area forward of the baffle.

With a belt sander, shape the bottom of the box to the curvature of the deck. Install the box by screwing cleats to the deck so that the box sits over the cleats. Be sure the cleats do not block the scuppers. Bed the edges—including the baffle—with polyurethane sealant and screw the box to the cleats. Install wooden bungs to hide the screws and trim the plugs. Lightly sand the box and finish it to match the other wood on deck.

MOVING THE FURNITURE

Adapting an old boat to your dream may involve changing the accommodations. In an earlier chapter I mentioned a 34-footer with nine bunks. If I possessed such a boat, there is little doubt that I would tear out most of the interior and start all over. Fortunately, most of us find ourselves with boats whose accommodation plan *almost* works for us, if we could just . . .

Before you destroy the old accommodations, you should carefully evaluate the changes you plan. It is not easy to accurately assess changes that only exist in your mind. If you are too hasty, you may end up with accommodations that are less comfortable than the original ones.

Before you start making major changes, buy a few sheets of the cheapest grade of 1/4-inch plywood and a dozen construction grade 1 × 2's to mock up each cabin and try out your ideas for space and function. If that seems like wasted effort and unwarranted expense, allow me to report that most of the major renovations I have been aboard are *less* functional than the original plan and invariably the owner apologizes for the most glaring shortcomings with a sentence that begins, "I didn't realize . . ." Besides dismaying you with the discovery that you are personally dissatisfied with the results of your efforts, butchered accommodations will make resale difficult and have an adverse effect on the value of the boat. Not a good way to spend your winter.

None of this is to say that improvements are not possible. *Au contraire*, I have never been aboard a stock boat that could not benefit from some accommodation changes. Sometimes very small changes

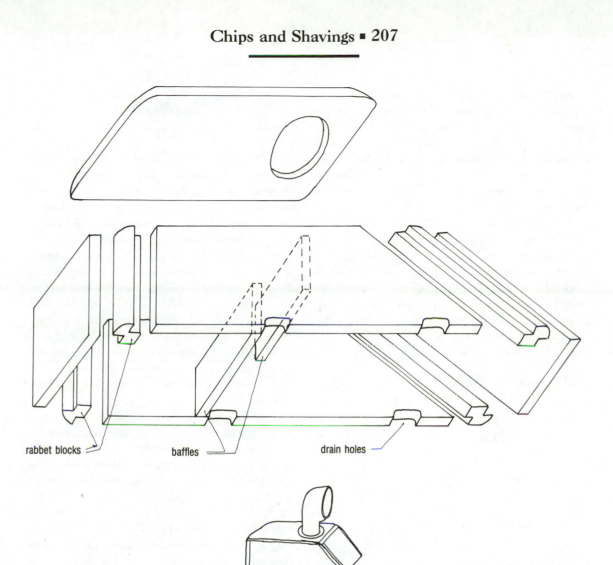

rabbet blocks   baffles   drain holes

an approximation of the finished item

Dorade box detail

can make a very big difference in comfort or convenience. Consider the lockers beneath the bunks and settees. Regardless of the size of the locker, most manufacturers of older boats used a standard template to cut access hatches. Fill such a locker with canned goods and someone aboard is going to spend hours emptying and repacking it in repeated searches for specific items. There are more enjoyable ways to exhibit great buns.

The solution: locker-size lids. Trace the perimeter of the locker on the surface of the top. Draw a second outline 4 or 5 inches inside the first. This is the size the lid should be. Radius the corners using a small paint can as a pattern. Check for wiring and plumbing by running your hand *inside* the locker beneath the outline. If the curvature of the hull causes the locker to be very shallow on one side, move that edge of the lid inboard a few inches. Make a plunge cut with your *sabersaw* and follow the outline. Support the lid to keep it from tearing free before you complete the cut. Lightly sand the cut edges.

Rip 1-inch-wide strips from a piece of ½-inch plywood for seating cleats. Cut the strips into appropriate lengths and glue them in place against the underside of the top of the locker. About ⅜ inch of the cleats should extend beyond the edge of the opening. If you do not have a sufficient number of clamps, use screws driven from inside the locker to hold the cleats while the glue dries.

As for the original lid, you can leave it unaltered or you can screw or glue it to its cleats. If the new lid is too big to be convenient, cut it in half and install a divider in the locker, or support the joint with a piece of 1 × 2 bridging the opening. Ideally, the space beneath a 6-foot-long bunk or settee should be divided into either three or four separated lockers, each with its full-size lid.

THE HARD STUFF

If you are still with me at this point, you are in possession of adequate woodworking skills to make

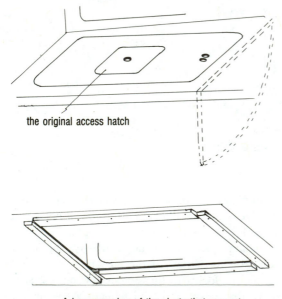

the original access hatch

A bean-can view of the cleats that support the lid.

A new locker lid

any repair or bring about any change to the wooden portions of your old fiberglass boat. Let's take on the installation of a new galley and you will see what I mean.

First, you need to recognize that the top of a cabinet is nothing more than a shelf, the sides no more than dividers. Add a front piece to the shelves and dividers and you have the basic box. And you thought the box section was long because I was just short on ideas. Aren't you ashamed?

As with any complex project, the best place to start is with a pencil and paper. Sketch out what you have in mind and get the rough measurements down. Decide where the sink goes. Will there be an ice chest? Can you incorporate a garbage bin into the top? Will you have drawers or lockers or some combination of both? Will the stove be gimbaled? Do you need mounting space for foot pumps? How will the cabinet be finished, and how will it be trimmed?

In this example, the new galley attaches to an existing bulkhead at one end and requires a new partial bulkhead at the other. The first challenge is to match the new bulkhead to the contour of the hull. Use the *stiff wire* method described earlier to transfer a close approximation of the contour to a piece of ¾-inch plywood, cutting the bulkhead to shape but a couple of inches too wide. Holding the slightly oversize bulkhead in place, use your compass to transfer the exact contour to the piece, and trim the bulkhead along this line. Check again for fit, then glue a polyurethane or PVC foam pad to the edge (to prevent the bulkhead from forming a hard spot in the hull), finally trimming the inboard edge as appropriate. Tab the new bulkhead to the hull, taking great care to keep it parallel to the existing one.

All that is required to complete your "box" is the front and the top. Fabricate the front first, using ½-inch plywood and squaring the top edge with the two sides. Install cleat stock on the bulkheads to act as glue blocks for the joints between them and the front. Screw the front temporarily into position.

To support the top, install cleat stock to the in-

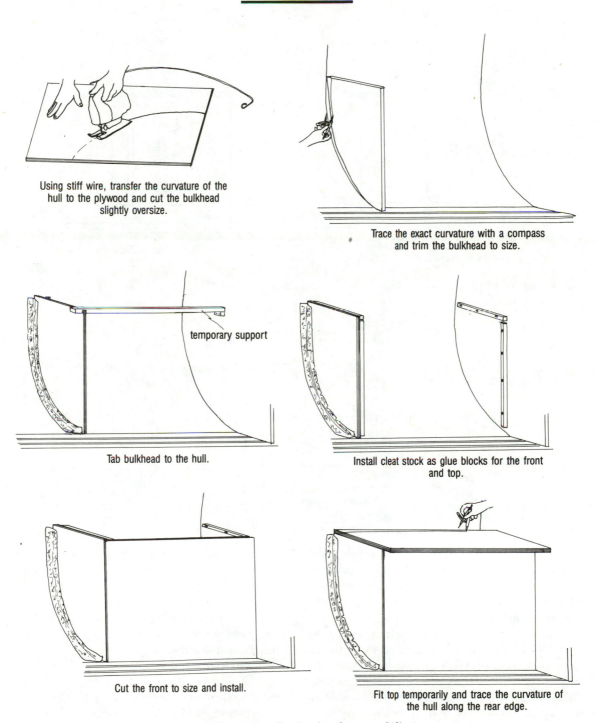

Using stiff wire, transfer the curvature of the hull to the plywood and cut the bulkhead slightly oversize.

Trace the exact curvature with a compass and trim the bulkhead to size.

temporary support

Tab bulkhead to the hull.

Install cleat stock as glue blocks for the front and top.

Cut the front to size and install.

Fit top temporarily and trace the curvature of the hull along the rear edge.

Building a new galley (continued on page 210)

Draw all necessary cut-outs. Plunge cut with
the sabersaw and make cut-outs.

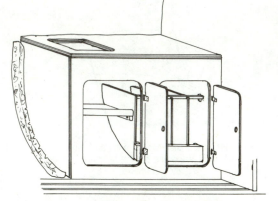

Install dividers and shelves.

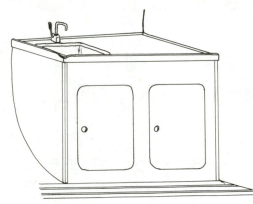

Paint, varnish, oil, or cover with laminate.
Cover raw edges with molding.

Building a new galley (continued)

side of the front flush with its top edge and along the
bulkheads toward the hull, using your square to
keep all the surfaces square. Do not carry the cleats
all the way to the hull, to allow for the tabbing between the hull and the top.

The top is fabricated from ¾-inch plywood. As
you did with the bulkhead, rough cut the outboard
contour, leaving an extra inch in width. Position the
top and trace the exact contour with a compass.
Trim along this line and attach a strip of foam. With
the top in position, mark the location of the front
edge and trim the piece to size.

There is little that is new from here on out. For
example, you need a cutout for the sink. Outline the
cutout and make it with your sabersaw exactly as
you did the enlarged access hole for the under-bunk
locker or the bin opening in the forepeak bulkhead.
The same procedure applies to cutouts for bins,
lockers, and drawers.

Fitting and installing shelves and dividers for a
cabinet you have built is no different from fitting and
installing them in existing cabinet work. Install full
dividers first, cleating them to the front and the top
and tabbing them to the hull. It may make the job

easier if you finish all of the interior features of your new cabinet before permanently installing the top. Tab it to the hull and screw and/or glue it to the cleats.

You will probably surface the top—and the sides if they are not hardwood plywood—with plastic laminate, a process we examined back in Chapter 7. Fiddle rails for the counter are fabricated just like those for a shelf. Wood trim can be purchased, or you can cut your own. For example, put a 1/2-inch by 1/2-inch rabbet in the edge of a length of 3/4-inch-thick solid wood, then rip a 3/4-inch strip from the rabbeted edge and you have a length of 3/4-inch corner molding. Fit molding together with miter cuts at the corners.

If your cabinet will have drawers, you will need to install guide rails. There are numerous options, but I prefer the plastic glide that is screwed to the rear of the drawer and slides on an (inverted) T-shaped rail *above* the drawer. The glides and the hardwood rails are available from lumber suppliers.

If the drawer is large or will contain heavy items,

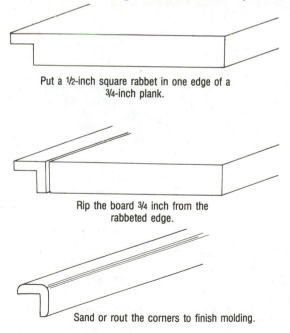

Put a 1/2-inch square rabbet in one edge of a 3/4-inch plank.

Rip the board 3/4 inch from the rabbeted edge.

Sand or rout the corners to finish molding.

Making corner molding

side rails are a better option. For a single drawer, cleat two lengths of straight 1 × 2 to the inside of the cabinet front, the 2-inch side flush with (or just slightly recessed from) the sides of the drawer cutout, half the width of the rails above the bottom of the drawer cutout, half below. The other ends of the rails are attached to the hull or to vertical framing installed just for this purpose. The rails must be square (in both directions) with the front and parallel to each other. Three-quarter-inch cleat stock is glued to the inside face of each rail about 1/8 inch below the level of the bottom of the cutout. This creates a pair of L-shaped rails that will support the drawer and align it.

The reason the cleat stock is 1/8 inch lower than the cutout is that the drawers you build will be notched in the front so they have to be lifted to open; otherwise they will slide out when the boat heels. A wooden turn button attached to the inside of the drawer at the rear will keep you from accidentally pulling it all the way out. You will also need "tip" rails above the drawer to keep it from tipping downward when it is opened. If you have a tier of drawers, the support rails of the drawer above may also serve this function. For a tier of drawers, substitute plywood dividers for the 1 × 2 side rails.

The drawers themselves are nothing more than a box. Cut the sides from 3/8-inch plywood. The end pieces are square cut and rabbeted to a depth of about 1/4 inch. Rabbeted corners will be strong enough for normal use, but if you are so inclined, you can buy a dovetail jig for your router and dovetail the drawer joints. A dovetail joint will last forever.

The bottoms are 1/8-inch hardboard or plywood. The drawers will be much stronger if the bottom panels fit into groves. Set the saw to a depth of about 1/8 inch and use a square cutting guide to groove the inside face of all four pieces about 1/4 inch from the bottom. When you assemble the drawer, do not glue the bottom panel into the groove—it should be able to expand and contract without affecting the joints.

With the drawer assembled, set the saw depth to 1/2 inch and stand the drawer on its front face. Set

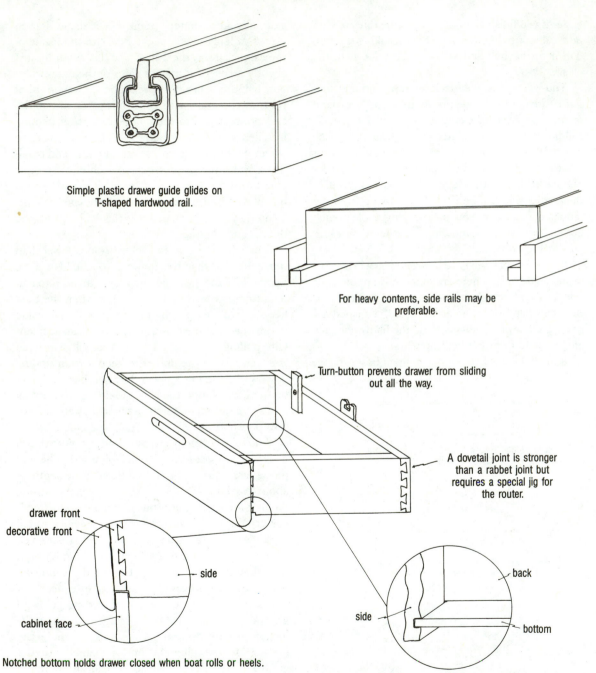

Simple plastic drawer guide glides on
T-shaped hardwood rail.

For heavy contents, side rails may be
preferable.

Turn-button prevents drawer from sliding
out all the way.

A dovetail joint is stronger
than a rabbet joint but
requires a special jig for
the router.

drawer front

decorative front

side

cabinet face

Notched bottom holds drawer closed when boat rolls or heels.

back

side

bottom

For strength, the bottom should fit into a groove in all four sides
of the drawer.

Drawer construction

the guide so that the saw will remove ⅛ inch from the bottom of the front. This will create the notch necessary to hold the drawer closed until you want it open.

The simplest drawer face is a piece of solid wood an inch or so larger than the cutout. Round the front edges with a router and glue the face to the front of the drawer. Protruding knobs and handles are dangerous on a boat, so make a slot instead. In the center of the face, a couple of inches from the top, bore a pair of 1-inch holes about 4 inches apart. Make two parallel cuts between the holes with your saber saw, creating an inch-wide slot with radiused ends for gripping the drawer to open it. Round the edges of the slot with your router and the face is finished.

Laminate-covered plywood with contrasting wood edging and a recessed wooden pull (purchased) also makes a simple and attractive drawer face. With seating cleats at the top and the bottom of the cutout, flush drawer faces are possible, but a close-fitting flush face will prevent the drawer from being lifted, so an alternative to the notched bottom must be used to hold the drawer closed. "Bird" cabinet latches are the usual choice, released through an open hole or slot pull. Because the flush drawer will not have a slot, the support rails must be flush with the bottom of the cutout, not ⅛ inch below.

Cabinet doors also present you with numerous choices, but there are two basic types: solid and paneled. A solid door is constructed exactly like a solid drawer front. A paneled door is composed of a frame—like a picture frame—surrounding a panel of some other material. We have already been through the process of fabricating a miter-cut frame in the discussion of speaker enclosures. A cabinet door frame is identical, but with a thin panel of laminate-covered plywood, or hardwood plywood, or slats, or louvers, or woven wood, or stamped aluminum (bletch!), or cane, or whatever.

To withstand the rigors a cabinet door is prey to, using the substantially stronger end-lap joint is a good idea. The ends of all four pieces of the frame have rabbets cut into them the width of the adjoin-ing piece. The depth of the rabbet is half the thickness of the material. It may be easier to mill the large rabbet required in an end-lap joint with a router, rather than cutting it with a saw. All four pieces can be rabbeted at the same time if they are clamped together, ends flush. You will get better results with a guide clamped across the wood instead of using an edge guide attached to the router because you can lay a fifth piece of the same stock in front of the ends to support the rear half of the router, helping you keep it level. A second setup will be required to mill the opposite ends.

When you assemble the frame, clamp it to a flat surface until the glue dries; this will insure that the frame does not warp. You cannot cut the rabbet (unlike mitered pieces) for the interior panel in end-lapped frame pieces before the frame is assembled. After the frame is assembled, rabbet the perimeter of the interior with the router. You will have to

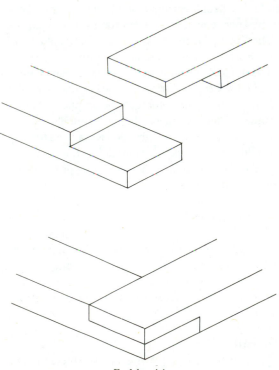

End-lap joint

square the corners with a chisel. The width and depth of the rabbet will depend upon the center panel.

If you want to use cane, a ⅜-inch by ⅜-inch rabbet will be about right. Cut the cane about 2 inches oversize and soak it in warm water for a couple of hours. Stretch it evenly–watch the alignment of the pattern–and tack the cane in place with brass brads through quarter-round molding pressed into the corner of the rabbet. While it is still soft, trim the excess with a razor knife. An alternative method is to rout a ¼-inch groove around the frame and secure the cane by stretching it over the groove and pounding *caning bead* into it. Either way, when the cane dries, it will be drum-tight.

ON DECK

The original brightwork of your old boat is almost certain to be mahogany or teak. If it is mahogany and it has been neglected for a long time, it is likely to be split, checked, or even rotten. If it is unvarnished teak, on the other hand, you should hope that it *has* been neglected. Every time a previous owner lovingly scrubbed or sanded the teak in preparation for a treatment of oil or sealer, another layer of the wood departed through the scuppers. After a couple of decades of scrubbing, handrails are too thin to be safe, not enough wood remains in toerails to hold bungs, and the mounting screws through wood coamings are on islands standing proud above the eroded surface.

Replacing the wood on deck is typically a matter of removing the old piece and using it as a pattern to cut a new one. While much of the work below involves plywood, solid wood is the dominant material on deck. You will need to pay attention to the direction of the grain, and you may need to join short or narrow pieces to make longer or wider ones.

Toerail

Fabricating and replacing wooden toerail is not very difficult. Determine the height and width that you want and buy your lumber as close to those

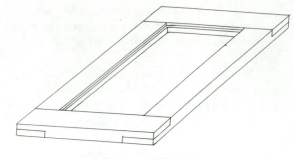

End-lapped door frame

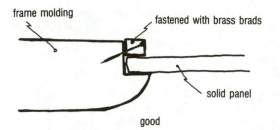

Solid panel installation

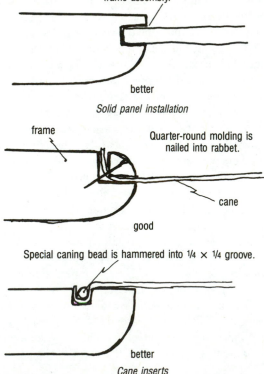

Cane inserts

dimensions as possible. To get the length required will necessitate joining more than one board. These pieces must be joined with scarfs.

If the glue line between two pieces of wood is perpendicular, you are looking at a butt joint. If that line is at 89 degrees, I suppose that is technically a scarf, but the angle of a true scarf—one that forms a strong joint—is more likely to be between 5 degrees and 10 degrees. Scarfs are not described by their angles but by a ratio of the length of the joint to the width of the material. For example, the joint of a 12-to-1 scarf between two lengths of 2-inch-wide lumber would be 24 inches long. For a toerail, 8-to-1 is ample.

The strength of a scarf depends upon the accurate fitting together of the parts. A jig is required. Cut two matching planks of 1/2-inch plywood at least 2 inches wider than the height of the toerail and several inches longer than the scarf will be. Align the two pieces and nail them together temporarily. Set the boards to an angle of about 7 degrees with the saw blade and cut the two pieces, starting at a corner. This cut is simple with a sliding top; otherwise, nail a small spacer to the boards near the

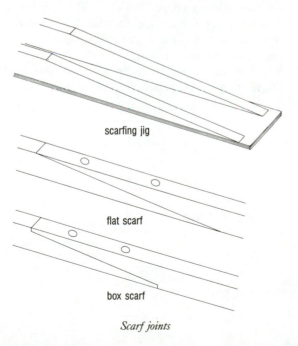

scarfing jig

flat scarf

box scarf

Scarf joints

rear so that when their forward corner and the spacer are held against the rip fence, the boards are at the desired angle. The fence must be twice as long as the pieces you are cutting.

Separate the two pieces and glue them to either side of a straight plank slightly wider than the toerail, forming a beveled channel. Place the wood for the toerail into the channel and trace the bevel onto the wood. Be sure you orient the wood correctly; the scarf should run from top to bottom, not side to side. Rough-cut the wood with a saw and then clamp it into the jig so that the surface of the cut is just below the sides of the jig. Put a straight-cut bit in your router and set the depth to about 1/4 inch. With the base plate sitting flat on the beveled sides of the jig, run the router around the perimeter of the cut, then back and forth across the center until the entire surface is flat.

A second piece prepared in the same way can be glued and clamped to the first one to form a joint as strong as the wood. Be careful about making up a single piece the length of your boat or it may snap of its own weight when you are handling it. Glue the joints together as you install the rail, putting at least two mounting screws through each joint.

High rails are often laminated, eliminating the need for scarf joints. Instead, the joints in each laminate are staggered to fabricate a long section. If the toerail is higher than it is wide and it is *not* laminated, a box scarf is preferable. The difference is that the scarf does not run all the way from top to bottom, but begins with a notch in the top and ends with a matching square end at the bottom. Assembled, the joint looks like a long, skinny Z.

All that remains is to shape the toerail and attach it. Shaping is accomplished by inclining the saw blade and running the wood against the rip fence. The top edges are radiused with a sander or router. Unless the rail is through-bolted, do not try to reinstall the mounting screws in the same holes. Carefully fill the old screw holes in the deck with resin putty and drill new ones through the rail as you bend it into place. Start at one end and drill and install one screw at a time. After all the screws have been installed, remove them, coat the deck and the bottom of the rail with polyurethane sealant, and reinstall it permanently. Coat the bungs with glue and tap them in place, taking care to align the grain. Trim the bungs, sand the rails, and coat them as you prefer.

Coamings

Cut to size. Shape. Screw in place. If you cut a replacement coaming from a single plank, these are the only instructions required, but if the coaming is high it can be difficult to find teak or mahogany of sufficient width. The solution is to edge-glue more than one piece of wood.

Rather than being less desirable, this alternative has a distinct advantage. A single board can be prone to warp and to split, but a coaming made up of several pieces properly assembled is not likely to exhibit either tendency.

Choose boards less than 4 inches wide with straight, smooth edges. If the edges are not perfect, run the board through your saw carefully to straighten them. Now look at the end of each piece to determine whether the grain curves up or down and reverse every other board to offset any warping tendency. Coat the edges with epoxy glue and clamp them together, taking care to keep the boards flat and flush. Dowels used to be commonly used when edge-gluing, but the strength of modern adhesives makes dowels unnecessary.

If you do not have sufficient pipe or bar clamps to apply even pressure, assemble the boards against a straight board nailed to a flat surface and apply clamping pressure with a number of wedge clamps as described earlier in the construction of a mitered frame. If you edge glue the boards in this manner, be sure to put a layer of waxed paper between them and the flat surface. Do not wipe the excess glue; slice it away with an old chisel after it dries.

When the glue dries, sand both surfaces. This is when a belt sander is very useful. If you are using a belt sander, be sure you keep it moving to keep from dishing the surface. With the panel assembled and surfaced, you already know the rest. Cut to size. Shape. Screw in place.

Handrails

I am particularly fond of handrails because they look so complicated and they are so easy to make. Begin with a solid plank about 1¼ inch thick and having a width twice the height of the old handrail, or not less than 5½ inches. You only need a single board for a pair of handrails; you will be constructing two at the same time.

Draw a line down the center of the board. Now if you are replacing a handrail, lay the old one on your board with the standoffs against the line and mark the location (both sides) of each standoff on the line. If you are not replacing but adding, divide the length of the handrail equally and mark the line where you want the standoffs to be. Measure along

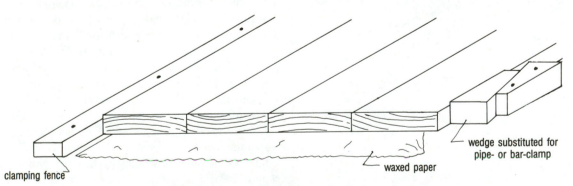

clamping fence

wedge substituted for pipe- or bar-clamp

waxed paper

Alternate the curvature of the grains to offset tendency to warp.

Edge gluing

the centerline 1½ inches from each side of the standoffs and mark these points on the line. Bore a 3-inch hole at each of these marks. With access to a drill press you can cut the holes with an expansion bit; if you are using a hand-held power drill, you need a hole saw. Bore from one side until the pilot drill penetrates the bottom, then turn the piece over and finish the hole from the opposite side.

Using your sabersaw, make parallel cuts between pairs of holes—exactly as you cut the slots for drawer pulls. Don't get confused and cut between the wrong holes; where the holes are close together is a standoff and you do not want to cut there. If you have done this correctly, you have a board with one or more—depending on the length of the handrail—

long slots with radiused ends in the center with 3 or 4 inches of solid wood between the slots.

Using the old handrail as a pattern, or selecting a radius you find pleasing, use the sabersaw to put an identical contour on each corner of the board. Now round all the edges, including the slots, with a router and a 3/8- or 1/2-inch corner-round bit. Finally, set the rip guide and rip the board down the centerline. Shazam! Two finished handrails.

Well, almost finished. To keep them from rocking after they are mounted, the base of each standoff should be *slightly* hollowed. This is accomplished by setting the saw blade about 1/16 inch above the table and clamping the fence diagonally (about 30 degrees will be fine) behind the blade. The distance

Draw a line down the center of a board twice the width of the desired handrail height. Mark the location of the standoffs. Put a dot 1½ inches from the edge marks for the standoffs.

Bore a 3-inch hole at each dot.

Make parallel cuts between pairs of holes.

Saw a radius on the ends.

Round edges with router or sander.

Saw down the centerline. Shazam—two rails!

Hollow the base by running the bottom of the handrails diagonally (30 degrees) across the saw blade.

Making a handrail

from the fence, measured perpendicularly, to the highest tooth on the blade should be half the thickness of the material you are cutting. Start the saw and run a scrap of material *slowly* along the fence and diagonally across the blade. Adjust the blade up or down to leave about ⅛ inch of material, on either side of the hollow, untouched by the saw. When the setting is right, run the bottom of the handrail over the blade.

Handrails should always be through-bolted. Get a helper to hold the rail in position while you bore the mounting holes from inside the cabin. A matching handrail inside the cabin attached to the overhead with the same bolts makes a yachtlike and functional installation. Fabricating the handrails in pairs assures perfect alignment.

Gratings

The big problem with gratings is the cost. After you price the necessary teak, you may decide to skip this enhancement. But cost is the only thing that should keep a determined owner from fabricating a cockpit grating.

A table saw and a dado blade greatly simplify the process, but it can be done with a router. Begin with the widest ¾-inch-thick stock you can obtain. You are going to cut ¾-inch dadoes *across* the board, ⅜ inch deep and ¾ inch apart. After all the dadoes have been cut, you will rip the board into ¾-inch-wide strips. Turn half the strips over and perpendicular to the other half and they will interlock into a grating. All that is left to do is put a drop of glue at each intersection, build a frame the size of the cockpit, and cut and rabbet the grating to fit the frame.

The difficulty comes in getting all these cuts precise. I strongly suggest that you make a grating for the wet locker or the refrigerator before taking on a cockpit grating.

The first step is to square the end of the board by trimming it on your sliding table. Install a ¾-inch straight bit in your router and set it to a depth of ⅜ inch. Now use contact cement to glue a foot-long batten ¾ inch wide and ¼ inch thick to the base of your router. The batten must be exactly ¾ inch from the closest edge of the cutter.

With the batten flush against the end of the board, make the first dado across the board. Now put the batten in the dado you just cut and make a second dado. If you positioned the guide correctly, the two dadoes will be exactly ¾ inch apart. Move the guide to the next dado and continue making cuts until you reach the end of the board.

Set the rip guide on your saw table to exactly ¾ inch and rip the board into strips. It is essential that the cuts have the correct width and depth and that the strips are a snug fit in the dadoes, so try out each new cut on scrap material before you begin making expensive teak or mahogany sawdust.

Assemble the grating with glue at every joint. Assemble a frame from wood the same thickness and at least two inches wide. Connect the pieces with end-lap joints. It will be easier to make the frame straight on all sides and trim it to fit after it is assembled. Put a ¾-inch-wide and ⅜-inch-deep rabbet on the bottom of the frame around the perimeter of the inside—just as in making a panel door.

Cut a scrap of plywood or door skin to tightly fit the rabbeted cutout. Using this as a pattern, cut the grating to size. Clamp a straight board to the router (to bridge the ends of the grating) and route a ¾-inch-wide by ⅜-inch-deep rabbet in the top of the grating around the perimeter. Check it in the frame for fit, then glue the two together. What else is there to say? Grate.

TEAK DECKS

I don't approve of teak decks on an old fiberglass boat. It isn't that I don't like the way they look; I do. And it isn't the maintenance they require; it's not that bad. What it is is all the screws through the deck. The decks of most old boats have plywood sandwiched between layers of fiberglass. It is hard enough to keep water from finding its way to the plywood and destroying it without drilling a thousand holes through the top laminate. So I pass.

Not that I expect you to care. If teak decks get your juices flowing, the risk of a spongy foredeck some years hence probably won't be much of a

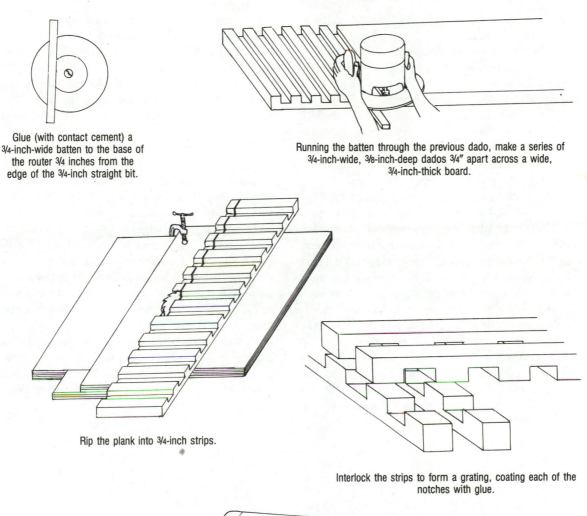

Glue (with contact cement) a ¾-inch-wide batten to the base of the router ¾ inches from the edge of the ¾-inch straight bit.

Running the batten through the previous dado, make a series of ¾-inch-wide, ⅜-inch-deep dados ¾″ apart across a wide, ¾-inch-thick board.

Rip the plank into ¾-inch strips.

Interlock the strips to form a grating, coating each of the notches with glue.

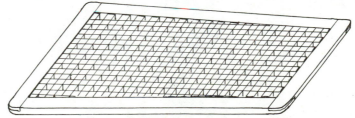

Build a half-lapped frame to fit the cockpit and rabbet the inside edge. Cut the grating to fit the rabbet, rabbet the edges of the grating, and glue the two assemblies together.

Building a cockpit grating

deterrent. So if you want to install a teak deck, can you do it? Absolutely.

The covering board—the wide plank nearest the rail—is cut to the curvature of the hull. To accommodate the curve, short pieces are joined with a box scarf—a joint you are familiar with.

The planks are straight lengths of $3/4$-inch-thick teak no more than 2 inches wide. Along the top of one edge is a $1/4$-inch-wide and $1/4$-inch-deep rabbet which provides the caulk groove when the planks are laid edge to edge. Nothing new here.

To get the planks to assume the contour of the covering board requires a great deal of clamping pressure, but what do you clamp *to*? Remember those wedge clamps we ripped out of scrap and used to clamp door frames and edge-glued planks? That's right. Screw half to the deck (what's a few more holes?) and drive the wedges in place to force each board against the previous one. You will need a couple of friends to hold the boards *down* while you are doing this or the board will spring loose and slap you crosseyed.

The king plank—the zigzag piece in the middle of the deck that the ends of all the other planks butt against—is cut to shape with a sabersaw. How do you determine the shape? Parallel pencil lines on either side of the centerline of the deck define the maximum width of the king plank. Where those lines intersect the outboard edge of each plank, use a square to draw a perpendicular line across the plank. This is where each plank will be cut and the staggered ends provide the outline for the king plank.

Drill and counterbore every hole, and screw the sprung planks to the deck. Wooden bungs hide the screws and you already know to line up the grain, to cut the bung off well above the surface, and to pare them smooth from the lowest edge.

I am not trying to suggest that laying a teak deck is easy; it isn't. There is more involved than the half-dozen steps outlined above—things like setting the deck in a generous bed of polysulfide, dealing with narrowing side decks, trimming around deck features, and of course caulking. A teak deck may be the most difficult woodworking project you are likely to take on in renovating your old fiberglass boat. And therein lies the point of the last few paragraphs. I'm not really trying to tell you how to lay a teak deck. I don't even approve, remember. I just want you to recognize that you can.

ELEVEN

Amps and Volts

Results! Why, man, I have gotten a lot of results. I know several thousand things that won't work.
–THOMAS A. EDISON–

The is something terribly romantic about the golden light of kerosene lamps spilling out into the harbor through bronze portholes. The soft glow speaks of the independence of the crew aboard– free of noisy generators or yellow umbilical cords. It was just this kind of independence–leaving behind the excesses of modern life ashore–that first attracted me to boating.

My first boat had electric cabin lights, but away from the dock there was no way to charge the battery that powered them. Rather than add some kind of charging equipment, I chose to install kerosene lamps–lovely fixtures of polished brass with smoke bells on gracefully arched supports. When I lit those lamps, I was transported to Tonga or Tahiti even though the boat was still tied securely in her slip.

Then I took the boat on a cruise through the Bahamas. I nearly went blind trying to read by the reflected yellow light of those beautiful lamps. It was impossible to sit near them because of the heat they generated, and if they were turned up to give off a reasonable amount of light, they so heated the cabin that it was uninhabitable. On more than one warm tropical night I risked becoming a late-night shark snack in a desperate effort to cool off.

I saw the light, so to speak. Kerosene cabin lamps, even the pressure kind that do generate enough light to read by, make poor shipmates south of Mason-Dixon. An electrical system capable of *brightly* illuminating the cabin became my top priority. If *your* boating dream includes a wardrobe lim-

ited to bathing suits, an adequate electrical system will also be one of your priorities.

Of course the same power source that lights the cabin can also start the engine, pump the bilge, pressurize the water system, lift the anchor, cool the refrigerator, illuminate channel markers, gauge the depth, transmit your voice tens or hundreds of miles, let you "see" through fog, make you visible at night, bring you Beethoven, and tell you exactly where you are. You will no doubt find at least some of these other uses appealing.

THE SHOCKING TRUTH

Mention electricity to a lot of people and they tell you about their Uncle Elbert who was up in the attic repairing a wire when Aunt Minnie came home early from Bingo and flipped on a switch, sending poor Elbert into the next life. The point of their lamentable tale is that messing around with electricity is just asking for it.

Where the electrical system of a boat is concerned, nothing could be farther from the truth. Adding and repairing electrical circuits on your boat exposes you to the same shock risk as replacing the batteries in a fluorescent lantern–none. Here I am talking about the battery-powered 12-volt system on your boat, not circuits that are connected to shore power, or AC circuits powered by an onboard generator. AC power–110- or 220-volt–is dangerous whether the circuit is in an attic, on the dock, or in the galley. But except for a short segment on shore power, this chapter is about 12-volt electrical systems. Twelve volts is simply inadequate to give you a dangerous shock, so let Uncle Elbert rest in peace.

The absence of shock risk does not relieve you of the need for caution. A badly overloaded circuit can generate enough heat to start a fire. An electrical spark in combination with propane or gasoline fumes inside the boat can have you bunking with Uncle Elbert. A rapidly charging battery gives off hydrogen—the same gas that filled the Hindenburg. Perhaps the greatest danger is from the sulfuric acid solution inside the batteries. It can cause blindness if you inadvertently get it in your eyes.

Just being aware of these dangers should be sufficient to prevent them, like knowing that dropping a 100-pound battery can smash the hell out of your foot, that you can cut yourself stripping insulation off a piece of wire, and that touching the tip of a hot soldering iron will lead to a painful burn. I don't mean to be flippant, but working on a 12-volt electrical system is no more dangerous than crossing the street. Your mom gave you the key to being safe; look both ways.

THE BASIC CIRCUIT

Connecting an electrical appliance—such as a cabin fan—to a battery is a matter of connecting one wire to the positive terminal and one to the negative terminal. When the circuit is completed in this way, the fan runs.

Why is it called a circuit? Because it creates a path for free electrons to flow between the positive and negative plates in the battery. Think of a battery as a high-school gymnasium packed with teenagers, boys at one end, girls at the other, separated by a partition. Hormones are pumping; the battery is fully charged. The circuit is an outside corridor that connects the two ends of the gym. Someone opens the door to the corridor and the guys, being more aggressive, race out of the gym, through the corridor, and back into the gym at the girls' end. This

"flow" will continue until the boys and girls have all paired off. When the gym is full of happy couples, our battery is dead.

To carry this sophomoric analogy a step further, if there is a turnstile in the corridor, as each boy passes through it, it spins—much like our fan. The turnstile stops when we interrupt the flow by closing the door or when we run out of randy boys. The same is true for the fan; it will continue to run until we disconnect it or until the battery loses its charge.

TERMINOLOGY

A case can be made for crediting an unknown Italian frog with the discovery of electric current. George Washington still had almost three years to go in his first term as President of the United States when Luigi Galvani, untroubled by animal rights concerns, hung the hapless croaker on an iron hook and stuck in a copper probe, noting that the frog's muscles contracted convulsively. Galvani did not understand the discovery—although it's likely the frog did, briefly. Yet to this day the flow of electric current between dissimilar metals immersed in a conductive liquid (Ugh!) is called galvanic action. Go figure.

It took another 10 years before fellow Italian Alessandro Volta finally deduced what the frog knew intuitively. As unfair as it may seem, the martyred frog was quickly forgotten, but not Volta, whose name now appears on virtually every item of electrical equipment.

After Volta came a whole gallery of scientists, inventors, and engineers who expanded on the frog's discovery, each carrying it a step further. For their contributions, most were honored by having some unit of measurement named in their honor. Besides the volt, you need to be familiar with the ampere, (named after a man named Marie!), the ohm, and the watt. German scientist George Ohm did make a number of important discoveries in the field, but James Watt, famous for his development of the steam engine, had about as much to do with electricity as his recent namesake had to do with conservation.

The *ampere*, commonly shortened to amp, is a measurement of the *rate* of the flow of electric current. It indicates the number of electrons that pass a point in a given time. Back to our analogy: If we counted the number of boys passing through the turnstile in a minute, we would come up with a rate. If we counted 120, we might say that the "current" was 120 boys per minute. But if we had a term that signified 100 boys per minute—let's call it a frog—we would then rate the current at 1.2 frogs. Big deal, right? Except that when we are counting electrons we are dealing with much larger numbers. How big? One ampere is equal to a flow of 6,280,000,000,000,000,000 electrons per second. Would you rather say 5 amps or 31.4 billion billion electrons per second? Amps it is.

The *volt* is a measurement of force. It is what causes the current to flow. Voltage is a measurement of what is called *potential*, a term easily understood from our analogy. For example, if both sides of the gymnasium were filled with boys, there would be no flow through the corridor; the flow occurs because the boys are attracted to the girls. Potential. We could raise the potential by filling one end of the gym with sailors who have been at sea for a year and putting their wives and girlfriends at the other end. If you suspect that this increase in potential would also increase the rate of the flow of the boys through the corridor, you would be right.

The *ohm* is a measurement of *resistance*. If the corridor is nice and wide, the flow of boys from one end to the other is uninhibited. But if the corridor is narrow, only so many boys can pass through at a time. Smaller wire inhibits the flow of electrons in a similar manner. The small corridor may not be a problem for the lower potential of the high schoolers, but the sailors are going to push and shove trying to get through the small hall. More will get through, but things are likely to heat up. So will a wire too small for the job.

The last of the essential terms is the *watt*, which is a measurement of *power*. The only reason we are interested in electricity is to get it to do work for us; the watt is the rate of doing work. We could tap the power of our gymnasium battery by taking a few turns of line around the turnstile and connecting the loose end to a weight, converting the turnstile into a windlass. Every time someone passed through the turnstile, he would move the weight. The more guys passing through the turnstile in a given time, the higher the *rate* of work. We can see that the rate of work is directly related to how many guys are moving through the corridor—current—and how motivated they are to get through the turnstile—potential.

A PAIR OF USEFUL FORMULAS

Fun's over; it's formula time. The direct relationship among power and current and potential is expressed by the formula P = EI, where *P* stands for power in watts, *E* stands for potential in volts, and *I* represents current in amps. *E* is short for EMF, or electromotive force, another term for potential. *I* comes from the concept that currents are *induced* to flow.

P = EI is a very useful formula. If you know any two of the elements, you can solve for the third one. For example, you know that the voltage of most boat appliances is 12 volts. If a particular appliance shows a current rating of 2 amps, you can determine the wattage of the appliance by multiplying 12 by 2.

A more common occurrence is that you know the wattage and you want to know how many amps the appliance will draw. For example, typical incandescent cabin lamps have bulbs rated at 25 watts. How many amps do these bulbs require? You can reconstitute the formula by dividing both sides by E to get I = P/E. Divide 25 watts by 12 volts and you find that each 25-watt cabin light requires 2.08 amps in use.

A second formula that will help in matching the various components of your electrical system is E = IR, with *E* and *I* representing potential and current respectively, exactly as in the first formula, and *R* representing resistance in ohms. This is called Ohm's Law and, like the previous formula, it is more useful in a different form. You are typically going to be interested in determining the current so the formula would be I = E/R. This relationship was alluded to when we mentioned the narrow corridor. Ohm's law simply states that current will increase with an increase in potential, and it will decrease with an increase in resistance; i.e., current is directly proportional to voltage and inversely proportional to resistance. Remember this stuff; unlike high school algebra, you'll actually use these formulas—and soon.

REDDY KILOWATT AND YOU

If you decide that a room in your home is too dark, the solution is simple: install higher-wattage bulbs or add additional lamps. The latest generation of electric kitchen gadgets features under-counter mounting—not low power consumption—because Madison Avenue knows that purchases are limited by counter space, not electricity. Even when you do consider consumption, as in the purchase of a refrigerator or an air conditioner, the reference is to other, comparable appliances, not to the power available. For all practical purposes, electricity is unlimited.

This is not the case with the electrical system on your old boat. You are not just the consumer; you are also the electric company. You must generate every amp that is consumed by the appliances you decide to put aboard.

Thinking of yourself as the electric company can be illuminating—no pun intended. You should be familiar with kilowatt-hours, the unit power companies use to calculate your electric bill. A kilowatt is 1,000 watts, and a kilowatt-hour represents 1,000 watts of power consumption for a period of one hour. It might also be 500 watts for two hours, or 100 watts for 10 hours. My electric company charges me about seven cents for every kilowatt-hour I use.

What will a kilowatt-hour that you generate cost? Recalling that I = P/E, you can convert from watts to amps by dividing by the voltage. Dividing 1,000 watts by 12 volts yields 83.3 amps, but we are converting kilowatt-*hours*, so the answer is 83.3 *amp-hours*. Amp-hour (Ah) is a common term in any discussion of 12-volt electrical systems; 1 Ah simply represents a current of 1 amp flowing for one hour.

The cost to generate 83 Ah depends upon your generating equipment. A standard engine-mounted alternator might have an output of 35 or 40 amps. With such an alternator it would take more than two hours of engine time to generate a kilowatt-hour of power. What does it cost to run your engine for two hours?

The operating cost, however, is not generally the controlling issue. The real issue is capacity. How much power can you generate? How much are you *willing* to generate, i.e., how many hours each day do you want to run the engine? And how much power can you store? When the load exceeds the capacity of your generating or storage equipment, the cost to increase capacity can be substantial. So before you place additional demands on your old boat's electrical system, you need to do a few load calculations.

Calculating Loads

A few years back, I shared an anchorage with a small cruising catamaran whose electrical system defined simplicity and low cost. From the broken taillight of a junk car the skipper had stripped a single light socket and mounted it inside a discarded plastic Rolaids jar. The 10-watt bulb lit the tiny cabin admirably.

Using the formula I = P/E, divide the wattage of the bulb by the voltage, i.e., divide 10 by 12, to find that the bulb draws about .8 amps. The load is calculated by multiplying the current the appliance requires (in amps) by the amount of time the appliance is in use (in hours). In this case, the cabin light was used about four hours *per day* so the *daily* load of the light was 3.2 Ah.

Since the one light was the only electric appliance on the cat, 3.2 Ah was also the *total* daily load. Total daily load is the sum of the daily loads of all the electric appliances aboard. An estimate of the total daily load aboard your old boat is where you should start any changes to the existing electrical system.

Make a list of every electrical appliance presently aboard your boat and the number of each. Beside each appliance, note its current rating in amps. If it is a light, the bulb will show the wattage—which can be converted to amps by dividing by the voltage (12). Motors, such as pumps, fans, and refrigerators, usually have a plate that shows the draw in amps. Electronics will have a similar plate or the specifications will be listed in the owner's manual. If you cannot find any indication of the power requirements of a specific item, look up similar equipment in a catalog; power consumption is almost always given.

Next to the current rating, estimate the number of hours each day the item is, or could be, in use. Your estimates should be liberal; like your electric company, you want to be able to handle even the highest-demand day.

Finally multiply the amp ratings by the hours to get the daily load of each item. Add all of the individual loads together to get the total daily load.

Continue your list by writing down every additional electrical item that you are considering. Obtain amp ratings from catalog listings and estimate daily hours of usage. Calculate the daily loads, and add them to the previous total to estimate the total daily load of all the equipment you plan to have aboard your boat. Your list should look similar to the table at right.

Without some frame of reference, these calculations have little significance. Recalling that 83.3 Ah at 12 volts is equivalent to 1 kilowatt-hour, you might be led to conclude that a couple of hundred amp-hours—less than 3 kilowatt-hours—is no big deal, especially when you compare it to home consumption. For example, my electric company tells me that my average daily home use of power is about 27 kilowatt-hours. But home consumption is not relevant; the electric company isn't supplying the power used, you are. And 200 Ah may be a very big deal.

The typical power source aboard an old boat is a single engine-driven alternator. Under the most ideal conditions, a 40-amp alternator will take five hours to supply 200 Ah of power, but for reasons that we will see shortly a more realistic estimate is 10 hours of engine time. However, regardless of the size of the alternator, it is usually the batteries that

Daily Power Usage.

Appliance	Number of Units ×	Amp Rating ×	Time Used	= Daily Amp-Hours
Cabin lights	3	2.1	5	31.5
Cabin fan	1	1.2	6	7.2
Pressure water	1	6	.5	3
Running lights	3	1.2	2	7.2*
Anchor light	1	.8	8	6.4
Bilge pump	1	15	.1	1.5
Starter	1	300	.01	3
Depth sounder	1	.2	16	3.2
VHF-Standby	1	.5	16	8
VHF-Transmit	1	5.5	.3	1.7

Current Total Daily Load in Amp-Hours 72.7

Reading lights	2	1	2	4
Cabin fan	1	1.2	6	7.2
Tape deck	1	1	4	4
Loran	1	.5	16	8
Windlass	1	90	.15	13.5
Refrigerator	1	5.5	12	66 **
Radar	1	3.5	16	56

Projected Total Daily Load in Amp-Hours 231.4

*Additional use of running lights would be partially or wholly offset by decreased use of anchor and cabin lights.

**Electric refrigerators cycle off and on, typically running about half of each hour.

supply the power; the function of the generating equipment is to recharge the depleted batteries. So the batteries must have sufficient capacity to supply the electrical demands between chargings. Let's take a look at what that means.

Battery Capacity

When two dissimilar metals are immersed in an electrolyte (a conductive liquid), a voltage develops.

Devices that supply electrical energy from a chemical reaction are known as voltaic cells.

The voltage of a cell depends upon the metals and the electrolyte. Stick a strip of zinc and a strip of copper into an olive and you will probably measure a potential of about half a volt. A "dry" cell has a voltage of about 1.5 volts. Four dry cells are combined in a 6-volt lantern battery, and there are six inside a 9-volt radio battery. "Wet" cells have a voltage of slightly more than 2 volts; when six wet cells are combined inside a plastic case they become a 12-volt battery.

Determining the capacity of a battery is not as easy as determining the voltage. Even defining capacity presents some problems. For example, if a battery manufacturer specifies that a particular battery has a capacity of 100 Ah, it is probably safe to assume that the battery can handle a 1-amp load for 100 hours, but can the same battery supply 100 amps for one hour? It looks like the answer should be yes, but it is almost certainly *no*. It is more likely that the maximum load that could be sustained for one hour will be closer to 50 amps. So is it a 50-Ah battery or a 100-Ah battery?

The answer is complicated by the absence of an industry-wide standard in rating capacity. Many, but not all, battery manufacturers specify the amp-hour capacity based on a constant discharge over a period of 20 hours, resulting in a voltage drop to 10.5 volts (1.75 volts per cell). By this standard, a battery capable of supplying 5 amps for 20 hours will be rated at 100 Ah. But the same battery will not supply 10 amps for 10 hours.

While a full water tank with a 30-gallon capacity yields 30 gallons regardless of how quickly you pump it out, battery capacity is more complicated because the energy is being *produced* by a chemical reaction going on inside the battery. The more rapidly the energy is removed, the less efficient is the process. Subject the 20-hour-rated battery above to a 10-amp load and the true capacity of the battery will be about 90 percent of the rated capacity. A 20-amp load will discharge the battery in less than four hours—around 75 percent of the advertised capacity. True capacity drops below 50 percent of the rating when you discharge the battery in one hour.

Marine interests find the waters muddied further by the absence of standard capacity ratings in favor of *cold cranking amps* (CCA) and *reserve capacity. Cold cranking amp* refers to the discharge in amps that can be maintained for *30 seconds* at 0 degrees Fahrenheit before battery voltage drops to *7.2* volts. *Reserve capacity* is the number of *minutes* that the battery will supply a constant 25 amps. Both ratings were conceived for automotive batteries and provide no useful information for marine applications unless the battery will be used *exclusively* to start the engine. For all other uses, you are only interested in the amp-hour capacity.

If you don't know the capacity of a battery, the direct relationship between capacity and the amount of plate material the battery contains will allow you to *estimate* the 20-hour capacity by weighing the battery. The results may surprise you. From a modern battery in a lightweight polypropylene case, expect about 1.25 Ah per pound of battery weight. This is also a good way to check the manufacturer's claims. You should be skeptical of a 50-pound battery claiming 100-Ah capacity. It just ain't so, Skip.

Since you're after ample battery capacity to handle your *daily* electrical demands, the 20-hour rate is generally the most useful—but not as useful as you might think. If your projected daily consumption is 100 Ah, you may have the silly notion that you need a 100-Ah battery. Snap out of it! If you draw 100 Ah from a 100-Ah battery, what do you suppose is going to happen when you hit the starter button? Is that your answer or the sound you expect the starter to make?

Even if you have a dedicated battery for starting the engine, a battery with a capacity equal to the projected load is still inadequate. Fully discharging a battery damages it, and doing so repeatedly will *severely* shorten its life. Imagine donating a gallon of blood instead of a pint and you get the idea. If you want the battery to last, you should not discharge it below about 50 percent of its rated capacity.

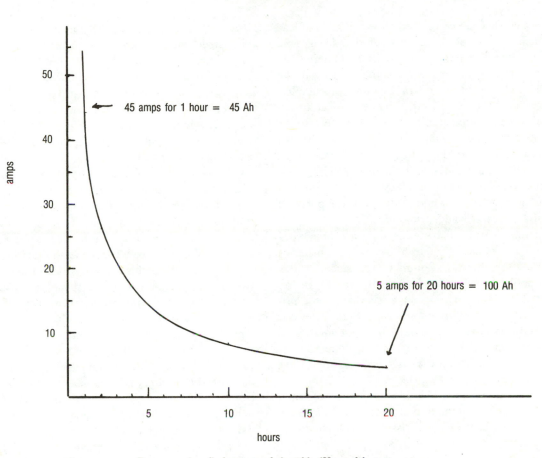

45 amps for 1 hour = 45 Ah

5 amps for 20 hours = 100 Ah

Representative discharge graph for 100-AH-rated battery.

Now you are closing in on what will constitute *sufficient* capacity. You don't want to be buying new batteries every couple of years, so you are going to limit the discharge to 50 percent of rated capacity. Which means that for a 100 Ah load, you should need 200 Ah of battery capacity. Except that it is difficult (for reasons we will shortly examine) to *fully* charge storage batteries; you will be doing extremely well to bring them up to 90 percent of their rated capacity. This reduces usable capacity to 40 percent of the rated capacity; 200 Ah of battery capacity will handle only an 80-Ah load. You need 25 percent more. Here is the rule: Calculate the actual battery capacity you need by multiplying your projected consumption *between charges* by 2.25.

Applying this rule to the 231.4 Ah from the load calculation illustration suggests a battery capacity of around 520 Ah. Cost per amp-hour of capacity will range from about $2 for heavy-duty deep-cycle marine batteries down to about $1 for cheap imitations. A thousand dollars in batteries is something to think about. And remember the capacity-to-weight ratio (1.25 Ah per pound)? Five hundred twenty amp-hours of battery capacity will weigh more than 400 pounds. What does your engine weigh? It might be a good idea to make this calculation now using *your* load projections. Reducing the load may be a more palatable alternative.

Choosing batteries. All 12-volt batteries (suitable for our purposes) are lead-acid batteries, meaning that they are comprised of lead plates and lead dioxide plates submerged in a sulfuric acid solution. Lead-acid batteries are called *storage* batteries because they appear to *store* electricity. Actually the electricity is produced by an internal chemical process—as in every other battery. What distinguishes a storage battery is that you can reverse the chemical process by passing a current back through the battery, restoring it to its fully charged state. Recalling the gymnasium full of couples, if a chaperon shows up and forces all the boys back through the corridor to their end of the gym, the potential will be reestablished. Same idea.

Among lead-acid batteries, there are three types that you should be aware of. Automotive batteries have been the most common type since Charles Kettering installed the first electric starter on the 1912 Cadillac. Starting the engine is still the primary function of an automotive battery. They are called upon to deliver several hundred amps for a few seconds, then they are immediately recharged. High currents mean the chemical reaction inside the battery must take place rapidly, dictating the need for thin plates. This concept may be easier to understand if you think of dissolving ice in water; 5 pounds of shaved ice will dissolve much more rapidly than a 5-pound block. But even if you grind away on the starter for a minute or two—an eternity when you are trying to start an engine—the total discharge will only be 10 or so amp-hours. The demands of headlights and other electrical equipment are simultaneously offset by input from a generator or alternator that operates when the car is in use. Deeply discharging a battery designed for the perpetually charged environment of automotive use damages it.

The so-called deep-cycle battery is a different concept. It is designed to be deeply discharged over a period of time before requiring a recharge. The thicker plates reduce the amount of time that a deep-cycle battery can supply very high currents (relative to automotive batteries), but allow the battery to be deeply discharged without damaging it. If a quality deep-cycle battery is not discharged below

about 50 percent of its rated capacity, it may be discharged and recharged as many as several *thousand* times. Deep-cycle batteries are often called "marine" batteries in recognition of their suitability for the typical demands of onboard use.

Gel batteries are a relatively new entry into the field. They derive their name from the form of the electrolyte. A similar technology is the *absorbed* electrolyte battery that contains the electrolyte in "wet" microporous separators between the metal plates. Such sealed batteries cannot spill, never need water, can be mounted in any position, and give off no gas during normal charging. All these qualities are advantages aboard a boat to be sure, but it is the way sealed batteries—especially gel batteries—combine the characteristics of automotive and deep-cycle batteries that merits examination. Design and chemistry differences allow a quality gel battery to be deeply discharged repeatedly—like a deep-cycle battery—and at the same time to accept a high-speed charge—like an automotive battery. In fact, the regimen for a badly discharged gel battery is to completely discharge it (similar to Ni-Cad batteries) before recharging. Some gel cells will accept a charge so quickly that the battery can be fully charged in 30 minutes (although a charging current of about *five times* battery capacity would be needed—i.e. 500 amps for a 100Ah gel battery).

The idea of a battery that can be discharged deeply and recharged rapidly has instant appeal. But wait. Before you run out and replace your aging deep-cycle batteries with gel batteries, take a closer look. The plates inside a gel battery are thin and closely spaced, making it essentially an automotive-type battery. Gel batteries derive their ability to survive numerous deep discharge cycles not from robust plates, but by eliminating strength-adding antimony from the thin lead plates. Battery-destroying corrosion during the discharge/charge cycle is reduced by substituting calcium for the antimony. Oversize negative plates may also be a feature, so that the negative plate is never fully charged and the generation of hydrogen (gassing) is avoided.

These changes do give gel batteries deep-cycle capacity far superior to that of an automotive battery; instead of 40 cycles, expect 400 from a gel battery. Some gel batteries are "rated" at up to 1,000 deep (50 percent) discharge cycles, but such longevity depends upon the battery's not being rapidly charged. Compare this with a true thick-plate deep-cycle battery; the best of these will deliver more than 2,500 deep (50 percent) discharge cycles. This disparity is even greater if the gel batteries are subjected to any of several common abuses, such as incorrect voltage regulation, partial discharge, or the mild overcharge associated with leaving the batteries connected to a charger.

Choosing the best battery for your boat depends upon how it will be used, but most boat owners will be best served by good-quality deep-cycle batteries. Quality deep-cycle batteries don't come cheap, but if they are treated well they can last a decade or longer. Be leery of discount-store "marine" batteries; too often they are little more than an automotive battery with a rope handle.

Automotive batteries do have their place on boats. Any battery that is used exclusively to start the engine could be the automotive type. Many boats have two batteries, one to start the engine and one to supply all the other power requirements. However, unless you boat in very cold weather where excessively high starting currents are required, or your engine is difficult to start, a pair of deep-cycle batteries may provide greater flexibility. With this configuration, both batteries can be used to supply ship's power as well as start the engine.

Suitable sealed batteries can cost 25 percent to 50 percent more than the best deep-cycle batteries, and they have a life expectancy of $1/4$ to $1/3$ that of quality deep-cycle batteries—even less if subjected to chronic under- or over-charging. But they may be used to advantage, especially the gel type, if your charging equipment is capable of rapidly recharging them. Some also have a very slow rate of "self-discharge," meaning they can be stored for a year or more without damage; a quality gel battery could be an outstanding backup.

Recharging. We are going to look at various methods of recharging the batteries aboard your boat. But before we do, we need to establish the relationship among charging capacity, storage capacity, and consumption. I don't mean the sequential relationship (charge, store, consume, charge, etc.), but how to determine how much charging capacity is enough.

The maximum absorption rate of an automotive (thin-plate) battery is no more than 50 percent of the rated capacity of the battery, i.e., a 100-Ah automotive battery will accept a charging current of up to 50 amps. However, a battery charged this rapidly will start to *gas* (bubble) and to get hot by the time the battery is 50 percent charged. If the current is reduced to about 25 percent of battery capacity, the battery will reach 75 percent of its charge before the gassing begins. To fully charge the battery, the current must be decreased to five percent or less of battery capacity. In concept, this is much like pouring a carbonated drink into a glass. Pour it fast and, when the foam dissipates, the glass is only half full; pour it slowly and you can fill the glass to the top.

Gassing, besides filling the battery locker with highly explosive hydrogen gas, depletes the acid in the battery. Excessive heat damages the plates and separators inside the battery. Both conditions will kill a battery in short order.

Deep-cycle batteries have a much slower absorption rate than thin-plate batteries. A deep-cycle battery should never be subjected to a charging current higher than 25 percent of the battery capacity, and even this current will cause the battery to begin gassing long before it is fully charged. This means that if your total battery capacity is 100 Ah, a 25-amp alternator is all you need. A 50-amp alternator will provide the *maximum* charging current for a pair of 100-Ah batteries.

This is where sealed batteries hold some advantage. Their natural absorption rate is about the same as standard automotive batteries—about 50 percent of capacity—but their construction allows them to be charged at an even higher rate without generating hydrogen or overheating. A totally discharged 100-

Ah sealed battery might be fully charged in half an hour, but the inefficiencies of such overcharging would require a charging current of about *five times* the capacity of the battery—not very practical and brutal on the battery. Without abusing it, a gel battery can safely be charged twice as fast as a deep-cycle battery.

There is a degree of inefficiency in the charging process even if you are not exceeding the absorption level of the battery. Generally speaking, you must replace about 20 percent more power than you removed to return a battery to a fully charged state. In other words, a 50-Ah discharge will require that you put 60 Ah back into the battery.

You can measure the level of charge with a voltmeter, but the voltage difference between a fully charged and a fully discharged battery is only one volt (12.7 volts to 11.7 volts). Even more relevant, the difference between fully charged and half-charged is just *0.5 volts*. An expanded-scale voltmeter, sometimes called a condition indicator, can provide a general idea of the level of charge, but voltage is not a very reliable indicator of a battery's state of charge.

Specific gravity (SG) of the electrolyte *is* a reliable indicator and you can buy a battery hydrometer for a couple of bucks. Squeeze the bulb and stick the flexible tip into a cell, drawing enough electrolyte into the clear tube to float the little overboard pole inside. How deeply the little pole floats indicates the specific gravity of the electrolyte. Normally a reading of 1.265 indicates fully charged, 1.190 about half charged, and at 1.120 the battery is flat, although these values can vary among batteries. It is a good idea to check the SG of your batteries when you know they are 100 percent charged. SG values are for a temperature of 80 degrees Fahrenheit and must be corrected if the temperature is significantly different; add .004 to the measurement for every additional 10 degrees or subtract that amount for every 10 degrees less. Once you have checked a cell, squeeze the electrolyte back into the *same* cell and check the next cell. All the cells should be checked and they should all read about the same. Be careful with the acid.

Alternators

Alternators have almost completely replaced generators on marine engines, and for good reasons. They are more efficient, they are more dependable, they are lighter, and they do not spark. But the main reason is that they can endure higher RPM, which allows them to have higher engine-speed ratio. As a result, they have a higher output when the engine is running at idle speed.

Typically, alternators develop rated output between 5,000 and 6,000 RPM. To get this speed when the alternator is driven by a slow-turning diesel engine, the alternator pulley is smaller than the crankshaft pulley. If the crankshaft pulley is three times the size (in circumference) of the alternator pulley, 2,000 engine RPM will turn the alternator at 6,000 RPM.

When you are cruising or living aboard, you do much of the charging at idle speed. There is a temptation to change the pulley ratio to make the alternator turn faster, but all alternators have an upper limit (usually 10,000 RPM) and if the change will cause the alternator to exceed this limit at maximum engine RPM, you are likely to damage the alternator. A better alternative for this situation may be to select an alternator that maintains its output at lower RPM. At 2,000 RPM, the output of some alternators is less than 30 percent of the rated output, while others generate around 80 percent of their rating. Those made by Motorola have notably good performance characteristics.

Most boat owners will find that their involvement with their alternators will be limited to adjusting belt tension and removing the unit to take it to a repair shop when it develops a problem. Good move. Alternators do not lend themselves to amateur repair efforts.

The number of terminals on the back of the alternator can be confusing, especially since some of them may not have a wire attached. Before you disconnect the wires to the alternator, sketch the features of the back—chart fashion—and locate each of the terminals on the sketch. Note on the sketch which wire—by color—is connected to which terminal; reinstallation will be a breeze.

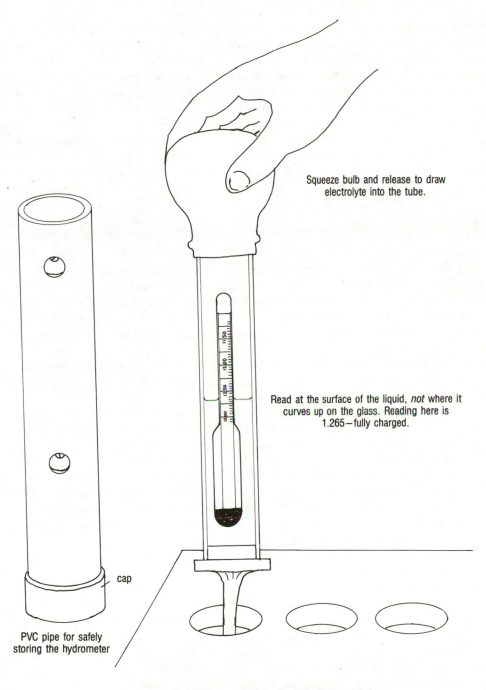

Squeeze bulb and release to draw electrolyte into the tube.

Read at the surface of the liquid, *not* where it curves up on the glass. Reading here is 1.265—fully charged.

cap

PVC pipe for safely storing the hydrometer

Leave the tip in the cell while checking. Squeeze all the electrolyte back into the cell after reading the specific gravity. Check each cell.

Using a hydrometer

If you are replacing the alternator with a larger one, or a different type, take your old alternator and your sketch with you when you buy the new one so a technician can show you how the new one should be connected. This is not all that complicated—there are typically only three wires—but you want to make sure they are on the correct terminals.

Sizing the alternator depends entirely upon the battery capacity and how fast you want to charge. The maximum charge rate for deep-cycle batteries is 25 percent, so if you have 200 Ah of deep-cycle capacity, the maximum charge rate is 50 amps. If the alternator is only charging the batteries, you need a 50-amp alternator. But if you have other equipment on during charging, the alternator should have enough capacity to supply the equipment and still deliver the maximum current to the batteries. This could be a few additional amps for cabin or running lights that happen to be on, or it could be 40 or 50 amps for the concurrent operation of an electric refrigerator.

You should also be aware of the horsepower required to run an alternator under load. In a perfect world you could convert one horsepower of mechanical energy into 746 watts of electrical energy. (You could also trust your senator with your tax money and your daughter.) A closer approximation is achieved by cutting your expectations in half (in both cases). Alternator output voltage will be around 14 volts. Multiplying this voltage by the rated current yields the power in watts—700 watts for a 50-amp alternator. Dividing wattage by 373 (½ of 746) reveals that the alternator will require around 1.9 h.p. The belt and pulleys consume an additional 1 h.p., so a 50-amp alternator reduces the power to the prop by about 3 h.p. A 150-amp alternator will require close to 7 h.p. under full load. I sure hope you don't have a 10-h.p. engine.

Regulators

When a 50-amp alternator is running at the rated rpm, it puts out 50 amps—period. But we have already noted that if you have a 100-Ah deep-cycle battery, you *never* want to charge it with a current greater than 25 amps. And as it approaches full charge, the charging current should not exceed an amp or two.

Limiting the output of the alternator is the job of the voltage regulator, but the name is misleading since it actually regulates the current. It works much like a thermostat, only instead of sensing room temperature, it senses battery voltage. When the voltage is low, the regulator turns on the spinning alternator by passing current to the field winding. When the alternator raises the voltage in the charging circuit to a preset level—usually between 13.8 and 14.4 volts—the regulator cuts the current to the field winding, turning the alternator off. (It continues to spin, of course.) The voltage in the circuit drops and the regulator senses it, turning the alternator back on.

In a solid-state regulator, this off-and-on switching takes place hundreds of times *per second,* and the output current is an average of the current *pulses* this switching causes. As the battery voltage rises, it takes less and less time for the alternator to elevate the voltage in the charging circuit to the cutout voltage. The "on" times become shorter and shorter, reducing the amount of current the alternator generates.

The voltage regulator is almost always the weak link in a boat's electrical system, limiting the *available* electrical power to far below the potential of the other components and shortening the life of the batteries in the bargain. Consider how a deep-cycle battery should be charged. Charging current should never exceed 25 percent of capacity, but the battery will accept the maximum until it is about 80 percent charged. The battery voltage will be around 14.4 volts and the cells will be gassing. At this point the alternator should maintain a constant voltage of 14.4 and allow the current to fall naturally. When the current drops below 5 percent of battery capacity, a constant *current* of about 5 percent should be fed into the battery until battery voltage stabilizes at its highest level (typically around 16 volts). This is called *equalization.* Once the battery is fully charged, the alternator voltage should be reduced to about 13.5 volts and held constant to *float* the batteries, maintaining the full charge. In actual practice, the equalization step is usually omitted because it takes up to four hours to raise the battery from 95 percent charged to 100 percent. The batteries should be equalized periodically for their health.

So for your half-discharged 100-Ah battery, you would like to have a 25-amp current until you have pumped about 36 amps (30 amps to raise the charge level from 50 percent to 80 percent plus another six amps for battery inefficiency [around 20 percent]) into the battery—about one hour and 25 minutes. If you continue the charge, you want 14.4 volts until the battery is 90 percent to 95 percent—at least an additional hour. You would normally terminate the charge at this point, but if you continue to run the engine—it does turn the prop, you know—you want the alternator to cut back to 13.5 volts.

How does a standard regulator actually perform? It depends on the cutout voltage, which is traditionally around 13.8 volts. Sensing a low voltage, a regulator set for 13.8 volts starts the charge with a current of about 35 amps, exceeding the recommended charge rate (25 percent). This excess lasts only a few minutes before the regulator begins to reduce the current. After an hour, the battery is only 70 percent charged, and charging current has dropped below 10 amps and still declining. It takes another hour and a half to reach the 80 percent level. At 13.8 volts, to raise charge level to 90 percent will take *several hours* of additional charging time. And when the battery is fully charged, a continuous voltage of 13.8 volts results in mild overcharging.

Two and a half hours to reach an 80 percent charge level and more than five hours to reach a 90 percent charge means that the battery will only get fully charged when you are under power for a long period. The rest of the time the battery will be *undercharged*, resulting in sulfation—the main cause of battery death.

To avoid this problem, regulators intended for marine use often have the cutout voltage elevated, up to a maximum of 14.4 volts. This cuts charging time dramatically, but it can damage the batteries in a different way. A 14.4-volt regulator starts with a current of more than 40 amps and abuses the battery for close to 40 minutes before the steadily declining current drops below the safe 25 percent rate. The battery reaches an 80 percent charge level in about one hour and 40 minutes, 90 percent in an additional hour—not much longer than the ideal. But if you continue to run the engine, the 14.4-volt setting will result in serious *overcharging*, boiling away the electrolyte and corroding the positive plates. Corrosion of the positive plates is the number two cause of battery death.

If voltage regulators do such a lousy job, why does every boat have one? Because boat owners are stupid. Just kidding. Regulators are standard fare because they are simple, *cheap*, dependable, foolproof, and manufactured in the zillions every year for automotive use—where, by the way, they do a darn good job. And if you run your engine a lot, they will do the job for you.

If you don't run your engine a lot, at the very least you need your regulator to be set to 14.4 volts. You can determine the setting of your regulator by measuring the voltage across the battery terminals while the engine is running at charging speed, but the battery must be *fully* charged (check it with a hydrometer). Some regulators have an adjusting screw, some have a multi-position switch, some have output terminals for differing voltages, but *most* are not adjustable. In this latter case, if you need a higher setting than your test reveals, you will have to replace the regulator.

High-output regulators are not without problems. Undercharging your batteries is more damaging—not to mention frustrating—than is some overcharging, but continuing to apply 14.4 volts to fully charged batteries will definitely shorten their lives. The batteries will tolerate being charged occasionally for several hours with a 14.4-volt regulator as long as you pay attention to their water level. But if you motor a lot, the high-output regulator will be doing a number on your batteries. A different solution is indicated.

Alternator controllers. One such solution is a manual alternator controller. Instead of pulsing the field current (switching it on and off) to control alternator output, alternator output can also be controlled by setting the field current to a specific level. Alternator controllers use a variable resistor—a rheostat—to adjust the field current.

Alternator controllers, also known as bypass devices, are a popular add-on when a boat owner wants to charge the batteries as quickly as possible. By turning the knob on the controller, the current can be set to the desired level—exactly as you use a dimmer switch to adjust the light level in a room. In fact, an old-style lamp dimmer—a rheostat, not the Triac-based solid-state units sold today—can be used as an alternator controller.

The idea is to *peg* the current at the maximum level—around 25 percent of capacity—and hold it there until the batteries begin gassing vigorously. At this point, the batteries will be around 80 percent charged and the control is adjusted to a lower current, or control is simply returned to the regulator. Because the controller is not actually "regulating" alternator output, voltage will vary with any change in rpms.

Alternator controllers work quite well *if they are closely monitored*. But if you relax vigilance, you will fry your batteries and destroy your alternator. The batteries might even explode—a revolting development—and the controller may overheat so badly that it starts a fire. For these reasons, most manual controllers have disappeared from the market, replaced by controllers with an automatic cutout that returns control of the alternator to the regulator when the voltage in the charging circuit has reached the preset level. The best known of these is the AutoMAC, manufactured by SpaCreek.

Installation of a bypass device is straightforward. It is connected parallel to the original regulator, hence the name bypass. A two-position switch installed on the source side allows you to choose between the manual controller or the regulator. The automatic cutout on semi-automatic models performs the same function. If you install a bypass with an automatic cutout, monitor the cutout voltage and the temperature of your batteries carefully the first time you use the unit. Such units are notorious for having widely varying cutout points.

Monitoring is essential whenever a manual controller is in use. An ammeter is required to allow you to determine the proper setting and to make sure you are not putting excessive demands on the alternator; most alternators are at risk if operated continuously at more than 75 percent of rated capacity. A voltmeter should also be included in the circuit.

Manual controllers, when monitored carefully

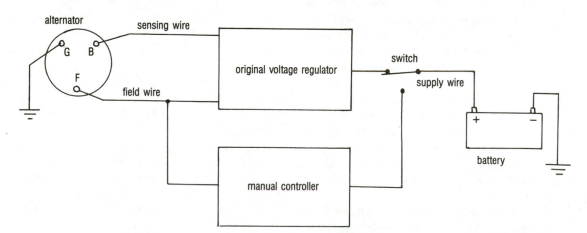

Wiring a manual controller

and adjusted properly, allow you to maximize the capacity of your alternator and to charge your batteries in the shortest possible time, but with a strictly manual controller, there is a very real danger of severely overcharging the batteries. Oddly enough, cranking a commercial controller with a cutout feature to the maximum output—the tendency of many users—is almost certain to result in chronic *undercharging*. This is because the rapidly rising voltage activates the cutout. The automatic cutout does largely reduce the risk of overcharging.

Smart controllers. Totally automatic controllers are also on the market. These sophisticated controllers are "programmed" to charge the battery in steps—typically providing a constant current until the battery voltage reaches 14.4 volts, then a constant voltage of 14.4 until the charging current drops below 5 percent of battery capacity, and finally a lower voltage (13.5 volts) to float the batteries.

The biggest advantage of smart controllers is that they require no manual intervention. Like conventional voltage regulators, they monitor voltage (some also monitor amperage) and increase or reduce alternator output accordingly. Because of the "stepped" charging sequence, smart controllers should give batteries the best treatment. One such controller can even provide a low-level fixed current to equalize the batteries, further contributing to long life.

What about charging performance? The answer may surprise you. In a *Practical Sailor* comparison of two prominent automatic controllers with a standard Delco automotive regulator, the regulator provided about 34 amps to a half-discharged 100-Ah battery in 90 minutes. The two controllers bettered that number by only 4 or 5 amps. Looking at the same results in a different light, the controllers achieved a charge level of around 88 percent in 90 minutes; the regulator took about 20 minutes longer.

Whether this level of improvement justifies the considerable expense of an automatic controller and the associated monitors is an individual call. Of course, we should not ignore the controller's third stage, cutting output voltage to a float level—but there are other, less expensive ways to achieve similar results.

Dual regulators. One alternative is dual regulators. Solid-state regulators are relatively inexpensive. Two regulators, one with a 14.4-volt setting and the other a 13.5-volt unit, connected in parallel with a two-position switch on the source side—exactly like the manual bypass connection—will allow you to switch to float voltage whenever you run the engine for a long period of time.

Almost all regulators are temperature compensated, losing as much as 10 millivolts (0.010 volts) per degree centigrade increase in temperature. Primarily because of the charging characteristics of "no-maintenance" automotive batteries, today's automotive regulators are set as high as 14.8 volts. But when the engine compartment rises by 50 degrees Centigrade, voltage drops to 14.3.

For a dual regulator setup, select the highest-output regulator readily available as one of the units (but it should not result in a charging voltage above 14.4 volts at normal operating temperature). For the float voltage, you will have difficulty finding a 13.5-volt regulator, but the heat of the engine compartment will reduce the actual voltage of a 13.8-volt unit to an acceptable value.

Dual voltage regulator. Another way to skin the same cat is through deception. By installing a resistor in the sensing wire of the regulator, you induce a voltage drop and fool the regulator into thinking that the voltage in the charging circuit is lower than it actually is. As a result, the regulator compensates by increasing the output of the alternator.

Adding resistance sufficient to achieve a 0.6-volt drop in the sensing wire will cause a 13.8-volt regulator to behave like one set to 14.4 volts. If you install a switch around the resistor, the same regulator can provide a regulated charge at 14.4 volts or 13.8 volts depending upon the switch setting.

Sizing the resistor depends upon the amount of current in the sensing wire. Sensing currents are typically a milliamp or less, so try a 500-ohm resis-

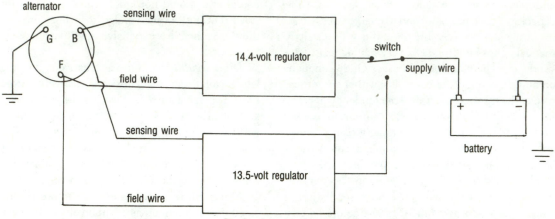

Dual voltage regulators

tor as a starting point and with full batteries, check the charging voltage. You can simplify the task by using a variable resistor. Adjust it until you get the output voltage you want, then measure the resistance setting and replace the variable resistor with a fixed one. You may be tempted to leave the variable resistor in the circuit, but that causes the regulator to imitate a manual controller—with the attendant risks. A fixed resistor gives you a dual-voltage regulator that requires no attention unless you are motoring for a long time.

Field Disconnect

If all this seems too complicated, just replace your existing regulator with a 14.4-volt unit and protect against overcharging with a simple field-disconnect switch. A switch installed on the battery

side of the regulator (*not* in the sensing wire) interrupts power to the alternator field, turning the alternator off. (If your regulator does not have a battery connection, you may need technical assistance.) The 14.4-volt regulator will provide good charging performance—only 15 percent to 20 percent off the pace of the best specialized controllers—and if you find yourself with full batteries and still motoring, just flip the switch. There is a lot to be said for simple and cheap.

Battery Chargers

The engine-mounted alternator is not the only device for maintaining the charge on the batteries. Battery chargers convert AC input from a shore power connection or a generator into DC power.

Battery chargers ought to be simple. Buy the size

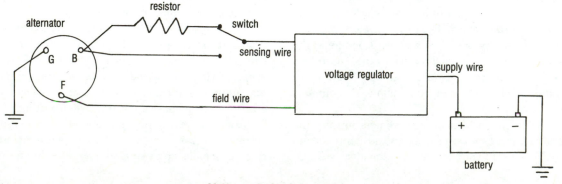

Making a dual-voltage regulator

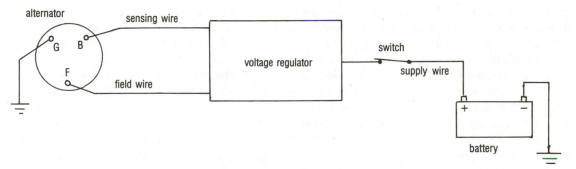

Field disconnect switch

you want, connect the red wire to the positive terminal of the battery, the black to the negative terminal,
the power cord to a convenient outlet, turn the
charger on, and forget about it.

Bad move, Skipper.

All chargers are not created equal. And it is difficult to ascertain *from a retailer* the differences in
various chargers. Ignore faceplates that say "50
amp" and "automatic," and advertising copy that
claims "will not overcharge." Pay no attention to
anything except the specifications.

Most battery chargers operate on the principle of
maintaining a constant voltage—exactly as the voltage regulator on the alternator does—and they suffer
from the same drawbacks as the regulator. The
usual setting of 13.8 volts results in a very low rate
of charge. Before the batteries are even 75 percent
charged, the actual output of a so-called 50-amp
charger will be less than 5 amps and declining.

If your charging pattern is to connect the charger
on Sunday night and disconnect it a week or two
later—the next time you use the boat—perhaps the
slow rate of charge is not a problem, but overcharging definitely is. Leaving a constant-voltage charger
operating for weeks at a time will murder your batteries. After such a charger has been on for 24
hours, you can be sure that it is doing *more harm than
good*. Turn it off.

A crude but effective way to safely use a constant
voltage charger unattended is to connect it to a common lamp timer (one of those gizmos that turn
lights on in your house so burglars think you're
home). Set the timer to turn the charger on one

hour a day. For the initial charge of *discharged* batteries, set the clock so that the on/off cycle is at least
12 hours away, then use the manual switch on the
timer to turn the charger on; it will turn off automatically at the end of the on/off cycle. The charging
circuit should have a blocking diode to prevent the
"off" charger from draining the battery.

"Automatic" chargers represent another, although
not necessarily better, alternative. Automatic chargers sense the battery voltage and turn off the charger
when the battery reaches a set level. The automatic
feature does tend to prevent overcharging, but automatic chargers typically never fully charge the batteries, which is bad, very bad.

Some chargers provide a constant current rather
than a constant voltage. *Trickle* chargers generally
fall into this category, providing a current of one to
three amps. Trickle chargers, because of the low
current levels, are almost always unregulated, but
even a current of just one amp can damage your
batteries over a period of time. Used with a lamp
timer, an inexpensive trickle charger with a 2- or 3-
amp output can meet the needs of many boat
owners.

Another constant-current type is the high-output
boost charger. The output can be set to a specific
amperage and turned down manually when the battery begins to gas. Boost chargers require constant
attention or they will cook your batteries. Most
come equipped with a timer switch to prevent the
charger from being left on inadvertently for too
long.

The best chargers match output to the requirements of the batteries. They work just like the best alternator controls. The output current is constant until the batteries reach about 14.4 volts, then the voltage is maintained until the current drops below five percent of capacity, when the voltage is reduced to 13.5 volts to safely float the batteries. Unfortunately, such chargers are also the most expensive, but unless you are powering the charger with an onboard AC generator, such quick-charging capacity is probably unnecessary.

The choice of a battery charger depends upon how it will be used. For unattended dockside use, I would choose a constant-current charger connected to a timer although a constant-voltage unit on a timer will do about the same job, but not if it has an automatic shutoff feature. The main thing is not to leave either continuously charging for more than a day.

Discount-store automotive chargers are perfectly adequate, *provided* they are overload protected and they are *isolated*. If the charger does not include an isolation transformer, it can cause *severe* electrolysis and you may even be at risk for an electric shock. Isolation is easy enough to check with an ohm-meter or a continuity tester. With one probe across both prongs of the plug, touch the other probe to every output wire or terminal. If nothing happens, reverse the probes to make sure a diode is not blocking the circuit one way. If the meter moves or the tester lights in either test, the charger is unsuitable for use aboard a boat. If the charger is UL approved, it is supposed to have an isolation transformer.

As for capacity, the charger should be capable of replacing your average daily consumption in 24 hours. A 5-amp constant-current charger will handle a 100-amp daily load, including the 20 percent battery inefficiency, but you need a 15- or 20-amp constant-voltage charger for the same load because the charger is going to severely reduce its output as the battery reaches higher levels of charge.

For liveaboard use, a constant-voltage charger will be the most convenient. It should have ample capacity to meet the *maximum* average demand. If

lights, fans, refrigeration, the stereo, and pressurized water are likely to place a 25-amp drain on the battery, a 25-amp charger will be about right. There is no point in having a charger with an output higher than 25 percent of your total battery capacity. If you turn off all the appliances, turn off the charger as well.

For use with an AC generator, choose a fixed-current charger capable of providing 25 percent of your battery capacity. These chargers can be as much as 90 percent efficient; voltage-regulated chargers waste up to 45 percent of the energy in heat. If you do not want to monitor the charge, then take out a loan and buy a charger that switches automatically from constant current to constant voltage to float voltage.

Wind Generators

Wind-powered generators are an increasingly popular alternative power source. There are numerous different units on the market, but they all fall into two basic types. They are either self-exciting alternators or permanent-magnet DC motors converted into generators. The most obvious difference in the two types is in their output characteristics. Commercially available alternator-type units typically generate about two amps in 15 knots of wind, while the DC motor type will put out four times that—around eight amps—in the same wind. If you have high current demands, capacity may be the deciding factor, but before you decide that is all you need to know, read on.

The DC motor type is a lot like a manual alternator control in that it requires constant attention when it is in use. Because the magnetic field is created by permanent magnets rather than a current passing through a field winding, there is no practical method of regulating the output of the generator. In 20 knots of wind, the generator is going to be pumping 15 amps into the batteries regardless of their condition. You cannot reduce the amount of current; when the batteries are above 80 percent full, your choices are overcharge or no charge (leaving the battery undercharged).

The consequences of overcharging are more immediate, so you have to stop the charge, but you cannot simply disconnect the charging circuit. That will remove the load from the generator, allowing it to spin freely—like a pinwheel. Burnout is likely as output climbs beyond capacity, and if the blades are even slightly out of balance, they may self-destruct. To stop the current flow, you have to *physically* stop the generator from turning, generally by turning the blades away from the wind and securing them with a strap once they stop.

Even under load, DC-motor-type generators have a propensity to self-destruct in high winds. If you are ashore and a squall passes through the anchorage, when you get back aboard you are not going to be a happy camper. So most sailors do not leave an expensive wind generator of this type running unattended. And even if you are aboard, a sudden storm can damage the generator before you can react. Think of it as getting caught flying too much sail.

Every sailor I know that has used a DC-motor-type generator for any time has at least one horror story. Most nevertheless praise the units, but they are conservative in how they use them. The point is that if the wind generator is disabled at night and anytime the crew is away from the boat, the *daily* output will be a lot less than you might expect by multiplying the 15 knot output by 24 hours. And when the generator is in use, the batteries must be carefully monitored.

The alternator-type wind generator, on the other hand, will survive any winds that most sailors are likely to encounter, especially if the stator coils have iron cores (as opposed to "air-filled"). This feature makes the alternator self-limiting, meaning that it cannot produce more than the rated output, and that eliminates the possibility of the unit's burning out in high winds.

Alternator-type wind generators can also be regulated with a simple device called a *shunt regulator*. A normal regulator will not work since these alternators are enabled with permanent magnets. Instead of reducing the output (like a regular voltage regula-

tor) when it senses increasing voltage, the shunt regulator diverts—shunts—some of the output into a "dummy" load where it dissipates as heat. Shunt regulators do not work well on the more powerful motor-type generators because current levels can rise too high.

High-wind capabilities and a means of regulating the charge mean that an alternator-type wind generator can be mounted permanently and more or less ignored. Average daily output *can* be estimated at 24 times the rated output.

One other factor often overlooked is the noise these units make. Alternator-types are typically powered by a turbine—a fan with five or six flexible blades. Motortypes are most often equipped with two (sometimes three) rigid wooden blades reminiscent of the blades of an airplane propeller. The turbines are relatively quiet, but twin-blade propellers can make you think you are on an airboat in the Everglades instead of a sailboat in a previously quiet anchorage. Some units are much worse than others, and while you may eventually become deaf to the howl, the boats around you won't. In Germany, they are experimenting with commercial wind generators with a *single* blade that whips around like a berserk Samurai wielding a 40-foot sword, with a scream to match. I pray this technology never comes to marine generators.

Tapping the Sun

The *potential* of solar power is impressive. In just 15 minutes, the sun bombards the earth with more energy than all of humanity consumes in a year. In the same 15 minutes about 6,000 watt-hours of energy falls on the deck of a 30-foot boat, enough to *fully* charge *five* dead 100-Ah batteries. Unfortunately, the best commercial panels are only about 12 percent efficient at converting sunlight to electrical energy. Still, cover the deck with photovoltaic cells and they will convert enough energy *in a single hour* to fully charge a pair of 100-Ah batteries. We only need a fraction of this area to get the same output in a day, so why aren't solar cells the dominant source of electricity on boats?

Let's look at *daily* output. Nontracking solar arrays reach their peak output when the sun is directly overhead. Output drops slightly at first, then dramatically, as the sun arcs downward toward the horizon. Total daily output varies with latitude, season, and the weather, but even in the best circumstances, daily output will not exceed five times the rated peak output. In other words, a panel rated at 50 watts will deliver no more than 250 watt-hours of power daily, even during a summer cruise along the Baja California coast.

The amount of solar energy available per square meter of surface area is about 1000 watts. A 12-percent-efficient module 1 square meter in size would yield 120 watt-hours at peak periods and no more than 600 watt-hours daily. To get daily amp-hours, divide by the rated voltage ($I = P/E$) *of the panel,* typically around 15 volts. So in ideal conditions, daily output per square meter will not exceed 40 Ah. To replace 100 Ah of consumption, plus 20 percent battery inefficiency, will require about three square meters of solar cells—almost exactly the area of a full sheet of plywood (4×8 feet). Size is the first problem.

The second problem is cost. Here there is good news and bad news. The good news is that since solar panels first came on the market two decades ago, the cost per watt of solar-generated power has dropped to a tenth of what it was. (In the mid-1970s, a panel capable of resupplying the power consumed by two miserly 8-watt fluorescent cabin lights cost around $600.) The bad news is that the cost is still around $7 per peak watt, or more than $20 per daily amp-hour. A solar array capable of handling a 100-Ah daily load will cost at least $2,500.

This would seem to suggest that solar power is still a bit expensive to meet all your onboard electrical requirements, but, in some applications, it is a clear winner. The most obvious is maintaining the battery aboard any boat stored on a mooring. An appropriate size solar panel can provide a constant float charge, avoiding harmful self-discharge and significantly prolonging the life of expensive batteries, without the risk of electrolysis associated with a constant shore connection. In sunny climates, a small panel can handle the modest battery drain of a boat used on weekends as effectively as a battery charger. And for cruising, a modest array can cut engine running time dramatically.

Of the three types of silicon-based solar cells on the market, single crystalline cells produce the most power in optimum conditions, with modules typically having an efficiency of around 12 percent. Polycrystalline modules are less expensive to produce and slightly less efficient—about 11 percent. Amorphous, or thin-film, cells are the cheapest to produce, but the best are only about nine percent efficient and they quickly lose as much as 20 percent of their efficiency before stabilizing at around seven percent. (A new thin-film cell made of copper-indium-diselenide [CIS] will soon double this efficiency; you heard it here first.) Both types of crystalline modules are rigid, while thin-film modules can be flexible. In fact the military is experimenting with tent material laminated with thin-film solar cells, an intriguing concept for boat awnings.

Obviously solar cells have to be exposed to the sun. On a boat, exposure will be less affected by the constant movement if the panels are mounted horizontally. To the extent possible, they should be clear of any shadows, even the seemingly inconsequential shadows of lines and rigging. The cells in shadow will practically cease to operate, and they will resist the flow of electricity from the other cells still in the sun, severely reducing total output. The reduction is less pronounced with thin-film modules because they are less affected by low light levels. In overcast conditions, thin-film modules may actually outperform, in total daily output, more efficient crystalline modules.

As incongruous as it seems, it is essential to keep solar panels cool. How essential? If the panel temperature reaches 120 degrees—not hard to imagine at noon on a 95-degree day—output may drop by as much as 25 percent. To avoid excessive heat buildup, panels should be mounted with air space beneath them. Select higher voltage panels (more cells) to compensate for the inevitable loss of output due to heat.

On this subject, a panel designed to charge a 12-volt battery may have from 32 to 37 cells in it. The voltage of an individual cell is about 0.45 volts, so the panel voltage varies from 14.4 volts to 16.7 volts. Manufacturers are fond of calling modules with 32 or 33 cells "self-regulating." Right; so is my bank account. With the voltage drop from elevated temperatures and from the blocking diode (meant to keep current from flowing the wrong way during darkness), a 33-cell panel will have insufficient potential to fully charge your batteries. Count the number of cells and don't buy a panel that has less than 36.

Solar-panel connections are basic. If the output of the panel is less than 0.5 percent of your battery capacity, it can be connected directly to the battery without regulation. Assuming normal self-discharge of about two percent daily, such a panel will float the batteries effectively. If the output of the panel is higher, regulation is required. It can be done manually by covering or disconnecting the panel, or automatically by feeding the output through a shunt regulator. If neither the panel nor the regulator includes a blocking diode in its circuitry, such a diode must be added between the solar panel and the battery or the panel will drain the battery at night. Don't forget to include a fuse in the positive cable as near the battery as possible.

TOOLS OF THE TRADE

To check and connect the various components of your old boat's electrical system, you need three special tools: a wire stripper, a soldering iron, and a multimeter.

It is quite possible to strip the insulation from the ends of electrical wiring with a pocket knife, but unless you are very careful you will nick the wire. The nick weakens the wire, is susceptible to corrosion, and increases the voltage drop. A wire stripper cuts through the insulation without damaging the wire. Besides being better than a knife, a stripper is cheaper than a decent knife, vastly easier to use, and eliminates the risk of thumb amputation.

Most household wiring is connected with wire nuts, plastic-covered metal cones that are threaded onto the twisted wires to hold them together. In the moisture-rich environment aboard a boat, twisted wires soon corrode and if the connection is not broken altogether, it assuredly *resists* the flow of electricity. Wire nuts should never be used on a boat and all wire-to-wire and wire-to-terminal connections should be soldered. A 50-watt soldering iron will handle most onboard soldering jobs, but higher wattage can make the job easier. The pencil type is smaller, easier to store, and generally handier, but whether you choose a pencil- or pistol-type iron is up to you. There are also 12-volt and butane models for use away from the dock.

Buy the least expensive multimeter you can find. You will use it on your old boat for two basic functions—measuring DC volts and checking continuity—and there is no value to having 30 or 40 different settings. An added advantage of a cheap meter is that you will not be afraid to use it. The only requirements are that the meter have a 0- to 15-volt DC scale and that it have virtually any ohm-meter scale—typically 0 to 1K (1,000 ohms). I bought my own multimeter for less than $10, and that was 14 years ago when meters were a lot more expensive than they are today.

Using a Multimeter

Don't imagine that meters are complicated. Checking the voltage in a circuit is no different from checking your speed on the turnpike except that the needle points to 12.6 volts instead of 65 m.p.h.

To measure voltage, plug the black lead into the common socket (marked – or COM) and the red lead into the socket marked 15V (or, if the meter has a dial, set it to 15V). Always make sure the range is higher than the reading you expect; i.e., don't set the meter to a 0- to 10-volt scale and attempt to check the voltage in 12-volt circuits.

The meter will tell you both voltage and polarity. Hold the black probe against the negative post of one of your batteries and, watching the meter, *tap* the red probe to the positive post. You just want to touch it for an instant. The needle should start up the scale. That tells you that you have the meter connected correctly and that the red probe is touching the positive side of the circuit. Now hold the probe against the post and read the voltage. If the battery is fully charged, the reading will be around 12.6 volts.

What happens if you connect the meter in reverse? Try it. Hold the red probe against the negative post and *tap* the black probe to the positive post. The needle tries to deflect the wrong way, although it is prevented from moving very far. This tells you that you have the polarity reversed. When-

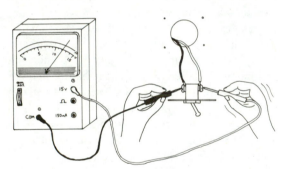

Testing voltage: Tap the positive probe to make sure scale and polarity are correct.

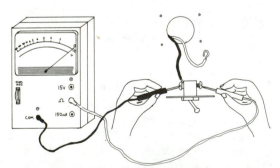

Testing continuity: Zero ohms indicates continuity. To check the switch, flip it; the needle should return to the left, indicating an open circuit. Always disconnect a component from its circuit when checking for continuity.

Using a multimeter

ever you use a multimeter, *always* tap one of the probes first to confirm that you have the meter connected correctly before you take the full reading. Tapping can also warn you that the meter is set to the wrong scale. If the meter moves in the correct direction, but the needle takes off like a shot, check the scale you are using. If the meter is on the 2.5-volt scale and you are checking 14 volts, a tap will not injure the meter, but a solid connection will "peg" the needle and probably damage the meter. Tap and you will never have a problem.

Use your voltmeter to locate problems with the wiring of your old boat. If you touch the probes to the positive and negative sides of any circuit, the meter will measure the voltage of the circuit *at that point*. Try it with a 12-volt outlet somewhere on the boat. Ideally, the meter should read the same voltage measured at the battery terminals, but if the outlet is some distance from the battery, there may be a slight voltage drop. The maximum acceptable drop is three percent. In other words, if you measure the battery voltage as 12.6 volts, the reading should be at least 12.2 volts on every circuit. Less and the wiring is too small or you have a poor connection somewhere in the circuit.

Anytime an electrical item fails to work, check the voltage at the terminals of the item. If there are no exposed terminals or connections, you can push the pointed probes through the insulation of the wiring. (It is advisable afterwards to seal probe punctures with a dab of silicone.) A good reading tells you the problem is with the item; no reading tells you the problem is with the circuit.

No voltage in a circuit should send you immediately to the main electrical panel to check the fuse (or the breaker, but breakers are not common in *old* boats). A bad fuse or poor contact in the fuse holder is usually the problem, but if this is not the case, then there is a break in the circuit and you will have to locate it.

Begin by opening the panel and checking the voltage between the *output* terminal of the fuse and the negative *buss bar*—the copper strip with all the black wires connected to it. If you read 12 volts, the break must be between the panel and the faulty appliance; 0 volts indicates that the fuse holder is bad. Check across another fuse holder to make sure there is voltage in the panel; it is embarrassing to discover that the whole problem is that you failed to turn on the battery switch.

Use the voltmeter also to determine the correct polarity when you are installing new equipment. The polarity does not matter to some items, particularly lights, but correct polarity is essential for DC motors and all electronics. Twelve-volt outlets should all be wired the same—with the positive side of the circuit to the larger pin.

WARNING: We are *only* measuring 12-volt DC circuits. The meter, set properly, will also measure AC voltage, but you must be *extremely* careful when you are working around 110-volt AC circuits.

Switch the multimeter to the ohmmeter setting and it is used to determine resistance. A battery in the meter introduces a tiny current at a known voltage into the circuit being tested. The meter actually measures the current through the circuit, but the markings on the face of the meter are calibrated to convert the current into resistance in ohms—the smaller the current, the greater the resistance. Before measuring resistance, you must calibrate the meter by holding the probes tightly together and turning the calibration knob until the meter reads zero, which is all the way to the right on the ohms scale.

Unlike voltmeter use, there must *never* be *any* voltage in a circuit being checked by an ohmmeter. If there is, the meter will be damaged, so the circuit being tested must be isolated by removing it from any power source. Individual devices should be removed from the circuit entirely to insure that the meter is measuring just the device and not the circuit.

Your primary use of an ohmmeter is likely to be to determine continuity. Touch the probes to the ends of a fuse and if the needle swings across the scale, the fuse is good. If the needle does not move, the fuse is blown. Connect the probes to the two terminals of a switch. Flip the switch one way and

the needle moves; flip it the other way and the needle returns to the left. If the needle fails to move, the switch does not work, and if the needle stays to the right on both switch settings, the switch is shorted out. Check runs of wire, light bulbs, and motor windings in exactly the same manner.

WIRING

If you didn't know anything at all about electricity, you might wonder why the wires on your boat are all different sizes, ranging from rope-size battery cables to hairlike leads for the compass light. Finding out that they all carry the same voltage—12 volts—just makes the variety of sizes more confusing. The simple answer is that the more current you expect to pass through a wire, the larger it needs to be. In principle, it is the same reason firefighters don't arrive with garden hoses.

The actual size of wire that is appropriate is also influenced by how far you expect it to carry the current. The longer the run, the greater the resistance of the wire. To avoid detrimental voltage drops, the higher resistance of extra length is offset by the lower resistance of wire with a larger diameter.

I know you would prefer that I provide the conductivity of copper—the only material appropriate for boat wiring—so you can compute the resistance of the wire from its length and cross section and calculate the voltage drop. Unfortunately, someone else has already done the calculations and put them into a table. From the load on the circuit (in amps) and the distance *to and from* the device, the table tells you the minimum wire size (by gauge) to limit voltage drop to three percent. Higher voltage drops (read smaller wires) are tolerable in light circuits, but not particularly advisable.

Wire for boat use should always be multi-strand. Solid wire, predominant in house wiring, will work-harden from movement or vibration and eventually break. It should never be used aboard a boat, even for AC circuits.

Tinned wire is far more corrosion-resistant than bare copper and well worth the extra pennies it

Conductor Sizes for 3 Percent Drop in Voltage.

(Total current on circuit in amps.)	(Length of conductor from source of current to device and back to source—feet)																		
	10	15	20	25	30	40	50	60	70	80	90	100	110	120	130	140	150	160	170
12 volts																			
5	18	16	14	12	12	10	10	10	8	8	8	6	6	6	6	6	6	6	6
10	14	12	10	10	10	8	6	6	6	6	4	4	4	4	2	2	2	2	2
15	12	10	10	8	8	6	6	6	4	4	2	2	2	2	2	1	1	1	1
20	10	10	8	6	6	6	4	4	2	2	2	2	1	1	1	0	0	0	2/0
25	10	8	6	6	6	4	4	2	2	2	1	1	0	0	0	2/0	2/0	2/0	3/0
30	10	8	6	6	4	4	2	2	1	1	0	0	2/0	2/0	3/0	3/0	3/0	3/0	3/0
40	8	6	6	4	4	2	2	1	0	0	2/0	2/0	3/0	3/0	3/0	4/0	4/0	4/0	4/0
50	6	6	4	4	2	2	1	0	2/0	2/0	3/0	3/0	4/0	4/0	4/0				
60	6	4	4	2	2	1	0	2/0	3/0	3/0	4/0	4/0	4/0						
70	6	4	2	2	1	0	2/0	3/0	3/0	4/0	4/0								
80	6	4	2	2	1	0	3/0	3/0	4/0	4/0									
90	4	2	2	1	0	2/0	3/0	4/0	4/0										
100	4	2	2	1	0	2/0	3/0	4/0											

(Wire sizes in AWG)

costs. To counter the damp environment, select wire that has an insulation designation of either THWN (thermoplastic, heat resistant, wet locations, nylon jacket) or XHHW (cross-linked polyethylene, high-heat resistant, wet locations). Because circuits invariably require two wires, a "hot" wire and an insulated return, duplex wire—two insulated wires sheathed together—is the most convenient to use. However, the most common multistrand duplex wire—lamp cord—is not suitable for marine use.

Connections

There is almost always more than one way to do any job on a boat, but in the case of making electrical connections, the only choice is to solder them. Every other method is inferior and leads to trouble. When copper wires are exposed, they eventually corrode, and any electrical connection formed by holding the wires in contact with each other suffers from such corrosion. That includes wires twisted together, crimped into fittings, or compressed under the head of a screw.

In contrast, any corrosion that might form on an exposed soldered connection will have little effect on the passage of current since the connection is actually *encased* in the solder. The two wires are, in effect, fused into a single conductor.

Anyone can make perfect solder joints every time. The only requirements are good-quality electrical solder, a properly tinned soldering iron, shiny clean wires, and three hands.

Solder for electrical connections must always be *rosin-cored*, never acid-cored. Solid solder can be used, but it requires separate rosin flux (the flux is inside the cored solders) and it is more difficult to get consistent results. Choose solder that is designated 60/40, meaning it is 60 percent tin and 40 percent lead. Some solders seem to flow better than others; I have always had good results with Kester.

Tinning a soldering iron is nothing more than coating the tip with solder, but if you heat the iron and touch solder to it, the solder will simply roll off in silver drops. First you must clean the tip thoroughly with a file or a piece of emery cloth; this will be a lot less painful if you do it *before* you heat the iron. Dipping the tip into soldering paste after you file it will help to get it completely clean. Now heat the lightly coated tip and touch the solder to the iron. If you have cleaned the tip well, the solder will coat it entirely—as if you had dipped the tip into shiny, silver paint. Wipe away any excess with a damp cloth, and the iron is ready to use.

When you strip the insulation from the wire ends to be soldered, the wire should be bright and clean. This is normally not a problem, but in an old boat, you may be working with old wires. If the copper is tarnished, it will not take solder. The best option is

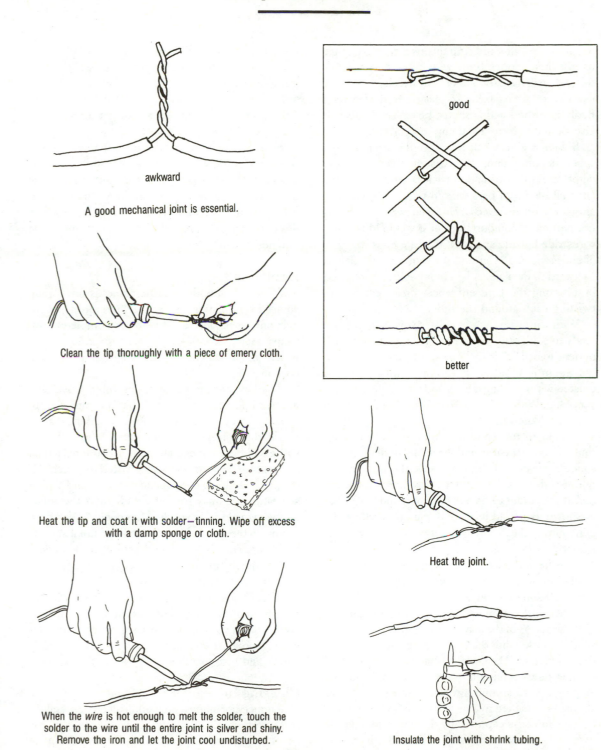

awkward

A good mechanical joint is essential.

good

better

Clean the tip thoroughly with a piece of emery cloth.

Heat the tip and coat it with solder—tinning. Wipe off excess with a damp sponge or cloth.

Heat the joint.

When the *wire* is hot enough to melt the solder, touch the solder to the wire until the entire joint is silver and shiny. Remove the iron and let the joint cool undisturbed.

Insulate the joint with shrink tubing.

Soldering

to cut off the ends and strip the insulation to expose untarnished copper. If the wire is too short to allow this, you will have to sand or scrape it clean. (Do *not* use the soldering paste to clean electrical wires.) Badly tarnished wiring should be replaced–period. Use tinned wire to avoid any reoccurrence.

Solder is a very soft metal, so the strength of a splice depends upon the twisting together of the wires. Strip the insulation back far enough to give yourself plenty of bare wire to work with; you can always cut off any excess. How you twist the wires is not particularly important, but if you hold the two wires side by side and twist the bare ends together like a grapevine, you end up with a splice that is awkward to insulate. A less bulky splice is achieved by crossing the bare ends near their centers and twisting each around the other.

With the wires tightly twisted together, you are ready to solder the joint. The only trick to getting a perfect joint is that the *wire* must melt the solder, not the iron. Hold the hot, tinned iron against the twisted wires, sliding it back and forth if the splice is very long. With your other hand, touch the solder to the *wire*. When the wire is hot enough, the solder will begin to melt and flow into the splice. Continue to move the iron and the solder until the entire splice is silver and shiny. Remove the iron and do not disturb the splice until it cools. *Shininess is essential*. If the solder turns dull or lumpy, you have what is known as a cold joint, and you must reheat the joint until the solder is shiny and flows out smoothly.

The heated wires have a tendency to melt the insulation near the joint, releasing chemicals from the insulation that can lead to corrosion. Snip a pair of 2-inch disks from an aluminum can and cut the disks about 2/3 of the way across. Spread the cut and slide the disks onto the bare wire against the end of the insulation. The disks will act as heat sinks.

It is rarely advisable to make a connection by looping a wire around a terminal screw. The wire should be attached to a ring terminal fitting, and the fitting should be captured by the screw. Joining the wire to the terminal fitting by crimping forms a good mechanical bond, but it is a vulnerable electrical connection in the marine environment. Terminal fittings must always be soldered to the wire. Be sure to heat the fitting sufficiently for it to melt the solder; otherwise you are certain to get a cold joint, which will be prone to failure.

Fork terminals are less desirable than ring terminals because they have a tendency to slip off the retaining screw; ring terminals cannot come loose unless the screw is removed entirely. Spade terminals are perfectly appropriate for items that must be disconnected periodically, but they must be watched carefully for corrosion.

Insulation

Electrical tape, despite the name, is not a good choice for insulating wire splices and terminal connections. Invariably it partially or completely unwraps itself . . . unless you want to remove it, in which case it becomes a solid, sticky, impenetrable cocoon.

The best choice is heat-shrink tubing. Available in assorted sizes, this product permanently reinsulates the splice. Select a size about twice the diameter of the wiring–large enough to slip over the splice–and cut a piece an inch or two longer than the splice. *Before* the wires are twisted together, slip the piece of tubing onto one of the wires and push it several inches away from the end. After the splice has been made and the solder has cooled, center the tubing on the splice. Heat the tubing until it shrinks tightly onto the joint. A hair dryer is recommended, but it is usually more convenient to play the flame of a lighter underneath the tubing.

Heat-shrink tubing also works well on wire-to-terminal connections. For insulating odd-shaped connections, you can buy heat-shrink tape, which is used like regular electrical tape, but then heated to shrink and fuse together.

Plugging In

Connecting a household appliance is generally a matter of simply plugging it in. Plugging in has never caught on with 12-volt appliances, and most will be "hard-wired" into the electrical system. This distinction aside, there is little reason to be any more concerned about connecting a fan you purchase for your boat than you would about a fan you purchase for your home.

Fans, lights, pumps, electronics—virtually every 12-volt item that you are likely to put aboard—will have *two* wire leads. The red wire gets connected to the positive side of the circuit, the other wire (often black) gets connected to the negative side. That's it.

If you are replacing an old piece of equipment, the wiring is already in place. Remove the old item and, with power to the circuit, determine which of the two wires is positive by touching the voltmeter probes to them. Turn the power to the circuit off by removing the appropriate fuse in the main panel, turning the battery switch to off or disconnecting the battery cable. Check the circuit with your voltmeter to be sure the power is off. Now, twist the red (or otherwise identified as positive) lead to the positive wire, and the other lead to the negative wire; solder and insulate. Reestablish the power to the circuit and switch on the appliance.

Plug connectors can be convenient on boats, particularly for items that are portable, such as spotlights, vacuum cleaners, and televisions. Many of these devices are equipped with plugs designed (with widely varying degrees of success) to obtain power from an automotive cigarette lighter socket. Installing a cigarette lighter aboard to accommodate such plugs is not a particularly good idea. Equipping your boat with two-prong sockets and replacing the lighter plug with a two-prong plug is a much better approach.

ring terminal   fork terminal   captive fork terminal   spade terminal

Terminal fittings

Be sure you wire every socket consistently—with the positive side to the larger pin—to avoid accidentally reversing polarity when you plug an appliance into a different socket. To determine how to connect the new plug to the appliance, bare a small spot on one of the wires near the cigarette lighter plug, set your multimeter to the ohmmeter setting, hold one of the probes to the bare spot, and touch the other to center contact of the lighter plug. The center contact is the positive one, so continuity indicates that the bared wire is positive; mark it. If the meter doesn't move, the other wire is the positive one. Confirm your findings by touching the probe to the side contact (negative) to make sure that you get the opposite results. Once you have identified the positive lead, cut off the lighter plug and install the two-prong plug, connecting the positive lead to the larger pin.

Two-prong household sockets can be used for 12-volt connections, but it is not a good idea, especially if you have any shore-power outlets aboard, because of the risk of accidentally plugging a 12-volt appliance into a 110-volt socket. Ka-boom! Stick with round-pin plugs and sockets for 12-volt connections. For on-deck use, choose the English-manufactured Dri-Plugs, which use an O-ring to seal moisture out quite effectively.

Adding a Circuit

New appliances may require a new circuit. All this means is that instead of connecting the leads at the appliance, you are going to extend them with additional wire and connect them at the distribution panel. This reverses the traditional way of looking at adding a circuit, but illustrates that there is no real distinction between replacing and adding. Whether you connect the new wiring to the appliance before or after you make the connections at the panel is immaterial.

Finding a route for the wiring can be troublesome. The original wiring probably runs across the top of the headliner, sandwiched between the headliner and the deck, out of sight but inaccessible. You will have to find a different route for new (or even replacement) wiring. Generally the wiring can be routed through lockers to keep it out of sight, but

if the locker will contain hard or heavy items, fasten the wires to the *top* of the locker or run them through plastic conduit.

If you are fortunate enough to have an unused fuse in the panel (fat chance), all that is required is soldering the positive lead to the output side of the fuse holder and the negative lead to the negative buss bar.

Since it is unlikely you'll have an open fuse, what about sharing a fuse that is already in use? It depends. When you connect several appliances in parallel—like the rungs of a ladder—the voltage in the circuit is unaffected by each additional appliance (rung), but the amperage is the *sum* of the amperages of the individual appliances. So if the appliance already connected to the fuse is drawing 10 amps and the new appliance draws 10 amps, what do you suppose is going to happen to a 15-amp fuse when you turn both items on at the same time?

No problem. Just replace the 15-amp fuse with a 25-amp version. *Wrong!*

Anytime only one of the appliances is on, the 25-amp fuse offers virtually no protection to the appliance. There could be a fire risk besides, since you undoubtedly sized the wire to carry only 10 amps, but it could be subjected to 2 1/2 times that current before the fuse blows. If a 15-amp fuse is the correct size for the existing circuit, you cannot arbitrarily change it.

On the other hand, if you are just adding a light that draws an amp or two and is unlikely to overload the 15-amp circuit, and the wire you are using is capable of carrying 15 amps without overheating, you may be able to share a fuse with another circuit.

Almost always, the preferable solution is to fuse the circuit separately. This means the addition of an auxiliary distribution panel with additional fuses, or the use of in-line fuse holders. If you use an in-line fuse holder, be sure it is in the positive side of the circuit, and locate it near the panel, not near the appliance, so that all of the wiring will be protected.

FUSES OR BREAKERS

A lot of newer boats are equipped with breakers rather than fuses. Twelve-volt breakers work like their 110-volt cousins in the breaker panel in your kitchen or garage. They perform the same function as fuses, opening the circuit when it becomes overloaded for any reason. The advantage of a breaker is that once the problem that caused the overload has been corrected, reestablishing the circuit is merely a matter of flipping a switch.

There is a tendency to think of fuses as old fashioned and somewhat inferior to breakers. Actually, in the marine environment, the fuse has a number of advantages. With no mechanical component, it cannot corrode and fail to trip. If it fails, it always fails open, protecting the circuit. A fuse panel can be custom configured by simply changing the sizes of the fuses in the various holders. And the cost of fuses and panels is about a quarter of the price of breakers.

If your old boat is equipped with fuses, there is no reason to change. And if you add an auxiliary panel, buy a fuse panel and spend the money you save on something else.

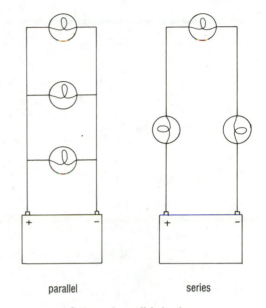

parallel   series

Series and parallel circuits

SWITCHES

Most equipment you install has its own switches, but occasionally you may need to install a separate switch in the circuit. The switch for an electric bilge pump comes to mind.

Switches are always installed in *series* with the device they control, and they are always installed on the positive side of the circuit. Maybe you are not clear on this series/parallel thing. *Parallel* means that more than one device is connected between the positive and the negative side of the circuit—like ladder rungs. The current branches; i.e., it can follow more than one path. *Series* means that the devices are connected end to end—like link sausages—and the current passing through the circuit must pass through every device in the circuit.

We install a switch in series by cutting the positive wire of the circuit and connecting the cut ends to the two terminals on the switch. When the switch is open (off), the entire circuit is open, and no power reaches the pump. Close the switch (on), and current passes through the switch and to the pump, causing it to run.

Suppose you want the pump to operate from a float switch most of the time, but you want to be able to turn the pump on manually in case the float sticks—which it will eventually do—and to turn the pump off altogether. You need a three-position switch.

Such a switch will have three terminals. If you check with your ohmmeter, you will find that when you flip the switch to the right, it connects the center terminal to the right terminal; when you move the switch to the middle, none of the terminals are connected; and when the switch is positioned to the left, the center terminal and the left terminal are connected. But when you cut the wire that connects the panel to the positive lead of the pump, you only have two ends.

Connect the end that is coming from the panel to the center terminal, and connect the other end to either of the other terminals. When you flip the switch to that side, the pump will run, but—stay with me—you want the pump to be "on" when you flip the switch to either side. (Forget about the float switch momentarily.) You can accomplish this simply enough by splicing a second wire to the positive

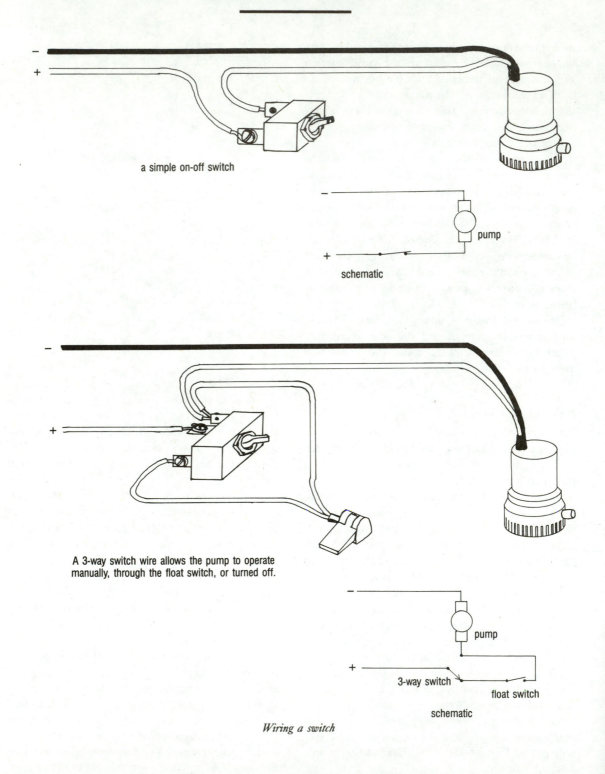

a simple on-off switch

pump

schematic

A 3-way switch wire allows the pump to operate manually, through the float switch, or turned off.

pump

3-way switch

float switch

schematic

Wiring a switch

lead of the pump and connecting it to the other terminal on the switch. Off is still off, but left or right sends the current to pump.

Now the float switch. You already know—I just told you—that a switch has to be installed in series. If you cut the hot wire between the three-position switch and the pump—you have two hot wires, so take your choice—and you connect the two ends to the float switch, the float switch will control the pump. But this only happens when the three-way switch is positioned to include the float switch in the circuit.

Are you with me so far? Can you also see that instead of splicing a second wire to the lead from the pump, then cutting it to insert the float switch, you could have accomplished the same thing by connecting the leads from the float switch directly to the right and left terminals of the three-position switch? If your answer is yes, you are not likely to encounter many problems in the 12-volt system on your old boat that you will be unable to comprehend and correct.

The Big Switch

Every boat should have a battery-disconnect switch, and those with more than one battery should be equipped with a battery-selector switch. The reason for the disconnect is to be able to turn off all power to the boat's electrical system— advisable any time the boat is left unattended, and essential in the event of an emergency such as a short circuit or an electrical fire. The selector, or isolator, switch serves the additional function of isolating two or more batteries from one another, allowing the separate banks to be discharged independently and charged in tandem.

Selector switches generally have four positions and three terminals. Heavy battery cables—#4 or #6 wire for reasonable run lengths—independently connect the positive terminals of the two batteries (or twin battery banks) to two of the terminals on the switch. Typically, several wires will be attached to the third terminal: a heavy cable leading to the starter solenoid to carry the high starting currents, a

smaller wire to the ignition switch to energize the solenoid, the output lead from the alternator, and a cable leading to the distribution panel to supply all the boat's other electrical requirements. The negative cables from both batteries are commonly joined and led to a bolt on the engine and to the negative buss bar in the distribution panel.

Because the switch isolates the batteries, only one battery will receive a charge when the engine is running unless the switch is turned to the "BOTH" setting. But when the engine is stopped, both batteries will be discharged by any load—planned or inadvertent—placed on the electrical system, unless the switch is turned to remove one of the batteries from the circuit. If you forget to turn the switch to the appropriate setting, the result may be the total discharge of one or both batteries.

BATTERY ISOLATORS

To avoid the necessity of operator intervention, you might consider installing a battery isolator. Instead of connecting the alternator output to the selector switch, you connect the output directly to the isolator. The isolator has dual (or more) outputs, so anytime the engine runs, both batteries receive a charge. The batteries nevertheless remain independent because the isolator contains diodes—electrical check valves—which allow the current to flow in one direction but not in the other. You can observe this function by checking a diode with your ohmmeter; you will get continuity one way but when you reverse the probes the circuit will appear to be open.

Adding an isolator is not always such a good idea. Diodes create a voltage drop of at least 0.6 volts— often considerably more—and such a drop can alter your ability to fully charge your batteries. For example, if your regulator is controlling alternator output to 13.8 volts, the drop across the diodes means that the voltage delivered to the batteries is only 13.2 volts or less. Such a low charging voltage is certain to result in perpetual undercharging of the battery, with all the bad consequences that are attendant.

If your regulator is adjustable, you may be able to

compensate by raising the voltage setting. Otherwise, this problem may be overcome by taking the regulator sensing wire directly to the positive terminal on the battery, but this causes the regulator to sense the condition of only one battery and may result in the other battery being undercharged. You cannot connect the sensing wire to both batteries or they will no longer be isolated. There are some other options, like putting a similar diode in the sensing circuit to equally reduce the sensed voltage, but buying a battery isolator and connecting it between the alternator and the batteries without somehow compensating for the inherent voltage drop is almost certain to cause more problems than it solves. Personally, I just turn the old selector switch.

FIELD DISCONNECT

If you "unload" the alternator by accidentally turning the switch to the "OFF" position, you are certain to fry the diodes in the alternator. On some older switches, as the selector was turned between batteries the momentary disconnect was enough to blow the alternator, but all brand-name battery switches currently on the market connect *before* they disconnect, eliminating concern about switching between batteries while the engine is running. You will still smoke the alternator if you pass through the "OFF" position on the way from battery one to battery two—unless the switch has an alternator *field disconnect* feature.

Field disconnect was mentioned earlier in connection with avoiding battery overcharging when using a regulator set to 14.4 volts. All that is required is inserting a switch into the battery side of the field circuit so the current to the field can be interrupted, which will turn off the alternator. (On alternators with an integral or internal regulator, identifying the field wire can present some problems and you should seek professional assistance.) Generally, you disconnect the source wire to the regulator (not the sensing wire) from the battery and connect it to one side of the field disconnect switch.

Connect the other side of the switch to the battery. The field-disconnect switch may be independent, to allow you to turn off the alternator when the batteries are fully charged, or it may be combined with the battery selector switch to avoid damage to the alternator by turning off the alternator *before* the battery switch is turned to "OFF." In either case, the same wiring applies.

SCHEMATICS

It is often helpful to draw out a circuit before you work on it. Electricians call such drawings schematics, but don't let the term put you off; it is just a map of the wiring.

Solid lines represent wires, dots are junctions, a zigzag is a resistor, a curlicue is a light, a wave is a fuse, and a little doorway is a switch. Almost all the standard symbols will be clear to you if you look at them for a few minutes, but for your own drawings, use whatever symbols you want. Circles or boxes with the name of the item written in are as good as zigzags and curlicues every day of the week.

If you make major changes in the electrical system aboard your boat, diagram the wiring and make the drawings a permanent part of your notebook. The drawings will save you a lot of effort in tracing circuits if you have problems or make additional changes at some future date.

Using color-coded wire and noting the colors on your schematic can also be helpful. The American Boat and Yacht Council long ago established a recommended color code for various applications. If your manufacturer followed those recommendations during the construction of your boat, identifying and tracing existing circuits will be infinitely easier, but don't get yourself too excited over this possibility.

ELECTRONICS

The array of electronic equipment available today and intended for boat installation is mind-boggling. The basic complement of a direction finder, a depth sounder, and a VHF radio have given way to Loran, SatNav, GPS, radar, autopilots, depth plotters, weather FAX, SSB, ham radio, and computers.

Adding various electronics is a common enhancement to old boats. The installation of electronics differs from the installation of a light or a fan by at least one additional connection—from a transducer, a sensor, or an antenna.

Even with this added complication, most marine electronics can successfully be installed by the owner. In fact, the manufacturer expects you to install the equipment and includes installation instructions with every unit. The equipment is calibrated and aligned at the factory and rarely requires technical adjustments during or after installation. If you follow the manufacturer's instructions carefully, your results should be at least as good as what you can expect from hiring someone to do the installation for you.

Power connections present no problems; positive lead to the positive side of the circuit, negative to negative. Always protect the equipment with a fuse in the positive side of the circuit; the instructions will tell you the correct size. Electronic equipment can be very sensitive to insufficient voltage, so make sure the wire size is adequate for the current demands of the item. Using wire a size larger than the chart indicates will assure adequate voltage, even in marginal conditions.

Give appropriate thought to *where* you are going to locate the piece of equipment. I once installed the control portion of an autopilot on the cabin side at the forward end of the cockpit and periodically it would deviate from the designated heading by 20 degrees or 30 degrees while at other times it worked perfectly. The problem turned out to be a hand-held compass mounted inside the cabin opposite the autopilot. When the hand-held compass was in its bracket, it deflected the compass in the autopilot.

Regardless of manufacturer's claims about how waterproof or weatherproof a particular unit is, mount it as though a single drop of water could ruin it—because it can. High and dry is the order of the day. Radios should be mounted up against the head-

liner, or at least under the side deck, not in a cutout in the face of a settee. When you get a little water below and onto the wrong tack, you will immediately understand why putting them there is not a good idea. You should also make every effort to keep electronics out of direct sunlight, and away from engine heat and vibration.

Most electronic equipment has a second piece—a transducer, an antenna, or the like—and where and how you install this item is also critical. Depth sounder transducers, for example, are adversely affected by turbulence and should not be located too far forward or too far aft. Best results are usually obtained when the transducer is mounted nearly amidships, or just slightly aft. A fairing block is usually required to position the face of the transducer parallel with the sea floor. And despite what you may have heard, installing the transducer *inside* the hull—in a water- or oil-filled box, or bonded directly to the hull—is always inferior, reducing the range of the sounder by 50 percent or more.

Speed-log impellers need to be mounted clear of interference—not behind an existing through-hull fitting, for example. The same need for uninterrupted flow applies to wind instruments.

Generally speaking, the higher you mount VHF antennas, the better; but the highest possible mounting location is not necessarily an advantage for other types of antennas. For example, there is no particular advantage to elevating antennas receiving signals from overhead satellites, i.e., SatNav and GPS. SSB ground transmissions over a short distance could benefit from a high antenna, but long-distance transmissions are accomplished with sky waves and the height of the antenna has little effect (but the length is critical). Loran reception may be enhanced more by making sure the antenna is not near other antennas than by mounting it on the highest spot on the boat. The manufacturer will suggest the best antenna locations, but with Loran especially, you may want try various locations before making the installation permanent.

The various impellers, sensors, and transducers invariably come with a length of cable to attach them to their associated piece of gear. The connection is made by inserting the plug on the end of the cable into the provided socket in the rear of the equipment. Excess cable is simply coiled out of sight. Antenna connections are made in a similar way, but often the coaxial cable must be cut to length and connectors installed on the ends. Solderless coaxial connectors should not be used on a boat, even if the manufacturer supplies them. Methods of installing properly soldered connectors differ for different types of coax, but the essential concerns are that the braid is soldered to the shell, the conductor to the contact sleeve, and that there are no loose strands of the braid that might touch the conductor and cause a short.

Some electronics, notably ham and SSB radios and Loran, require special grounding systems. Up to 100 square feet of copper or bronze screening located somewhere in the boat may be recommended. At the very least, the equipment will have to be grounded to the engine with a heavy copper strap. Hull-mounted porous bronze ground plates marketed for this purpose will likely prove inadequate, particularly for ham and SSB transmissions. The ground plane is the base from which your signal is launched; it cannot be too large.

All wires and cables to your electronic equipment should be routed carefully to keep them out of wet areas and to avoid chafing of the insulation from the motion of the boat. Capture the wiring every foot or two with plastic clips screwed in place or with nylon cable ties; if you use electrical tape, you will regret it. Do not bundle antenna or transducer cables with electrical wiring or you risk introducing electrical interference. In fact, keep antenna leads as far from electrical wiring as possible.

Even when the cables are all run separately, electrical interference can be a big problem with many electronic items. Loran-C is particularly susceptible to stray signals generated by the various components of the boat's electrical system, and such "noise" will render the Loran inoperable. The ignition systems of gasoline engines are especially likely to generate electrical noise, but alternators, fluorescent lights, and even a spinning prop shaft can be sources of interference.

The sources of radiated noise can be hunted down with a transistor radio tuned to a blank spot on the band and used like a geiger counter. The charging circuits and fluorescent lighting are the most common sources. You can turn off the lights—the engine, too, I suppose. I know more than one sailor who makes no effort to use his Loran when the engine is running. A better solution is to shield the offending wires, or replace them with shielded cable. The shielding must be grounded. Some types of noise are best eliminated by installing a filter in the positive lead, or a capacitor (typically 1 uf, 200 volt) between the hot lead and ground. If your electronics appear to be suffering from interference and you don't have the foggiest idea what the hell I'm talking about, get someone to help you who does.

AC CIRCUITS

An old poet said that a little knowledge is a dangerous thing, and this is especially true when it comes to AC circuits, particularly in the potentially damp environment of a boat. I would like to advise you to leave your shore power system alone, but there is an equal likelihood that ignorance of the system you already have represents just as great a danger. So here are the rules. There are no exceptions.

Rule 1. If you are bringing power aboard with any two-wire conductor, STOP. If the hot wire connection inside your old power drill touches the case and you touch the case, this project is over for you. By the time the breaker way back up at the dockmaster's office recognizes the short and trips, your heart will be acting like Galvani's frog. Your family and friends will miss you, but eventually they will mostly recall how stupid your death was. It is a sorry way to be remembered.

Rule 2. Buy a polarity checker and use it before you plug into any shoreside socket. The black wire is hot and, as pointed out above, if you touch it and you are grounded, *you* will complete the circuit. The white wire is neutral, but that does not mean it does not carry current. On the contrary, the white wire is the negative side of the AC circuit, completing the circuit back to the generating plant. Still, because the white wire is grounded at the plant, you would not normally get shocked if you touched it. But all that is required to change this is for an electrician to accidentally connect these two wires to the wrong sides of an outlet. Suddenly the innocent white wire with the benign "neutral" name can be deadly. The circuits of some battery chargers, for example, connect the negative side of both the AC and the DC sides of the transformer. If the AC polarity is reversed, the negative DC output wire you expect to have zero potential is charged with 110 volts—an extremely dangerous situation. (This is also why all battery chargers used aboard need to be isolated.)

Rule 3. Make sure every 110-volt socket on your boat is properly wired and grounded. With the power cord disconnected and coiled in the locker, trace the shore power circuit from the initial receptacle to every outlet. In a properly wired AC circuit, the black wire is always hot, the white always neutral, and the green (or bare) wire is always ground. Pull the plate off each receptacle and check that the black wire is connected to the brass screw, the white wire to the silver screw, and the green wire to the green screw. If there is no ground wire, do not use the outlets until they are properly wired.

Rule 4. Connect the green wire also to your boat's *common ground point*, usually a bolt on the engine to which the *negative* battery cable and the negative lead to the distribution panel are attached. (The engine is normally grounded to the water through the prop shaft, but if you have a flexible shaft coupling, a heavy cable to some underwater metal part such as a through-hull or a grounding plate is required to complete the ground.) The purpose of the ground wire is to provide a path for stray currents to ground, protecting you from shock, and the damp environment aboard boats is conducive to stray currents. If the ground in the dock outlet fails—an all too common occurrence—you are left totally unprotected from any short circuit. Grounding to your boat's common ground point eliminates that risk.

There are a couple of problems that come with Rule 4. The first is that in the event of a short to ground, although you would be protected, any swimmers near your boat could be at risk. Fortunately, the number of swimmers in a marina is usually pretty small. The second problem is that grounding the green wire to your boat's grounding point greatly increases the likelihood that the metal parts on your boat will suffer galvanic corrosion from stray currents—either from your own electrical system or attracted to the ground from the electrical systems of nearby boats.

There are means of avoiding both problems, but omitting the connection of the green wire to the boat's common ground is *not* one of them. The best approach is to install an isolation transformer. Basically, this unit provides AC power without any *electrical* connection to shore, so grounding does not complete the circuit. You must touch *both sides* of the circuit to get shocked. The risk of shock is vastly reduced. Since there is never any flow of electricity to ground, the isolation transformer also eliminates the risk of electrolysis caused by such currents.

An isolation transformer is always a good idea, but unless you are living aboard, you may want to avoid the expense by simply disconnecting the shore power cord when it is not in use. Unless the currents are quite high, stray current corrosion is a relatively slow process. Being plugged in for a day is not going to eat away your prop. If you want to constantly float your batteries, buy a solar panel for that and avoid the problems associated with continuous shore power connections altogether.

Rule 5. Treat AC circuits with respect. You can experiment all you want with 12-volt DC circuits; if you get the wires crossed, the only real risk is to your equipment and if it is properly fused, even that risk is minimal. But don't mess around with 110-volt circuits. Especially around water, AC kills.

TWELVE

Going with the Flow

Oh, a sailor travels to many lands;
any place he pleases.
But he always remembers to wash his hands
so he won't catch no diseases.
–PEEWEE HERMAN–

Y ou would likely freak out if someone called you and told you there was 2 feet of water *inside* your hull, but guess what? There is! The ocean is standing 2 feet deep inside the galley drain line, in the cockpit drain hoses, in the cooling water lines, in the head connections, and in every other hose that is connected to an underwater through-hull fitting. If you doubt it, pull one of those hoses off and see for yourself.

So? Did you ever hear the old saying that a chain is only as strong as its weakest link? While you are blissfully content that the extra-thick solid laminate hull of your old boat is a veritable fortress against any breach by the ocean, the truth is that the only thing that is keeping your old boat off the sea floor is 1/16 inch of flexible rubber–the wall thickness of the various hoses. Strong, supple new hoses are invariably up to the task, but old hoses become brittle and split or crumble.

Old boats have old hoses.

HOSES

Checking Hoses

How can you tell the difference between a hose that is perfectly good and one that isn't? You *squeeze* them. If you also have a piece of new hose to squeeze, differences will be immediately apparent. But even without a piece of new hose for comparison, you can identify questionable hoses.

Suspect any hose that you *cannot* squeeze, unless it is reinforced with helical wire. If it is not obvious whether the hose has wire in it or not, you can check by examining one of the cut ends. When an unreinforced hose is rock-hard, that generally means it is brittle inside. Aside from the risk of its rupturing, it may be shedding flakes of brittle rubber. If this is the inlet hose for your engine cooling water, those flakes can lodge in the narrow passages of the heat exchanger or inside the engine, resulting in overheating or worse. Replace hard hoses.

At the other end of the spectrum is the spongy hose. If the hose feels like foam rubber, heat or chemicals have attacked the inside of the hose. Soft hoses may also appear swollen, especially where they attach to the fitting. Replace spongy hoses.

Always check your hoses in good light. When you squeeze or flex the hose, examine the surface closely; cracks suggest that the hose is beyond its useful life. Look for flattened, kinked, or collapsed hoses. Check hoses carefully where they pass over other items or through bulkheads for any signs of chafe. Use a small screwdriver to "dig" at the *end* of the hose to determine if it is still supple or has turned brittle. If anything about a piece of hose, particularly one connected to a through-hull fitting, raises the slightest doubt about its integrity, replace it. A split hose is just as dangerous as a split hull and far more likely.

Replacing Hoses

Conceptually, hose replacement is little different from changing socks; pull the old one off, slide the

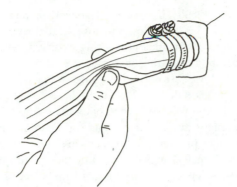

Squeeze: The hose should not be too hard or too soft.

Look: Replace swollen or spongy hoses.

Flex: If the surface shows cracks, replace the hose.

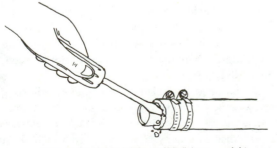

Poke: If the end is brittle, or if it flakes . . . right.

Checking hoses

new one on. And in ideal conditions, it offers a similar level of difficulty. But you should have sensed by now that when it comes to working on a boat, especially an old boat, ideal conditions are rarely encountered.

Unlike your socks (one assumes), hoses tend to adhere to the fittings on which they have spent some time. This is an admirable quality in a piece of hose, sealing it to the fitting and preventing leaks. Admirable, that is, until it comes time to remove the hose. This problem is made worse by the same principal that makes Chinese handcuffs work. You remember those woven pink and yellow tubes you used to have as a kid; you stuck your fingers into the ends and the harder you tried to pull them out, the tighter the tube gripped. When you try to *pull* a hose from its fitting, it also tends to grip even more tenaciously.

Perhaps I am getting ahead of myself. The first step in hose removal is to stop the flow to the hose. That means to close the seacock if you are removing the hose from a through-hull fitting, to drain the coolant below the level of the engine hose you are replacing, or to shut off the flow from freshwater tanks. If the water tanks are higher than the hose and you have no valve in the line, flow may be stopped by clamping the vinyl hose with a pair of vise-grip pliers. Do not grip the hose directly with the pliers; use them to sandwich the hose between two scraps of wood.

The next step is to release the hose clamps. While your old sweat socks are right there at the end of your legs, hose connections too often are almost inaccessible. Use the largest screwdriver that will fit the clamping screw and the space available, and release the clamp until it can be slid along the hose out of the way. There should be dual clamps on all through-hull connections.

If you cannot turn the clamp screw with a screwdriver, see if the screw has a hexagonal head. If so, use your socket wrench to apply as much force as necessary to release the clamp. Don't worry about breaking the clamp; if it is frozen with corrosion you are going to replace it anyway. If all else fails, cut the clamp with snips.

Now grip the hose and *twist* it. If it breaks free and turns, you should be able to remove the hose from the fitting by pulling on it as you twist it back and forth. If it doesn't break free easily, don't look for ways to increase your leverage. You don't want to unscrew the fitting or damage it. Take a short break and put a kettle of water on the stove.

After a soothing cup of tea, pour the rest of the boiling water over the stubborn connection. The heat will soften the bond and expand the hose slightly. Using a cloth or gloves to protect your hands, try twisting the hose again. If it still won't budge, and you can apply pressure to the end of the hose, try *pushing* the hose off the fitting; alternatively, *push* the hose further onto the connection. The trick to the Chinese handcuffs was to get someone to push the ends toward each other, which made the tube expand in diameter. Push and twist.

No? Desperate measures are called for. If the hose is being replaced, the easiest approach is to use a very sharp razor knife to slice the hose free of the fitting. Wield the knife like a surgeon, not a butcher, and don't slice all the way through though; you don't want to risk cutting a channel into the fitting. Instead, slice the hose twice, on opposite sides, as deeply as feels safe. Twist again. The hose is almost certain to come free. If not, carefully finish one of the cuts and peel the hose free.

A wire-reinforced hose will be very difficult to split, and you will not want to cut any hose that you intend to reuse. (You may be replacing what the hose is attached to rather than the hose itself.) When the end of the hose is accessible, you may be able to work an awl, or an ice pick with the point ground off and rounded, between the hose and the fitting, breaking the grip. If not, your only choice is to cut the hose from the fitting, but if the hose is long enough, you may still be able to use the shortened piece.

Getting the new hose on the fitting generally presents fewer problems. If the hose does not go on easily, hold the end in a pan of boiling water for a couple of minutes. Now coat the fitting with a little dishwashing liquid and the hot hose should slip on without difficulty. If it doesn't, suspect that you have the wrong size hose. Push the hose on all the way to the base of the nipple. If the fitting is barbed, center the clamp; if the fitting has a ring, the clamp should grip the hose just beyond the ring.

If you slide the clamp onto the hose before you install it, you will not have to open the clamp fully. In an emergency, any clamp that will fit around the hose can be pressed into service; you can even combine two small clamps (by inserting the end of each into the screw of the other) into a large clamp. But when you are fitting new clamps, select the clamp specified for the hose diameter because the radius of the base of the tightening screw varies. Tighten clamps adequately to assure that the connection will not leak and cannot slip apart, but keep in mind that overtightening can actually cut the hose.

Dual clamps are imperative on both ends of any hose connected to a through-hull fitting, and they are a very good idea on all hose connections. If a hose clamp fails on your car, it lets the water *out;* the worst case is that you will find yourself walking. When the wrong clamp fails aboard your boat, it lets the water *in,* and you could find yourself swimming. How far can you swim? That is the farthest from shore you should sail until you have dual clamps on all hoses that have the ocean running through them.

Clamps can vary widely in quality, and despite the fact that they are stainless steel, they do corrode. I was mildly surprised once to discover a loose clamp on the short piece of hose between the stern tube and the stuffing box. Surprise changed to shock when each of the other three clamps tore loose as I checked them for tightness. From the top all four clamps looked brand new, but the drip of the stuffing box had caused all of them to corrode on the bottom where the corrosion could not be seen. Naturally!

Automotive hose clamps use a plated adjusting screw which quickly rusts in a salt-rich environment. Be sure to buy clamps that are *all* stainless. Even "marine quality" clamps, when you look at them critically, turn out to have not a great deal of metal between the notches for the screw and the edge of the clamp. The Swedish Abba clamps are not perforated; the screw tightens against indentions in the band. This makes the clamp less prone to corrosion failure, and the smooth inner surface and rolled edges eliminate the risk of cutting the hose by overtightening. I like everything about them except the fact that they cost about three times as much as the perforated types.

Occasionally I still see spring-type hose clamps on boats. It must be because they last so long. Spring clamps are loops of spring wire that are released by squeezing together the turned-out ears of the overlapping ends. They are fine for light-weight bilge blower hoses, or for holding the filter element in your air cleaner, but not for any water hose connections. Spring clamps are designed to be used in tandem with special fittings and on any other type of connector they exert inadequate compression on the hose for a secure connection. If you have any spring-type clamps aboard, replace them.

You can hold hoses clear of chafe by clamping them to bulkheads. Copper pipe straps—available at any hardware store or plumbing supply—are ideal for this use. When chafe cannot be avoided, protect

the hose by cutting a short section of the same size hose, splitting it lengthwise, and fitting it around the hose you want to protect. To hold it in position, run a couple of beads of silicone around the inside of the short section before installing it. Chafe protection is especially critical where a hose lies against the engine.

Hose Choices

I purchase hose from a commercial hose supplier in my city at about half the price charged by marine chandlers (guess where *they* buy their hose?), and at first I was intimidated by the vast array of hoses available. I soon discovered, however, that when I described the use of any hose I was replacing, I almost invariably went out the door with one of three types of hose.

Hoses connected to through-hull fittings need foremost to be tough. If the hose might also be part of the cooling system of the engine, heat resistance is also important. Automotive *heater hose* is designed for high-temperature use. Built much like a tire, with a center ply of woven nylon, heater hose is also very tough. Silicone rubber heater hose is the best choice for most raw water and cooling water hoses. The most common size aboard is $3/4$-inch inside diameter (ID), and standardizing as many fittings as possible will allow you to carry a single length of hose as an emergency backup.

The construction of standard $1\frac{1}{2}$-inch *radiator hose* is usually different from that of heater hose. Radiator hose is often wire-reinforced; the inner and outer layers of the hose capture a coil of spring wire. The woven reinforcement of heater hose prevents the hose from expanding when subjected to heat and pressure, but the stiff wire reinforcement of radiator hose also serves to keep the hose from collapsing when it is used on the suction side of a pump. For most $1\frac{1}{2}$-inch applications—cockpit drains, head discharge lines, high-capacity bilge pumps—radiator hose is a good choice. Try to select hose with a smooth inner wall to minimize flow resistance.

For the freshwater system, choose *nontoxic clear*

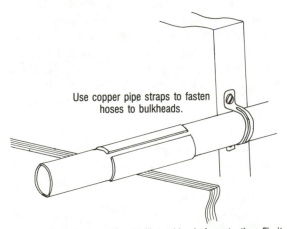

Use copper pipe straps to fasten hoses to bulkheads.

A short length of split hose will provide chafe protection. Fix it in position with silicone sealant.

Protecting hoses from chafe

vinyl hose. Be sure it is FDA-approved for potable water systems. If you have water under pressure or hot water, the hose must be reinforced; you will be able to see the crisscross of nylon threads inside the walls of the hose. The standard size to fit most pumps and faucets is ½-inch ID. I also prefer reinforced clear vinyl hose on the outlet side of bilge pumps, especially those that operate automatically, so that I can observe the flow when the pump is operational.

Clear vinyl hose is never a good idea for any line that carries seawater, especially the head inlet or a galley saltwater supply line. Aside from questionable strength, it has another problem: the light passing through the hose will encourage all manner of marine life to set up housekeeping inside the hose. The colony may go unnoticed as long as the line gets daily use, but if you leave the boat for a couple of weeks, much of the marine colony dies in the stagnant water, and the next time you pump the head or the saltwater pump in the galley, the odor will send you scurrying for the companionway. Pray you are not already offshore and a little queasy. The short-term solution is to go over the side with a squirt bottle of bleach and squirt it into the through-hull fitting while someone aboard operates the offending pump until the smell of bleach is overpowering inside; give the bleach 20 minutes to do its job, then flush the system with some vigorous pumping. The long-term solution is to replace the clear hose with an opaque variety.

There are some other types of hose you may need. If you have a wet exhaust system, flexible hose can be used downstream of the water injection. For this application, you need wire-reinforced exhaust hose. It may also be called steam hose, but be sure it is petrochemical resistant. Exhaust hose looks similar to radiator hose, but it will be rated for higher temperatures.

You might save a little money selecting ribbed, thin-wall PVC hose for a long run from the manual bilge pump to the bilge. This hose is usually white or grey and you may be familiar with it as vacuum cleaner hose, or (in other colors) as the hose on a swimming pool vacuum. The resistance caused by the ridged interior of the hose will somewhat reduce the capacity of your bilge pump. If the hose does not have molded cuffs, special cuffs will be required for a leakproof seal. The cost of the cuffs can offset the savings on the hose.

Thin-wall PVC hose is also regularly installed on the discharge side of head installations. Bad. Very bad. It is invariably odor-permeable, and the ridged interior holds an ample supply of odor-generating matter. If your head smells like a construction-site outhouse and the toilet is connected with thin-wall PVC hose, suspect the hose. You can check it by wiping the hose with a clean rag and then—I'm sorry—sniffing the rag. If the cloth smells, the hose has to go.

Special nonpermeable sanitation hose is available for head discharge use. True sanitation hose has a heavy wall and a smooth interior. Most radiator hose is also nonpermeable and works just as well for this application. When the installation requires a tight bend in the discharge hose, a *preformed* radiator hose can often be used to advantage.

Special hoses are also required for oil or gas lines. Hot oil is especially hard on hoses and any flexible oil lines should be regularly checked. Replacement hose must be designed for this use. Hydraulic lines must be rated for the pressures of the system they are part of. A high-pressure rating is also essential for thermoplastic propane hose. Refrigeration hose is specially compounded to contain refrigerant (Freon), which will pass right through the walls of any other type of hose you might be tempted to substitute. Except for refrigeration hose, which may be connected with special hose clamps, most oil and gas lines will require machine-installed end fittings. The supplier will be able to fabricate the hose to your required length.

RIGID ALTERNATIVES

To avoid the problem of hose deterioration altogether, you might well ask why boats can't use the kind of rigid piping that is used in our homes and seems to last for half a century or longer. Good question.

You don't need a great deal of imagination to figure out what would happen if you connected your fidgety engine to the intake through-hull with a rigid pipe. And if you are going to isolate the pipe from the engine with a short length of hose, you may as well connect the hose between the engine and the through-hull.

Vibration is not the only concern. Suppose the sole of the cockpit is 3 feet above the hull, and the connection between cockpit drains and through-hull fittings is rigid. Now take the boat for a rigorous sail. Any movement of the hull or the cockpit sole will apply significant leverage to the through-hull fittings. Hose would simply flex.

Once you think about a rigid pipe trying to tear your through-hulls loose, we can probably agree that rigid piping to through-hull fittings is ill-advised. But why not in the freshwater system? Wouldn't copper or rigid PVC pipe be better than vinyl hose? Generally speaking, no.

Rigid piping is far more difficult to install than hose. Every piece must be cut to a precise length, and each turn in the run requires an elbow and two connections. Unlike those in houses, the "walls" in a boat are not straight and square, and unless the piping has some flexibility, it will not accommodate the necessary curvature. Even when the run is straight, the restricted spaces of a boat often make it impossible to install the pipe as a single piece.

Soft copper tubing, because it has some flexibility, eliminates some of these problems. A freshwater system plumbed with copper is definitely top drawer and should last the life of the boat, but copper tubing is relatively expensive and the fittings to join the tubing to other components add additional expense and complication. And they have an annoying tendency to leak.

Another problem with rigid piping is that most plumbing components for boats are manufactured with hose fittings. Such fixtures can only be installed in a rigid-pipe system with hose-to-pipe adapters. If you are forced by design to have some

hose in the system, why not all hose? Clear vinyl hose may not have the class of copper plumbing, but it excels in value and ease of installation. As for life expectancy, the vinyl hoses on my own boat have given more than 20 years of trouble-free service.

If you decide to install some rigid piping—occasionally there are situations when it is clearly the superior choice—PVC plastic pipe is the easiest to work with. Unless you have a reason for selecting something else, use PVC Schedule 40 (CPVC if the line will carry hot water). Cut the pipe to length with a hack saw and use a sharp knife to remove any burrs and to put a small chamfer on the inside and outside edges of the cut end. It is advisable to dry-fit the pipe and fittings and check the assembly for fit before you glue the pieces together. Mark the depth and orientation of each fitting with your knife before disassembling; any other type of mark will be lost in the cleaning process.

All you need to join the pipe to the various fittings is PVC cement. PVC cement is actually a solvent that melts the surfaces of the pipe and the fitting and fuses the two together. Buy commercial strength (usually grey instead of clear), and be sure you get the right kind of cement for the kind of pipe you are using. Also buy a can of cleaner; cleaning the pipe and fittings first will assure a good joint. Coat the clean pipe generously with the cement, and coat the inside of the fitting more sparingly. *Immediately* slide the two parts together, turning the pipe about a quarter turn to evenly distribute the cement. An even bead should appear all the way around the joint. Align the knife marks and hold the joint in position for about 30 seconds. Leave it undisturbed for about three minutes before you cement the next joint. The pipe can be put into service in an hour.

Rigid copper pipe is joined to fittings by soldering, called a sweat joint. To make a sweat joint, clean the pipe and the fitting thoroughly with a wire brush or a piece of emery cloth until the surfaces are bright. Brush a light coat of flux over both cleaned surfaces and assemble the joint. Play the flame of a

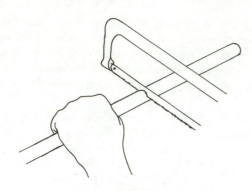

Cut the pipe squarely with a hacksaw.

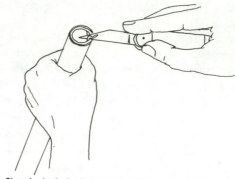

Chamfer both the inside and outside edges of the cut end.

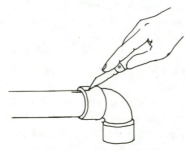

Dry-fit the parts and mark the
orientation with a knife.

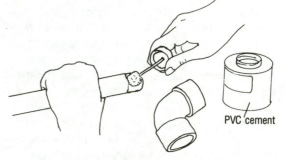

PVC cement

Swab the mating surfaces with cleaner, then coat with
PVC cement.

propane torch over the joint, touching the joint with
the tip of the solder (50-50 tin-lead solder, *not* acid
or rosin core) periodically to determine when the
joint has been sufficiently heated. When the solder
melts on contact with the pipe and fitting at the
joint, stop heating the joint and continue feeding
the solder until a bead of solder appears all the way
around the joint. Allow the joint to cool before disturbing it. If you have done it correctly, capillary
action will have drawn solder into the joint, fusing
the two pieces rigidly together.

Flexible copper can also be connected with
sweat joints, or connections may be mechanical—flare or compression fittings. Instructions for
such mechanical connections are provided in
Chapter 13.

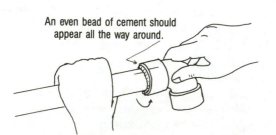

An even bead of cement should
appear all the way around.

Slide the parts together, twisting ¼ turn to distribute the
cement. Align the knife marks and hold in position for
30 seconds.

PVC connections

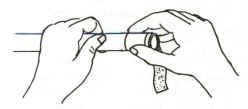

Clean the pipe with emery cloth.

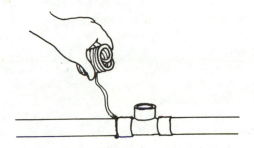

Clean the fitting with a wire brush. Coat mating surfaces with flux.

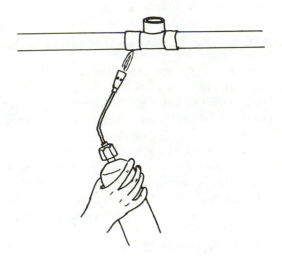

Join the components and heat the joint with a torch.

When the pipe is hot enough to melt the solder remove the heat and feed solder to the joint until it is silver all around and begins to drip.

Sweat joint

CHOOSING A FRESHWATER SYSTEM

Your old boat may or may not be equipped with a pressure water system. There are valid arguments on both sides of this issue. A lot of boat owners think the convenience of pressure water outweighs the potential for waste and the modest electrical demands that accompany a pressure system. Others find prematurely empty tanks far more inconvenient than pumping water.

I come down strongly on the side of this latter viewpoint; pressure water wastes an intolerable amount of water. But while hand pumps *may* save water, I cannot stand the irritation of trying to wash one hand at a time, or washing dishes one-handed. In my view, the only reasonable water delivery system aboard a boat with limited water capacity is the foot pump.

To those who contend that pressure water is not necessarily wasteful, I suggest you imagine what your daily consumption ashore might be like if you had to pump every drop used. In light of droughts, unrestrained development, and water shortages all over America, maybe I'm on to something. Environmental considerations aside, the simple fact is that you *will* use more water with a pressure system. This may not be a big issue for weekending, but it can be if cruising is in your future.

Pump Installation

Regardless of the type of pump you select, installation and connection are not difficult. Hand pumps are installed through an appropriate size hole in the counter and held in place by tightening a nut from the bottom against the underside of the counter. The installation is completed by slipping the supply hose (from the water tank) onto the single hose fitting and clamping it.

Foot pumps can be somewhat more difficult to install, not because of the plumbing but because of the mounting. Of course, there are different types of foot pumps available—some that mount through the sole, some that mount on the sole, and some that

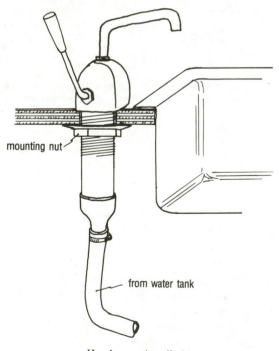

mounting nut

from water tank

Hand pump installation

mount inside a cabinet and are operated by a lever. The lever type, typified by the original (and still the best) Irish-built Whale Gusher, is the most versatile, the most popular, and the most difficult to mount. Since these pumps are invariably mounted with the lever protruding through a hole in a cabinet, one wonders why the pumps do not mount to the cabinet; four wood screws and *voila!* Too obvious, I guess. Instead they come with mounting brackets on the bottom—perfect for a scow or a johnboat, but not worth a damn in a sailboat.

The mounting brackets were in the same location back in 1974 when I installed my first foot pump. I installed two side by side; one to deliver fresh water and one to deliver salt water. I first decided where the pumps should go and cut two slots in the face of the galley cabinet tall enough to allow full travel of the lever. Then I simply epoxied a small board to the hull inside the galley cabinet and screwed the two pumps to the board. Sixteen years later the pumps are still securely mounted, but if the thickness of the board will locate your pump lever too high above the sole, an alternative is to make a mounting plate from a small rectangle of stainless steel. Mark the location of the pump's mounting tabs on the steel plate and drill the plate for the largest mounting screws possible. Insert the screws from the bottom of the plate and lock them in place with a nut and a star washer. Seat the plate on a layer of saturated mat and cover it with two layers of fiberglass cloth extending several inches out onto the hull, taking care not to get resin into the threads of the mounting screws. When the fiberglass cures, the pump can be placed over the screws and secured with nuts and washers.

A foot-pump installation also requires a spout mounted over the sink. The spout is mounted through a hole in the counter and held in place by a nut on the underside. The supply hose is clamped to the inlet side of the foot pump. A second length of hose connects the outlet side of the pump to the hose fitting at the bottom of the spout.

The simplest and least expensive pressure system merely substitutes a small electric pump for the

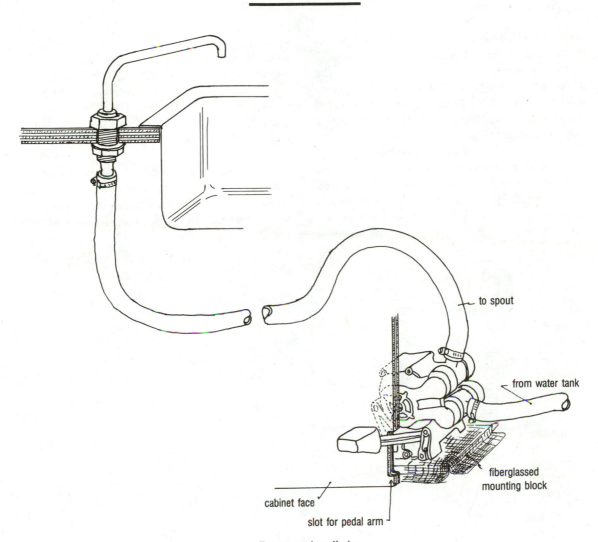

Foot pump installation

foot pump and routes the power to the pump through a switch near the spout. Turn the switch on and you get a fixed flow; turn the switch off and the flow stops.

The ability to control the flow requires a faucet *and a pressure-relief switch*. The pressure-relief switch senses the pressure on the outlet side of the pump, and if it exceeds the setting of the switch, the switch opens the circuit, turning off the pump. Without the pressure relief, if you closed the faucet with the pump on, back pressure would either dam-

age the pump or blow the line (centrifugal pumps excepted). From a plumbing standpoint, the switch is connected with a tee into the line between the pump and the faucet. Electrically, the pressure-relief switch replaces the manual switch. When the faucet is opened, pressure falls and the switch turns on the pump. When the faucet is closed, pressure rises to the switch setting and the switch turns off the pump.

Happily, most pumps intended for pressurizing a freshwater system have an integral pressure switch.

A faucet is substituted for the spout (and installed in the same manner) and the plumbing is identical to that of the foot pump. One advantage is that the pressure pump can be located virtually anywhere on the boat that is convenient. Wiring is a matter of connecting the positive and the negative leads to a fused circuit in the distribution panel.

There is also a nonelectric method of having pressure water. A small tank is installed high in the boat—up against the overhead or on deck. The tank is filled on a daily basis by manually pumping water from the main tank. A second hose connects the day tank and the faucet, and when the faucet is opened, water flows by gravity. This system seems to me to combine the *worst* of both systems; it is as wasteful as a pressure system and as inconvenient as a manual one. If I am going to pump the water anyway, it seems to me better to pump it when I need it, and only as much as I need. In sunny climes, a black deck tank can be a good way to have *hot* water.

The right pump. Different pumps operate on different principles, and there may be occasions when understanding *how* a pump works will assist you in selecting the right pump for your specific need.

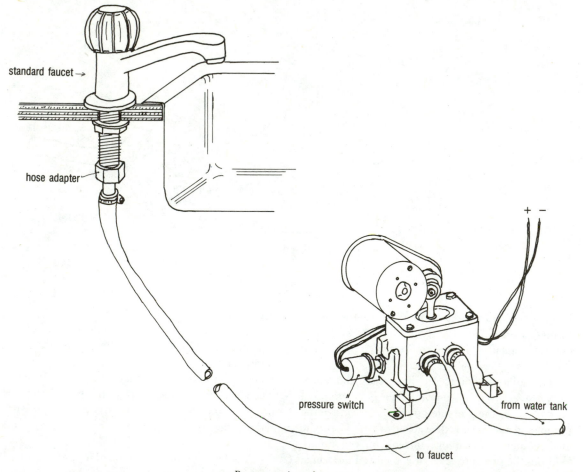

Pressure activated pump

Most hand pumps operate on a piston principle—similar to the operation of a bicycle pump. When the piston inside the hand pump is lifted, the vacuum formed in the cylinder sucks water from the supply line into the cylinder, where it is trapped by a check valve at the inlet. The downward stroke opens a second check valve in the piston, allowing the water to flow from the bottom of the piston to the top. On the next upward stroke, the piston simultaneously forces the water on top of the piston out the spout and sucks a fresh fill of water from the supply line into the cylinder. The downward stroke transfers the water to the top of the piston and every upward stroke pumps water.

Foot pumps are almost always diaphragm pumps. The principle of operation is similar to that of a piston pump. The pump is basically a short cylinder with a rubber lid—the diaphragm. A handle is attached to the center of the diaphragm. The chamber has two openings, an inlet and an outlet, both fitted with check valves. When the handle is lifted, the increase in interior volume of the chamber causes a vacuum and sucks water into the chamber, just as your lungs suck in air when you expand them. When the diaphragm is depressed, the pressure forces the inlet check valve closed, but the outlet valve opens and the water is pumped out of the chamber through the outlet. When the handle is lifted again, the suction closes the outlet check valve and opens the one on the inlet side, again filling the chamber. And so on.

A check valve is often no more than a rubber flap attached on one side. It is like a door without a knob; going one way, you simply push the door open, but you cannot pass through the door going the other way. When the flow is the correct way, the flap opens, but any reverse flow closes the flap and holds it against its seat.

If the pump is configured with the diaphragm in the middle of the chamber, in effect creating two chambers, and each chamber has its own inlet and outlet, you have a *double-action* pump. As the diaphragm expands the volume of one of the chambers, it simultaneously decreases the volume of the opposite chamber. Such a pump delivers water on every stroke. The Whale Gusher and similar lever-action foot pumps work on this principle (although for design reasons they actually have two diaphragms operating in tandem from the same lever).

Electric pumps will almost always be one of three types: diaphragm, flexible impeller, or centrifugal. Electric diaphragm pumps operate just like manual diaphragm pumps except the diaphragm is actuated by a connecting rod from an electric motor.

Electric flexible impeller pumps are similar to the raw water pump on your engine. The rubber vanes on the impeller divide the interior of the pump into a half dozen or more small chambers. A flat spot in the otherwise round pump body is located between the outlet and the inlet openings and compresses the vanes together as the impeller spins. Any water in the chamber between two compressed blades is squeezed out the adjacent outlet. As the vanes pass the flat spot, they spring apart, increasing the volume of the chamber and drawing in water from the inlet.

Centrifugal pumps work like a squirrel-cage blower, moving water instead of air. Water in the center of the vanes is slung out to a chamber around the rigid impeller. This flow builds pressure in the chamber and forces the water to flow out the outlet opening.

Knowing that a hand pump is probably a piston pump, or a foot pump is probably a diaphragm pump, may not be very important since you probably have no alternative. But in choosing a pump for a pressure system, understanding the different types is essential.

For example, centrifugal pumps can run with the flow inhibited without damage and without generating excessive output pressure. This characteristic makes it possible to omit the pressure switch, even with the pump connected to a flow-restricting faucet. (An on-off switch is still required.) Centrifugal pumps can also run dry without damage. In fact, centrifugal pumps are almost trouble-free. And they are the least expensive of the three common types. What keeps them from being the pump of choice in

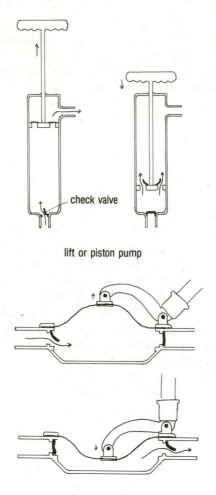

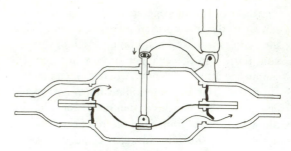

double-action diaphragm pump

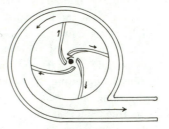

centrifugal pump

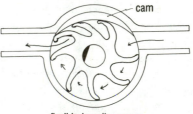

diaphragm pump

flexible impeller pump

Various pumps

most pressure water systems is that centrifugal pumps are *not* self priming. To work, the pump has to be full of water to start. Generally, that means that the pump must be mounted *below* the water tank (so water flows to the pump by gravity), quite a challenge on most boats.

Both flexible impeller pumps and diaphragm pumps are self-priming, and may be mounted in almost any convenient location. Both will also be damaged by excessive flow restriction and require a pressure switch to protect the pump. What sets

these two types apart is that when a flexible impeller pump is allowed to run dry for even a few seconds, it will be damaged—usually shedding the vanes of the impeller. A diaphragm pump can run dry indefinitely without damage.

Why would the pump in a pressure water system run dry? Because the tank is empty (which is—take my word for it—going to happen a lot more often with a pressure delivery system, Skip). When the tank is empty, there will be no pressure on the output side of the pump, the pressure switch will automatically turn the pump on, and it will continue to run until you manually turn it off at the electrical panel. Meanwhile, a flexible impeller pump is likely to be damaged. Consequently, an electric diaphragm pump is generally the best choice for a pressurized freshwater system.

Accumulator Tanks

The pressure switch in a pressure water system will cause the pump to cycle on and off when a faucet is open. If the faucet is wide open, the pump may run continuously, but if the water is being used more frugally, pressure will build up in the restricted line and shut the pump off momentarily until the pressure drops again. The cycling can be quite rapid, but except for wear on the pressure switch, it really does not hurt anything. The pump is going to be subjected to about the same amount of total run time to deliver a tank-full of water whether it is in intermittent trickles or a constant flow.

If the rapid cycling bothers you, you can reduce the cycling somewhat with the addition of an accumulator tank. Sometimes accumulators have an inflatable bladder inside, but the kind normally seen on boats is simply an empty tank with a single opening in the bottom fitted with a tee connector. The

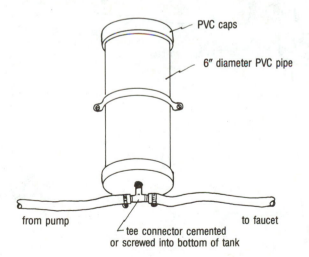

Constructing and installing an accumulator tank

hose on the discharge side of the pump is cut, and the cut ends slip over the two exposed barbs of the tee on the bottom of the vertically mounted tank.

Once the accumulator is in the system, when the pump runs, it also fills the accumulator tank. Since it is filling the tank from the bottom, the air in the tank is trapped and compressed. When the pump shuts off, the pressure of the compressed air continues to deliver water until the pressure drops below the cut-in point for the pump. One advantage of the accumulator is that the pump will not necessarily run at all when you open the faucet to draw a small amount of water. It can be an important advantage to a crew member asleep with his head next to the pump.

Accumulator tanks are available reasonably priced, or you can make your own if you can pick up a foot-long scrap of 5- or 6-inch PVC pipe. (Ask a plumber or try a construction site.) Buy two PVC caps from a plumbing supply and generously cement the caps to both ends of the pipe to make a tank. Drill a hole in the center of one of the caps and thread or glue a 1/2-inch hose connector into the hole. Connect the tank into your discharge line with a tee connector and a length of hose.

Filters

Water supplies are sometimes questionable, and even good water stored in a tank for a long time can get pretty disgusting. The solution is a filter.

There are some filtration systems on the market that filter out the tiniest particles, but such fine filtration severely restricts the flow of water through the filter, especially as the element becomes clogged by the particles it is removing. In shoreside plumbing, the high pressure will continue to force water through the filter, giving the element a reasonable life span, but in the low-pressure environment of a boat, an extremely fine filter element will have to be replaced much more often. Such filters cannot be used at all in a system using manual pumps.

For taste and sediment removal, an activated charcoal filter is usually satisfactory. The most convenient type have a plastic canister that can be unscrewed easily for cartridge replacement. Don't pay extra to get it from a marine supply; these units are available inexpensively from any hardware store, or even Sears. The inlet and outlet will be threaded for home use, so you will need ⅜-inch NPT (National Pipe Thread) to ½-inch hose adapters. Install the filter in the line between the pump and the spout or faucet. If you try to install a filter on the inlet side of a pump, the suction may cause the hose to collapse. Because the filter has to be on the inlet side of a hand pump, you may find that your hand pump simply will not work properly with a filter in the line. It is just another good reason not to have hand pumps.

Water Heaters

When the water heater at home shows signs of cashing in, it sends a chill through the spines of ordinary men. It is big, heavy, awkward, wired to a 220-volt circuit, soldered into the plumbing lines, and has 30 or 40 gallons of water inside it. By comparison, replacing or adding a typical marine water heater is child's play.

A boat owner who lives aboard or cruises from marina to marina might select a large unit (marine water heaters are commonly available up to 20 gallons), but most others will find a 6-gallon heater more than adequate unless they have an abnormally large freshwater capacity. Regardless of the size of the heater, the connections are basically the same.

The power requirements of a water heater are too high for battery operation and most have a 110-volt heating element. That makes them useful only when a boat is hooked to shore power or has a 110-volt generator of adequate capacity to supply the power. To counteract this limitation, marine water

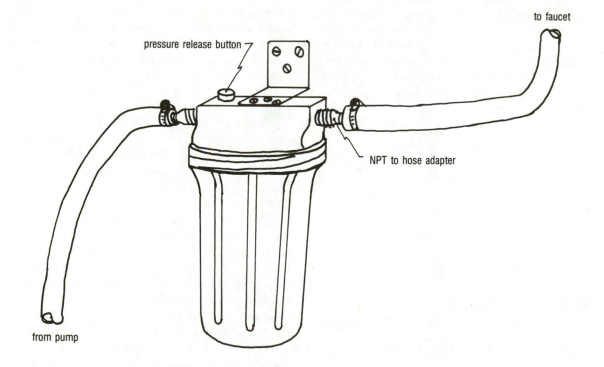

pressure release button

to faucet

NPT to hose adapter

from pump

Charcoal filter installation

heaters also contain a heat exchanger so that the heat generated when the engine is running can be transferred to the water in the tank.

The three-wire electrical connection (hot, neutral, and *ground*) is not difficult, but it must be made with care. If you put a breaker in the circuit—highly recommended—be sure it is a *two-pole* breaker, not the more common single-pole variety. If polarity is ever reversed, a tripped single-pole breaker will break the neutral side of the circuit, meaning that

there would still be power to the appliance—an extremely dangerous situation. The two-pole breaker opens both the hot and the neutral sides of the circuit. You also need a switch in the *hot* side of the circuit to turn the heater off and on; a common wall switch works well.

If you are not absolutely sure what you are doing, get an electrician to do the 110-volt wiring for you. Don't take any chances! And once the water heater is wired, be sure that you do not turn it on until the

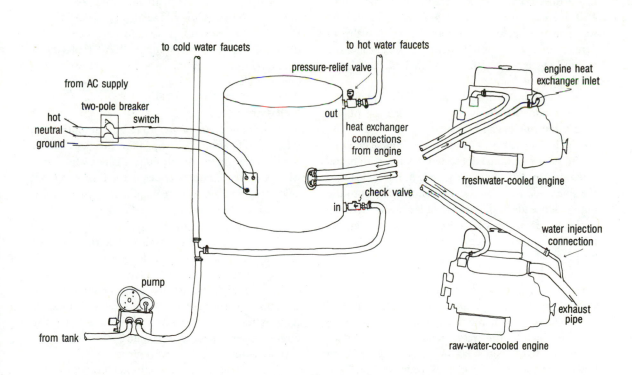

Water heater installation

unit is also plumbed and full of water. Turning on the heating element when the tank is empty will burn out the element in a matter of minutes.

How you connect the water heater's heat exchanger will depend on the cooling system your engine has. If the engine is raw water cooled, disconnect the cooling water hose from the injection point on the exhaust pipe and connect it to one side (the inlet side if it is marked) of the heat exchanger. Attach a second length of hose to the other side and connect it back to the exhaust pipe. If your engine is freshwater cooled, disconnect the *freshwater* hose from the inlet side of the engine's heat exchanger and connect it to the inlet side of the heat exchanger in the water heater. Connect a second hose from the outlet side of the water heater exchanger back to the inlet side of the engine's exchanger. If your engine has a high operating temperature (let's say above 180 degrees), this configuration may overheat the water in the heater and cause the safety valve to vent. In that case, connect the water heater into the cooling system *after* the engine's heat exchanger rather than in front of it.

To make the freshwater connection, install a tee connector in the discharge hose from the pump. The same pump can pressurize both the hot and cold sides of your system. If you have an accumulator in the system, install the tee downstream of the accumulator. A hose from the tee connector leads to the inlet side of the water heater. A hose from the outlet side leads to the hot water faucet. Be sure the outlet hose can handle the heat. Multiple faucets may be supplied by tee connections in the outlet hose.

Many hot water heaters are factory-equipped with a check valve on the inlet side to keep the hot water from migrating back toward the pump, and with a safety valve on the outlet side in case pressure rises too high. If the water heater you install does not have these features, you will need to install both devices in the respective lines near the inlet and outlet ports.

If water usage is a concern, mount the water heater as close to the galley as you can. The water in the hose will be cool, and if the hose is long you will waste a lot of water waiting for the hot water to arrive.

Based on our type of boating–cruising–we enhanced our old boat by *removing* the hot water heater. It cut our water consumption, but on the other hand, it reduced our water capacity by 6 gallons. To compensate, we added extra tankage in a more appropriate location. The accessible space previously occupied by the water heater is more useful for gear and supply stowage.

As for hot water, we heat a full kettle of water each morning at breakfast and pour it into a *pump* thermos mounted near the galley sink. It is still hot enough 24 hours later to precipitate an oath from the careless. We find heating a kettle is less onerous than running the engine, and we make coffee every morning anyway. Mixed with cool water, two quarts of near-boiling water is adequate for our daily usage. Pumping the hot water is no hardship since we also removed the pressure water system, replacing it with a pair of foot pumps–one for fresh water and one for salt water.

Saltwater Pumps

For economizing on freshwater consumption, no other modification will help more than a saltwater pump in the galley. Admittedly, it is not very useful when you are tied up to a dock in the East River, but anywhere the water is pure enough to swim in, it can be used for dishwashing as well.

The choice of pumps is up to you. I prefer the foot pump, but you can install an electric pump just as easily as a manual one, as long as you select one that specifies that it can be used in a saltwater system. In fact, a pressure saltwater system makes better sense than a pressure freshwater system since there is no concern for how much salt water you pump. Power consumption could be a consideration if your battery capacity is modest.

Do not install a new through-hull fitting to supply salt water to the galley. Install a tee connector in the hose supplying raw water to the engine, or in the head inlet hose (provided the inlet is on the opposite side of the hull from the outlet), and run a length of hose from the tee to the saltwater pump. You will need a separate spout (or faucet) at the sink.

Tanks

A common enhancement is to increase the water-carrying capacity of an old boat by adding tanks. There are three basic options: build your own tank from plywood and fiberglass, have a tank custom built from stainless steel or Monel, or purchase an off-the-shelf rigid or flexible tank.

Sailors often consider converting the space beneath the Vee-berth to water storage. From a performance standpoint, adding 300 or 400 pounds of water (at about 8 pounds per gallon) high up in the eyes of the boat is a bad idea. Extra tankage ideally should be located low and near the center of the boat. But if this were an ideal world, the damn boat would have enough water storage to begin with. Besides, if the tank replaces 250 pounds of canned goods, how much effect is it really going to have? Put extra tankage somewhere else if at all possible, but if the Vee-berth is the only choice, strike a compromise by using the water from that tank first. Empty, the tank is the *best* thing to have in the bow.

With a fiberglass hull, there is a temptation—especially in the bow—to use the hull as part of the tank. The addition of one side and a top is all that is necessary to complete the tank. An added benefit occasionally mentioned is that the integral tank acts as a watertight compartment in the event of holing the bow. Hmmmm.

There are three serious problems with integral tanks. Because the hull flexes, integral tanks sooner or later leak. The fiberglass—even after it has cured for 20 years—gives the water a bad taste, and while the taste can be controlled with filtration, I strongly suspect that the taste is only symptomatic of an unhealthy level of toxic chemicals that water sloshing around in a fiberglass tank likely contains. And even if your personal health is not at risk, integral tanks are definitely risky for the health of your boat. The 1988 hull blister study done by the University

of Rhode Island concluded that allowing water to stand *inside* the hull will hasten laminate *saturation*, leading to serious and potentially disastrous blistering. As for the waterproof bulkhead aspect, if you hit something hard enough to punch a hole in the hull, I wouldn't count too heavily on four or five layers of tabbing surviving the impact.

If you insist on integral tankage, at least coat the hull with 10 mils of epoxy before you tab the additional sides to the tank, and use several extra layers of tabbing, taking care not to cause a hard spot in the hull with the new bulkheads and baffles. Better yet, build a tank separately to the shape of the space beneath the berth and fiberglass or strap the finished tank in place.

Plywood tanks assembled and completely coated inside with fiberglass are adequately strong for water storage. To avoid the damaging momentum of sloshing water, baffle the tank into compartments no larger than 18 inches square. Tab the baffles in place as strongly as the exterior sides of the tank. An inspection port is essential for cleaning the tank, and with a framework of baffles, more than one port may be desirable. Glassing the top in place with internal tabbing is usually impossible, and *always* difficult, and screwing it in place is rarely adequate. Attach the top with several exterior laminates of fiberglass, but first seal the top edges of the sides and the inside of the top with several coats of penetrating resin. Then seat the top on a heavy bead of polysulfide sealant and glass it in place.

A well-built fiberglass tank eliminates the hull saturation risk, and hull flexing will not cause the tank to leak, but it still gives the water a horrible taste. I have heard that if the tank is constructed of epoxy resin rather than polyester, the taste is not as bad. I do wonder what "not as bad" means, but I confess to having no firsthand experience with epoxy tanks.

I do have experience with Monel, and water stored in a Monel tank tastes great, even after six months. Metal tanks are not a do-it-yourself item, but having a tank custom built of stainless steel or Monel can be well worth the money if you plan to own the boat for a few years. Monel costs twice as much as stainless, but it is far more resistant to corrosion. Have the fabricator baffle the tank and provide a large clean-out opening. The inlet, outlet, and vent connections should all be in the top, or high in one end. The pickup pipe should be an inch or so short of reaching the bottom so that it does not pick up any sediment that settles out of the water.

A less expensive alternative is an off-the-shelf tank. The rigid ones are usually polyethylene, and the flexible ones are nitrile or PVC coated nylon fabric. Rigid polyethylene tanks are lightweight, strong, relatively inexpensive, FDA approved, and *usually* taste free. They should be strapped securely to prevent abrasion. Split hose can be used to protect the corners.

High-quality flexible tanks are also taste free. Instead of being strapped in place, they must be tied in place with lines led to grommetted tabs. Flexible tanks are especially susceptible to chafe, so before you install one, line the locker it will go in with 1-inch-thick closed-cell foam.

Every tank requires three connections: the fill, the vent, and the outlet. A hose from the fill is usually led to a deck plate, although the fill plate is sometimes installed directly in the top of the tank to simplify the installation and avoid the risk of salt-water contamination. For the same reasons, it is almost always advisable to terminate the vent line inside the boat. Run the line as high as possible and turn the end down (like a candy cane) to keep anything from falling into the vent. Unless the vent line

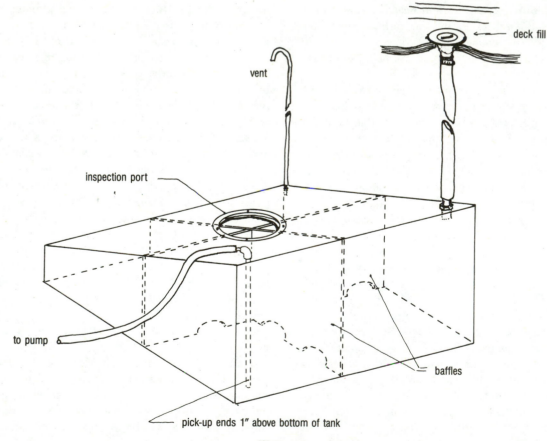

deck fill

vent

inspection port

to pump

baffles

pick-up ends 1″ above bottom of tank

Water tank

is higher than the deck fill, it is likely to pour water every time you fill the tank, so don't terminate it above the SSB.

A hose from the tank outlet would normally lead to the freshwater pump, but the pump is already connected to the original tank. The simplest way to plumb the new tank into the system is to attach the outlet hose to the hose leading from the old tank with a tee or Y connector, but this is not a good idea because any contamination will taint the entire water supply.

I watched a skipper at the fuel dock in Staniel Cay pump several gallons of diesel fuel into his water supply before he realized he had the wrong deck fill. Water in the Bahamas cost 20 or 30 cents *per gallon* at the time, a substantial expense just to fill his tanks, much less to give them the thorough rinsing that was likely to be required to rid them of the fuel contamination. Fortunately (perhaps wisely is a better term) his tanks were not interconnected and he simply drained the contaminated tank and had it steam cleaned when he returned to the states. The consequence of his error was a few gallons less water aboard for the remainder of his cruise.

Instead of a tee connector, connect multiple tanks to the inlet side of the pump with a Y valve.

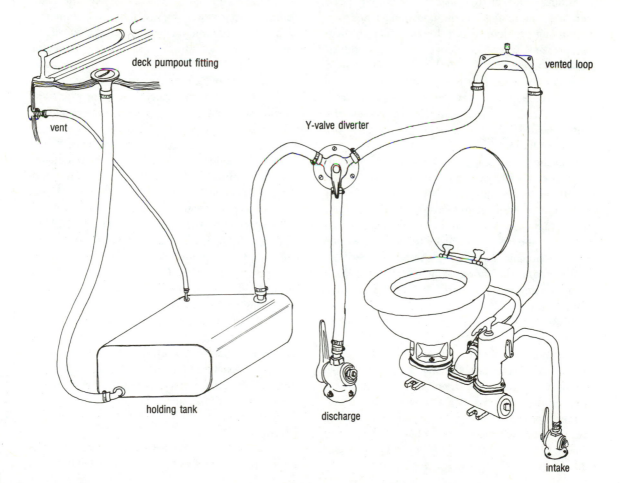

Head and holding tank installation

An inexpensive dual-hose adapter (for connecting two garden hoses to a single faucet) will do the job. You want a *plastic* one with dual shutoff valves. Install the appropriate hose connectors (the kind you buy to repair a garden hose) on the ends of the hoses. The hoses from the two tanks connect to the two valved branches and the hose supplying the pump connects to the tail of the Y. By turning the two valves, you can supply the pump from one tank and isolate the other one from the system. A third tank can be plumbed in with another adapter.

Showers

Adding a shower to a boat that is not equipped with one is more of an accommodation change than a plumbing problem. From the plumbing perspective, pressure water may seem essential, and indeed it is if you want a hot shower. But if you do not have hot water aboard, a foot pump can supply water to the shower head very effectively. In either case, plumbing a shower is a matter of connecting the shower head to the pump or to the hot and cold water supply lines.

It is the drain that represents the larger challenge. A sump is required to collect the water, and too often it is a shallow pan with a drain hole that leads directly (or through a hose) to the bilge. With this system, hair, scum, and unmentionable gradú ends up in the bilge, eventually rendering the bilge pump inoperable and putting the boat in peril.

Water from the shower should be captured in a separate sump and pumped overboard. The sump can be remotely located—it can even be located in the bilge—but it should either contain its own float-operated electric discharge pump or it should be large enough to hold the water from the shower, to be pumped overboard afterwards with a manual pump. A strainer in the drain will dramatically cut down on the problems with a shower drain system.

For tropical cruising, a pressurized garden sprayer makes a miserly and effective freshwater shower. On chilly evenings, a kettle of boiling water added to the tank provides a hot shower.

Municipal Supply

If you do not have pressure water aboard, you cannot tie into the municipal system because the water would flow through the pumps and out the spouts continuously. But if your on-board water system is pressurized, there is no reason that you cannot use city water pressure when you are tied to the dock. More than one manufacturer offers special deck fittings that contain a regulator that drops the high municipal pressure to a more manageable 40 PSI. Regulators are also available that simply screw onto the faucet before the hose is attached.

In addition to a regulator, you are also going to need at least one check valve. Connect the shore water into your system by installing a tee connector in the hose between your pump and the faucets. A hose from the inlet fitting leads to the tee connector. Between the tee connector and the pump, install a check valve to make sure the pressurized water cannot flow back through a leaky valve in the pump and overflow your tanks. (If you have an accumulator tank, it is not necessary for it to be in the system when you are on shore pressure; the check valve and the tee connector should be on the outlet side of the accumulator.) If the regulator does not contain one, a second check valve installed at the inlet fitting will allow you to disconnect the hose without being sprayed by the pressure in the system.

It is risky to leave your boat unattended when connected to a municipal water supply. You can imagine what happens if a hose blows off a fitting. Turning off the faucet is all that is required, but doing this repeatedly becomes a chore if you are living aboard. One alternative is to install a water timer at the faucet. Made to turn off sprinklers, this inexpensive gizmo turns off the water after so many gallons (adjustable) have passed through it, limiting the amount of water that will flow into your boat in the event of a hose failure.

Heads

This used to be an easy subject. The head that came with your old boat was almost certainly a manual unit, operating with a few strokes of a lever or a handle. Regardless of the manufacturer—Wilcox-Crittenden, Groco, Raritan, or whoever—manual heads all operate on the same principle. A double action piston pump supplies raw water to the bowl and at the same time pumps the sewage out of the bowl.

A ³/₄-inch hose connects the inlet to a ³/₄-inch through-hull fitting and a 1¹/₂-inch hose connects the head discharge to a 1¹/₂-inch through-hull. A valve at the inlet fitting allows the operator to stop the inlet flow. With the valve open, the upward stroke of the piston pumps raw water above the piston into the bowl while the suction beneath the piston as it rises draws the sewage from the bowl into the pump cylinder. The downward stroke closes the check valve in the bottom of the bowl and forces the sewage from the cylinder through a second check valve (the joker valve) and into the discharge hose, at the same time drawing fresh raw water into the cylinder above the descending piston. After the head has been pumped several times, the inlet valve is closed, and a couple more strokes pump the bowl dry.

Manual heads worked great until they were overwhelmed with the enormity of the crap that comes out of politicians. If bodily excretions pumped from boats are polluting our oceans, maybe we should back off the ban on whaling—or force the whales to avail themselves of (nonexistent) pumping stations. Inane or otherwise, zero discharge inside the 3-mile limit is the law—unless you mix the effluent with *chemicals*. Now there is a concept that is clearly well considered.

In any case, the discharge hose from your head can no longer be legally connected directly to a through-hull fitting unless you never bring your boat inside the 3-mile limit. The inlet plumbing is unaffected, but you have two choices on the discharge side. You can install an *approved* device that grinds up any solids, mixes them with a bacteria-killing chemical like chlorine or formaldehyde, and pumps the combination overboard. Or you can connect the discharge hose to a holding tank and carry the sewage around with you until a pumpout facility is handy or cruise out beyond the 3-mile limit and pump it overboard yourself.

I am satisfied that the crude chemical treatment of a Type I MSD (marine sanitation device—bureaucratese for head) is environmentally more harmful than untreated effluent and suggest that you choose the equally intelligently named and environmentally more sound Type III MSD, the holding tank. How you ultimately dispose of the effluent I leave to your own conscience, but please don't pump any more chemicals into the oceans and bays.

Holding tank connections. Holding tanks are typically provided with three hose connectors. The basic installation is to remove the head discharge line from the through-hull fitting and connect it to the 1¹/₂-inch inlet fitting on the top of the tank. From the 1¹/₂-inch outlet fitting located near the bottom of the tank (or with an internal pickup tube running to the bottom), a new discharge hose is connected to a special deck fitting to allow the tank to be vacuumed out at a pumpout station. The third tank connector takes a ³/₄-inch hose led to a vent fitting on the deck or through the hull up near the rail. The vent is necessary to let smelly and *explosive* methane gas escape from the tank.

Unless there is a pumpout facility near you, and your boating never takes you away for more than a few days (depending on the size of your holding tank), this bean-counter-envisioned configuration will not be satisfactory. You are going to need some other way of emptying the tank. Divide the discharge hose from the tank with a Y valve that can divert the waste into two directions. Connect the hose from one side of the valve to the deck-mounted pumpout fitting. The inlet side of a manual diaphragm pump is connected to the other branch of the valve. A hose from the outlet side of the pump connects to the seacock on the discharge through-hull fitting (previously connected directly to the head discharge). Set the valve in one direction and you can empty the tank at a pumpout sta-

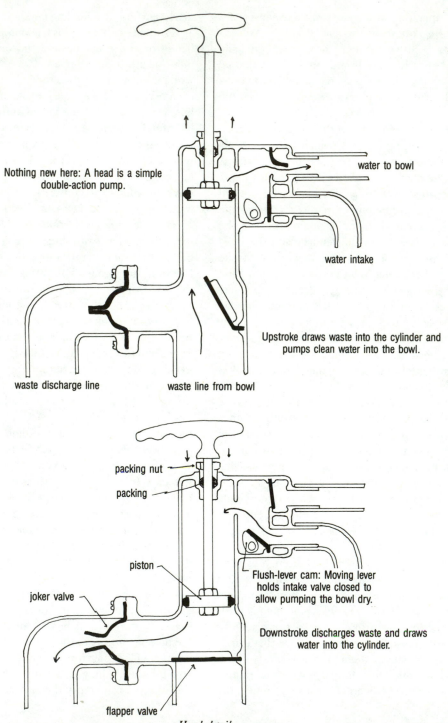

Nothing new here: A head is a simple double-action pump.

water to bowl

water intake

Upstroke draws waste into the cylinder and pumps clean water into the bowl.

waste discharge line

waste line from bowl

packing nut

packing

piston

joker valve

Flush-lever cam: Moving lever holds intake valve closed to allow pumping the bowl dry.

Downstroke discharges waste and draws water into the cylinder.

flapper valve

Head detail

tion; turn it in the other direction and you can pump the contents directly overboard. An electric pump cannot be used to empty the holding tank unless it is specifically intended for this function. Such pumps cost four to five times as much as a manual pump, consume 15 or more amps, and necessitate reducers in the discharge line or a new through-hull fitting. A hand pump is less complicated to install and it will empty a 20-gallon tank in less than two minutes.

Away from U.S. coastal waters, there is little point in emptying the head into a holding tank only to discharge the effluent overboard with another pump. The law prohibits your head from being connected directly to an overboard discharge fitting, but it can be connected to a Y valve with one side of the valve leading to the tank and the other side to a through-hull fitting. An oft overlooked aspect of this proviso is that inside the 3-mile limit, the valve must be *secured* in the holding tank position. Padlocking the handle or securing it with a nylon wire tie to an eyebolt is acceptable, but wiring or taping it in position is not. If your installation is missing this feature, it can cost you up to $2,000.

If you have been paying attention, it may have occurred to you that the through-hull discharge fitting is already occupied with the overboard discharge line from the holding tank. You have at least three options. The most obvious one is to install an additional through-hull fitting, but another hole in the hull is *never* a good idea if it can be avoided.

Option number two is to make the through-hull fitting available by dispensing with the overboard discharge from the tank altogether. The tank is only used when pumpout facilities will be available. Otherwise, the head is flushed directly overboard, bypassing the tank altogether. The unvarnished truth is that there are thousands of installed holding tanks that have never contained anything but air. They are installed only to comply with the law, not to be used. When the objective of the installation is only compliance, an overboard discharge from the tank is an unwarranted complication and expense.

If you want the capacity to discharge both the head and the tank overboard, the only additional item required is a $5 Y connector. Through it, both discharge hoses may be connected to the same seacock.

Vented loops. A head installed aboard a sailboat may or may not be above the waterline when the boat is upright, but it almost always dips below the waterline when the boat heels on one tack or the other. The head is below the waterline on many powerboats as well. Any time the head is below the waterline, it has the potential to sink your boat. Scores of boats sink needlessly for this very reason.

The reason is simple: water seeks its lowest level. When the ocean is higher than the head and you connect the two with a hose, you have created a saltwater bidet. Looping the hose above the waterline does not necessarily stop the inward flow since filling the hose when flushing is likely to set up a siphon action. The two check valves—the joker valve in the discharge line and the flapper valve in the bottom of the bowl—may initially prevent back siphoning, but their ability to seal tightly declines with age. The solution is a siphon loop.

A siphon loop is an inverted U-shaped pipe with a small flapper valve installed at the high point of the loop. To be effective, the siphon loop must be mounted so that it is above the waterline on all points of heel. The discharge line from the head connects to one side of the loop. From the other side of the loop, a hose connects to the discharge seacock in the case of a direct discharge head, or to the Y valve in the case of a holding tank installation.

Siphon loops have two serious problems. The valve has a tendency to clog shut, rendering the loop ineffective, or it sags open, filling the head compartment with noxious fumes. To avoid the first problem, the loop should be removed every time the head is serviced and flushed with water under high pressure to dislodge any grunge that may be blocking the vent. Before you stick the garden hose nozzle in one end of the loop and pull the trigger, try to remember why it is called a loop. In between servicing times, unscrew the vent and wash it in warm, soapy water. To avoid the foul odors that often come from a vented loop, attach a hose to the vent and run it to a deck-mounted vent fitting.

From a safety standpoint, it is also a good idea to install a vented loop in the intake line. Practically, however, you may decide against it. A loop in the inlet has a negative impact on the operation of the head. Because the loop is on the suction side of the inlet pump, pumping *opens* the vent (it closes it on the discharge side) letting in air and reducing the suction in the line. Several vigorous strokes of the pump are required at the beginning of each flush to draw the water into the line and over the loop, and each stroke pumps less water than an unvented line. And unlike the discharge side of the head, the inlet side does not depend on a pressure-controlled check valve to prevent unwanted flow. The head has a positive-action valve that stops the inlet flow. If there is any flow past this valve, it is likely to be very small, and if the valve begins to allow the bowl to fill from the inlet side, the head requires servicing.

Whether you have siphon loops or not, *always* close both head seacocks when you leave the boat unattended.

Maintenance. Rebuilding a marine head is more a matter of mechanics than plumbing. The exact procedure for rebuilding your head will depend upon the make and model, but manual heads are very simple machines and you are not likely to encounter many difficulties. Kits are available, or you may find that you only need to replace a specific part or two.

Dismantle the head by releasing all the screws and nuts, paying attention to how the parts are assembled. Once disassembled, the base of the head may need to be "boiled" out with a 10 percent solution of muriatic acid. Be very careful if you do this, and after the acid loses its fizz, flush the body thoroughly to remove loosened deposits and all traces of the acid.

There are a few general rules that apply to virtually all manual heads and may help you to avoid problems. Weighted flapper valves always have the weight up, and flapper valves always open to give the least restricted flow, i.e., they should always be oriented so the widest opening faces the outlet. The bill on a joker valve always points in the direction of the flow. The walls of the pump cylinder should be polished clean and lubricated lightly with petroleum jelly. If the piston uses leather cups, two are required facing opposite each other. Clean all mating surfaces thoroughly of old gasket compound or sealant. When you reattach the bowl to the base, tighten the four nuts evenly and not too tightly or you will crack the china. A bit of flexible gasket compound will help to seal the bowl without overtightening, and will help you to avoid weeping around the pump base and the discharge manifold as well. Wait until you have reinstalled the head to tighten the pump-rod seal, then tighten it only enough to keep it from leaking.

Bilge Pumps

Somehow water always manages to find its way inside a boat, collecting in the bilge, and every boat must have some means of pumping it back outside again. The plumbing for any bilge pump is pretty basic—a hose from the bilge to the pump, a hose from the pump to an overboard discharge. And if you select a submersible electric bilge pump, the only plumbing required is from the pump to the overboard discharge. So what's the big deal?

For one thing, you need to know what you expect from a bilge pump before you select and install one. I always thought of the bilge pump primarily as essential safety equipment, there to keep me from becoming shark fodder if the hull suddenly began to leak. Capacity was the only significant consideration; bigger was better. So I installed the largest submersible bilge pump I could afford, connected it to a float switch and, except when the float stuck, forgot about it for a decade.

The fact that there was always a couple of inches of water in the bilge never concerned me. There was supposed to be water in the bilge, right? Why else is the term "bilge water" in the language? Then along comes the University of Rhode Island study concluding that the likelihood of destructive blisters in the hull laminate increases dramatically if water is left standing in the bilge. To quote the report, "prolonged stagnation of bilge water is the *surest* method for destroying hull integrity." That is bad news for high-capacity bilge pump installations.

Perhaps you're wondering what the capacity of the pump has to do with how much water stands in the bilge. Glad you asked. It isn't the pump; it's the discharge hose. On my old boat, the most direct route from the pump to the overboard discharge requires about 9 feet of hose—probably shorter than the norm. The high capacity pump necessitates 1½-inch hose. What do you think happens to the column of water in the discharge hose when the pump shuts off?

A check valve might initially keep the water from draining back into the bilge, but deposits of debris and detritus from the bilge water will soon prevent the valve from sealing. Besides, a check valve in a bilge pump discharge line is a *bad idea* because it reduces the output and introduces a real risk of blockage.

The only way to minimize the amount of water draining back into the bilge is to keep the run as short as possible and to use the smallest hose you can. Discharging the water through a ½-inch hose rather than a 1½-inch hose reduces the amount of water that drains back by 89 percent! Unfortunately, it also reduces the amount of water you can pump *out* by the same percentage. Reduce the 1½-inch discharge hose on a 3,500 gallons per hour (g.p.h.) pump down to ½ inch and you cut the output to less than 400 g.p.h. This is woefully inadequate for any serious breach.

If a 1½-inch through-hull fitting 6 inches below the waterline sheds its hose, it will admit the ocean at the rate of about 1,900 g.p.h. To stand a chance against such a leak, the discharge hose of a high-capacity pump must match the pump outlet, but even with a 1½-inch discharge hose, a pump rated at 3,500 g.p.h. will probably fail to keep up with a

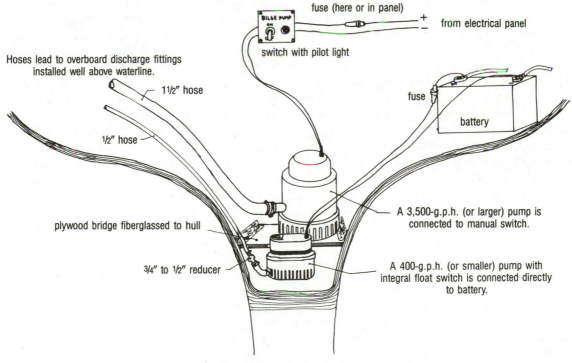

fuse (here or in panel)

from electrical panel

switch with pilot light

Hoses lead to overboard discharge fittings installed well above waterline.

1½″ hose

½″ hose

fuse

battery

plywood bridge fiberglassed to hull

A 3,500-g.p.h. (or larger) pump is connected to manual switch.

¾″ to ½″ reducer

A 400-g.p.h. (or smaller) pump with integral float switch is connected directly to battery.

Dual bilge pump installation

1,900 g.p.h. leak. Centrifugal bilge pumps are rated at their theoretical maximum delivery with *zero lift*. If this is not dishonest, it is certainly misleading. Never expect a centrifugal pump with 5 or 6 feet of lift to expel water from your boat at more than half the rated capacity.

Where does all this leave you? You can let your boat either delaminate or sink. What kind of choice is that?

The fact is that you cannot accommodate both objectives–dealing with serious flooding *and* keeping the bilge dry of errant rain and stuffing-box drips–with a single pump. Two pumps are required. The good news is that there is almost no additional cost for this dual-pump system. Honest.

The key is the purchase of a small (400 g.p.h. or less) pump with an *internal* float switch. Such a pump costs only a few dollars more (in some cases actually less) than a float switch for the high-capacity pump–a switch you are going to omit. In the event of major water intrusion, you will manually switch on the high-capacity pump with a clearly labeled toggle switch near the companionway. The money you don't spend on a float will (almost) pay for the small automatic pump.

Shouldn't the high-capacity pump also have a float switch? When you are aboard it clearly does not matter, but let's consider what happens if a hose fails while the boat is unattended. The 400 g.p.h. automatic pump will have very little effect. With 1,900 g.p.h. pouring in, a 30-foot sailboat will sink in less than six hours.

Connect your high-capacity pump to a float switch and it may be able to keep up with the leak– but for how long? The pump draws 15 amps. It will drain a 100-Ah battery in 6 hours. Then the boat begins to fill.

But won't someone notice? If you mean notice the pump running, probably not; boats all over the marina are discharging water from generators or air conditioning units. If you mean notice the boat sinking, someone probably will notice if it happens in the daytime. And if you are really lucky, they will try to stop it. But by the time another sailor notices

your boat settling and calls, or breaks in, a float-switch operated pump has already run for hours and drained the battery. On the other hand, if the high-capacity pump is *not* on a float switch, and if the batteries are still above water, the emergency pump can be turned on, arresting the problem and providing several hours to correct it. If you insist on installing a second float switch, connect it to an alarm horn to make sure the trouble does get someone's attention.

Install the 400 g.p.h. pump in the *lowest* part of the bilge and wire it through a fuse directly to one of the batteries. The pump will have a 3/4-inch outlet, but insert a reducer in the line and run 1/2-inch hose as directly as possible to a discharge fitting installed in the hull just below the rail. It is imperative to have the discharge clear of the water on all points of sail or the ocean will siphon in when the pump shuts off. Try not to locate the discharge where you come aboard from the dinghy.

Several inches higher, and *not* directly above the small pump, fiberglass a plywood bridge across the bilge. Mount the high-capacity pump to the plywood bridge and wire it to the main panel, properly fused and with a conveniently located and clearly labeled toggle switch in the hot line. If you wire the pump to the panel, either of the battery banks can supply the power to run the pump. Connect the pump to a second discharge fitting with 1 1/2-inch hose. The size of the hose is no longer a concern; if the pump is used, any water that drains back into the bilge will be removed by the smaller pump.

This dual-pump installation will result in a bilge that is bone dry if you maintain the stuffing box. The small pump, because of its size, pumps the water level lower to begin with, and the small discharge hose minimizes the amount of water that drains back. The shallow puddle that does remain soon evaporates, absorbed by the air instead of the hull. An added advantage of this arrangement is that the expensive high-capacity pump, because it sits high and dry, should never require replacement.

An engine-driven alternative. The inadequacy of even a large electric bilge pump might lead you to consider an engine-driven pump to deal with major water intrusion. Relieving the high-capacity bilge pump of the need to operate automatically makes an engine-driven pump a viable alternative. Such a pump will operate for as long as you can keep the engine running, and the capacity of large engine-driven pumps puts electric bilge pumps into the "wimpy" class. A commonly seen model from Jabsco is rated at 4,980 g.p.h., and will deliver close to that even with 6 feet of lift. If you have to be there to throw the switch anyway, it might as well be for a pump that has half a chance against a major leak.

If you go this route, make certain that the pump you select is self-priming. A manual clutch is a better choice than an electric one because it keeps the pump independent of the electrical system. Belt-driven pumps can be remotely mounted, but the oscillation of the engine will subject the belt, the pump bearings, and the engine bearings to damaging shock loading. So find a way to bracket the pump directly to the engine. Mock up a mounting bracket from scrap plywood and have the mockup duplicated in heavy gauge mild steel. The mount will have to be adjustable or an idler pulley will be required to achieve the appropriate belt tension. Size the pulleys correctly to get maximum output from the pump.

Engine-driven pumps are usually flexible-impeller types and don't handle solids well, so the pickup hose should lead into a strum box—a strainer. Keep in mind that you are not trying to *dry* the bilge with this pump; that job is left to the small electric pump. So you do not want a box with holes only in the bottom; you want a strainer that is unlikely to clog. Traditional bronze strum boxes are expensive, but you can fabricate an excellent strainer from a 12-inch piece of 3-inch PVC pipe. Cap one end and fit the other end with a 2-inch adapter and a 1 1/2-inch hose connector. Now drill the bejeezus out of the pipe with a sharp 3/8-inch bit. Settle in; you are not finished until there are more holes than plastic.

You cannot ignore an engine-driven pump as you can a submersible. Fill the bilge and run the pump occasionally, or at least turn it by hand to keep the impeller from taking a set. If you run it, don't let it run dry. Open the pump and check the impeller once a year, replacing it if it is cracked or shows any signs of hardening. Lubricate the chamber with Vaseline.

Manual bilge pumps. If you are out for a pleasant sail and rising water gets over your batteries before you realize you are sinking, neither electric nor engine-driven pumps are likely to do you any good. Regardless of how many other pumps you have aboard, the only one that is certain to work when you need it is a manual pump. No boat should be without one.

But don't put all your faith in a manual pump. The biggest ones around (Edson) are rated at 30 g.p.m. That sounds like 1,800 g.p.h., but before you come to that conclusion go down to the spa and see how long you can last on the rowing machine. A sizable crew can keep a manual pump pumping at capacity for a long time, but one or two people aboard are not going to last very long at 30 strokes a minute. And somebody has to be trying to locate the leak and stop it, not to mention sailing the boat. A manual pump is not a substitute for a tireless electric or engine-driven pump. But it is your last line of defense and you should install the largest and least tiring pump you can find.

Rotary and piston-type pumps are incapable of efficiently moving a serious quantity of water. The only reasonable choice for a manual bilge pump is the diaphragm-type. Besides high capacity, corrosion resistance should influence your choice. Ease of access to the valves—to clear any jams—is also a plus, although diaphragm pumps are amazingly tolerant of trash. If the intake hose leads to a strainer, jams are not likely.

Exhaust Plumbing

Early engine installations commonly used a so-called dry exhaust system. Appropriately named, they were indeed dry because when the engine was running, the exhaust system became red hot. Many a good boat burned as a result. Jacketed exhaust systems followed, standard equipment aboard almost all older fiberglass boats. This system cools the exhaust pipe by routing the engine cooling water, on its way overboard, through a water jacket around the exhaust pipe. Jacketed exhausts were an immense improvement but by no means the end-all solution. They have numerous problems.

To begin with, they are heavy and bulky. Both the weight and the rigidity make jacketed systems subject to vibration fracture, particularly when bolted to the notoriously fidgety small marine diesel engine. Usually made from copper, jacketed systems are also expensive. And since they are nothing more than exhaust pipes with cooling jackets around them, jacketed systems do not muffle the exhaust noise.

But the most serious shortcoming is that jacketed systems are subject to undetected failure of the inner jacket wall. Copper is not a good material for a diesel exhaust system, and the sulfuric acid in the exhaust eats through the inner jacket wall. This failure is undetectable when the engine is running because the pressure of the engine exhaust carries any leaking water with it, but when the engine is stopped, water in the cooling jacket flows through the holes in the jacket wall into the exhaust pipe and back into the engine. We once had to do a very expensive major overhaul on a diesel engine after only 1,000 hours due to this very problem.

If the boat is at risk with a dry exhaust, and the engine at risk with a jacketed exhaust, what is the solution? The answer is the waterlift exhaust system. This is no more than a canister with an inlet and an outlet, the outlet pipe extending inside the canister almost to its bottom. The engine cooling water is injected into the exhaust line near the exhaust manifold. Water from the wet exhaust fills the canister above the bottom of the outlet pipe, effectively blocking the outlet. When sufficient pressure builds up in the canister, the water and exhaust gases are literally "blown" out of the submerged outlet pipe, and the cycle begins again. Boats equipped with waterlift systems are easily detectable by the bursts of cooling water from their exhaust pipe instead of a continuous flow.

They are also detectable by how quiet they are.

That was brought home most effectively to me one cold December morning shortly after we installed a waterlift exhaust. Friends on a sistership with the identical engine and the original jacketed exhaust had stopped at our dock for the night. As they prepared to leave, I also started our engine. From the back deck of the house, 50 feet away, I could only hear the *splash* of our own exhaust, but as our friends motored away from us on the river, I could hear their exhaust clearly for almost 20 minutes!

A waterlift exhaust is incredibly easy to install. Once water has been injected into the system, exhaust lines downstream may be rubber exhaust hose. With flexible hose for exhaust pipe, the engine can jump around all it wants without damaging the exhaust system. As long as the water injection point is at least 6 inches above the waterline, and the waterlift muffler can be mounted lower than the manifold, the only hot exhaust line is a short section between the manifold and the water injection point. A threaded exhaust pipe flange will allow you to fabricate this section from galvanized pipe fittings available from any plumbing supply or hardware store. You need three short nipples (lengths of pipe threaded on both ends), a 45-degree elbow, and a tee connector with a hose fitting for the injection line. Exhaust hose connects the exhaust pipe to the inlet on the canister, and a second piece of hose runs from the outlet to the overboard discharge fitting.

Most sailboat auxiliaries are, unfortunately, located below the waterline. If the muffler can still be located lower than the exhaust manifold, the only real accommodation that sailors have to make is to loop the cooling water discharge line well above the waterline and equip it with a vent at the top. The usual installation uses an anti-siphon valve, but they are notorious for packing up with salt and seizing. If they seize in the closed position, they will not break the siphon and the engine could fill with raw water. If they seize open, it is like a saltwater sprinkler going off in the engine room. Instead of an anti-siphon valve, use a 1/4-inch vent line led overboard. This is a cheap and troublefree alternative, although it may weep a bit.

In both of these installations, the exhaust line

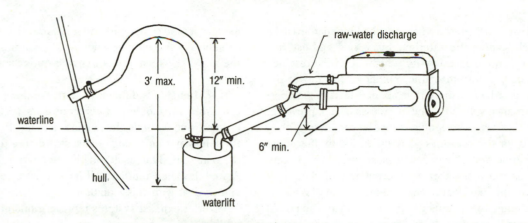

water injection point at least 6" above the waterline

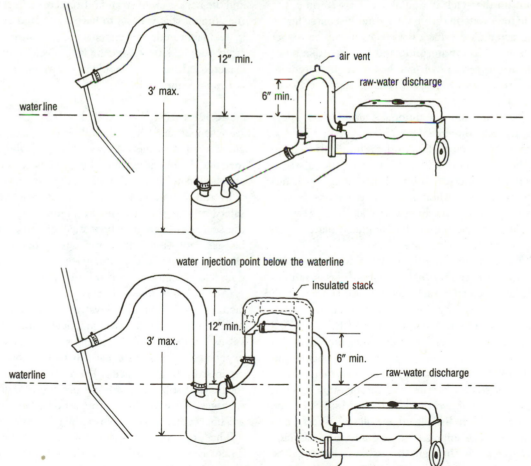

water injection point below the waterline

waterlift muffler above the exhaust manifold

Exhaust plumbing

from the waterlift muffler must be looped at least 12 inches above the waterline. In a very deep boat, this may require an excessively high lift. If the distance from the bottom of the muffler to the top of the exhaust loop is more than about 3 feet, engine performance will suffer due to excessive back pressure. In this case, the muffler must be mounted higher.

If for this reason, or any other, the muffler must be mounted above the exhaust manifold, precautions must be taken to prevent the muffler from draining back into the engine. A dry stack is required to, in effect, raise the exhaust manifold above the muffler. If, as a result, the water injection point on the stack is well above the waterline, the need for a vent on the cooling water discharge line is eliminated. A dry stack is easy to custom construct with galvanized water pipe and elbows. Like a dry exhaust, the riser will get hot enough to require insulation, but it does not pass through lockers or the hull.

There are some additional cautions that apply equally to all three configurations. The first is to be certain that the waterlift muffler is firmly attached to the boat. Do not let its light weight, particularly in the plastic variety, fool you. Remember that it fills with water and when full will have considerable momentum in a pitching or rolling boat. (By the way, despite the seeming incongruity, plastic mufflers work perfectly.)

The second caution is to try to avoid mounting the muffler to the side of the engine. This is particularly important for sailboats because so mounted, on one tack the muffler is elevated relative to the exhaust manifold. At large angles of heel, residual water in the muffler could flow into the engine. If possible, mount the muffler aft of the engine and close to the centerline of the exhaust manifold.

Sailors should be sure the through-hull exhaust outlet is well above the waterline. More than one skipper has seen his idle engine fill with water when following seas engulfed his exhaust port, forcing seawater back through the exhaust lines to the engine. A valve in the exhaust line is the best protection from this disaster, but you must remember to close it (and to open it) and it is somewhat inconvenient. A flap might be effective, depending upon the angle at which your discharge outlet exits the hull.

If your engine is difficult to start, you have a special problem. Cooling water continues to fill the muffler, but without the engine actually running, there may not be enough exhaust pressure to blow the water out. The result can be water in the engine. A well-designed muffler will have a drain to allow you to deal with this situation.

Waterlift exhaust systems represent one of those oddities where cheaper is better. A waterlift canister and the necessary hose and fittings cost a fraction of the amount that it costs to have a jacketed exhaust system fabricated, or even repaired. If you are repowering your old boat, or simply suspicious of your jacketed exhaust (you should be), a waterlift system is the best alternative.

Seacocks and Through-hulls

Seacocks and through-hull fittings have to be considered together. Every through-hull fitting installed below the water line needs a seacock attached to it. Tens of thousands of boats have been delivered without regard to this most basic tenet of safety, but the guy who made the decision to omit the seacocks from your boat was concerned about his ass, not yours. If a previous owner has not already equipped every through-hull with a seacock, doing so should be a top priority.

Seacock selection. Twenty years ago, if manufacturers opted to install valves on the through-hulls, they had only two practical choices: gate valves or tapered-plug seacocks. Seacocks were expensive, gate valves cheap, so a lot of boats were equipped with gate valves. There are other options today, yet I still see new boats every year delivered with gate valves on the through-hulls. Gate valves are unacceptable for a marine installation.

The problems with gate valves are numerous. There is no way to know if the valve is open or closed without turning it, and even then turning the handle does not assure you that the valve is closed.

For example, despite cranking the handle clockwise until it stops—the only confirmation that the valve is fully closed—the valve will still be open if a bit of trash has found its way under the gate. "Closing" the valves when you leave the boat does not provide the measure of security you may be expecting. Most gate valves are also brass and quickly corrode in sea water. They may look bright and new, but the corrosion is internal and sinister. When you need to close the valve, you will find that the threaded shaft that raises and lowers the gate has dissolved and the valve is useless. Lastly, lacking a mounting flange, gate valves are invariably mounted by simply threading them onto the through-hull fitting.

In contrast, the orientation of the handle instantly tells you whether a traditional seacock is open or closed. A tapered plug with a hole in the center allows the water to flow through the valve, or with a quarter turn the hole (and the handle) are turned perpendicular to the flow, stopping it. If trash in the valve interferes with its operation, you will know immediately because you will be unable to move the handle to the off position. Traditional seacocks are bronze, not brass, and unless attacked by electrolysis they can last for decades. The flanged base allows the seacock to be strongly fastened to the hull.

As good as it is, the traditional tapered-plug seacock has a number of shortcomings. For one thing, it requires an inordinate amount of maintenance, beginning with the need to be completely dismantled and serviced at least once a year. If it is to seal properly, the valve must be *lapped* by smearing the plug and the seat with (automotive) valve grinding compound and turning them against each other until they fit perfectly. Be sure to remove all the grinding paste thoroughly before reassembly.

With age, corrosion eventually takes its toll on the tapered plug, causing it to become wasp-waisted around the hole. When this happens, lapping will not correct it, and the valve will no longer completely stem the flow of water in the closed position.

Less dramatic imperfections are accommodated by packing the valve with waterproof grease, but if the seacock is turned often, the grease is displaced and water soon begins to seep between the plug and the body of the seacock. Crank the nut that holds the tapered plug in the valve tight enough to stop the leak and the valve is impossible to open and close. Loosen the nut and water trickles down the hull. Even adjusted "just right," opening and closing the valve a few times soon gets it out of adjustment. But fail to operate it regularly, and it tends to seize and cannot be turned at all when the need arises.

I have heard sailors advocate permanently installed grease fittings, but nipples leak and such fittings almost always introduce a dissimilar metal to the seacock. A *bronze* grease *cup* can be used successfully, but considering that cars have not had grease fittings for two decades, why would you want them on your boat?

Tapered-plug seacocks have long been a mainstay, but high maintenance, corrosion, weeping, and seizing have always plagued the design. One effort to overcome these failings is a type of bronze seacock substituting a cylindrical neoprene plug for the traditional tapered bronze one. A threaded T bar located opposite the plug handle is tightened against the end of the neoprene plug, forcing the plug to swell in the middle and creating a very effective seal. Before the seacock can be opened or closed, the T bar must be unscrewed several turns to release pressure on the neoprene plug.

I have always found this type of seacock less prone to leak or weep, and the only maintenance required is cleaning and greasing during haul-out and occasionally oiling the threads of the T bar. However, rubber-plug seacocks are not recommended for sink or head discharge lines because certain chemicals attack the rubber, causing the plug to swell and making it difficult or impossible to turn the valve.

The best seacocks, by a wide margin, are ball valves. The port, rather than going through a cylindrical rubber or tapered bronze plug, passes through a ball sandwiched between two circular seats. Bronze ball-type seacocks have a hard chrome-plated bronze ball turning in Teflon seals. Ball-valve

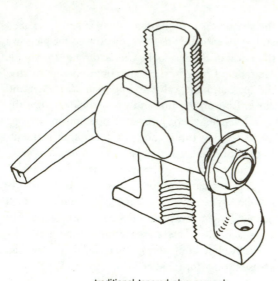

traditional tapered plug seacock

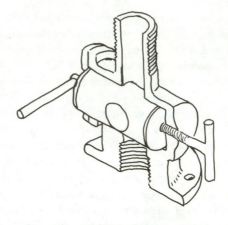

T-bar/rubber plug seacock

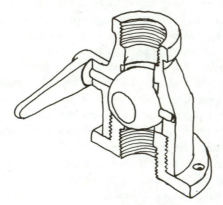

ball-valve seacock

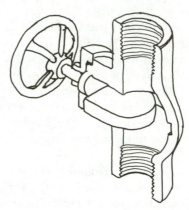

gate valve—leave ashore

Seacocks

seacocks are virtually maintenance free, requiring only a light application of petroleum jelly to the ball annually to keep them turning easily.

Plastic seacocks made their first appearance more than 20 years ago and seemed a natural for plastic boats. I had several plastic ball-valves aboard, and in marked contrast to the bronze seacocks aboard, the plastic valves *always* operated freely, required no maintenance, and never leaked a drop. But the plastic used in the manufacture of those early plastic valves became brittle with age, and after several years all required replacement.

A new generation of plastic seacocks has gained wide acceptance in the last decade. Not to be confused with their predecessors, today's plastic seacocks are molded of incredibly tough and durable glass-reinforced nylon. Completely corrosion free and relatively inexpensive, glass-reinforced nylon seacocks exhibit a single shortcoming: they will melt in a fire. However, so will the hose attached to a bronze seacock, and unless you are braving the flames to close all the seacocks, this seems to me to be less than a critical flaw. For aluminum or steel hulls, where bronze seacocks (and through-hulls) represent an electrolysis threat, nylon fittings are ideal. Maintenance of these plastic ball valves is limited to turning them occasionally and lubricating the ball annually. As for aging, it is hard to tell the difference between a valve just installed and one put into service five years ago. Just how long they will actually last is still anybody's guess, but the seacock assassin, corrosion, has no effect on these valves.

Through-hull and seacock installation. There is rarely a genuine need for an additional through-hull fitting in an older boat; most have far too many holes in the hull already. Only if you cannot find a way to avoid drilling another hole in the hull by installing a tee connector in an existing inlet or discharge line should you add a through-hull fitting. Installing a new through-hull fitting differs from replacement only in the need to drill a hole in the hull.

Locate the new seacock where it will be readily available. Check the location carefully both inside and outside the hull to make sure, for example, that inside there will be ample room to throw the handle, and that outside the new fitting is not going to set up turbulence in front of your depth sounder or speed-log impeller. From inside the hull, drill a small pilot hole and check the location one more time.

Select a hole saw the size of the fitting you are installing. Cut the required hole by first drilling from the outside of the hull until the pilot drill in the hole saw penetrates the hull, then finish the hole by drilling from the inside. Clean up the edges of the hole with emery cloth.

If the hull is cored rather than solid laminate, you will have to dig out the core around the hole to hollow an area at least as large as the flange of the seacock you are installing. Fill the hollow area with epoxy putty and allow it to fully harden before proceeding. The epoxy provides a solid base for the through-hull and prevents water from reaching the core material.

If you are replacing a through-hull fitting, first release the nuts on the bolts through the mounting flange. Use a hammer and a punch to drive the bolts out of the flange, and extract them from the hull. With the help of a pipe wrench, if necessary, unscrew the seacock from the through-hull. If the through-hull has been installed with polyurethane sealant, it will be very difficult to remove from the hull. Obtain a large ($3/8$- or $1/2$-inch) bolt about 4 inches longer than the through-hull, along with a nut and a pair of washers too big to pass *through* the fitting. Slide one of the washers onto the bolt and from inside the boat pass the bolt through the fitting, seating the washer flat on the fitting. Outside the hull, pass the bolt through a hole drilled in a short length of 2 × 4 and fit the second washer and the nut. Now support the length of wood on both sides of the fitting with a couple of wooden blocks. As you tighten the nut, the bolt will pull the fitting from the hull. With a razor knife, scrape away all sealant residue and wipe the area around the hole—both inside and outside the hull—with toluene or acetone.

Once the hole is prepared, the remaining steps are identical for either installing a new seacock or replacing an old one. With your sabersaw, cut a circle of $3/4$-inch plywood 2 or 3 inches larger than the flange of the seacock. Use your hole saw to cut out the center of the circle, forming a ring. Now with a rasp or a belt sander, shape the bottom of this ring to the inside curvature of the hull around the hole until the ring sits flat against the hull. The ring serves to reinforce the hull around the hole and to provide a flat surface for the seacock flange. Mark the ring so you will be able to orient it correctly later.

Next dry fit the parts. From outside the hull, insert the new through-hull fitting. Inside, slip the wooden ring in place and thread the seacock onto the through-hull. Never attempt to install a plastic seacock on a bronze through-hull, nor a bronze seacock on a plastic through-hull. The seacock and the through-hull must *always* be the same material. Tighten the two parts together. A wedge of steel plate—most yards have one around—is inserted against the "ears" inside the fitting to hold it from turning. A wedge cut from a scrap of wood will do the same job.

With the seacock tightened snugly—not too tight—you should have plenty of threads inside the seacock, but the length of the through-hull should not prevent the base of the seacock from tightening against the plywood ring. If the through-hull is too

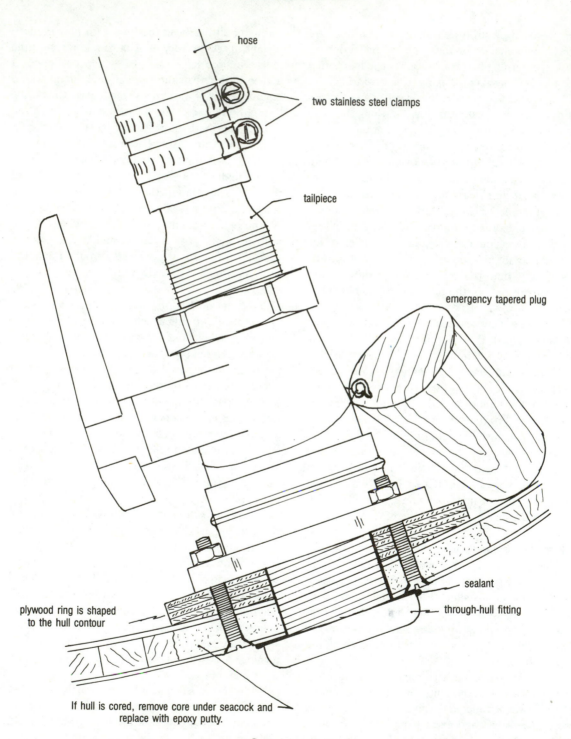

hose

two stainless steel clamps

tailpiece

emergency tapered plug

sealant

through-hull fitting

plywood ring is shaped
to the hull contour

If hull is cored, remove core under seacock and
replace with epoxy putty.

Seacock installation

short, replace the 3/4-inch-thick ring with a new one cut and shaped from 1/2-inch plywood. If it is too long, add an additional ring cut from 1/4-inch plywood. Ideally, the through-hull should be just short of bottoming out inside the seacock.

Position the seacock the way you want it and make sure you can turn the handle without risking tetanus. If the seacock has a drain plug, try to orient it on the low side of the valve. Once you are satisfied with the position, drill the mounting holes through the hull from inside the boat, using the holes in the mounting flange as a drill guide. If the flange is not predrilled, drill three evenly spaced holes through the flange and the hull. From outside the hull, countersink the three holes. Now unscrew the seacock and remove the through-hull.

Having seen dozens of backer blocks turn to the consistency of damp toilet tissue from the constant weeping of a seacock, I strongly recommend that you give the plywood rings two or three coats of clear polyurethane before finishing the installation.

Wipe the hole one more time with acetone. Put a heavy bead of polysulfide or polyurethane (preferred) sealant around the shoulder of the through-hull and coat the threads less heavily. Insert the through-hull, put the plywood ring in position, and insert the mounting bolts through the hull and far enough into the plywood to prevent it from turning. Tighten the seacock until it seats snugly on the ring and the mounting holes are in alignment. Remove the mounting bolts and coat them heavily with sealant, then reinsert them and install washers and nuts on the bolts where they extend through the flange of the seacock.

If the seacock is bronze, be sure the mounting bolts are also bronze. Either stainless steel or bronze bolts may be used to mount plastic seacocks. Tighten the nuts, but don't try out your Wheaties on them. Bronze bolts especially will stretch if you crank them too tight.

Tightening the flange bolts tends to push the through-hull out of the hull as the wooden backer conforms and compresses. After the mounting bolts are tight, use the wedge tool to check the through-hull for tightness. Sealant should be squeezing out all around the fitting and the mounting screws. With your finger, use some of the excess sealant to fair over the heads of the screws.

If bolting the flange to the hull seems unnecessary to you, allow me to relate an incident with a bronze seacock simply threaded on a bronze through-hull. This was the raw-water inlet for the engine. Impeller failure and a dying breeze necessitated an offshore pump repair, but when I tried to close the barely accessible seacock, it wouldn't budge. Undeterred, I braced my feet against the bulkhead and gave a mighty tug. Instantly I found myself lying on the cabin sole, seacock in hand, looking between my knees at a 6-inch-high column of water spouting through the hull and into the engine room. Unseen corrosion inside the through-hull had severely weakened it. The lowering sun was refracted by the clear water outside the hull, giving the unstemmed flow a rainbow of colors, but my admiration was fleeting. Diving back into the engine room, I held out the ocean with my bare hand.

Which brings me to the final step. A seacock installation is not complete until you have a tapered softwood plug attached to it with a piece of light twine. Imagine if the little Dutch boy had whipped out a mallet and a wooden plug from his hip pocket and tapped the plug into the hole. It would have ruined a good story, but who can doubt that the little Dutch boy would have been a lot happier?

It is not easy to feel terribly smug when your thumb is in the dike, particularly when you are responsible for the hole, but it's possible. Tied to the seacock still hanging from the intake hose was the appropriate wooden plug and the necessary hammer to tap it into place was close at hand. Hardly enough water came in to activate the automatic bilge pump.

All that is required to put your new seacock into service is to fit it with a tailpiece (using thread sealant) and attach the appropriate hose. And don't forget to use dual clamps on all hose-to-seacock connections—which is either *deja vu*, or pretty close to where we came in.

THIRTEEN

A Cold Day in August

There's booze in the blender
And soon it will render
That frozen concoction that helps me hang on.
–JIMMY BUFFETT–

About 15 years ago, on a sweltering August day in the Bahamas, I asked a crew member below to check the temperature of the refrigerator. The two guys on the only other boat in the anchorage threw their necks out of joint as that magic word drifted across the tepid water. Within a matter of seconds their dinghy was alongside and they were offering to trade all the fresh lobster we could eat for a six-pack of cold beer–and they would furnish the beer. Refrigeration aboard a sailboat back then was the ultimate luxury. While happy hour on other cruising boats usually consisted of warm rum and Tang, we served iced drinks to our guests. We were very popular.

Those days are gone forever. Today half the boats in every anchorage will have some kind of refrigeration. And the other half is planning to join the club–probably including you.

And why not? Marine refrigeration has made quantum leaps in the last decade. A 12-volt system only draws about 50 Ah per day. With a 100-Ah battery, you can go two days before you need to run the engine and then your 100-amp alternator will recharge the battery in an hour. With a decent wind generator and a 10-knot breeze, you can forget about running the engine altogether, and if the wind isn't blowing, you will let the solar panels take care of it.

NOW HOLD ON A MINUTE, MR. PRESIDENT. Not a single statement in the last paragraph is true, not even the part about quantum leaps. Marine refrigeration *advertising* has made quantum leaps–we all want refrigeration aboard–but the physics involved has remained unchanged. It is true that there are many more choices today, and today's systems are often extraordinarily dependable. But the main objection to onboard refrigeration, other than cost, is exactly the same as it was 15 years ago: refrigeration consumes a lot of energy.

When this truth is considered, many boat owners find that refrigeration aboard their boat is not a particularly good idea. Boats that see only weekend use may not benefit at all from refrigeration. Ice is cheap and simple, and often required anyway to transport supplies between home and the boat. Refrigeration would only serve to add complexity and place additional demands on the boat's electrical system. At the other end of the spectrum is the liveaboard; refrigeration is a fundamental requirement aboard a boat used as a home. Between these two extremes, the decision is more complicated.

If you plan to live aboard your old boat, if you are only interested in refrigeration when you are tied to the dock, or if you keep an onboard generator running constantly, energy consumption will not be high on your list of concerns. In fact, you can skip this chapter altogether; in less time than it will take you to read it, you can have refrigeration aboard and already chilling the shrimp cocktail. That is because the only sensible choice for you is a 110-volt unit. Such refrigerators are cheap, they require no complicated installation, they are virtually trouble-free–after a couple of hundred million units, the manufacturers have worked out most of the bugs–and they are available from your local department store or discount house. Size and cost will be your only two considerations.

If you do not, or will not, have a constant source of 110-volt power available, and you still want to have refrigeration aboard, read on. In this chapter, we will examine marine refrigeration. Our objective is to give you sufficient understanding of the various types of refrigeration and the suitability of each for various applications. We will place particular emphasis on the factors that determine the efficiency of a particular installation. Keep in mind that marine refrigeration gobbles up energy like William Perry gobbles up party franks. And you thought they called him the "Refrigerator" because of his size! Regardless of the optimistic claims of the five-color brochures you have been studying, add install-it-in-your-existing-box, 12-volt refrigeration to a normally equipped 35-foot sailboat and the daily drain on the ship's batteries triples. That power must be replaced by some onboard power source. This fact pushes energy consumption to the front of the list of considerations when choosing a system. A carelessly selected and poorly executed refrigeration system, rather than being a source of pleasure, will quickly become an expensive disappointment.

THE BOX

Because the energy required for marine refrigeration depends so heavily on the design of the box it is installed in, how big the box is and how well insulated, box design is where our discussion must start. If the one aboard your boat is only nominally smaller than the cockpit locker, or if it is separated from the engine room by only a half-inch of plywood, get used to the sound of your engine. Or plan to make some changes.

It is a relatively simple matter to test the efficiency of your box. Heat always transfers from a hotter object to a colder object and what we want to determine is how much heat passes through the insulation into the box. The unit of measurement we will use is the Btu (British Thermal Unit), the amount of heat required to raise one pound of water one degree Fahrenheit. The change of state from ice to water requires a great deal more energy than a simple temperature rise—it takes 144 Btus to change a pound of ice into 32-degree water—and it is this fact that allows us to test the box.

Begin by getting the interior of the box cold by loading it with block ice. If you already have refrigeration, you can use it to chill the box, but *not* if it is a holding plate system. Once the box is at about 40 degrees, take the ice out and weigh it, then return it to the box and close the door. After 24 hours, weigh the remaining ice to determine the amount of ice that has melted. Multiply the number of pounds by 144 to determine how much heat has passed through the insulation.

Let's assume that your box melts 24 pounds of ice (to make the arithmetic easy) in 24 hours. That is 3456 Btus per day or 144 Btus per hour, a number consistent with what we might expect of a medium-size (9-cubic-foot) box insulated with two inches of polyurethane foam. This is the amount of cooling required *just to keep up with heat leak*.

If you install an electric refrigerator into this box, how much power is it going to require? Without getting into the math and the efficiency assumptions, a useful estimate is that you can remove about 3.5 Btus of heat per watt of electrical power. So 144 Btus divided by 3.5 gives us about 41 watt-hours. From Chapter 11 you know to divide watt-hours by the battery voltage (12 volts) to get amp-hours—about 3.4. This means that the *daily* current requirement to offset this leak is going to be about 80 Ah. But you have not cooled anything yet, or opened the door—or thought about ambient temperatures.

Suppose the outside temperature during this test is about 80 degrees. The temperature difference between the inside and the outside of the box will be 40 degrees. Take your old boat south where the ambient temperature is 100 degrees and what happens? The relation between temperature differential and heat leak is direct. A 60-degree temperature differential will yield 1.5 times the leak of a 40-

degree differential: 5,184 Btus daily in this case, requiring 120 Ah of power to offset.

Aboard our boat, five of the six sides of the refrigerator box are inside the engine compartment and we use half the box as a freezer, holding 0 degrees. With an engine room temperature of 120 degrees, this configuration for the test box would yield a leak number close to three times that of the original test and more than 200 Ah would be required daily just to keep up with leak.

Part of the solution is insulation. Assume the test box has 2 inches of insulation. Increasing the insulation to 4 inches (lid included) will cut the leak in half; increasing it to 6 inches will cut the leak to a third of its original amount. Note that the effect is the fractional relationship of the old insulation to the new and thus the benefit is a decreasing one. In any case, the same box with 6 inches of insulation now requires only 48 Btus per hour to keep up with insulation losses—about 27 Ah of current. But you still have not actually refrigerated anything, and you certainly have not made ice.

Another solution is a smaller box. The equation for calculating leak directly relates Btus to the surface area of the box, conventionally the outside surface area. Your 9-cubic-foot box will have an outside surface area (insulated) of about 35 square feet. Cutting the interior size by 50 percent, to 6 cubic feet, reduces the surface area to about 26 square feet—a reduction of about 25 percent with a similar reduction in leak.

When you actually refrigerate something, you have additional power requirements. For example, the six-pack we cooled in exchange for fresh lobster required about 280 Btus. Cooling the lobster required another 300 Btus. (Darn right, we took it!) And about 50 Btus fell out of the box every time we opened our front-opening door. Assuming that you are cooling drinks, putting fresh food in the box, and opening it occasionally, you can expect to require at least another 2,000 Btus of refrigeration, probably more. Applying the 3.5 Btus per watt, we need about 48 Ah to handle the load, so even a small, 6-cubic-foot box insulated with 6 inches of

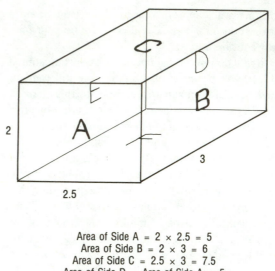

Area of Side A = 2 × 2.5 = 5
Area of Side B = 2 × 3 = 6
Area of Side C = 2.5 × 3 = 7.5
Area of Side D = Area of Side A = 5
Area of Side E = Area of Side B = 6
Area of Side F = Area of Side C = 7.5
Total Surface Area = 37

Calculating surface area

polyurethane foam—assuming an ambient temperature of 80 degrees—is going to draw 68 Ah daily. The same system is going to drain 100 Ah daily from the batteries in use in the tropics.

TWELVE-VOLT REFRIGERATION

The calculations above refer to refrigeration systems that utilize a 12-volt compressor to circulate a refrigerant, usually Freon 12, through an evaporator inside the box. The Adler-Barbour ColdMachine is the most common system of this type, but there are numerous manufacturers building similar units.

Twelve-volt refrigeration is easily the most popular choice among sailors. It is not difficult to understand why. The initial cost is low. With only two major components, the evaporator which goes inside the box and the compressor/condenser unit which goes outside, installation is simple. The units are efficient and trouble free.

Unfortunately, as we have seen from the calculations above, power requirements often place excessive demands on the battery and charging capacity of the typical sailboat. This is perhaps 12-volt refrigeration's only disadvantage, but it is a serious one. If you cannot provide 60 to 100 amps per day, you will not have refrigeration. Many owners discover too late that special charging equipment is required to keep up with the electrical demand of the refrigerator. This ancillary equipment can easily double or triple the cost of the refrigeration system. Perhaps more important, the additional equipment adds to the complexity of your boat.

Also, unless a dedicated battery is used, 12-volt refrigeration can actually put the boat at risk with its unrelenting demand for electrical power; more than one captain has experienced the failure of the engine to start at a critical moment because the refrigerator has drained the batteries. Do not be misled by the "low voltage cutout" feature mentioned in some brochures; that is for the protection of the compressor. By the time it shuts down the system, the battery will be far too low to start any engine.

Most 12-volt units are comprised of an hermetically sealed compressor, an air-cooled condenser, and a box-shaped evaporator—the only configuration some manufacturers offer. But in the tropics, run-time will be dramatically reduced with a water-cooled condenser, a serious consideration if a southern cruise is in your future. Manufacturers who offer this feature may supply both types of condensers with their systems, or they may require that you select one or the other.

Differences in evaporators might also be significant for your particular installation. Instead of the standard box-shaped evaporator, some manufacturers can also supply flat evaporators, or L-shaped

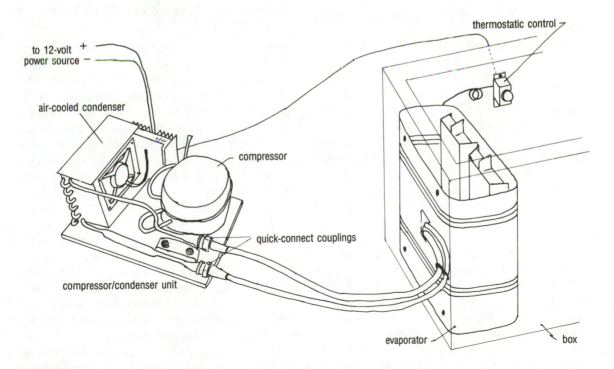

12-volt refrigeration

units designed to fit into one corner of the box. Such evaporators can be especially valuable if your box is small or has an irregular shape.

Twelve-volt refrigeration is typically operated dockside by simply plugging in the battery charger. However, for weekend sailors not wanting to empty the fridge on Sunday night, running the unit all week long this way may not be the best treatment for the boat's battery. If this is how you anticipate using your refrigerator, you should consider selecting a unit with an AC/DC compressor. When the shore-power cord is connected, these units switch automatically to AC.

THERMOELECTRIC REFRIGERATION

Another type of 12-volt refrigeration that you will encounter is thermoelectric refrigeration, often called "solid state." The technology of thermoelectric refrigeration has been around since 1834, when Frenchman Jean Peltier applied voltage across two dissimilar metals and noted that one of the metals became cool to the touch while the other heated. Thermoelectric units have no refrigerant and no moving parts, other than a small fan to dissipate heat. They are virtually silent in operation. Module life is about 250,000 hours of running time—you can will the unit to your children. Installation requires only cutting a hole in the side of your box, screwing the unit in place, and making the electrical connection. These features combine to make thermoelectric refrigeration seem ideal for marine applications. And in some cases, it is.

However, thermoelectric refrigeration is not very energy efficient. A typical unit will require about 100 amps per day to cool a box of less than 2 cubic feet. And thermoelectric refrigeration has limited cooling capacity, capable of reducing the box temperature only about 40 degrees below the ambient temperature. If cabin temperatures get above 90 degrees, a common occurrence in a boat in southern waters, the temperature inside the box will approach 50 degrees, no longer sufficiently cool to

safely preserve meats or dairy products. Ice is out of the question.

Thermoelectric refrigerators are useful in cooler climates, and portable units—some with power requirements closer to 50 amps per day and priced well under $100—offer weekend sailors a convenient alternative to the ice chest. Eliminating the need for ice, a small thermoelectric unit will cool as many items as a much larger ice chest while weighing less and occupying less space.

Another potential use for thermoelectric is a refrigerated medicine cabinet. Storing medicines, particularly in the tropics, can be a problem. A tiny, well-insulated medicine cabinet using the smallest available thermoelectric unit could provide a solution for the sailor needing to carry a supply of prescription drugs.

THE ELECTRICAL SYSTEM REVISITED

When you get away from the dock, the bottom line on any 12-volt refrigeration system is how often and how long are you going to have to run the engine. How often depends upon your battery capacity. As a starting point, let's assume a pair of batteries in the 110- to 120-Ah range. As we saw in Chapter 11, a battery rated at 120 Ah is not designed to deliver 120 Ah of current; if you want the battery to have a reasonable life, it should not be discharged below about 50 percent of its rating. So a pair of 120-Ah batteries *combined* provide about 120 Ah of usable current, only a little more than what we have already calculated as the daily demand of your refrigerator in a warm climate. You need 200 Ah of available current just for refrigeration if you want to go two days between charges. Refrigeration manufacturers usually suggest a dedicated battery bank for the refrigerator; this is an excellent idea, but it will not reduce the daily engine-running requirement.

How long the engine will need to run each day depends upon your charging system. We have already seen that the life of deep-cycle batteries is shortened if we charge them at more than 25 percent of their amp-hour capacity, so to put 100 Ah back into a *pair* of 120-Ah batteries is going to take about two hours at the maximum charge rate of 60 amps (30 amps per battery). (Recall that battery inefficiency requires you to put back about 20 percent more current than what was consumed.) If you have not modified your charging system, the standard regulator is not going to keep the alternator at 60 amps throughout the charge cycle, cutting back to 30 amps or less as the batteries reach about 70 percent of their charge, and continuing to decline. At the end of two hours the batteries will be around 80 percent charged; to take the charge above 90 percent will require an additional hour. Most of us will conclude that three hours of engine time daily to refrigerate a small, well-insulated box is unacceptable although we may be perfectly content with the unit for weekend use in a temperate climate.

Does all this mean you may as well turn off the refrigerator if you cross the tropic of Cancer? And a freezer is out of the question south of the Mason-Dixon? Not at all.

Since the amount of time required to charge batteries is dependent upon their percentage of discharge, not their total ampere-hour capacity, increasing battery capacity is usually step one in the search for a solution. We have already concluded that a pair of 120-Ah batteries discharged to 50 percent of capacity will take close to three hours to charge. Double the battery capacity, discharge it to 50 percent, and you can still recharge in about three hours. So if your refrigerator draws 100 Ah per day and you have 480 Ah of capacity, you can now go two days between charging, making your *average* engine time 1½ hours per day—assuming that your charging system is up to the task.

That is a big assumption. For the first hour of the charge, you need an alternator capable of an output of about 25 percent of your battery capacity—around 120 Ah in this case. Since alternators should generally not be operated continuously at more than 75 percent of rated capacity, the needed alternator should be rated at 160 Ah. The alternator fitted to most sailboat auxiliaries is rated closer to a third of that output. High-output alternators are available

and the installation of one is frequently step two. A special regulator to make more efficient use of the high output alternator is step three.

Still, the limiting factor is going to be the batteries. Regular deep-cycle batteries will be damaged if you try to charge them too quickly, so you are stuck with running the engine for about three hours. Maybe you can find a place for a couple more batteries and go three days between chargings, but then you will need a 240-amp alternator. Cost becomes prohibitive.

Sealed "gel" batteries offer some advantages since they can be charged much faster than their conventional deep-cycle counterparts. Assuming a charge rate of 50 percent of capacity for a gel battery, our original 240-Ah capacity system could theoretically be recharged in one hour, but would require at least a 180-amp alternator and a special regulator. Two days between charges and you need a 360-amp alternator—and 15 h.p. to drive such an alternator. The more realistic 180-amp unit is going to take two hours to bring the batteries up.

MOTHER NATURE

An average of one hour of engine time per day is more palatable, but why can't you eliminate the engine altogether? What about solar panels? Can't you run your 100 Ah refrigerator from the sun?

You can, but you probably won't. From our examination of silicon photovoltaic cells in Chapter 11, we already know that with the best solar arrays available commercially, we can expect about 130 watts per square meter of solar panel. Output voltages vary, but are generally around 15 volts, so the output current is 8.7 amps (130 divided by 15).

This is peak current; the *optimum daily output* will be about five times the peak current or 43 Ah per square meter. To get the necessary 120 Ah per day (including the 20 percent battery inefficiency) requires about three square meters of cells—an area the size of a full sheet of plywood. Even if you can find the space for that large an array, expect the cost to exceed $2,500.

The wind is another possibility. To supply 120

Ah per day, you need a wind generator with at least a 5-amp output. A typical alternator-type unit will require a wind velocity of 23 knots to delivery the necessary amperage. In 15 knots of wind, output will be down to 2 amps.

Permanent magnet-type generators do provide a much higher output, generating the necessary 5 amps in 12 knots of wind. But if the wind drops to six knots, output will be down to 1 amp. The propensity of this type of wind generator to self-destruct in a squall makes it a risky proposition to leave one running overnight. That reduces running time to 16 hours a day, in turn raising the required output current to 7.5 amps. Now it will take more than 15 knots of wind to generate that output. A consistent 15 knot wind is unlikely outside of the trades. One advantage of wind power is that equip-

ment capable of supplying the amp-hour requirements in optimum conditions is about a third the cost of an equivalent solar array.

You could install two wind generators, or a combination of solar panels and a wind generator, but even after this added expense and added complication, on many days you will still be running the engine. This fact leads many to accept engine running as a necessary refrigeration by-product.

ENGINE-DRIVEN REFRIGERATION

Instead of trying to minimize engine time with additional or more powerful charging equipment, an alternative approach is to avoid the whole battery charging issue by running the refrigerator directly

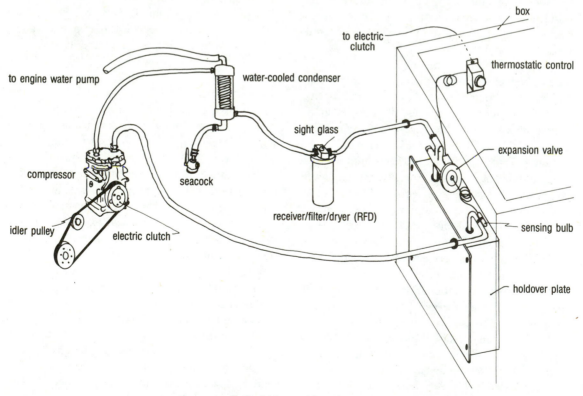

Engine-driven refrigeration

from the engine. If you want a freezer, one measured in cubic feet, this is probably your only reasonable choice.

Engine-driven systems are not dependent upon the boat's electrical system. They are very powerful, easily capable of maintaining a sizeable freezer as well as a large refrigerator. They are inherently more efficient because they avoid the conversion of energy from mechanical to electrical and back to mechanical. Battery inefficiency is also avoided.

But engine-driven systems have a high initial cost, two to three times that of a 12-volt refrigerator. They are relatively complicated and often more trouble-prone because of it. And they almost always require running the engine every day.

How long are you going to have to run the engine? Again, much depends upon your box. It also depends upon the size and efficiency of your holdover plates, and to a lesser degree on the size of the compressor.

An engine-driven system cools in exactly the same manner as a 12-volt unit, or a 110-volt unit, for that matter. A liquid refrigerant (Freon) is pumped through tubes inside the box. The low boiling point of the Freon enables it to absorb a large amount of heat as it changes in state from a liquid to a gas. The gas flows back to the compressor, where it is compressed under high pressure and sent to the condenser. Working like a radiator, the condenser allows the heat the refrigerant is carrying to dissipate into the surrounding air (or water in the case of a water-cooled condenser.) The now liquid Freon flows again into the box to absorb more heat. The process is continuous as long as the compressor is running.

Therein lies one of the differences. The 12-volt

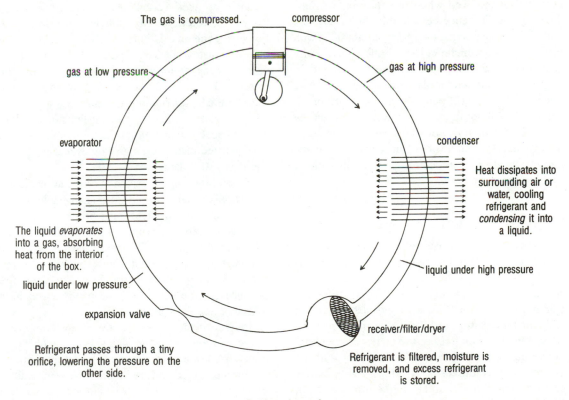

Refrigeration cycle

compressor cycles on and off as the box alternately warms and is cooled, typically running at least 20 to 30 minutes of every hour. The engine-driven compressor runs only once or twice a day, depending upon the efficiency of the system and the owner's preference.

It is the other difference, the holdover plate, that provides the flexibility to run the compressor only once a day. The Freon passing through the tubes of the evaporator of a 12-volt refrigerator is cooling the air inside the box. In contrast, the evaporator tubes of an engine-driven system run through a metal box filled with a fluid—the holdover plate—extracting the heat from the fluid and causing the fluid to freeze.

The effect of freezing the holdover plate is similar to loading the box with ice. As the solution inside the plate melts, it absorbs heat from the box; the heat is later removed when the compressor runs. The biggest difference between the holdover plate and a block of ice is that the plates are not filled with plain water but contain either a brine solution or a glycol mixture, which typically freeze at around 26 degrees for a refrigerator plate and at 0 degrees for a freezer plate. A tray of water sitting on a block of 32-degree ice will not freeze, but the same tray sitting on a 0-degree holdover plate will soon freeze solid. The greater the volume of frozen solution inside the refrigerator, the longer the box will stay cold without running the compressor.

THE FREEZER

Before looking more closely at holdover plates, let's recalculate the daily Btu requirements of a typical installation, this time including a freezer. We have already calculated an hourly leak of 36 Btus for a 6-cubic-foot box with 6 inches of insulation and an ambient temperature of 80 degrees. If we also assume a 6-cubic-foot freezer, the higher temperature differential will yield a leak of 72 Btus. With an ambient temperature of 100 degrees, leak numbers go to 54 and 90, or a total of 144 Btus per hour, 3,456 Btus per day.

Keeping the refrigeration load the same at 2000

Btus, let's assume that all you use the freezer for on a daily basis, other than keeping the already-frozen stuff frozen, is to make a couple of trays of ice. A tray of ice weighs about a pound, so two pounds of water cooled from 100 degrees to 32 degrees requires 136 Btus (2 × 68). Freezing requires another 288 (2 × 144), so your total freezer load is 424 Btus—make it 550 to allow for opening the door three or four times during the day. The total combined load is about 6,000 Btus per day (3,456 + 2,000 + 550).

If you want the system to hold over for two days, you need plates capable of absorbing 12,000 Btus. The brine solution inside commercial holdover plates varies with manufacturer and with the purpose of the plate (refrigerator or freezer), but we will not be far off if we assume that a gallon of frozen brine will absorb about 1,000 Btus. That means you are going to need 12 gallons. At 231 cubic inches per gallon, you need 1.6 cubic feet of frozen solution inside the box. Unfortunately the tubing inside holdover plates takes up about 30 percent of the internal space, so for 1.6 cubic feet of solution, the plates will occupy 2.1 cubic feet of the interior space of the box. Looking at it another way, a 12″ × 18″ × 3″ plate contains about 2 gallons of solution. You will need *six* such plates. You are more likely to opt for three plates, enough holdover capacity for one day (6,000 Btus).

Most of the engine-driven systems available are enough alike that parts are interchangeable. Compressors are the same; fittings, hoses, driers, and controls are standard; condensers may differ slightly in design, but not in function. Assuming ample compressor displacement, how quickly you can freeze the plates is dependent mostly upon the internal structure of the holdover plates. Here there are real differences in design.

Some manufacturers place the greatest emphasis on the solution inside the plates, insisting on a true eutectic solution. An eutectic solution freezes at a fixed temperature and maintains that temperature until it completely thaws. (The alternative, a glycol solution, warms as it thaws.) Water is the eutectic solution of choice, with salts added to lower the freezing temperature. A brine solution is as much as 30 percent more effective at absorbing heat than a glycol solution but it is highly corrosive, necessitating that brine-filled plates be constructed entirely of zinc-coated or stainless steel.

However, there is more to holdover plate efficiency than heat absorption. How quickly the heat can be removed from the plate is just as important to the user. This is a function of the construction of the plate. If you compare the internal structure of holdover plates from two different manufacturers, you may find the cooling coil in one to be as much as four times the length of the coil in the other. Fins on the coil further enhance heat transfer. The solution in contact with the tubing freezes first, insulating the rest of the solution from the refrigerant, so the greater the surface area of the cooling coil, the quicker the plate can be frozen. But more internal structure also reduces the volume of brine and thus the holdover capacity of the plate. Tubing length and size are a compromise between maximum heat transfer and maximum holdover capacity.

Heat transfer is also enhanced if the plate is made of a heat-conductive material, such as cast aluminum. Internally finned and cast aluminum plates will be glycol-filled.

Holdover plates of the kind typically used in marine refrigeration have a practical pumpdown limit of about 1,500 Btus per hour. If our example box has a single plate, we are looking at four hours of run time (6,000 divided by 1,500) daily under heavy use conditions. Because the capacity of the compressor is greater than that of the plate, multiple plate systems are generally more efficient, but are not a multiple of single-plate efficiency. Three properly designed and connected plates might be pumped down at the rate of 2,500 Btus per hour, cutting the run time to 2.4 hours.

If you don't want to run the engine for 2½ hours a day, you must increase the number of holdover plates (and maybe the compressor size) or reduce the load. After insulation and size, the way you use the box has the most load reduction potential.

The goal is usually an hour of run time per day. This is quite possible with an efficient refrigeration system installed in a well-insulated box and used judiciously, but as our calculations show, less easily achieved when the system also includes a sizeable freezer.

Running the engine an hour each day may not seem onerous, but this daily obligation may present some unanticipated difficulty if you are refrigerating for a cruise and your plans include overnight (or longer) sightseeing trips away from the boat, or an occasional flight home. And if you spend a lot of time in marinas, running the engine once (or more likely twice) a day is going to be a vexation—to you and your neighbors. While virtually every holdover system manufacturer offers a shore power option, expect it to add 50 percent to the already high initial cost.

DOUBLE DUTY

Operating an engine-driven system from shore power typically involves the expense of a separate 110-volt compressor. Some manufacturers simply parallel the engine-driven compressor with the electrical one, sometimes even claiming higher efficiency because the holdover plate has a single circuit. That is doublespeak for "We didn't want to spend the extra five bucks on our holdover plates to install a separate circuit for the shore power option." The circulating refrigerant also carries the lubricating oil for the compressors, and due to the potential for the oil to migrate and leave one of the compressors without sufficient lubrication, two compressors should never be connected to the same circuit. If you are planning to operate your holdover-plate system from shore power as well, select a manufacturer that provides his holdover plates with the needed independent circuit. As for holdover plate efficiency, the 110-volt compressor circuit is typically a single loop of tubing having no noticeable impact on the capacity of the plate; this circuit is not as efficient as the main circuit, but with all the resources of the electric company at the other end of the power cord, that is not really a concern.

If you will be at the dock more than at sea, you might consider a system that approaches the shore-power problem from the opposite direction. Instead of being engine-driven, the compressor is belted to a 110-volt motor. Away from the dock, a special alternator supplies the power to run the motor when the engine is running.

ABSORPTION REFRIGERATION

There is yet another type of refrigeration that occasionally finds its way aboard boats. The ice cream vendors who ply their trade in the Tuileries Gardens in Paris push wheeled carts made distinctive by a large black ball on a pole sticking up above one corner. That ball is part of a refrigeration system that keeps the ice cream frozen solid even on sultry summer days, seemingly without any power source. When I first encountered this system many years ago, I immediately thought I had discovered the end-all solution to marine refrigeration. But things that appear too good to be true usually are.

The system is called absorption refrigeration, and what I discovered when I investigated further was that at the end of the day, the vendors prepared their carts for the next day by heating the ball over a flame for a couple of hours. My enthusiasm waned.

Absorption refrigeration uses ammonia rather than Freon as the refrigerant, and a heat source rather than a compressor puts the refrigerant in motion. Absorption refrigerators are built by a number of manufacturers for the RV trade. An LPG or kerosene flame usually provides the heat. Silent operation, virtually no power drain (safety sensors and perhaps a circulating fan), and no engine-running requirement are all seductive characteristics, but the danger of an unattended open flame aboard a boat cannot be ignored. And it isn't, not by insurance underwriters—most will not insure a boat with absorption refrigeration aboard.

Nor is the danger ignored by absorption refrigeration manufacturers. No U.S. manufacturer that I know of will knowingly sell his product for use aboard a sailboat. They sight the imperative of proper venting of the flame as one difficulty with marine installations. (Like a heater, an unvented refrigerator in a closed boat can be a killer.) And in order to function properly, the refrigerator (or at least the plumbing) must remain level, particularly unlikely aboard a sailboat—with the possible exception of a multihull.

In concept, absorption refrigeration has great appeal. Its advantages have been touted over the years by numerous cruising luminaries, including the almost legendary Eric Hiscock. But even Hiscock acknowledged the risk, and aboard the various *Wanderers,* the refrigerator was operated only in port, never while underway. I suspect a constant flame aboard is more palatable in the cold dampness of Hiscock's home waters around Great Britain than it would be in the already-oppressive heat of, say, Baja, California. That consideration aside, the potential for disaster of a surreptitiously installed RV refrigerator, improperly vented and casually monitored, leads me to only one possible conclusion: Forget about it!

PREPARING THE BOX

The success of any refrigeration system depends upon the box it is installed in. An efficient box is the key. In a great box, even a marginal refrigeration unit will shine. It is imperative that you test your box using the method outlined earlier and correct any deficiency before you even consider the refrigeration system you will install. Every pound of ice that melts represents about 3.4 Ah of electrical demand just to cool the box, not the contents. Even if a simple ice chest is adequate for your current needs and you do not plan to install refrigeration, improving the efficiency of the box will dramatically lengthen the amount of time the ice will last.

If the test block in your *stock* box (snicker) loses more than (snicker, snicker) 6 pounds (snort) in 24 hours (guffaw), you should suspect (shriek) that it has insufficient insulation (gasp!). You are more likely to have just enough ice left to chill a Scotch. Good idea. Now find a way to dismantle one side of the box and find out why the ice melted.

It is not uncommon for the factory ice box in an

older boat (new boats, too, for that matter) to have no insulation—zero, nada. If it is insulated, the insulating material is often fiberglass batting, okay for slowing the melting of a block of ice over a long weekend, but woefully inadequate for an efficient marine refrigeration installation. Corrective measures are required.

If you can get around the original box—all the way around it—and if there is room to insulate it with 4 to 6 inches of rigid polyurethane foam, and if it is top loading and not larger than the head, adding the insulation and properly sealing the lid may be all that is necessary to prepare the box for refrigeration. If not, which is more likely, plan on building a new box.

The first step is to determine the capacity of the box. It should be no larger than absolutely necessary. Do not be unduly influenced by the interior size of the original box; it was probably designed to hold 50 to 100 pounds of ice in addition to the food.

Unless you are planning on rearranging the accommodations, the size of the box is going to be determined by the space the existing box occupies. Measure the length, width, and depth of the space available. If the space lies against the curvature of the hull, your measurements should be for the largest cube that will fit into the space. These measurements are for the outside of the box.

To determine the inside measurements, subtract twice the thickness of the insulation from each of the dimensions. Begin with the assumption that your insulation will be 6 inches thick, so subtract 12 inches. Multiply the remaining length, width, and depth together to get the interior space in cubic inches, and divide that number by 1,728 (12 × 12 × 12) to determine the cubic feet of interior space your new box can have. You may be shocked by the results.

Suppose your existing cabinet is 28 inches long, 24 inches wide, and 30 inches deep. With 6 inches of insulation, the interior dimensions (making no allowances for wall thickness) would be 16 inches by 12 inches by 18 inches, or 3,456 cubic inches of interior space—exactly 2 cubic feet. Before you con-clude that this is absolutely, positively too small, let me share with you a simple truth about marine refrigeration: *you are a thousand times more likely to be dissatisfied because your box is too large than because it is too small.*

A judicious selection of cold foods and drinks adds immeasurably to the pleasures of being on the water, but such pleasures are diminished by dead batteries or listening to the engine for hours. All other things being equal, the larger the box, the more power and/or engine time required to keep it cold. If these are concerns, keep the box as small as possible.

Two cubic feet may be too small for an ice chest, since 50 pounds of ice will occupy almost half the space. But 2 cubic feet may be more than adequate for a refrigerator. Volume beyond what is required to contain the things that need refrigeration does not contribute to the convenience of refrigeration, only to inefficiency.

How do you determine if the properly insulated box that can be constructed in the space available on your boat is large enough? Try it. Mock up the compartment by modifying a cardboard carton, then fill the carton from your home refrigerator. Include only those items that you expect to have aboard. Maybe it will hold everything if it is absolutely full? Perfect. You don't want to be refrigerating air. By the way, you can put more than 10 six-packs in a single cubic foot of space. Not that that matters to *you*.

If you are planning on installing an engine-driven system, be sure you make allowances for the hold-over plates. They come in all shapes and sizes, but for preliminary estimates expect the plate to reduce the usable capacity by about 0.4 cubic foot.

So far, we have been focusing on refrigeration. Twelve-volt systems typically have a box-shaped evaporator, providing about 0.3 cubic foot of freezer space—enough to make a couple of trays of ice and to keep a pair of Porterhouse steaks and a package of chicken breasts frozen. A holdover plate system allows you to divide the box into refrigerator and freezer according to whatever ratio best suits your needs, or to have an entirely separate freezer. As with the refrigerator, you do not want any more freezer space than is necessary to contain the items you plan to carry.

The way refrigeration is used—to store fresh foods and perishables—means that, generally, refrigeration requirements are not related to how long you will be on the boat, but more to the variety of fresh foods you want on hand. A freezer compartment, on the other hand, relates directly to the length of time between supply ports. If long-term cruising is your objective, a freezer twice or three times the size of the refrigerator might be desirable—a dramatic departure from the Frigidaire at home in the kitchen.

BOX CONSTRUCTION

Exactly how you go about building a new box will depend upon the specifics of your boat, but there are some principles that will aid you in the construction.

Begin the job by sketching out the space available and calculating the size of the compartment after you make allowances for 6 inches of insulation. If the resulting box will be too small, you can reduce the thickness of the insulation to 4 inches, but not less than that. Even reducing it this much will add about 17 percent to your daily power consumption and/or engine time.

If one side of the box is defined by the hull, do not be tempted to let one corner of the liner approach the hull in order to increase the interior volume. Six inches of insulation all around means *all around*. You might shape the liner to the contour of the hull, but a more practical approach is to put a step in the liner, making the box shallower near the hull, deeper near the face of the cabinet.

A lot of older boats had front-opening iceboxes. A front opening is to be avoided if at all possible. Try this little experiment and you will see why. Fill a sink with cool water and two small glasses with ice-cold tea. Holding your hand over the top of each glass, submerge both and remove your hand, sitting one upright to simulate a top-opening refrigerator, and laying the other one on its side to simulate front

opening. The tea allows you to *see* what is happening. After 15 seconds, lift both glasses out of the sink and compare the color of the liquid in the glasses. If you still are not convinced, stick your finger in the one with color; it will still be cold.

When you open the door of a front-opening refrigerator, the cold air pours out. Occasionally someone suggests that the easier access of a front-opening box reduces the amount of time the door is open and may actually result in less heat intrusion than digging around for the horseradish from the top. To that I say horseradish! There is no appreciable difference in trying to find an item in the *bottom* of the box or in the *back* of it. But if the only option that does not involve a naval architect is a front opening box, do not despair. The negative aspect of front opening is minimized if the box is small and full. A piece of heavy, dodger-window plastic attached over the opening inside and cut into 2-inch strips (like fringe) can help to keep the cold in when you open the door. Reach through it for the items you need. I have happily (more or less) coexisted with a front-opening refrigerator and freezer for 18 years. Life is full of little compromises.

Assuming a top-opening box, begin by removing the top of the cabinet in which it will be installed, and extracting the old ice chest. Remove all traces of the old insulation and sheath all of the interior surfaces with a layer or two of fiberglass matting wetted out with epoxy resin. Next, buy a roll of heavy-duty aluminum foil—the thicker variety—and line the interior surfaces with it, including the hull, setting the foil in wet epoxy resin. Conventional wisdom is that the shiny side should face the source of the heat—the outside of the box. From the hardware store, buy a roll of 4-mil (or thicker) polyethylene sheeting and cover the foil with the plastic, again using epoxy resin as the adhesive. Overlap all seams at least one inch and leave a couple of inches at the top to provide overlap when the top of the cabinet is screwed into position. The foil acts as a heat reflector and the plastic sheeting provides a vapor-proof barrier.

The appropriate insulation is rigid polyurethane

foam, not styrofoam or any other less efficient insulation. Polyurethane foam is available either in sheets or as a two-part liquid. The density you want is 2-pound. Using the sheet foam is straightforward, but the liquid can be tricky. If your box is regular in shape, use sheet foam. You will usually find it in 4 × 8 sheets in either 1- or 2-inch thicknesses.

Cut the foam to size with a sabersaw, or a fine-toothed hand saw. Cut it *slightly* oversize so that all the joints are tight. Notch the foam to accommodate any cleats joining the sides of the cabinet.

Do not lay 6 inches of sheet foam in the bottom of the box, then insulate the sides. Heat leaks into your box are most likely to occur at the joints in the insulation, so you do not want straight butt joints making it easier. Lay one layer of foam in the bottom, then insulate the sides with one layer. Glue a second layer in the bottom, then a second layer on

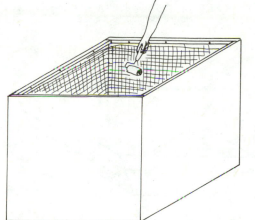

Sheath the interior surfaces of the cabinet with fiberglass wetted out with epoxy resin.

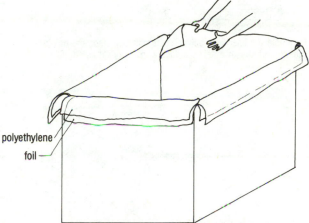

polyethylene

foil

Line the box with foil, then with 4-mil polyethylene sheeting. Set the foil and plastic in epoxy resin. Leave several inches at the top to overlap when the top is installed.

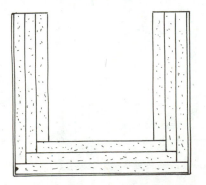

Insulate the box with 6 inches of polyurethane foam, alternating bottom and sides to achieve staggered joints.

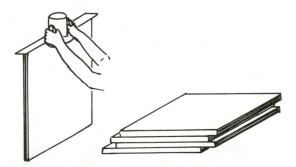

Cut the plywood pieces for the inner liner and cover one side and the top edge with plastic laminate.

Constructing an efficient box (continued on page 306)

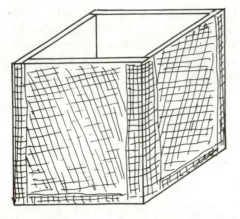

Assemble the liner with polyurethane adhesive. Tape the outside joints and sheath outside surface with epoxy-saturated glass.

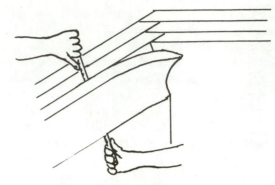

Mark the top of the box on the foam and carefully cut a bevel in the foam above the line.

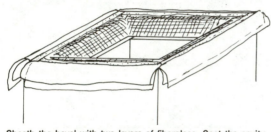

Sheath the bevel with two layers of fiberglass. Coat the cavity with epoxy and install the liner.

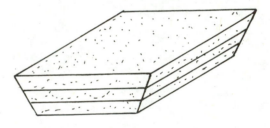

Build up a foam block and cut a beveled plug to fit the opening.

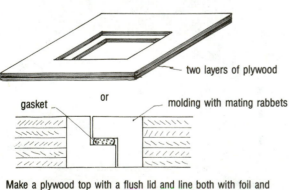

two layers of plywood

gasket   or   molding with mating rabbets

Make a plywood top with a flush lid and line both with foil and plastic. Glue the beveled block to the lid and sheath it with fiberglass.

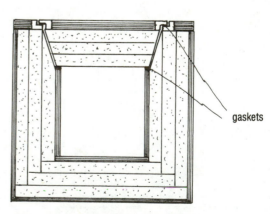

gaskets

Fold the extra foil and plastic over the foam and install the top. The lid should seat on dual gaskets.

Constructing an efficient box (continued)

the sides. Continue in the same sequence until the desired thickness has been achieved. This will result in all the corner joints being staggered. Have a can of aerosol insulation—that canned foam sold at hardware stores to insulate around door jambs—on hand to fill in any spaces in each of the joints as you proceed. Glue the foam sheeting in place with epoxy resin.

How you construct the liner will depend upon whether the box is an ice chest or a refrigerator, but the initial steps are the same. From ³/₈-inch plywood, cut the bottom and the four sides to build a box that fits tightly into the cavity formed by the insulation. The top edge of the sides should be 6 inches short of the top of the foam.

If you are constructing an ice chest, assemble the box, joining the parts with epoxy and holding them together with finishing nails until the glue dries. Next the exterior of the box, especially across all the joints, is sheathed with two layers of fiberglass cloth for strength. Then the interior is lined with two layers of mat and a layer of finishing cloth to make the interior of the box both durable and watertight. Use epoxy resin, not polyester; the epoxy is more flexible, making it less likely to crack when you drop a 50-pound block of ice onto it, and epoxy is less likely to flavor the food. To deal with the latter, after the liner is installed and the ice chest completed, pour 5 gallons of boiling water into the chest, close the lid, and let it sit for several hours. Paint the interior, preferably with two-part urethane.

For a refrigerator and/or freezer, plastic laminate (Formica) is better, yielding an attractive, long lasting, and easily cleaned surface. Choose a horizontal grade in a bright white. Cover the five pieces of plywood with laminate (one side only) before assembling the parts. Also cover one edge of each of the sides, the edge that will be at the top of the box. After the laminate has been applied and trimmed, assemble the pieces into the liner, this time joining them with polyurethane adhesive (3M #5200 or equivalent) instead of epoxy resin. Hold the parts together with finishing nails. Drag a damp finger along each of the joints inside the liner to shape the excess sealant

into smooth, watertight fillets. Trim away the excess outside the liner after the sealant cures.

The outside of the liner could sweat, resulting in some risk of rot. You don't want to do this again, so sheath the outside surfaces with a layer or two of epoxy-saturated mat. Strengthen the liner with two or three layers of 4- or 6-inch fiberglass tape over each of the joints.

After the resin kicks, tie two lengths of heavy fishing line (50-pound test) around the liner—under the bottom and across the top—and slip the liner into the insulation cavity to check for fit. Trace the top of the liner onto the insulation, then remove the liner. Now you know what the two lines are for.

Because the lid will be almost 7 inches thick and hinged on the top, the insulation has to be beveled for the lid to open or close. Even if you do not plan to hinge the lid—you will lift it—it should still be beveled. You should think of the lid more as a beveled plug than as a simple access hatch. To prepare the box for this plug, you need to bevel the insulation. That is where the line you just drew marking the top of the liner comes in. It marks the bottom of the bevel. Unless the lid is very small, a bevel of about 2 inches will be about right, so the first or second joint in the insulation (depending upon whether you use 1- or 2-inch foam) marks the top of the bevel. Using a hacksaw blade (without a handle) cut into the foam until the blade is exiting the top of the foam at the 2-inch joint line and exiting inside the cavity at the trace line. Carefully keeping the saw on both lines, cut a bevel all the way around the cavity.

To protect the foam, sheath the bevel with two layers of fiberglass cloth, carrying the cloth an inch or so beyond the bevel on the top of the insulation and the same distance into the cavity. Once the resin kicks, coat the interior of the cavity with epoxy resin and install the liner permanently.

The top of the box is usually ³/₄-inch plywood with a hole cut out for the lid; you may be able to use the original countertop. Sheath the underside of both the counter and the lid with foil and polyethylene sheeting. The cutout should be at least an inch larger all around than the top of the beveled opening in the foam.

There are any number of ways of making the hatch fit flush, beginning with cleats screwed to the underside of the counter and extending into the opening. A better method is to make the counter from two layers of plywood, and make the cutout in the bottom layer smaller. It is sometimes easier to fit and trim the lid at the same time by cutting a 3/8-inch by 7/16-inch rabbet in a length of 3/4-inch teak or mahogany square stock. The opening is framed with the rabbet up and the lid with the rabbet down, providing the mating surfaces for a flush fit. The extra depth of the rabbet (7/16 inch instead of 3/8 inch) is to allow for an 1/8-inch rubber gasket. If you go this route, apply and trim any laminate that you intend to use *before* you tack and glue the lip trim in place. And don't forget to install a lift ring before it is time to see how snug the fit is.

Fold the extra foil and plastic from the sides over the foam and install the countertop. With the top on and a lid that fits and seats on a rubber gasket—closed-cell, adhesive backed weatherstripping makes an adequate gasket—all that remains is to insulate the lid and provide it with a second, inner seal. Begin gluing together pieces of foam to make a 6-inch-thick block slightly larger than the beveled opening. Next tape scraps of plastic laminate to the bevel to simulate clearance (the foam "plug" is also going to be sheathed with fiberglass), and tape 1/8-inch-thick strips of wood or hardboard on the top edges of the liner to provide allowance for the second seal.

Measure the widest part of the beveled opening and draw the opening on one side of the foam block. Measure the narrowest part of the opening and duplicate it on the other side of the foam block, taking care to align the two rectangles. With your hacksaw blade, cut along both outlines simultaneously. The plug that results should match the beveled opening. Sand and trim the plug until it seems to fit flush and does not prevent the lid from seating properly. With the foam plug in place, coat the top of it with epoxy resin, put the lid in place on the

plug, and take a break. When the resin hardens, the plug should come up with the lid.

Almost finished! Sheath the plug with a layer or two of fiberglass, extending the cloth out onto the plywood lid. Remove all the spacers and stick weatherstripping tape to the top edge of the liner. It is imperative that the lid have two gaskets, or it will leak heat; sweating is a sure sign that your gaskets are not sealing properly. If you have done everything correctly, the lid should close with a satisfying *woosh*.

If the lid will be large, it may be advantageous to hinge it in the middle so that only one half needs to be opened at a time, yet the whole lid can be removed when necessary. A split lid should be joined with piano hinge and have dual gaskets between the two halves to prevent heat leak when the lids are closed. If, despite my authoritative and irrefutable warnings, you are constructing a big box, you will not want to lift off the entire top. In this case, build the liner with a sixth side, cutting an adequate access hole in the top. Insulate the top around the hole, tapering the insulation to accommodate the lid.

If the shape of your box dictates the use of poured foam, the process differs only slightly. The liner has to be built first and suspended in the center of the cabinet with temporary framing until the foam has been poured around the bottom and part way up the sides. Then remove the framing to prevent it from compromising the insulating qualities of the foam.

Two-part foam begins life innocently enough as a couple of syrupy liquids which you mix together with a drill-powered paint mixer. It lets you know it is ready by changing color temporarily. When the *flash* occurs, it is time to pour the foam, and you don't have any time to waste. Like some creature from a fifties horror movie, the foam bubbles and fumes, giving off a foul odor and expanding rapidly and with tremendous force. If you pour too much at once, it is easily capable of turning your neat cubic box into an angular ball. Large pours are also subject to efficiency-robbing voids in the insulation, especially in corners. You should begin by mixing a very small batch and doing a bit of hands-on experimenting. Even after you get the hang of it, you will be wise to limit the quantity of each pour to no more than a pint. Horror stories abound, so go slowly.

If only one side of the cavity is irregular, for example a box next to the hull, there is no reason that you cannot insulate with sheet foam—which has slightly better insulating qualities— and use the liquid only to fill the one side. After it cures, poured foam can be cut and shaped just like the sheet variety.

Stainless steel is sometimes used in box construction, and it makes an attractive and easy-to-clean liner, albeit an expensive one. However, as opposed to being an efficient insulator, metal is an efficient *conductor* of heat. The negative effects of that property are minimized if the liner is totally insulated from the outside, but steel liners are usually part of a steel counter or a stainless front surface, often with a matching stainless steel lid or door. Not good. The steel is pumping heat from your cabin right into the box. It is best to avoid metal altogether in icebox construction.

If your box will be used as an ice chest, it will need a drain in the lowest corner. The drain should be large enough not to clog instantly—not smaller than $1/2$ inch in inside diameter—and installed in such a way that it is unlikely to leak. A straight length of PVC pipe epoxied into a drilled hole will work, but there may be a tendency for the joint to crack, allowing water into the insulation. A better choice is a *flush-mount* plastic through-hull fitting carefully bedded in polyurethane sealant before the liner is installed. Fit the hose to the barb and thread it through the hole in the insulation as the liner is glued in place. Use quality PVC hose because hose replacement will be very difficult.

The drain line cannot be straight or the cold will pour out along with the melted ice. A water trap is essential. If you are using poured foam, it is a simple matter to bend the hose into a reclining S before pouring the foam. Water stands in the trap, preventing cold air from falling out of the box. It is more

difficult to form the trap inside the insulation when you are using sheet foam, and most amateur builders opt to put the loop in the line after it exits the insulation. This represents some loss in efficiency since it provides a direct path to the outside of the box, insulated only by the thickness of the hose. If the trap is outside of the box, insulating the line to the trap has merit.

The only effective way to prevent a drain from allowing some of the cold to escape from the box is not to have one. Refrigerators and freezers should *not* have drain lines—period. Spills may be more difficult to clean up, but you really don't want the spilled milk running into the trap anyway. Trust me. Perhaps a drain seems like a good idea so that you can put ice in the box in case the refrigeration packs in. If the box is well insulated, the ice is only going to melt to the tune of about 2 quarts per day—a couple of good slurps with the bilge pump for the dinghy. A teak grating in the bottom of the box to keep everything from sliding around on the liner— and just because it looks great—will also, in an emergency, keep the ice from sitting in the water. No drain!

REFRIGERATOR/FREEZER

Beyond a small compartment, as mentioned earlier, you are unlikely to have much of a freezer with a 12-volt system—certainly not large enough to justify a separate box. A marine freezer is almost invariably chilled by holdover plates connected to an engine-driven compressor.

There are numerous ways to configure a refrigerator and freezer, beginning with a single compartment with the plate in the bottom. Frozen items are kept on the plate, unfrozen items are placed on a shelf or in a basket in the "warmer" air near the top of the box. But a single compartment usually results in the unwanted thawing of frozen items, and the equally undesirable freezing of fresh items.

The best configuration is dual compartments in the same insulated cabinet, each compartment insulated from the other with 2 inches of foam. One or more holding plates in the freezer compartment maintains the temperature below zero. (Don't forget that holding plates intended for a freezer are designed to freeze at least 20 degrees colder and as much as 50 degrees colder than a plate intended to provide refrigeration and two trays of ice.) With an adjacent freezer, no holding plate is required in the refrigerator. Two 2-inch holes are bored between the two compartments and a tiny thermostatically controlled fan is installed in one of the holes. When the refrigerator warms up above the set temperature, the thermostat turns on the fan, bringing cold air into the refrigerator; the circulation through the second hole makes the exchange more efficient. When the refrigerator is cold enough, the fan shuts off. The cold removed from the freezer is replaced the next time the engine runs.

INSTALLING THE HARDWARE

Not that long ago, almost all onboard refrigerators were custom-built. For those so inclined, it is still possible to assemble a completely satisfactory engine driven system from scratch, using an automotive air-conditioning compressor, standard controls from a local refrigeration supply house, and a home-constructed holdover plate. But today the broad array of professionally engineered and manufactured marine refrigeration systems makes the do-it-yourself alternative less attractive, particularly if your prior experience with refrigeration is limited to Coors Light. Most of us determine what type of system best satisfies our requirements, then shop around for what we believe to be the best system of that type. If you buy a complete system, it will come with comprehensive installation instructions, and the manufacturer will have support personnel familiar with your system only a telephone call away. In fact, buying a system from some manufacturers is almost like joining a club. If your sailing plans will take you beyond the horizon, that could be a prime consideration.

It seems to me a waste of printer's ink to detail here a typical installation, but an understanding of the relationship of the various components might be helpful in your decision to tackle the installation yourself, or leave it to someone with experience.

The easiest installation is the 12-volt system epitomized by Adler-Barbour's ubiquitous ColdMachine. These systems typically have only three parts, come precharged, and can be installed by an average boat owner or an above-average baboon in an afternoon. The most difficult part is finding the right location for the compressor unit so that it gets adequate circulation of *cool* air. You mount the evaporator unit inside your just-reconstructed box with four screws, along with the thermostat.

Connecting the system is no more difficult than mounting it. Inside the box, uncoil the capillary tubing from the thermostat and clamp it to a special bracket on the evaporator. Route the two refrigerant tubes and a wire through a hole in the box (reinsulate and seal holes where wires and lines pass through the walls) from the thermostat to the compressor. Plug the wire into a socket at the compressor and screw the refrigeration tubes to couplings in a manner similar to the way you attach a hose to your dockside faucet. Tightening the couplings opens internal poppet valves, allowing the charge of refrigerant to circulate. Make electrical connections—properly fused and with a switch in the hot side—to the battery. Click. Whirr.

The installation of an engine-driven system is somewhat more challenging. A system typically comes in about a half a dozen major pieces, plus hoses, tubes, special fittings, and—most distressing of all—several cans of R-12 refrigerant (Freon). Good news, Skipper. It looks a lot more complicated than it is.

The first challenge is finding a way to mount the compressor. It should be hung on the engine—like the alternator—but finding a mounting spot on some engines can be nearly impossible. The system manufacturer may offer brackets for the most popular engines, or a "universal" (would that it were only true) bracket, but if your engine is not among the chosen, you will have to have a special bracket fabricated. And even if the furnished bracket fits, there still may not be room in your engine compartment to mount the compressor *that* way.

Although not recommended, it is possible to mount the compressor off the engine—bolted to the engine bed, for example. There is some risk to the crankshaft bearings and the compressor bearings from the side loading caused by the independent motion of the engine, but it is minimal since the engine actually moves *around* the crankshaft; at the crankshaft pulley where the compressor drive belt will attach, the engine is essentially motion free. Unfortunately, when the compressor is rigidly mounted to the hull, it tends to introduce vibrations when the refrigeration system is running, particularly if the compressor is a reciprocal type. Swash-plate compressors are much smoother and better suited to off-engine mounting.

Reciprocal compressors are the big, square ones that look like lawn mower engines. Almost all are made by either Tecumseh or York. The cast-iron Tecumseh compressor (Yorks are almost identical but made of aluminum) has proven to be an incredibly durable unit in the hostile environment of a boat engine compartment. Swash-plate compressors are the round ones, not much larger than an alternator. They now dominate auto air-conditioning and a swash-plate compressor made by Sankyo is usually the "standard" compressor with most commercially available marine refrigeration systems.

Swash-plate compressors are smoother, lighter, cheaper, and more compact than reciprocal compressors, but they also have a higher incidence of failure. Because they do not have an internal oil supply, swash-plate compressors are entirely dependent upon oil circulating with the refrigerant for lubrication. If the refrigerant leaks out of the system and the compressor runs, damage is likely. In a freezer installation, the compressor may pull the system into a deep vacuum, resulting in reduced refrigerant circulation and correspondingly less lubrication. A low-pressure cutout switch will protect a swash-plate compressor from damage due to lost refrigerant (such a switch is a good idea regardless of the compressor type), but for a freezer instal-

lation, a reciprocal compressor is a better choice.

Once the compressor is mounted and belted to the engine, giving attention to pulley size and belt tensioning, the next step is to mount the water-cooled condenser. Water-cooled condensers come in numerous forms, but the principle is always the same: raw water flows over a coil carrying the refrigerant. Installation requires only mounting the condenser to a convenient bulkhead. Typically, the cooling water is supplied by cutting the hose from the inlet strainer to the raw-water pump on the engine and clamping the two cut ends to the hose fittings on the condenser. Refrigeration line connections wait until all the components are mounted.

Mounting is similarly easy for the receiver/filter/drier (RFD), a round canister that serves as a reservoir for surplus refrigerant, filters out any foreign particles, and removes any moisture from the refrigerant. A sight glass—a tiny window to monitor the flow of the refrigerant—is an essential feature of the RFD. All driers are similar, but Grunert's inclusion of isolating valves on the drier to allow drier replacement with minimal refrigerant loss is worthy of special note. Convenience aside, this is an environmentally conscious feature that you should demand from whatever manufacturer you select. Refrigerant—R-12 or R-22—belongs to a class of chemicals known as chlorofluorocarbons, or CFCs, and scientists now tell us that CFCs released into the atmosphere are damaging the protective ozone layer. The release of some refrigerant into the atmosphere is an unavoidable consequence of servicing marine refrigeration, but it can be significantly reduced with RFD isolating valves.

Mount the holdover plate (or plates) inside the box, typically with four screws. An expansion valve, which controls the flow of refrigerant through the plate, may already be mounted to the plate; otherwise, thread it to the inlet fitting of the plate. Clamp the sensing bulb—attached to the valve by a thin, flexible capillary tube—to the plate's outlet tubing. Some systems use special self-contained expansion valve units that mount on the *outer* wall of the box.

An expansion valve eliminates the need for a

thermostat, although some systems also include one. An externally mounted timer switch is now more common. As mentioned earlier, the inclusion of a low-pressure switch in the system drastically reduces the risk of compressor damage in the event of refrigerant loss, and it will also shut the system down when the expansion valve has sensed that the plate is frozen and has restricted the flow of refrigerant. The low pressure switch is often combined with a high-pressure switch to shut the system down in the event of pressure-raising blockage. A high-temperature switch (sensing compressor temperature) may also be included. All of these switches are simply wired in series in the hot wire between the electric clutch on the compressor and the power source.

Making Connections

Once the various components are mounted, they must also be connected. The manufacturer may supply refrigeration hoses with special end fittings, or they may supply a coil of copper tubing and the fittings to fit that. Both hose and tubing are satisfactory. Hose is generally superior for connections to the compressor because it is immune to vibration while the tubing may work-harden and crack. For all other connections, tubing is usually preferred.

Hoses will normally be supplied "made up," that is, with factory installed end fittings. If you are doing your own refrigeration system from scratch, barbed hose fittings and special hose clamps are available from refrigeration suppliers. For those on a tight budget, when you buy the compressor from the junkyard (old Ford products used Tecumseh and York compressors), take all the hose—with the fittings—that you can get. Even if you shorten the hose, snip away the ferrule and you can reattach the end fitting using a hose clamp. It isn't pretty, but it's cheap.

By the way, when you are removing the compressor and the hose, if the system doesn't hiss when you crack the fittings, find another one; when all the refrigerant has leaked out, that means that moisture has probably leaked in. Clean the fittings before you open them, and immediately seal them with tape to keep out moisture. Take the mounting bracket and the idler pulley with the compressor, but leave the drier; you need a fresh one.

Copper tubing is attached with either compression fittings or flare fittings. A square-cut end is essential for either and is easily achieved with a good-quality tubing cutter. To use a tubing cutter, place the tube in the V formed by the two rollers and turn the knob until the cutting wheel *just* touches the tube, clamping the cutter in position. Rotate the cutter around the tube, then give the knob a quarter turn and rotate the cutter again. Continue tightening the cutter a quarter turn at a time until the cut is complete. If you try to hurry the process by tightening the cutter too quickly, you will cause a ridge on the inside of the tube. The cutter usually has a V-shaped blade for reaming the inside of the cut, but the possibility of introducing copper chips into the system makes reaming refrigeration tubing risky. Reaming is essential for a tube that will be flared, but skip this step for a compression fitting.

Compression fittings are the easiest to make, and the double ferrule type (Swagelok) are especially leakproof. Slip the nut over the end of the tubing, followed by the compression ferrule—or both ferrules in the case of a double-ferrule fitting. Insert the tubing into the recess in the fitting body until it rests firmly on the shoulder in the recess, slide the ferrule and nut to the fitting, and tighten the nut. Tightening compresses the ring around the tubing, forming the seal.

Good flare fittings begin with a good flare tool, not one from Woolworth's 99-cent counter. Before flaring the tube, slip a long-nosed flare nut over it, then place the tube in the clamp block with the end protruding by a third of the depth of the bevel (more for larger tubes) and tighten the wingnuts on the clamp. Put a little refrigeration oil on the cone and position it over the end of the tube. To form the flare, screw the cone down into the tube, but not too tightly. If you have done it correctly, the flare should be round and even, and it should just fit inside the nut. If the flare distorts or cracks, cut it off and try it

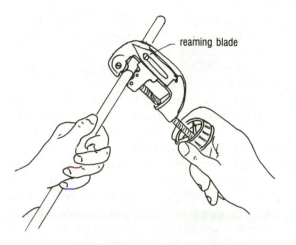

Always cut with a tubing cutter.

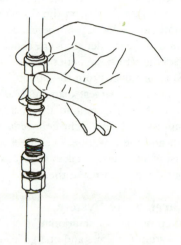

Assembling a double-ferrule (Swagelok) connection. Snug, then tighten 1¼ turn.

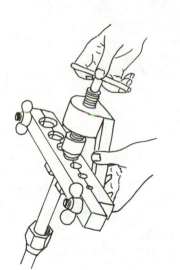

Flare fittings require a *good* flaring tool. Ream the inside lip before flaring, taking care not to leave shavings in the tube.

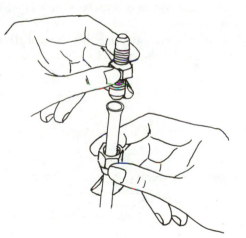

Assembling a flare connection.

Tubing connections

again, this time heating the copper with a lighter first to make it more malleable. Assembling the fitting requires only that you seat the flare and tighten the nut.

Solder fittings are also possible if you have expe-rience with sweat fittings, but on the plumbing for your expensive refrigeration system is not the best place to learn by your mistakes.

The manufacturer will provide specific instruc-tions for which line connects to which fitting, but the sequence of the connections follows a regular pattern. A line connects the discharge side of the compressor to the top of the condenser. From the bottom of the condenser, a line connects to the inlet side of the RFD; the outlet side is connected to the expansion valve. From the outlet side of the hold-over plate, the largest diameter line in the system returns the refrigerant to the suction side of the compressor. That's eight connections if I counted right, and there will be a couple more if you have pressure switches. It takes almost as long to write about them as to make them.

Charging the System

Getting an air-conditioning technician to check the system for leaks and charge it initially is not a bad idea, but if you are going to have engine-driven refrigeration aboard and you are going to depend upon it, you better learn how to put refrigerant into the system and how to determine when it contains the right amount.

A set of refrigeration gauges is *not* essential, but for 30 or 40 bucks, they can tell you what is happening inside the system if trouble develops. And the valves that are part of the manifold make charging somewhat easier. You do need a refrigerant can tap and one charging hose. (For the gauge set, three hoses are required.)

Buy your refrigerant in 14-ounce cans from your local discount store. A can will cost less than $2, under a buck on sale, and cans are much easier for the amateur to use than bulk tanks. Wipe the top of the can before slipping the tap in place and moving the lever that clamps it to the top of the can. Screw the valve body down until the rubber gasket at the bottom is tightly in contact with the can, but don't screw it down so tightly that you distort the top. Now turn the tee-handle clockwise until it stops, piercing the top of the can with the needle inside the valve and simultaneously closing the valve. If any hissing comes from the tap/can connection, tighten the valve *body* slightly to stop it. Connect a service hose to the tap, making the end with the metal piece in the center the free end.

Your compressor will have either Schrader or Rotolock service valves, and they will be marked

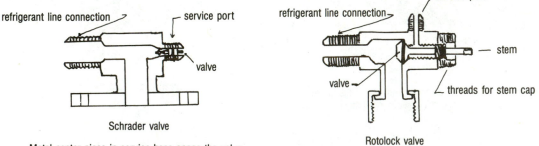

Schrader valve

Metal center piece in service hose opens the valve.

Rotolock valve

Shown in the "back seat" position—service port is closed. Turning the stem allows both ports to be open (mid-position) or the compressor to be isolated from the line (front seat).

Service valves

SUCTION and DISCHARGE. Schrader valves are easy to identify because they have a single cap, while Rotolock valves have two caps—a large one covering a square valve stem and a small one sealing the port. Schrader valves are spring-loaded, exactly like tire valves, and you can remove the cap without losing the refrigerant charge, but if you remove the small cap on a Rotolock valve without first turning the square stem fully *counterclockwise* to close the service port, you will blow the entire charge. The valve would normally be in this "back-seat" position except during servicing, but some systems tee-connect the pressure switches to the service port, necessitating that the valve be open during normal operation. Be sure you know which kind of valves you have before you start adding refrigerant.

Prepare for charging a system with Rotolock service valves by removing the large cap covering the square stem on the valve marked SUCTION and turning the stem fully counterclockwise; do *not* turn the valve fully clockwise—the "front-seat" position—as this closes the suction line. With the valve back-seated, remove the cap on the service port. If you have Schrader valves, removal of the cap is all that is required. Be sure you are opening the SUCTION port; if you connect the can to the wrong port the high pressure can actually blow the can apart—giving you quite a surprise! Attach the service hose to the SUCTION port, but just turn it about two threads. You need to purge the hose before you tighten it.

Open the valve on the tap and refrigerant should begin to hiss out around the loose connection. The refrigerant is non-toxic and will not hurt you (I cannot say the same for its effect on coming generations), but it can freeze your skin so exercise some caution. Open the valve a couple of turns so the hose is pressurized and the R-12 is escaping vigorously, then tighten the hose-to-port connection to stop the leak. All the air and moisture will have been expelled from the hose. If you have Schrader valves, tightening the connection (be sure the end of the hose on the valve is the one with the metal center) depresses the valve pin and you are now putting refrigerant into the system. Close the valve on the tap to stop the flow. Rotolock valves do not admit refrigerant until you turn the stem about one full turn clockwise. Use a 1/4-inch open-end wrench on the stem, or buy a special square ratchet wrench for your tool box.

Leak test a new system by putting about half a can of refrigerant into it. Open the valve on the can, and the Rotolock valve if you have one, and invert the can until it is about half empty. *The only time you should ever charge the system with the can inverted is when the compressor is not running.* If liquid refrigerant enters the compressor while it is running, the compressor will be damaged. With half a can of refrigerant in the system, close the valves and check all of your connections for leaks. Big leaks can be located by soaping all the fittings with a 50-50 mixture of dishwashing liquid and water and watching carefully for bubbles, but this is rather crude and not terribly sensitive. The best detector for the amateur is a halide torch, a special fitting for a standard propane torch that reacts to the presence of refrigerant with a color change in the flame. A pick-up hose allows you to pinpoint the point of the leak. A halide detector is sensitive and cheap (about $25). If you find a leak, it can usually be stopped by tightening the fitting.

Before the system can be fully charged for the first time, it must be evacuated. This takes a special vacuum pump which is probably too expensive to purchase, but you may be able to rent or borrow one. If not, hire this job done.

The technician will have refrigeration gauges, and so should you. The blue gauge measures the low-pressure side of the system and the blue hose from the fitting on that side of the manifold is always connected to the SUCTION side of the compressor. The red gauge measures high pressure, and the red hose connects to the DISCHARGE side of the compressor. It is not necessary to connect the red hose for evacuating or charging the system; it is used for more advanced troubleshooting than we have room to get into here. The center hose of the manifold is normally connected to the refrigerant

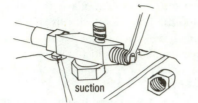

Remove the stem cap and back-seat the valve by turning it counterclockwise.

Clamp the tap to the refrigerant can and screw the body down to seat the gasket. Turn the T-handle to pierce the can.

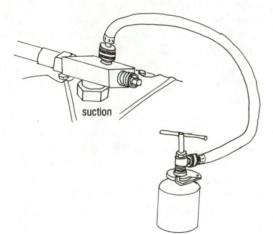

Remove the service port cap and connect the service hose to the port and to the can tap.

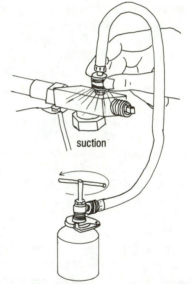

Turn the T-handle counterclockwise to let refrigerant into the hose. *Loosen* the service port connection, allowing gas to escape vigorously and purging the hose of air. Tighten the connection.

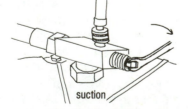

Open the service valve by turning the stem 1½ turns clockwise. Start the system. Refrigerant is being added. Caution: Keep the refrigerant can upright.

Watch the sight glass on the dryer. When it runs clear the system is full. Shut down, back-seat the valve, close the tap, disconnect the service hose and replace both caps. Cool!

Foam indicates low charge.

Stationary bubbles are normal.

Clear may indicate empty or full. Look closely to see the liquid refrigerant flowing.

Adding refrigerant

supply, but for evacuation it is connected to the vacuum pump. The two valves on the manifold connect the center hose to each corresponding side. The gauges read the system pressures regardless of the position (open or closed) of the valves.

With the blue hose connected to the SUCTION port (and the Rotolock valve open, if applicable) and the center hose of the manifold unconnected, crack the valve on the low-pressure (blue) side of the manifold to let the refrigerant in the system escape. You want to let it escape slowly so that it does not carry any refrigeration oil with it, although a little oil loss is unavoidable. When the hissing stops and the gauge reads zero, close the (blue) valve on the manifold, connect the center hose to the vacuum pump, start the pump (make sure the pump's exhaust port is not capped), and slowly reopen the same valve all the way. The blue gauge should indicate a vacuum of more than 20 inches of mercury within about ten minutes. Depending on the capacity of the pump, pulling the deepest vacuum will take 15 to 30 minutes. If the system does not leak, the vacuum should approach 29 inches.

After the pump runs for 30 minutes, close the valve first, then turn off the pump. Observe the vacuum gauge for the next 15 minutes; it should not lose more than 1 inch every five minutes, or you have an undetected leak in the system that you will need to find and correct.

With the system evacuated and holding vacuum, tap a can of refrigerant (you can start with the half of a can that you have left from leak testing) and connect the tap to the center hose on the manifold. Open the valve on the tap, then purge the center hose by loosening its connection at the manifold, letting air and refrigerant escape for a few seconds. Tighten the fitting. Open the (blue) valve on the manifold and the R-12 will flow into the evacuated system. Invert the can and hold it above the compressor to hasten this initial charge. When you have about half a can of refrigerant in the system again, close the manifold valve.

If the can is empty, you can change cans without the need to again purge the supply hose by closing the tap valve until it stops. Now unscrew the valve body. Since the needle is protruding beyond the

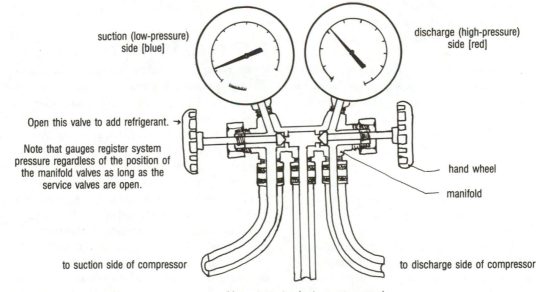

suction (low-pressure) side [blue]

discharge (high-pressure) side [red]

Open this valve to add refrigerant. →

Note that gauges register system pressure regardless of the position of the manifold valves as long as the service valves are open.

hand wheel

manifold

to suction side of compressor

to discharge side of compressor

to refrigerant can tap (or to vacuum pump)

Refrigeration gauges

gasket, be sure to unscrew the body until the *needle* clears the top of the can, then unclamp the tap. Clamp it onto a new can and screw the body down until the gasket seals the connection. The needle will pierce the can before the gasket touches the top, but the needle will seal its own hole. After the gasket seats, open the tap valve several turns. If you seat the gasket first, then pierce the can, you will have opened the center hose to the atmosphere and it will have to be purged. More bad news for the ozone layer.

Start the engine and set it to about 1,200 rpm. Turn on the compressor, then open the valve on the manifold to let more refrigerant into the system. From here on, keep the can upright so that the added refrigerant enters in a gas state. Warming the can with your hands will hasten the transfer. (When a venting can is no longer cold, it is empty.) Within a minute or two, the gauge should read about 30 psi and be slowly decreasing. When the holdover plate gets very cold, the gauge will dip into a slight vacuum.

If you have the high-side gauge connected, it may start at over 200 psi, but after a minute or two it should read between 150 and 180 psi and also be decreasing. If the high side reading exceeds 300 psi, shut the system down and make sure there is a water flow through the condenser.

You determine how much R-12 to put into the system by reading the sight glass. Initially it will be full of foam, but as the amount of refrigerant in the system increases, the sight glass will become clear. Watch the glass carefully, and as soon as it clears, add only an additional 1/4 of a can of refrigerant to the system, then close the valve on the manifold. Do not add any more refrigerant than this; overcharging will result in damage to the system. If the red gauge climbs over 200 psi, you have almost certainly overcharged the system.

Once the system is properly charged and the manifold valves closed, back-seat (by turning counterclockwise) the Rotolock valve and remove the service hose. With Schrader valves, just remove the hose. If you also have a service hose on the high-pressure side, shut the system down and wait a few minutes for pressures to equalize before removing it. Cap the service ports and the (Rotolock) valve stems. If the pressure switches are connected through the service ports of your Rotolock valves, turn the valve shafts about a turn and a half clockwise before capping the stems.

The sight glass will tell you the status of the charge during operation as well. Engine-driven compressors often leak a little around the shaft seals, necessitating the occasional addition of refrigerant—like adding water to your batteries. As we've seen, some foaming in the sight glass when the system is first turned on is normal, but after the system has been running for several minutes, the foam should be replaced with a clear stream of liquid refrigerant. The liquid may have a few stationary bubbles, but these do not indicate a low charge. If you don't see any bubbles at all, right from the start, the system could be empty instead of full. Be careful. An absence of refrigerant will damage a swashplate compressor very quickly. If the glass is filled with foam and does not clear up, add refrigerant until it does clear, then add an additional 1/4 of a can. Then add a six-pack.

THE COLD TRUTH

Refrigeration does add to the complexity of a boat, although perhaps less than you initially imagined, but I cannot imagine cruising without refrigeration. There is no sweeter symphony to my ear than the susurration of wavelets running along the beach of a deserted cove mixed with the ringing of ice cubes in slender glasses. But every year, particularly in southern waters, we encounter sailors that have spent hundreds, sometimes thousands, of dollars to equip their boats with refrigeration only to be bitterly disappointed with the performance. The truth is that electric refrigeration is going to use close to 100 Ah per day in the tropics. The acceptability of that will depend upon your ability to replace that current drain. And an engine-driven system is going to obligate you to running the engine for an hour or more *every* day. Day in and day out. Are you and your engine up to that?

If you are planning to install refrigeration, you can easily determine what to expect from it by testing your box honestly. If the results of your calculations are unacceptable, there is little point in "hoping" that it won't actually be that bad. It will be, so you either will have to spend the time and money the solutions require, or do without. It's a cold world.

FOURTEEN

Brush and Roller

*Painting, n. The art of protecting flat surfaces
from the weather and exposing them to the critic.*
–AMBROSE BIERCE–

Some years ago, I shared a seawall with an old Pearson with a chalky blue hull. The gloss had long since disappeared from the hull of my own boat, but next to this partly cloudy Pearson my boat still looked good. Then one weekend I arrived to find the Pearson in a cradle on shore, her owner sanding away on the hull. The next time I saw the boat, the hull looked as though it was coated with blue mercury. The paint was a new product, something called Awlgrip, and never had I seen such a beautiful finish. In a week, this old boat had been transformed from scratched glass to polished diamond. I never looked at my own hull through the same eyes again.

Nothing has a more immediate impact on the way a boat looks than putting a mirror finish on the hull. Thanks to space age technology, doing just that is within the capability of almost any boat owner. But before you take on refinishing the hull, you need to develop, at the very least, a certain rapport with a brush, sandpaper literacy, and an adequate grasp of the essentials of surface preparation.

PAINTING 101

The place to start any painting project is an inconspicuous spot. How about the inside of a locker? Most old boats can benefit from a coat of paint in the lockers. And most boat owners can benefit from a painting project where runs and brush marks will be of little consequence. You are more interested in the locker being clean, and in some cases in protecting the raw fiberglass, than in a flawless finish.

You can paint the inside of the lockers on your old boat with two-part polyurethane (Awlgrip and similar) if you want to, but except as an exercise in applying this kind of paint, it is not a very good idea. Aside from the expense, success with polyurethane requires meticulous preparation. Save this effort for surfaces that show.

The paint of choice for lockers, and for most other interior surface applications, is *alkyd enamel*. Alkyd enamel is quite durable, it is less sensitive to temperature and humidity, it does not require strong solvents, it goes on easily and has good flow characteristics (i.e., brush strokes tend to disappear), and minimal preparation is required. Additives such as silicone and acrylic may improve gloss retention and color.

Choosing from among the hundreds of different brands and formulas of alkyd enamel can be intimidating, but it need not be. Trot down to your local paint store—I am talking house paint here—and ask them for a gallon of their best alkyd enamel. House paint? Absolutely. Marine enamels are formulated for maximum gloss retention despite the effects of sun, salt and weather. Gloss is not a high priority inside a locker; in fact, a semi-gloss or low lustre paint will look good longer. And presumably the surface will have minimal exposure to sun, salt and weather. Wall enamel, on the other hand, is typically formulated for toughness and washability—just what you want in the bottom of a locker.

There are two other advantages to choosing wall paint. Alkyd enamel, regardless of the actual composition, will cost about twice as much if the can has a picture of a boat on it. I find that I am about twice as likely to apply a generous second coat when the paint costs $20 a gallon rather than $40 a gallon.

The second advantage is color selection. Topside enamels tend to be available in white, black, several shades of blue, and perhaps a dark green and a strident red; the manufacturer may offer more colors, but few retailers stock them. The neighborhood paint store, meanwhile, stocks a broad array of soft colors suitable for interior decor and can mix almost any color while you wait.

Color is a matter of personal preference, but lockers almost always benefit from light colors. Settee lockers and the space inside the galley cabinet tend to look best when they are painted bright white. The white imparts a clean look and makes the locker look larger, but the biggest advantage is that the white brightens the locker, making dark lockers less so.

For some reason, painting the inside of cockpit lockers and lazarettes a pastel shade rather than white seems to update an older boat, and the pastels are almost as effective as white at brightening the locker. Whether you choose powder blue, butter yellow, mist green, or heather pink, the touch of color adds a bit of unexpected gaiety every time the locker is opened. To make the most of this effect, the underside of the hatch should be painted the same color as the locker.

In addition to a gallon of pastel alkyd enamel, pick up a gallon of mineral spirits—it is much cheaper by the gallon—and a quart of acetone. You also need a brush, a roller and a tray, and a few sheets of sandpaper.

BRUSH BASICS

I have heard the virtues of synthetic brushes extolled, but I have never used a synthetic brush that I liked. Conversely, I have rarely been disappointed with the performance of a natural bristle brush, even the cheap, throwaway variety. Most natural bristle brushes are made from hog bristle and are called China (or Chinese) bristle because China is the principle hog bristle supplier. Ox and camel hair are also used in better quality brushes, and the finest brushes are made of badger bristle.

What makes natural brushes superior is split ends. This splitting or "flagging" on the ends of the bristle works like the split tip of a drawing pen, allowing the bristle—and the brush—to hold more paint and to give it up more uniformly. The natural taper of the bristle also serves to give the brush a lighter touch at the tip. Toward this end, better brushes are also trimmed to a point—called a chisel trim. Less expensive brushes are straight at the tip, or only slightly rounded.

The best quality brush is not always the best brush for a given job. For example, to paint the inside of a locker, an inexpensive natural bristle throwaway brush is preferred over an expensive ox or badger brush because the expensive brush has to be cleaned. Cleaning a brush thoroughly is a time-consuming and messy job and requires quite a bit of solvent. Aside from the cost of the solvent, there is the question of how to responsibly dispose of it. Actually, if you allow the used thinner to sit undisturbed (in a sealed container to retard evaporation) for a couple of days, the paint will settle to the bottom and most of the thinner can be carefully poured off to be reused for brush cleaning. But few people seem inclined to go to this trouble to reuse thinner, and tossing the brush when you are finished is infinitely easier. Sending a brush to the landfill seems to me more environmentally conscientious than dumping a pint of used thinner behind the shed. And for the inside of a locker, a throwaway brush is entirely adequate. You will probably find a 2½- or 3-inch width about right.

If the locker is large, a more appropriate method of applying the paint is with a roller. Like brushes, roller covers come in a variety of compositions, thicknesses, and even sizes. For use on the relatively smooth surfaces of a boat, a generic 9-inch short-nap roller is indicated. Throwaway rollers are almost always preferred for the same reasons that make throwaway brushes attractive, especially since rollers are even more difficult to clean adequately.

To use a roller, you also need a handle and a paint tray. Select a handle with a birdcage frame; changing rollers is simpler with this type of frame. Buy the cheapest tray, then line it before each use with a layer of heavy-duty foil. When you are finished, discard the foil and the tray is ready for the next job.

SANDPAPER SAVVY

You are likely to encounter six or eight different *kinds* of sandpaper in a dozen different *grits*. To prepare almost any surface for painting, you are only interested in two kinds of paper and three or four grits. The type and grit will be printed on the back of each sheet.

Most of your sanding will be done with dry (or *production*) paper, and the kind of production paper you want is *aluminum oxide*. Aluminum oxide is a tough, long-lasting abrasive, and aluminum oxide paper is brown in color. Avoid lighter-colored flint paper or red garnet paper; both are too soft to last on fiberglass. You will usually need 80-grit and 120-grit for initial preparation and 220-grit for sanding between coats.

The other type of sandpaper you are likely to use during a painting project is *silicon carbide*. This is the charcoal-colored paper you may know as *wet-or-dry*, or by the trademark Carborundum. Wet-or-dry sandpaper is used to sand between coats of paint or

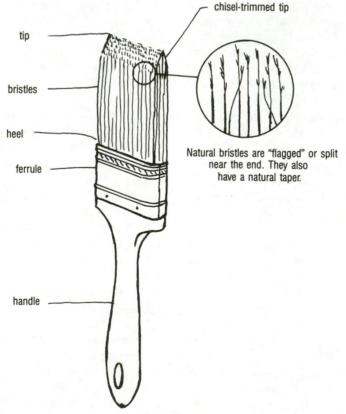

tip

bristles

heel

ferrule

handle

chisel-trimmed tip

Natural bristles are "flagged" or split
near the end. They also
have a natural taper.

Brush features

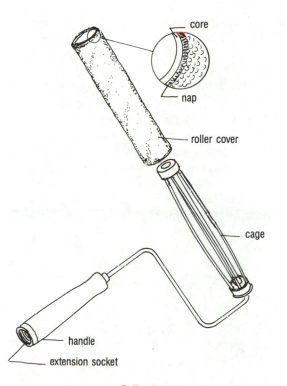

Roller features

Labels: core, nap, roller cover, cage, handle, extension socket

the locker down thoroughly with the acetone, turning the cloth to a clean side frequently. If you recall way back in Chapter 6, the final layer of fiberglass is finishing resin containing a wax that floated to the surface, or, if it was laminating resin, it was coated with a wax to seal it so that it would fully cure. Either way, the surface is coated with wax, old wax though it may be, and you have to remove the wax in order for the paint to adhere. *Do not* sand first because the sandpaper will pack the wax into every tiny scratch it makes and getting the wax back out will be difficult.

If the surface has been previously painted, the preparation is the same, with the added step of testing for compatibility. Soak a cloth with mineral spirits and lay it against the old paint for 10 minutes. As long as the old paint doesn't soften and lift, you can paint right over it. If the old coating is peeling, you will have to remove all the loose paint; if it is peeling badly, stripping may be your only choice.

After the surface has been wiped with acetone, sand it. Sanding before painting serves two functions. The first is to smooth the surface, knocking down high spots and fairing low ones. When you are painting the outside of the hull, getting the surface flawlessly smooth is critical, but right now you are painting the inside of a locker. The only smoothing you are interested in is rounding any points or sharp edges.

The second function of sanding is to give the paint or varnish a good surface to grip. Paint will not adhere to a mirror-smooth, glossy surface. Sanding removes the gloss and puts tiny scratches in the surface, vastly improving adhesion. Improving adhesion is the only reason for sanding the inside of a locker.

Because the inside surface of the hull is probably rough, sanding will not be very effective; the sandpaper will tend to ride across the high spots of the roving or weave. As long as you have already removed all traces of oil and wax from the surface, this hit-or-miss sanding will be adequate. It is the high spots that will be most subject to abrasion after you paint, but the paint on these spots will adhere

varnish when a very fine finish is desired. For this use, 340- or 400-grit should be selected. You might also use coarser grits wet as a substitute for production paper to minimize dust—when sanding toxic bottom paint, for example.

MEANWHILE, BACK AT THE BOAT

With supplies in hand, it is time to paint. Begin by emptying the locker and scrubbing away all the dirt and oils with trisodium phosphate (TSP, available in a box from your hardware store) dissolved in water. Use a brush to clean the weave of the fiberglass cloth or roving surface. Rinse the locker *thoroughly*. Satisfied? Rinse it again. If you are painting a cockpit locker, use the dock hose to rinse it.

While the locker dries, put on your rubber gloves and saturate a clean cloth with acetone. Now wipe tenaciously because the high spots will have received the brunt of your sanding efforts.

You have three basic choices of *how* to sand the locker surfaces. You can use a disc sander, in effect grinding the surface much as you would to prepare the surface for fiberglass work. If you try this, a soft foam disk will be superior to a hard, stiff disk, allowing the paper to conform somewhat to the contours of the surface. You might also use an orbital finishing sander. If the surface is relatively flat and the sander armed with 80- or 100-grit paper, it will prepare the surface very quickly. The third choice is hand sanding, which in the case of a small locker,

tight corners, or pronounced curvature of the hull surface, may be the best. For hand sanding, some people fold a half-sheet of sandpaper into thirds (never grit to grit), but I find I can read braille and open safes after an hour with a piece of folded 100-grit. I use an unfolded quarter-sheet, gripped with my thumb, but with the fingers applying pressure to the smooth side of the paper. An alternative is a rubber sanding block—which you can purchase or cut from a scrap of closed cell foam. Attach the paper to the block with sanding disk adhesive.

As a general rule, you should prepare a surface for painting or varnishing by sanding it with 120-grit

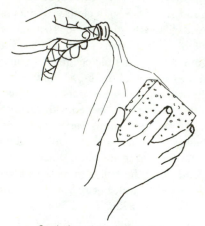

Scrub the area to remove dirt.

acetone

Wipe with solvent to remove wax.

Sand to remove imperfections and to provide *tooth* for good paint adhesion.

Pick up all sanding dust with a tack cloth.

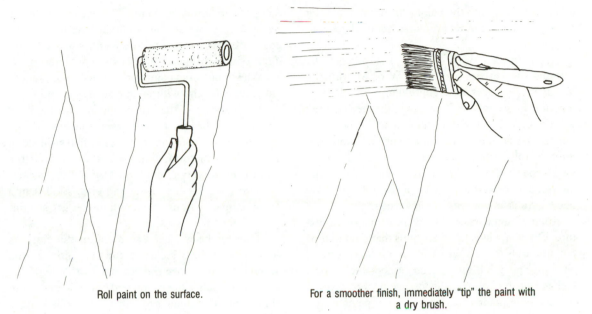

Roll paint on the surface.

For a smoother finish, immediately "tip" the paint with a dry brush.

Six basic painting steps

production paper. This grit promotes good adhesion while the scratches left behind by 120-grit will be completely hidden by the flow of the paint or varnish. Paint obscures scratches better than varnish, and will usually hide 100-grit, or even 80-grit marks, but it is usually not worth the risk. You may initially sand the surface with 80- grit paper for more rapid smoothing, but you should follow with 120-grit to make sure the 80-grit marks do not show by removing them before you paint.

However, you need not work to such exacting standards when recoating a locker. Sand that sucker with 80-grit and stop there. Brush away the sanding dust—the only legitimate use I have ever found for a synthetic brush—or, better still, vacuum away the dust. Wipe the surface one more time with acetone and you are ready to paint.

Proud Mary

Time to do a little rollin'. You should have had the paint shaken at the paint store, but if not, then stir it thoroughly with a flat stirrer. Line the paint tray with heavy-duty foil (you can also buy inexpensive plastic tray liners). Use a paint opener (the store will give you one or sell it to you for a few cents), not a screwdriver, to pry open the lid. The opener lifts the lid while a screwdriver tends to unroll the lip. Work your way around the lid, taking care not distort it or to bend the lip. Pour some paint into the well of the paint tray, then use your brush to clean out the rim of the can, wiping the brush against the inner lip to return the paint to the can. Once most of the paint is removed from the lid, wipe away any residue with a piece of paper toweling and reinstall the lid. Do not hammer the lid in place; push it into the groove with your thumbs, again working all the way around the lid. Keeping the lid closed will keep the paint fresh.

Slip a new cover onto the cage of the roller handle and roll the cover into the paint. Lift it out and roll it over the sloped part of the tray several times, dipping the roller into the paint again as necessary to get paint evenly on all sides of the cover. After initially loading the roller, the process to reload the roller is to dip it into the paint, then lift it and roll it two or three times *down* the slope, but not back into the paint.

Applying paint with a roller usually begins by painting the surface with a big W or M with the freshly loaded roller, then continuing to roll the area until it is fully covered. The size of the area covered will typically be about a 3-foot square. The direction of the stroke is not important, and you may want to roll a rough surface in two directions to insure total coverage. If the roller fails to cover the uneven surface of the interior of the hull, you may need a roller cover with a longer nap.

Rolling usually leaves the paint with a slight texture. On paints like alkyd enamels that tend to flow out smoothly, the surface will dry to the texture of an orange peel. This is perfectly acceptable inside a locker, but to eliminate this orange peel texture on more visible painted surfaces, tip the paint with a brush. Try tipping the surface of the locker. Immediately after you have rolled on the paint, lightly drag the tip of a dry (meaning not dipped in paint) brush in long, uniform strokes across the painted surface. Do not drag the brush across the same area more than twice. Roll the next area, then tip it, dragging the brush back into the previously tipped area. Do not stop the brush, but lift it to minimize brush marks.

On a small locker, it may be preferable to use a brush only to apply the paint, and even when the locker is large enough to justify the use of a roller, a brush will be required to trim the paint into the corners or around hardware. Never paint right out of the can the paint came in. Aside from exposing the paint to the air, causing it to begin to thicken, you also expose it to contamination from bristles and old paint. Pour as much paint as you need into a clean tin can or plastic container, then clean and close the paint can.

Dip only the tip—never more than a third of the length of the bristles—of the brush into the paint, then draw the brush across the edge of the container to unload the paint from one side. If the job is large, I punch two holes near the top of the container (before pouring paint into it) and run a piece of coat hanger wire through them. The wire gives me a straight edge rather than a curved one to drag the loaded brush across, and the paint is less likely to find its way to the outside of the container.

When you apply paint with a brush, you want to do it quickly, and with as few strokes as possible. Use only the tip of the brush, angling the handle of the brush in the direction of travel—like leaning into a strong wind. You want to spread the brushload of paint into a uniform, thin coat, then stop. If the paint is not covering, don't try to put it on thicker; you are going to need a second coat. Skill with a brush comes with practice. When you get it right, you'll know it.

Thus far I have failed to mention thinning. As long as you have ideal weather conditions, you should be able to use the enamel as it comes from the can—which is to say you had better learn how to thin paint. The thinner for alkyd enamel is mineral spirits—sometimes labeled as "Paint Thinner"; they are the same thing.

Almost everyone has trouble when he starts mixing in thinner. When the paint is too thick, the brush (or roller) drags, the paint does not flow out, and every brush stroke shows. But if you thin it too much, it runs and drips, and the gloss is destroyed.

You don't have to be smart to get the proportion of thinner just right. You just have to be *patient*. The trick is to creep up on the correct viscosity by adding the thinner in very small, measured portions. Add just a few drops too much thinner and you will render the paint useless—unless you have some unthinned paint left to save it. For this reason, thin only the paint you are using, not the entire can.

A vertical scrap of window glass is the ideal surface to test the paint on before you start painting. If the brush strokes fail to disappear, add a few drops of thinner, mix thoroughly, and try again. Continue to add thinner a few drops at a time until the paint flows out the way you want it to. If the paint develops a tendency to run, you have gone too far. You will need to add more paint, but keep in mind that it will take a cupful of paint to offset the effect of a capful of thinner.

What do you do when nature calls or you suffer a

Prepare a clean container with a piece of stiff wire across the open end near the top.

Stir the paint thoroughly.

Pour up a small quantity of paint. For best finish, filter the paint through a mesh filter or discarded pantyhose.

Dip the tip of the brush—no more than 1/3 of the bristles—into the paint.

Unload *one* side by dragging the brush over the wire.

Test the flow of the paint on a test surface. A scrap piece of glass is ideal because it can easily be wiped or scraped clean for reuse.

If the brush drags, add a *small* amount of thinner. If the paint runs or sags, you have added too much thinner.

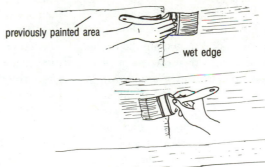

previously painted area — wet edge

lift

Begin brushing with the loaded side of the brush to the surface. Brush back toward the previously painted portion. Flow out the paint with as few strokes as possible. Finish with a stroke into the previously painted area, lifting the brush while the stroke is still in motion.

Brushing technique

Big Mac attack? The answer is to wrap the paint roller and the brush in plastic kitchen wrap. Also pat a layer of plastic onto the surface of the paint in the tray, including the wet paint on the slope. Protect the paint in the container you are using with your brush the same way—by covering the surface of the paint with plastic. When you are ready to start painting again, just peel away the plastic and your roller, brush, and paint will be as fresh as when you left.

When storing a half can of paint, or less, you can extend the life of the paint by covering the surface of the paint with plastic before sealing the can. The plastic will protect the paint from the air in the can and keep the top from forming a skin. To use the paint, remove the plastic and mix the paint, thinning if necessary.

More Than Skin Deep

Painting the interior of the hull can serve more than a cosmetic function. As I noted in Chapter 12, the University of Rhode Island study concluded that water standing *inside* the hull contributed to hull blistering. Actually, the study was somewhat more forceful: "prolonged stagnation of bilge water is the *surest* method for destroying hull integrity." The bilge pump installation detailed in Chapter 12 will eliminate most of the water in the bilge, but not all.

The study recommended protecting the *outside* of the hull from saturation with two coats of alkyd enamel. Presumably, such treatment would provide the same protection for the *inside* of the hull. Because the paint is likely to be constantly wet, select a marine paint. The study cited an alkyd-urethane-silicone blend as the least permeable. Epoxy paint will also protect the hull from saturation and will probably be more durable than the enamel . . . if you can stand to spend a day or two in the bilge with epoxy fumes.

Put on your rubber gloves and scrub the bilge *thoroughly* with TSP or some other strong detergent, using a stiff brush and plenty of elbow grease. Rinse the area, then scrub it a second time; 20 years of bilge slime will not clean away easily, but the bilge must be squeaky clean for the paint to adhere.

Rinse away all of the detergent, using the scrub brush as you rinse to dislodge all the residue from the crevices of the weave. After the fiberglass is completely dry, wipe it down thoroughly with a clean rag soaked in acetone. Twice. This is a good time to run a fan; the acetone fumes concentrated in the confines of the bilge can dissolve brain cells as readily as it dissolves oil and grease.

Sand the surface of the bilge with 80-grit production paper, then wipe it again with acetone. In order for this effort to keep the bilge dry to really be effective, the laminate needs to be dry before you paint it. The best chance of accomplishing that in a northern climate is to prepare the bilge at the end of the season, when the boat is hauled for the winter, applying the paint just before spring launch. If you sail in southern waters where there is no winter haulout, select a time when the boat will be out of service for at least a couple of weeks, preferably longer. In both instances, a dehumidifier will help the process. If the boat is in the water, wrap the shaft and rudder post stuffing boxes with a towel to keep the occasional drip from falling into the bilge. Put a tag on the ignition switch that says: "WAIT! There is a towel around the stuffing box!" If your memory is like mine, it ain't what it used to be. So don't trust it. Make the tag.

After you have let the bilge dry out as long as you can, wipe it down one more time with acetone, then give it three coats of alkyd enamel. If you decide to use epoxy instead, application is basically the same. Mix the two parts in the ratio specified on the can and apply with throwaway brushes (bristle or foam) or foam rollers. For the epoxy to be effective, it needs to be 10 mils thick. Each coat will be about 2 mils thick, so plan on applying at least five coats. Do not use a primer with either coating.

Recoat time is critical with epoxy. If you wait too long—usually any more than two hours—you will have to sand the surface before applying the next coat. Unless you just enjoy sanding while standing on your head, get each successive coat on within the recoat time specified for the epoxy you are using. You shouldn't need a calculator to see that putting

10 mils of epoxy on the surfaces of the bilge is going to require an entire day.

By the way, keep that fan running. A few specks of dust in the paint is a small price to pay to avoid the loss of 10 or 20 points on your IQ. If you're thinking "What?", it's already too late.

Out of the Closet

Now that you have the driest bilge and the whitest, or pinkest, lockers in the marina, it is time to try your skills on more visible surfaces. The tops of the settees and bunks—that area beneath the cushions—is invariably painted. If the old paint is a bit dingy, this is a good time to freshen it. Scrub the surface, then wipe it lightly with an acetone-soaked rag. Check the old paint for compatibility by putting a mineral- spirits-soaked rag on it for a few minutes. Use your palm sander loaded with 120-grit production paper to prepare the surface for painting. Wipe it one more time with acetone.

Again, you will usually get the best results by rolling on the paint and tipping it with your brush. Only one or two passes with the brush are required, and remember to tip *back* into the previously coated area.

If the surface has removable hatches, remove them and paint them separately. If you leave the hatches in place, the edge of the hatch will work just like the edge of the paint container, unloading the brush into the crack. Removing the hatches eliminates this problem and allows you access to the edges of the hatch and opening and to the cleats. Anytime you are painting to an edge with a brush, stroke *off* of the surface, not onto it.

A New Decor

Before plastic laminates came along, bulkheads were either varnished (or oiled) wood or they were painted. Plastic laminates were both a blessing and a curse. When they were used as a substitute for paint, they offered definite advantages; as a substitute for teak or mahogany, they were a bad joke.

The best way to refinish a laminate-covered bulkhead is to glue a new layer of laminate over the old one, but to do it properly requires the careful removal of all molding as detailed in Chapter 7. An easier alternative is to paint the bulkhead and, if done with care, there is no reason why a painted bulkhead should not look as good as or better than one covered with laminate.

Plastic laminate presents a stable and nonporous surface, an ideal base for paint. However, paint will not adhere well to the Melamine surface of plastic laminate. The solution is thoroughly sanding the surface. Load your palm sander with 80-grit sandpaper and sand the surface you intend to paint until it is uniformly dull. The 80-grit paper will cut the tough surface of the laminate more quickly than a finer paper will. After the hard gloss of the laminate has been removed, load your sander with 120-grit paper and sand the surface again to remove the 80-grit marks and prepare the surface for painting.

Painting will be neater and somewhat easier if you mask all the wood trim with masking tape before you begin painting. You also need to apply a coat of primer to any surface that has not been previously painted. The primer is not as essential for good adhesion on a synthetic surface such as fiberglass or plastic as it is for metal and wood surfaces, but it does cover some surface imperfections and it is especially helpful when you are painting a light color over a dark one.

If you are wondering why primer did not come up earlier, I purposely omitted priming in the lockers since you were, after all, painting the insides of lockers. Priming the fiberglass surfaces of the lockers might have marginal benefits to adhesion and coverage, but if you omit the undercoat, the first coat of enamel serves as the primer. However, all unpainted wood, even inside a locker, *should* be primed before it is coated with enamel.

Use the primer recommended by the paint manufacturer—it will be specified on the label of the enamel. Treat the primer just like the enamel, stirring it thoroughly and pouring it into the foil-lined paint tray. Instead of a fiber roller cover, you may find that you get better results on a very smooth surface with a foam roller. Use the roller to coat the sanded and acetone-wiped bulkhead surface completely. It is not necessary to tip the primer with a brush; you are going to sand the prime coat to a smooth surface before over-coating it with alkyd enamel.

Primers are typically fast-drying. After allowing the drying time specified on the can, sand the primer evenly with 120-grit production paper. Brush or vacuum the surface to remove the sanding dust, then wipe the surface with a clean, damp cloth. You can use a tack cloth—available from your paint supplier—but I am always concerned about the tack cloth leaving something behind that will interfere with the adhesion of the paint. I know the damp cloth will not do that—as long as I give the surface a few minutes to dry before painting.

No tack cloth eliminates airborne dust, so remove dust generators, such as cushions, and vacuum the entire cabin before applying the top coats. I use an old Fantastic spray bottle filled with water to mist the surfaces near where I am painting to hold the dust down. I also mist my clothes, but this particularly fanaticism has its drawbacks when the mercury dips below 40 degrees. It should go without saying that all fans must be turned *off*, and hatches that *face* the wind should be closed.

Before you paint the bulkhead between the cabins, the one everyone sees when they first come below, experiment on the engine room bulkhead, or some other less conspicuous laminated surface. You may find the slightly textured surface that will result from applying the paint with a foam roller attractive; if you examine plastic laminates closely, you will find that many have a similar texture. If you want a smoother finish, tip the paint with a brush. You will probably be unable to smooth the finish with the relatively coarse bristles of a throwaway brush; you need a soft, well-flagged, and chisel-trimmed China, camel, or badger brush to achieve a perfect finish.

A semi-gloss or a satin-finish paint will not highlight the imperfections, they will be easier on the eyes, and they will impart a softer, warmer look to the cabin. White is traditional; trimmed with teak or mahogany, it is no wonder that it remains popular. Many find off-white or beige more pleasant, and there is really no reason why color cannot be introduced into the cabin with paint rather than cushion covers. The only rule is that lighter colors will make the cabin appear larger, darker colors will make it close in.

Once the paint on your test surface is dry and you are satisfied with the results, damp-wipe the remaining surfaces and apply the paint. If you apply the second coat within the recoat times specified, you will not need to sand the surface between coats; the "green" surface of the previous coat will be softened by the solvent in the fresh paint, forming a chemical bond. If you are unable to get a subsequent coat on within the time specified, you will have to sand the surface with 120-grit production paper or the second coat will not adhere to the first one.

If, after the paint has started to set, you notice an error—a run, a sag, or obvious brush strokes—do not try to correct it with your brush or roller; you will only make it worse. Wait until the paint is thoroughly dry (usually at least 24 hours), then remove the blemish with 120-grit sandpaper and repaint. For best results, sand and recoat the entire bulkhead.

The ease with which the surface may be recoated is one of the major advantages of painted bulkheads. If the color that looked so great in your mind's eye assaults your sensibilities when you actually get it on the bulkheads, a few minutes of sanding and a coat of a different color will make things right. Sticking to white generally eliminates this kind of problem.

THE PAPER CASE

There is little reason why paper and fabric wall coverings cannot be used as successfully on a boat as they are in fine homes. The conditions in the main cabin of most boats will be easier on wallpaper than, say, the steamy environs of most bathrooms, yet paper of all types is a common bathroom wall covering. This is a commentary on the tenacity of modern wallpaper glues.

The concept of wallpaper on boats is not a revolutionary one. Luxury yachts have been using fabric and vinyl coverings on bulkheads for years, to good effect. The same coverings can likewise enhance the interior of your old boat.

The array of wall coverings that you will encounter in any large wallpaper outlet is mindboggling. Many you can probably eliminate immediately as unsuitable: untreated paper, flocks, foils, murals, and florals all seem to belong to this group. Vinyls are the most durable, and some of the fabric coverings are strikingly elegant. On the small (by wall-size standards) spaces of a bulkhead, solid colors will almost always be preferable to patterns. As with paint, light colors will make the cabin appear larger.

For the most secure adhesion, you should prepare the laminate just as if you were going to paint it. Sand it first with 80-grit, followed by 120-grit, then prime the surface with an alkyd undercoater. Sand the primer and, using a brush or a roller, coat the surface with *resin sealer*. Resin sealer provides a surface the paper will "glide" onto in the hanging process and at the same time provides the "tooth" needed by the adhesive. Resin sealer is available from the wallpaper supplier, and it is superior to the more commonly used wallpaper size. A quality resin sealer will adhere to most plastic laminates without the need to sand and paint, but preparing the surface removes any doubt. Allow the sealer to dry.

Aside from the wall covering and the resin sealer, you need a mildew-resistant paste of the type recommended for the covering you have chosen, a 6- or 8-inch flexible nylon scraper (usually superior to the old-fashioned smoothing brush), a trimming knife (the type that uses a single-edge razor blade), a 10-inch drywall knife (also for trimming), and perhaps a seam roller.

Since the concept of level is dubious aboard a boat, align the covering with a vertical feature of the bulkhead, such as a passageway, by measuring away from the vertical feature one inch less than the width of the covering and, with a pencil, drawing a parallel vertical line from the top to the bottom of the bulkhead. The edge of the first strip of covering will lie on this line.

Prepare the first piece of covering by cutting a piece from the roll long enough to extend a couple of inches beyond the top and the bottom of the bulkhead. Lay the covering face-down on a protected flat surface. Coat the back of the strip with paste, then fold each end of the strip to the middle—paste to paste—and set the strip aside for several minutes. This is called "booking" the paper. Normally you would coat several strips while the first one cures, but if this is your initial experience with wallpaper, don't get fancy.

After the strip sits for about 10 minutes, unfold it and spread it onto the bulkhead, aligning it with the line you drew. It should overlap the top and the bottom, and the vertical feature you measured from initially. By putting your palms flat on the strip, you will be able to slide it around on the bulkhead until you are satisfied with the alignment. If you are hanging a vinyl, use the nylon scraper to work out all the bubbles by stroking the paper in a starburst pattern from the center. Do not apply much pressure; you are trying to expel the bubbles, not the glue. If the covering is cloth, you may have better success smoothing it with a clean paint roller. Try not to stretch the covering; it will shrink as it dries, opening the seam with the next piece.

Once the strip is in place, trim away the excess. Trimming against a straight corner or a straight piece of molding is not difficult; use the drywall knife to hold the paper into the corner between the bulkhead and the molding, and draw the blade of the trim knife along the edge of the drywall knife. Reposition the drywall knife and continue the cut until it is complete.

Trimming around curved molding is more difficult. On an outside curve, you may be able to use the trim knife with the edge of a putty knife to follow the contour. On an inside curve, force the covering against the molding with something blunt but hard enough to leave a crease. Lift the paper and trim

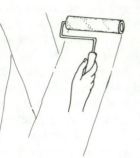

After sanding and priming, coat the surface with resin sealer and allow to dry.

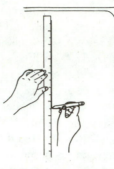

Measure away from a vertical feature 1 inch *less* than the width of the covering and draw a parallel vertical line.

Cut a strip of the covering long enough to extend beyond the top and bottom of the bulkhead and coat the back surface with paste.

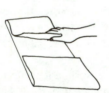

"Book" the strip by folding each end to the middle—paste to paste. Allow to sit for several minutes.

Unfold and apply the fabric to the bulkhead, sliding it to align with the vertical line.

Smooth the panel from the center with a nylon scraper, a smoothing brush, or a clean paint roller.

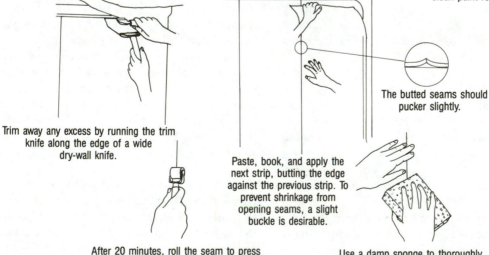

Trim away any excess by running the trim knife along the edge of a wide dry-wall knife.

Paste, book, and apply the next strip, butting the edge against the previous strip. To prevent shrinkage from opening seams, a slight buckle is desirable.

The butted seams should pucker slightly.

After 20 minutes, roll the seam to press the edges together and to the bulkhead.

Use a damp sponge to thoroughly remove any glue from the surface of the covering.

Applying fabric coverings

along the crease with scissors. Smooth the trimmed covering back into place.

Measure and cut the next strip from the roll. On the assumption that a printed covering has not been selected, there are no concerns about matching patterns. Paste and book the strip, and while the glue cures, use a wet sponge to remove the paste from all the surfaces where you trimmed the covering. Keep rinsing your sponge and scrubbing until all the paste is gone; if you fail to remove the paste while it is still wet, it will be difficult to get it off. If you taped the trim before priming the bulkhead, you can avoid most of this mess by leaving the tape on until you are finished hanging the covering, to protect the trim from paste as well.

Butt the second strip against the edge of the first one. Because the covering will shrink slightly, the joint between the two strips should be just slightly buckled. Smooth and trim the second piece. Continue the process until the bulkhead is covered. After a strip has been in place for about 20 minutes, go back to it and run a seam roll over the seam between that strip and the prior one to press the two edges together and against the bulkhead. If the roller marks the covering you have selected, use a

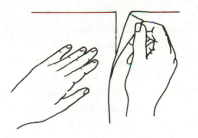

Overlap the adjacent strips, matching the pattern if there is one.

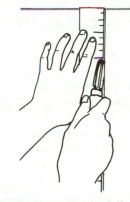

Use a straightedge and trimming knife to cut through both layers in the center of the lapped seam.

Carefully peel off the outer strip severed by the cut.

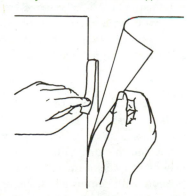

Lift the fabric and peel away the inner strip. Smooth the cut edges together, forming a perfect seam.

Double-cutting a seam

sponge instead to compress the seam. Wash off any paste that gets onto the surface of the covering.

INTERIOR WOOD

If you are lucky enough to have bulkheads covered with honest wood veneer, your interest is not in covering the bulkheads, but in uncovering them. The cure for dull, drab interior woodwork—whether full bulkheads or molding and trim—depends upon whether the wood is oiled or varnished to begin with, and whether you want it to be oiled or varnished.

The first step in resurfacing brightwork is the same as the first step in painting—cleaning the surface. Interior woodwork tends to harbor mildew in the pores and is subject to a greasy buildup from the galley. Both can be removed at the same time by mixing a cup of detergent and a cup of household bleach into a gallon of water and wiping the wood with this solution. Wear rubber gloves, and use an old towel rather than a sponge. Wring out the towel—if it is too wet, it will raise the grain—and wipe down all the wood surfaces. Allow the solution to stand on the wood for 30 minutes, then use a clean towel wrung out in fresh water to thoroughly rinse the wood. When the wood is thoroughly dry, it should be clean, but it will also seem rather dull and lifeless. That's good.

If you want a natural finish, all you need to do is wipe the wood with *lemon oil*. Lemon oil will not stand up to the rigors of exterior exposure, but it is the ideal treatment for natural interior wood, highlighting the beauty of the wood. It feeds the wood, replacing lost natural oils, it is poison to mildew, it is not sticky when it dries, subsequent applications will absorb surface grease, and it smells good. Apply lemon oil (not lemon wax or lemon polish) with a cloth, rubbing it into the grain of the wood. Do a second application in a week. After that, wipe down the interior wood with lemon oil about once a month, depending upon how much use your boat sees. Keep in mind that the interior wood is like fine furniture; if you want it to look good, you have to give it *some* care.

EXTERIOR TEAK

We will come back to the interior woodwork when we get to the subject of varnishing, but first let's look at refinishing the exterior wood naturally, which requires a somewhat different regimen. The only woods that do well naturally in exterior applications are oily woods, and aboard a boat that is almost exclusively teak. Other woods require a protective finish or they will split and crack. Lemon oil can be used effectively on virtually any wood that may be in your cabin, but when we talk about oiling exterior wood, we are talking about teak. Let's outline the process, beginning with black, unmaintained teak, and you can follow only the steps that apply to your own exterior brightwork.

Jet fuel, air pollutants, street grime, and the effects of weather and the sun necessitate more vigorous cleaning than wiping the wood with a detergent-and-bleach-dampened cloth. Numerous "patented" teak cleaners are on the market. The two-part cleaners use a powerful acid that literally eats away the top surface of the wood; if you use this type of cleaner often, cap-rails will soon dissolve to veneer and handrails to the diameter of a pencil. The acids will also etch your gelcoat or paint if you are not extremely cautious. Anyway, I am pretty sure I don't want any chemical on my wood that has to be "neutralized."

One-part cleaners—liquids, creams, and powders—may be strong detergents, or mild acids, or a combination of both, but they will be easier on the wood. And harder on you. One-part cleaners require scrubbing, which also tends to remove some of the wood. Whatever type of cleaner you use, after a few years hardware on the teak seems to be sitting on top of an island as the wood around is eroded. If you clean the wood *before* it is in such bad shape, a mild *soap* can be used, preserving whatever teak remains.

But we are starting with neglected teak, so mild soap will not get the job done. If you are going to use a teak cleaner, select one of the less powerful single-part variety. Exercise is good for you, Skip. An equally effective and significantly less expensive cleaner is TSP (trisodium phosphate), the same crystals you used to clean the bottom of the lockers. Two or three spoonfuls in a bucket of water will give you a bucket full of cleaner for a few cents, which contrasts sharply with the niggardly amount of commercial cleaner $10 buys. And the active ingredient is just as likely to be TSP, so you are paying about $9.80 for a quart of water; it should at least be Perrier.

I find that a synthetic scrubber is the best for cleaning teak. A janitorial service used to save the center piece from heavy-duty floor buffer pads for me; otherwise, they punched out and discarded them. If you don't know anyone who uses a floor buffer, buy a new pad (the most dense) and cut the whole pad into a supply of scrubbers. A lot of sailors scrub the teak with a brush, but I never was satisfied with any brush I tried. Bronze wool is excellent if you have already come into your trust fund. Never use steel wool; it leaves behind little particles of steel that will rust and stain the wood.

Wet the teak, then apply the TSP mixture. You can dip the scrubber into the bucket to get the cleaner on the wood, but for teak trim, try a spray bottle. Don't mix a bucket full and then pour it into a bottle. Toss about a half a teaspoon of TSP into the empty spray bottle, fill it with water (Perrier, if you like), and shake it well. Spray the teak heavily and scrub. Wear rubber gloves. Give the resulting foam about four or five minutes to lift the surface dirt and oil—no more than that or it will also lift the pulp—then rinse away every trace of the cleaner by flooding the wood and scrubbing it lightly with a clean scrubber.

If the wood does not come totally clean, try a second application. Bleaching the wood damages the surface and should be avoided if at all possible. This includes use of the so-called brighteners, which are bleach solutions—usually oxalic acid. If the teak is badly stained and cleaning does not restore it, try an oxalic bleach, but use it sparingly and rinse it thoroughly.

The various cleaning chemicals will eventually eat away the soft pulp of the teak, leaving the harder lignin standing proud and looking rough. The only treatment for rough teak is to sand it. Use a finishing sander and 120-grit production paper to restore a smooth surface to the wood. Brush or vacuum away all the sanding dust and wipe the wood with a rag soaked in mineral spirits to remove any embedded dust; any dust you leave behind will darken the color of the wood when you oil it.

Oiling Teak

Oiling teak—any wood, for that matter—is good for the health of the wood, restoring some of the natural oils and resins. Unfortunately, oiling is like a workout; the beneficial effects are lost unless you do it regularly.

There are basically two types of oil that are suitable for exposed teak, and one or the other is found in virtually every teak oil on the market. The less expensive of the two is linseed oil (which ought to be called flax-seed oil). Linseed oil is an excellent preservative, but tends to turn the wood dark, a problem that is exacerbated by the resins that are usually combined with the oil in most teak oils to make them more durable.

The second type is tung oil, derived from the fruit of the Chinese tung tree. (Don't you wonder exactly what a tung fruit looks like?) Tung oil will not turn the wood dark, and it is more water-resistant than linseed oil, a significant advantage aboard a boat. If a teak oil is tung-oil based, it will say so in big letters because tung oil is significantly more expensive than linseed oil. If the teak oil does not state the ingredients, assume that it contains linseed oil.

The unfortunate truth is that neither oil will last more than a few weeks on a vertical surface, and as the sun carbonizes the oil on the surface, the oil turns black. The surface must be scrubbed to remove the dirt and blackened oil, and another coat of oil must be applied to the wood. To reduce the frequency, most teak oils contain one or several synthetic and natural resins. They also contain driers to hasten drying, UV filters, and mildew retardants.

The best way to select a teak oil is to ignore advertising claims and the "independent" tests. Simply find a boat in your marina that has teak that looks the way you want yours to look and ask the owner what product he uses. Teak oils that are widely praised in some regions are just as widely maligned in others. Climate is a major factor. Also ask your marina neighbor how often he applies it; your own teak will not look as good unless you follow a similar schedule.

Oil can be applied with a cloth, but is easier and less messy to apply with a brush. For the first coat, there may be some benefit to thinning the oil about 20 percent with mineral spirits or turpentine to encourage it to penetrate the wood as deeply as possible. For the same reason, apply the oil in the sun. Teak will initially exhibit a thirst that might impress Dean Martin, but after three or four coats, the oil will begin to stand on the surface. Excess oil must not be allowed to dry, but must be wiped off the wood immediately with a cloth. Continue to oil the wood until it refuses to accept any more. Then the wood should have a matte finish with no sign of a gloss anywhere.

The resins in most teak oils will stain your gelcoat or paint, so apply the oil with the same care you would show if you were painting the wood. Any drips or runs should be wiped up with a cloth soaked in mineral spirits. Watch for runs under the sprit or down the hull that may not be visible without looking for them. Once the resins dry, the stain will be almost impossible to remove.

SEALERS

Another approach to the "natural" finish is the application of a sealer. Sealers do not feed the wood but, as the name suggests, they seal the surface, holding the natural oils and resins in and the moisture and dirt out. An effective sealer can be concocted by thinning varnish 50 percent with turpentine or mineral spirits. The sealer, like oil, is applied with a brush without any concern for the quality of the brush or the direction of the brush strokes.

Since the natural oils and resins have already been lost, applying only a sealer is not an effective treatment for old teak—like closing the gate *after* the livestock have escaped. If you plan to seal the teak,

oil it first to restore the wood; you will be unable to oil it after the sealer has been applied. Allow the oil to dry for a couple of weeks, then wash the wood and remove the surface oils with a rag soaked in acetone before applying the sealer.

In commercial teak products, sealers and oils are often blended in an effort to combine the durability of a sealer with the rejuvenating effect of oil. Such products are often called dressings or treatments, and some are enormously popular. These coatings are maintained by washing the wood and applying a fresh coat every two to three months.

VARNISHING

The secret to having beautifully varnished brightwork is not the brand of varnish, although some are undoubtedly better than others. It is not the brush; anyone can buy a good brush. It is not the number of coats. It is not keeping the varnish bubble free. It is not the grit of sandpaper selected for the final sanding. It is not wrist action, or the way you hold your mouth. All of those things—except maybe the one about the mouth—are important, even essential, but the secret to *having* beautiful varnish is *vigilance*. You must touch up every nick and scratch immediately, and you must recoat the varnish regularly and at the first sign of deterioration. If you fail to notice, or fail to act, even for a week or two, the consequence can be stripping the surface back to bare wood. Good varnish, good brush, good preparation, and good technique will not count for a thing.

Why am I telling you this? Take a stroll down the dock and look at the varnished brightwork. When it is maintained, it adds an air of elegance, even opulence, to the most humble boat. But when the varnish has been neglected, even sweet lines are disgraced by the peeling and blackened wood. Which effect will varnishing have on *your* boat? Deciding to varnish—particularly exterior brightwork—is not a one-time decision but a long-term commitment. Exterior surfaces will have to be sanded and a fresh layer of varnish applied at least twice a year—three times a year on horizontal surfaces. Unless you are both able and willing to accept this responsibility, save yourself a lot of grief and just oil or seal the wood. Stripping varnish is a job you only want to do once.

STRIPPING

If the varnish on your old boat is in bad shape, there is good news and bad news. The good news is that most of the original wood thickness is probably still there since the wood has not been scrubbed every eight weeks for 20 years. (That alone is a good reason to elect to varnish.) The bad news is that all the old varnish has to come off.

Stripping old varnish with a scraper is the cleanest, safest, and sometimes the easiest method. If you have never used a scraper, buy one and give it a try before resorting to one of the other methods of varnish removal. You need a 4- or 5-inch *cabinet scraper*, which is nothing more than a flat piece of hard steel. You can buy a handle for the scraper, but it is often easier to use without one. The edge of the scraper has a microscopic burr, which acts as a cutting edge. Hold the scraper at an angle of about 75 degrees to the wood surface and pull it toward you. The tiny edge, in effect, planes the old varnish from the wood. In skilled hands, a scraper can put a remarkably smooth finish on wood.

Eventually the scraper will lose its edge, but it is a simple matter to renew it. Clamp the blade in a vise and draw a mill file across each edge several times to make the edges flat and square. Holding the blade perpendicular, whet each edge on an oilstone, using a circular motion. With each side of the blade flat on the stone, make several circular passes to remove any burrs from the filing. Lay the blade flat on the edge of your worktable and use the round shank of a Phillips screwdriver to burnish the edges of the face by placing the shank almost flat on the blade and stroking it with heavy pressure. Burnish all the way around both sides. Put the blade back in the vise and burnish the edges by drawing the horizontal shank heavily across each edge about a dozen

times. Now tilt the shank about 10 degrees so that it forms an angle of about 80 degrees with the face of the scraper and draw the shank along the edge twice to form the burr. Tilt the shank the other way and put a burr on the other side of the same edge. When you have done all the edges, you will have eight fresh cutting edges. You should be able to resharpen a scraper by simply burnishing away all traces of the dull burr and burnishing on a new one two or three times before draw-filing is necessary.

Sanding is another method of stripping old varnish. On large, flat surfaces a belt sander can make short work of it, but it can also make an irreparable gouge before you can say, "Oh fudge." If you try the belt sander, use a fine-grit belt, apply light pressure, keep the sander in perpetual motion, and be very, very careful.

A finishing sander with 60- or 80-grit paper is slower but much safer. If you leave the sander in one place, it will heat the varnish, softening it and causing it to gum up the paper. You just can't do this job without moving your arms. If you remove the varnish by sanding, much of it will have to be done by hand.

Chemical strippers can take much of the work out of removing old varnish, but such strippers are not selective; get any on a painted deck and it will remove the paint just as effectively, and some are strong enough to damage gelcoat. Mask all surrounding surfaces; a single layer of newspaper will be insufficient. Strippers also attack skin, so wear rubber gloves.

Buy the heaviest-bodied stripper you can—the consistency of molasses. Pour a little into a can, not onto the wood. Dip your brush, but do *not* wipe it. Apply the stripper with a single stroke, probably no more than 4 inches. Dip and apply the next 4 inches, and so on. It is the vapors from the stripper that do the work and if you brush back and forth, you release them into the air, reducing the effectiveness of the stripper by as much as 80 percent!

To give the stripper longer to work before it dries, try to avoid working in the sun. After it has been on the surface about 30 minutes, use a wide putty knife to scrape off the softened varnish. Be careful where the curls fall; they can still damage other finishes. Use bronze wool for curved and hard-to-reach areas. Where varnish still remains, repeat the process. Once all the varnish has been removed, wipe the wood with clean cloths soaked in denatured alcohol or lacquer thinner to remove the wax left behind by the stripper as well as all stripper and varnish residue.

Scraping and sanding may result in a surface that has a uniform color, but not necessarily. Chemical stripping is almost certain to leave a surface that is stained and mottled, yet a consistent surface is essential for the new varnish. Stains sometimes respond to the mild bleaching agents in one-part teak cleaner, but if after you scrub the wood thoroughly it

still exhibits stains and multiple shades, bleaching may be your only option. Bleaching is hard on the wood and the bleach can etch the gelcoat and paint, so do not bleach wood except as a last resort.

If the teak cleaner failed to remove the stain, Clorox is not likely to do the job either. The bleach you need is oxalic acid, which you can obtain in crystal form from your hardware store. While you are there, buy a box of soda ash or borax to use as a neutralizer. Stir oxalic acid crystals into warm water until they stop dissolving to make up the bleach solution. Paint or wipe this carefully onto the wood, taking great care not to drip or spill it onto any other surface, and let it dry completely. Vacuum away the powder that remains, or brush it into a dustpan.

Mix a cup of the soda ash or borax into a bucket

Draw a mill file across the edge to square it.

Whet each edge on an oil stone.

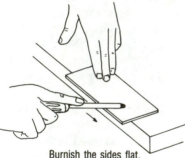

Burnish the sides flat.

With heavy pressure, burnish the edges at 90 degrees.

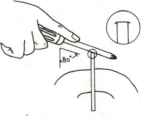

Tilt the shank about 10 degrees and burnish one corner of the edge to 80 degrees. Tilt the shank the other way and burnish the opposite edge.

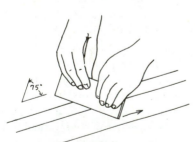

Use the scraper by holding it about 75 degrees to the work and drawing it toward you, shaving the surface.

Sharpening and using a cabinet scraper

of water and wet all of the bleached wood generously with this solution. Thoroughly rinse the wood, and all areas around the wood with the dock hose; scrubbing is recommended. Treat the wood again with the neutralizing agent, followed by a vigorous second rinse. When the wood dries, it should be uniform in color. Remaining dark spots can be retreated with bleach and neutralizer, although it will be difficult to achieve consistency spot-bleaching.

Bleached or not, sand the wood thoroughly with 100-grit paper. When you are sanding for varnish, always sand *with* the grain; scratches across the grain will show through the varnish. If the wood has been bleached, this initial sanding dust could still harbor some acid, so rinse it away thoroughly. Of course, the rinsing may again raise the grain, so one more application of sandpaper is called for. If the wood is teak, stick with 100-grit paper to provide good tooth for the varnish. For mahogany, 150-grit will contribute to a better finish. Somewhat finer paper should be used on interior furniture; 120-grit for teak and up to 220-grit for mahogany and other hardwoods—always with the grain. Wipe the wood down with a rag soaked in mineral spirits and you are ready to varnish.

CHOOSING A FINISH

For exterior use, select a varnish loaded with UV inhibitors; it is the sun that kills varnish. Spar varnish traditionally has more UV protection than other varnishes. It is also softer and retains its flexibility longer, which reduces cracking and splitting. However, you are not assured of either of these characteristics just because a product is labeled spar varnish. Here again, the best approach is to identify a boat with the finish you are after and ask the owner what kind of varnish was used.

Spar varnish, because of its softer surface, may not be the best choice for interior furniture. Less subject to the killing effects of the weather, interior finishes are murdered by abrasion. A hard varnish should be selected. Some UV inhibitors are still

required. The choice of gloss or satin finish is a matter of taste.

Clear polyurethanes, often called urethane varnish, have a well-earned reputation for releasing their grip on the wood and peeling off in sheets. The clear urethanes commonly sold in paint and hardware stores usually contain no UV inhibitors and are patently unsuitable for use on a boat. There are some new blends on the market, but none have the history of user satisfaction that comes with marine or spar varnish. Unless you have reliable information—not advertising copy—about a particular polyurethane, stick with real varnish.

Urethane varnish is also not to be confused with clear two-part urethane. Two-part urethane is the same product—without a color-adding pigment—that has revolutionized boat painting. Handled properly, two-part urethane has the *potential*, and I emphasize potential, to put a finish on exterior brightwork that will last for four or five years without attention. This is, however, an exacting and relatively expensive process fraught with great potential for problems. Even if your application is perfect, instability of the wood can reduce the life of the finish to that of plain varnish. And it is virtually inevitable, sooner or later, that the finish will have to be renewed. When that happens, the incredible toughness of two-part urethane will switch from blessing to curse and you may come to regret your choice. We will come back to this, but let's first look at varnishing.

Laying It On

The first thing you need is a supply of cat food cans. You do not want to expose the varnish to the air any longer than necessary before you flow it on, so you want to pour up a small amount at a time, sealing the varnish can each time. You don't have a cat? So mix the stuff with a little celery, onion, and mayo and make sandwiches for a dock party. Who will know?

You also need a supply of good weather. Moisture in the form of rain, dew, and fog will ruin the surface of fresh varnish, so don't varnish when rain is threatening (or falling!), begin late enough and stop early enough to avoid evening dampness, and pay attention to fog conditions. Ironically, bright sunlight can also cause problems, accelerating the drying so much that the varnish blisters; put up the awning before you start and try to work in the shade. The biggest weather nemesis is wind, which loads the wet varnish with swirling dust; when the wind picks up, so should you.

And you need a good brush. Badger hair is not too good for a truly perfect finish, but if you don't want to spend 25 bucks on a great brush, a quality Chinese bristle brush will do the job *almost* as well for 1/3 the cost. Unlike throw-away brushes, a good brush requires cleaning after *every* use. *Do not* simply leave the brush soaking in thinner. The thinner removes the natural oils from the bristle and before long your expensive brush will be no better at laying on varnish than a 50-cent throwaway.

Between coats, you can safely leave your brush soaking in kerosene. Don't leave it standing on the bristles or the delicate chisel tip will be deformed; a pair of pencils or dowels clamped around the handle with rubber bands will allow you to suspend the brush with the ferrule just below the surface of the kerosene. Rinse the brush twice in mineral spirits before you use it. When the job is finished, rinse the brush at least three times in thinner (clean thinner each time, not three times in the same thinner), spreading the bristles gently to make sure all the varnish has been removed. Comb the brush into shape, then dip it into a container of clean motor oil (30W seems to be the favorite) and let it soak for a few minutes. Wrap the bristles in stiff paper and hang the brush or store it flat. A brush treated this way will last until you wear away the bristles with a few million strokes. Rinse the brush twice in thinner before you use it again.

To avoid brush cleaning, which is messy and time-consuming, lay on the first three or four coats of varnish with a throwaway brush. A fine varnish job will require at least six coats, perhaps a couple more, and it is only in the final coats that the better brush makes a difference. If you cannot get throw-away bristle brushes that do not exhibit a tendency to shed bristles into the work, try foam brushes. Some people have such good luck with foam brushes that they use them right through the finish coats.

With well-prepared wood, a quality varnish, and a good brush, only three things stand between you and a flawless finish. The first one is dust. It is impossible to totally protect varnished surfaces from dust, but you can eliminate 98 percent of it. If you are varnishing below, remove all cushions and other dust generators, then vacuum and damp-wipe *all* interior surfaces. Mist your clothes, or eschew them altogether. Ventilation is essential, but try to avoid dust-disturbing drafts.

For exterior brightwork, scrub the deck before you start, and damp-wipe the entire deck after every between-coat sanding. Varnishing at anchor is better than at the dock, and try to avoid windy days. I will leave how you dress to your judgment.

The second barrier to the flawless finish is air—in the form of bubbles. Disturb varnish as little as possible; *never* shake varnish, and if stirring is required—to add thinner, for example—stir slowly and gently. Any bubbles in the varnish will end up encapsulated in your finish. Gently pour the varnish for the first coat through a paint filter or a double layer of panty hose into a clean container. Filter the varnish even if the can is new; blobs of gum and little flakes of dried varnish will ruin the finish. Do not clean the rim of the varnish can with a brush and wipe it back into the can; that is just another way of introducing bubbles. Use a rag or paper toweling to clean the rim. Seal the varnish can.

The third barrier is impatience. All the steps outlined below are required for consistent results. Don't look for shortcuts or the "quick" way. In the long run, laying on the first application of varnish with great deliberateness will be the quick way, but you can only know the truth of this by following another course. Don't.

Often sealers are recommended as a base coat before the varnish is applied, but sealers can introduce more problems than they solve, and they often give the varnish an off color. On teak and mahogany, if you thin the first coat of varnish adequately to insure good penetration, a separate sealer is not required. Thin the varnish about 50 percent (the exact ratio is not critical) with mineral spirits or turpentine, then lay on the first coat quickly and without fuss. The wood will change color, but most of the varnish will be absorbed. A second coat, thinned about 25 percent, should be applied with the same speed as soon as the first is dry to the touch.

Allow the second coat to dry overnight, then sand it lightly with 180-grit sandpaper (220-grit for interior varnish) to remove surface roughness and provide tooth for the next coat. It is possible to apply subsequent layers of varnish without sanding between coats (you just did this between the first and second coats) as long as you apply the coat within the recoat time specified on the can. However, for the best finish, sand between coats.

Varnish, with the exception of "quick-drying" formulas, which are not recommended, should always dry overnight before being sanded. Allowing it to dry longer is fine, but when you do, wipe the varnish *before* you sand with a thinner-soaked rag to remove any pollutants that may have settled on the surface. After sanding, wipe the surface thoroughly with a damp cloth or a tack rag. You can make an excellent tack cloth for varnish work by wringing out a clean cotton cloth soaked in warm water and sprinkling it with turpentine, followed by a spoonful of your varnish. Wring the cloth again to distribute the varnish and store it in a Zip-loc bag between uses. Toss it when the job is finished.

The third coat should be thinned about 10 percent and the fourth coat applied unthinned. After

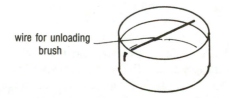

wire for unloading brush

One tuna can holds a small amount of varnish, limiting the air exposure before the varnish is applied.

The second can is used to wipe both sides of the brush *after* each varnish application to expel particles, loose bristles, and bubbles.

Two-can varnishing method

the fourth coat, it is time to start exercising care. This is where the cat food cans (or tuna cans) come in. Be sure they are clean and dry, then punch two holes near the rim of one of the cans and insert a piece of coat hanger wire, as described earlier. Decant an inch or so of varnish into the can with the wire, filtering it through panty hose.

Dip just the tip—about a third—of the brush into the varnish and give it time to become fully saturated; if the brush is not saturated, it will lay on bubbles instead of varnish. Unload one side of the brush by dragging it *slowly* across the wire. If you unload the brush on the rim of the can, bubbles are likely. Lay the varnish on with smooth, continuous strokes, taking care not to put it on so thickly that it runs or sags. When the brush is "dry," use it to "tip" the varnish you just applied, stroking back into the previous varnish and gently lifting the brush clear of the surface. Once the varnish has been tipped, leave it alone. Plan to sand out any mistakes—and to learn from them.

Before you dip your brush back into the varnish, wipe both sides of the brush on the lip of the second can to remove loose bristles or any particles the brush picked up from the wood and to expel any bubbles from the bristles. Dip the tip of the wiped brush back into the container of varnish, allow it time to saturate, unload one side gently against the wire, and continue to lay on the varnish.

When only a small amount of varnish remains, do not use it, but pour it into the can you are using to wipe your brush, or into some other container. You can save it to use for initial coats on other brightwork, but it should not be used for the final coats. Never pour *any* varnish back into the original can.

Decant fresh varnish into your varnish container and continue laying it on until all surfaces are coated. When you are finished, suspend the brush in kerosene and throw away the two small cans. If you have applied the varnish with care, the surface should be almost flawless. Allow the fifth coat to dry overnight, longer if you have any sags or runs.

Six coats are almost always enough—if the var-

nish is *too* thick it is prone to cracking—so this is the coat that separates the artists from the house painters. Sand the fifth coat (180-grit outside, 220-grit below) to remove any mistakes and to provide a smooth, uniform surface for your final coat. Wipe the wood and all surrounding surfaces completely dust-free. Clean the brush twice with thinner, and prepare one of the two *new* tuna cans with a wire. Fanatics open a fresh can of varnish for the final coat. Pour the varnish through pantyhose into the tuna can and apply it exactly as you did the fifth coat, except without the mistakes you made on that coat.

Your final coat isn't flawless? Don't get crazy. Everyone, no matter how much experience they have, can show you mistakes in their own varnish work. If you can bring yourself to call it "pretty good," everyone else will think it is great. Stop. Don't even think about "just one more coat." You will get another chance in six months when it is time to lay on a fresh coat. Just hold onto that sense of dissatisfaction and apply the fresh coat with care when it is time.

One good thing about varnish—external varnish—is that you never have to look at your mistakes for longer than a few months. If it is an interior surface you are unhappy with, go ahead and correct it now. Interior varnish should last five to 10 years before recoating, too long to look at a curtainlike sag across the main bulkhead.

When you are through, clean and oil the brush and set it aside for future varnish work only. If you ever use it for paint, you will spoil it forever for varnish use. Empty and rinse (with thinner) a nail polish bottle or a paste bottle—the kind with a brush in the lid—and funnel it full of varnish for immediate nick and scratch repair. Rubber-band a few squares of 220-grit paper around the bottle to complete your first-aid kit. If you are vigilant in touching up and follow a schedule of regularly recoating, exterior varnish can look as beautiful a decade later as the day the first application was completed. If you neglect the finish, you will be repeating this whole process next year, or opting for the oiled look. Store the remaining varnish upside down so that it will skin on the bottom.

The Clear Polyurethane Alternative

The failure of varnish, invariably from neglect, has led some to seek a system of coating wood that is unaffected by neglect. Properly applied, clear two-part polyurethane will withstand neglect for a number of years.

A characteristic of varnish that is both an advantage and a disadvantage is that it is semi-permeable. While the varnish may not seal *out* moisture as well as other coatings, it allows the wood to "breathe." Polyurethane, on the other hand, seals the wood. On a humid day, lay a place of clear plastic on deck in the bright sunlight and it will soon form droplets on the underside. A similar thing happens when you coat moisture-containing wood with clear plastic. The moisture tends to cause the polyurethane to lose its grip on the wood, a problem that is exacerbated by the natural oils in the wood. Two-part clear polyurethane should never be applied directly to bare wood.

There are two ways to use clear polyurethane on brightwork with a better likelihood of success. The wood can be first sealed with three or four coats of saturating epoxy. The epoxy is a much better glue than the polyurethane and will be less affected by moisture, but all surface oils will need to be removed for the epoxy to adhere. Oils can be removed by wiping the wood vigorously with acetone, but a more effective treatment is to bleach the wood with oxalic acid. Two applications of neutralizer and final sanding are required before coating with the epoxy.

Epoxy is very sensitive to the mixing ratio; if you do not combine the two parts correctly, the epoxy will fail to harden and become a mess. Follow the manufacturers' instructions exactly for mixing the two parts of the epoxy.

Epoxy also tends to have a short recoat time, so sanding between coats may be necessary. However, cured epoxy has a very hard surface, so it is usually advisable to limit the application to only as much

wood as can be coated within the recoat time so that subsequent coats may be applied without sanding, or with only light sanding to scour the surface. Wipe the surface with acetone or toluene before recoating.

While some epoxies will cure underwater, some epoxy coatings are sensitive to humidity. If you are in a humid climate, select a coating that is tolerant of moisture. Also try to apply the epoxy when the temperature is mild. Use a foam brush to lay on the epoxy just like the varnish. After three coats, allow the epoxy to cure for a least one day, then sand the surface with 180-grit production paper.

The chemicals and solvents in two-part polyurethanes are highly toxic and must be handled with great care. In the section on refinishing the hull that follows, we will describe the health risks and the process of working with polyurethane paint in greater detail, but the general procedure for applying a clear polyurethane coating over epoxy-sealed wood is to first wipe the surfaces with the solvent recommended by the manufacturer of the polyurethane you are using. Be sure you have adequate ventilation and protect your skin from the solvent. Mix the clear urethane according to the manufacturer's instructions, and lay it on with a foam brush, tipping the surface with a "dry" badger or quality Chinese bristle brush. Tip the surface immediately and only once, stroking back into the previously coated surface. For large areas, use a foam roller rather than a foam brush. Throw away the foam brush, but clean the badger brush immediately and thoroughly in the solvent.

Allow the first coat of urethane to dry overnight, then *wet* sand the entire surface with 340-grit wet-or-dry sandpaper. Wet sanding is exactly what it sounds like. The simplest way is to keep a trickle of water from a hose on the surface work as you sand, but you can also simply dip the paper in a bucket of water often enough to keep the paper and the surface wet. You can use a rubber block or just the pressure of your fingers.

Wet sanding polyurethane produces a scum that must be removed. When all the surfaces have been sanded, wash them thoroughly with fresh water and a clean cloth or sponge. You can hasten drying by toweling the surfaces, but be sure all joints and cracks are moisture free before proceeding. Wipe the surfaces with the recommended solvent, and apply the final coat of polyurethane with a foam roller or brush, tipping it out to a perfect finish with a dry brush.

Polyurethane over an epoxy base can last five years or longer, but in sunlight the lack of UV inhibitors in the epoxy can result in a much shorter life. The wood is left unprotected from the sun and the epoxy tends to darken with age and may even degenerate.

Polyurethane may also be applied over a base coat of *cured* varnish. The advantage of this combination is that the UV inhibitors in the varnish protect the wood and stabilize the color of the finish while the clear polyurethane provides a long-lasting and abrasion-resistant top coating. Apply six coats of varnish as outlined above and allow the varnish to age for at least three months. The aggressive solvents in the polyurethane will attack the varnish if it is still "green." Prepare the surface by sanding with 180-grit paper and wiping with solvent. Apply two coats of polyurethane as previously detailed.

Whether you apply clear polyurethane over an epoxy base or a varnish base, chances are very good that eventually the coating will fail. When that happens, you are in for a very difficult job. For this reason alone, varnish alone is still the brightwork finish of choice for most boat owners.

REFINISHING THE EXTERIOR

While clear polyurethane has not displaced varnish, two-part polyurethane paint is today the only sensible choice for restoring the gloss to an old fiberglass hull. Remember the old Pearson I mentioned? On the day I saw her owner sanding the hull, in my ignorance of the finish he was about to apply I motored out the channel feeling sorry for him. I *knew* that once you gave up on the gelcoat and painted a boat, even if you used the very best topside enamel available, you were doomed to repaint it every other year. Polyurethane changed all that.

Two coats of properly applied two-part polyurethane should still have most of its gloss after five years and may last twice that long. And, as with varnish, if the first application has been done with care, when the time finally does arrive to repaint, it is basically a matter of sanding the surface and laying on a fresh coat.

Perhaps you have heard that polyurethane is expensive, dangerous, and finicky. All true, but don't be put off. Take expensive, for example. Polyurethane costs two to three times the price of the most expensive enamels, and it requires special primers and pricey solvents. But expensive is relative. Think of a 20- or 30-thousand dollar purchase price. *All* the materials necessary to put a mirror finish on the hull and deck of an old 30-foot boat will cost $200, and that seems reasonable. From an investment standpoint, refinishing with polyurethane—if done well—adds thousands in value. Even compared to the cost of enamel, the life of the polyurethane makes it the cheapest in the long run, not to mention the savings in labor.

The reputation for danger is not exaggerated; polyurethane can kill you. However, when the paint is applied outside with a brush or a roller, protecting yourself from risk involves no more than wearing

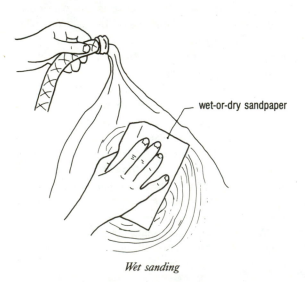

wet-or-dry sandpaper

Wet sanding

gloves and eye protection. The most serious hazards are associated exclusively with spray applications. The solution is simple: NEVER spray polyurethane. (Professional refinishers who do spray polyurethane wear protective suits and use positive pressure respirators.) I have yet to see a paint job that would have been worth dying for. And the flow characteristics of polyurethane are so good that I defy you to tell the difference between a sprayed coating and one carefully applied with a roller and tipped with a brush.

What about finicky? Polyurethanes don't like high humidity, and they should be applied when the temperature is between 50 degrees and 85 degrees. They prefer shade to direct sun, and any significant wind, aside from blowing trash into the finish, will actually set up tiny wave patterns in the free-flowing paint. You can do most of the preparation in any weather, but you need a couple of dry, moderate, still days, preferably with a high overcast. If you pick the right season to take on this project, these requirements should not represent a particular hardship. If a spell of uncooperative weather forces you to stay in the yard a week longer than you planned to get the two days you need, so be it. Applying polyurethane in less than ideal conditions is almost certain to yield less than ideal results.

Should you take on this project at all? If you are willing to devote the time and have the patience, there is little reason why you should not attempt it. It is, after all, painting, not cutting holes in the hull. If you don't like the way it comes out, you can sand it down and do it again.

The question of *who* does the job may be academic anyway. Professionals in my part of the country charge about $100 per foot to refinish a hull and $200 per foot for the deck. Not everyone can afford those prices. And even if you can afford it, you may find yourself less than enthusiastic about paying $9,000 for a job that you can do yourself for $200.

Preparation

The first step is to select the *brand* of paint you are going to use. Optimum results are only assured if you follow the instructions of the specific manufacturer, including using the proprietary preparatory products (say that backwards three times!) that they recommend. Differences in chemical composition may make one manufacturer's primer less compatible with a different manufacturer's finish coat. There is really no way of knowing if a different brand is compatible, so play it safe and buy fillers, primers, paint, and thinner from the same manufacturer.

If the hull of your old boat has been previously painted with anything other than a polyurethane, the aggressive solvents in the urethane are likely to affect the old coating like paint remover. If the surface is in good shape, a "conversion" coating can be applied to protect the old finish from the urethane, but if the old paint shows any signs of poor adhesion, it should be removed. Stripping a painted hull back to the gelcoat is never a bad idea unless the old coating is polyurethane.

Wash the hull (and/or deck) thoroughly to get it as clean as possible, then wipe it down with the specified solvent to remove all traces of wax. Fill all scratches and gouges in the gelcoat with the epoxy filler the paint manufacturer recommends and allow the epoxy to cure. Block-sand the repairs with 80-grit production paper, then sand the entire surface with 120-grit paper. A finishing sander is ideal for this step. Not long ago, when I stopped to talk with a couple refinishing their hull, I was astonished that they both had finishing sanders. The best ideas always seem to be so obvious!

If your gelcoat is in perfect shape, you need only wipe down the hull with solvent and lay on the polyurethane, but the gelcoat of few old boats is in such shape. Keep in mind that polyurethane, unlike alkyd enamel, goes on very thin and will not cover any flaws. In addition, the extreme gloss of polyurethane will actually highlight imperfections. To achieve a beautiful finish, the surface must be flawless, but the gelcoat of a neglected old boat is likely to be porous and perhaps crazed. The solution is epoxy primer.

After the gelcoat has been sanded and thoroughly wiped down with solvent, apply a coat of epoxy primer—the specific primer called for by the manufacturer—with a brush or a foam roller. Sand the cured primer with 120-grit paper, then inspect the surface closely. If all crazing and porosity are not filled, apply a second coat of primer. Once the prime coat has been sanded perfectly smooth and all traces of sanding dust wiped away with solvent, you are ready to apply the urethane.

Painting the Hull

Follow the manufacturer's instructions for mixing and thinning the paint, using cups or spoons for accurate measurement of smaller quantities. More than any other single aspect, thinning the paint with the *perfect* amount of solvent will lead to the perfect finish, but because of varying conditions, you cannot just add a specified amount of solvent. Some experimentation is required to get the paint thinned properly. When I painted my own hull, I painted the hull of my hard dinghy at the same time (including all the preparatory steps), making most of the mistakes on the dinghy before I touched a bristle to the hull of the boat. One of the great characteristics of two-part polyurethane is that you will know almost immediately if you have it right. If the paint runs, it is too thin; if it fails to level out, you need to add solvent. The coating also needs to stay "wet" long enough for overlapping sections to flow together; if the paint sets too quickly, the temperature or the humidity may be too high. Pinholes or little craters in the paint indicate that the surface is still porous and you need additional primer. "Fish-eyes" indicate wax or other contaminants on the surface.

If you don't have a hard dinghy, maybe someone you know would accept a free paint job on theirs. If not, do your experimentation on the transom. Keep your testing area small and if problems do show up you can remove the paint immediately with a solvent-soaked rag.

Two-part polyurethane has a pot life of about eight hours, but it remains stable for only about two hours before you have to start adding solvent to maintain the viscosity. You can mix enough paint in the morning to last the day, but pour up only what you will use in two hours and refrigerate the rest; refrigeration will extend the stable time and mini-mize the amount of additional thinning that will be necessary. Determine the amount of paint to mix by measuring the surface you intend to paint.

Before you begin painting, wet down the ground around the boat thoroughly to hold down the dust. Tape off the rail and the boot stripe or the bottom paint with "Fine-Line" masking tape. Try to paint each side of the hull when it is the shady side, i.e., one side in the morning and the other side in the afternoon.

Pour the paint into a paint tray and roll the coating on thinly with a special foam roller intended for use with polyurethane paints. (The solvents in polyurethane will dissolve standard foam rollers, leaving you with a flocked hull.) Immediately tip out the paint with a dry badger hair (or other high-quality) brush; one or two even strokes back into the previous section will be sufficient. With two people painting, one rolling the paint onto the hull and the second following behind, leveling the paint with the tip of the brush, the side of a hull can be coated in a matter of minutes. And the results are stunning.

Two-part polyurethanes are always applied in at least two coats. The second coat, if applied within 48 hours, can be applied over the first coat without sanding, but *don't do it*. Allow the first coat to dry overnight, then wet sand the entire surface with 340-grit wet-or-dry sandpaper. Flush away the resulting scum with plenty of fresh water. When the surface is totally dry, wipe it down with solvent and apply the final coat of polyurethane. Now look at your reflection in the hull with that stupid grin on your face. Try not to be too smug. Anybody can paint the flat expanse of a hull. When you can put the same flawless finish on the multi-faceted surface of a deck, then you are entitled to brag.

Restoring the Deck

Preparing and painting the deck is the same as for the hull, with two important distinctions. The deck surface is interrupted by handrails and hardware, not to mention portholes and hatches. And the integrity of the nonskid surface that covers much of the deck must be protected.

For the best refinishing job, remove as much of

the deck hardware as you can. Removal has several benefits. First, it makes sanding and painting easier. Because it simplifies flowing out the paint, removal also tends to reduce lap marks and breaks in the finish that may result from painting *around* a cleat or handrail. It allows more of the surface to be initially coated by rolling, which yields a more uniform coating and a better finish than brush application. And it reduces the number of exposed edges; the reinstalled hardware sits *on* the new coating. Any deck hardware or features that will not be removed must be masked.

How you treat nonskid surfaces will depend upon the condition of the original texture. While some later molded-in patterns had sufficient definition not to be compromised by a coat or two of polyurethane, most early nonskid was only marginally effective to begin with. Two coats of high-gloss paint added to two decades of wear yields a surface more suitable for ice skates than deck shoes. You may also want the nonskid to be a different color from the rest of the deck.

Assuming that the nonskid requires special treatment—either to enhance the nonskid characteristics or to provide a contrasting color—the smooth portions and the nonskid portions of the deck will have to be painted separately. No such segregation is required for surface preparation. Once the entire deck has been de-waxed, filled, primed, and sanded as required, carefully mask the nonskid areas and apply two coats of polyurethane to the smooth areas.

There are two reasons for painting the smooth surfaces first. Typically the smooth areas are white, while the nonskid has color; color covers white better than the other way around. The second reason is that if the final masking is done on the nonskid rather than the smooth surface, a sharp line between the two will be difficult to achieve.

After coating the smooth surface, mask it and paint the nonskid panels. The nonskid properties of a painted surface are enhanced by adding grit to the paint in one of two ways. Paint manufacturers usually offer a nonskid additive—typically polymer beads—that is mixed into the paint providing a rough surface as the paint is rolled on. (There is no reason to tip nonskid paint.) This method is effective, but because the beads tend to settle almost immediately to the bottom of the paint tray, the resulting texture is usually irregular.

Shaking the grit onto the paint coated surface provides a more uniform grit pattern. Sand, pumice, or ground walnut shells are the traditional grits, but the plastic spheres and beads of nonskid additives can also be applied this way. Apply a coat of epoxy primer and, while it is still wet, cover the surface entirely with grit sifted from your fingers or a large shaker. When the epoxy kicks, use a soft brush to gently sweep up the grit that did not adhere (it can be reused on another nonskid area). Roll on two coats of polyurethane, encapsulating the grit.

Nonskid Overlay

For secure footing, rubberized nonskid such as Treadmaster M is superior to any painted or molded nonskid surface I have ever encountered. It even provides better footing than raw teak.

Before the rubber overlay can be applied over an old nonskid surface, the molded-in texture has to be removed. Usually most of the texture can be quickly ground away with a grinder or a belt sander and 50-grit belt. Be careful not to let the sander get outside the textured area. It is not necessary and usually not desirable to sand away all of the texture. Rather, fill the remaining depressions with epoxy putty, and fair the surface when the epoxy cures. Paint the deck, including an inch or so into the nonskid areas, before proceeding.

Start by making patterns from heavy (kraft) paper of each of the nonskid panels. Panel sizes will be limited by the sheet size of the overlay, usually 3 feet by 4 feet. For drainage and appearance, leave at least a 1-inch gap between panels and 2 inches between the nonskid and any vertical surfaces (cabin sides, rails, coamings, etc.). Cut the paper oversize, place it on the deck, and use a pencil to draw the exact outline. A flexible wooden batten will help you to parallel the curvature of the rail and other features. Use a lid or a can to put a uniform radius on the corners of the panels.

Carefully tape around the nonskid areas with masking tape.

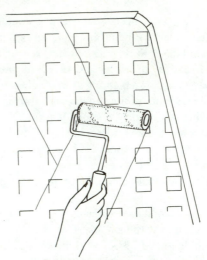

Roll on a coat of epoxy primer.

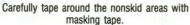

While the primer is wet, sift grit over the entire area. A paint can with holes punched in the bottom makes an adequate shaker.

After the epoxy kicks, sweep up the grit that did not adhere with a *soft* brush.

Roll on two coats of polyurethane.

Painting a nonskid surface

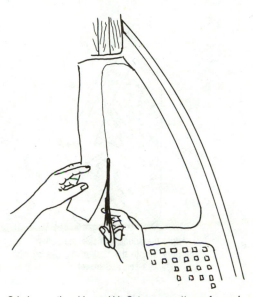

Grind away the old nonskid. Cut paper patterns for each nonskid panel.

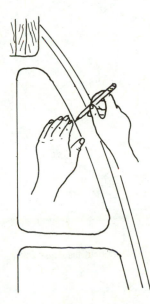

Draw around each pattern to outline the area to be coated with adhesive.

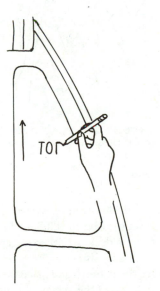

Draw a line parallel to the centerline of the boat and write "top" on each pattern.

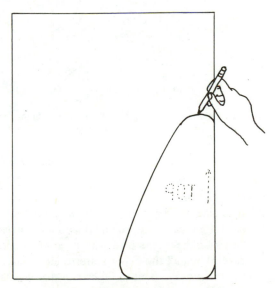

Turn the pattern over and place it on the *back* side of the overlay. Trace.

Installing nonskid overlay (continued on page 350)

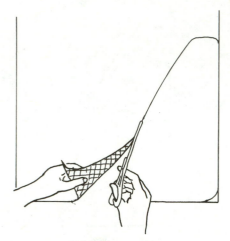

Cut out the nonskid panel.

Apply the adhesive inside the outline
on the deck and to the back of the overlay with
a serrated trowel.

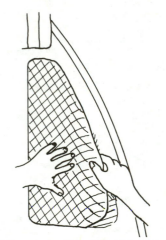

Position the overlay and press it in place. Flatten it to the deck,
working from the center.

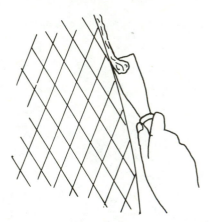

Use a putty knife to pick up any excess adhesive that squeezes
out around the edges. Clean the residue away with solvent.

Installing nonskid overlay (continued)

Take your time to get the patterns right, then cut them to size and tape them temporarily in place. Write TOP on each pattern and draw a line parallel to the centerline of the boat with an arrow toward the bow. When all the paper patterns are in place, look at the overall effect to be certain that you are satisfied. Do not cut patterns for only one side with the intention of reversing them for the opposite side; boats are almost never symmetrical and hardware is certain to be in different locations. Trace each pattern on deck to outline the area that will be covered with adhesive.

Remove the patterns and place them *upside down* on the *back* side of the sheets of overlay. Align the pencil line you drew with the long side of the sheet to insure the correct orientation of the nonskid's design. Move the patterns around to make the most effective use of each sheet. Trace each pattern onto the overlay, then cut out each piece with shears, snips, or heavy scissors.

If the overlay manufacturer does not recommend a different adhesive, glue the nonskid to the deck with epoxy. Use a serrated trowel to apply the glue to both the back of the covering and to the area inside the pencil outline. Carefully position the section of overlay and press it to the deck. Be sure the overlay lies flat on the deck, working from the center toward the edges. Use a flat screwdriver or a putty knife to pick up any epoxy that squeezes out, and clean away the residue with acetone or toluene. Apply each section in turn. When the epoxy dries, your tread is good for 50,000 miles. At least.

PAINTING THE BOTTOM

If you have just put a mirror finish on the topsides, how much of a challenge can painting the bottom be? Not much. Sand the old coating smooth and roll on a couple of new coats. But if you have never done a bottom job before, a bit more exposition might help your confidence and improve your results.

Coating the bottom of your boat with even the most potent antifouling paint is a waste of time and money if the paint starts flaking off as soon as the boat goes back into the water. As with every other paint job, success depends upon surface preparation.

Rake and Scrape

Getting ready to paint begins as soon as the keel clears the surface of the water. While the bottom is still wet, the slime and growth will be relatively easy to remove. If you let the stuff dry, it will takes a chisel to remove it. I am not making this up. Scrape and scrub the bottom growth-free the instant it comes out of the water.

Fortunately, most boatyards now have a pressure washer at the lift (or ramp) and will blast all the little sea critters off your hull while it hangs from the slings. A few passes with long-handled scrapers takes care of the mussel colony on the bottom of the keel. If bits of bottom paint flake off under the pressure of the washer nozzle, have the yard worker make another pass to remove as much of the loose paint as possible. If the yard you are planning to use does not have a power washer, suggest that they get with the program, or find another yard. By the time the yard workers block and level your hull, the bottom should be completely clean.

The safest way to prepare the hull for a fresh coat of poison is to scrape it. Scraping does not raise a cloud of toxic dust to be ingested into your lungs, and it peels away the old, dead paint like peeling an apple. You need a 3-inch paint or hook scraper, available in any hardware or paint store; any wider will bridge the curvature of the hull. Hook scrapers usually have a reversible blade attached to a handle with a wing nut. Unlike a cabinet scraper, which can be used in either direction, you always *pull* a hook scraper. Sharpen the scraper by drawing a mill file across the edge and chasing the edge with a whetstone. Do *not* burnish a burr onto the edge of a hook scraper.

Sanding is the second choice. The paint has probably lost much of its potency or you would not be in the yard, but the *under* layers of paint are still plenty toxic and you want to keep the dust out of your lungs and off your skin as much as possible. TBT-based copolymers are particularly hazardous. Wear long pants and long sleeves, with the cuffs banded inside your gloves. Goodwill and other thrift stores are a good source of loose-fitting clothes that can be discarded at the end of the day. If you don't have a full hood, at least wear a hat and goggles, especially if you are using a grinder.

Before you sand bottom paint, you need a tight-fitting respirator, the rubber kind with replaceable filters. Paper masks are as useless as paper condoms. If you don't believe me, blow your nose after sanding for an hour in a paper mask. The blue tissue tells you you have just barnacle-proofed your nasal passages. Tain't funny. This stuff can turn you into a rutabaga. Invest the 20 bucks in a respirator—3M makes an excellent one—and use the thing.

A grinder and 80- or 100-grit disks in skilled hands can prepare a hull for recoating relatively quickly. Be sure the disk is on a foam pad, and do not apply too much pressure; let the grinder do the work. Keep the grinder moving and keep in mind that a high-speed grinder can chew its way through paint and gelcoat and into the laminates in an instant. A drill motor a with foam-backed sanding disk is perfectly adequate for spot sanding, but drill motors are not designed for continuous service. If you are going to grind, you need a grinder.

A powerful finishing sander, like the Makita, loaded with 80-grit paper, is slower, but safer for the hull. I would not try to remove several layers of paint with one, but a finishing sander is perfectly suited for smoothing and feathering sound old paint.

Leave the belt sander in the locker. A belt sander is designed exclusively to make things *flat* and that is the effect it will have on your hull.

If the old paint is beginning to lift, or if you are putting on a new paint that is incompatible with the old one, you will have to do more than sand the surface. The old paint will have to be removed. The only sensible way to strip a bottom back to the gelcoat is with a chemical stripper—but not just any chemical stripper. Many chemical strippers, when they have had their way with paint, will proceed to dissolve the gelcoat as well. This is a disaster of the first order, so be sure that you use a stripper that is clearly labeled for use on fiberglass.

Using the fiberglass-safe stripper to remove bottom paint is no different than removing varnish with a chemical remover. Apply a thick coat of the stripper to the paint without brushing back and forth. Allow the remover to soften the paint, then scrape away the softened paint with the push of a putty knife. Use the hook scraper to remove the stubborn "islands" that the putty knife leaves behind. For a decade of bottom paint, multiple applications may be necessary.

Sandblasting bottoms has become a popular way to strip away bottom paint and is probably the best way to strip a metal hull. But despite the fact that it is today a common practice, fiberglass hulls should *never* be sandblasted. Sandblasting destroys the integrity of the gelcoat, making it porous and almost certainly leading to hull blisters. Even if you are planning on sealing the gelcoat after stripping, sandblasting is still a bad idea; if the nozzle is not held at a low angle to the surface, no more than 30 percent, the underlying laminate will also be damaged. Sandblasting is popular because it is easy, not because it is smart. Stick to mild chemical strippers and the scraper.

The Final Prep

If you have stripped the hull back to the original gelcoat, wash it with a TSP solution, then flush the surface thoroughly with water to remove loose particles and all traces of the stripper. Invest in a quart of de-waxing solvent and wipe the hull down, turning your cloth to a clean section often. Unless this was done before the original commissioning dealer applied the first coat of bottom paint—fat chance—there is still mold release wax on the hull and it will still interfere with the adhesion of your paint.

The next step depends upon whether or not your old boat has hull blisters and whether you are worried about getting them. If your hull has a case of

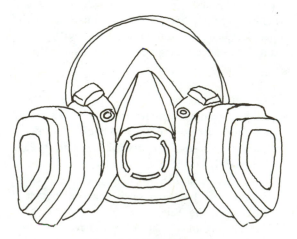

Twelve buck life insurance.

Cartridge respirator

boat-pox, you need to open, drain, clean, dry, and fill each of the blisters. The specifics of blister repair are detailed in Chapter 6. A 20-year-old boat that has never had a blister is not likely to have a rash pop up this year either unless you damage the gelcoat by sandblasting, using the wrong stripper, or sanding too enthusiastically. If your hull has had boat pox, the "cure" is to dry the hull and seal it. Preventing the recurrence (or the initial occurrence) depends upon keeping moisture out of the hull laminate.

There is no point in sealing a saturated hull. That simply traps the moisture inside the hull and makes the situation worse. Drying the hull, getting the saturation level below 50 percent, is essential before sealing the hull. In 100-degree weather, the hull will dry sufficiently in two weeks out of the water, but the lower *average* temperature and the high humidity typical of a Florida summer will retard the drying so that two months out of the water are required. In a northern climate where the average temperature is closer to 50 degrees, the hull needs to be out of the water for at least five months. Tenting and using a dehumidifier will reduce these times.

With the blisters repaired and the hull dry, you have two choices for sealing the hull. The one most widely used is to coat the hull with at least 10 mils of epoxy. At about 2 mils per coat, this means rolling on at least five coats. Sanding between coats is unnecessary as long as you recoat the surface within two hours. One problem with the epoxy treatment is that if water does manage to permeate, the interaction of the epoxy coating with the underlying polyester resin tends to promote blistering.

This problem is absent in the other alternative: painting the hull with alkyd enamel. Three coats of alkyd enamel, preferably an alkyd/urethane/silicone blend, seal the hull as well as epoxy and provide a good base for the antifouling bottom paint. Select an enamel formulated for marine use, and roll it on, lightly sanding between coats. No primer is necessary.

Whether the surface is enamel or epoxy, old bottom paint or bare fiberglass, preparation for the application of antifouling paint is the same. Sand each of these surfaces lightly with 80 grit production paper. To keep the dust down, a preferable alternative for old bottom paint is to wet sand it with 120-grit wet-or-dry paper. Flush the surface with fresh water: after it dries, wipe it down with acetone. Mask the boot stripe with Fine-Line tape.

Choosing a Bottom Paint

With the recent ban of the highly toxic TBT (tributyl tin) as an antifoulant on boats under 82 feet, less effective but environmentally more sound copper is once again the active ingredient in virtually all bottom paints. This pretty well levels the playing field and makes bottom paint selection relatively uncomplicated. The more copper a paint contains, the more effective it is likely to be.

There are a couple of other factors worthy of consideration. Some bottom paints are soft, using pine resin (rosin) as a binder. As the binder erodes, the cuprous oxide is exposed, gagging the little critters that are trying to set up housekeeping on your hull. Soft paints dissolve away whether the boat moves or not, but they tend to be effective for a relatively short period of time, often only a few months.

Harder paints, with an epoxy or a vinyl binder, tend to release their toxicant more slowly, making them somewhat less effective initially, but they keep their antifouling characteristics for a longer period of time—up to 18 to 24 months for those with the highest copper content. Most of these are contact-leaching paints, meaning that the binder becomes porous, allowing the copper to leach to the surface; but some are *ablative*, dependent upon motion through the water to release the copper.

Many of the now-banned TBT-based paints were copolymers. In copolymers, the toxicant, rather than being a powder that is simply mixed into the paint, is chemically bound to the paint. As long as the paint lasts, it has antifouling chemicals. Some copper-based copolymers are appearing on the market, but whether they will have the multi-year effectiveness of their tin-based predecessors is doubtful.

Another consideration is what is already on your

hull. The different types and brands of paints are often incompatible. You cannot put anything over a soft paint except another soft paint, and vinyl paints cannot be applied over anything except vinyl. But soft paints can be painted over anything and hard coatings over anything but soft paint. And some copper paints should not be applied over a tin-based paint. If you don't know what is on the hull, you are well advised to strip the old paint and start all over.

When you look at all the different cans on the shelf, how do you decide? Your choice will depend on whether your sailing season is short or endless. It will depend on whether you haul every year or only when you have to. It will depend on whether your boat sees little or a lot of use. And it will depend on what has been used on the bottom of your old boat in the past. Once again, your neighbors in the marina will be your best source of information about which antifouling formulas work best in your waters.

How much paint do you need? A rough estimate of wetted area can be calculated by multiplying the LOA times the beam times 0.90. The paint label will specify the coverage per gallon.

The Final Step

The copper in bottom paint tends to settle into a solid lump, and vigorous stirring with a flat paddle is required. You can slosh $50 worth of paint out on the ground while you stir, or you can pour half the paint into another container—your choice. Keep digging and stirring with the paddle until the bottom is clean and all the copper is distributed through the half remaining in the can. If the other half is in another container, pour it back into the original can slowly while you continue to stir; if it is in the dirt, just leave it there.

Adding thinner to bottom paint is generally not recommended. The paint depends upon thickness for its effectiveness. If you apply the paint on a hot, windy day, some thinner may be required to get the paint to flow out, but normally you will use the paint as it comes.

For longer-lasting protection, apply two coats. The second coat can usually be applied in a contin-

uous operation, i.e., by the time you have finished painting the hull, the paint on the area where you started will be dry enough to recoat. Even if you apply only one coat, use any leftover paint to apply a second coat at the waterline where the scrubbing action of the water tends to remove the paint more quickly.

Save a little paint to coat the bottom of the keel and the areas under the screw pads or wedges when the boat is back in the slings. Don't even consider backing off a screw. Never mind that your boat is likely to do a little pirouette and fall over, squashing you like a roach. *My* boat could be sitting next to yours in the yard.

You can put on bottom paint with a brush, but it is much easier with a roller, brushing only the areas the roller misses. Use only throwaway brushes and rollers. A short-nap roller will provide a smoother surface, weigh less (copper paint is heavy), and sling less paint on the ground and you. Use an extension on the roller handle and you should be able to paint the hull in a white linen suit (*not* recommended).

Roll on bottom paint as quickly as you can. Unless you are racing your old boat, there is little reason to consider tipping out the coating with a brush. It is difficult to do effectively anyway because the solvent in most bottom paints tends to flash, leaving the paint almost immediately tacky. You will invariably get a smoother job just rolling. It is easier to roll up and down, but racing sailors concerned with the ridges that may form where strokes overlap sometimes roll bow to stern. The tiny ridges left behind by the roller will have no noticeable effect on the performance of a pleasure boat, but for competitive use, select a hard paint and wet-sand or burnish (with bronze wool) the paint to a slick finish.

BOOTSTRIPE

Perhaps the easiest way to apply a bootstripe—that narrow strip of black or gold or whatever that separates the topsides from the bottom and gives the bottom paint a finished look—is to use a bootstripe tape. The vinyl tape intended for bootstripe use is

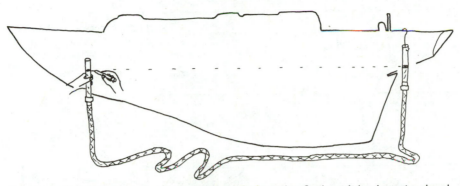

Use a water-filled garden hose to mark the location of the bootstripe. Sections of clear hose at each end will allow you to see the water level. Mark the hull every foot, closer where the hull is changing shape. Mark both sides of the stripe.

Mask the stripe with Fine Line tape, carefully making a fair curve through the marks.

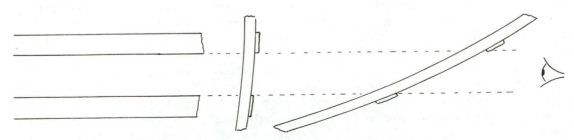

Note that the space between the tape—the width of the stripe—will vary depending on the shape of the hull, but viewed from the side, the *apparent* width will be uniform.

Painting the bootstripe (continued on page 356)

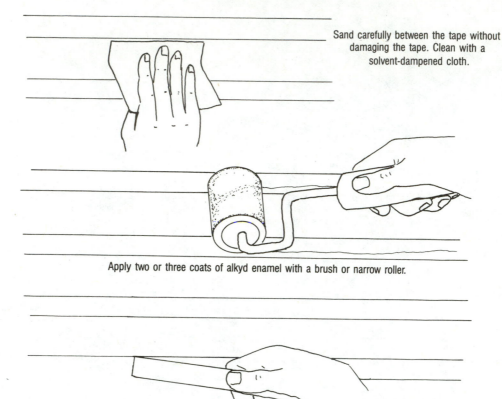

Sand carefully between the tape without damaging the tape. Clean with a solvent-dampened cloth.

Apply two or three coats of alkyd enamel with a brush or narrow roller.

When the top coat is dry, or slightly tacky, peel the back upon itself and slightly downward (upward for the top strip).

Painting the bootstripe (continued)

amazingly durable and it is available in multi-stripe effects as well as a variety of widths and solid colors. The drawback to bootstripe tape, particularly for use on a sailboat, is the fact that it is a uniform width. Because of the curvature of the hull, in order for the bootstripe to *appear* to the eye to have a uniform width, it must actually be wider as the hull surface becomes less vertical. Hold up a strip of tape or a narrow piece of paper and slowly rotate it from vertical to horizontal to understand what I mean.

Painting on the bootstripe allows you to vary the width of the stripe so that when the boat is viewed from the water, it will appear to have a uniform

width. The top of the stripe is a fixed distance *higher* than the bottom of the stripe.

Regardless of how you intend to apply the stripe, the first step is to establish the waterline of your boat. Newer boats occasionally have a molded-in line, or even both lines for the stripe, but old boats rarely do. Yards occasionally score the line so it is not lost when they are repainting the bottom. Of course the old stripe, if there is one, will mark the waterline. If the exact location of the waterline is in question, you will need to establish it some other way.

An easy way to locate the waterline is to do it while the boat is afloat. Pick a mirror calm morning and check the trim of your boat with a borrowed carpenter's level. Use the cabin sole to check fore-and-aft trim and span the cockpit seats with the level to check for list. Redistribute equipment and supplies until the boat sits level in both directions. From a dinghy, or in the water, use a knife to score the hull at the surface of the water at the bow and at both corners of the transom.

Once in the yard, you need to have the yard workers level the hull. Again use the carpenter's level on the sole (or galley counter) and across the cockpit seats. Once the boat is level, marking the waterline is easy. All that is required is a garden hose half again as long as your boat and about 3 feet of clear ³/₄-inch vinyl hose. You also need a couple of garden hose replacement fittings, one male and one female. Put the fittings on either end of the clear hose, then cut the hose in half. Now screw the two pieces to the garden hose to provide each end with about 18 inches of clear hose.

With a piece of line or wire taped to one of the clear sections, hang it from the rail so that the waterline mark you made, or any other reference waterline, crosses the clear hose approximately in the middle. Hold the other clear hose above the waterline and fill the hose completely with water from a bucket or another hose. Once the hose is full, lower the free end until it is level with the waterline, spilling out some of the water. Raise the hose again, and you will notice that the water level in both clear sections is exactly at the waterline. (If it isn't, add or spill a little water until it is.)

Since water seeks its own level, you can walk around the boat with the loose end and hold it against the hull to mark as many points as you like that are level with the control point. Because the hose is flexible, the internal volume may vary as you move it around the boat, so it is advisable to have a second person at the control location to raise or lower the hose if necessary to make sure the water level is exactly at the reference line before you mark each spot. Some oscillation will also occur as you move the hose; allow the water to settle before marking the hull. Mark the hull every foot, closer

where the hull is changing shape quickly—as it does under the stern.

You probably do not want the boot stripe to lie exactly at the waterline. Immediate fouling will occur if the boat is slightly out of trim, and even wave action can keep the stripe wet enough to foul. The bootstripe should be at least an inch and as much as 2 inches above the *load waterline*, with the antifouling paint carried up to the bottom of the stripe.

You should also keep in mind that the load waterline moves up the hull as you put fuel, water, gear, supplies, and people aboard. You can estimate the amount of movement by calculating the pounds-per-inch (PPI) immersion factor. The PPI can be precisely determined by multiplying the water plane area by 5.33, but for this purpose an approximation calculated by multiplying the waterline length by the waterline beam by 3.4 is adequate. My old Seawind, with a 24-foot waterline and a 9-foot beam, has a PPI of approximately 735 pounds (24 × 9 × 3.4). Eight fathoms of ³/₈-inch chain (9 pounds per fathom) will sink my waterline an inch. So will 90 gallons of water. Or a crew of four.

If you are using bootstripe tape, once you have determined the location of the bottom of the bootstripe and marked it all the way around the hull, all that remains is to carefully align the bottom of the tape with the marks and press it onto the hull. For a painted stripe, decide the *apparent* stripe width you prefer and, on a vertical part of the hull, measure that distance above the first mark. Hang the controlling end of the hose across this higher mark and add water to the hose until the water level in both ends is even with the mark. Use the loose end to make a second series of marks around the hull.

There is no need to pencil the waterline onto the hull; you are going to connect the marks with masking tape. However, if you want to scribe a permanent line, use a plastic-laminate scoring tool and a flexible batten. A second pair of hands will be helpful.

To mask the bootstripe, use only Fine Line tape, which will not wick paint like cheap tape and will give a crisp, sharp edge to the stripe. Don't ruin the stripe to save a couple of bucks on tape. Wide tape— an inch or more—will be easier to keep straight.

Be sure the bottom paint has had a day to dry, or the tape is likely to lift some paint when you remove it. Start anywhere on the hull and tape along the marks you made with the water level (or along the old stripe if you are just recoating), sighting along the top of the tape to keep it straight and touching the tape to the hull only lightly. When you have finished, check the fairness of the line from the side, from the bow, and from the quarter and correct any hills or valleys. Once you are satisfied, run your thumb along the edge of the tape to seal it and assure a clean line. Mask the topsides for the top of the bootstripe in the same manner.

Lightly sand the area between the tape, taking care not to damage the tape, and clean it with an acetone-dampened cloth. Alkyd enamel is the usual choice for painting the stripe. Apply the enamel with a brush or a narrow roller. As soon as the enamel dries, apply a second coat. When the top coat is dry or only slightly tacky, immediately remove the masking tape, pulling it in the direction you are peeling and slightly downward (upward for the top strip).

GRAPHICS

Most boatowners hire a sign painter to put the name on the stern of their boat. A few use plastic letters. And computer generated vinyl graphics are becoming more popular. But there is no reason why a skillful painter like yourself cannot put the name on the stern. All you need is a large piece of paper, a can of brushable or spray mask, and a pounce wheel, all of which may be purchased from an art supply store.

You are going to draw the name on the paper, erasing, correcting, and experimenting as necessary until you get it right. The only thing you need to be aware of is that the curvature of the transom (or the hull if your boat has a canoe stern or is a double-ender) will curve the alignment of the letters. If you draw the name straight on your paper, it will have a

smile or a frown, depending on the configuration of the stern. A curve in the name may look quite nice, but if you want the name to be straight on a curved transom, an offsetting curvature has to be part of your pattern.

How do you know how much of a curve and which direction? If you are still in the yard, drag out the old garden-hose level. Tape your pattern paper to the hull. Make two holes in the paper and two pencil marks on the hull so you can realign the paper later. Decide where you want the name and use the hose to put a *level* series of marks across the paper, connecting them into a level line. It will be helpful to make a second line where the *top* of the letters will be. If you cannot decide on the exact height of the letters until you lay out the name, draw two or three lines at different heights. Also draw the lines for the hailing port.

If the boat is not in the yard, the lines can be drawn by measuring up from the surface of the water. A reverse transom complicates this process, but a level fastened to a wooden square nailed together from two lengths of 1 × 2 will allow you to accurately mark the vertical height from the water.

For reference, measure across the transom and mark the center of each of the lines. Remove the paper and take it home to do the artwork. You can use a stencil to draw the letters on the paper, or copy any lettering style you like. Graphic-arts books will show you how to enlarge letters accurately. Use a straight edge and a French curve to achieve clean, sharp lines. Be sure each letter is perpendicular to the base line.

When you are satisfied with your artwork, place the paper on the carpet or a blanket and follow the lines with the pounce wheel, perforating the pattern. You may have to lightly sand the back of the paper to fully open the holes.

Buy a can of *spray* enamel in the color you want. Pick a calm day and take the paint, the pattern, the can of spray mask, and a razor knife (an X-acto works well) to the boat. You will also need some newspaper and masking tape.

Wipe down the transom, then mask the surface with tape and newspaper, leaving uncovered only the area where the name will be. Spray the uncovered area with the spray mask. The mask forms a thin plastic film that protects the surface and can be peeled away easily. Now tape the pounced paper stencil to the stern, aligning it with the two reference marks you made earlier. Tape over the reference holes.

Lightly spray the stencil with your paint to transfer the outline of the letters to the hull. (You can also use pounce powder, if you prefer.) Release the bottom of the stencil and look underneath to make sure that all the letters are fully outlined. If not, tape the stencil back down and spray the areas indicated. Remove the stencil.

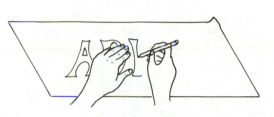

Draw the name on a large sheet of kraft paper.

Follow the outlines with a pounce wheel, perforating the paper and creating a stencil.

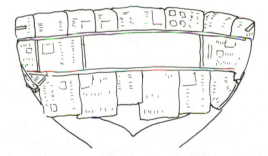

Protect the transom with newspaper and masking tape, leaving only the area where the name will be exposed.

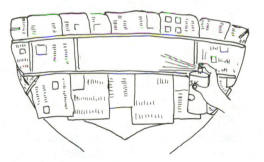

Spray the uncovered area with spray mask.

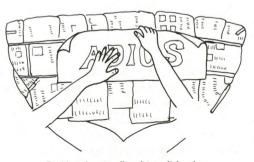

Position the stencil and tape it in place.

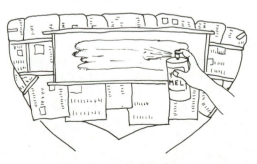

Spray the stencil with paint.

Painting graphics (continued on page 360)

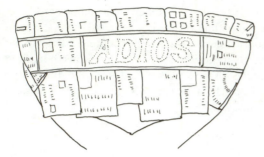

Check to be sure all the letters are fully outlined with paint dots, then remove the stencil.

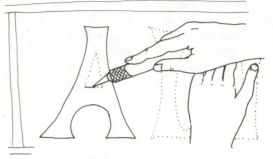

With a razor knife (X-acto), carefully cut the spray mask along the dotted lines. Peel away the inside of each letter.

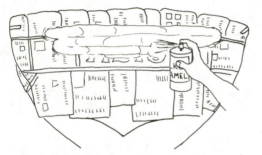

Spray the cut-out mask with several coats of enamel.

When the paint is dry, peel away the tape, paper, and mask.

Painting graphics (continued)

Use your razor knife, with the help of a straight-edge and a French curve, to cut the spray mask along the dotted lines. Light pressure will be sufficient to cut through the mask. As each letter is cut out, peel it away. Any slips of the knife can be repaired with Fine Line or cellophane tape and re-trimmed. When all the letters have been cut out, spray the mask *lightly* with paint. Spraying too heavily will cause the letters to run or sag. Apply four or five light coats, allowing the paint to dry between coats—usually a matter of a few minutes. When you are satisfied with the coverage, give the paint several hours to dry and peel away the tape, paper, and mask. Pretty nice!

You can do special effects with a little more effort. For example, if you want each letter outlined in a contrasting color, pounce the outline of the letter and the outline of the border on the stencil. Cut out the mask along the outer dots and spray the border color. On large letters, spray around the outline of the letter to concentrate the paint in the border areas. Let the paint dry overnight, then spray the surface again with mask. Respray the stencil and this time cut out the letters along the inner dots. Spray the surface with your primary color. After the paint dries, peel away the mask and you will have bordered letters. The same process can be used to achieve shadowing or any other multicolor effect.

With her wood glowing, her topsides blinding, and her name freshly painted on the stern, your old boat should be looking pretty sharp by now. Nothing has a more immediate impact on the look of a boat than paint and varnish, making even a tired old dowager suddenly seem young and fresh. But don't stop with cosmetics. It is time to give the old girl a new wardrobe.

FIFTEEN

Material Things

Clay is molded to make a vessel,
but the utility of the vessel
lies in the space where there is nothing.
–LAO TZU–

The enhancement possibilities for your old boat represented by a few yards of canvas or other fabric and some basic sewing skills are virtually limitless. There are the obvious improvements, like new upholstery on the cushions and a bright new sail cover on the boom. There are features you admire on other boats, like a sun-deflecting Bimini or bum-cradling cockpit cushions. There are cruising essentials like windscoops and harbor awnings. And there are unexplored ideas like storage pockets and canvas tool rolls.

The skills required to accomplish all of these things are amazingly few. A machine does all the hard work; all you have to do is cut the fabric to the appropriate dimensions and guide the pieces through the machine. A reasonable analogy can be drawn between running a piece of canvas through a sewing machine and a piece of plywood through a band saw. The big difference is that if you get off your line with the sewing machine, the material is not ruined; you can simply remove the errant stitches and do it again.

Of all the traditional marine crafts, canvas work is my personal favorite. I *love* to sew, and I make no excuses for that sentiment. It is a creative, artistic, and therapeutic activity. It provides a sense of satisfaction similar to the one you get fashioning a lump of wood into a thing of beauty or utility, but without risk to fingers and eyes. Like painting and varnishing, it yields the gratification of immediate visual enhancement, but without dust and fumes. A missed stitch is not going to let the mast go over the side or the ocean flow into the cabin. Canvas work

doesn't leave you itching, like working with fiberglass, or grimy, like mechanical repairs. Weather is not a factor. Projects can be done at a single sitting, or as time permits over a period of weeks or months. But the main reason I enjoy it is that it's just plain fun.

THE SEWING MACHINE

Many years ago—back when the Japanese were making cheap imitations of American products instead of the other way around—I traded an old black-and-white television for a Japanese sewing machine. The other party to the trade could hardly control her glee as the deal was consummated, but I got the last laugh. For the next decade, while, according to the Nielsens, "The Dukes of Hazard" was the number one show on television, I coaxed a hundred yards of upholstery material and canvas through that sorry machine, saving hundreds of dollars outright and adding thousands of dollars to the value of the old boat I owned at the time.

Today I own a much better sewing machine, a commercial-quality tailor's machine, and if I tried to claim that the old machine did as good a job as the new one, I would be lying. The new machine, which is also Japanese, by the way, does most things better and everything easier. If it didn't, what would have been the point in buying it? But with that old machine, I did manage to sew awnings and sail covers and settee cushions and every other fabric project I attempted. The point is that almost any domestic sewing machine, even one of doubtful virtue, can do the job if you will help it along. A *good* domestic machine should not need much help.

If you do not have a machine and you are going to buy one, there are a few features that you should look for. For canvas, particularly acrylic canvas, the longer the stitch the better. Look for a machine that will sew a straight stitch at least four millimeters long. A zigzag stitch is rarely needed for canvas work, and you can often buy an older heavy-duty straight-stitch machine cheaply. However, if you want to do any sail repair or construction, a wide zigzag is almost essential. A width of six millimeters is *just* adequate.

Adjustable foot pressure is mandatory, and a wide feed dog—the toothed claw that pulls the fabric through the machine—will make some jobs easier. Some machines have interchangeable feed dogs and matching needle plates—the polished plate around the dog. More underarm space is always better than less.

What you don't need is a machine that does 20 different decorative stitches. And avoid machines with slant needles. When you start looking around, don't ask a blue-haired lady in a sewing center at the mall. Find a commercial outlet or a reputable repair shop and tell them you want a cheap, sturdy machine without any bells and whistles. Emphasize cheap. They often take trade-ins or have unclaimed repairs that can be purchased reasonably. Classified ads and flea markets are also good sources. Take a piece of acrylic canvas with you, and before you pay your money, make sure *you* can make the machine stitch through six layers. It is not unusual for a canvas item to be six layers thick in the corner, and if the machine will handle this test, it will probably handle every canvas project you are likely to attempt.

My own machine, as a matter of reference, will sew through more than a dozen layers. If you expect to be messing about in boats for decades to come, I strongly recommend that you do your homework, then spend the extra dollars for a quality sewing machine. Like any quality tool, it will return the investment many times over. But first use the machine you have, one you borrow, or one you obtain inexpensively to do a few of the projects that follow to determine your interest and aptitude.

OTHER TOOLS

A pair of *sharp* scissors is a pleasure to use. Don't dig out the old rusty pair you use for paper and gasket material. Treat yourself to a new pair just for canvas work. The new generation of lightweight, vanadium steel scissors with bright plastic handles (Japanese-made, of course) are generally excellent and 9-inch scissors, a convenient size, cost less than $10.

While you are buying scissors, pick up a seam ripper. This is a little gizmo that resembles an undersize fountain pen when the lid is in place. Under the lid is a metal shank that ends in what looks like a thumb and a pointing index finger; the metal "skin" between these two digits is razor sharp. Slip the finger under a stitch and push the ripper forward and it slices right through the thread.

A measuring tape and a straight yardstick are essential for the initial layout, and a carpenter's square can be useful. A lead pencil or chalk should be used to mark the material; a marker or a pen will bleed through the fabric.

Grommets are a common feature of many marine canvas items, and a special die set is required to install them. Washer grommets are sold in hardware stores and chandleries, and are commonly used in amateur canvas work. They are adequate for light duty, but *spur* grommets, which have a heavy rolled edge and a half dozen spurs that lock the grommet to the cloth, are infinitely superior. The installation of spur grommets is identical to that of washer grommets, and the cost difference between the two is pennies. So why would anyone use washer grommets? Beats me. Probably because washer grommets are more readily available and often sold in a kit that includes a setting tool and a hole cutter with the grommets.

A spur grommet die set should cost $25 to $35, depending upon the size; that is about twice what a washer grommet kit costs, but at the risk of sounding like a broken record, a good tool will last a lifetime. As for the cost of the grommets, buy them by the gross and they are inexpensive. They won't spoil.

The most common sizes (measured as the diameter of the hole through the grommet) are 3/8-inch and 1/2-inch. In washer grommets, these sizes are designated as #2 and #3, respectively. For some reason that undoubtedly has a logical basis, spur grommets in these two sizes are designated as #2 and #4. Unless exceptional stress is likely, or you need the larger diameter, the smaller size will serve most purposes.

Mechanical fasteners are also commonly used in boat canvas. As we will detail later, twist fasteners are installed with a heated knife and a pair of pliers, but snap fasteners require a special tool for correct installation. An adequate snap fastener installation tool will cost around four bucks.

One final item that you may find very helpful if you are a novice is a roll of transfer tape. Transfer tape looks a bit like a narrow roll of brown packing tape. Once it is applied to the cloth, the paper is then gently lifted and peeled away, leaving only the adhesive behind. Transfer tape allows you to assemble two pieces of fabric, or form a hem, before you take the fabric to the sewing machine. The parts may be peeled apart and repositioned as necessary. It is used mostly to assemble the slick Dacron or nylon panels of sails, but it is equally effective on acrylic canvas and other marine fabrics. Basting seams with transfer tape before you attempt to stitch them can make the difference between frustration and disdain.

GETTING STARTED

The first step in canvas work is a familiarity with your sewing machine. If you have a manual, read it carefully and locate every guide and screw and lever. If you don't have a manual, try to get one; it not only details the major components, but it will show you how to thread your particular machine and where to oil it—both essential for good results.

Oiling is a good place to start. Don't think a couple of drops of oil in holes in the top of the machine is all that is required. My manual shows 42 specific oil points for my machine. If you don't have a manual, put two drops of oil in every hole in the top, sides, and base of the machine. Open the hinged cover on the presser foot end of the machine and put two drops on every round shaft or bushing you see. Tilt the machine on its back and apply two drops to every round shaft or bushing and to any exposed gears. With no thread and the presser foot up, run the machine to distribute the oil, then wipe the exterior of the machine. Always oil the machine before you start a project.

It is important to thread the machine correctly. If you do not have a manual, get someone to show you how to thread your machine and draw a sketch so you do it the same every time. Virtually all machines pass the top thread around the tension knob and up through the take-up arm before it goes through a guide on the needle clamp and through the eye of the needle. But there are various fixed and spring guides that the thread must pass through in the proper direction and sequence. Even the orientation of the eye of the needle can vary, with the thread passing through the needle from front to back on some machines and from left to right on others.

Needle size will depend upon the weight of the fabric you are attempting to sew. As a general rule, the heavier the fabric, the larger the needle. Needle designations are logical, i.e., the larger the number designation, the larger the needle. For very light fabric such as spinnaker cloth, a #11 needle works well. For medium-weight or loosely woven fabrics such as corduroy, chintz, or oxford cloth, try a #14 needle. Heavy, tightly woven fabrics such as canvas—both natural and synthetic—and sail cloth require a #16 or #18 needle, sometimes a #20.

A #16 needle is a good choice for most marine-related work. You want *ball-point* needles, which tend to gently shoulder the weave aside rather than pierce the yarns. Buy plenty of needles; they will bend, break, and dull regularly, which is perfectly normal. In fact, anytime you begin to have problems with your machine, the *first* thing you should do is *change the needle*.

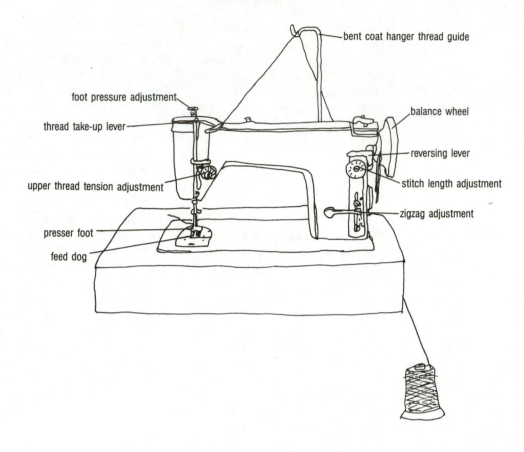

foot pressure adjustment

thread take-up lever

upper thread tension adjustment

presser foot

feed dog

bent coat hanger thread guide

balance wheel

reversing lever

stitch length adjustment

zigzag adjustment

Typical threading sequence

Heavy-duty thread is required for canvas and upholstery work, not the brightly colored spools of *spun* polyester found in variety stores and fabric shops. Fabric shops usually carry some heavy, cotton-wrapped polyester which is reasonably strong and has the advantage of sewing easily because the cotton surface pulls through the tension devices in a more consistent way.

Polyester fiber thread is much stronger and more durable and is better suited to outdoor applications. Unfortunately, the relatively "slick" surface of polyester can lead to tensioning problems, especially with cheaper thread. It is difficult to tell whether a thread will sew well or not by looking at it. Heminway and Bartlett thread has a good reputation. If you

plan to use polyester thread, which you should, and your fabric supplier carries a different brand, I strongly suggest you buy a small cone (1 ounce—about 1,000 yards) and try the thread before purchasing a large amount. A 1-ounce cone will cost $3 or $4. If you like the way the thread handles, you may want to invest in a 16-ounce cone ($25 to $35 dollars), which will last you a very long time. White is the only color you need.

V-69 thread is a good all-around weight that can be used to sew both light and heavy fabrics, but I prefer the extra strength of V-92 thread. You want "bonded" polyester, not a "soft" finish. You also need "left-lay," which is more or less standard; it will also be called Z-twist. (Right-lay is called S-twist and will not sew well on your machine.) Do not buy thread that is not twisted. And do not buy monofilament thread.

Unlike spools of dress thread that sit over the pin on the back of the machine and spin as the machine pulls thread from them, cones of industrial thread do not spin. The thread is pulled from the top of the cone. Commercial machines are outfitted with special thread stands, but sitting the cone on the floor and feeding the thread to your machine over a coathanger-wire guide works equally as well.

FABRIC

There are thousands of fabrics available in various weights, colors, patterns, weaves, and compositions, hundreds of which are suitable for marine use. Almost any fabric that would be suitable for heavy use as a living room sofa cover can be used for cabin upholstery, provided it is mildew- and stain-resistant. Textures, colors, and patterns are more a matter of taste than suitability.

Outdoor fabrics are more limited. Among the materials that you are likely to use are nylon spinnaker cloth, clear vinyl, and open-weave vinyl-coated nylon, but canvas is still the dominant marine fabric. Most of the projects that follow are constructed of either treated (natural) or synthetic canvas.

Natural canvas is a wonderful material. Even though it is tightly woven, natural canvas "breathes," preventing the condensation that breeds rust, rot, and mildew. Yet when the natural fiber—usually cotton—gets wet, it swells, making the cloth completely waterproof. This last part sounds a lot like the way traditional wooden hulls seal. And like wooden hulls, natural canvas requires special care. It is highly susceptible to mildew and rot, particularly in the marine environment. Other materials are almost invariably a better choice.

One alternative is *treated canvas,* natural cotton canvas treated to resist rot and mildew. Treated canvas has most of the best attributes of natural canvas without the deficiencies. The best-known treated canvas is Vivatex, but it is not the only one. Your

supplier may carry Terrasol, Permasol, or Graniteville. Vivatex and Terrasol are available in "natural" colors: natural (off-white), pearl gray (looks green to me), and khaki. Permasol and Graniteville offer a wider variety of colors and patterns.

Synthetic canvas is similar in weave and weight to natural canvas, but instead of cotton, the fiber is a synthetic. Nylon is used to make some strong, lightweight canvaslike materials—Cordura and Oxford come to mind—but nylon has a very short life in the sun. Polyester (Dacron) is also subject to UV damage, although deterioration can be delayed with a UV coating. The biggest problem with polyester canvas is that it does not accept dye readily and tends to fade quickly in sunlight.

The best fiber, by far, for maintaining its strength and color despite constant exposure to the sun and other elements is acrylic. The fade resistance and long life of acrylic canvas has revolutionized the marine canvas industry. I recently replaced two acrylic sail covers, the fiber finally degrading after *16 years* of continuous exposure to the Florida sun; but the color was still bright. Acrylic canvas once seemed to come in only one color, the ubiquitous sail-cover blue, but today it is available in dozens of colors and patterns. The original acrylic canvas fabrics were Sunbrella and Yachtcrylic—identical fabrics except that Sunbrella came in 30-inch width while Yachtcrylic was 40 or 46 inches wide. Today these two are joined by others like Argonaut, Diklon, and Sun Master.

There is a tendency to think that when canvas is indicated, acrylic canvas is always superior. Not true, Skip. Treated canvas has three noteworthy advantages over synthetic canvas. It is waterproof, while synthetic canvas is "water-resistant"—a major distinction when *you* are sitting under the drip. Natural fibers are less susceptible to chafe damage than acrylic fibers. And the cost of treated canvas is about half the cost of acrylic canvas. As for life expectancy, I have a set of Vivatex harbor awnings that have seen 17 years of intermittent use and show no sign of needing replacement any time soon.

Our initial project will be constructed from 10

ounce treated canvas because it is a relatively inexpensive material to learn on and because it is the best material for this particular project. You will need from 1 to 3 yards of 31-inch (the most common width) material, depending upon the dimensions you choose, but I suggest that you buy a couple of extra yards which will eventually be put to good use. If your supplier carries wider material, fine. Ask about end-rolls and remnants; when they are available they can save you quite a few dollars.

A REAL TENSION HEADACHE

Before you start a project, you need to get the sewing machine adjusted for the material and thread you are using. That is generally not very complicated since you will normally be concerned with only four adjustments.

The first one is the dial that adjusts the length of the stitch. Set it to the highest number and forget about it. Shorter stitches are for sissy stuff like taffeta and chiffon, not the two-fisted fabrics you will be sewing. Acrylic canvas, which tends to pucker from the penetration of the needle, especially benefits from long stitches.

The second adjustment is presser-foot pressure. It is adjusted by pushing a button or turning a knob on top of the machine above the presser foot. You won't need to adjust it unless you are having feed problems. Light materials require light presser-foot pressure or the feed dog will pucker the material rather than feed it. But if the foot pressure is too light, heavy materials will feed unevenly—causing irregular stitches—or stop feeding altogether. Domestic machines often will not feed regularly without some help from the operator no matter what adjustments are made, but increasing presser-foot pressure can help. If your machine allows you to set the height of the feed dog, raising it will also improve the machine's ability to feed heavy material.

Another problem that might relate to improper presser-foot pressure is skipped stitches in heavy material. A sewing machine operates by forming a loop in the thread at the end of the needle which is picked up by a hook on the rotating shuttle. The loop is formed as the needle lifts, leaving the thread behind. In heavy, tightly woven fabrics, the needle may jam in the fabric, causing the fabric to lift with the needle. When this happens, no loop is formed and the stitch is skipped. Increasing foot pressure keeps the material from lifting.

Bobbin tension is the third adjustment. First be sure you have the bobbin in the bobbin case correctly; the loaded bobbin winds clockwise on some machines, counterclockwise on others. Bobbin tension is adjusted by turning the tiny screw in the flat spring on the bobbin case. With the wound bobbin in the case and the thread leading out from under the bobbin tension spring, pull on the thread. It should pull out smoothly, but with some resistance. If the thread has little or no resistance, tighten the screw. If the thread is hard to pull, or feeds in jerks, loosen the screw *slightly*. This is an initial setting and you may have to readjust the bobbin tension after you see how the machine sews.

The last adjustment is the upper thread tension and, after the initial adjustment of the other three, upper tension is usually the only adjustment that will be necessary each time you change materials unless the change is drastic. Upper tension is adjusted by looking at the way the machine stitches. Time to stitch.

If you have never run a sewing machine before, getting someone to show you the basics will be easier than my instructions. For those of you in isolation, after you have the machine threaded, a loaded bobbin in the case, and the case installed, the first thing is to pick up the bobbin. You do this by holding onto the end of the upper thread and rotating the machine by hand (the top of the balance wheel turns *away* from you) through one stitch. When the needle is back at its highest point, pull on the thread and it will bring up the bobbin thread. Both threads should *always* trail behind the foot about 3 inches before you start to sew.

You normally use scrap material to adjust the thread tension, but since you don't have any scrap yet, cut about four inches of canvas from the end of the piece you bought. Cut or fold the strip into thirds so you will be sewing through three layers. Slip the material under the needle and lower the presser foot onto the material. Be sure the thread leads through the slot and under the foot, not over the top of it. Now step on it, Dude. If the machine just hums, either sing along or give the balance wheel a little help with your hand to get the needle started.

It is not necessary to sew as fast as the machine will go. You will have better control if you sew slowly. After you sew 4 or 5 inches, stop. Rotate the needle back to the highest position or just beyond it, then raise the presser foot. Remove the fabric to the left, pulling about 3 inches of thread from both the needle and the bobbin. Snip both threads close to the fabric and brush them toward the back of the machine and you are again ready to sew.

Check the stitching to see how to adjust the thread tension. When the tension is correct, the

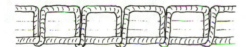

Tighten upper thread tension (or loosen bobbin tension).

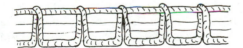

Loosen upper thread tension (or tighten bobbin tension).

Whoa! Don't touch anything.

Adjusting thread tension

stitching on the top and the bottom of the fabric should look exactly the same. If the bottom thread just looks straight, like a piece of wire, with the top thread looped around it, you need more upper thread tension. Turn the tensioning knob clockwise. If it is the top thread that is straight, with the bottom thread looping over it, the upper tension is too tight. Make a small adjustment and sew another line of stitches. Keep testing and adjusting until the interlock between the two threads is buried in the center of the material. There is no other way to adjust thread tension, so just take your time and get it right.

A lot of sewing problems that seem to relate to thread tension are actually caused by using too small a needle. With cotton-wrapped polyester or V-69 polyester thread, start with a #16 needle. If you are using V-92 thread, you should have a #18 needle in the machine. If you seem to be unable to get both threads to pull into the material, try a larger needle.

If the thread starts breaking or the material puckering before you get enough upper tension to pull the lower thread inside the fabric, then your bobbin tension is too tight. Loosen it and start all over. On the other hand, if the thread forms a "bird's nest," or you can pull the layers apart and expose the stitching, the bobbin is too loose. Again, adjust and start all over. When you have a tight, regular stitch with the interlock buried, you are ready to make something.

THE FLAT SHEET

An astonishing number of canvas marine items are basically flat sheets of cloth with the edges hemmed. This is where we are going to start, beginning with a fender skirt. No, I am not talking about a car part found on low riders in East L.A. The kind of fender skirt I have in mind I saw on a 60-foot gold-plater tied up at Pier 66 in Fort Lauderdale. If it is good enough for the idle rich, it ought to be good enough for you. And after all the work you just put into that great finish on the hull, you are going to appreciate my observant nature.

The fender I am referring to is the kind that keeps your hull off the pilings, but fenders have a bad habit of scuffing the hull. Colorful terry-cloth covers have become popular, and coordinated with sail covers and canvas tops they do look nice. But against a creosote piling, a fabric cover works exactly like a paint roller, painting your previously pristine hull black. At low tide, the cloth picks up bits of barnacle and other crustaceans, and as the fender rotates, the sharp bits of shell grind into your hull. Bad. Very bad.

The solution is a fender skirt—a flat piece of canvas that hangs from the rail between the fender and the hull. No matter what the fender gets into, the hull is always protected. The gold-plater had a single piece about 25 feet long that protected one entire side of the hull from all of the fenders, but if you only have two fenders aboard, 50 feet of canvas skirt seems like a bit of overkill. The skirts were also acrylic, matching the sail covers, the dodger, and the jet-ski cover—naturally. Barring vanity, treated canvas is a better choice. Aside from the savings, the natural fiber will sustain the chafe of the fender better and it will be easier on the hull.

The size of the skirt is up to you, but to protect the hull from a single fender, a skirt 3 or 4 feet long and somewhat less than the distance between the rail and the water in width should be adequate. Add about 4 inches to both dimensions to allow for a $1\frac{1}{2}$ inch hem on all sides. If the math here bothers you, a 4-inch allowance gives you $1\frac{1}{2}$ inch hems because the additional $\frac{1}{2}$ inch is turned under to hide the raw edge.

The hem, which is nothing more than turned-under fabric, not only gives the edge a finished look, but reinforces the edge as well. It also provides reinforcement for grommets and fasteners, which are normally installed in the hem area.

To put a $1\frac{1}{2}$-inch hem in the canvas, fold over 2 inches of the material and rub the fold firmly with the back of your scissors to crease the canvas. You may want to press the crease in with an iron, but be sure the iron is only warm if the material is synthetic.

Run a row of stitching about $\frac{1}{4}$ inch inside the fold to hold the hem in place. It is not necessary to draw a line on the cloth to keep the row of stitching straight. Use a reference on the machine. For example, the edge of the presser foot may be about $\frac{1}{4}$ inch from the needle, so just keep the fold even with the edge of the foot and the stitches will be where you want them. Many needle plates have reference lines engraved into them that you can use the same way. Or mark the plate with a pencil or a piece of masking tape as a reference.

When your row of stitching is 3 or 4 inches long, stop the machine with the needle buried in the fabric and turn the hem behind the foot over to check the stitching. You adjusted the tension for three layers of fabric and you are only sewing two. If a tension adjustment is necessary, make it and continue sewing. It is a good habit to check the stitching every time the thickness of what you are sewing changes.

It is always a good idea to lock the stitches when you start and finish sewing by taking a few stitches in reverse. Locate the needle $\frac{3}{4}$ inch from the edge of the material and depress the reverse lever on the machine, stitching back to the edge. Release the lever and run the row of stitching to the opposite edge. Depress the reverse lever and backstitch about $\frac{3}{4}$ inch. If your machine has no reverse lever, you can accomplish the same thing by stitching from the edge $\frac{3}{4}$ inch, then lifting the needle and the foot and, without cutting the thread, repositioning the needle to the edge and stitching over the first few stitches. Finish the same way, backing up the needle and over-stitching the last $\frac{3}{4}$ inch.

As long as the feed dog pulls the material through the machine, all you need to do is guide the fabric. I find it easiest with my right hand actually holding the hem just in front of the foot and my left hand palm-down on the fabric to the side of the needle. This allows me to both direct the material and to slide it.

If the material is heavy and the piece large, it may overpower the feed dog. In that case the place for the left hand is behind the needle, pulling the material while you feed it from the front with your right hand. You do not want to pull hard enough to slide the material, only hard enough to help the dog move it. It is a skill acquired with practice.

Another skill acquired with practice is keeping the top and the bottom of the hem (or any seam) feeding at the same rate. While the feed dog is clawing the bottom layer of fabric forward, the presser foot is rubbing heavily against the top layer, impeding its movement through the machine. As a result the top layer tends to "crawl," resulting in a wrinkled hem (or an uneven seam). Experienced machine operators learn to counter this tendency, but the easiest solution for the amateur is basting the hem with transfer tape before you sew it. An alternative is to pin the hem with straight pins every 6 or 8 inches, removing the pins as they reach the front of the foot.

Back to the skirt, after the first row of stitching is in the hem, you want to turn 1/2 inch of the raw edge under and crease it by rubbing the edge— consequently a hem that is folded twice is called a *double-rubbed* hem, or just a *double* hem. Baste this fold if it helps you and run a second row of stitches 1/4 inch inside the fold to complete the hem. You are now sewing through three layers, so check the stitching to make sure the thread tension is correct. You may have better results if you make this second row of stitches with the fold *underneath*. If the feed dog of your machine is sufficiently wide, it will engage both the bottom layer and the underside of the top layer, feeding both evenly.

You are going to hem the other three edges the same way. Hem the opposite edge first, then the two ends. When you do the end hems, it may surprise you to discover that where the inner edge of the end hem crosses the inner edge of the side hem, you have *nine layers* of material to sew through. Fortunately this is a very short section—only three or four stitches—so it should not present any serious problems. You may have to help your machine across this ridge by turning the balance wheel by hand.

All that remains to be done is to install grommets in the two top corners. In the center of the square formed by the overlapping hems, make a hole with the cutter that accompanied your die set. Note that overlapping hems provide four layers of cloth, which will reinforce the grommet installation. The usual instructions are to place the material on a piece of wood and hit the cutter with a hammer, but you will greatly extend the cutter life if you simply twist it back and forth on the material rather that pounding on it. A sharp cutter will slice through several layers of cloth with only a slight twisting action. Never let the edge of the cutter touch anything but fabric or wood. If you're a wimp, protect the palm of your hand with several layers of folded cloth—uh, so I've heard.

Seat the male half of a grommet on the die and put the hole in the cloth over the grommet. Put the ring portion of the grommet on top of the cloth over the male half. Insert the grommet setter, making sure the grommet is still seated in the die and the setter is vertical. *Lightly* tap the setter with a hammer to roll the edge of the grommet and compress the two halves together. Finally, hit the setter a little harder to set the grommet. If you are using a ring grommet, set it firmly enough so that the grommet will not twist in the cloth, then go back and read the section on spur grommets.

With the two grommets installed, the skirt is ready to use. Hang the skirt with lengths of line "stopped" in the grommets with figure-8 knots. If you decide to make a long skirt, additional grommets spaced along the top hem will be necessary to support the middle of the skirt. The treated canvas will protect your hull from stains and scratches, but you can make the skirt even easier on the hull by lining one side with terry cloth.

Hem a piece of terry cloth to the size of the skirt, then hold the two pieces together and stitch them along both ends and across the top; leaving the two pieces open at the bottom will make washing the skirt easier and more effective. It is not necessary to turn under the raw edge of the hem in the terry cloth except at the bottom since the other three edges will be hidden when you sew the terry cloth to the

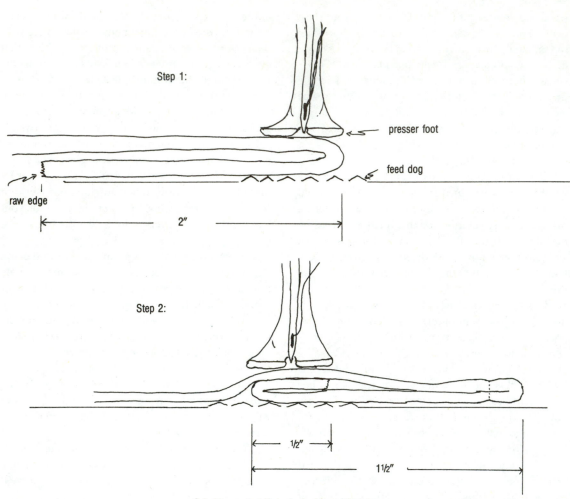

Step 1:

presser foot

feed dog

raw edge

2"

Step 2:

1/2"

1 1/2"

Stitching a 1 1/2-inch double-rubbed hem

canvas. Also leave the terry unstitched above the grommets, running a U-shaped row of stitches around the bottom of the grommets instead. This will allow you access to the grommet to attach the mounting lines and the terry will protect the hull from the grommets.

LEE CLOTHS

For staying securely in my bunk at sea, I prefer leeboards, but leeboards are not easy to install on all bunks. And for a boat that is only occasionally underway overnight, lee cloths have the advantage of stowing completely out of the way when not in use—which is most of the time.

There are only subtle construction differences between the fender skirt above and a lee cloth. Again 10-ounce treated canvas is a good choice, although the more mildew-resistant acrylic canvas might be less affected by the often-damp environment of under-bunk stowage. Phifertex—the vinyl-covered screenlike material that now dominates outdoor furniture—is another good choice for lee cloths, especially in the tropics, because it does not inhibit air circulation.

Typically a lee cloth should be a couple of feet shorter than the bunk and stand about 18 inches high in use. That means for a 6½-foot bunk with a 5-inch-thick cushion, you need a piece of canvas 4½ feet long and 23 inches wide, plus hem allowances. Actually, you probably need a couple of inches more width to allow for the cloth to be screwed down to the bunk.

Hem the canvas just as you did the fender skirt, but with one change. To make the attachment to the bunk very strong, stitch a length of 1½-inch-wide nylon webbing inside the hem. Nylon webbing—seat belt material—is available from most fabric suppliers. If you can buy only 1-inch webbing, reduce the bottom hem to 1 inch. To seal the webbing and prevent it from ravelling, cut it with a soldering pistol or a hot knife. Install grommets in the two upper corners of the hemmed cloth.

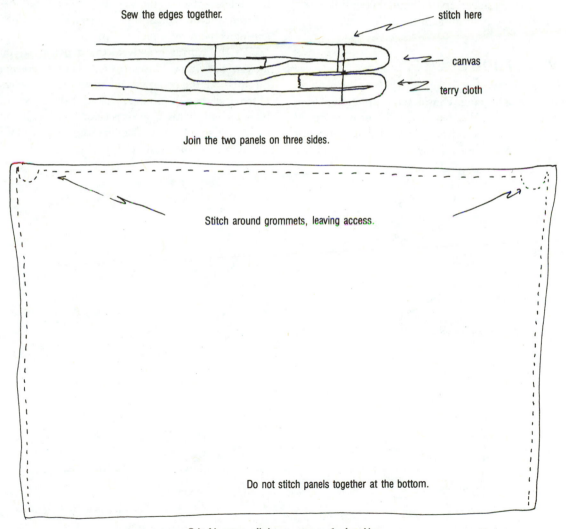

Sew the edges together.

stitch here

canvas

terry cloth

Join the two panels on three sides.

Stitch around grommets, leaving access.

Do not stitch panels together at the bottom.

Stitching terry lining to canvas fender skirt

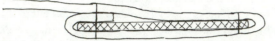

Strengthening a hem by stitching webbing inside

Install the finished lee cloth by screwing the reinforced hem to the bunk with oval-head screws and finishing washers. Space the screws approximately every 6 inches. Heat the tip of an ice pick to punch the mounting holes in the hem of the canvas; the hot tip is not necessary for natural fiber, but it will cauterize the hole through the nylon webbing.

WEATHER CLOTHS

Enclosing the cockpit with weather cloths can provide the occupants considerable protection from wind and spray. Weather cloths also provide a good deal of additional privacy. And a lot of sailors just like the way they look. If the weather cloths will be a permanent feature of your boat, the constant exposure makes acrylic canvas the best fabric choice; but if they will only be rigged for inclement weather or offshore sailing, treated canvas is a less expensive alternative.

To determine the size, measure the distance between stanchions and from the caprail to the top lifeline (or the underside of the handrail). A single cloth may pass around several stanchions if you choose. If the stanchions are not vertical—where the lifelines attach to the stern pulpit, for example—measure the horizontal distance at several stations and note them on a piece of paper.

Cut the canvas exactly to the dimensions you measured, with no allowances for a hem. Following this method, the completed cloth will have 2 inches of space all the way around it, allowing the canvas to be stretched tightly when it is laced in place. If you prefer less space, add to the dimensions of the cloth accordingly before you cut it to size.

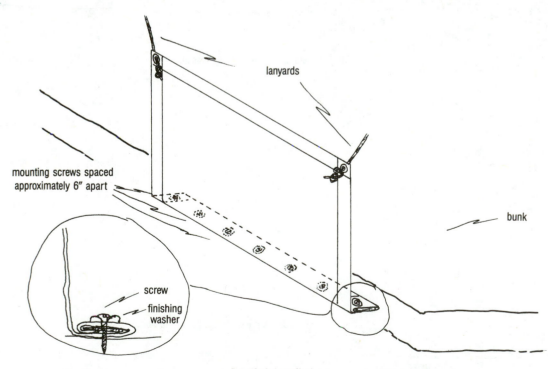

Lee cloth installation

Hem the four edges of the weather cloths with double-rubbed hems exactly like those on the fender skirt. Even if one end of the cloth attaches to a curved railing, try to keep the hem of the cloth straight, accommodating the curve with the lacing. Because of the stiffness of canvas, curved edges are difficult to hem.

A convex curve can be hemmed by making evenly spaced darts—small, triangular pleats—in the hem to take up the extra material that accrues when the curved material is folded back on itself. With a curved hem, the sequence of stitching also changes. First, fold the raw edge over 1/2 inch and sew it down, putting darts in the folded edge as necessary to get it to lie flat. Then fold the 1 1/2-inch hem and stitch it 1/4 inch from the edge. Finally, a third row of stitches will be required along the inside edge of the dart, stitching down regular and evenly spaced darts at the same time.

A concave curve is more difficult to hem because the problem becomes a shortage of material, not an excess. The solution is a second piece of material. Using the curve of the cloth as a pattern, cut a similarly curved strip of material 2 inches wide. Along the convex side of the strip, fold the raw edge over 1/2 inch and stitch it down, putting darts as necessary. Now with the stitched fold on top, lay the curved strip on top of the weather cloth so that the curved edges exactly match. Stitch the two pieces together 1/2 inch from the edge.

With your scissors, somewhere along this curved edge make a perpendicular cut to within about 1/8 inch of the row of stitches you just made. Make a similar cut every inch along the curve; if part of the edge is straight, slashing is not necessary in the straight portion. Be very careful not to cut any closer to the stitching than 1/8 inch. The slashes will allow the edge of the cloth to expand when you fold it and make the seam lie smooth.

Now fold the strip over to the other side of the cloth. If you have done it correctly, the seam between the two pieces now forms the curved edge, which appears finished from both sides, and the raw edge of the strip is between both pieces. Stitch the

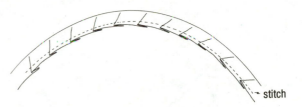

Step 1: Fold over raw edge and sew down evenly spaced darts.

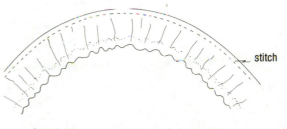

Step 2: Make second fold and stitch near fold.

Step 3: Form excess cloth into evenly spaced darts and stitch down.

Hemming a convex curve

inner edge of the strip down to finish the hem. Hemming the piece in this manner reduces the hem allowance from 2 inches to 1/2 inch—the amount of weather cloth that is actually turned under.

This same method, instead of darts, can be used to put a neater hem on a convex edge. The difference is that you need to slash the raw edge of the strip rather than sewing darts into it, and after the strip has been sewn to the cloth, make a series of 90-degree V-cuts in the edge rather than slashes. The V-cuts remove excess fabric that will otherwise bunch up inside the hem. The best approach is to

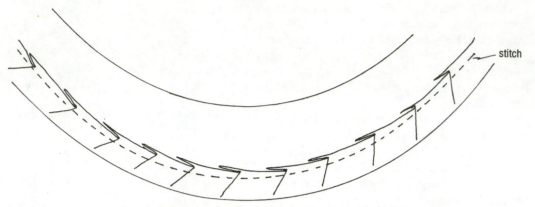

Step 1: Hem the convex edge of a 2-inch-wide curved strip of cloth.

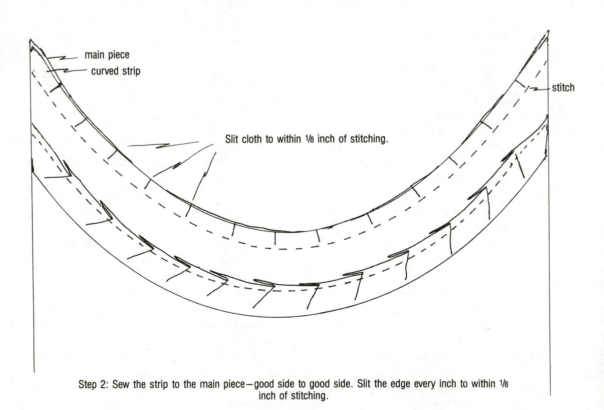

Step 2: Sew the strip to the main piece—good side to good side. Slit the edge every inch to within ⅛ inch of stitching.

Hemming a concave curve (continued on page 375)

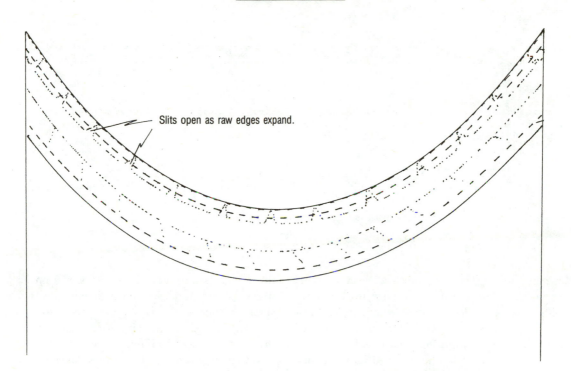

Slits open as raw edges expand.

Step 3: Fold strip over at seam line and stitch it down along both edges.

Hemming a concave curve (continued)

keep those hems straight and you won't have to get into this at all.

Finish the weather cloths by installing grommets in the corners and spaced 6 to 8 inches apart along all four edges. Position the grommets by dividing the distance between the corner grommets into equal spaces. The weather cloths are installed by simply lacing them to the stanchions and lifelines. Eye straps screwed to the deck or the inside of the cap rail provide the attachment point for the lower lacing. The eyes should be positioned between the grommets.

FLAGS

Flags probably do not qualify as boat enhancements, but they do illustrate another flat-sheet canvas project and can give you an opportunity to tune your sewing skills productively.

Flags can be made from almost any fabric. Commercially produced flags are usually made from nylon because it is light, strong, and accepts dye well. Four-ounce oxford cloth is a good choice for signal flags or pennants.

Aside from the material, a single-color flag differs from a fender skirt or a weather cloth mostly in the size of the hems. There is no standard size for flags, but a common size aboard boats is 18 inches (on the hoist) by 24 inches (on the fly). The hems on three sides need not be any larger than $1/2$ inch, but on the hoist where the grommets will be installed, you will need at least a 1-inch hem. Taking the additional $1/2$ inch that will be turned under to hide the raw edges into account, for a finished size of 18 × 24, you need to cut the cloth 20 inches by $26^{1}/_{2}$ inches.

Begin by hemming one of the long sides. Fold $1/2$ inch of the cloth over, then fold the raw edge under by folding the cloth again $1/2$ inch. Sew the hem

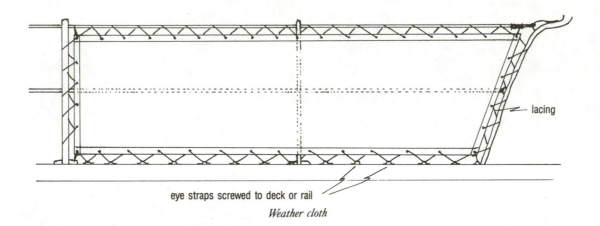

lacing

eye straps screwed to deck or rail

Weather cloth

down by stitching as close to both edges of the hem as you can. Hem the opposite edge in the same manner, then put a $1/2$-inch double hem on one end of the flag. When you hem the end, you can make the corner neater by putting a diagonal fold on the ends of the hem. Make the first fold for the hem, then fold the two corners at a 45-degree angle. Now make the second fold to complete the hem and stitch down both sides and the diagonal ends of the hem.

This is a good place to learn to change directions when you are sewing. Stitch along one side of the hem until you are near the end, then make the last two or three stitches by turning the balance wheel by hand. When the needle reaches the stitch line you want to sew—usually $1/4$ inch from the edge of the material, but in this case less—stop the machine with the needle buried in the cloth. Lift the presser foot and turn the material, using the needle as an axis, until the new stitch line lines up with the needle. Lower the presser foot and continue to sew. In this case, since the distance along the diagonal edge of the hem is slightly more than $1/2$ inch, continue to operate the machine by turning the balance wheel with your hand. When you reach the stitch line on the opposite side of the hem, stop with the needle down, raise the foot, rotate the cloth, lower the foot, and sew along the edge of the hem until you reach the other end. Turn again to sew this end, and stitch

the straight seam one more time to end up back where you started. Sew an inch onto the initial stitching, then back-stitch a few stitches to finish.

Your flag will last much longer if you reinforce the hoist seam with webbing. Enclose a length of 1-inch webbing inside the hoist seam, just as you did for the bottom hem in the lee cloth. Try installing the webbing by first placing it so that $1/2$ inch of the webbing is lying on top of the raw edge of the flag, then stitching down the center of this overlap. Now flip the webbing over onto the cloth, then flip it again. The webbing should be enclosed inside the cloth. Stitch around the perimeter of the hem, about $1/4$ inch in from the edges. All that remains to finish the flag is to install grommets about an inch from either end of the hoist hem.

There may be a minor shortcoming in the above instructions. Of the 40 flags and pennants in a set of international flags, only one is a single color. Fortunately it is the Q (quarantine) flag, which will serve you well if you are going foreign . . . until it is time to hoist the flag of your host nation. Want to guess how many countries have single-color flags?

Intricate designs are usually embroidered or appliqued onto a flag of the basic color. Applique is not terribly difficult, involving cutting out the design (twice) and stitching it to both sides of the flag, usually with a zigzag stitch to finish the raw edges. Fortunately, most flags have simple designs—two

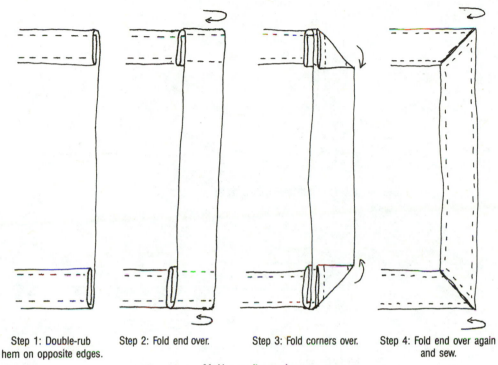

Step 1: Double-rub hem on opposite edges.

Step 2: Fold end over.

Step 3: Fold corners over.

Step 4: Fold end over again and sew.

Making a diagonal corner

colors, stripes, or checks—and these are best made by stitching together the material into the appropriate pattern, then hemming the piece into a flag.

The easiest way to join two pieces of fabric is to overlap their edges and stitch them together. This is called, simply enough, an overlap seam, but it leaves the raw edges exposed and they will ravel—unless they happen to be the ravel-resistant factory edges called selvages. Cut edges should be joined with a *flat-felled* seam, especially where both sides of the material being joined will be visible.

To join two pieces of cloth with a flat-felled seam, place one on top of the other so that the two edges you want to seam together are even. Now slide the top piece back so that ¹/₂ inch, or slightly less, of the bottom piece is visible, then sew the two pieces together with a row of stitches ¹/₂ inch inside the edge of the top piece of fabric. Fold the flap of bottom fabric up over the top fabric, then fold the top fabric over this flap, pulling it as far as the origi-

nal stitching will allow without stretching the seam. Finish the seam by stitching along both edges. Transfer tape makes flat-felled seams much easier to do.

CURTAINS

Boat curtains are yet another flat-sheet item. Typical boat curtains have some type of track above and below the portholes and tabs sewn to the curtain slide in (or on) the track. By equally spacing the tabs, when the curtains are open, they fold into attractive pleats. If the curtains are made longer than the track, they will also have a pleated look when they are closed.

Fabric choices for curtains are extensive. To ward off the confusion, we generally go to a department store or two and look at their curtains and drapes, pick something we like, then buy the smallest panel available. For some unknown reason, packaged

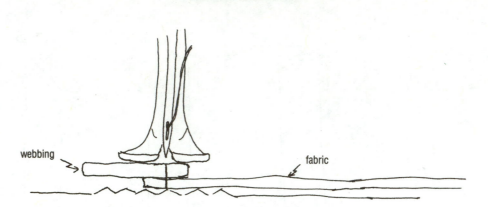

Step 1: Overlap webbing ½ inch and stitch to fabric.

Step 2: Flip webbing once.

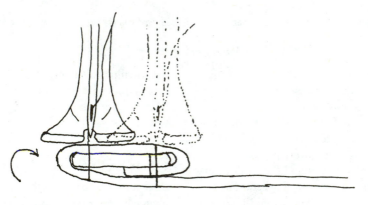

Step 3: Flip webbing a second time and sew along both edges of hem.

Installing reinforcing webbing in a double-rubbed hem

draperies are often cheaper than the price of an equivalent amount of material from a fabric shop. Washable material is a good idea, but because our curtains are also over the galley, we give priority to fireproofing and usually select a fiberglass material.

The dimensions of the material will depend upon the length of the tracks, their distance apart, and whether the curtains will be a single panel or multiple panels. The width of a simple slide-pleated curtain should normally be twice the length of the track, but if the material you are using is very heavy, such curtains can appear bulky when they are open. With bulky material, you may choose to reduce the width to 1½ times the length of the track or less.

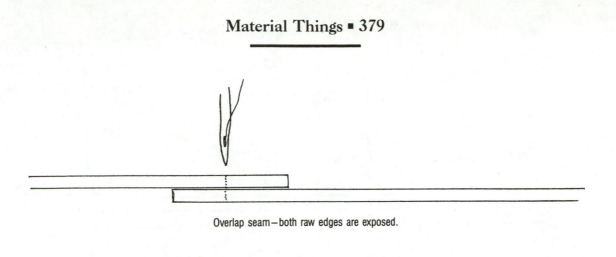

Overlap seam—both raw edges are exposed.

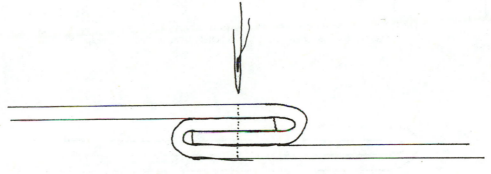

Flat-felled seam—both raw edges are concealed.

Two types of seams

Less width also makes sense for curtains that will rarely be closed.

If the porthole (or portholes) will be covered with two panels meeting in the middle, each panel would obviously be 1/2 the total length. Curtains for tandem portholes often look nice divided into three panels, one at each end and one that covers the fiberglass between the portholes. Making each panel 1/3 of the total gives the best look when the curtains are open, but do not be surprised that when they are closed, the panels do not meet in the center of the portholes. If that upsets your sense of symmetry, then make the center panel 1/2 the total length and each of the side panels 1/4.

The height of the panels depends upon the distance between the upper and lower track. Typically, the curtains should extend about an inch above and below the tracks. For all of these measurements, I am assuming preinstalled tracks. If you do not have tracks, numerous track systems are available. The tracks should extend beyond the portholes about 10 percent of the total length (20 percent if the curtain will be a single panel)—enough to allow the curtains to gather off the porthole.

To the dimensions determined above, add hem allowances. Side hems need not be wider than 1 inch, so a 3-inch allowance (don't forget the extra 1/2 inch that turns under) for each panel is about right. The size of the top and bottom hems will depend upon height of the curtains. For curtains covering portholes, 2-inch hems are appropriate, requiring a 5-inch hem allowance. Curtains for large saloon windows will look better with 4-inch hems.

You may want to line the curtains if the material you have chosen is an open weave. If you bought a packaged curtain and it is lined, you can use the

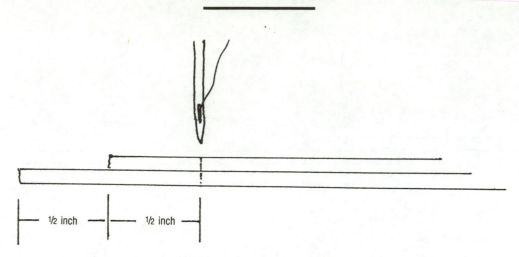

Step 1: Stitch two pieces together with bottom fabric protruding ½ inch.

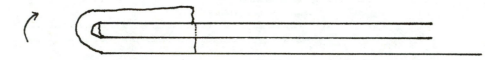

Step 2: Fold bottom fabric up over top fabric.

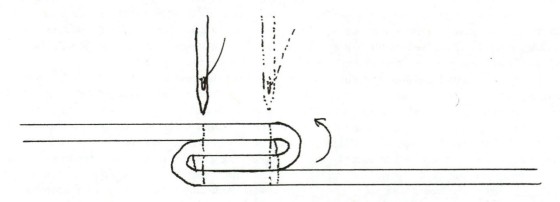

Step 3: Fold top fabric over folded flap. Sew both edges of seam.

Forming a flat-felled seam

lining material. Otherwise, you can buy lining material at most fabric shops. Lining curtains adds some complexity, but not much. Cut the lining to the same dimensions as the curtain fabric and stitch the two together with a row of stitches 1/4 inch from the raw edges around the perimeter of the panel. Fabricate the curtain exactly the same as if it were not lined.

The secret to getting the tops of the curtains to stand up is a size-stiffened cotton or linen material called buckram. Another advantage of buying a packaged drape is that you can often press the buckram it contains and reuse it; otherwise, you will need to purchase a length of this stiffener. It usually comes in 4-inch widths, but you are more likely to need half that. No problem. Cut it to the width you want.

The buckram goes inside the top and bottom hems. For curtains 10 to 20 inches high, a 2-inch stiffened hem is about right. The easiest way to install the stiffener is similar to the installation of reinforcing webbing. Place the curtain fabric and the buckram side by side, with the curtain fabric face down. The top (or bottom) raw edge of the curtain should butt against the buckram. Lift the edge of the buckram and slide it onto the fabric 1/2 inch and stitch down the center of the overlap. With the fabric still lying flat, flip the buckram over onto the fabric. Flip it again. You now have a hem, albeit unstitched, with the stiffener inside. Run a row of stitches 1/4 inch from the inside edge of the hem; it is not necessary to stitch along the outside edge and the curtain will have a better appearance without the second row of stitches. Turn the panel around and install the stiffener in the opposite edge in the same manner.

Hem the two sides and the curtain is finished. All that remains is to attach the slides to the curtain. Place a series of equally spaced marks between 3 and 5 inches apart on the stiffened hems; the exact distance can be determined by pleating the panel with your fingers to see what size pleat looks best to you. Be sure the marks are even and the correct distance from the top and the bottom of the panel

for the slides to fit into the tracks, then sew the slides in place.

If the curtains will be closed often, you can make the pleats self-adjusting with a length of ribbon or bias tape. Before you sew the slides to the curtain, cut the bias tape to the length the panel should be when it is closed and write down that length. Now count the number of *spaces* between the marks for the slides on the curtain. Divide the length of the bias tape by the number of spaces, using the result to mark the tape into the same number of spaces. Pin the tape to the curtain, matching each of the marks. Now sew the slides in place, sewing the tape to the curtain at the marks at the same time. When the curtain is open the pleats are always even because the space between the slides is the same—no space. The tape holds the slides evenly spaced when the curtains are closed, maintaining even pleats.

Curtains that attach to a single track or a rod and hang free at the bottom are constructed in the same manner, with some minor differences. First, the buckram is omitted from the lower hem so the fabric will hang naturally. Second, pleats are often formed by sewing them into the top hem rather than as a result of the location of the slides.

Both pinch pleats and box pleats begin in the same manner. The stiffened upper hem is marked into equal divisions of around 2 inches. Starting at one edge, the hem is folded so that the first mark is face-to-face with the third one. (The second mark will be in the center of the fold.) From the top of the hem, stitch straight down through the two marks, joining them permanently. The stitching should extend about 1/2 inch beyond the bottom of the hem. Fold the hem to join the fourth and sixth marks, and sew in the next pleat. Do the same for marks seven and nine, and so on until the hem is completely pleated.

To make the pleats attractive, they need to be stuffed, boxed, or pinched. Stuffed is just what it sounds like. A roll of stiffener, or a bit of cotton or foam, is inserted into the pleat to give it body. Boxed pleats are formed by flattening the pleat so

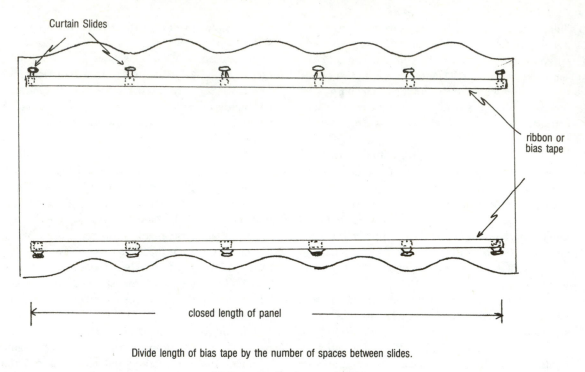

Curtain Slides

ribbon or
bias tape

closed length of panel

Divide length of bias tape by the number of spaces between slides.

Making self-adjusting curtain slides

that the original fold lies against the *vertical* seam (the center of the pleat), and tacking the edges of the pleat to the curtain at the hem stitch line with a couple of hand stitches. Pinch pleats are made by accordion-folding the single pleat into three smaller pleats and hand-tacking the pleats together, again at the hem stitch line.

Lining free-hanging curtains is also slightly different from lining dual-slide panels. Instead of cutting the lining to the same size as the curtain fabric, omit the hem allowances for the *height* dimensions. Put a 1-inch hem in the bottom edge of the lining. With the unlined curtain already hemmed at the bottom (and the buckram in the top hem, but not stitched down), align the two bottom hems, turned-under side to turned-under side, with the bottom of the lining about ¹/₂ inch shy of the bottom of the curtain. The side edges of the lining should match the edges of the curtain and the raw top edge should overlap the stiffened and as yet unstitched top hem.

Trim the lining as required to reduce this overlap to ¹/₂ inch. Lift the enclosed buckram and let the raw edge of the lining fall under it, then place the edge of the hem back on top of the lining. Making sure the lining is still aligned with the ends of the curtain and ¹/₂ inch short of the bottom, sew the hem down, capturing the lining at the same time. Finish installing the lining by stitching both sides ¹/₄ inch from the edge. The lining is not attached at the bottom, allowing it to hang independently of the curtain. Complete the panel by hemming the sides and pleating in the manner you prefer.

WIND CHUTES

Everyone has a favorite wind chute and mine happens to be a flat sheet. Besides being easy to make, its advantages are that it is big (funneling in the lightest zephyrs), it is easy to rig, it is easy to store, and when rain comes unexpectedly, I can close the

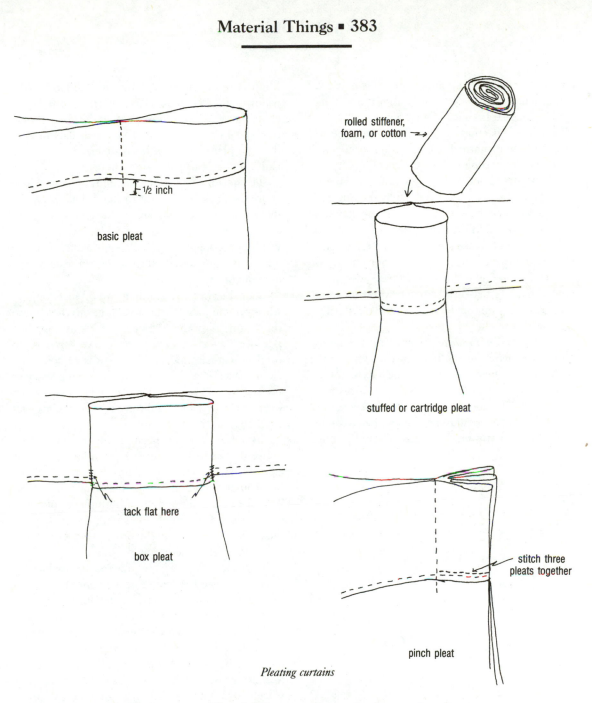

Pleating curtains

hatch without involving the chute. The disadvantage is that the boat has to face more or less into the wind, a problem at the docks and in anchorages subject to strong currents. Despite that, this design has done an admirable job of cooling our cabin in the tropics for two decades.

The best material for a wind chute is 1.5 spinnaker cloth because it is strong, light, and fills easily. The only drawback to spinnaker cloth is that it tends to be noisy, particularly when it is new. If the rattle of the chute might annoy you, this particular chute, because it gets its shape from the way it is rigged, can also be made from canvas.

To adapt this chute to your boat, open the forward hatch to its normal open position, or to about 45 degrees if the support is adjustable. Place a piece of stiff paper—about 3 feet wide will probably be about right—on the top of the hatch and slide the paper down until the edge touches the deck behind the hatch. Now fold the paper down on either side of the hatch and crease it with your fingers where it touches the deck. Cut the paper along the crease line. You should end up with a three-sided paper lean-to that sits flat on the hatch when the three sides are sitting on the deck. This is the pattern for one end of the chute.

Measure the *perpendicular* distance from the top of the open hatch to the deck just forward of the hatch opening—perpendicular to the hatch, not the deck. If the hatch is open to 45 degrees, this measurement will be about 0.7 times the side length of the hatch—as you would know, if you had been listening back in trig class instead of daydreaming.

Flat-sheet wind chute

Multiply this measurement by 2 and add to that the width of the hatch to arrive at the width of the chute. For a 20-inch-square hatch, the chute should be about 48 inches wide. Add a 4-inch allowance for the side hems. As with horseshoes and hand grenades, close is usually good enough.

The height of the chute depends upon how high above the deck you want it to stand. I generally use the scientific method: since the spinnaker cloth comes in 41-inch width, not wide enough for the width or the height of the chute, I make the chute 82 inches high—less whatever is lost in seaming and hemming.

Start the chute by seaming two 52-inch long (or whatever you measured across your own hatch plus the seam allowance) pieces of cloth together. Because the edges of the cloth have selvages, an overlap seam is fine. The slickness of spinnaker cloth makes it a pain to sew, so be sure you use transfer tape on this seam and all the hems. Overlap the two pieces 1 inch and run a row of stitches near each edge of the seam.

If you have a zigzag machine, this is a good place to use that capability. Set the stitch for the widest zigzag, then run a row of stitches down the center of the seam to secure it. Now stitch along both edges. The needle should penetrate both pieces of fabric on one side of the stitch and should be just beyond the edge of the seam on the other. This is the same way your sails are assembled.

You now have a piece of material approximately 81 × 52. Place the center of the paper pattern on the center of one end of the material and trace the angled sides of the pattern onto the cloth. With a straightedge, extend these angled lines to the edges of the cloth. If your hatch support is not adjustable, the chute will set better if you add about 3 degrees to these angles when you redraw them with your straightedge. Cut the material along the two lines, which will trim off the two corners.

Put a 1½-inch double hem in both sides of the chute. Enclosing strips of webbing in the three hems at the bottom of the chute will provide additional reinforcement for the grommets that you are going to install.

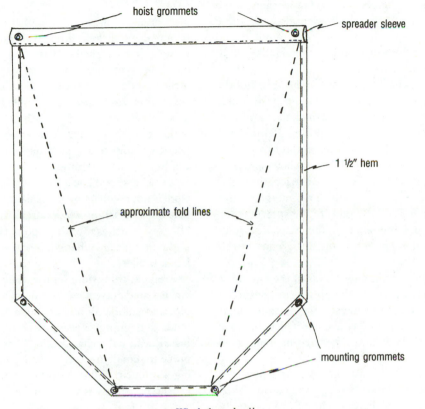

Wind chute detail

The top of the chute requires a spreader. A length of ³/₄-inch aluminum tubing, ¹/₂-inch (ID) PVC pipe, or 1-inch wooden dowel will all work, but a flat spreader, like a sail batten, will not. You can stitch the spreader inside the spreader sleeve, but I prefer a removable spreader. A 2¹/₂-inch sleeve should accommodate your choice of spreader, but check to make sure before you stitch it.

A spreader sleeve is nothing more than a hem with the ends open. Fold over 3 inches of material and run a row of stitches ¹/₄ inch from the fold. Do not omit this row of stitches; it will help to stabilize the sleeve and keep it from wrinkling. Normally you would fold under ¹/₂ inch of the raw edge and stitch it down to finish the hem/sleeve, but for the moment leave the inside edge of the sleeve loose.

To prevent the chute from "bunching" on the spreader and at the same time take advantage of the inherent strength of the spreader as an anchor point for the hoist lines, these lines should pass through grommets in the spreader sleeve. Install grommets approximately 1 inch from each end of the sleeve and the same distance from the stitching along the fold. If the spreader is hollow, grommets in one side of the sleeve (at both ends) will be adequate. A solid spreader demands grommets on both sides of the sleeve; when the sleeve is flat, the two grommets should be in alignment. Now turn the raw edge under and sew it down, finishing the sleeve.

All that remains is to install grommets in the bottom hem of the chute in each of the *four* corners, the corners formed where the angled edges intersect the sides and the bottom. Install brass S-hooks on these four grommets, closing the top of the S slightly to secure the hooks.

To mount the chute, you need four small strap

eyes screwed to the deck at the four corners of the hatch. If my instructions have been adequate, these eyes will correspond with the four grommets and hooks at the bottom of the chute. Hook the S-hooks onto the eyes.

At the top, cut the spreader to the length of the sleeve and file or sand away any sharp edges. Slide the spreader into the sleeve and mark the location of the end grommets on the spreader. Remove the spreader and drill 3/8-inch holes at the two marks. Drill only through one wall of a hollow spreader. Reinsert the spreaders and thread two lengths of 1/4-inch Dacron line through the grommets and the drilled holes and out the ends of the spreaders (or out the second grommet in the case of a solid spreader). Put a figure-8 knot in the ends of the lines.

Put bowlines in the other ends of the two hoist lines and attach them to the jib halyard, snapping the halyard around the forestay at the same time. Hauling the halyard hoists the chute which, because the bottom folds around the hatch opening, now appears funnel-shaped.

There are other hoist options. Attaching the lines to a single piston snap or spring snap rigged with a loop for the halyard shackle can simplify putting the chute up. A triangular piece of cloth sewn to the front of the spreader sleeve with a single grommet in its apex can eliminate one of the hoist lines; you will have to stitch or tie the spreader into the sleeve. The problem of a roller-furling headsail can be overcome with a 12-inch piece of canvas hemmed into a wide canvas strap (4 inches should be wide enough) with grommets or D-rings in the ends for the lines from the chute and a lift ring stitched to the top of the strap to allow it to be hoisted against the furled headsail. The spinnaker halyard may be substituted for the jib halyard.

Adjust the length of the hoist lines until the chute is tight and lies flat on the top of the hatch. In effect, it becomes an extension of the open hatch, but with approximately 10 times the wind-gathering capacity. With this chute flying, you are going to need extra glue for your toupee.

AWNINGS

The simplest of awnings is a flat sheet of canvas, hemmed on all four sides, with grommets on the corners. It is installed by stretching it over the main boom and tying the corners out to the rigging or the lifelines. More complex designs have spreaders, center lifts, and side curtains, but they all begin life as a flat sheet.

Despite the proliferation of synthetic fabrics, when it comes to a boat awning I remain solidly in the treated canvas camp. Lightweight nylon awnings snap and pop like a flag court in a gale. Dacron cloth is not much quieter, and neither of these materials offers much protection from the sun's harmful UV rays, which is the whole point of the darn thing in the first place. What good is an awning that acts like a broiler?

Weblon, that white on top, blue on the bottom vinyl-coated polyester that is popular for power boat tops and sailboat Biminis, is not a bad choice, but it tends to be more satisfactory on tops than on awnings. Because the vinyl coating does not breathe it is prone to remaining damp, making folding and stowing a problem and mildew a given.

Acrylic canvas is an excellent awning material, but with four serious drawbacks. It is usually selected as much for its vivid colors as for its durability, but color is the first liability. Anyone contemplating a sun awning constructed from royal blue, Kelly green, chocolate brown, or any other dark-colored canvas has never sat under such an awning in the tropics. The heat under a dark awning is nauseating. Any color absorbs the heat, conducting it to the air below the awning, but the lighter the color, the less heat absorbed. It is the same reason you wear light-colored clothes in the summer, but you already know all this stuff.

Why not acrylic canvas in a light color? Good idea. My personal favorite is striped material, half white and half a *pale* shade of yellow or green or what have you. The stripes look nice and halve the heat absorption. But a moderate-size awning will require 25 or 30 yards of fabric, perhaps twice or three times that for a *set* of curtained awnings to

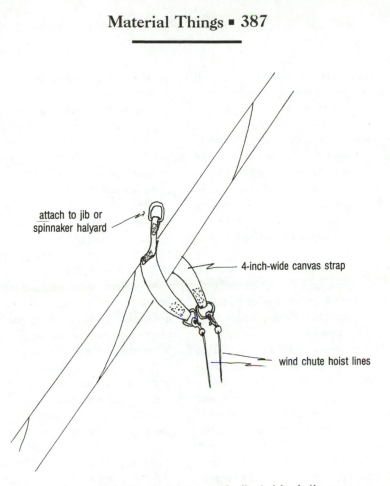

attach to jib or
spinnaker halyard

4-inch-wide canvas strap

wind chute hoist lines

Strap for hoisting wind chute around roller-furl headsail

shade the entire boat. If the difference in cost between treated canvas and acrylic canvas is $4 to $5 per yard . . .

An acrylic canvas awning will be watertight when it is new, but after a couple of years it will leak like Snuffy Smith's roof. It can be reproofed with a spray treatment, but the need is still a demerit.

The fourth impropriety of acrylic canvas is its susceptibility to chafe damage. Awnings often lay across or against something, and if the contact goes unnoticed or the awning is left unprotected, a patch will be required in short order.

Treated canvas is chafe-resistant, waterproof, relatively inexpensive, and readily available in a heat-reflecting, glare-reducing natural (off-white) color. It dries quickly for easy stowage. It provides excellent UV protection. And it is strong enough to survive high winds, durable enough to last a decade or more, and mildew resistant. The defense rests.

The first step in building any awning is to settle on a design. Will it be a tent awning supported by the boom and tied to the lifelines? Will external spreaders be used to reduce the pitch of the awning and improve headroom? Will it be a flat awning, held rigid with spreaders inside sleeves? Will the awning extend from the mast to the backstay or will it be shorter? Are the aft lower shrouds in the way? What about the topping lift? How will you make it easy to rig? Will it be strictly a harbor awning or used underway? (I cannot estimate how many miles we have logged under the cruiser's rig—genoa and main awning.) Awning designs are as varied as the boats they shade and you will need to resolve all the design considerations before you start.

The next step is to arrive at the dimensions. If the awning will be supported by the boom, measure the length along the top of the boom. Less chafe and more headroom will result from stretching the awning above the boom. To determine the length of such an awning, tie a line between the mast and the backstay (or between the masts on a ketch or yawl) at the height you want the ridge of the awning. Measure along this line from the mast to the topping lift. The maximum length of the awning is several inches shorter than this dimension to allow for some inevitable stretch.

If the end of the boom is sufficiently short of the backstay, it may be advantageous to design the awning with a hole for a lift that can be disconnected, or a slot for one that is permanently attached, so the awning can extend beyond the lift.

Width dimensions are determined by measuring from the ridge rope to the lifelines. Again the maximum width will be at least 3 or 4 inches less than the measured dimension to allow for stretch and sag. If the awning will have spreaders, the width of the awning will be determined by the length of the spreaders (or vice-versa). On our 10-foot-wide boat we spread a 12-foot awning with external spreaders.

As you measure for your awning and decide how it will be shaped and attached, sketch it on a piece of paper and note the measurements. Awnings should be given generous hems; 2½ inches should be adequate. If the ends of the awnings will have sleeves for internal spreaders, the sleeves will be at least 7 inches wide. Add the appropriate allowances for hems and/or sleeves to your dimensions.

Begin the actual construction by sewing together panels to form a sheet of canvas large enough for your awning, including the hem allowances. Treated canvas typically comes in 36- or 42-inch widths. Cut the panels to the width dimension of the awning including allowances, plus 3 inches, which I will explain later. Join the edges in athwartship seams to achieve the needed length. Flat-felled seams are appropriate, but since the edges have selvages, I prefer to join the panels in the same manner as the panels of a well-made sail—with a triple-stitched

overlap seam. Overlap the panels 1 inch and stitch down the middle of the overlap with your widest zigzag stitch. Run the second row of stitches along the edge of the top panel, with one side of the stitch penetrating both panels and the other side just beyond the edge of the panel. Turn the material over so that the other edge of the overlap is visible and run a similar row of zigzag stitches along this edge.

Once the panels are stitched together, cut a 3-inch-wide strip from one side and set it aside, then trim the awning to your cut size. Fold over the hems (and sleeves) on all sides and press the folds to mark them, but do not stitch them.

A well-built awning should be almost bullet-proof, which means it needs to be reinforced at every point of stress—specifically at the attachment points. Typically an awning is attached in at least six locations: at the center of both the front and rear edges and at each of the four corners. It may have additional attachment points spaced along the sides, and some awnings have a lift point—sometimes two—in the middle of the awning along the centerline. Each of these points will benefit from reinforcement patches.

Again, let's take a lesson from the sailmaker. Triangular patches in the corners and half-circle patches along the edges will avoid stress concentrations and make the awning set better. Two additional layers of material should be adequate. The awning can be sandwiched between matching patches, but the awning will have a better appear-

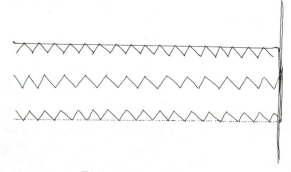

Triple-stitched overlap seam

ance if you keep the patches on the underside, cutting one an inch or so smaller than the other.

The patches will have a reduced tendency to wrinkle if the "grain" or weave of the patch matches the grain of the awning. From extra material, cut two 4-inch squares and two 5½-inch squares along the weave then cut the patches corner-to-corner diagonally to make eight triangular patches in two sizes. Place a smaller patch in one of the corners, aligning the equal sides with the fold lines; the hem will later be stitched on top of the patch. Use transfer tape or pins to hold the patch in place. Place a larger patch on top of the first one, aligning it the same way; the diagonal edge should extend about 1½ inches beyond the first patch. Turn ½ inch of the diagonal edge under and ¼ inch from that edge

run a row of stitches across the patch to attach it to the awning. One inch from the first row of stitches, run a parallel line of stitching, sewing both the top patch and the one underneath to the awning. Reinforce the other three corners the same way. There is no reason to sew the other two edges of the patches; they will be sewn when the hems are sewn in.

For edge patches, cut two half-circles, one about 2 inches larger than the other; 4 and 6 inches will be adequate. Turn ½ inch of the circular edge of the larger patch under and sew it down, spacing darts evenly for a smooth hem. Center the smaller patch over the attachment point—the eventual location of a grommet—aligning the straight edge of the patch with the fold line for the hem. Place the larger patch on top (raw edge turned under) and stitch the rein-

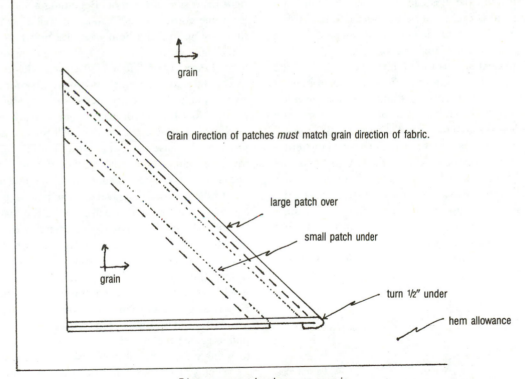

grain

Grain direction of patches *must* match grain direction of fabric.

large patch over

small patch under

grain

turn ½" under

hem allowance

Edges are sewn when hems are sewn in.

Corner reinforcing patch

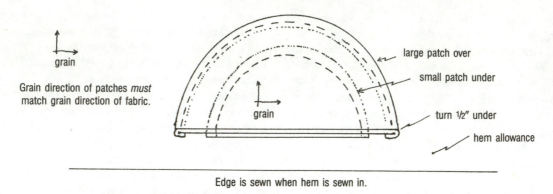

Grain direction of patches *must* match grain direction of fabric.

grain

grain

large patch over

small patch under

turn ½" under

hem allowance

Edge is sewn when hem is sewn in.

Edge reinforcing patch

forcement to the awning with a line of stitching ¼ inch from the circular edge. Run a concentric line of stitching 1 inch from the first row to sew both patches to the awning.

Lift-point patches can be rectangular, but truncating the corners will better distribute the stress. As with the corners and edges, use two patches with the larger one covering the smaller.

The next step is to stitch the hems down. The awning will be much stronger if it is roped all around. This feature represents virtually no additional work—the hem has to be sewn anyway—and adds less the $10 to the initial cost of a 100-square-foot awning, yet it makes the difference in whether an awning lives or dies in a squall. Use ¼- or ⅜-inch, three-strand *Dacron* rope; nylon rope has too much stretch, causing high stress to be borne by the canvas. Determine the length of the rope by measuring around the entire perimeter of the awning; then add about 6 inches.

You need a zipper foot to sew the rope inside the

hem. A zipper foot has a notch in one or both sides, allowing the machine to sew right up against a zipper or a bolt rope. If you have an adjustable foot, adjust it so that the needle runs in the notch on the right-hand side of the foot. Beginning a yard or so from one corner on the leading or trailing edge of the awning, fold the hem over the bolt rope and stitch right against the rope, capturing it inside the hem. Leave about 1 foot of the rope sticking out where you start. Continue stitching right around the awning until the entire perimeter is roped, stopping about 1 foot before you reach your starting point.

Stitching around the corners will present some problems because the front of the foot encounters the rope before the needle reaches the new stitch line. If your machine has adequate space under the foot to allow the foot to travel *over* the bolt rope, you can make the corner as usual, pivoting the material around the buried needle. Most domestic machines will have insufficient clearance. (In fact, when you are finished sewing in the bolt rope, you may have to *remove* the foot to get the material free of the machine.) In this case stitch around the corner as closely as possible, then when you are a couple of inches beyond the corner, tug on the rope enough to pull it against the corner stitching, but not enough to wrinkle the material or to risk losing the end.

When you are back where you started, you want to join the two ends of the rope. The seamanlike way is to cut them with about 5 inches of overlap and join the ends with a short splice. If you are less

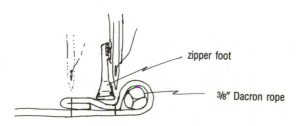

zipper foot

⅜" Dacron rope

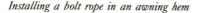

Installing a bolt rope in an awning hem

zealous, cut and seal the ends so they mate, then hand-stitch them together with a dozen or so long loops of waxed twine. Finish stitching the rope into the hem. With the regular foot back on the machine, turn under the raw edges of the hem and stitch them down.

If your awning will not be supported by the boom, a ridge rope should be sewn into the awning to provide support. Again the rope must be Dacron, and 3/8-inch rope will provide more rigid support than smaller line does. If you are going to use this line to attach the awning to the mast and the back-stay, you will need several extra feet of line at each end. My own experience is that the various lanyards wear out long before the awning does, so I don't like the idea of major surgery on the awning every time a piece of line chafes through on the backstay. A better approach is to splice both ends of the ridge rope around stainless thimbles and tie lanyards to the thimbles.

The usual method of installing a ridge rope is to fold the awning in half—underside to underside— slide the rope into the fold, and run a row of stitches against it. It is a popular method because it is easy. Perhaps it is adequate for a light-duty awning, but all the stresses on an awning with a ridge rope installed in this manner will be concentrated on the row of stitching. To get an idea of what I mean, pull on the ends of a piece of note paper to see if you can pull it apart. Now fold the paper in half and run a row of staples 1/2 inch from the fold. Unfold it and pull on it again. If you're lucky, your expensive awning will fail less dramatically.

To avoid this problem, leave the awning flat and

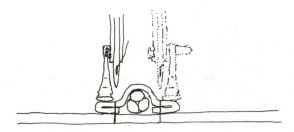

Installing the ridge rope

enclose the ridge rope under a separate piece of material. This is where that 3-inch-wide strip of canvas you set aside earlier comes in. Turn the raw edges of the strip under and tape or stitch them to make a 2-inch-wide strip with finished edges. Turn under one end.

Fold the awning exactly in half and run a pencil inside the fold to mark the location of the ridge rope. Open the awning and stitch one side of the strip to the underside of the awning so that the center of the strip will be centered over the pencil line when the strip encloses the ridge rope. This will be easier to accomplish if you temporarily place the rope on the line and position the strip over it, marking the correct location of one of the edges. Draw a second line through that mark and parallel to the center line, place the edge of the strip on that line, and stitch it to the awning with a line of stitching 1/4 inch from the edge. When you near the end, cut off any excess and turn the end of the strip under before completing the seam. Put the ridge rope between the strip and the awning and, using the zipper foot this time to place the line of stitches against the rope, sew down the other side of the strip.

All that remains to complete the awning is to install grommets in the reinforcing patches and to rig the lifting point if you are using one. Most awnings can benefit from being hoisted in the center. The traditional method of rigging a lift point is to install grommets on either side of the ridge rope and reeve a strop that passes under the rope; but the grommets are, in effect, holes in the roof when it rains. I prefer to use 3-inch-wide canvas folded twice to make 1-inch-wide, triple-thickness strapping. (Try to use a selvaged edge for the raw edge, and turn under the ends before making the folds.) Two straps are required and they should be the same length as the reinforcing patch you installed. You could use 1-inch webbing, but it will have to be replaced in a couple of years because of the sun.

Position the two straps on *top* of the awning and over the reinforcing patches, one on either side of the ridge. Sew 1/3 of each of the straps to the awning

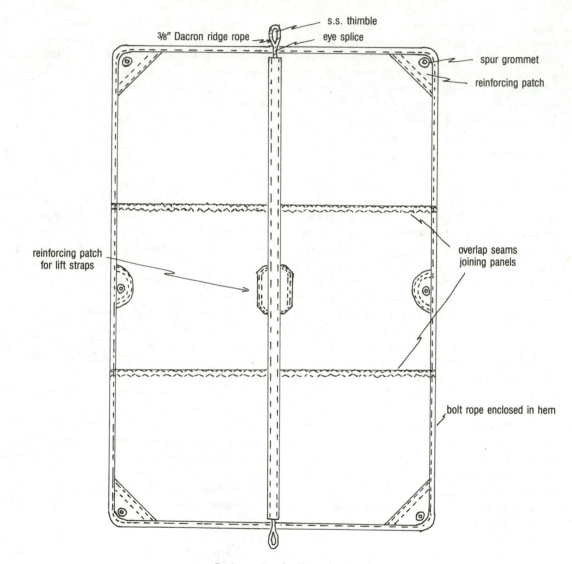

Basic awning detail—underside

as close to the ridge rope as possible, using a boxed X pattern (exactly what it sounds like) for the stitching. Slip a 1-inch brass ring over the two straps and cross them. Again position the ends on either side of the ridge rope, but on the sides opposite their stitched ends. Sew the loose ends down with a matching boxed X, still as close to the ridge rope as possible. The middle third of the two straps should

form an X over the ridge rope with the brass ring at the cross point. Your awning is ready for a decade of loyal service.

When spreaders are required, I prefer external spreaders because they allow the awning to peak, making it less prone to pocketing water; they also subject the awning to less chafe. There are innumerable ways to attach external spreaders, but none

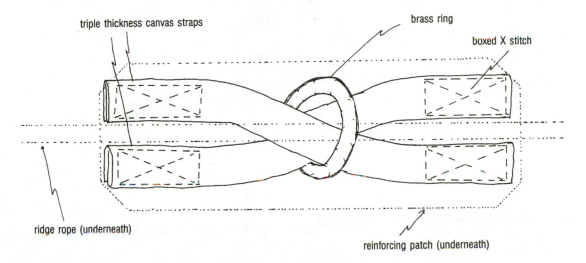

triple thickness canvas straps

brass ring

boxed X stitch

ridge rope (underneath)

reinforcing patch (underneath)

Awning lifting straps

simpler than the method I use. One inch from each end, drill a hole the size of the lanyard line (usually $1/4$ inch) completely through the spreader. The holes must be on the same axis, not twisted in relation to one another. From the end of the spreader, make two saw cuts to the drilled hole, forming a slot the width of the hole diameter. Sand or file the slot smooth, taking the sharp edge off the remaining half-circle of the drilled hole, and flaring the front of the slot somewhat to make slipping a line into it easier. A couple of inches from where each lanyard attaches to the awning, tie in a figure-8 knot. The lanyard is simply stretched over the end of the spreader and dropped into the slot; the knot will hold it in place. Tie off the loose end of the lanyard to a stanchion or the rail or whatever. Hoisting the awning will tighten the fit.

When I first developed this system, my spreaders were $1^{5}/_8$-inch wooden closet rod, available from lumber yards in 12-foot lengths. Since then I have converted to telescoping aluminum tubing to get the stowed poles off the deck. A tubing supplier can sell you two sizes that will slide together; a bolt or a clevis pin holds them extended. To prevent the tubing from cutting the lanyards, I cut off 3 inches of the solid ends of the old spreaders and turned half of each down to fit into the ends of the tubing; solid

aluminum ends would be better. Solid ends are not necessary for heavy-wall PVC spreaders, but the flexible plastic does not work well as an *external* spreader.

For internal spreaders, sleeves are required. The end sleeves present no problem since they are simply larger hems with the ends left open. Sleeves for spreaders across the middle of the awning are fabricated in a manner similar to the way the bolt rope is captured. A strip of canvas wide enough to accommodate the spreader is stitched to the bottom of the awning. Turn the raw edges of the strip under before sewing it to the awning. To avoid the necessity of sewing across the ridge rope, make center sleeves in two sections, leaving several inches of the middle of the spreader exposed.

A tip that will make grommet attachment easier is to allow for *both* the sleeve *and* a hem at the ends. If you need a 5-inch sleeve, allow $7^{1}/_2$ inches of material. Fold the allowance over and stitch along the fold, then 2 inches from the fold to form the hem. Turn the raw edge under and stitch it down to form the pocket inboard of the hem. Grommets can be installed in the hem.

If a hole is required for the topping lift, protect the edges of the hole from chafe with a binding of leather. Binding simply means folding a strip of

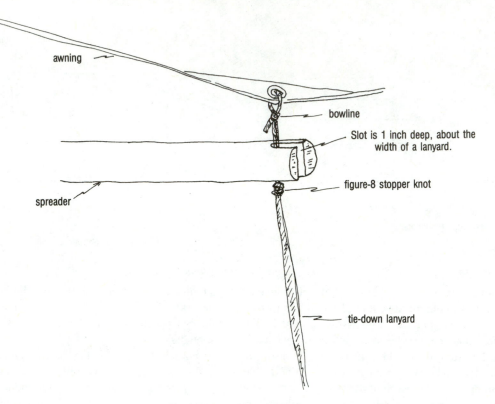

awning

bowline

Slot is 1 inch deep, about the
width of a lanyard.

figure-8 stopper knot

spreader

tie-down lanyard

External spreader attachment

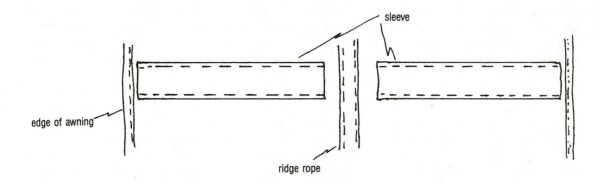

sleeve

edge of awning

ridge rope

Divide center sleeve into two sections.

Center spreader sleeve detail

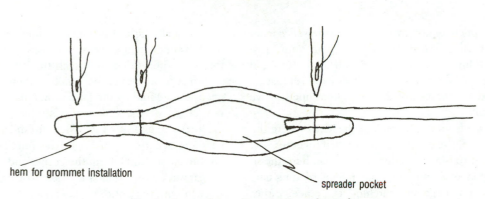

hem for grommet installation

spreader pocket

Forming hem and spreader pocket for end spreaders

material—vinyl, cloth, or in this case leather—over the raw edge and stitching it. The binding will both finish the edge and protect it.

A slot for a permanently attached lift can be closed with snaps, twist fasteners, or a zipper, but if you can still tie your own shoes, the strongest and easiest may be a simple lacing between two rows of grommets. Whatever method you use, a flap with a Velcro edge is required over the slot to prevent it from leaking.

Thousands of variations and modifications are possible. Zip-on or snap-on (or lace-on) side panels can keep out the afternoon sun. Screen panels can provide protection from insects. Trapezoid foredeck awnings can lower cabin temperatures and allow the forward hatch to remain open even when it is raining. And a hose fitting in the lowest spot of an awning can allow you to catch that often-precious rain and direct it to your tanks. Give your own use ample thought before you start, then make the awning that satisfies your requirements.

THE ENVELOPE

There are a number of useful canvas items that are nothing more than folded flat sheets with the sides hemmed together—envelopes.

The simple storage pocket typifies the canvas envelope. Dimensions will depend upon what the pocket will contain and where it will be mounted, but the measurements are not necessary to understanding the concept. Put a double-rubbed hem in

all four edges of a rectangle of canvas. Now fold the rectangle in half—well, not exactly in half. Instead of bottom edge to top edge, the bottom edge should be about 3 inches below the top. Run a line of stitches on either side to stitch the "halves" together. Put grommets in the top corners and hang the pocket against the hull or inside a locker, perfect for pot lids or pantyhose.

The choice of fabric for a storage pocket depends upon its use and location. The most versatile fabric remains treated canvas because of its durability, but the vivid colors and UV resistance of acrylic canvas make it a good choice when the pocket will be visible or outside. Some upholstery materials have the prerequisite stability to make at-

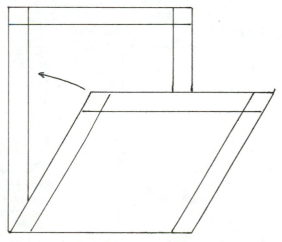

From flat sheet to envelope

tractive pockets and may make an exposed pocket less obtrusive. For the stowage of light items, 1.5-ounce spinnaker cloth is hard to beat. Linens and clothes will benefit from the unrestricted ventilation afforded by storage pockets sewn from open weave Phifertex.

To cut down on the bulk of the hems where the two sides of the envelope are stitched together, you may want to bind the edges rather than hem them. Binding involves no more than folding binding tape over the raw edge and stitching it in place. Either cloth (usually Orlon) or vinyl binding tape may be used. If your machine will sew a zigzag stitch, that is the best stitch to use to attach the binding.

Bind the bottom edge—which becomes the front edge—before folding the fabric, then bind the three raw edges of the envelope, stitching the sides together at the same time. The bottom corners will be more secure if you begin the binding on the bottom about 1 inch from the corner and end it in a similar way on the other side. Alternatively, you may elect to bind the entire perimeter of the envelope,

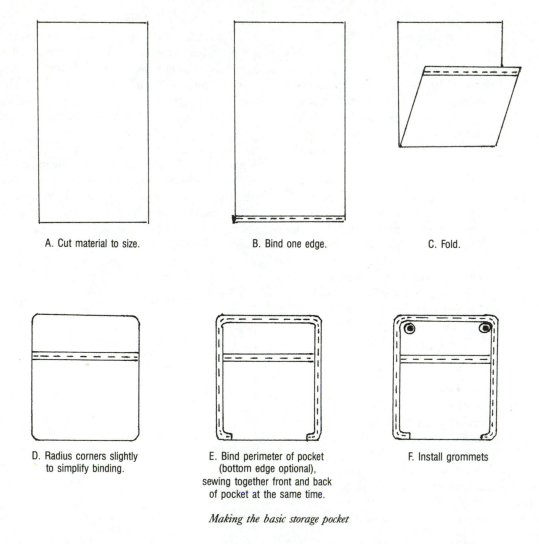

A. Cut material to size.

B. Bind one edge.

C. Fold.

D. Radius corners slightly to simplify binding.

E. Bind perimeter of pocket (bottom edge optional), sewing together front and back of pocket at the same time.

F. Install grommets

Making the basic storage pocket

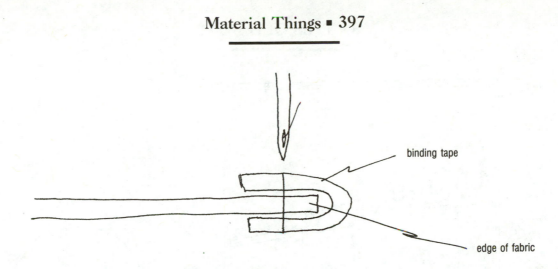

binding tape

edge of fabric

Binding a raw edge

including the folded bottom. Binding may be easier if you radius the corners. The edge where the tape overlaps itself will be less noticeable if you cut the tape end on a diagonal before stitching it down.

Tool Rolls

The best way to stow hand tools on a boat—better than boxes, racks, or drawers—is in canvas tool rolls. Rolls are easy on the tools, keep them quiet, provide instant accounting, and can be stowed almost anywhere. The only fabric choices are natural or treated canvas. Wipe the tools with oil and the cotton fiber will absorb the oil, protecting the tools from rust. Acrylic canvas will not absorb the oil and the sharp edges of tools soon chafe through the fabric.

The tool roll is a basic envelope with vertical dividing seams to separate the tools, but there are some modifications to the standard pattern that will make the envelope better suited for tools. Let's make a roll for a set of wrenches.

Lay the wrenches out side by side, and use a cloth measuring tape—or mark a strip of fabric—to measure the distance from the supporting surface over the wrench and back to the surface at the widest part of each wrench. Add ½ inch to each of these measurements to provide some extra room in each pocket, then add all the dimensions together, plus a 2-inch hem allowance (1 inch will be adequate

if you are binding the edges) to arrive at the cut width. The cut length will be approximately three times the length of the longest wrench in the set.

Fold the material into thirds and rub the folds to crease them. Place the wrenches on the material in size order with the bottom of each aligned along the top fold. Slip a straightedge between the wrenches and the fabric, defining a line across the throats of the wrenches just below the jaws. Remove the wrenches, slide the diagonal straightedge up 1 inch to provide the hem allowance (not necessary if you are binding the edge) and mark the fabric. Unfold the material and cut it along this line. Sew a ½-inch double hem on all four sides.

On the back face of the material—in this case the face opposite the hems—and near the longer of the two sides, mark a spot midway between the two fold creases. Over this mark and parallel to the creases, stretch a length of shoe lacing (or similar flat cord) and stitch it to the canvas for about 2 inches.

Refold the diagonal end along the original crease and run a row of stitching along both sides to form the envelope, taking care not to accidentally stitch over the lacing flopping around somewhere underneath. Mark the folded edge with the width of the individual pockets that you originally derived, and use a square to lightly mark perpendicular lines to the top of each pocket. Complete the roll by stitching along each of these lines, backstitching to start

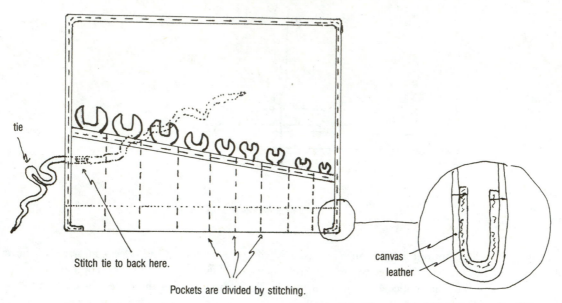

tie

Stitch tie to back here.

Pockets are divided by stitching.

canvas

leather

Leather strip sewn into fold will increase durability.

Tool roll

and finish. Insert the wrenches, fold the flap over them, roll them tightly, and tie the roll closed with the lacing.

For a large set of wrenches, the size of the flap can get out of hand. In such a case, the bulk of the roll can be reduced by cutting the flap parallel to the angle of the pocket rather than square.

Lining the bottom of the pocket with leather will add years of life to a roll for heavy tools. Before the final folding and stitching, center a 2- or 3-inch-wide strip of soft leather over the fold crease and stitch it down all the way around. Then complete the roll as above.

Tool rolls are equally well suited to the storage of chisels and punches and screwdrivers and pliers. I even keep my socket set in a canvas roll.

Sheet Bags

The basic envelope made from acrylic canvas can also be a useful pouch to keep sheets contained and out of the way. A slightly altered envelope makes for a somewhat neater installation on flat surfaces. Instead of folding the canvas and stitching two sides to form the envelope, in this case you are going to cut the front and back separately and seam them together on three sides.

The dimensions will depend upon the bulk of the sheets you want the bag to hold, but I recently looked at a 17-inch-wide by 9-inch-deep bag at the chandlery for $31.75. You can build a much better bag for less than $7.

For the back piece of a 17 × 9 bag, or any size sheet bag, you want about 3 inches of extra *height* to provide flanges for mounting the bag. To determine the cut size, allow for a $1/2$-inch, double-rubbed hem on the sides, 1 inch at the bottom, and a 2-inch hem at the top. If you are getting the hang of this by now, you came up with a cut dimension of 19 × 16.

For the front piece, it is extra *width* that you need—to give the pouch volume. Four inches should be adequate. The sides and bottom get a $1/2$-inch double hem, with a 1-inch hem at the top. Let's see. Four and seven and carry the one . . . How does 23 × 11$1/2$ sound?

Hem the back according to the above sequence—2 inches at the top, 1 inch at the bottom, 1/2 inch on the sides—and put it aside. Because the front piece is going to have elastic in the top, you will need to hem its sides in a specific sequence. Begin by putting the hem in the bottom edge, then turn 1/2 inch of the remaining three raw edges over and baste or stitch them. Finish the top by folding the edge over again 1 inch and sewing it down. Do *not* stitch along the fold as you might a regular hem; this is a sleeve (or casing) for the elastic and you want it to bunch, which stitching down the fold will inhibit.

You can use waistband elastic for the next step, but unless you are one of those kinky types, you know how quickly the snap goes out of your drawers. If your machine will stitch over it, use 1/4-inch bungee cord. Otherwise buy 1 1/2-inch elastic and fold it in half. Tape the bungee (or elastic) to a piece of straight wire and thread it through the sleeve. With several passes of the needle, secure one end of the bungee close to the edge of the fabric. Now pull on the bungee and bunch the sleeve until its width is 1 inch more than the width of the back piece. Holding this adjustment, sew down the bungee near the edge of the fabric and snip off the excess cord.

The elastic top is not going to keep out rain and spray, so drain holes are essential. It is much easier to install them before you assemble the bag. All that is required is a pair grommets in the front piece as close to the bottom seam as you can locate them without any part of the grommet on the seam. They should also be located near the sides (so they will be in the corners of the bag when it is completed), but do not place them so they will interfere with your ability to pleat the bottom.

Placing the bottom of the front piece 1 inch above the bottom of the back piece—the hems of both pieces should be underneath—put the second fold in the side hems of the front piece and stitch the pieces together. On both ends of the bottom of the front piece, fold the material into equal pleats. They will be about 1 inch wide and should be formed so that the folds align with the sides of the bag and the bottom hem lies flat on the back piece. Run a row of stitches across the bottom to finish the bag.

The bag *can* be mounted with screws, but snap fasteners allow the bag to be removed when not in use, greatly extending its life. The male half of the fastener should be installed on the boat first. Decide on a location for the bag and pencil its outline on the surface. Locate fasteners inside each corner and evenly spaced every 4 to 6 inches across the top. Drill holes and screw the fasteners in place. Use the installed fasteners to mark the correct position on the bag for the female halves.

To install snaps in the canvas, use a heated punch to melt a small hole for the barrel. Place the button in the die and place the material over the barrel of the button. Be sure the button is on the correct side of the fabric. Slip the socket over the protruding barrel, then position the setting tool on the barrel and tap the tool lightly with a hammer to set the snap.

Here is one more idea thrown in for free. Find a spot inside the locker to install a second row of snaps and stow the sheets by unsnapping the bag and resnapping it inside the locker.

Small-parts Stowage Bag

One final envelope before we move on. I saw this one mounted inside the door of a mechanical contractor's van and it is too good not to pass on.

As an example, let's make a nine-compartment bag for small-parts stowage, but in practice you can make as few or as many compartments as you need. Arbitrarily, the back of the bag has a finished size of 15 inches wide by 20 inches tall and is made from acrylic canvas.

For the front of the bag, you will need 0.020 clear vinyl, the material in dodger windows. The type sold from a roll will be cheaper and is adequate for this application. A piece of clear vinyl 18 inches by 27 inches is required. The 18-inch dimension is the height, allowing 1 inch of canvas above and below for the installation of grommets or other mounting hardware. The 27-inch dimension is the

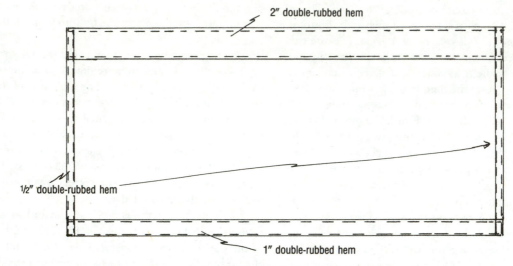

2″ double-rubbed hem

½″ double-rubbed hem

1″ double-rubbed hem

A. Cut back piece to size and hem edges.

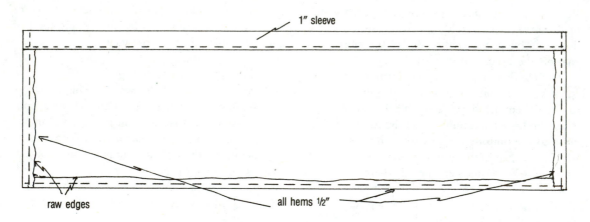

1″ sleeve

raw edges

all hems ½″

B. Cut front piece to size. Hem three sides and put sleeve in top.

Making a sheet bag (continued on pages 401, 402)

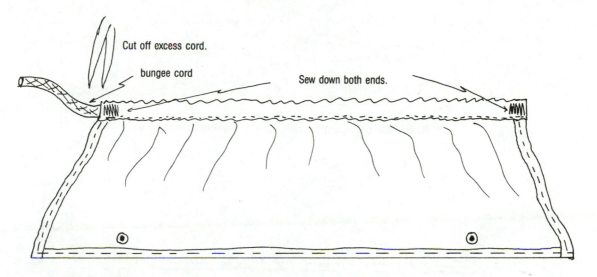

C. Thread bungee cord into sleeve and gather top edge to the same width as the back piece. Install grommets as drain holes.

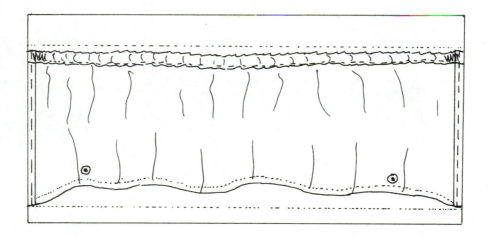

D. Stitch front piece to back piece along both sides.

Making a sheet bag (continued)

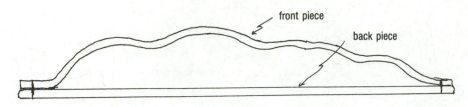

E. Bottom after sides have been sewn together. (Hems omitted for clarity.)

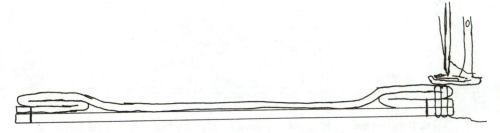

F. Bottom ready to be stitched with similar pleats on each side of front piece.

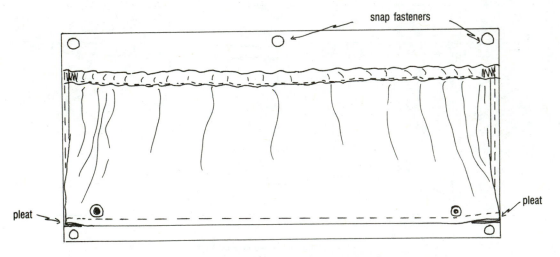

G. The finished bag with snap fasteners installed for mounting.

Making a sheet bag

width, determined based on the number of pockets *across,* in this case three (as you will see shortly). Three equal pockets across 15 inches of canvas means each pocket is 5 inches wide. As with the sheet pocket, 4 inches of material are added to give the pocket fullness, so each pocket requires 9 inches of material, or 27 inches for the three. A wonderful feature of (unreinforced) vinyl is that it does not require hemming or hem allowances; cut pieces are ready to use.

On the front (hems on the back) of the canvas, draw two light lines dividing the width into three 5-inch sections. Draw two similar lines on the vinyl, but dividing the wider vinyl into 9-inch sections. Center the vinyl on the canvas 1 inch from the top and the bottom. Align the edges on one side and stitch the two pieces together. If your presser foot has a tendency to stick to the vinyl, rub the top surface lightly with talcum powder, which you can wash off later.

From the unstitched edge of the vinyl, split the 18-inch dimension into three 6-inch strips, cutting right to the stitch line. Keeping the strips together (edge to edge) and centered on the canvas, align the ends with the other side of the canvas and stitch the strips to the canvas.

Because of the extra length of the vinyl, it will be rather full. The next step is to divide that fullness. Place the pencil lines on the vinyl on top of the pencil lines on the canvas and join the pieces here with a row of stitching. Do the same on the second pair of lines, dividing the vinyl strips into thirds.

Finally, you are going to form three accordion-fold pockets from each strip by pleating the strips in the same manner that you pleated the bottom of the sheet bag. Each pocket will have a 1-inch-wide pleat on either side, and the top fold of the pleat will line up with the edge of the bag, or the row of stitching between pockets, depending upon the location of the pleat. Hold the pleats in position, or make them as you go, and run a line of stitches across the bottom of the strip. Do the same across the bottom of all three strips.

The results are nine clear pockets that are ideal for holding a variety of items. The same principle can be used to make smaller or larger pockets, depending upon your stowage requirement. Grommets at the top and bottom will allow you to screw, hook, or lace the bag in position.

THE ONE-PIECE BAG

The next level of complexity is the one-piece bag. There are a number of ways to fold and stitch a piece of canvas into a bag and we are going to look at three of them. It may be easier to think of this as making an open box out of canvas and putting handles on it.

Boat Bag I

I was going to call this Ice Bag I, but with your new refrigeration system, who needs an ice bag? However a few sturdy canvas bags can greatly simplify getting equipment and supplies to and from the boat. Off cruising, the boat bag is essential since the nearest market is inevitably miles from the harbor. If you are wondering what boat bags, other than hauling tools and brushes to the boat yard, have to do with refurbishing your old boat, bear with me. There is a method to my madness.

For clarity, let's do a cubic-foot bag. The fabric of choice is 10-ounce treated canvas. You need a piece 3 feet long and 2 feet wide, plus hem allowances. A 1½-inch hem around the top of the bag adds 4 inches to the 3-foot dimension, and ½-inch bound seams on the sides add 1 inch to the width.

Fold the material in half across the long dimension and stitch the two halves together on both sides with a row of stitches ½ inch from the edge, forming an envelope. Bind the raw edges with binding tape, using a zigzag stitch if you have it.

Measure in along the fold 5½ inches from the stitching and draw a line on the fabric parallel to the stitching; make the line about 6 inches long. Now measure along the stitched edge 5½ inches from the fold and draw a line from the stitched edge to the first line, this one parallel to the fold. Cut from the side and from the fold along these lines to the point

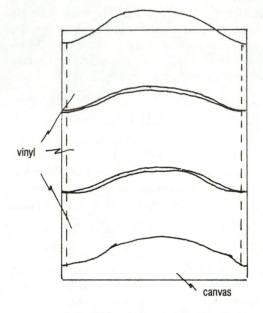

A. Sew strips of clear vinyl to canvas back.

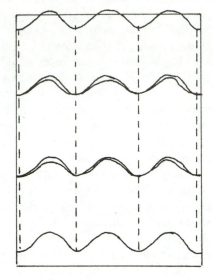

B. Divide fullness of vinyl equally with two seams.

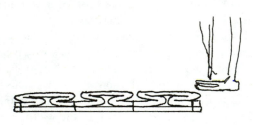

C. Pleat and sew down the bottom of each vinyl strip.

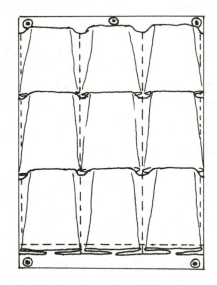

D. Install mounting grommets in top and bottom of canvas.

Small-parts stowage bag

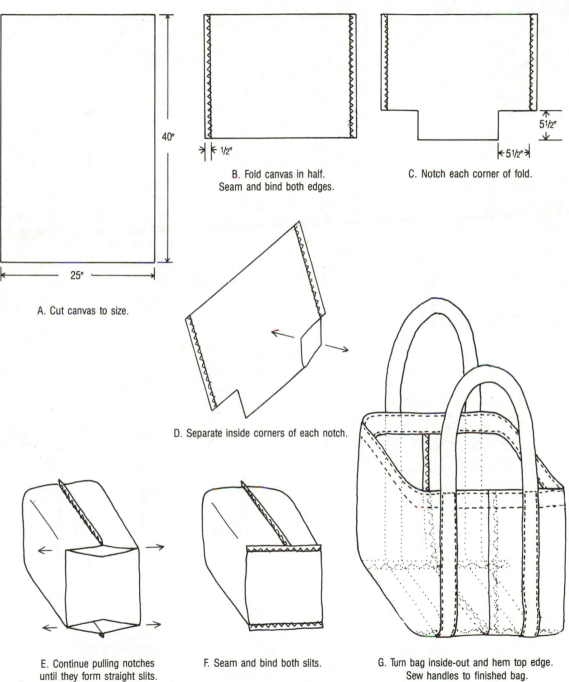

A. Cut canvas to size.

40″

25″

B. Fold canvas in half.
Seam and bind both edges.

½″

C. Notch each corner of fold.

5½″

5½″

D. Separate inside corners of each notch.

E. Continue pulling notches
until they form straight slits.

F. Seam and bind both slits.

G. Turn bag inside-out and hem top edge.
Sew handles to finished bag.

Boat bag I

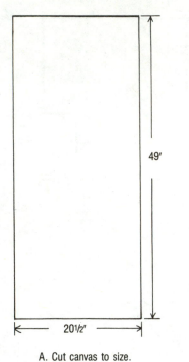

49"

20½"

A. Cut canvas to size.

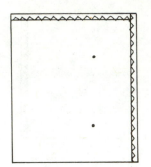

B. Fold canvas in half. Seam and
bind two edges. Mark four dots
equidistant from fold line
and stitch lines.

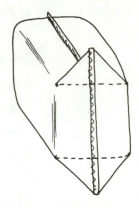

C. Open bag and shape bottom into square
with dot at each corner. Stitch between dots
across triangular "ears."

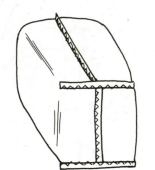

D. Trim off ears and bind raw edges.

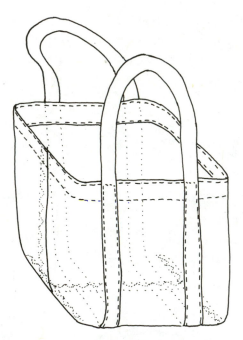

E. Turn bag inside-out and hem top edge.
Sew handles to finished bag.

Boat bag II

where they intersect, making a square notch in the corner. Measure and cut a similar notch from the opposite corner.

Gripping the two layers of fabric separately at the inside corner of one of the notches, pull the layers apart. The four edges of the hole in the fabric resulting from the notch should form a diamond shape. Continue pulling, narrowing the diamond until the hole closes and you only have two edges, one above the other. Sew these edges together with a row of stitching, then bind the raw edges. Handle the second notch in the same manner.

I hope it does not come as a shock to you that you suddenly have a canvas bag. Put a 1½-inch double-rubbed hem around the top of the bag, then turn the bag inside out. All that remains is stitching on a handle. Short handles can be attached to the top hem, but for the most durability, the handles should go completely under the bag. I prefer 1½ inch webbing for the handles and about a 10-foot length is required for a cubic-foot bag. Draw two parallel lines 5 or 6 inches apart from one lip down the side, across the bottom, and back up the other side. Sew the webbing over the lines, allowing about 2 feet on each side—a foot-high loop—for the handles. Sew down both edges of the webbing.

Boat Bag II

An alternative method of constructing the same bag requires a piece of canvas 4 feet by 1½ feet plus allowances. Add 1 inch to the 4-foot dimension for a bound seam. To the 18-inch dimension add 2½ inches for a 1½-inch top hem and a ½-inch bound seam across the bottom.

Fold the fabric in half across the long dimension and stitch the layers together on *one* side and across the edge opposite the fold. Bind the raw edges.

The final step will be easier with reference marks on the fabric. Put a dot 6 inches from the stitch lines of the two seams. Put a second dot 6 inches from the fold and an equal distance from the stitching of the adjacent seam. Stick pins straight through these two dots and turn the fabric over, marking a second pair of dots where the pins protrude.

Stand the bag up and open the unstitched end. Flatten the bottom and shape it into a square with the reference dots at each corner. You should end up with triangular-shaped ears sticking out on two sides of the bag with the bottom seam running from apex to apex. Run a straight line of stitches across each of the triangles from reference dot to reference dot. One half inch beyond the stitching, cut off the triangles. Bind the raw edges. Put a 1½ inch hem around the top of the bag, then turn the bag inside out and sew on the handles. Another bag in the bag.

Boat Bag III: Hatch Cover

The third one-piece bag is best illustrated with a hatch cover. Acrylic canvas is the material of choice. Determine the fabric dimensions by measuring the length and width of the hatch. Add twice the height of the hatch to both dimensions, plus an additional 3 inches for a 1-inch double-rubbed hem on all sides. A 20-inch hatch 2½ inches high requires a 28-inch square of canvas.

Center the canvas on the hatch, letting the excess drape equally over all four edges. Crease or mark the fabric around the edges of the hatch, making certain that corner locations are clear. At the sewing machine, fold each corner diagonally on a line from the position of the corner of the hatch (as indicated by creases or markings) to the actual corner of the material. With the raw edges of the material perpendicular to the line of stitching, sew a straight row of stitches from the raw edge to the fold, crossing the fold slightly wide of the mark for the hatch corner. This pinches the excess material at the corners into a triangle—something like the corners of a tablecloth.

Check the cover for fit before proceeding. It should be snug, but not so tight that it will be difficult to install. Adjust the location of the corner seams if necessary, then cut off the excess material and bind the raw edges. Put a 1-inch double-rubbed hem all around the cover and one-piece box number three is finished.

A common way to hold the hatch cover in place is with snaps in the hem. One snap in each side is

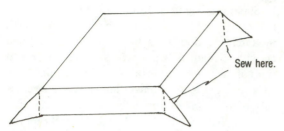

A. Drape canvas over hatch and pinch corners. Seam as shown, trim away excess and bind seams.

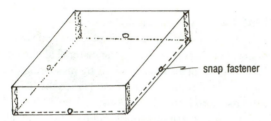

B. Turn inside-out, hem bottom edge to finish, and install snap fasteners to hold cover in position.

C. Detail of alternative drawstring attachment method.

Boat bag III: hatch cover

adequate on small hatches, two snaps on larger covers.

An alternative that eliminates screws into the side of the hatch is the drawstring. Cut the original material 2 inches longer and wider so the hem extends below the bottom of the hatch. When you hem the cover, stitch along the fold but do not stitch down the raw edge. First install eight grommets in the loose flap of the hem, two on each side of the cover, all located about two inches from the corners. Now finish the hems.

Using a piece of stiff wire, feed a length of 1/8-inch flag halyard into the hem, exiting the grommet before every corner and re-entering the grommet after the corner. Canvas, because it is stiff, will not gather well with a drawstring; but installed this way, the drawstring "cuts" the corners, passing under the corners of the hatch and securing the corners of the cover. The loose ends of the line lead out the two grommets at one corner, where they are tightened and secured with a bow knot, then tucked up under the cover. Bungee may be threaded through the hem as well, eliminating the need to tie the cover each time, but with some loss of security.

THE TWO-PIECE BAG

For any shape but square or near square, the two-piece bag is appropriate. I will detail two such projects, but as you will quickly see, they are almost identical.

The Obligatory Ditty Bag

What kind of canvas-work instructions would these be without a ditty bag? I could have my license revoked. The truth is we only have one such bag aboard, but it contains our clothespins and sees daily use when we are aboard. One bag, that is, if you don't count the sail bags or the canvas bucket.

Any sturdy material can be sewn into a ditty bag, but smaller bags shape and draw better if they are made of a softer material like oxford cloth. The two pieces you need for a two-piece bag are the bottom—which can be any shape—and the main piece which forms all the sides and is almost always rectangular.

For a ditty bag you need a circle of material 1 inch larger than the finished size of the bag, and a rectangular piece with a length of 3.14 (π) times the finished diameter of the bottom, plus 1 inch, and a width 2 inches greater than the finished height of the bag. The allowances are for bound seams and a 1-inch hem around the top of the bag. For a clothespin bag 6 inches in diameter and 8 inches deep, cut a 7-inch circle and a 10-inch by 20-inch (rounding 19.84) rectangle.

A grade-school compass will enable you to draw small circles, but what about a large circle? You need a pin, a piece of thread, and a pencil. Put two

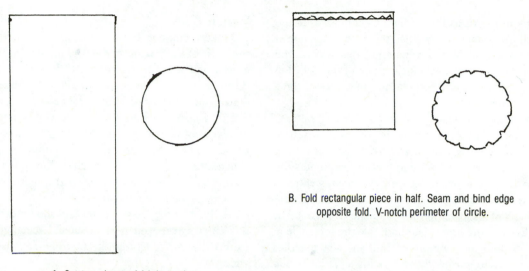

B. Fold rectangular piece in half. Seam and bind edge
opposite fold. V-notch perimeter of circle.

A. Cut two pieces of fabric to size.

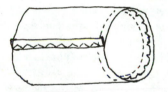

C. Open tube and sew circle into one end.
Bind seam for a better finish.

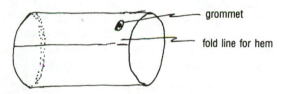

grommet

fold line for hem

D. Turn bag rightside-out and install grommet below
the fold line for the top hem.

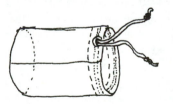

E. Thread both ends of drawstring through grommet.
Hem top of bag over drawstring. Put stopper
knots in ends of string.

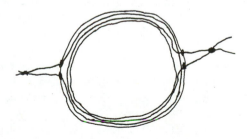

F. Detail of dual drawstrings for large bags.

Ditty bag

loops in the thread, separated by the *radius* of the circle you want to draw. Stick the pin through one of the loops and into the material; this will be the center of the circle. Stick the point of the pencil in the other loop, and, pulling the thread taut, trace the desired circle.

Round is the usual shape for a ditty bag, but you can just as easily fabricate the bag with a square bottom. The circular shape is not just a tradition; the curved seam of a round bottom distributes the load evenly, while a square bottom concentrates most of the stress in the corners. But a radius on the corners of a square bottom eliminates this concern.

Back to the project at hand, fold the rectangle in half (across the long dimension) and sew together the edges opposite the fold with a 1/2-inch-wide seam. Bind the raw edges. Open this fabric "tube" and fit the circle into one end, mating the edge of the tube to the edge of the circle. Pin or baste the two pieces together. Run a row of straight stitches 1/2 inch inside these flush edges, joining the two pieces. Bind the raw edges. Turn the bag right side out.

If you are sewing stiff material it may be easier to get the round piece to turn out smoothly if you make a few evenly spaced V-cuts with your scissors in the hem allowance of the circle. Limit the cuts to about 1/4 inch deep. Staples in the hem allowance may be easier than pinning and more secure than basting with transfer tape, but be sure to remove them before you bind the edges.

A drawstring completes the bag. Rub the hem down to mark it, then install a single grommet just below the crease. Encircle the bag with a piece of light line, threading both ends through the grommet. A heavier drawstring may necessitate two grommets placed side by side, one for each end of the drawstring. Fold the hem over to encase the line and stitch the hem down, taking care not to accidentally stitch the line.

Larger bags, such as sail bags, will close much more easily with two drawstrings exiting the hem on opposite sides of the bag. Pulling on the opposing drawstrings in effect chokes the bag. Four grommets and two separate lengths of line are required for this arrangement.

Winch Cover

Make a ditty bag, but with the drawstring around the waist of the bag instead of the mouth, and you have a winch cover. Or omit the drawstring altogether and tack a tie to the outside of the bag for drawing in the waist. Too crude? Then try this one.

Add 1 inch to the diameter of the winch to determine the cut size of the top. Don't forget to take into account any self-tailing mechanism fitted to your winch. Measure the overall height of the winch and add a 1 1/2-inch seam allowance for the width of the rectangle. The length will be 3.14 times the diameter of the winch, plus a 1-inch seam allowance. For this fancy cover, you need a second rectangle of cloth the same length as the first one and half as wide.

Put a 1/2-inch double hem along one edge of the large rectangle, then fold the rectangle in half and stitch the ends together to make the skirt. Pay attention to right side and wrong side so both the hems and the seam will be on the wrong side. Bind the raw edges of the seam.

Put a *1-inch* double hem along the edge of the small rectangle, but stitch only the inside edge of the hem, not along the fold. Thread a length of 1/4-inch bungee (or heavy-duty waistband elastic) through the hem, then fold the piece in half and stitch the ends together, starting the stitching from the unhemmed edge. Stop the machine with the needle buried when the front of the presser foot reaches the hem. Pull on both ends of the bungee cord, helping the hem to gather with your other hand, until the original diameter is reduced to about half. Holding the bungee, complete the seam, sewing back and forth across the bungee (inside the hem) several times to secure the ends. Snip off the excess cord.

Slip the large skirt *inside* the smaller one and align their raw edges. Fit the circle into this end and mate its edge with the raw edges of the two skirts, stapling it in position. Run a row of straight stitches 1/2 inch inside these flush edges, joining the three pieces. Bind the raw edges. Turn the cover right side out. Reach inside the cover and spread the inner skirt over the winch when you install the cover. The elastic around the waist of the winch will hold the cover in position.

THE BOX

The box is the last of the five basic configurations that make up the majority of the canvas items found aboard boats. The box is nothing more than a *three-piece* bag – a two-piece bag with a top. Sew a circle or a square in each end of the ditty bag design above and you have a box. You also have a problem. There is no way to turn the box right side out. Anytime a fabric is sewn together with hidden seams, there must be some opening in the box to allow it to be turned inside out. It is fabricating the opening that represents the only significant difference – other than the third piece – between a two-piece bag and a box. Read on.

Cockpit Cushions

The most common application of the fabric box is as a cushion cover. Let's start in the cockpit. My original experience with cockpit cushions was a typical set constructed of polyurethane foam covered with reinforced vinyl (Naugahyde) and closed with a metal zipper. A more worthless combination I cannot imagine. While the vinyl was ineffective at keeping the water out, it was great at keeping it in; within days the foam was full of water and was never again dry. The soaked cushions were as heavy as lead, and only slightly softer. The always-clammy vinyl was uncomfortable to sit on, impossible to sleep on, and a ready source of second-degree burns in summertime. It tended to adhere to the deck with such tenacity that whenever the cushions were peeled up, bits of gelcoat came with them. The zipper quickly dissolved into green powder, two shades lighter than the mildew rioting inside the covers on the cloth backing of the vinyl. I pitched the cushions and swore never to have cockpit cushions again.

Then came closed cell foam. My first closed cell cushions I coated with vinyl – like a ski-belt – eliminating zippers and fabric, but the vinyl was still

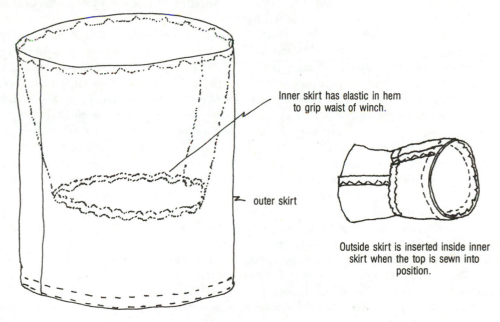

Inner skirt has elastic in hem to grip waist of winch.

outer skirt

Outside skirt is inserted inside inner skirt when the top is sewn into position.

finished cover

Winch cover

clammy and sticky, and downright treacherous when wet. Covers were needed, and open-weave Phifertex was the fabric we chose.

Cockpit cushions made of closed-cell foam and covered with Phifertex do not absorb water and surfaces dry very quickly. Spills and stains are no problem, and we often throw our cushions over the side for lounging in the water. Color choices were more limited when we purchased the fabric than they are today and we selected white. It turned out to be a wise selection, although the fabric does tend to yellow slightly with age.

Acrylic canvas also makes excellent cockpit cushion covers, drying quickly and resisting stains and mildew. But as with awning fabric, dark colors make the cushions intolerable in the tropics. Acrylic canvas in a light color is perhaps the best choice for both appearance and durability.

If your old boat is without cockpit cushions, the first step is to cut the foam. Use heavy paper to make a pattern for each cushion in order to get the angles and relationships correct. Closed-cell foam comes in sheets of various sizes, and the number and shape of the cushions may be influenced by how to use the sheet most efficiently. It also comes in various thicknesses; 2-inch foam makes very luxurious cockpit cushions. Closed-cell foam cuts easily with a *sharp* knife. Put a razor edge on your fillet knife, and draw it across the foam several times without a great deal of pressure to get the cleanest cut. Closed-cell foam tends to shrink, so cut the cushions about 1/2 inch oversize.

If you cut paper patterns, use them to mark the fabric for cutting, adding an allowance for 1/2-inch seams on all sides. Otherwise, place the foam on the fabric and trace the outline. If the cushion is not square on all sides, be sure to align any stripe or other pattern in the fabric with the edge that is square. Cut the material to the size of the foam, without allowances (you cut new foam 1/2-inch oversize anyway); this provides for a tight fit, but you need to be aware that it also reduces both the length and the width of the cushion.

We have already determined that the box requires a bottom *and* a top, and unless the cushion has a beveled edge (which we will consider later), both pieces are the same size. If the material has a right and wrong side—reinforced vinyl, for example—the two pieces need to match wrong side to wrong side, but this is not a concern with Phifertex or acrylic canvas.

While the two pieces are stacked, cut a series of notches in the seam allowances. Notch both pieces at the same time every 6 to 8 inches around the entire perimeter. If corners are radiused, cut three evenly spaced notches in each corner. The biggest problem with boxed cushions is getting the orientation of the top and the bottom twisted, and these notches will help you to avoid that.

The third piece in a boxed cushion—the piece that was the main piece of fabric in the ditty bag and the skirt for the winch cover—is called, appropriately enough, boxing. Twice the width plus twice the length of the cushion gives you the approximate length of the boxing. The width is the thickness of the foam plus a 1-inch seam allowance. For a slightly better fit, reduce the width of the boxing by about 1/4 inch.

You will generally fare better if you can cut the boxing first, reserving one edge of the material for this purpose. If no opening was required, the boxing might be single strip, but an opening is necessary to turn the cover inside out and, just as important, to get the foam inside the cover. For this latter purpose, the opening should be as large as possible, generally the full length of the back side of the cushion. The cut length of the boxing will be the calculated length from above less the length of the opening. For your first cushion, allow an additional 6 inches to accommodate hems and overlap. If your fabric is not long enough to allow you to get the length you need in a single strip, you can seam shorter pieces together, but try to avoid any seams in the front edge of the cushion.

I have seen cushions fabricated with snaps and occasionally Velcro to close the opening, but the only closure that will give the cover a tight, consistent fit is a zipper, and the only zipper that you

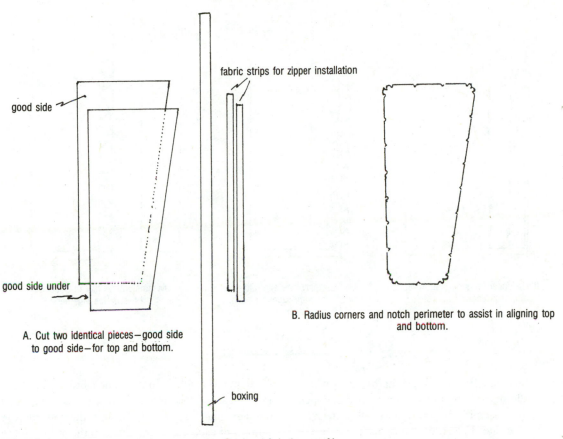

good side

good side under

fabric strips for zipper installation

A. Cut two identical pieces—good side to good side—for top and bottom.

B. Radius corners and notch perimeter to assist in aligning top and bottom.

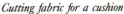

boxing

Cutting fabric for a cushion

should use is a YKK #10 Delrin zipper. These zippers are the industry standard, providing extraordinary strength with immunity to corrosion. You can buy assembled zippers (jacket zippers) in a variety of lengths, but buying zipper tape by the yard is generally cheaper. The sliders on assembled zippers are metal, and for marine use, especially outdoor use, they should be replaced with plastic sliders. Buy only plastic sliders for use with zipper tape, and remember that it takes 2 feet of tape to make a 1-foot-long zipper.

To convert zipper tape into the remaining length of boxing requires two strips of fabric the length of the opening. The width of each of the strips is 1/2 the cut width of the rest of the boxing plus 3/4 inch.

Assemble the fabric and the zipper by positioning the zipper tape on top of the fabric, aligning the rear edge of the zipper (*not* the toothed edge) with the edge of the fabric. Sew the two pieces together with a straight row of stitches 1/4 inch from the flush edges. Now turn the assembly over and fold the fabric back until the teeth of the zipper tape are just exposed. Run a row of stitching 1/2 inch from the fold, sewing through two layers of fabric and the zipper tape. This second row of stitching should be on almost the same line as the first row. Make up the other side of the zipper in a similar manner, then assemble the two halves with a plastic slide.

Place the boxing on the good side of the zipper assembly with one end flush and seam the two

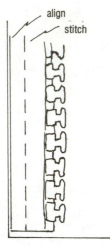
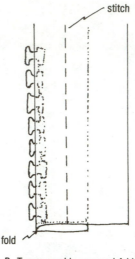
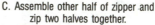
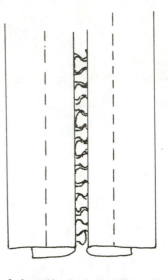

A. Place zipper on good side of fabric strip, align edges, and stitch.

B. Turn assembly over and fold good side of fabric up, exposing teeth. Stitch.

C. Assemble other half of zipper and zip two halves together.

Installing a zipper

pieces together. Run the machine by hand where the needle may encounter the teeth of the zipper, moving the assembly as necessary to allow the needle to penetrate. Fold the boxing back so that the seam becomes an overlapping hem and run a second row of stitches across the boxing and zipper assembly. You now have a single strip long enough to box the cushion.

You need one more component before you are ready to assemble the cover. For a professional look, piping is required. Piping is the round welt that is sewn into the edge seams to hide the stitching. Molded vinyl piping, purchased by the yard, requires no preassembly, sews easily, and works well with Phifertex. If the fabric is white, a piping in a color that matches your other canvas can provide a little extra flair. For canvas covers, a welt assembled from 1/8-inch braided Dacron cord and binding tape, or strips of canvas, is more appropriate. Whether you make the piping the same color as the cushion or a contrasting color is a matter of taste.

To make a welt from the same fabric as the cushion, cut the fabric into 1 3/8-inch strips. You need enough total length to go around the top *and* the bottom of each cushion. Join all of the strips end to end with 1/4-inch seams, taking care to keep the raw edges always on the same side. Fold the strip over the braided cord and, holding the edges flush, use a zipper foot to run a line of stitches next to the cord. The welt is ready to use.

Place the zipper assembly, good side down, on top of one of the cover pieces (good side up), with the edge of the assembly flush with the fabric edge that will be at the rear of the cushion. Center the zipper end to end, on the back edge. Slip the welt assembly in between the two parts so that all the raw edges are flush. Using the zipper foot, start a couple of inches from the unattached end of the zipper assembly and sew the three parts together, placing the stitches as near the welt as possible. You may find it easier to get the boxing to follow the contour of the fabric around corners if you make a

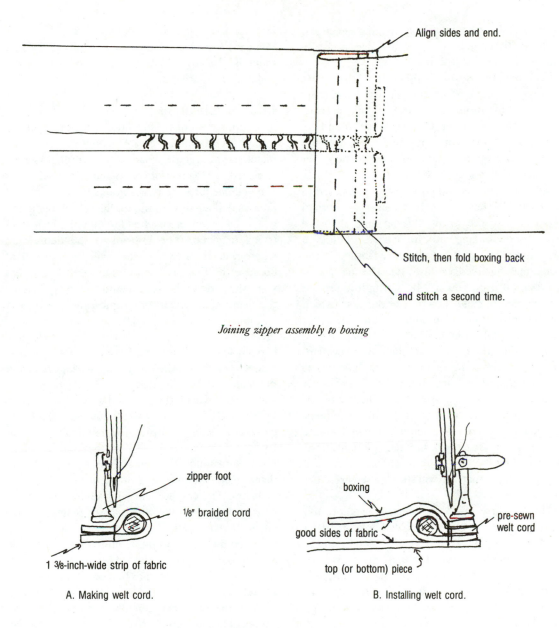

Align sides and end.

Stitch, then fold boxing back

and stitch a second time.

Joining zipper assembly to boxing

zipper foot

1/8" braided cord

1 3/8-inch-wide strip of fabric

A. Making welt cord.

boxing

good sides of fabric

pre-sewn welt cord

top (or bottom) piece

B. Installing welt cord.

Welt cord

few shallow slits in the seam allowance. Sew right around the perimeter of the cover until you near the loose end of the zipper assembly, a few inches short of your starting point. Cut off any excess boxing, leaving enough to overlap the end of the zipper assembly by about an inch plus 1/2 inch to turn the raw edge under. Fold the raw edge and slip the folded boxing between the unstitched end of the zipper assembly and the piping, aligning the edges, and finish the seam. Binding the raw edges is unnecessary since they will be inside the cover.

The next step is to take precautions to prevent the top of the cushion from being twisted in relation to the bottom. Remember the matching notches you put in the two pieces. Go all the way around the stitched-on boxing, notching the raw edge of the boxing *exactly* opposite the notches in the cover piece the boxing is already sewn to.

Make sure the second cover piece is oriented to match the notches in the first piece—not turned around or with the wrong side up—and align the notches in the boxing with the notches around the fabric. Insert the welt between the fabric and the boxing, making all edges flush. Because the assembly is turned over, you will be sewing the second seam in the opposite direction to the first (which contributes to the cover's tendency to twist), so start the seam a couple of inches from the folded edge of the boxing in order to finish stitching at the overlap.

Pay attention to the alignment of the notches as you stitch around the cover. If they start to get out of alignment, stretch the bottom fabric slightly as you sew to get them back in alignment. If the alignment goes out badly around a corner, stop and pull out the stitching, then resew the corner to get it right. Basting or stapling (be sure to remove them afterward) will help, but the material will still shift if you are not vigilant.

When you arrive back at your starting point, stop stitching before you reach the folded boxing. Adjust the fold to be square with the sides, then finish the seam. It is not necessary to stitch the fold down across the zipper, but to keep the slide from going too far, take a few hand stitches across the teeth, or distort a couple of teeth with the side of a heated knife blade.

Unzip the cover and turn it inside out. Use your fingers inside the cover to shape the corners, taking care not to cut yourself if the welt is molded vinyl. Insert the foam; sometimes it is easier to insert the foam folded in half and unfold it inside the cover. Work the foam into all the corners with your hand, then zip the cover closed. Place the cover in the cockpit. Turn around. Sit down. Ahhh.

Interior Cushions

Interior cushions differ little from those in the cockpit. The differences are mainly related to the materials you will use. Foam is an example. As great as closed-cell foam is for cockpit cushions, it is not a good choice for settees and bunks because it compresses deliberately. In the middle of the night you will feel as if you are packed for shipping instead of trying to sleep. The bottom of the depression where you are now chocked will be stone hard because the foam is compressed, and if you claw your way back to the surface and change positions, the depression remains for some time.

Interior cushions should be constructed of polyurethane foam, and be certain to buy quality foam—bargain foam will not be a bargain. Poly-foam is graded by density; the higher the grade, the firmer the foam will be. Anything under 40 pounds and your elbows will hit the plywood when you roll over. Foam rated between 50 and 60 pounds will provide good, firm support. Spray the foam heavily with Lysol before you cover it, and periodically afterwards, and mildew—which seems to like polyurethane foam—will not be a problem.

Fabric choices are virtually unlimited. Fortunately, demon vinyl, which boat manufacturers once thought the only suitable fabric for cushion covers, is no longer common. Herculon, a demon in its own right, replaced vinyl. Herculons have poor shape retention and tend to be hot. Herculon actually refers to the fiber and I have to admit to encountering some very nice Herculon (and other Olefin) fabrics. The problem is that both vinyl and Herculon are popular mostly because they are waterproof and stain resistant. Maybe I am just a wild and crazy guy, but what about comfort?

As I indicated earlier, a fabric that you might

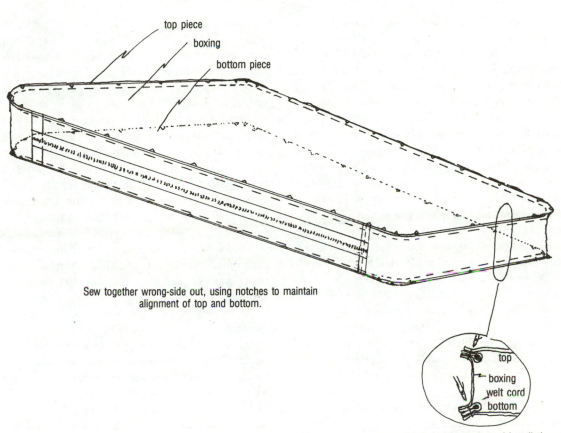

top piece

boxing

bottom piece

Sew together wrong-side out, using notches to maintain
alignment of top and bottom.

top
boxing
welt cord
bottom

detail showing welt cord installation

Assembling a cushion cover

select for your sofa at home is also a candidate for interior cushions. That includes synthetic fabrics of acrylic, polyester, or nylon—such as acrylic canvas, polyester and cotton blends, and velvets. For pure comfort, cotton is hard to beat. Natural canvas gives an interior a traditional look. Heavy corduroy is another excellent choice. Spray-on stain guards and mildew treatments can help you to avoid the two biggest problems with natural fibers. Try an automotive fabric outlet for a selection of durable, stain resistant, and unique fabrics especially suited to the heavier demands of boat interiors.

If you select a fabric with a bold pattern, keep in mind that you will have to match the pattern from cushion to cushion. This often results in quite a bit of wasted material, and while matching the patterns is not particularly difficult, if you fail to do this, or do it badly, you will wish you had selected a different material.

It is just as important to use plastic zippers on interior cushions as it is for those in the cockpit. You can save a few dollars by using the smaller YKK #5 zippers if you like. Piping is the same inside and out, but you can achieve different looks with different size welts. If a bunk is made up of more than one cushion, you may elect to omit the piping.

Bunk cushions often lie against the hull, requiring a bevel on the back edge of the cushion. Use a bevel gauge to duplicate the angle when you are cutting your foam. In order to make the boxing come out right, the boxing on the beveled side—generally the zipper assembly—will have to be a separate piece and run the full length of the beveled side. Note that the boxing on this side will also be wider; determine the width by actually measuring the foam after you cut it. Join the two pieces with angled seams located at the intersection of the beveled side and the square ones. You will achieve the smoothest transition if you make these seams as you are sewing the boxing to the top and bottom pieces.

When the cushion is beveled, the top and bottom pieces will be two different sizes. You can mark them by tracing both sides of the foam. To cut the alignment notches, align the front and sides of the two pieces and notch the seam allowances. Then slide the smaller piece back, aligning the *rear* edges and the two sides. Cut matching notches in the rear edge.

Unless you have chosen canvas, the upholstery fabric you are using for interior cushions probably has a right side and a wrong side. Be sure that the pieces are right side to right side when you notch them. When you are seaming pieces together, they should always be right side to right side.

Instead of boxed cushions, you might prefer the softer look of bull-nosed cushions. The shape of the foam determines the shape of the cushion, and the front of the foam is given a round front edge. You can do this with shears or by shaving the foam with a very sharp knife.

As for the cover, there is nothing new here. Measure the front-to-back circumference of the cushion, plus a 1½-inch seam allowance, to arrive at the cut width of the fabric. The cut length is equal to the side-to-side dimension of the cushion plus a seam allowance. Instead of folding the fabric in half and stitching the ends together, as you might for a two-piece bag, sew the two ends to a zipper in the same manner that you sewed the boxing strips to the zipper, i.e., edge to edge, then folding the material to expose the teeth and topstitching the resulting hem.

Trace the outline of the end of the cushion onto the fabric, using a compass to make the rounded front uniform, and adding ½ inch for seam allowances. Cut out two pieces. Fit the end pieces into the open ends of the cover, centering the zipper line on the square ends of the end pieces. Stitch the parts together with a row of stitching ½ inch from the flush edges. Unzip the cover and turn it inside out and it is finished.

If you want to pipe the cushion around the ends and across the back, make the back edge a separate piece of fabric. Build a zipper assembly, just as with any boxed cushion, and cut the main piece only wide enough to reach from the rear edge at the top, around the front of the cushion and to the rear edge at the bottom, plus a 1-inch seam allowance. Cut

angled seam (both corners) Note: Top and bottom pieces have different width dimensions and rear strip of boxing is wider than front and sides.

Giving a cushion a beveled edge

A bull-nosed cushion

the side pieces an inch or two longer so they will overlap the zipper assembly. Stitch the pieces together with piping between the cover and the boxing. Alignment notches will help you keep the ends from twisting.

A center-welt cushion is yet another look. Remember the one-piece hatch cover? If you make two such covers the size of the cushion (but only half the width) and sew the raw edges together with a welt between the layers, and install a zipper where the two covers join in the back, you have a center-welt cushion. This design gives a comfortable, over-stuffed look, but a softer fabric is required. For a puffier look, instead of darting the corners and cutting off the excess material, fold the material into a number of evenly spaced pleats, trimming the fabric only to maintain a straight edge around the corner.

Backrests are not always loose cushions. They may have a plywood back. In such a case, cut a single piece of boxing long enough go around the cushion—a zipper is not required—and wide enough to allow at least an inch of material to turn over the back. Marking the boxing where it should fold over the wood will make it easier to get the tension even. Sew up the cover, then install it by folding the boxing over the plywood and holding it there with closely spaced staples. Use Monel staples or they will rust and damage some fabrics in the process.

Covers for plywood-backed backrests may not be boxed at all. A flat piece of material is simply folded around the foam and plywood and stapled

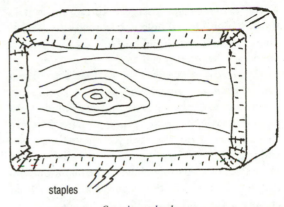

staples

Covering a backrest

down. Again, a traced line marking the desired location of the folds will help you to get the piece on straight. Corners have to be worked with patience to fold the excess material over smoothly and evenly.

Buttons are another common feature in boat upholstery. The buttons help to stabilize a cushion, especially to keep the fabric in a backrest from sagging. The biggest drawback is that they have to be removed any time you want to remove the cover. You can buy button "blanks" that you cover yourself, or you can have them done by an upholsterer who will have a machine that does them quickly and easily. If you do your own, try to find blanks with the ring or eye attached to the button rather than to the back.

In a loose cushion, buttons on either side of the cushion are tied together with waxed sail twine. Put the doubled twine through the ring of the button, then spread the bight of the twine and pass it over the top of the button to put a bale sling on the ring. Thread both ends of the twine into a needle and push it through the cushion. Remove the needle and pass both ends through the ring of the second button. Pull the thread to obtain the tuck you desire, then wrap the ends around the shaft or throat of the ring—where the ring attaches—twice in opposite directions and finish with a couple of square knots. Buttoning a plywood-backed backrest

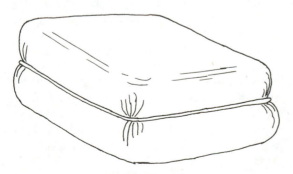

Center-welt cushion

is the same except that the thread must pass through a pre-drilled hole in the wood and the two ends are threaded through two holes of a *backing button* and knotted together.

If you are re-covering cushions that are a different design from any mentioned above, take the old cover apart to see how it is cut and assembled. If you are trying to duplicate something you have seen on a friend's boat, see if they will let you unzip a cover and take a peek inside. Special shapes often are no more than extra batting glued to the foam, but you may find special flaps or ties inside the cushion that achieve a certain look.

One final comment on interior canvas work. When you are finished, if there is a small pucker in the corner, or a few ripples in the boxing, you are the only one who will notice them. The most effective treatment for these little flaws (professionally made cushions have them too, I assure you) is a couple of stitches—between your upper and lower lips.

CUSTOM CANVAS

Some canvas items found on boats do not fall into any of the categories I have listed. Such items require custom canvas work, but even here assembly and finishing will not differ from techniques in the projects we have already considered. Custom work is generally facilitated by fabricating the item from stiff paper, then trimming and adjusting and taping the parts together until the fit desired is achieved. The parts are then disassembled and used as patterns for cutting the fabric. More complicated items may be first constructed from inexpensive pattern cloth, then duplicated in canvas, making any adjustments required.

SAIL COVER

A cover for the furled mainsail is an essential item for any sailboat that leaves its mainsail furled on the boom. Otherwise the sail will be destroyed by the ultraviolet rays of the sun. The sail cover also serves to "dress" the boat, and most sail covers are constructed from brightly colored acrylic canvas.

There is little about a sail cover that is complicated. It may be helpful to think of a sail cover as two wedge-shaped pieces of cloth—wide at the mast and narrow at the end of the boom—seamed together along the top and snapped or laced together at the bottom and along the forward edge. Except for the fact that the top edge is generally curved, this description pretty well defines a sail cover.

To determine the length of the cover, measure from the center of the forward side of the mast around the bulk of the furled sail and to the end of the boom. The maximum height of the cover can be determined from the bottom of the gooseneck to a point on the mast about 3 inches above the reposed headboard. A stitched-on collar at the top, which lashes tightly around the mast to deflect most of the rain, will make the finished cover higher. Add 4 inches to the length and height for hem allowances.

The exact shape of the curved "spine" of the cover is laid out by measuring from the bottom of the boom to the top of the furled sail every 3 to 6 inches near the boom, and every foot or two once the slope of the furled sail becomes regular. Add 2 1/2 inches to each of these measurements for a 1/2-inch flat-felled seam at the top and a 1 1/2 inch double-rubbed hem along the bottom. Plot these measurements on the fabric, measuring from one of the finished edges, and connect them with a smooth line.

Laying out the second piece in the opposite direction and from the opposite edge will usually result in the most efficient use of the material. It is sometimes possible to lay out the two pieces in such a way that they adjoin along the straight length of the spine. Cut out the two halves of the cover.

Except for the smallest sail covers, the curved line of the spine is almost certain to run off the opposite edge of the fabric as it approaches the mast end of the cover. To achieve the required width will necessitate adding a piece of fabric. Cut a piece long enough to reach from the point the curve runs off the fabric to the mast end of the main strip. Hem the two pieces together, selvage to selvage. Unfold the two parts and fold the hem against the main strip

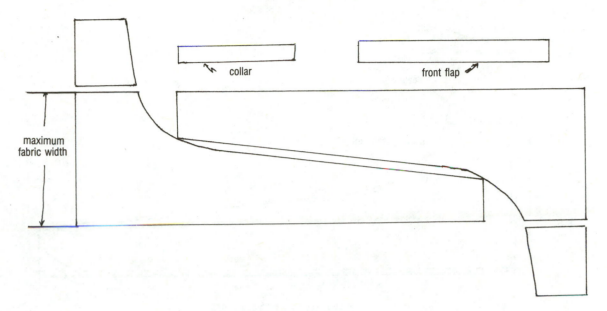

Cutting out a typical sail cover

of fabric. Make two parallel top stitches, catching both edges of the hem. The topstitching strengthens the hem, and it looks nice. Now finish plotting the curve of the spine and trim away the excess canvas.

Once the two sides are cut to size, the next step is to seam them together along the spine. A flat-felled seam is best, despite being a little troublesome to make in the curve of the spine. Place the two pieces together, sliding one down and forward slightly so that the spine edge of the bottom piece extends about 1/2 inch beyond the top piece. Pin the two pieces together to maintain this relationship. Fold the 1/2 inch onto the top stitch down the middle of the fold. In the curve, it may be necessary to cut slits in the fold to allow it to lie flat. Complete the seam by folding the top piece over the stitched fold and running two parallel lines of seams the length of the cover spine, just inside both edges of the seam.

Check the cover for fit by spreading it over the sail. If you are going to lace the front and the bottom, the edges should be a couple of inches short of meeting when hemmed. If you want to use twist fasteners, you need an inch of overlap. For a zip-

pered front edge, the hems should just touch. Make any necessary adjustments.

Hem all the raw edges except the top one with a 1 1/2-inch double-rubbed hem; put a 1/2-inch hem at the top. Leave the inside edge of the hem on one side of the front of the cover unstitched temporarily.

Cut a strip of canvas 6 inches wide and as long as the circumference of your mast plus 3 inches. Put a 1/2-inch double-rubbed hem in the sides and a 1 1/2-inch double hem in each end. After it is hemmed, the ends should be an inch short of meeting around the mast. This will be the collar and is sewn to the top edge of the cover. Crease it to mark the center, and align the crease with the spine seam. Overlap the collar about 1 inch so that the hem in the collar is just below the top hem in the cover, and sew the collar to the cover with two parallel rows of top stitching.

Cut a second strip of canvas 7 inches wide and 2 inches longer than the front edge of the cover—excluding the collar. This is the front flap. Put a 1/2-inch double hem on the ends and *one* side. Slide the other edge under the still-loose edge of the hem on one side of the front of the cover and sew down the hem. At the top you will encounter a problem with

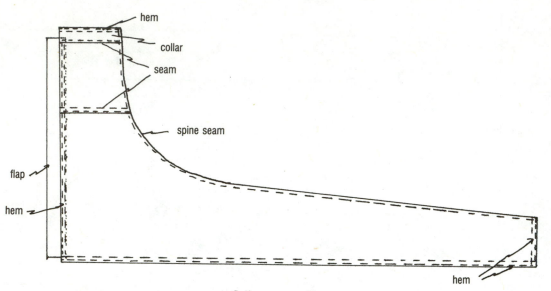

hem

collar

seam

spine seam

flap

hem

hem

Sail cover assembly

the stitching securing the collar; simply slit the raw edge of the flap to allow it be tucked under the hem on either side of the stitching.

If mast-mounted winches interfere with the fit of the cover, install sewn-in winch boots. Begin by constructing a cover for the winch, but without the elasticized inner skirt. Turn the boot right side out. Put the sail cover on the sail and carefully mark the location of the winch. Cut a circular hole in the sail cover *1 inch smaller* than the stitched diameter of the cover (or 2 inches smaller than the *cut* diameter of the end piece in the boot). Make a series of $3/8$-inch-deep slits about every inch around the entire circumference of the hole. Insert the winch cover into

the hole from the outside of the sail cover, folding the slitted perimeter in. Position the raw edge of the boot flush with the slitted edge of the hole and run a row of stitches $1/2$ inch from the edges. A second row of stitches to strengthen the attachment is recommended. Bind the raw edges with binding tape.

All that remains to be done is to install the closures. I prefer sail hooks opposite a pair of grommets in both the bottom and the front, allowing the cover to be laced tightly. The sail hooks can be sewn to the fabric or installed with rivets. Twist fasteners do not allow for any adjustment, but some sailors find they make the cover easier to put on. Twist fasteners are installed by melting slits for the prongs

Closing a cover with sail hooks and lacing

with the point of a hot knife, inserting the prongs through the canvas, and bending them over the backing plate or washer with pliers. Cut the canvas from the center of the *installed* eyelets with a hot knife.

Place fasteners every 6 inches on the front of the mast, every 18 inches along the boom. For a zippered front closure, you need a #10 jacket zipper (so it will separate completely). Sew the two halves of the zipper inside the front hems.

A pair of grommets in each end of the mast collar will allow you to use a cross-lacing of Dacron line to cinch the collar against the mast. Despite being open at the front, I find this collar is more effective than one that wraps and secures with an external tie.

If I left anything out, do what seems right. And if some step doesn't work for you, change it. It's your sail cover.

BIMINI

The Bimini top takes us back to where we started—with the flat sheet. A Bimini is nothing more than a flat sheet of canvas (or Weblon) hemmed on the sides and cut on either end to the contour of the supporting bows. A strip of fabric cut to the same contour is seamed—right side to right side—to each end, then folded over on the seam line and hemmed underneath to form a contoured sleeve at each end. This is the same as putting a curved hem on a flat sheet, described back in the section on weather cloths.

The top is installed by slipping the sleeves over the bows before they are assembled into the framework. If the top has more than two bows, hemmed strips are stitched onto the underside of the fabric in the appropriate locations to form additional sleeves. The top can be made removable by attaching one side of each of the pockets with a zipper instead of stitches.

It can be necessary for the straps that hold the frame in its unfolded position to attach to the top of the frame. This is accommodated by half-circle cutouts in the outer edges of the fabric strips that form

the front and rear sleeves. When the strips are sewn to the top, the cutouts end up on the underside of the bow, providing an exit for the tie-down straps.

A more professional look is achieved if "visors" are sewn into the front and rear of the top. Visors are simply folded strips of fabric that are stitched between the top and the bottom of the end sleeves in exactly the same manner as piping, and for the same reasons. Cut a strip of material 3 inches wide and 2 inches longer than the edge of the top. Fold the ends in 1 inch, then fold the strip in half lengthwise and run a line of stitching across each end. When you stitch the contoured sleeve to the edge of the top, put the visor between both pieces so that all raw edges are flush. When the sleeve is turned over and stitched on the other side, the visor forms an attractive skirt across the front (and rear) of the Bimini, hiding the bow sleeve and giving the top a finished look.

This is a treatise of canvas work, but the relationship between the Bimini (or dodger) and the support frame makes some comments in order. You can sail around in the bay with any kind of frame you like, but do not go offshore with a frame constructed of anything less rigid than $7/8$-inch stainless steel tubing. There is an unavoidable tendency to grab the frame for support, and aluminum tubing, if it doesn't pitch you over the side, will be rendered hopelessly out of shape. Aluminum end fittings should also be shunned; in a saltwater environment they corrode badly, becoming virtually impossible to remove from the tubing. Do I even need to comment on plastic fittings?

High quality stainless steel fittings are readily available, making custom frame configurations a snap. The only difficulty is in bending the tubing. For a dodger project, I priced a frame from a local top fabricator and was shocked when they quoted a price of $240. But my visit wasn't wasted when I saw the homemade plywood bender they used to bend the tubing. I found a supplier of stainless tubing, nailed together the bender in the sketch, and built the frame myself in a couple of hours for under $100.

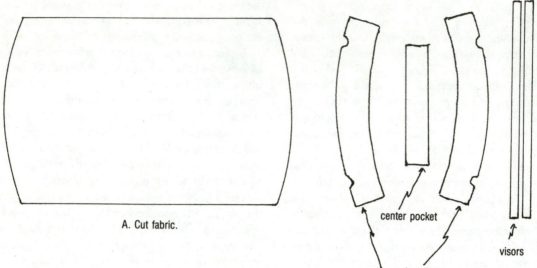

A. Cut fabric.

center pocket

end pockets

visors

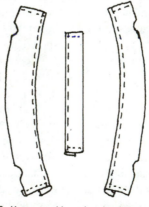

B. Hem one side and ends of pockets.

Making a Bimini top (continued on pages 425, 426)

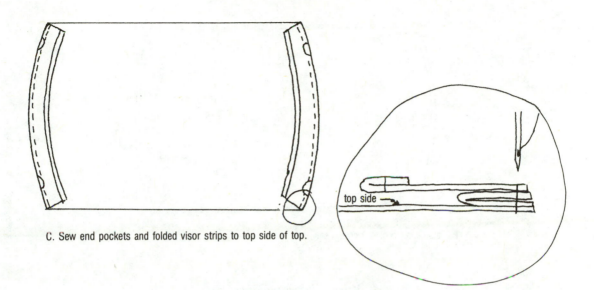

C. Sew end pockets and folded visor strips to top side of top.

top side

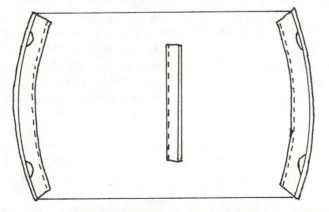

D. Turn top over and sew hemmed edges of end pockets to underside. Sew unhemmed edge of center pocket to underside of top.

Making a Bimini top (continued)

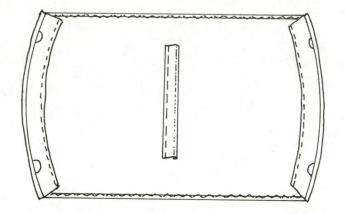

E. Fold center pocket over and sew down hemmed edge. Bind sides of top to finish.

Making a Bimini top (continued)

If you design and fabricate your own framework, be sure you have thought about where it goes when you want to fold it down. Will it interfere with the mainsheet? Can you still operate all the sheet winches? Can you get out of the cockpit to go forward without being a contortionist? If you have roller reefing, is the end of the boom going to sag onto the frame? Making up a trial frame from inexpensive PVC water pipe and fittings can show up problems that would otherwise appear only after the actual frame is completed. Then you can reuse the PVC for wind chute spreaders.

DODGER

I would like to say that a dodger is nothing more than a Bimini top with a windshield, and in some respects that is an accurate description. But because the dodger also has panels that enclose the side of the supporting framework, and because it must be attached to the deck, a dodger can be somewhat more complicated than a Bimini.

Replacing a dodger is easier than constructing one from scratch because the design work has been done for you. Simply take the old dodger apart, noting how the pieces are assembled, and use the old pieces as patterns for new canvas and vinyl.

If you are starting from scratch, the project is more involved, but not beyond the capabilities of anyone with modest skill on the sewing machine. If that describes you, Skip, even if "skill" may be just a bit of a stretch, read on. You need to start by answering most of the questions in the paragraph above concerning Bimini top frames, plus one or two related to access to the companionway; crawling in and out over the bridge deck wears more than your knees thin. Additionally, you have to engineer the attachment of the front of the dodger to the deck and across the main hatch.

Again a PVC mock-up of the frame is a good place to start. Angular connections can be made with duct tape. Fold the frame to see where it goes. Guy the bows to hold them in position and tape paper or fabric over them to get an idea how the dodger will look. Go below and come on deck to see if you lose any teeth or crush your skull. Reeve the headsail sheets and crank the winches; remember that the sides of the dodger will extend somewhat aft of the rear bow. Hoist the mainsail and slacken the topping lift to check the clearance. Stand at the

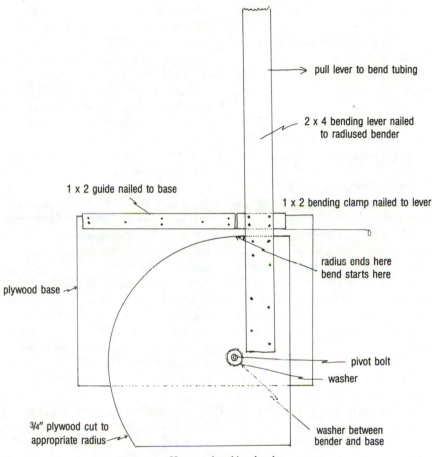

Homemade tubing bender

helm to be sure you can see *over* the dodger, which will be impossible to see through when it is coated with salt or spray. Now get off the boat and look at the dodger from every direction. How does it look? Would it look better shorter? Wider? Is the windshield too near vertical? Answer all these questions with paper and plastic pipe.

Build the frame and install it. If at all possible, put some curvature in the center of the bows to prevent the flat expanse of the top from "puddling" in the rain at anchor. A single curve from deck to deck makes a dodger that sheds water like an umbrella, and it looks attractive on some boats, but such a dodger tends to restrict the crew's ability to

wedge themselves in the forward corners of the cockpit. Be sure you can sit comfortably under the dodger.

Open the frame and guy each bow rigidly in position with webbing or light line. Make sure the two bows are the same height. Once again cover the frame with paper, this time taking greater care to get the paper over the frame smoothly. With tape and Kraft paper, make a paper dodger that looks exactly like you want the finished item to look. Tape the front piece to the deck and extend the side "wings" back along the coaming to the point where they will be anchored. Work out any fit problems, for example where the cockpit coaming attaches to the deck house, by cutting and fitting until you find a way that will work.

Outline on the front of the dodger what portion will be clear. Draw in the location of the zippers that will allow you to open the front panel. If the sides will have portholes, position them and sketch them in.

Decide how the front of the dodger will be attached to the deck. The most watertight attachment is a bolt rope inserted into an extrusion screwed to the deck. When this is not practical, twist-lock fasteners are generally used. Snaps cannot normally be used at the front of a dodger because the lifting stress would just unsnap them. Snaps are often used to secure the side flaps.

If your main hatch does not slide into a hood, attaching the front edge across the hatch may present a challenge. Sometimes a mainsheet traveller is providentially located in the right place. If not, blocks on either side of the hatch may be necessary to position the edge to allow the hatch to slide through a flapped slot.

Once you have the attachment problems worked out, draw the front and side edges of the dodger on your paper pattern. Now mark the seam lines along the front edge of the forward bow and the back edge of the aft bow. This should divide your pattern into the four basic pieces of a dodger—a football-shaped top, a similarly shaped front panel, and two triangular side "wings." Some additional pieces may be necessary to get the dodger to conform to the requirements of your particular installation; mark these seam lines also. Label each section and draw short lines across the seam lines to show how the pieces mate after they have been cut apart.

Take one more stroll on the docks to see if you are pleased with the effect. Now cut the pattern apart along the seam lines. Use the paper patterns to cut the canvas, making adequate seam allowances.

If the front panel is mostly clear vinyl, fabricate the assembly by framing the vinyl panels with hemmed strips of canvas. Fold the strips lengthwise, fold both edges inside, slip the vinyl between the folded edges, and stitch. This gives a finished edge both inside and outside the window. Hem the ends of the strips. Complete the front panel by installing zippers (they should open when you move the slide toward the top).

For the best visibility, buy 0.020 clear vinyl in sheet form. The optical qualities of polished sheet vinyl are far superior to the vinyl that is sold from a roll.

Using the top piece as a pattern, cut two 4-inch-wide canvas strips to form the sleeves for the frame bows. They should extend across the relatively straight length of the bows, stopping short of the side bends. Hem the ends of these two strips and if you want to be able to remove the dodger easily, sew one side of a #10 jacket zipper to the inside edge of each strip.

You should also cut a 3-inch-wide strip of leather or reinforced vinyl to the contour of the aft edge of the top. The aft bow of your new dodger will instantly become your most-used handhold, and it will soon be soiled, later worn out, if you do not protect it with a chafe strip. The strip should extend to just short of the attachment point of the side panels.

Round side windows are a popular feature, and not difficult to include in your dodger, provided you follow the correct sequence. Cut the circle of clear vinyl 2 inches larger in diameter than you want the window. Pin it to the inside of the canvas and run a row of stitching 1/4 inch from the edge of the vinyl. *Do not cut the hole in the canvas first.* After the window is sewn to the canvas, turn the assembly over and draw a circle 1 inch inside the circle of stitches. Cut this circle out, taking care not to cut or scratch the vinyl. Turn 1/2 inch of this raw edge under—slits in the edge may be necessary—and stitch the edge down with a row of stitches 1/4 inch from the fold.

All that remains is to sew the pieces together. Along the front edge, align the raw edge of the front assembly with the raw edge of the top, outside to outside. Place the sleeve strip on top of the two pieces, holding all of the raw edges flush, and sew these three parts together with a straight line of

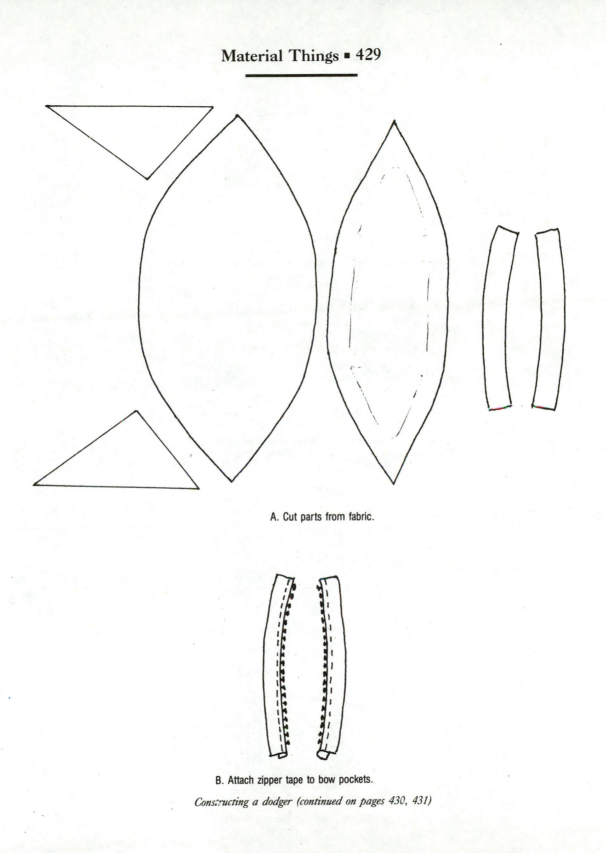

A. Cut parts from fabric.

B. Attach zipper tape to bow pockets.

Constructing a dodger (continued on pages 430, 431)

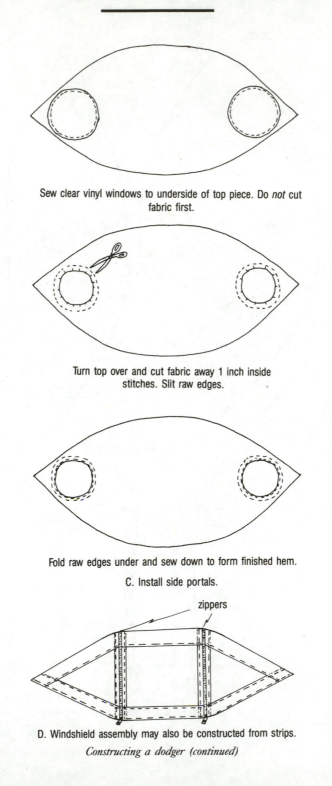

Sew clear vinyl windows to underside of top piece. Do *not* cut fabric first.

Turn top over and cut fabric away 1 inch inside stitches. Slit raw edges.

Fold raw edges under and sew down to form finished hem.

C. Install side portals.

D. Windshield assembly may also be constructed from strips.

Constructing a dodger (continued)

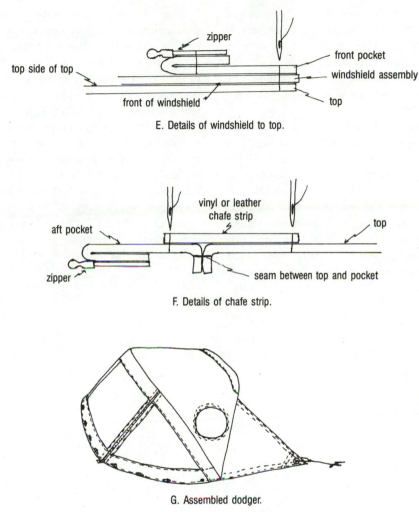

E. Details of windshield to top.

F. Details of chafe strip.

G. Assembled dodger.

Constructing a dodger (continued)

stitches ½ inch from the edges. Straps to secure the rolled front window should also be captured in this seam. Baste the parts to keep them from shifting during sewing. It's also best to stitch from the middle to each side to offset the tendency of the parts to shift or crawl. Turn the sleeve under and sew the edge or the other side of the zipper to the top.

Along the back edge, position the chafe strip on the top and sew around three sides, leaving the aft edge unstitched. Put the sleeve strip on top of the chafe strip, aligning the aft edges, and seam through the three layers. Turn the sleeve under and sew the edge or the zipper to the top.

Cut four triangular reinforcement patches and sew them to the inside of the aft corners of the side panels, then sew the side panels to the rest of the dodger. Bind any raw edges on the underside of the dodger.

Install the assembled dodger on the bows and mark the locations for the fasteners on the deck. Remove the dodger and install the fasteners on the boat at the marked locations. Reinstall the dodger and mark it for the mate to each of the fasteners. If you are using a bolt rope, this is also the time to position it. The bolt rope should not be sewn into the bottom hem of the dodger; rather it should be contained in a strip of fabric sewn inside the dodger at the bottom.

Install the various fasteners, including a grommet in the aft corner of each of the two wings. Put the dodger back on the frame and attach all the fasteners. Tie a lanyard to each of the grommets in the corners of the wings and reeve them through strap eyes screwed to the boat. The entire dodger is tensioned with these two lines, the reason for the reinforcing patches. If the wings do not extend far enough to tension the assembly, use tie-down straps to the aft bow, similar to the way a Bimini is rigged. Work the dodger with your hand as you tension it to get a smooth fit.

Not everyone should attempt to build a dodger, although the cost to have one built may lead you to rethink the matter. But few other canvas items aboard are so complicated or so exacting. Learning to hem a flat sheet and to fold it into an envelope opens a number of possibilities. Manipulating the fabric into a one-piece bag, or joining it with another piece to form a two-piece enclosure broadens the possibilities. Sewing a top on the two-piece bag gives you a fairly complete complement of canvas work skills, allowing you to duplicate virtually any item that you see that falls into one of these five categories—which includes 95 percent of the canvas items found aboard. Whether you go on to designing custom canvas items for your boat will have more to do with desire than skill.

SIXTEEN

A Lofty Project

Do or do not. There is no try.
–YODA–

Early in this century the hallmark of the small-boat sailor was self-sufficiency. He often built his own boat, rigged her himself, and even made his own sails. Sails of that era were made of cotton, and the shape of the sail was as much a product of how you broke it in and how you took care of it as it was of the way the sail was cut.

The hallmark of the cruising sailor of today is still self-sufficiency. Many still build their own boats. And as we have already seen, mechanical terminal fittings have made do-it-yourself rigging a snap for anyone so inclined. But it is extremely rare today for a sailor to attempt the construction of a sail. Sailors still haunt the woods looking for trees with just the right crook to use as ribs for a boat a-building, cast their own bronze fittings, and do intricate (and often beautiful) cabinet work. But sailmaking is left to the professionals.

For competitive sailing, you need the expertise of a professional. Finely tuned sails that deliver that extra tenth of a knot may well make the difference between winning or losing. But how important is this for a sail down the bay with good friends and a good wine? How essential is sail perfection to the cruising boat with a full keel, a three-blade prop, and towing a net bag of dirty diapers? And how perfect will that high-tech sail be three years from now? Six years from now?

Several years back, after thinking at length along these lines, I decided that I could see three good reasons to give sailmaking a try. The first was that sail years are like dog years and shocking though it was at the time, our 14-year-old genoa had rightfully expired. Reason number two was that despite two decades of sailing, I was not certain that I still understood exactly what made a sail tick and I figured that to make an efficient sail, I would have to learn what made a sail efficient. But the real reason was the third one; I hoped to save some money.

Once I had *almost* decided on this course of action, I made the rounds at the next boat show, going to seven different sailmaker's booths, asking for exactly the same sail. The results of this enterprise were very enlightening. Every sailmaker recommended a different approach. Some said to use 5-ounce cloth, some said 6.5-ounce. Some said to use soft cloth for the roller furling, some said hard for shape. Some said to cut it flat, others recommended fullness. There were sails with horizontal panels, sails with vertical panels, and even a radial cut genoa.

Like the sails, prices seemed to run the gamut. The cheapest price I encountered was around $800, the most expensive was just shy of $2,000. These were quotes for sails identical in dimension, similar in weight (depending upon the sailmaker's recommendation), all "computer designed," UV protected, hand finished, and triple stitched. The average price among all seven sailmakers was right in the middle of these two extremes, around $1,300.

I left the boat show determined to give sail construction a try. Instead of seven different designs, I figured there were eight. I was satisfied that mine would not be as good as some. Still, if it was not the worst, then it might actually be better than the choice I might have made since I had not a clue of how to select among the other seven. I selected my sailmaker—me.

Am I really suggesting that you make your own sails? Yes. And no. What I am suggesting is that you consider it. If the projects in the previous chapter seemed (or seamed) to go fairly well, you may be pleasantly surprised to discover that you are perfectly capable of building a very acceptable sail—and saving hundreds, even thousands of dollars in the process.

You will recall that the most basic canvas project from the last chapter was the flat sheet of canvas, hemmed along all edges, with grommets or bolt ropes in the hem. With a change in shape, a change in the location of the grommets, or a few reinforcement patches, the flat sheet was a weather cloth, a wind scoop, or an awning. Here comes the essential point of this chapter, so don't miss it. A sail is a flat sheet, hemmed along all edges, with grommets or bolt ropes in the hem. The fact that this particular sheet of cloth is triangular is, well, immaterial.

Wait a minute! you protest. Sails aren't flat. True. But the method of putting "shape" into a sail is so simple it is almost ludicrous. Knowing *how much* shape to put in is not so simple. But the truth is that shape is always a guess.

The ideal shape for 10 knots of wind is not so good in 20 knots. The ideal shape for sailing on the wind is less than ideal when the sheets are eased. Even with two identical boats, the way the boat is normally loaded, the skill (or attention) of the crew, the usual sail combinations, the number of different sails, the tension on the rigging, and the variety of wind and sea conditions can suggest sails with entirely different shapes. The sailmaker is going to guess at these factors, looking for a shape that gives you, *on average*, good performance. But the person who knows your boat, your skills, and your habits best is you. Borrow a few calculations from sailmakers gone before, and you are likely to be quite satisfied with the shape of your own sails.

PRELIMINARIES

This chapter differs somewhat from previous chapters in that it examines a single project—making a sail. No special skills are required beyond the basic ability to operate a sewing machine. Sails can be made with a straight-stitch machine, but the results tend to be significantly better with a zigzag machine. Unless the cloth is heavier than 8 ounces, the same V-69 bonded polyester thread that you used on the canvas projects from the previous chapter is the thread of choice. Transfer tape is not optional; for consistent results it is essential that you baste *every* seam with transfer tape before sewing.

Another essential is a "hot knife." Dacron sailcloth is burned along cut lines, which fuses the edges and prevents the material from raveling. You can buy a special hot knife, but if you have a soldering *gun*, it will have a blade-shaped plastic cutting tip, which does a fine job. A length of wood or high-pressure laminate is necessary to slide under the material when you are cutting to keep from burning the outline of the sail permanently into the floor.

In this project, as in the previous canvas projects, the emphasis will be on cutting the various pieces to the right size and stitching them together for a good fit. It is not my intent to instruct you in sail theory, although you will almost certainly understand sails much better after you go through the process of making one. Nor will we consider alternative sail designs and construction techniques. That would be to miss the point, which is that for most of the sailing most of us do, a basic design and standard construction techniques will produce a sail that will satisfy our needs.

If you understand and execute the steps that follow, the result will be a sail. And if you use a quality cloth and triple-stitch the panels together with commercial polyester thread, you can expect the same life from a sail you make as from one built professionally. How the performance of your sail might compare to that of the professionally built one will depend less on some special knowledge of the unfathomable mysteries of sail theory and more on how well you assess your particular requirements and how accurately you sew the panels together. I trust it won't come as a surprise to you that the sail loft employee who actually sews your sail together may not have a doctorate in fluid dynamics. It is also conceivable, however remote, that said person might actually be thinking about something else while stitching *your* sail. You won't be.

FABRIC

Except for spinnakers and very light drifters, the fabric you are going to choose is Dacron sailcloth. I am ignoring more sophisticated materials like Kevlar and Mylar. The basic sail does not benefit from these materials, certainly not enough to justify the considerable added expense. Stick with plain vanilla Dacron.

Choosing the weight of the cloth is the first of your educated guesses. As a starting point, divide the waterline length of your old boat by four. The result is a base cloth weight for the working sails of your old boat. For a 24-foot waterline, you need a main and working jib of 6-ounce cloth. If all your sailing is done in Long Island Sound in the summer, lighter cloth will make more sense. If you and your old boat are off for Patagonia on Tuesday, you won't regret selecting heavier material.

A medium-air genoa can be lighter cloth. A rule of thumb is to make the genoa 75 percent of the weight of the main. If you want to keep the genoa up until the turnbuckles start to elongate, make the darn thing the same weight as the main. If light air performance is the thing, so is light cloth. Are you getting the hang of this?

If your old boat sports a second stick, the mizzen *can* be lighter than the other working sails, but I always ask *why*? My tendency when the wind pipes up, like the tendency of a lot of other ketch sailors, is to give up the mizzen last. If it is the same weight as the main, its smaller size will allow it to handle heavier winds. No one thinks of a mizzen as a light-air sail, so what is the benefit of using light cloth? Make the mizzen from the same cloth as the main.

Sailcloth comes in different textures or "hands,"

from soft to very firm. Soft is easy to handle and less prone to wrinkle, but it does not hold its shape well, especially in light air. Firm sailcloth is like heavy paper—hard to handle and subject to wrinkles and permanent creases, but providing the smoothest surface when handled carefully and holding its shape well. Medium cloth is a good compromise, easy to handle while also holding its shape well. Unless you have a special need, select a stabilized Dacron cloth with a medium finish.

You will also encounter specialty cloths. For example, if you mention to your fabric supplier that you are making a mainsail, you may be offered mainsail cloth. Unless your main has an aspect ratio greater than three to one (the length of the luff compared to the length of the foot), decline the offer. Mainsail cloth has an "unbalanced" weave, meaning that the yarns that run across the cloth in one direction are larger than the ones that run in the other direction. That gives the cloth greater stretch resistance in one direction, but tends to reduce resistance to bias (diagonal to the thread line) stretch. Low-aspect mainsail cloth with less difference in the weft and warp yarns is also available, but your safest choice will usually be a cloth with a balanced weave.

Balanced-weave cloth is suitable for most sails, performing as well as the specialized weaves except under the most demanding conditions. It simplifies sail construction by eliminating concerns about which way the weft and warp run; you need only be concerned with grain, or the direction of the thread lines. Tightly woven fabrics of square (balanced) construction may be called genoa cloth. Do not be misled by this label. If the weight is correct, this cloth is suitable for all of your sails.

GETTING STARTED

The first step is to cover your dining room table with blank paper; blank newsprint is perfect and you can get end rolls from your local newspaper for free. On the paper, you are going to draw the sail to a scale of one inch to one foot, and make all the lofting calculations. This will allow you to go through the lofting process risk free, giving you the opportunity to make sure you fully understand what you are doing before you start cutting sailcloth. Going through this step first has the added advantage of yielding a scale drawing of the finished sail from which you will be able to take measurements quite easily.

The scale drawing will also allow you to calculate the amount of material you will need for the actual sail. An approximation of the number of square yards of cloth required is 0.15 times the area of the sail in square feet. The construction of a 100-square-foot sail, seam allowances, patches, and all, will require approximately 15 yards of 36-inch-width sailcloth. You calculate sail area by multiplying the luff length by the perpendicular length from the luff to the clew (LP) and dividing by two.

It would be redundant to describe the creation of the scale sail drawing, then to go through the identical process of laying out the sail to full size. Besides, the function of the scale drawing is to assist you in understanding the actual lofting process. So the description that follows is for lofting the sail full size, but do not omit this first step. It will keep you out of the quicksand.

The Loft

In my experience, the amateur sailmaker will encounter only two real problems during the construction of a sail, particularly a large sail. One of those problems is a loft.

To make a sail, you need a large, flat surface. On one occasion, I used a wooden deck attached to the rear of the house we owned at the time. In a later house, we removed or shoved aside the furniture in the living/dining room and I lofted the sail on the varnished oak floors. Very carefully, I might add. A garage, patio, or driveway will work perfectly if they are clean. Putting a fresh coat of sealer on the scrubbed concrete will reduce the likelihood of soiling the sailcloth, and you have probably been meaning to seal the surface anyway. Just another one of those intangible benefits of boat ownership.

If you cannot find a large enough space around the house, perhaps the school your children attend would let you use the gym one weekend. Or maybe your church has a recreation room you could borrow. Perhaps a real-estate agent friend could arrange access to a vacant warehouse or commercial space. Put your mind to it, and you can come up with the needed flat surface.

While I don't particularly recommend it because it adds considerable complexity and introduces additional error potential, it is possible to loft a sail in more than one part. When the wooden deck I planned to use to loft our genoa turned out to be smaller than the sail, I decided to try lofting it in two parts. It was more difficult, but the sail turned out perfectly. The secret to success is overlapping a full panel to assure a smooth transition between the upper part of the sail and the lower part. Consider this possibility only as a last resort; you will have a much easier time if you locate a sail-size space.

The Basic Triangle

Lofting is nothing more than drawing the sail to full scale on the floor. You need a tapemeasure, a ball of packaging twine, a roll of ¾-inch masking tape, and a pencil. You also need the dimensions for the luff, leech, and foot of your sail. If you are replacing a sail, simply take these three dimensions from the old sail. If you are adding a new sail to your inventory, you will have to obtain these dimensions from the sail plan for your boat, by making a scale drawing, or by establishing the position of the clew and measuring to the head and the tack locations.

Begin the lofting process by stretching a length of string longer than the luff of the sail across the floor, taping both ends down to provide a straight line. With two small lengths of tape, mark the length of the luff along this line. A helper will make the measuring process easier.

If the sail will have a headboard, position it next to the string and outline it with tape. While your helper holds the end of the tapemeasure at the other end of the luff, measure away from it by the foot dimension of the sail and swing a short arc, marking it with chalk or tape on the floor. Move the end of

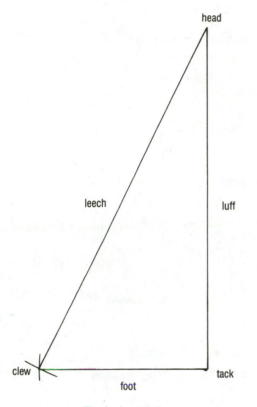

The basic triangle

the measuring tape to the other end of the luff, positioning it at the mark or, if you have outlined a headboard, at the leech corner of the headboard. Measure toward the arc by the leech dimension of the sail and strike a second arc. The two arcs intersect at the location of the clew. Connect this point to the marked ends of the luff line with two additional lengths of string, taping the ends to the floor. You now have a triangle the approximate size of your planned sail, with three perfectly straight sides. To avoid any confusion, label the luff and the leech.

Hollow Leech

Headsails rarely have battens anymore, thank God, but as a result the leech wants to flutter. One method of dealing with this is with a leech line, a light piece of line inside the leech hem, anchored at the head of the sail, cleated near the clew. Tightening the line puts a hook in the sail, quietening the leech.

The leech line is generally not required if you cut the leech of the sail slightly hollow. How hollow? In normal sailing conditions, you should get satisfactory results from a maximum hollow of two percent of the leech length, or slightly less. If the headsail will be used only in light air, a light genoa, for example, reduce the hollow to about one percent.

The curve of the hollow is not particularly critical, but it is still advisable to make it regular. Divide the leech line into quarters and put a strip of tape on the floor inside of the string at each of these stations. The maximum hollow will be in the center, or at the 1/2 station. On a 20-foot leech, for example, a 1.9 percent hollow will be about 4 1/2 inches. Calculate the maximum hollow for your sail and place a mark on the floor that distance inside the leech line at the 1/2 station. To achieve a "normal" curve, the offsets at the two 1/4 stations will be 70 percent of the maximum hollow—about 3 1/8 inches in the above example. At the 1/4 station and the 3/4 station, mark the appropriate distance inside the leech line.

Use the 3/4-inch tape to make a smooth curve on the floor from the intersection of the leech and luff through the three leech-hollow points and to the clew. Place the inside edge of the tape on the five points so the outside will mark the cut edge, automatically providing the hem allowance.

Roach

Unlike headsails, the leech of a mainsail (or a mizzen) is usually supported by battens. They allow the leech to be rounded rather than hollowed. The excess material is called roach and provides racing sailors with "free" sail area, but this extra area is only beneficial when sailing free. On the wind, roach has little effect on performance unless the weight of the battens tends to fold the sail, breaking the air flow and *reducing* the efficiency of the sail.

Except for racing—where you are forced to play by the rules—I think battens are a bad idea. Most

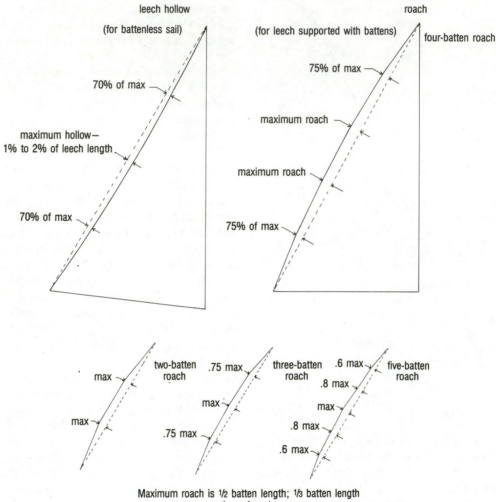

Lofting the leech

mainsail repair has to do with batten pocket damage, and battened mains have an annoying habit of getting entangled in the rigging, jamming the sail half up or half down, sometimes tearing it. A battenless mainsail is easier to handle, easier to furl, and will require far fewer repairs. If the lost sail area is a concern, increase the size of the headsail to compensate. The leech of a battenless main is cut hollow just like that of a headsail.

This viewpoint is neither new nor radical, nor, it would seem, catching on. On the assumption that despite their questionable benefit and obvious problems, you still want battens in your main, I am including the necessary instructions.

Batten lengths are generally dictated by rating rules, not by sail theory. You are, no doubt, replacing an existing main, so just use the old battens. Their original length may have been determined by a racing rule that limits intermediate battens to 12 percent of the length of the foot of the sail along the boom plus 12 inches and upper and lower battens to 10 percent plus 12 inches. In the absence of rule requirements, battens can be any length. In fact, full-length battens are currently enjoying a renaissance, but we will confine our discussion to traditional battens.

The maximum practical roach is about 1/3 the batten length. For example, if you have 24-inch battens, limit the roach to 8 inches. To loft the roach, divide the leech line equally by the number of battens and put strips of tape on the floor at each of these stations. This is similar to dividing the line into quarter stations, but this time the tape strips go *outside* the line. You are rounding the leech, not hollowing it.

If you have two battens, measure out from the leech line the full roach dimension—1/3 the length of your battens—and mark the points. With three battens, measure out the full distance at the center station, 75 percent of that distance at the other two stations. A four-batten roach will be at the maximum distance at the middle two stations, 75 percent at the other two. With five battens, mark the center station with the full roach dimension, 80 percent at stations two and four, and 60 percent at stations three and five.

Starting at the head and ending at the clew, connect all these points with masking tape. Unlike what you did for the leech hollow, *do not* make the roach a smooth curve. Join each pair of points with a straight line; in fact, the leech of your sail will be less likely to flutter if you will *slightly* hollow each of the lines between the points. Put the inside edge of the tape on the points so the outside will give you the cut dimension.

Luff Stuff

One of the ways you introduce fullness or shape to the sail is by rounding the luff. This was the main way when cotton was king. When the sail is hoisted, straightening the rounded luff, the excess fabric moves back into the sail, causing a certain amount of camber. The amount of camber depends upon the amount of luff round.

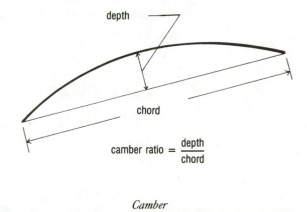

$$\text{camber ratio} = \frac{\text{depth}}{\text{chord}}$$

Camber

Camber is expressed as the ratio between the chord and the sail depth. Chord is the horizontal distance between luff and leech when the sail is set, and depth is the amount of bow in the sail. The appropriate camber for your sails depends upon your boat. Fat boat, fat sails. Flat boat, flat sails. The starting point is 10 percent—1 foot of depth for 10 feet of cord. For an easily driven boat with a fine entry, a chamber ratio closer to five percent (1/20) might give better performance. A heavy, bluff-bowed cruiser may benefit from the extra power of a 15 percent camber.

To introduce a camber of 10 percent to your sail, you are going to add cloth outside the luff line the equivalent of 2.7 percent of the chord of the sail at that point. If you want your sail flatter, reduce this percentage; 0.7 percent luff round will result in a five percent camber—a very flat sail. If you need more powerful sails, increase the percentage, but not beyond about six percent, which yields a very full sail with a camber near 15 percent. If you are unsure about this aspect, build your sails with a 10 percent camber, or vary the camber only slightly one way or the other depending upon whether you categorize your boat as easily driven, average, or heavy. A camber near 10 percent will provide good performance over a wide range of conditions.

Divide the luff line into quarters, marking the quarter stations. Measure horizontally (what will be horizontal when the sail is set) across the sail to the

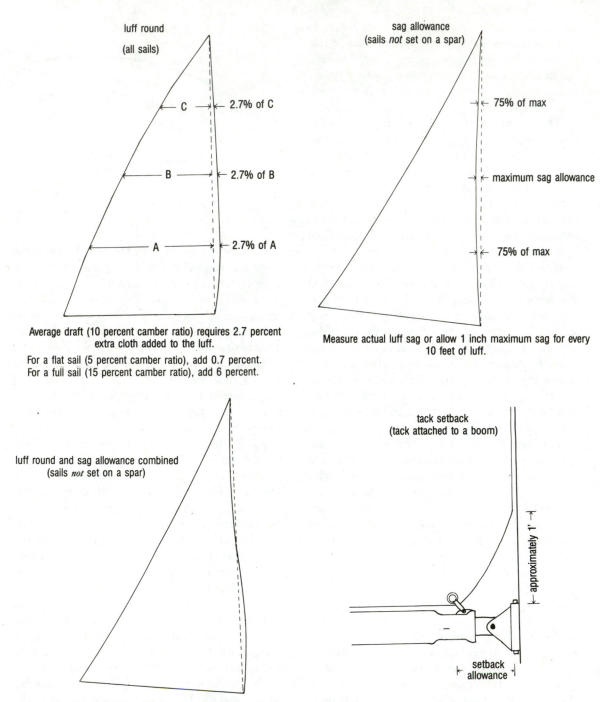

luff round

(all sails)

← C → 2.7% of C

← B → 2.7% of B

← A → 2.7% of A

Average draft (10 percent camber ratio) requires 2.7 percent extra cloth added to the luff.

For a flat sail (5 percent camber ratio), add 0.7 percent.
For a full sail (15 percent camber ratio), add 6 percent.

sag allowance
(sails *not* set on a spar)

← 75% of max

← maximum sag allowance

← 75% of max

Measure actual luff sag or allow 1 inch maximum sag for every 10 feet of luff.

luff round and sag allowance combined
(sails *not* set on a spar)

Note that when round and sag are combined, offsets may be inside the basic triangle at the top of the sail and outside in the lower part.

tack setback
(tack attached to a boom)

approximately 1'

setback
allowance

Luff offsets

leech. Multiply each of these measurements by 2.7 percent—or an alternate percentage you select—to arrive at the amount of luff round at each of the three stations. Mark these distances on the outside of the luff line, and perpendicular to it, at each of the stations.

If the sail you are making sets on a mast (a mainsail or a mizzen), you are through with the luff. Using the inside edge of the masking tape, make a new luff line from the head of the sail through the three points and smoothly back into the tack point.

If the sail sets on a wire or an extrusion, you need to compensate for sag before taping the line. A common rule of thumb for a hanked-on sail is to allow 1 inch of sag for every 10 feet of luff, but a roller-furling sail on a wire will sag more, one in an extrusion less. And obviously a great deal depends on how tight you have the rigging. I suppose you can tighten or loosen stays to make the rig fit the sail, but the closer the sail shape to your normal sag, the better.

To determine the sag, go sailing. Tape a ruler half way up the luff and hoist the old sail. Lead the spinnaker halyard to the bow (you can use the main halyard if it is the only other line from the masthead) to provide a reference. Put the boat close-hauled and note the amount of sag as indicated by the distance the ruler moves across the halyard. Use binoculars to read the ruler if necessary. Be sure to use only the *change* in the distance between the luff and the halyard, not the absolute distance. To measure the sag of a sail that hoists in an extrusion, it may be necessary to make an L-shaped cardboard scale to tape *near* the luff of the sail.

The sag allowance is applied in the opposite direction as the luff round. (Compensation for a flexible mast is handled in a similar manner, but *added* to the luff round.) At the 1/2 station, measure *back toward the sail* the full amount of the calculated or measured sag. At the other two stations (1/4 and 3/4), measure back 75 percent of the sag amount. The new 3/4 station point is almost certain to be inside the string line, and the mid-station point may be as well. Not to worry; this is normal. Tape a smooth curve from the head through these three points and to the tack. Typically this curve will have

an S shape—hollow in the upper part of the sail, rounded in the lower part.

I lied earlier. A mainsail (or mizzen) requires one more small adjustment to the luff shape. Look at the position of the tack attachment on your boom. Typically it will be a few inches from the mast. Measure the normal distance between the mast and the luff and the distance between the mast and the edge of the sail at the tack and subtract one from the other. This is the amount of setback your sail should have. Mark this setback distance on the foot of your triangle, measuring from the tack point. Peel up the tape marking the luff round for about 12 inches above the tack and reposition it to form a smooth curve to the new tack point. *Now* the luff is finished. Honest.

The foot of the sail is also rounded, but for different reasons, depending on the sail. Headsails are rounded at the foot to get more sail area and to get the bottom of the sail right down on the deck, reducing the amount of bypass flow at the foot. Usually you will want to put the maximum roach possible in the foot of a headsail. For offshore use, excessive roach may put the sail at risk of catching a wave, and a roller-furling sail may furl more smoothly if the roach is kept to a minimum or omitted altogether. Rounding the foot of the mainsail, on the other hand, is essential—not to add sail area, but to introduce draft into the sail at the foot.

Despite the different purposes, the shape of the foot of both types of sails will be similar. For a headsail, you can determine the maximum practical amount of roach by dividing the length of the foot (in inches) by 12. You may not want to put in the maximum roach if the sail will be used in moderate to strong winds; a roach of about 1/2 the maximum will likely be more satisfactory.

Calculate the appropriate roach. Following the above recommendation, a 10-foot foot would have a 5-inch roach. The curve of the roach is not critical, but the maximum depth should be slightly forward of the center of the sail, say 45 percent back from the luff. Use the inside edge of the tape to make a smooth curve from the tack through the point marking the maximum roach, and back to the clew.

Because the foot-round in a mainsail is for draft,

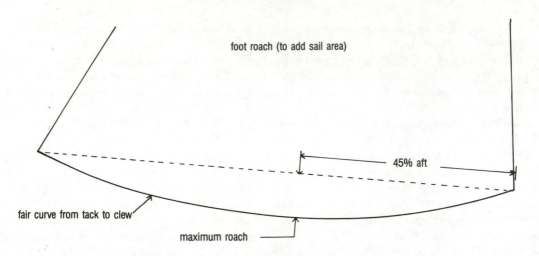

foot roach (to add sail area)

45% aft

fair curve from tack to clew

maximum roach

Maximum roach for a light air headsail is 1 inch per foot of foot length.

Maximum roach for a moderate or heavy-air headsail is ½ inch per foot of foot length.

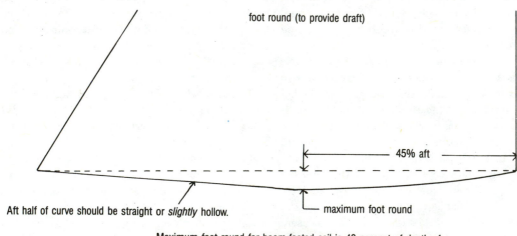

foot round (to provide draft)

45% aft

Aft half of curve should be straight or *slightly* hollow.

maximum foot round

Maximum foot round for boom-footed sail is 40 percent of depth of draft at the foot.

Maximum foot round for loose-footed sail is 80 percent of depth of draft at the foot.

Lofting the foot

the appropriate amount is determined by the camber of your sail. The exact amount of round will be 40 percent of the depth in the foot (about twice that percentage for loose-footed or shelf-footed sails). For example, if your sail has a camber of 10 percent ($1/10$) and is 12 feet wide at the foot, the depth will be 14.4 inches; the amount of foot round should be $5^3/4$ inches.

Like headsail roach, the maximum amount of foot round should be about 45 percent behind the luff. Connect the tack, the point marking the maximum round, and the clew in a smooth curve with the masking tape. The sail will be less likely to develop radiating creases at the clew if the aft half of this curve is absolutely straight, or even *slightly* hollow.

ON A ROLL

Your lofting is finished. The next step is to cover this full-size drawing of your sail with cloth. All of the panels will be *perpendicular* to the straight leech line (the string). It is imperative to make sure the panels are perpendicular to this line or the load on the leech will not be with the thread line, but on the bias (diagonally across the thread line), and the shape of the sail will be destroyed. It may be helpful to stretch a piece of string from the tack exactly perpendicular to the leech string as a reference.

Start covering the outline at the bottom of the sail. Place the bolt of cloth outside the leech and unroll it across the outline so that it is perpendicular to the leech and the bottom edge of this first panel intersects the tack. The resin-impregnated cloth is slippery and can be slid around easily to position it. Don't cut the panel from the bolt of cloth yet.

If you are making a headsail, measure perpendicular from the bottom edge of the panel to the tape marking the foot. If the maximum distance is no more than 15 inches at any point, you can save some fabric by splitting the bottom panel. Reposition this bottom panel, still (always) perpendicular to the leech, by sliding it down until it covers the foot tape by about $3^1/2$ inches. Using scissors—you can make all the rough cuts with scissors—cut the

panel from the roll, making certain there is at least 1 inch of cloth beyond the leech and cutting the material 3 inches beyond the luff. Now with your hot knife, split this panel down the center. Leave the top half on the outline and set the bottom piece aside.

If this is not the circumstance, i.e., the distance to the foot is more than 15 inches, or you are making a mainsail, leave the bottom edge of the initial panel on the perpendicular line from the leech to the tack. Cut the panel from the roll (with scissors) leaving an inch beyond the leech, 3 inches beyond the luff.

Whether your first panel is full or split, turn the bolt of fabric around and, starting from the luff, roll out a second panel above the first. The two panels should overlap by about $3/4$ inch. You will notice a faint blue line along both edges of the cloth; this line will help you to maintain a consistent overlap. Cut the second panel from the roll, maintaining the same amount of extra cloth at the ends—1 inch at the leech, 3 inches at the luff.

Reversing the bolt each time, continue to roll out and cut overlapping panels until the entire outline, except the foot area, is covered. By reversing the bolt for each panel, you will notice that you waste very little sailcloth.

If you are going to want numbers or an insignia on the sail, position them on the loose panels at this point, gluing them to the sailcloth. Now take the panel to the machine and zigzag the edges of the perimeter; this will be much easier to do on a single panel than on the assembled sail. Put the panel back over the outline.

Broadseaming

While luff round was sufficient to give canvas sails shape, the paperlike stiffness of resin-impregnated Dacron cloth tends to prevent the draft from moving back into the middle of the sail. This problem is overcome by broadseaming.

Broadseaming would better be named broadeningseam. As you seam toward the luff of the sail, you are going to increase the overlap of the panels,

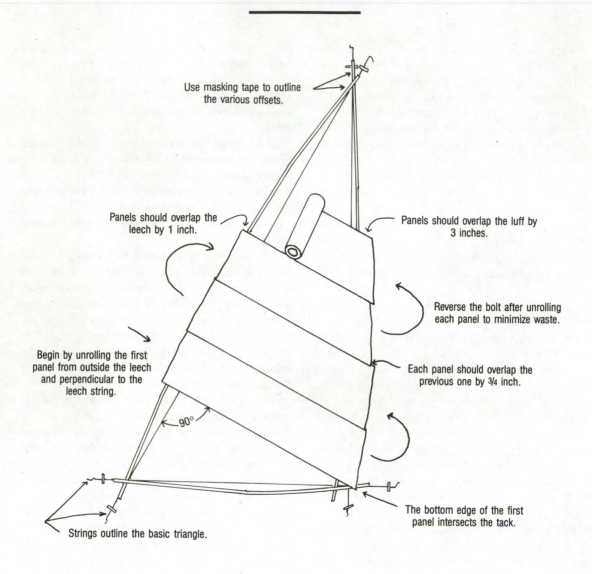

Use masking tape to outline the various offsets.

Panels should overlap the leech by 1 inch.

Panels should overlap the luff by 3 inches.

Reverse the bolt after unrolling each panel to minimize waste.

Begin by unrolling the first panel from outside the leech and perpendicular to the leech string.

Each panel should overlap the previous one by ¾ inch.

90°

The bottom edge of the first panel intersects the tack.

Strings outline the basic triangle.

Covering the plan with cloth

broadening the seam. This has the effect of removing cloth from the edge of the sail, meaning the center of the sail has more cloth than the edge. The exact position of this bagginess–draft in the finished sail–depends upon the location and shape of the broadseams.

The position and widths of the broadseams are two more of those educated guesses. Measure ⅔ of the way up the luff and mark the point. Measure out from the tack 45 percent of the sail width along the bottom edge of the bottom panel (along the top edge if you split this panel) and mark a second point. Mark a third point on the floor halfway between the tack and a point on the leech about 10

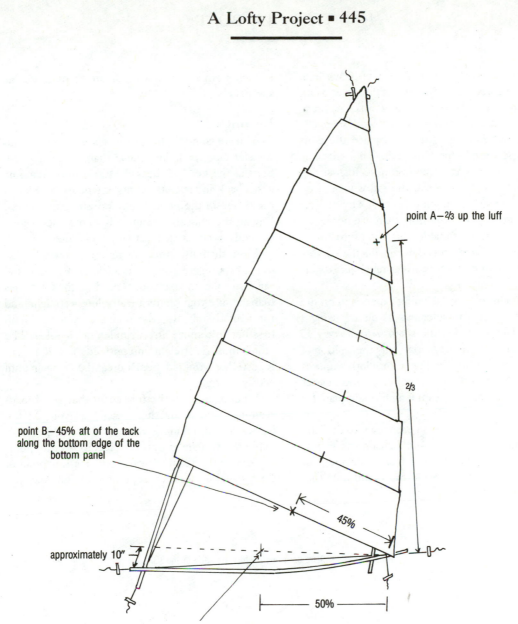

point A—2/3 up the luff

2/3

point B—45% aft of the tack
along the bottom edge of the
bottom panel

45%

approximately 10"

50%

Point C—halfway between tack and a point 10" up the leech

To position the broadseams, make a smooth curve through points A, B, and C. Mark each seam where the curve crosses it.

For a light-air sail, move the curve aft about 5 percent. For a
heavy-air sail, move the curve forward about 10 percent.

Determining broadseam locations

inches above the clew. With a piece of heavy line, connect the three points in a smooth curve. Mark every seam where the curved line crosses it; these will be the initiation points for the broadseams.

This broadseaming pattern will place the draft about 35 percent behind the luff. This shape is recommended as a good compromise for varying wind conditions. However, if the sail will be used mostly in light air, moving the draft back by moving this curve aft slightly—not more than five percent—may give you a more suitable sail. Windward ability in strong air will be improved by moving the curve—and the resulting draft—forward as much as 10 percent.

The amount of broadseaming depends upon the hand of the cloth you selected. If you are using a medium Dacron, widen the seam *1/4 inch every 15 inches* of seam length, measuring only the section of the seam you are broadening. Firm cloth requires more broadening—1/4 inch per foot. One-quarter inch every 18 inches of seam length is adequate for soft cloth.

Measure from the mark on each seam to the tape luff line and write the measurement on the excess cloth. Calculate the amount of broadseaming for each seam, using the above formula, and note that

at each seam as well. Now you are ready to join all the panels.

Basting

You are going to glue all the seams together with transfer tape, including those that get broadened. Start at the head of the sail. Turn the overlapping panel back and stick the transfer tape to the edge of the panel on the floor. Peel away the paper cover, leaving the adhesive behind. Keeping the overlap perfectly even, stick the two panels together.

More than any other single item, how you glue the panels together is going to determine how the sail turns out, so take your time. Use the blue lines to make sure your seams are absolutely straight, and run your thumb over the seams as you put them together to remove any wrinkles or bubbles. The seams must be straight and perfectly flat. If a seam is curved or wrinkled, peel it up and do it again until you get it right.

When you reach the first seam that gets broadseaming, tape it together exactly as you did the higher seams, taking great care to keep the seam perfectly straight from the leech to the point marked on the seam indicating the starting point of the broadseam. From this point to the luff line, you

Note that seam flairs as it approaches the edge of the sail.

	1/4	1/2	3/4	luff
start of broadseaming				

Approximate percentage of broadseaming at quarter stations:

	1/4	1/2	3/4	luff
Normal entry-	5%	25%	55%	100%
Flat entry-	8%	30%	65%	100%
Full entry-	4%	20%	45%	100%

Maximum broadening should be about 1/4 inch for every 15 inches of broadseam length (for medium Dacron cloth).

Broadseam detail

are going to increase the overlap so that the maximum increase—as you calculated and noted on the excess cloth by the seam—occurs exactly at the luff. Not before. Not after.

The shape of the broadseams is also important. You do not want the seam to have a wedge shape. It should flare near the luff, more like a golf tee. For a normal entry, the seam should only broaden about 5 percent of the total in the first $1/4$ of its length, and only about 25 percent at the halfway point. At $3/4$ of the length of the broadseam, it should be broadened slightly more than 50 percent, with almost $1/2$ of the broadening occurring in the last $1/4$ of the seam. A fuller entry is achieved with slightly lower percentages at the first three stations and more than half of the total in the last $1/4$. A flat entry results from higher percentages early and less than 40 percent of the total in the last $1/4$ of the seam.

Work each of the remaining seams carefully, taking pains to get the straight part of the seams straight and to get the broadseams to have smooth, gradual curves with the appropriate amount of flare. Broadseaming is going to cause the material in the middle of the sail to wrinkle. No problem. That is just the draft you are going through all of this to achieve.

While you are broadseaming, you can prevent a nervous leech if you tighten it slightly with a couple of broadseams. Pick a couple of seams, one about $1/3$ of the way up the leech and a second near the $2/3$ point and peel them apart back about 2 feet. Now reglue the panels, broadening the seams by about $1/8$ inch at the leech, no more. This will cause the leech to be under slightly more pressure than the cloth in front of it and should reduce its tendency to flutter.

The transfer tape holds pretty well, but as you have no doubt discovered, it can be peeled apart. To keep the seams from coming apart when you are handling the sail for sewing, which you are almost ready to do, staple each seam a couple of times on either end in the excess material. Put the staples close to the edge and you won't have to remove them; they will get trimmed away.

Sewing the Panels

With the panels glued together, it is time to sew. This is the other serious problem that making a sail presents to the amateur. The problem is not the sewing machine. It is the bulk of the sail. How do you sew down the center of a room-size sheet of stiff Dacron?

The answer is to roll the sail up tightly parallel to the seams, leaving only the topmost seam exposed. After you sew this seam, roll the sail from the top and unroll from the bottom until the next seam is between the two rolls. After each seam, roll the top, unroll the bottom. It will be like sewing down the dead center of a humongous scroll.

Because the cloth is stiff and slick, the rolls will make every effort to expand to the size of a small culvert as soon as you release your grip on either end. The solution is four strong spring clamps to clamp the ends of the rolls.

Sail lofts usually have the sewing machines level with the floor, the operator sitting in a well. It is a dynamite arrangement because the sail does not have to be lifted at all to go through the machine. If your machine is a portable, putting it on the floor will accomplish almost the same thing. Operate the foot control with your knee.

A table-mounted machine makes sewing the sail more difficult. Somehow you need to get the sail up level with the machine, both in front of the needle and behind it. A couple of long tables will work, or you can construct a pair of 8-foot chutes from a sheet of hardboard with 1×4 side rails. Support the chutes with chairs or what-have-you.

Do not try to sew the sail without a helper. Getting the sail to feed smoothly through the machine is a two-person job. Your helper should keep the unsewn end of the sail free until you near the midpoint of the seam, then move around to the other side of the machine to help the sewn end.

Use a "square" zigzag stitch—$3/16$ inch long and $3/16$ inch wide (or the widest your machine will make if it is less.) Make a few rows of practice stitches on scrap material to get the stitch size and the tension adjusted. Unlike canvas, Dacron sailcloth is too hard for the interlock between the top and bottom thread to pull into the cloth. Instead, when the upper tension is adjusted properly, the threads will form a tight knot at each stitch on the bottom of the fabric. This is perfectly normal. You will find the sewing goes better if you use a #18 or larger needle. For Dacron, the needles *must* be ball point.

Run the first row of stitches down one edge of the seam, with one side of the stitch right on the edge. The machine will feed better if the edge you are stitching is underneath so the feed dog engages both panels. When one edge is sewn down, flip the "scroll" over so that the two rolls are on the opposite sides of the needle from before. This puts the bottom side of the seam up. Run a second row of stitches along the unsewn edge of the seam. For maximum durability, run a third row of stitching between the other two down the center of the seam.

The Foot

With the panels sewn together, it is time to add the foot. Spread the sail back over the taped outline on the floor, properly aligned.

If you split the first panel back at the start, cover the foot portion of the sail with the 1/2 panel you put aside. Otherwise, roll out a new panel to cover the foot. Cut the panel long enough to overlap the leech by 1 inch and the luff by 3 inches. Trim the bottom to the shape of the foot, allowing 3 inches of extra material.

If one panel is not sufficient, reverse the bolt and continue rolling out panels until the foot is covered. Glue these panels together with constant overlaps, then trim them as above. Take this section to your machine and sew the seams.

If you are building a headsail, split the foot panel vertically into three nearly equal pieces, making the cuts perpendicular to the rounded bottom of the panel. You are going to sew the three pieces back together with broadseams. With the panels positioned on the floor, initiate the broadseams 3 inches inside the string marking the foot of the original triangle; the seams should achieve their maximum overlap at the tape line for the foot. Widen the seams 1/4 inch for every 3 inches of maximum foot roach. Glue the foot panel to the rest of the sail, broadseaming this seam according to the mark and calculations you made earlier.

The foot for a mainsail gets a different treatment. With a hot knife, cut the foot panel on a straight line from the tack to a point on the leech 10 inches above the clew. Sew the two pieces back together with a broadseam that begins halfway between the tack and the leech (unless you shifted the draft forward or aft) and widens 1 1/2 times the amount you used for all the other broadseams, i.e., 3/8 inch for every 15 inches of seam length if you are using medium cloth. Glue the foot panel to the rest of the sail, broadseaming from the 45 percent location you marked earlier. Broaden this seam *twice* the normal amount.

Once the foot panel is assembled and glued to the rest of the sail, triple stitch all the glued seams.

Trimming to Size

Position the sail one final time over your outline. Let the center wrinkle, but try to get the edges to lie flat. With a pencil, outline the finished size of the sail by tracing the inside edge of the masking tape. Along the leech also trace the outside edge of the tape to provide a hem allowance (the luff does not require one). Trace the outside edge of the foot tape as well if the foot will be hemmed, but not if it will have a bolt rope. (Almost all headsails will be hemmed along the foot; mainsails are likely to be roped.) With a hot knife—keeping a piece of wood or laminate under the sail to protect the floor—cut the sail along the outermost of your pencil lines.

Corner Patches

The corners of the sail require reinforcement patches. Cut them from the same material as the sail, taking care to align the weave of the patch to the sail weave. Three patches in each corner will be adequate. Sew them all on one side of the sail, with the largest patch outermost and each of the inner patches an inch or two shorter than the one above.

There is no hard, fast rule for sizing patches. A good starting point is to make the largest patch

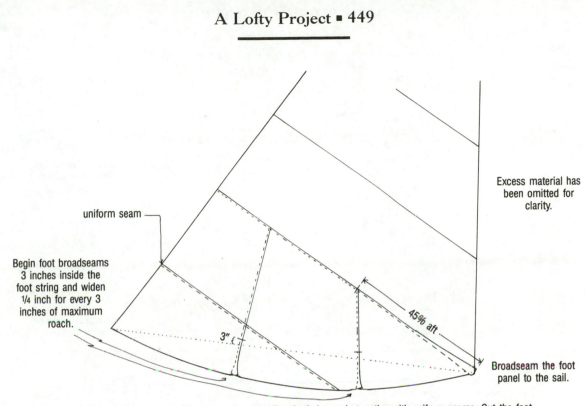

uniform seam

Begin foot broadseams 3 inches inside the foot string and widen ¼ inch for every 3 inches of maximum roach.

Excess material has been omitted for clarity.

45% aft

3"

Broadseam the foot panel to the sail.

Roll out material to cover foot portion of sail and stitch panels together with uniform seams. Cut the foot panel into three pieces and sew the pieces back together with broadseams. Sew the foot panel to the rest of the sail with a broadseam.

Headsail foot portion detail

extend along both edges of the sail 1 inch for every foot. In other words, a clew patch on a sail with a 20-foot-long leech and a 10-foot-long foot would reach about 20 inches up the leech, 10 inches along the foot. If a patch looks too tall and narrow, widen it. Make the inside edge of the patch straight or curved as you prefer.

Baste the patches to the sail, aligning them with the edge of the sail or the hemline as appropriate. Sew down the inside edge of the largest patch, using a zigzag stitch. You will be able to see the inside edges of the smaller patches through the cloth; run a line of stitching along the inside edges of both smaller patches. Leave the outer edges unstitched for now.

For a sail with reef points, additional patches along the luff and leech are required for the reef cringles. These should be cut and sewn to the sail at this time. Each reef should reduce the height of the

sail by 15 percent to 25 percent. Leading the reefing line a couple of inches aft from the leech reef cringle eliminates the need for reef points across the center of the sail. Instead of the traditional diamond patches with grommets for intermediate ties, sew short loops of webbing to either side of the sail. These loops may be used with lengths of bungee to contain the excess cloth at the foot.

If you plan to use a D-ring at the clew, now is the time to install it. Fold the sail and the largest patch out of the way and cut the corner off the inner patches to match the straight side of the D-ring. With your hot knife, cut three 1-foot-long lengths of 1-inch webbing. Fold all three in half around the straight side of the ring, sandwiching the inner patches between sides of the webbing. Align one piece of webbing with the leech, one with the foot, and position the third in the middle. Sew the webbing and sailcloth together in a boxed-X pat-

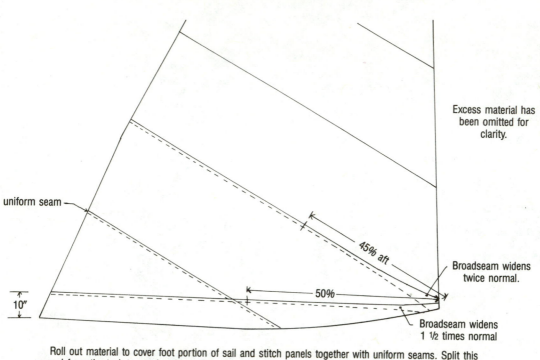

Excess material has
been omitted for
clarity.

uniform seam

45% aft

Broadseam widens
twice normal.

50%

10"

Broadseam widens
1 ½ times normal

Roll out material to cover foot portion of sail and stitch panels together with uniform seams. Split this
panel from the tack to a point about 10 inches above the clew and sew the two pieces back together with
a broadseam that widens 1 ½ times normal. Sew the foot panel to the rest of the sail with a broadseam
that widens twice the normal amount.

Mainsail foot portion detail

tern. Hand-stitch the webbing tightly against the flat side of the ring with waxed twine.

Hemming Leech and Foot

Fold the sail at the pencil line along the leech and the foot (if the foot has one) so that the hems fold over the top of the patches. Crease the fold and baste the hems down with transfer tape.

If you want a leech line in your headsail, lay a $1/16$- or $1/8$-inch braided Dacron line into the fold of the leech hem before you glue it. A sail with a lot of foot roach can benefit with a similar control line sewn into the foot hem. You can secure the control line to a button sewn to the sail, in which case you also need to install a small grommet in the hem near the clew for the leech line to exit, or near the tack for the foot line. Alternatively, use a leech line cleat,

which you will rivet to the sail later over a small exit slit in the hem.

Sew the edge of the hems down with a zigzag stitch, being careful not to stitch any control lines you may have installed. Anchor the line at the top of the sail by sewing across it several times. Anchor the foot control line at the clew.

Batten Pockets

Now you are going to wish you listened to me when I told you to omit the roach in your new mainsail. From the cloth you have left, cut batten pockets 4 inches longer than your battens. Make the pockets $1\frac{1}{4}$ inches wider than the battens, flaring about 5 inches from one end to twice that width. Put a $1/2$-inch hem in the wide end.

You need a few inches of wide waistband elastic,

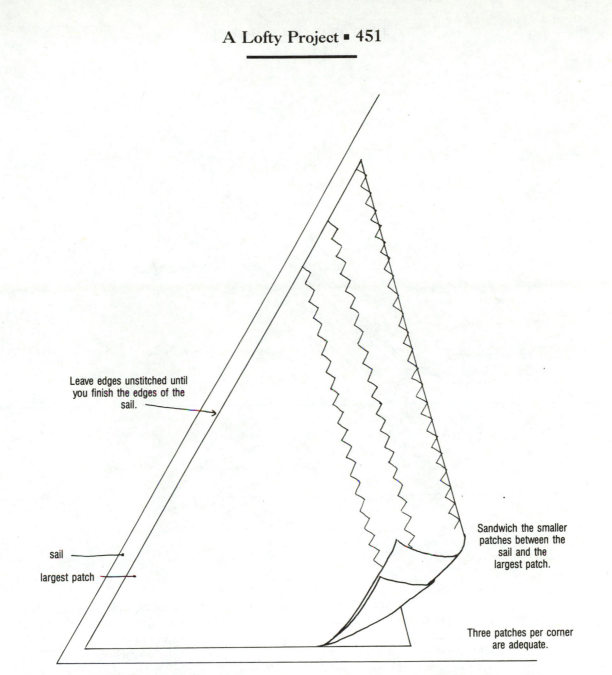

Leave edges unstitched until you finish the edges of the sail.

Sandwich the smaller patches between the sail and the largest patch.

sail

largest patch

Three patches per corner are adequate.

Patches should extend along the edge of the sail 1 inch for every foot of length of that edge.

Reinforcement patches

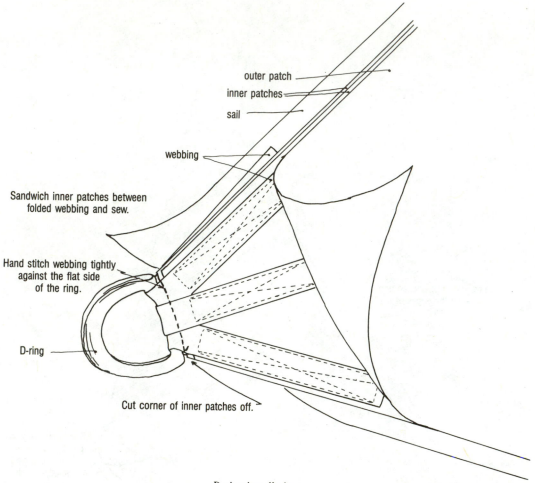

outer patch
inner patches
sail

webbing

Sandwich inner patches between
folded webbing and sew.

Hand stitch webbing tightly
against the flat side
of the ring.

D-ring

Cut corner of inner patches off.

D-ring installation

the wider the better. Cut a 3 1/2-inch strip of elastic for each of the pockets. Stitch one end of the elastic to the underside of the pocket (based on the hem you just made) about 5 inches from the narrow end, with the elastic extending toward that end. Fold 2 inches of the narrow end under and crease the fold.

Put the pocket in place on the sail, gluing the forward (narrow) end in position with transfer tape between the turned under portion and the sail. You should be able to identify the location of the battens by the change in direction of the leech at each point. Battens are perpendicular to the leech, except any located below reef points. These must be posi-

tioned parallel to the boom. Unfold the pocket and sew down all four sides of the flap. Now sew the other end of the elastic to the sail about an inch aft (toward the leech) of the stitched-down flap. This will form a loop of elastic to keep the batten pressed against the leech end of the pocket.

Position the pocket and glue the edges to the sail with transfer tape. Run a line of zigzag stitches around the entire perimeter of the pocket except the top half of the hemmed end; this is the opening for inserting the batten. (If the sail also has a leech line, be sure not to sew across it.) Double stitch the lower half of the open end of the pocket to resist the

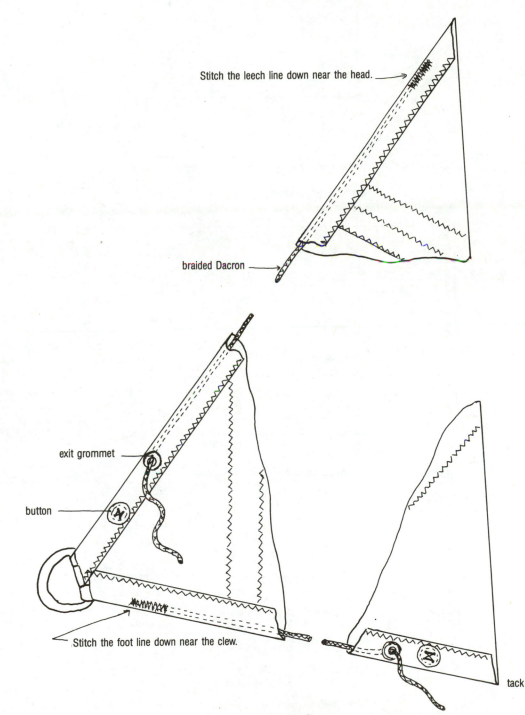

Stitch the leech line down near the head.

braided Dacron

exit grommet

button

Stitch the foot line down near the clew.

tack

Leech and foot lines

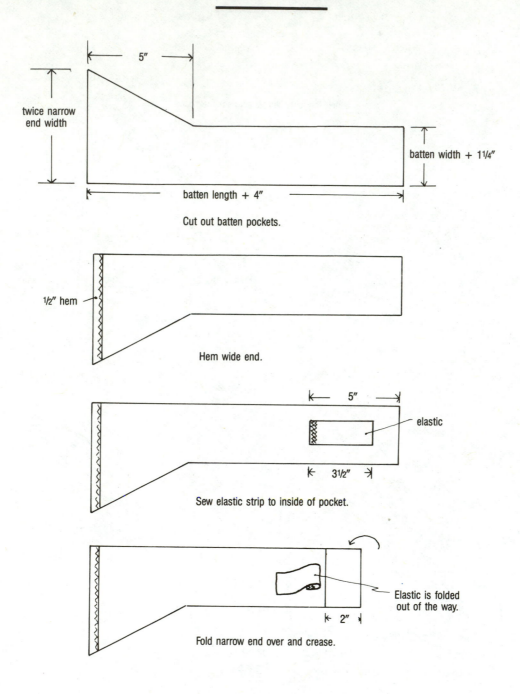

5″

twice narrow
end width

batten width + 1¼″

batten length + 4″

Cut out batten pockets.

½″ hem

Hem wide end.

5″

elastic

3½″

Sew elastic strip to inside of pocket.

Elastic is folded
out of the way.

2″

Fold narrow end over and crease.

Batten pockets (continued on page 455)

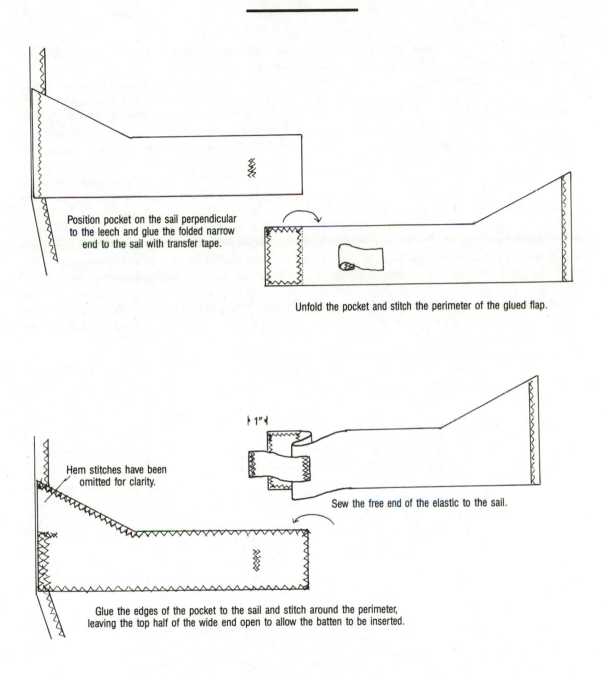

Position pocket on the sail perpendicular to the leech and glue the folded narrow end to the sail with transfer tape.

Unfold the pocket and stitch the perimeter of the glued flap.

Hem stitches have been omitted for clarity.

⊢ 1″ ⊣

Sew the free end of the elastic to the sail.

Glue the edges of the pocket to the sail and stitch around the perimeter, leaving the top half of the wide end open to allow the batten to be inserted.

Batten pockets (continued)

chafe of the battens. To make the battens more secure, stitch in from the leech about ½ inch at the bottom of the pocket opening.

Finishing the Luff

How you finish the luff will depend upon whether your sail is a headsail or mainsail, whether it is hanked on or feeds into an extrusion, and whether you want a rope or a wire for reinforcement.

Perhaps the easiest of the various possibilities is the continuous support tape required on headsails that feed into an extrusion. These tapes are prefabricated and come in half a dozen different sizes, so be sure to get the correct one for your extrusion. If the tape on your old sail is in good shape, you can reuse it. To install a support tape, position it on the luff, basting the flaps of the tape to both sides of the

sail. Sew it to the sail with two rows of zigzag stitches.

Sometimes hanked-on headsails are reinforced with two or three layers of Dacron tape sewn to the luff, but most will have a rope or wire in the luff. One quarter or ⁵/₁₆ inch rope will be adequate unless the sail is quite large; wire will typically be about half the diameter of rope, and should be plastic-coated. Which you choose is up to you—the method of attachment is virtually identical—but rope is somewhat easier to work with.

The critical factor in a rope luff support is to get the rope the correct length so that the rope rather than the cloth takes the stress. For all practical purposes wire has no stretch and you want the finished dimension of a wire luff reinforcement to be the length of the luff of the sail. Make a prestretched Dacron luff rope about 1 inch shorter than the luff

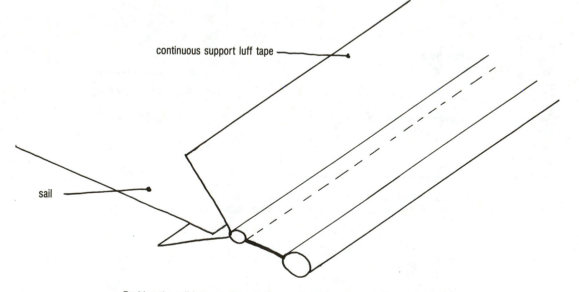

continuous support luff tape

sail

Position the sail between the two flaps and sew two rows of zigzag stitches.

Attaching luff tape

for every 15 feet of luff length. Regular Dacron and nylon have more stretch than is normally desirable in the luff of a headsail unless the sail is being used competitively. Different brands of rope have differing amounts of stretch, but making a regular Dacron luff rope 1 inch shorter than the luff for every 6 feet of luff length should allow the sail to set properly; shorten nylon 1 inch for every 4 feet. Cut the line at least a foot longer to allow ample length for spliced eyes at either end.

The luff rope will go inside a sleeve sewn to the luff of the sail. The simplest way to make the sleeve is with 5-ounce Dacron tape in 4-inch width. Crease the tape down the center and sew the sail to one side of the tape with the luff against the crease, placing the zigzag stitches near the edge of the sail. Lay a length of strong twine into the fold to serve as a messenger for pulling the luff rope through the sleeve. Fold the tape over the string and onto the sail and glue the edge down with transfer tape. You may have better results if you turn the sail over and baste the loose edge on the other side as well. Sew the tape down with a row of zigzag stitches 1 inch behind the fold and a second row along the inside edge.

If the reinforcement is rope, splice an eye around a stainless-steel thimble at one end. For a wire luff, strip the plastic from the end and put the wire around a thimble, securing it with a nicopress sleeve. Be sure no raw ends protrude beyond the nicopress sleeve and wrap the sleeve with plastic tape. Mark the rope or wire to the appropriate length determined above.

Attach the messenger string securely to the straight end of the rope or wire and pull it through the sleeve. Slide the sail far enough back, bunching the sleeve as necessary to allow sufficient rope or wire to exit for you to put in a second thimbled eye in at the mark you made. If you are using wire, wrap the sleeve with plastic tape.

With your hot knife, split the fold of the sleeve at each end to allow the eyes to recess into the sleeve. The center of the eye should be about where the respective edges of the sail would meet if they were extended. Trim away (with a hot knife) any of the sleeve that covers any part of the eye opening.

Starting an inch or more before the eye, whip the luff rope tightly against the front of the sleeve, using doubled, waxed twine and a sail needle. Pass the thread around the sail and through the sleeve just inside the rope. A sewing palm will make pushing the needle through the multiple layers of sailcloth easier. Pliers may also be useful. Pull each loop tightly, capturing the loose end of the thread under the first few loops. Continue the whipping up the inside leg of the eye until you reach the leech or the foot, finishing by tucking the end of the thread under the last two loops. If you are building a headsail, the installation of the luff rope completes the sail except for the handwork, which is detailed in the next section.

A rope is also used to reinforce the luff of a mainsail, but with a couple of differences. No eyes are required in the ends of the rope; the sail is normally anchored at the tack with a grommet and hoisted with a hole in the headboard. And the rope commonly continues around the tack and across the bottom of the sail to reinforce the foot as well as the luff.

Regular three-strand Dacron is the usual choice for the bolt rope in a mainsail. As indicated above, the Dacron rope should be about 1 inch shorter than the luff for every 6 feet of luff length. Use the same factor for the foot if two sides of the sail will be roped.

The sleeve for the bolt rope is installed exactly as above except that if the sail is also reinforced at the foot, the sleeve continues around the tack and along the foot of the sail to the clew. You will need to slit the sleeve to get it to make the turn at the tack. Be sure to run the messenger line inside the sleeve before stitching it closed. Leave a small section of the sleeve open at the tack to make installing the bolt rope easier.

Cut the rope to length, leaving several inches at either end to allow for some adjustment later, after you have had the opportunity to sail with the sail; the different stretch factors of different ropes may require some shortening or lengthening. Mark the calculated lengths on the rope, marking the luff length and the foot length separately and making a third mark where they meet; this mark will be placed at the tack. Use the messenger line to pull the bolt rope from the head out the open flap at the tack, then from the tack to the clew.

Position the tack mark on the rope at the tack, then with a sail needle and waxed twine doubled, make a series of 1/4-inch-long stitches just inside the rope, forcing the rope tightly into the fold of the sleeve. You may need a sewing palm and pliers. Begin at the tack and sew about 6 inches up the luff, then whip the bolt rope for an additional inch. The whipping passes around the outside of the sail and through the sleeve against the inside edge of the rope. Space the loops closely and pull each very tight, finishing by passing the end of the twine under the last two loops.

If only the luff is reinforced, put a second inch of whipping around the rope near the bottom of the sleeve. If the rope continues across the foot, start

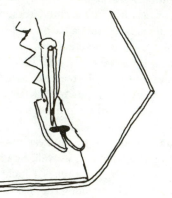

Crease 4-inch Dacron tape in the center and sew the sail to one side of the tape.

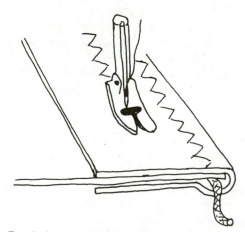

Turn the loose side down and stitch through all three layers, laying a messenger cord in the sleeve that is formed.

Creating a luff-rope sleeve (continued on page 459)

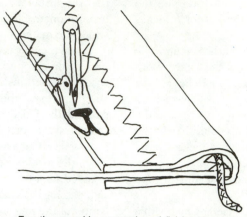

Turn the assembly over again and finish with a row of
stitches along the inside edge of the tape.

Creating a luff-rope sleeve (continued)

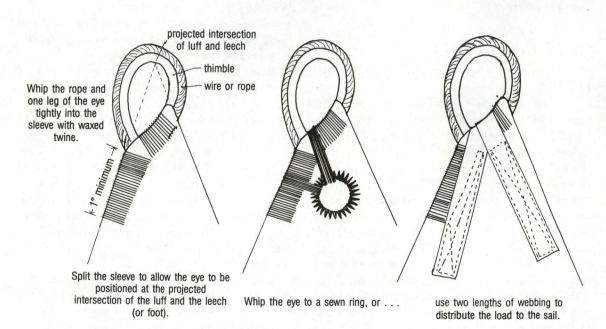

projected intersection
of luff and leech

thimble

wire or rope

Whip the rope and
one leg of the eye
tightly into the
sleeve with waxed
twine.

1" minimum

Split the sleeve to allow the eye to be
positioned at the projected
intersection of the luff and the leech
(or foot).

Whip the eye to a sewn ring, or . . .

use two lengths of webbing to
distribute the load to the sail.

Finishing the ends of a headsail luff rope

again at the tack and sew the bolt rope into the sleeve the same way you did the luff for 6 inches along the foot.

Pull on the rope at the head of the sail until the mark on the rope is at the end of the sleeve. With your sail needle and waxed twine, stitch behind the rope for 6 inches at the head of the sail—just as you did at the tack. Put 1 inch of whipping right at the top of the sail, and whip rope a second time at the other end of the stitching, about 6 inches lower. Position the mark for the other end of the rope at the end of the sleeve at the clew and secure the rope tightly the same way.

Take the sail to your sewing machine and with a zipper foot, run a line of straight stitches—the longest stitches your machine will make—against the inside of the luff/foot rope, forcing it against the front of the sleeve for its entire length. Work the wrinkles out of the sleeve as you sew. Where you whipped and hand-stitched the bolt rope, fold a length of Dacron tape over each area to protect it from chafe and sew it to the sail with two rows of zigzag stitches.

THE HARD STUFF

All that remains to be done to your sails is some handwork.

On a headsail, you will need to protect the sail at the clew. Pass a butterfly-shaped piece of leather through the D-ring, folding it onto both sides of the sail, and stitch down its inside edges. If your machine will sew through all the layers of various materials now at the clew, by all means machine-stitch this edge. Then use the time you save to write a testimonial letter to the sewing machine manufacturer. Most of us will have to hand stitch the edge of the leather. Join the sides of the leather along the leech and the foot with a baseball stitch—a stitch that looks just like the laces on your high-tops, Skip.

If your sail will have a grommet instead of a D-ring at the clew, you have a couple of choices. The easiest is to take the sail to a nearby loft and pay

them to install a stainless eye with their hydraulic installation machine. Or you can do sewn eyes, which are marginally stronger and a lot more work.

A sewn eye is actually made up of a brass ring, which you stitch to the sail, and a brass grommet that is pressed inside the sewn eye to protect the stitching. Installation is time consuming, but not particularly difficult. Position the brass ring on the sail at least $1/4$ inch from any edge and trace around the outside. Cut a hole in the cloth $3/4$ of the diameter of the inside of the ring. With a sail needle and doubled heavy waxed twine, whip the ring to the sail, passing the needle up through the hole and the center of the ring and down through the sail on the penciled circle.

Space the loops about $3/16$ inch apart all the way around the circle, and pull each loop as tightly as you can. If you don't pull the stitches tight enough, the sleeve won't fit inside the ring. Wrapping your index finger with several layers of masking tape will minimize nerve damage. Stitch around the ring a second time, placing the second row of stitches between the first ones on the circle. When the stitching is done, the sleeve is installed and flared like a grommet. This takes a special die, so you still may have to make a trip to the loft.

Sewn eyes are also appropriate for the tack of your mainsail as well as for the reef cringles. If you are not using a headboard, put a sewn ring in the head of the sail also. Use sewn rings at the head and tack of a headsail with a support-tape luff.

Sewn rings may also be used at the tack and clew of your headsail for securing the sail to the eyes of the luff reinforcement. For this use chafe is not a problem and the brass insert is not required. Position these two rings adjacent to the splice or nicopress sleeve that forms the eye in the luff rope, at least $1/4$ inch from the rope or the opposite edge of the sail.

Once the rings are sewn to the sail, join the rings to the eyes with three or four dozen loops of sail twine; make the loops snug, but not tight. Put an equal number of loops of twine around the luff of

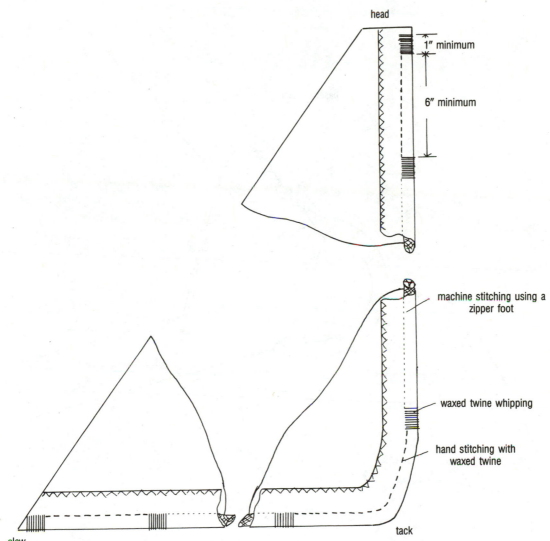

Securing the luff (and foot) rope in the sleeve of a mainsail

the sail and through the rings to reinforce the sleeve at the head and tack.

If you do not want to install sewn rings in the headsail, you can accomplish the same objective with a couple of lengths of webbing passed through each eye and sewn to the sail. From each eye, one strip should extend onto the sail parallel to the leech or the foot (depending upon whether the eye is at the head or tack) and the other strip parallel to the luff.

Install the headboard with rivets or by stitching, placing it tightly against the bolt rope, unless the rope feeds into a groove; in that case, set the headboard back about 1/8 inch. Cut out the hole in the cloth (for the halyard shackle) with your hot knife.

Rivet the leech line cleat to the sail, or sew a

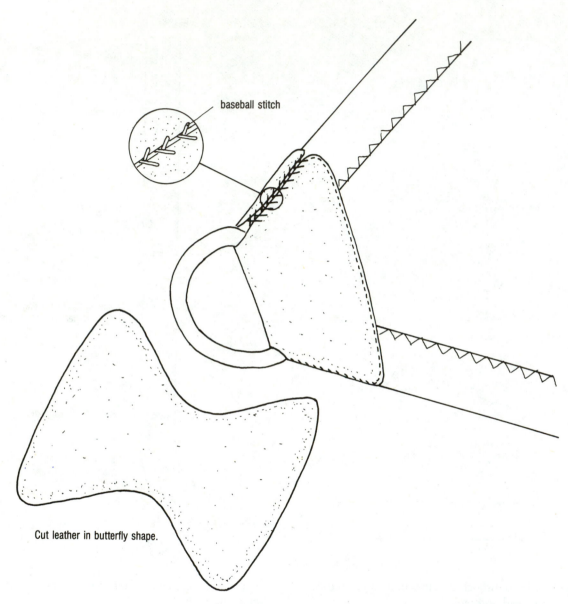

baseball stitch

Cut leather in butterfly shape.

Leather clew patch

plastic or leather button to the hem near the exit grommet. Sew a small cloth or webbing flap over the cleat or the button, leaving it unstitched along the outside edge. This flap will prevent the fitting from snagging on the rigging or lifelines.

All that remains to be done is to attach hanks or slides. How you attach them will depend on the type of hardware you are using and perhaps on your preference. Slides, in particular, are often sewn directly to the sail with twine or attached with short

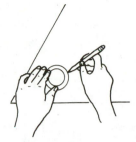

Trace the outline of the brass ring onto the sail.

Cut a hole in the cloth ¾ the diameter of the *inside* of the ring.

"Tick" the outline every ³⁄₁₆ inch to aid in getting the stitches uniform.

A leather sewing palm will make pushing the needle through several layers easier.

Whip the ring to the sail with heavy, doubled, waxed twine. Pass the needle up through the hole and down through each tick mark, pulling every loop tight.

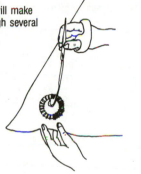

Stitch around the ring a second time, placing the second row of stitches between the first ones.

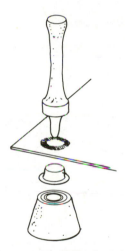

To protect the stitching from chafe, install a brass sleeve, using a special die set.

Installing a sewn ring

lengths of webbing sewn to the sail. Slides attached with cord binding or shackles and most jib hanks for big boats require a grommet in the luff.

Spur grommets are quite satisfactory for this use. To keep the luff from developing puckers, mount the grommets right against the bolt rope. Hanks and slides are typically spaced about 2 feet apart; it is a good idea to support the headboard with two sail slides.

That's about it. If I left out something, hey, I never claimed to be a sailmaker. Once you have the shape right, you ought to be able to figure out any other problems that crop up. If you need a particular feature, duplicate what was done on your old sail.

How long should all this take? Hard to say, Skip. I spent the better part of five days making that first sail. The next sail I made—a couple of years later—was a mizzen and it took less than three days. I

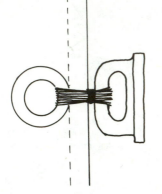

twine lashing through a grommet

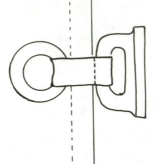

webbing through a grommet

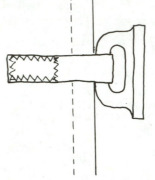

webbing sewn to the sail

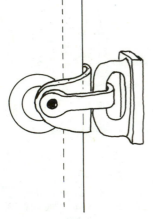

stainless steel or plastic shackle

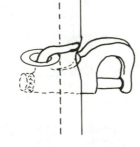

press-on jib snap

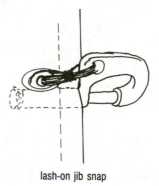

lash-on jib snap

Slide and snap attachment

didn't know if that was because I was "experienced," or simply because the second sail was a lot smaller. Subsequently I made a main which also took about three days—do-it-yourself workdays, not the union variety.

Are the sails I built as good as what I might have expected from a professional sailmaker? Maybe not. The professional certainly has the tools to achieve a better finish, but that is at least partially compen-sated for by the greater care I gave the project. Since I used materials identical to those used by the pros and I triple-stitched every seam, I have every reason to believe that my sail will last as long and hold up as well theirs. As for performance, I remain uncon-vinced that any differences in the shape of a profes-sionally built sail will add a tenth of a knot of speed to my boat in my hands. And I saved over $1,000 on that very first sail alone.

So where does all this leave you? Should you build a sail? I don't know. If you want a sail perfectly cut with a perfect set, the sail you build may not satisfy you. On the other hand, if cost is a big consideration, if you have time available, and if you are reasonably handy, it might be a worthwhile alternative. At the very least you will learn a great deal about what makes your old boat go, and you just may discover that sail perfection is not nearly as elusive as you imagined.

SEVENTEEN

Epilogue

Just Do It.
–NIKE–

Brion Toss, whose knowledge of rigging humbles ordinary sailors, relates in his book, *The Rigger's Apprentice*, a way of tying a bowline that he learned from Paul Newman. Okay, so he saw it in a Paul Newman movie; it's almost the same thing. Quit nit-picking and pay attention.

After you pass the line around the bollard or through the clew ring or whatever, hold the standing part of the line in one hand, and the end of the line—pointed back toward the bollard—in the other. Reach over the standing part, then dip your hand under it, forming a loop around your wrist. Now pass the end of the line beneath the standing part, pushing it under with your thumb, then reaching over the standing part to get a new grip on it. Still gripping the end, pull your wrist out of the loop. Draw the knot tight. That's a take.

Why am I telling to you this? Because although I

Hold the standing part in one hand and the end—pointed back toward the bollard—in the other hand.

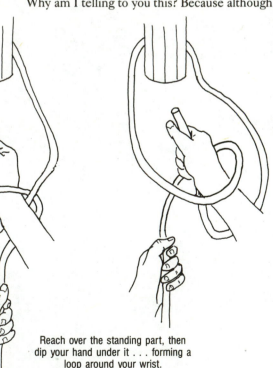

Reach over the standing part, then dip your hand under it . . . forming a loop around your wrist.

The Newman bowline (continued on page 467)

first learned to tie a bowline a quarter of a century ago, I still have the rabbit coming out of the hole, running around the tree, and going back into the hole every time I tie this knot. I have progressed to where I no longer have to say it out loud—but I still move my lips. Paul Newman's way is better than mine. It's quicker. It's easier. It has style. But the bowline that results is exactly the same as the one formed by chasing the rabbit around the tree.

Similarly, many of the changes detailed in the preceding pages can be accomplished in various ways. The methods I have elected to illustrate are either the simplest or the best *I know*—nothing more. In some cases, no doubt, there are quicker ways, easier ways, ways with more style. If you discover a better way to accomplish a particular enhancement, by all means do it that way. I'm tying bowlines differently, I can tell you.

The inspiration for *This Old Boat* was an unshakable conviction that refurbishing an old boat is a financially sound alternative to the escalating cost of new boats. In the free spending environment of leveraged acquisitions, obligatory BMWs, and the "art" of making billion dollar deals, I had some doubts in the beginning about whether there was anyone left out there who would be interested. Hell, the last President to suggest belt tightening to the American public was summarily tossed out of office. But the pendulum appears to be swinging in the opposite direction as last year's tycoons face bankruptcy court. Or criminal court.

No matter; boom or bust, old boats make sense. They have a lower initial cost and, in many cases, a lower operating cost than a new boat. It is essential to escape the automobile mentality that makes us think that something new is trouble free while

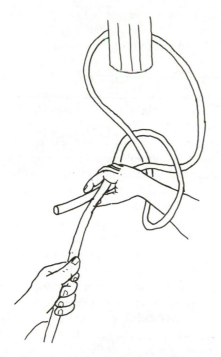

Pass the end under the standing part, pushing it under with your thumb, then gripping it again on the other side.

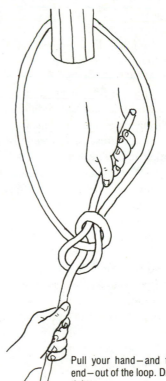

Pull your hand—and the gripped end—out of the loop. Draw the knot tight.

The Newman bowline (continued)

something old is "just asking for it." This kind of thinking doesn't apply to boats. While a five-year-old car may already be well on its way to the crusher, a *good* boat should give 50 years or more of dependable and pleasurable service.

Financial benefits aren't the only attraction. After 17 years of intimacy with the same old boat, she welcomes me and my wife aboard, embraces us like a sister, soothes us like a favorite slipper, pleases us but never surprises us. (Offshore, surprises I don't need.) She is a trusted partner, an accommodating host, a member of our family. I cannot imagine a reason for a new boat.

Putting an old boat back in service rather than purchasing a new one seems to me also to have ecological implications. Perhaps few boats end up in landfills, but those that are effectively discarded do end up clogging marinas and waterways. New boats just add to the problem. The sensible alternative is boat recycling.

Nor should we overlook the social benefit of matching unfulfilled dreamers with unused boats and getting them both away from the dock. In truth, it only takes a few dollars to get out on the water, yet how many forego sailing, fishing, or cruising altogether because the boats featured in the five-color ads in yachting magazines are unaffordable? (The back cover of the latest issue of one of America's oldest boating magazine features an ad for a 105-foot sailboat. Who buys a 105-foot sailboat?) Old boats being offered for sale today at a fraction of new boat prices were once featured in similar colored ads; today's new boats are tomorrow's old boats. Should that deprive us of the pleasures of boating?

So I set out to call attention to the potential of old boats and to create a single volume that would contain all the necessary information a motivated boat owner requires to put his or her old boat into better-than-new condition. Gathering and consolidating the broad array of information required to achieve such a lofty goal turned out to be considerably more challenging than I initially anticipated. I am not sure I will ever know how well I succeeded—but you will.

I do know that *This Old Boat* contains a vast amount of useful material. My own old boat, which has seen her share of enhancements and modifications in the 17 years she has owned me, has already benefited from this research, and a number of future projects have been penciled into the matrix. I also discovered some of my earlier efforts could have been substantially improved had I known then what I know now. Not that I regret that; the biggest mistake of all is being afraid to make a mistake.

Use *This Old Boat* as your initial source of information, but not your *only* source. When the information I have provided is inadequate, you may find a more comprehensive explanation in a specialized text on the specific subject. Magazine articles are an excellent source of information about the latest products and techniques. Other sailors with experience in the matter at hand can provide invaluable assistance. To raise your skill level, consider educational opportunities; local schools often offer courses (for credit or not) in carpentry, diesel mechanics, refrigeration, electricity, and even boat repair. And don't forget Paul Newman movies; you never know where the clarifying light may come from.

For my part, I have done the best I can; the rest is up to you. If you have honestly and judiciously evaluated your needs and expectations, if you have taken the time to visualize an unlimited image of your old boat, if you have drawn up a well-considered plan for making the desired modifications, if you have acquired quality tools, and if you have practiced each of the essential skills, you are separated from the boat in your vision only by time.

My parting advice is: don't let new-found skills cloud your perspective. Boats are to be enjoyed; that's why we call them pleasure boats. Working on them should not take precedence over using them. Likewise, writing about them. See you on the hook, Skip. I'm outta here.

Index